ROADWATCH

Wherever you're driving, call AA Roadwatch for the latest reports on roadworks and weather. Information is regularly updated throughout the day and night. Save yourself time and frustration— phone before you go . . .

NATIONAL ROADWORKS AND WEATHER

National motorways		0836-401-110
1.	West Country	0836-401-111
2.	Wales	0836-401-112
3.	Midlands	0836-401-113
4.	East Anglia	0836-401-114
5.	North-west England	0836-401-115
6.	North-east England	0836-401-116
7.	Scotland	0836-401-117
8.	Northern Ireland	0836-401-118
9.	South-east England	see below

LONDON AND THE SOUTH-EAST— TRAFFIC, ROADWORKS AND WEATHER

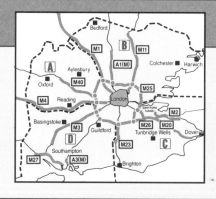

	Central London (inside North/South Circulars)	0836-401-122
A.	Motorways/roads between M4 and M1	0836-401-123
B.	Motorways/roads between M1 and Dartford Tunnel	0836-401-124
C.	Motorways/roads between Dartford Tunnel and M23	0836-401-125
D.	Motorways/roads between M23 and M4	0836-401-126
	M25 London Orbital only	0836-401-127
	London special events (certain weekends only)	0836-401-128

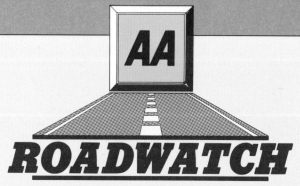

ROADWATCH

Messages are charged at a rate of 25p per minute cheap rate, 38p per minute at all other times.
Callers pay only for the time they use.

FREE COPY!

FOR YOUR FREE COPY OF THE FULL AA DIRECTORY OF RECORDED INFORMATION WRITE TO
AA INFORMATION SERVICES (DEPT BRA) CWI, FANUM HOUSE, BASINGSTOKE, HANTS RG21 2EA.

GREAT BRITAIN ROAD ATLAS

1:200,000
Approximately 3 miles to 1 inch

GUILD PUBLISHING
LONDON · NEW YORK · SYDNEY · TORONTO

4th edition September 1989
3rd edition October 1988
2nd edition October 1987
Reprinted April 1988
1st edition October 1986

ISBN 07495 0002 6

Printed by Graficromo SA, Spain.

The contents of this book are believed correct at the time of printing. Nevertheless, the publisher can accept no responsibility for errors or omissions, or for changes in the details given.

Mapping produced by the Cartographic Department of The Automobile Association. This atlas has been compiled and produced from the Automaps database utilising electronic and computer technology.

Every effort has been made to ensure that the contents of our new database are correct. However, if there are any errors or omissions, please write to the Cartographic Editor, Publishing Division, The Automobile Association, Fanum House, Basingstoke, Hampshire RG21 2EA.

This edition published 1989 by Guild Publishing by arrangement with The Automobile Association
CN 2517

GREAT BRITAIN ROAD ATLAS

Route Planning

The maps and charts at the beginning of this atlas are designed to help you plan your journey with ease and economy.

FINDING IT
Look for the placename you want in the index section at the back of the atlas. The name is followed by a page number and a National Grid reference. Turn to the atlas page indicated and use the National Grid reference to pinpoint the place.
The National Grid and how to use are explained on page XIV.

GETTING THERE
Having found your destination in the main atlas, find the nearest large town. This will also be shown on the Route Planning Maps, pages IV-XIII. These maps show the principal routes throughout Britain and a basic route can be planned from them. A special feature of these maps is that a key to the atlas pages is superimposed – making at-a-glance place location much easier. A more detailed route can then be worked out from the main atlas. Taking a note of road numbers and directions reduces the need to stop and consult the atlas on the way.

WHICH ROAD?
Motorways are quicker and more economical than other routes because you can maintain a consistent speed and avoid traffic delays.
Primary routes should be considered where you cannot use motorways. These are marked in green on the maps, and signposted in green on the roads. The shortest route is not always the quickest, and primary routes tend to take you round towns rather than through their centres, thus avoiding delays caused by traffic lights, one-way systems etc.

HOW FAR?
The length of the journey is a fundamental consideration when a journey is being planned. The mileage chart on page XV gives the distance between main towns and can be used to make a rough calculation of the total journey length. You should then be able to estimate the time needed for the journey.

RADIO
Frequent bulletins are issued both by national and local radio stations on road conditions, local hold-ups etc and these can be of great assistance to the driver.

ALERTNESS
Planning the journey in advance will ensure that the driver sets out feeling alert and confident. It will also make the journey less troublesome. Tired drivers are a hazard to themselves and other road users. On a particularly long journey allow extra time for short rest breaks. Always allow plenty of time for a journey.

Legend

Motorway	≡≡≡
Motorway under construction	≡≡≡
Primary route single carriageway	=
Primary route dual carriageway	=
Other A roads	—
Motorway junction	⓪
Motorway junction with limited entries or exits.	❼

Scale 16 miles to 1 inch

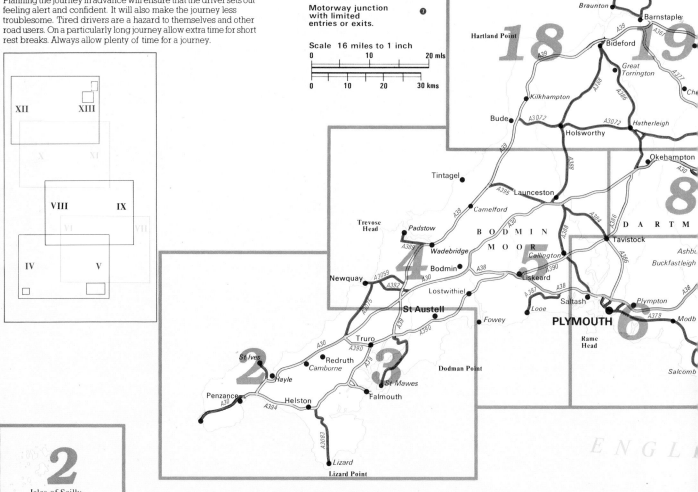

ENGLAND

ENGLISH CHANNEL

Guernsey

152

Jersey

FRANCE

V

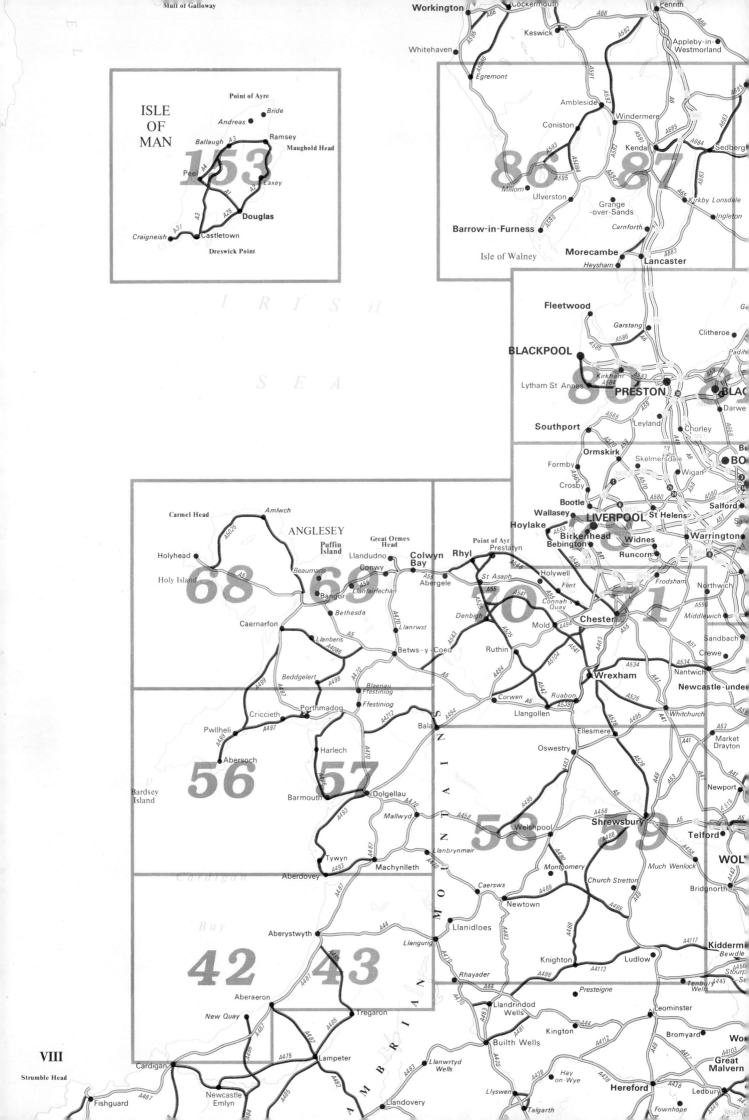

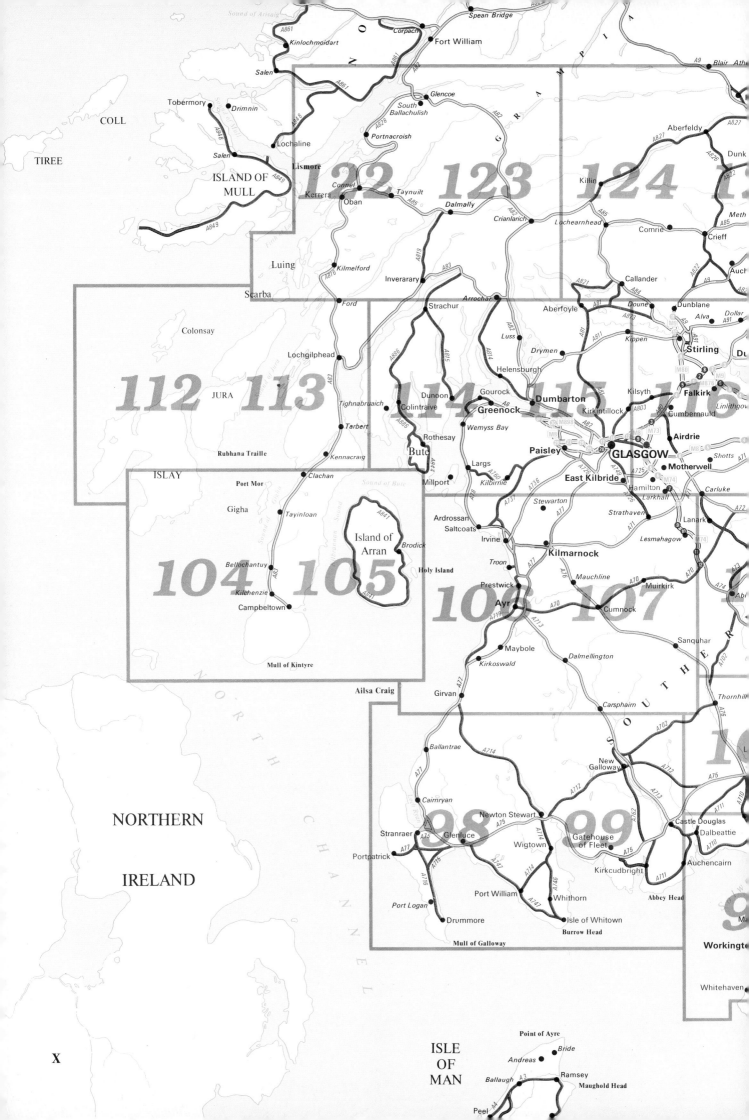

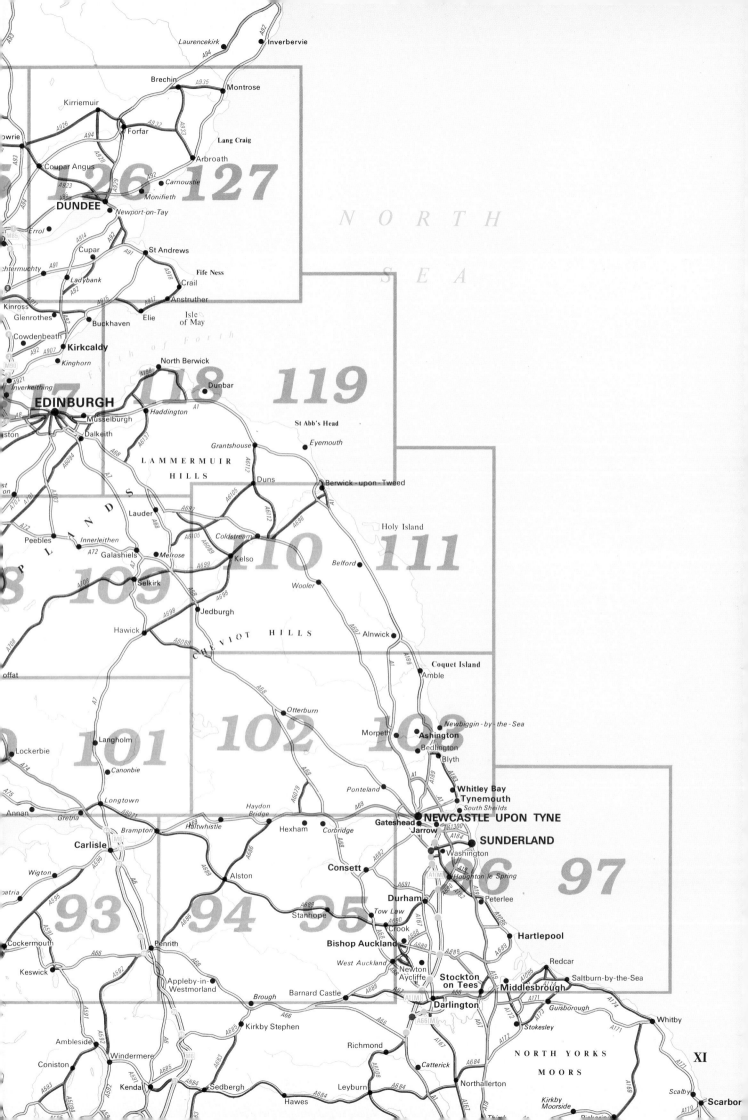

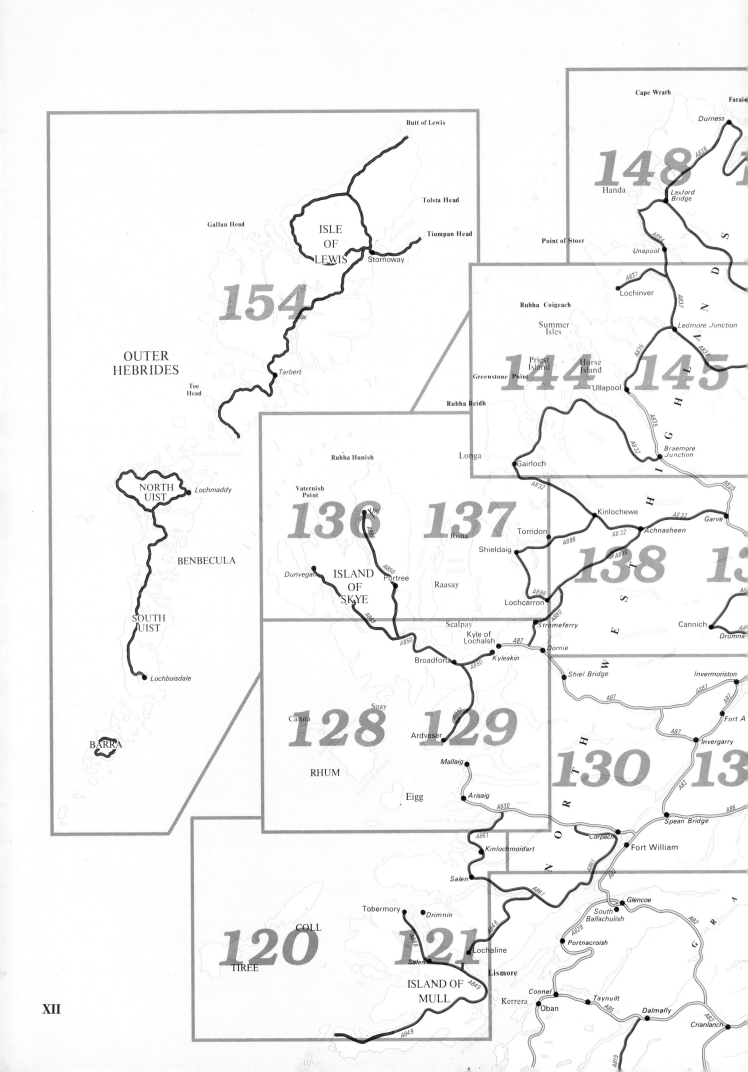

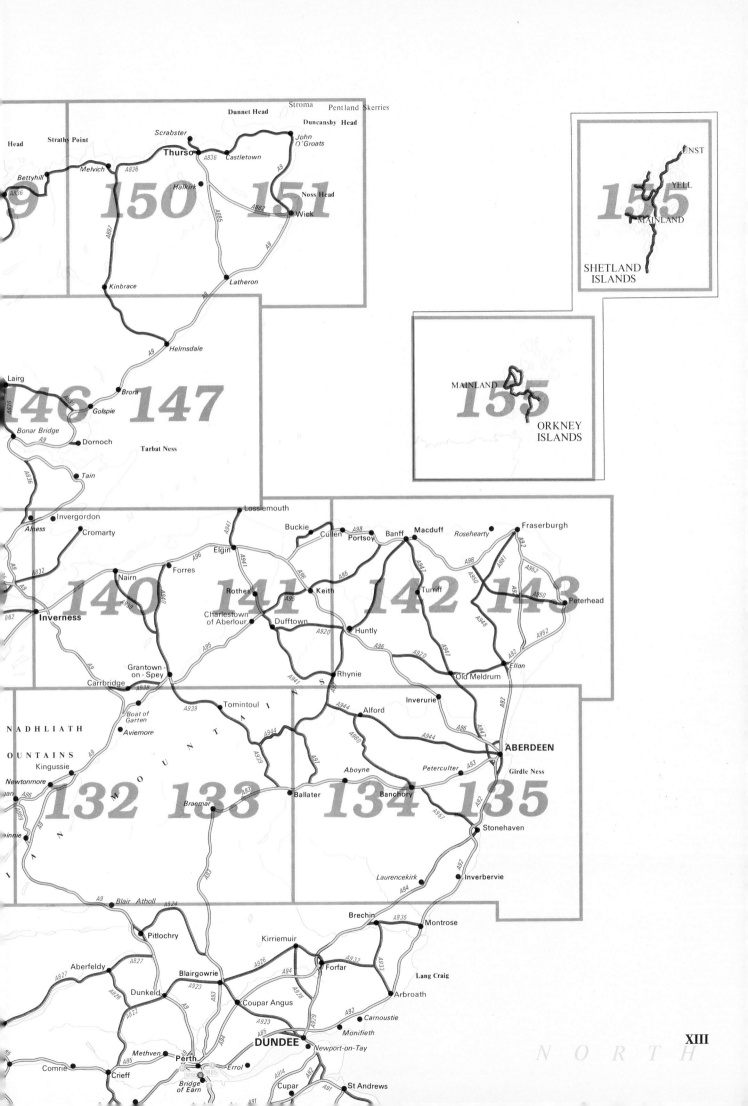

Place Location

To locate a place in this atlas, first look up the name of the town or village required in the index, which starts on page 208. Each entry is followed by the page number on which the place can be found and its National Grid reference.

eg: Hyssington   59   SO 3194
     Hythe (Hants)   13   SU 4207
     Hythe (Kent)   29   TR 1635

Hythe (Kent) is on page 29 with National Grid reference TR 1635.

When the required place name and its reference have been found in the index:
a) turn to the page number indicated
b) find the location using the last four numbers.
Taking Hythe (Kent) as our example: the first figure of the reference – 1, refers to the numbered grid line running along the bottom of the page. Having found this line, the second figure – 6, tells you the distance to move in tenths to the right of this line. A vertical line through this point is the first half of the reference.
The third figure – 3, refers to the numbered grid lines on the left hand side of the page. Finally the fourth figure – 5, indicates the distance to move in tenths above this line. A horizontal line drawn through this point to intersect with the first line gives the precise location of the place in question. See example below.

THE NATIONAL GRID

The National Grid provides a system of reference common to maps of all scales. The grid covers Britain with an imaginary network of 100 kilometre squares. Each square is identified by two letters, *eg* TR. Every 100 kilometre square is then sub-divided into 10 kilometre squares which appear as a network of blue lines on the map pages. These blue lines are numbered left to right ⓪-⑨ and bottom to top ⓪-⑨ These 10 kilometre squares can be further divided into tenths to give a place reference to the nearest kilometre.

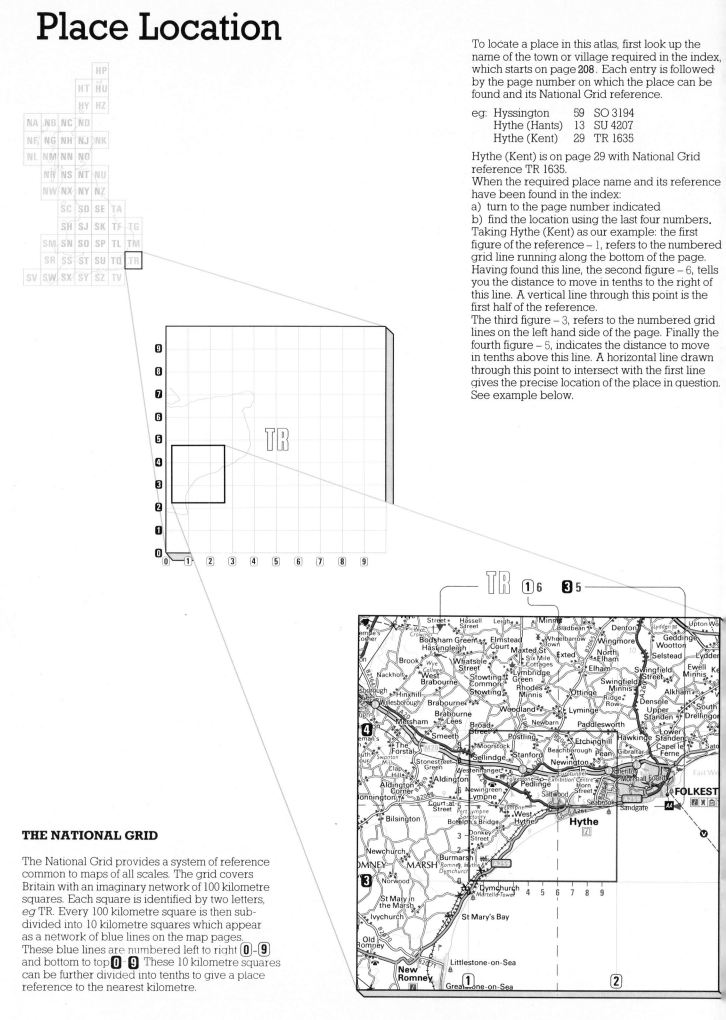

Mileage Chart

The distances between towns on the mileage chart are given to the nearest mile, and are measured along the normal AA recommended routes. It should be noted that AA recommended routes do not necessarily follow the shortest distances between places but are based on the quickest travelling time, making maximum use of motorways or dual carriageway roads.

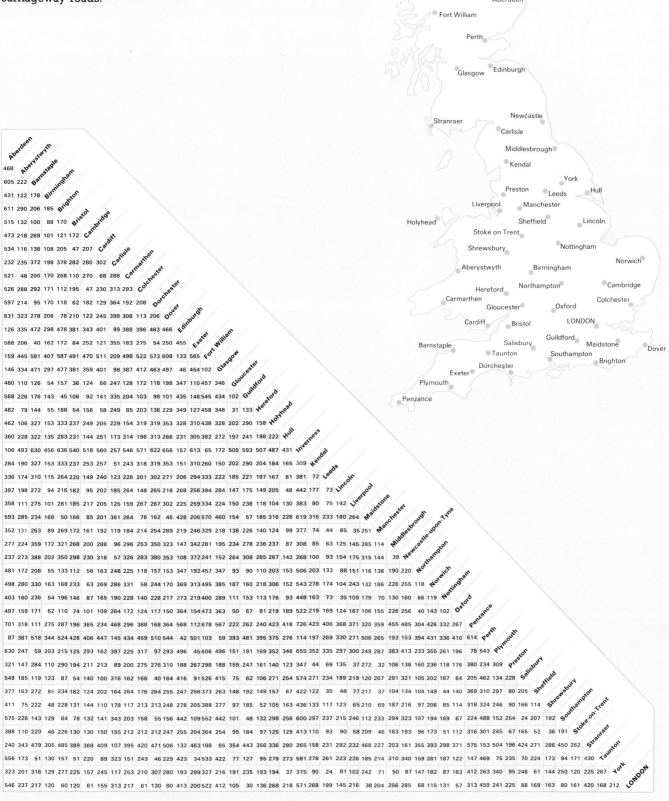

From \ To	Aberdeen	Aberystwyth	Barnstaple	Birmingham	Brighton	Bristol	Cambridge	Cardiff	Carlisle	Carmarthen	Colchester	Dorchester	Dover	Edinburgh	Exeter	Fort William	Glasgow	Gloucester	Guildford	Hereford	Holyhead	Hull	Inverness	Kendal	Leeds	Lincoln	Liverpool	Maidstone	Manchester	Middlesbrough	Newcastle-upon-Tyne	Northampton	Norwich	Nottingham	Oxford	Penzance	Perth	Plymouth	Preston	Salisbury	Sheffield	Shrewsbury	Southampton	Stoke-on-Trent	Stranraer	Taunton	York
Aberystwyth	468																																														
Barnstaple	605	222																																													
Birmingham	431	122	178																																												
Brighton	611	290	206	185																																											
Bristol	515	132	100	88	170																																										
Cambridge	473	218	269	101	121	172																																									
Cardiff	534	116	138	108	205	47	207																																								
Carlisle	232	235	372	198	378	282	280	302																																							
Carmarthen	521	48	200	170	268	110	270	68	288																																						
Colchester	526	288	292	171	112	195	47	230	313	293																																					
Dorchester	597	214	95	170	118	62	182	129	364	192	208																																				
Dover	631	323	278	206	78	210	122	245	398	308	113	206																																			
Edinburgh	126	335	472	298	478	381	343	401	99	388	396	463	466																																		
Exeter	588	206	40	162	172	84	252	121	355	183	275	54	250	455																																	
Fort William	159	445	581	407	587	491	470	511	209	498	522	573	608	133	565																																
Glasgow	146	334	471	297	477	381	359	401	98	387	412	463	497	46	454	102																															
Gloucester	480	110	126	54	157	36	124	66	247	128	172	118	198	457	110	457	346																														
Guildford	568	226	176	143	45	106	92	141	335	204	103	98	101	435	148	545	434	102																													
Hereford	482	79	144	55	188	54	156	58	249	85	203	136	229	349	127	458	348	31	133																												
Holyhead	462	106	327	153	333	237	249	205	229	154	319	319	353	328	310	438	328	202	290	158																											
Hull	360	228	322	135	283	231	144	251	173	314	196	313	266	231	305	382	272	197	241	198	222																										
Inverness	106	493	630	456	636	540	518	560	257	546	571	622	656	157	613	65	172	505	593	507	487	431																									
Kendal	284	190	327	153	333	237	253	257	51	243	318	319	353	151	310	260	150	202	290	204	184	165	309																								
Leeds	336	174	310	115	264	220	149	240	123	226	201	302	271	206	294	333	222	185	221	187	167	61	381	72																							
Lincoln	397	198	272	94	216	182	95	202	185	264	148	265	218	268	256	394	284	147	175	149	205	48	442	177	73																						
Liverpool	358	111	275	101	281	185	217	205	125	159	267	267	302	225	259	334	224	150	238	118	104	130	383	80	75	142																					
Maidstone	593	285	234	168	50	166	85	201	361	264	76	162	45	428	206	570	460	154	57	185	316	228	619	316	233	180	264																				
Manchester	352	131	263	89	269	172	161	192	119	184	214	254	289	219	246	329	218	138	226	140	124	99	377	74	44	85	35	251																			
Middlesbrough	277	224	359	172	321	268	200	288	96	296	253	350	323	147	342	218	195	234	278	236	237	87	308	85	63	125	145	285	114																	
Newcastle-upon-Tyne	237	273	388	202	350	298	230	318	57	326	283	380	353	108	372	241	152	264	308	265	267	142	268	100	93	154	175	315	144	39																
Northampton	481	172	208	55	133	112	56	163	248	225	118	157	153	347	192	457	347	93	90	110	203	153	506	203	133	88	151	116	138	190	220															
Norwich	498	280	330	163	168	233	63	269	286	331	58	244	170	369	313	495	385	187	160	218	306	152	543	278	174	104	243	132	186	226	255	118														
Nottingham	403	160	236	54	196	146	87	165	190	228	140	228	217	273	219	400	289	111	153	113	176	93	448	163	73	35	109	179	70	130	160	66	119													
Oxford	497	159	171	62	110	74	101	109	264	172	124	117	150	364	154	473	363	50	67	81	219	189	522	219	169	124	167	106	155	226	40	143	102												
Penzance	701	318	111	275	287	196	365	234	468	296	388	168	364	568	112	678	567	222	262	240	423	418	726	423	406	368	371	320	395	455	485	304	426	332	267											
Perth	87	381	518	344	524	428	406	447	145	434	459	510	544	42	501	103	59	393	481	395	375	276	114	197	269	330	271	506	265	193	153	394	431	336	410	614										
Plymouth	630	247	59	203	215	125	293	162	397	225	317	97	293	496	45	606	496	151	191	169	352	346	655	352	335	297	300	249	287	383	413	233	355	261	196	78	543									
Preston	321	147	284	110	290	194	211	213	89	200	275	276	310	188	267	298	188	159	247	161	140	123	347	44	69	135	37	272	32	60	138	160	236	118	176	380	234	309								
Salisbury	549	185	119	123	87	54	140	100	316	162	166	40	164	416	91	526	415	75	62	106	271	254	574	271	234	189	219	81	205	291	321	105	202	167	64	205	462	134	228							
Sheffield	377	163	272	86	234	182	124	202	164	264	176	264	255	247	256	373	263	148	192	149	157	67	422	122	35	48	77	217	37	104	134	104	149	44	140	369	300	297	80	205						
Shrewsbury	411	75	222	48	228	131	144	110	213	148	278	205	388	277	148	436	133	117	123	65	210	69	206	97	206	85	114	318	324	246	67	67	197	216	67	367	342	207	205						
Southampton	575	226	143	129	64	78	132	141	343	203	158	55	156	442	109	552	442	101	48	132	298	256	600	297	237	215	246	112	233	294	323	107	194	169	67	224	488	152	254	24	207	192				
Stoke-on-Trent	388	110	220	46	226	130	130	150	155	212	212	212	247	255	204	364	254	95	184	97	125	129	413	110	93	90	58	209	46	163	193	96	173	51	112	316	301	245	67	165	52	36	191			
Stranraer	240	343	479	305	485	389	368	409	107	395	420	471	506	132	463	188	85	354	443	356	336	280	265	158	231	292	232	468	227	203	161	355	293	298	371	575	153	504	196	424	271	286	450	262		
Taunton	556	173	51	130	157	51	220	89	323	151	243	46	229	423	34	533	422	77	127	95	278	273	581	278	261	223	226	185	214	310	340	159	281	187	122	147	469	75	235	70	224	173	94	171	430	
York	323	201	316	129	277	225	157	245	117	253	210	307	280	193	299	327	216	191	235	193	194	37	375	90	24	81	102	242	71	50	87	147	182	87	183	412	263	340	95	248	61	144	250	120	225	267
LONDON	546	237	217	120	60	120	61	155	313	217	61	130	80	413	200	522	412	105	30	136	268	218	571	268	199	145	216	38	204	256	285	68	115	131	57	313	459	241	225	88	169	163	80	161	420	168	212

Map Pages

Map Symbols

MOTORING INFORMATION : VERKEHRSINFORMATIONEN : INFORMATIONS ROUTIERES

Motorway with number
Autobahn mit Nummer
Autoroute avec numéro

Motorway junction with and without number
Anschlußstelle mit/ohne Nummer
Echangeur avec/sans numéro

Motorway junction with limited access
Anschlußstelle mit beschränkter Auf- bzw. Abfahrt
Echangeur partiel

Motorway service area
Tanken und Rasten
Aire de Service

Motorway and junction under construction
Autobahn und Anschlußstelle im Bau
Autoroute et échangeur en construction

Primary route single/dual carriageway
Hauptverbindungsstraße
1 Fahrspur/2 Fahrspuren
Route principale 1 voie/2 voies

Other A road single/dual carriageway
Andere Straße der Klasse A
1 Fahrspur/2 Fahrspuren
Autre route catégorie A
1 voie/2 voies

B road single/dual carriageway
Straße der Klasse B
1 Fahrspur/2 Fahrspuren
Route catégorie B 1 voie/2 voies

Unclassified road, single/dual carriageway
Nicht klassifizierte Straße
1 Fahrspur/2 Fahrspuren
Route non classifiée 1 voie/2 voies

Road under construction
Straße im Bau
Route en construction

Narrow primary, other A or B road with passing places (Scotland)
enge Hauptverbindungsstraße, 'A' bzw. 'B' Straße mit Aus-weichstellen (in Schottland)
Route principale étroite/autre route catégorie A ou B étroite avec places d'évitement (en Ecosse)

Road tunnel
Straßentunnel
Tunnel routier

Steep gradient (arrows point downhill)
Steigung/Gefälle (Pfeile weisen bergab)
Montée/Descente (à la flèche dirigée vers le bas)

Road toll
Straße mit Gebühr
Route à péage

Distance in miles between symbols
Entfernungen in Meilen zwischen Zeichen
Distance en milles entre symboles

Vehicle ferry – Great Britain
Autofähre – Inland
Bac pour automobiles en Grande Bretagne

Vehicle ferry – Continental
Autofähre – Ausland
Bac pour automobile – à l'étranger

Hovercraft ferry
Luftkissenfähre
Aéroglisseur

Airport
Flughafen
Aéroport

Heliport
Hubschrauberlandungsplatz
Héliport

Railway line/in tunnel
Bahnlinie/im Tunnel
Voie ferrée/sous tunnel

Railway station and level crossing
Bahnhof und Bahnübergang
Gare et passage à niveau

AA Centre – full services
AA-Hauptdienststelle
Centre AA principal

AA Road Service Centre – limited services
AA-Straßendienststelle – beschränkte Dienstleistungen
Centre-service routier auxiliare

AA Port Services – open as season demands
AA-Hafendienststelle – Öffnungszeiten von Jahreszeit abhängig
AA Centre-service de port – heures d'ouvertures varient selon la saison

AA and RAC telephones
AA bzw. RAC-Telefon
Téléphone AA et RAC

BT telephone in isolated places
Öffentliche Telefonzelle in abgelegenen Gebieten
Téléphone PTT aux endroits isolés

Urban area/village
Stadtgebiet/Dorf
Agglomération/Village

Spot height in metres
Höhenangabe in Meters
Altitude en mètres

River, canal, lake
Fluss, Kanal, See
Fleuve, canal, lac

Sandy beach
Sandstrand
Plage de sable

National boundary
Landesgrenze
Frontière nationale

Page overlap and number
Hinweiszahlen für die Anschlußkarten
Suite à la page indiquée

TOURIST INFORMATION : FREMDENVERKEHR : RENSEIGNEMENTS TOURISTIQUES

Tourist Information Centre
Informationsbüro
Syndicat d'initiative

Tourist Information Centre (summer only)
Informationsbüro (nur im Sommer)
Syndicat d'initiative (seulement en été)

Abbey, cathedral or priory
Abtei, Dom, Kloster
Abbaye, cathédrale, prieuré

Ruined abbey, cathedral or priory
Abtei-, Dom-, Klosterruine
Abbaye, cathédrale, prieuré en ruines

Castle
Schloss/Burg
Château

Historic house
Historisches Gebäude
Edifice d'intérêt historique

Museum or art gallery
Museum/Kunstgalerie
Musée/galerie d'art

Industrial interest
Von industriellem Interesse
De l'intérêt industriel

Garden
Gartenanlage
Jardin

Arboretum
Arboretum
Arborétum

Country park
Park auf dem Lande
Parc promenade

Theme park
Freizeitpark
Parc d'attractions

Zoo
Tiergarten
Zoo

Wildlife collection – mammals
Tierpark – Säugetiere
Réserve d'animaux sauvages/mammifères

Wildlife collection – birds
Tierpark – Vögel
Réserve Ornithologique

Aquarium
Aquarium
Aquarium

Nature reserve
Naturschutzgebiet
Réserve naturelle

Nature trail
Naturlehrpfad
Sentier de découverte de la nature

Forest drive
Waldstraße
Route forestière

Long distance footpath
Fernwanderweg
Sentier de grande randonnée

Hill fort
Prähistorische Festungsanlage
Colline fortifiée

Roman antiquity
Überreste aus der Römerzeit
Antiquités romaines

Prehistoric monument
Prähistorisches Monument
Monument préhistorique

Battle site with year
Schlachtfeld mit Datum
Champ de bataille et Date

Preserved railway/steam centre
Museumbahn/Dampflokomotivmuseum
Chemin de fer touristique/musée de la vapeur

Cave
Höhle
Grotte

Windmill
Windmühle
Moulin à vent

AA viewpoint
AA-Aussichtspunkt
AA-Panorama

Picnic site
Picknickplatz
Lieu pour pique-nique

Golf course
Golfplatz
Golf

County cricket ground
wichtiger Kricketspielplatz
Terrain de cricket important

Horse racing
Pferderennbahn
Hippodrome

Show jumping/equestrian circuit
Reit-und Springturnier
Saut d'obstacles/circuit equestre

Motor racing circuit
Autorennen
Courses automobiles

Gliding centre
Segelflugplatz
Centre de vol à voile

Coastal launching site
Slipanlage für Boote
Air de mise à l'eau

Ski slope – natural
Skigelände
Piste de ski

Ski slope – artificial
Skigelände – künstlich
Piste de ski artificielle

Other places of interest
Weitere Sehenswürdigkeiten
Autres curiosités

Boxed symbols indicate attractions within urban areas
Das Einrahmen eines Zeichens bedeutet: die Sehenswürdigkeit befindet sich in einem Stadtgebiet
Dans le cas où le symbole est dans une case, la curiosité se trouve dans une localité

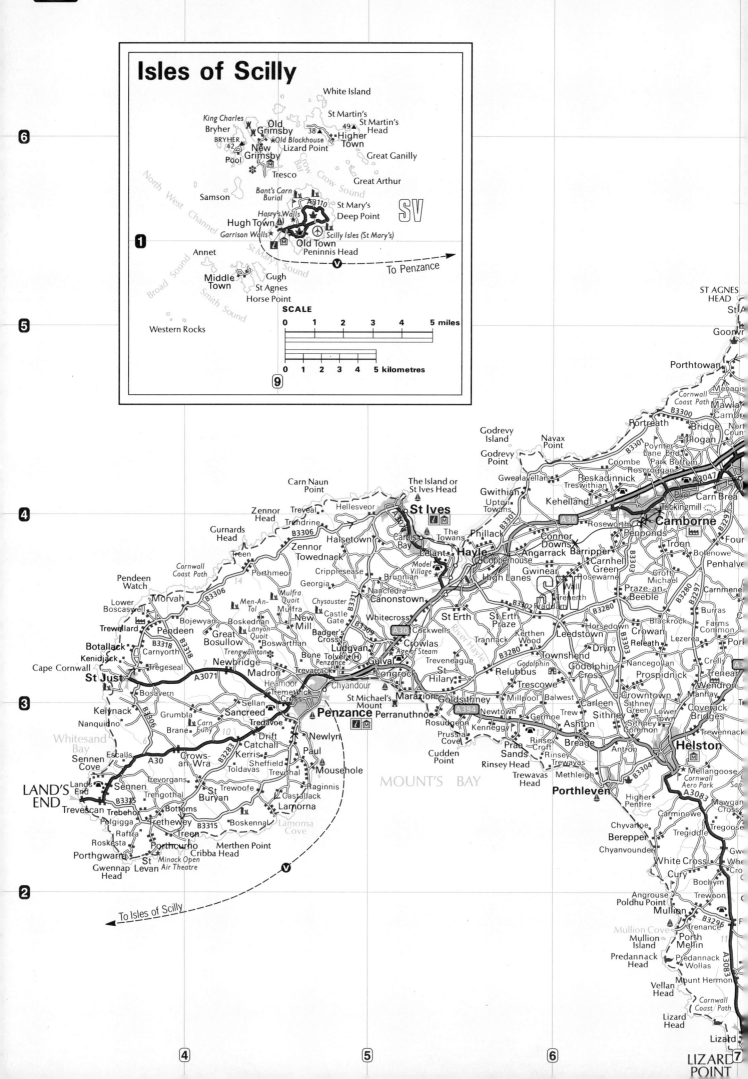

Isles of Scilly

White Island

King Charles
Bryher
BRYHER
42
New
Grimsby
Pool
Old
Grimsby
Old Blockhouse
Lizard Point
38
49
St Martin's
St Martin's
Head
Higher
Town

Great Ganilly

Tresco

Great Arthur

Samson

Bant's Carn
Burial

A3110
St Mary's
Deep Point

SV

Harry's Walls

Hugh Town
Garrison Walls
Old Town
Peninnis Head
Scilly Isles (St Mary's)

To Penzance

Annet

Middle
Town
Gugh
St Agnes
Horse Point

North West Channel

Broad Sound

St Mary's Sound

Smith Sound

Crow Sound

Crow Sound

Western Rocks

SCALE

0 1 2 3 4 5 miles

0 1 2 3 4 5 kilometres

9

ST AGNES
HEAD
St A
Goonvr
Porthtowan

Godrevy
Island
Godrevy
Point

Navax
Point

Gwealavellan
Treswithian
Kehelland

Coombe
Roscroggan

Portreath
Bridge
Nort
Coun

Cornwall
Coast Path

Menagis
Mawla
Cambr
B3300

Park Bottom
Poynter's
Lane End

B3301

B3047

Pool
Carn Brea
Tuckingmill
Roseworthy

Carn Naun
Point

Zennor
Head

Treveal

Trendrine

Hellesveor

The Island or
St Ives Head

St Ives

The Towans

Phillack

Roseworthy

A30

Connor
Downs

Camborne

Penponds

Troon

Four

Gurnards
Head

B3306

Zennor

Carbis
Bay

Lelant

Hayle

Angarrack

Barripper

Bolenowe

Penhalv

Towednack

Copperhouse

Carnhell
Green

Crofty
Michael

Carnmene

Treen

Porthmeor

Model
Village

High Lanes

Gwinear

Rosewarne

B3280

B3297

Pendeen
Watch

Cornwall
Coast Path

Cripplesease

Georgia

Brunnian

Nancledra

Praze-an-
Beeble

Burras

Lower
Boscaswell
Morvah

B3306

Men-An-
Tol

Mulfra
Quoit

Chysauster

Whitecross

Canonstown

St Erth

St Erth
Praze

Pladam

B3280

Crowan

Horsedown

Blackrock

Refrom
Common

Lezerea

Porl

Trewellard

Pendeen

Bojewyan

Boskednan

Mulfra

New
Mill

Castle
Gate

Ludgvan

Cockwells

Kerthen
Wood

Drym

Releath

Treneath

Botallack

Great
Bosullow

Lanyon
Quoit

Badger's
Cross

Crowlas

Trannack

Townshend

Nancegollan

Crelly

Kenidjack
Carnyorth

B3318

Boswarthan

Bone Tolver

Trevarrack

Age of Steam

Treneague

Leedstown

Godolphin
Cross

Godolphin

Prospidnick

Wendron

Cape Cornwall

Tregeseal

Newbridge

Trengwainton

Madron

Longrock

St
Hilary

Relubbus

Trescowe

St Just

Bosavern

Heamoor
Tremethick
Cross

Chyandour

Marazion

Goldsithney

Millpool

Balwest

Carleen

Crowntown

Coverack
Bridges

Kelynack

Sancreed

Sellan

St Michael's
Mount

Penzance

Perranuthnoe

Newtown

Trew

Sithney

Germoe

Ashton

Sithney
Green

Lower
Town

Manhay

Helston

Nanquidno

Grumbla

Tredavoe

Prussia
Cove

Rosudgeon

Kennegg

Ashton

Breage

Antron

Trewennack

Brane

Carn
Euny

Drift

Cudden
Point

Rinsey
Croft

Rinsey

Sithney
Common

Whitesand
Bay

Escalls

A30

Crows-
an-Wra

Catchall

Kerris

Sheffield

Trevithal

Paul

Mousehole

Rinsey Head

Trewavas

Methleigh

Mellangoose
Cornwall
Aero Park

Sennen
Cove

Sennen

Trevorgans

Toldavas

Newlyn

Trewavas
Head

Porthleven

Higher
Pentire

MOUNT'S BAY

Trengothal

St
Buryan

Trewoofe

Raginnis

Castallack

Carminowe

Tregoose

LAND'S
END

Land's
End

Trevescan

Trebehor

Bottoms

Lamorna

Chyvarloe

Berepper

Tregiddle

Polgigga

Trethewey

B3315

Boskennal

Lamorna
Cove

Chyvaunder

White Cross

Gw
Whe
Cro

Raftra

Treen

Merthen Point

Cury

Bochym

Roskesta

Porthcurno

Cribba Head

Angrouse
Poldhu Point

Trewoon

Porthgwarra

St
Levan

Minack Open
Air Theatre

Mullion

B3296

Gwennap
Head

Trenance

Mullion Cove

Porth
Mellin

A3083

To Isles of Scilly

Mullion
Island

Predannack
Head

Predannack
Wollas

Vellan
Head

Mount Hermon

Cornwall
Coast Path

Lizard
Head

Lizard

LIZARD
POINT

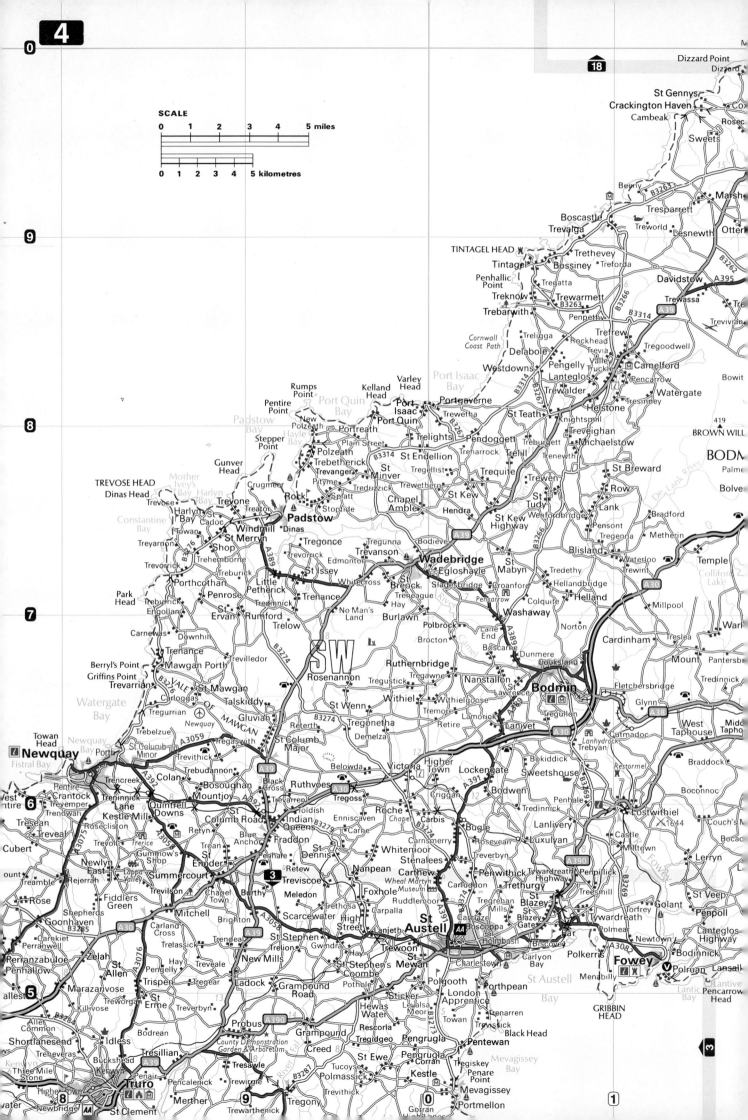

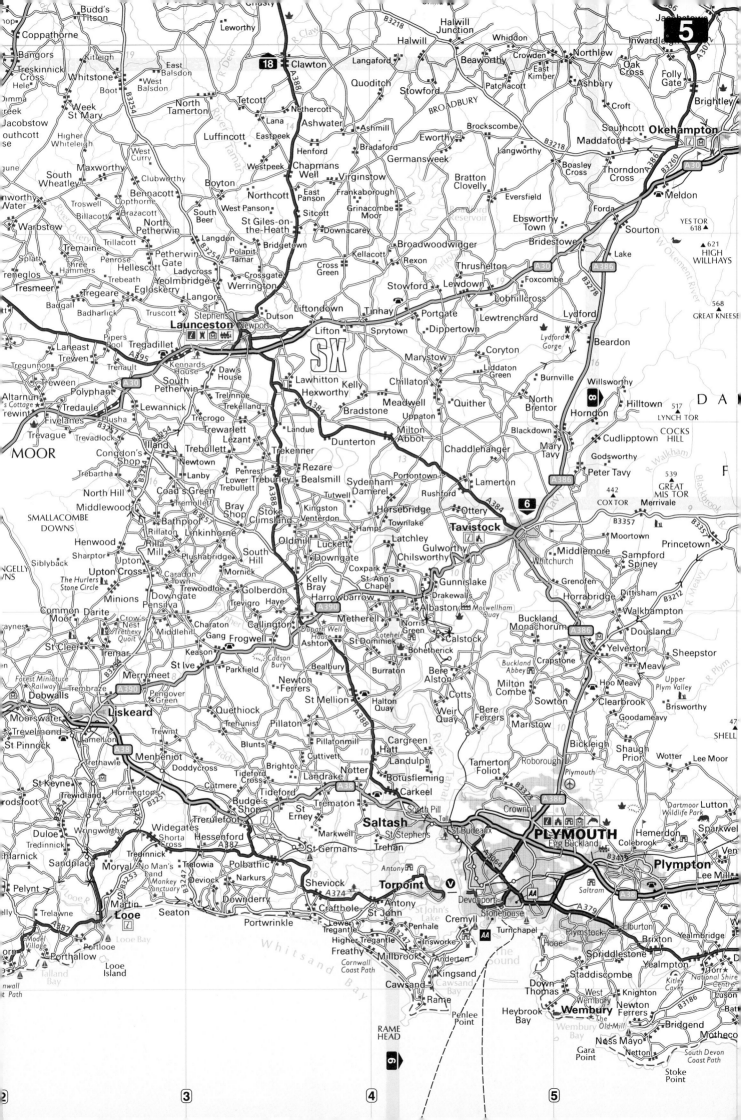

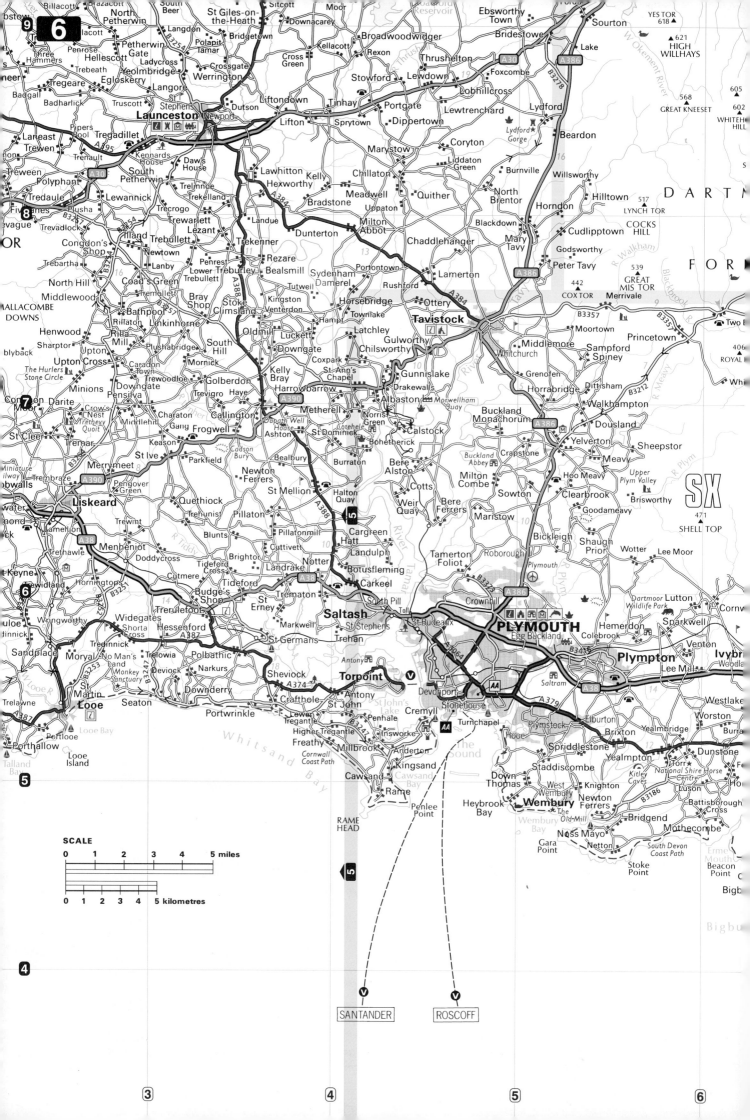

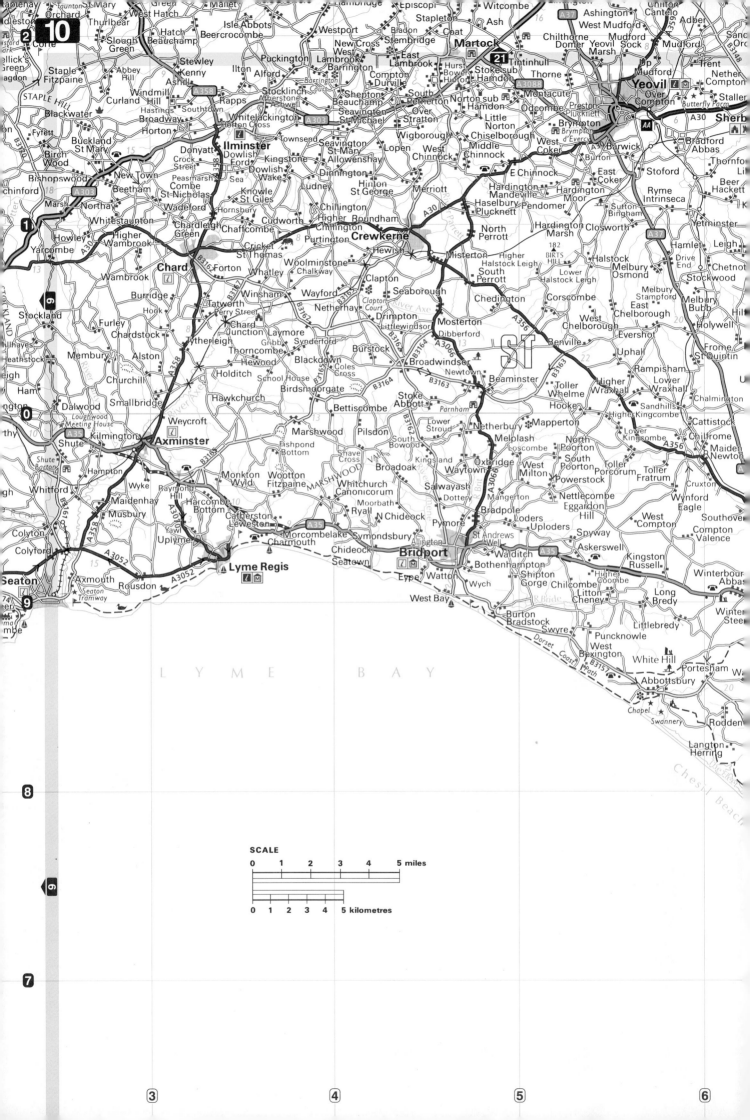

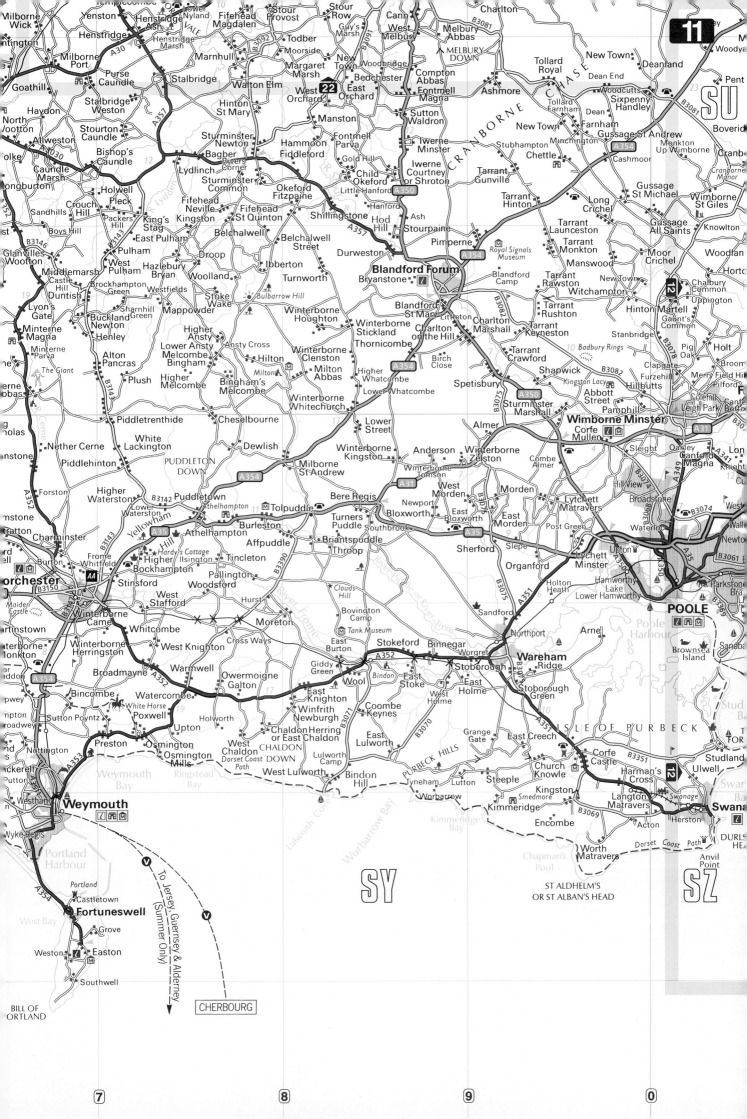

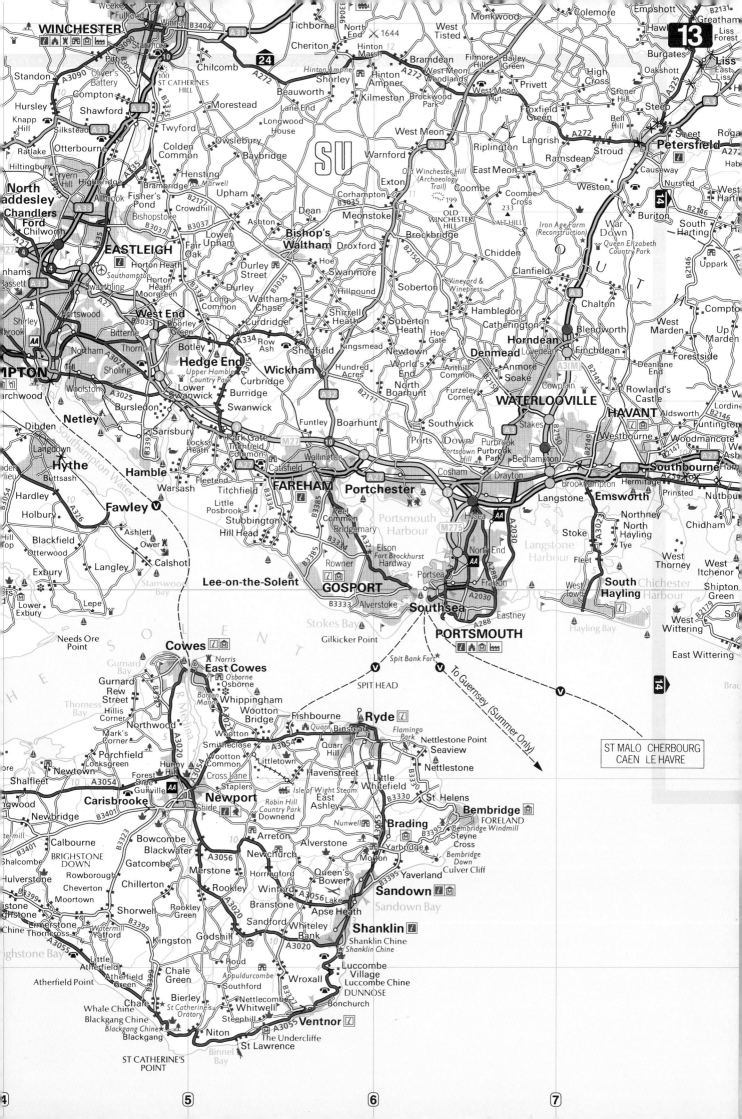

5

North West
Point

LUNDY
ISLAND

142

Marisco
Surf Point

SCALE

0   1   2   3   4   5 miles

0 1 2 3 4   5 kilometres

Bull Point

Morte Point

Rockham
Bay

Lee
Bay

Mortehoe

B3343

Woolacombe

B3231

Morte Bay

Pickwell

Baggy Point   Putsborough

Croyde Bay

Bu

George

Croyde Bay

Darracott   Knov

Croyde

Lobb

Saunton

B3231

Wraf

Braunton

4

BARNSTAPLE

OR

BIDEFORD BAY

Appledore

Westward Ho!   Northam

We

3

HARTLAND
POINT   Shipload
Bay

Eastlei

A386

Pil

Titchberry

Abbotsham

Bideford

Damehole
Point

Somerset and
North Devon
Coast Path

Brownsham   Clovelly
Court   Clovelly

Fairy
Cross   Ford

Yeo
Vale

A386

Landcro

Hartland   Velly   Sierra

Horns
Cross

Buck's
Mills

Woodtown

Littleham

Hartland
Quay   Stoke

B3248

Dyke

Buck's
Cross

Goldworthy

Saltrens

Spekes Mill
Mouth

Cranford

Parkham

Buckland
Brewer

Monkleig

Milford   Philham

Woolfardisworthy

Cabbacott

Elmscott

Parkham
Ash

Melbury

Frithelstock

2

Hardisworthy

Frithelstock
Stone

Taddipo

South
Hole   Ashmansworthy

West
Putford   East Putford

Thornehillhead

B322

Southcott

A388

Welcombe   Darracott

Meddon

Langtree

Mead   Woolley

East
Youlstone

Dinworthy

Colscott

Bulkworthy

Lan
We

Gooseham   Eastcott

16

West
Youlstone

Haytown

Stibb
Cross

Berry
Cross

Morwenstow

Higher Sharpnose
Point   Shop

Bradworthy

Abbots
Bickington

Newton
St Petrock

Lower Sharpnose
Point

Kimworthy

Alfardisworthy

Sutcombe

Venngreen

Milton Damerel

Steeple
Point

Kilkhampton   Darracott

Sutcombemill

Sandy
Mouth

Stibb

A39

B3254

Thurdon

Soldon

Soldon
Cross

Thornbury   Shebbear

Bucklar
Filleig

1

Northcott
Mouth

Poughill   Venn

Dunsdon

Holsworthy
Beacon

A388

Little
Lashbrook

Bradford

Priestacott

Dippermill

Bude

Maer

Hersham
Bush

Grimscott

Lana

Brendon

Cookbury

Hole

Flexbury

Stratton   Launcells

Kingford

Chilsworthy

Cookbury
Wick

Holemoor

Lashbrook

Black
Torrin

Bude   Bude
Bay

Launcells
Cross

10

Pancrasweek

Anvil
Corner

13

Lynstone

A3072

Red Cross

Holsworthy

Brandis
Corner

Upton   Buttsbear
Cross

Derril

Derriton

Whimble

A3072

Odham

Helebridge

Bridgerule

Chasty

Hollacombe

Chilla

Marhamchurch

Pyworthy

Widemouth
Bay   Budd's
Titson

Leworthy

B3218

Halwill
Junction

Box's Shop

Halwill

Whiddo

0

Millook

Coppathorne

R. Claw

Dizzard Point

Poundstock   Bangors

Kitleigh

19

Clawton   Langaford

5   Beaworthy

Dizzard   Penlean

Treskinnick
Cross   Hele

East
Balsdon

A388   Quoditch

Stowford

Patchacot

St Gennys   Coxford

mma

Whitstone   Boot

West
Balsdon

BROADBURY

ackington Haven   Tregole

Trenceek

Week
St Mary

B3254

th
Tamerton

Tetcott

Nethercott

Cambeak   Rosecare

Lana

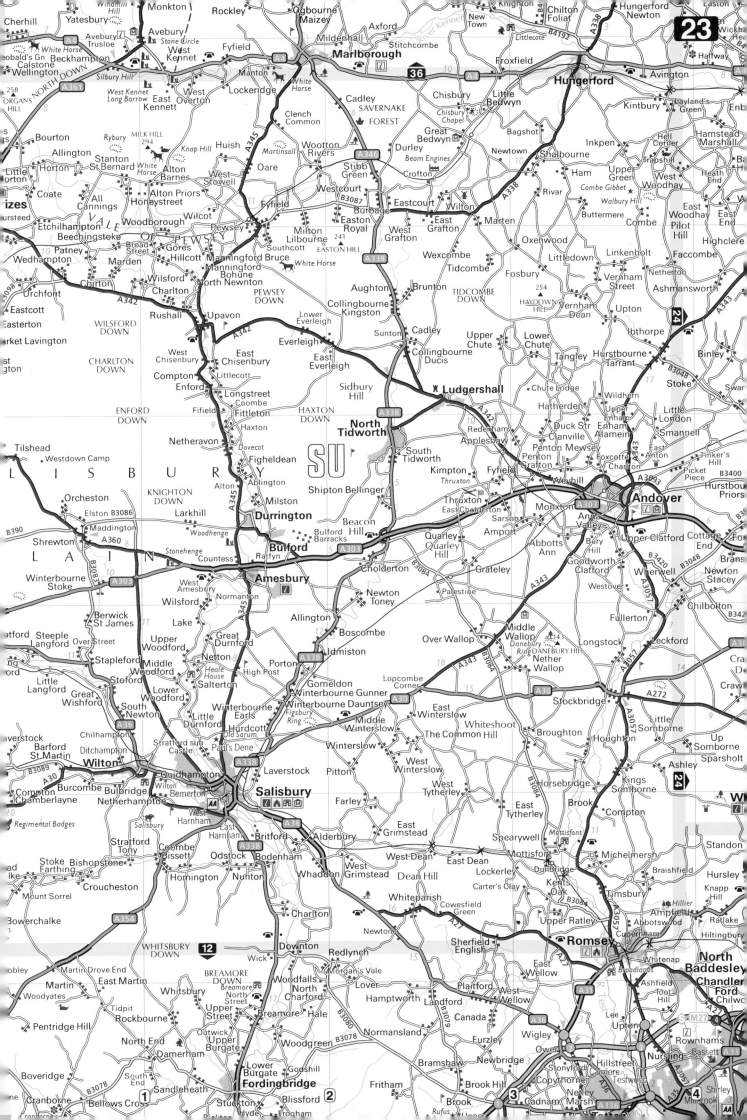

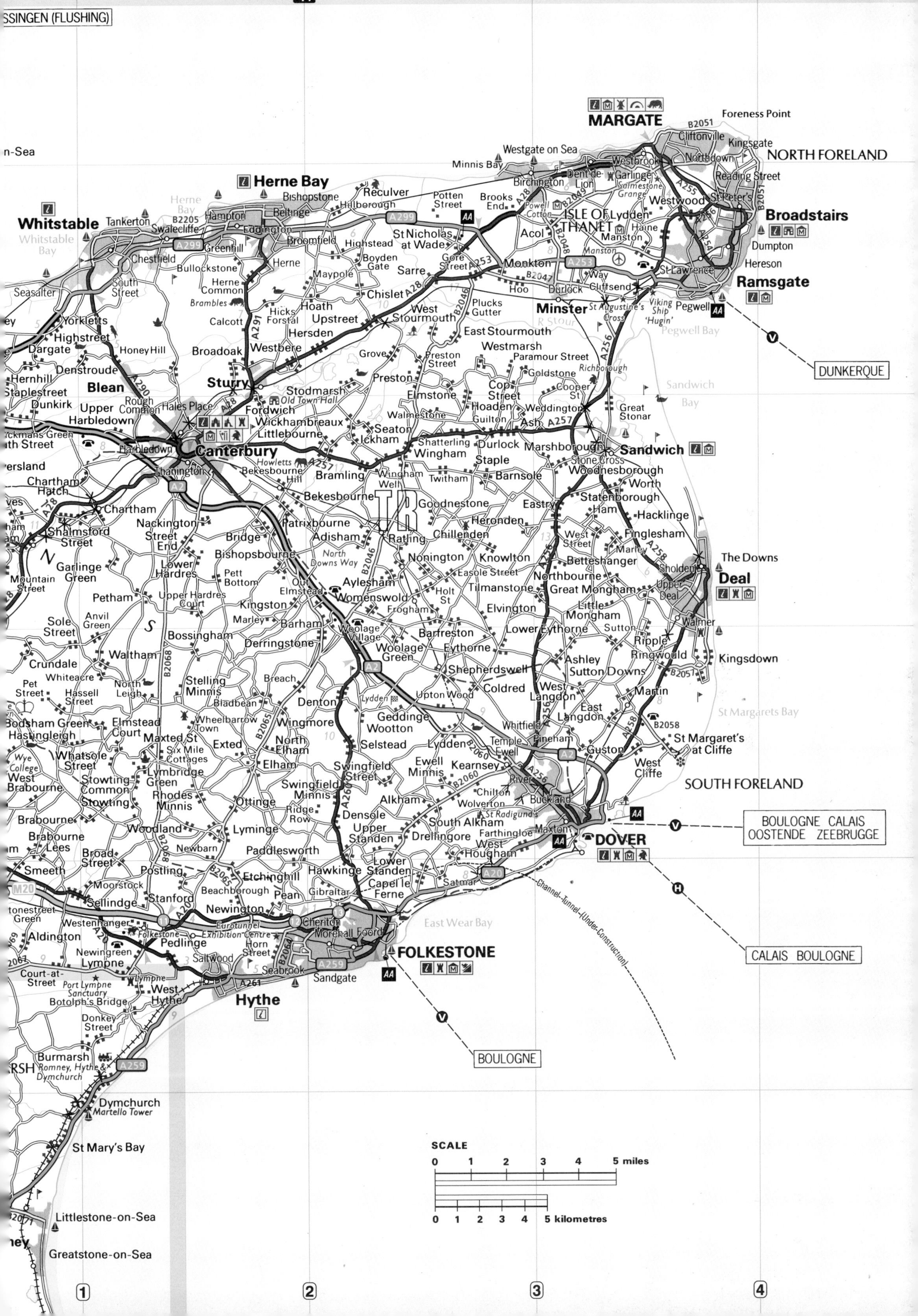

VLISSINGEN (FLUSHING)

MARGATE
Foreness Point
Westgate on Sea Cliftonville Kingsgate
Minnis Bay Westbrook Northdown NORTH FORELAND
Herne Bay Birchington Dent-de-Lion Garlinge Reading Street
Bishopstone Reculver Brooks End Powell St Peter's
Whitstable Hampton Beltinge Hilborough Potten Street Cotton Westwood **Broadstairs**
Tankerton Eddington ISLE OF Lydden Haine
Swalecliffe Greenhill Broomfield Highstead St Nicholas at Wade THANET Dumpton
Seasalter Chestfield Herne Gore Street Monkton Manston Hereson
Yorkletts Bullockstone Maypole Sarre Hoo Durlock **Ramsgate**
Highstreet Herne Common Hoath Chislet West Stourmouth **Minster** St Augustine's Cross Pegwell
Dargate South Street Hicks Forstal Upstreet Plucks Gutter Viking Ship 'Hugin' Pegwell Bay
Denstroude Brambles Hersden East Stourmouth Cliffsend
Hernhill Broadoak Westbere Westmarsh Richborough DUNKERQUE
Blean Honey Hill Grove Preston Street Paramour Street Sandwich Bay
Staplestreet Rough Common Stodmarsh Preston Goldstone Great Stonar
Dunkirk Hales Place Fordwich Cop Street Cooper St Sandwich Bay
Upper Harbledown Wickhambreaux Elmstone Hoaden Weddington
Littlebourne Walmestone Guilton Ash Woodnesborough **Sandwich**
Canterbury Seaton Ickham Shatterling Durlock Marshborough Worth
Harbledown Wingham Staple Barnsole Stone Cross Statenborough
Thanington Bekesbourne Hill Howletts Wingham Well Twitham Eastry Ham Hacklinge
Chartham Hatch Bramling Goodnestone Heronden West Marsh Finglesham The Downs
Chartham Bekesbourne Rathling Chillenden Marley **Deal**
Shalmsford Street Patrixbourne Adisham Nonington Knowlton Betteshanger Sholden
Nackington Street End Bishopsbourne Aylesham Easole Street Northbourne Upper Deal
Garlinge Green Bridge Pett Bottom Womenswold Holt St Tilmanstone Great Mongham Walmer
Lower Hardres Out Elmstead Frogham Elvington Little Mongham
Petham Upper Hardres Court Kingston Woolage Village Eythorne Lower Eythorne Sutton Ripple Ringwould
Sole Street Marley Barham Woolage Green Barfreston Ashley Kingsdown
Anvil Green Bossingham Derringstone Shepherdswell Sutton Downs Martin
Waltham Stelling Minnis Breach Coldred West Langdon
Crundale Whiteacre North Leigh Bladbean Denton Upton Wood East Langdon St Margarets Bay
Pet Street Hassell Street Wheelbarrow Town Wingmore Geddinge Whitfield St Margaret's at Cliffe
Bodsham Green Elmsted Court North Elham Wootton Temple Ewell Pineham Guston
Hastingleigh Maxted St Exted Selstead Lydden West Cliffe
Whatsole Street Six Mile Cottages Elham Swingfield Street Ewell Minnis SOUTH FORELAND
Stowting Common Lymbridge Green Rhodes Minnis Swingfield Minnis Kearsney Chilton
West Brabourne Stowting Ottinge Ridge Row Alkham Wolverton River Buckland
Wye College Woodland Lyminge Densole South Alkham St Radigund's
Brabourne Newbarn Upper Standen Drellingore Farthingloe Maxton Calais Boulogne
Brabourne Lees Broad Street Paddlesworth West Houghan **DOVER**
Smeeth Postling Etchinghill Hawkinge Lower Standen Satmar
Moorstock Beachborough Pean Capel le Ferne BOULOGNE CALAIS
Sellindge Stanford Newington Gibraltar OOSTENDE ZEEBRUGGE
Stonestreet Green Westenhanger Eurotunnel Exhibition Centre Cheriton East Wear Bay Channel Tunnel (Under Construction)
Aldington Folkestone Horn Street Morehall CALAIS BOULOGNE
Newingreen Pedlinge Saltwood **FOLKESTONE**
Lympne Seabrook Sandgate
Court-at-Street Port Lympne Sanctuary West Hythe **Hythe**
Botolph's Bridge
Donkey Street
Burmarsh Romney, Hythe & Dymchurch
BOULOGNE
Dymchurch Martello Tower
St Mary's Bay
Littlestone-on-Sea
Greatstone-on-Sea

SCALE
0 1 2 3 4 5 miles
0 1 2 3 4 5 kilometres

1 2 3 4

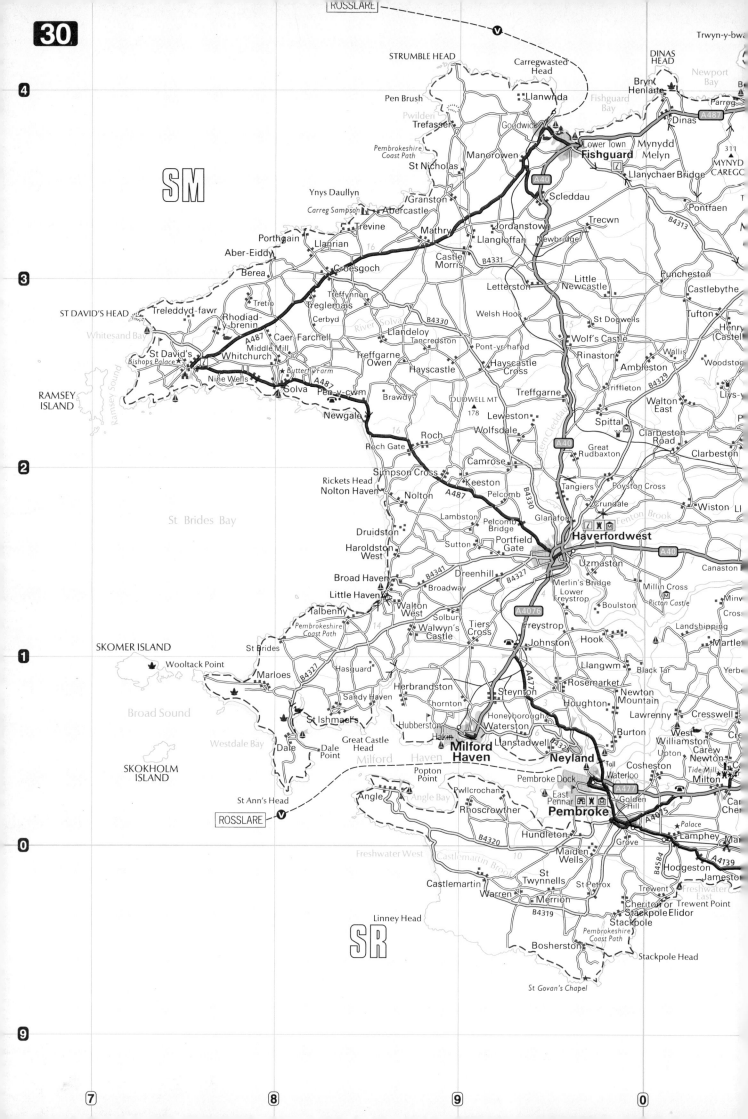

56

C A R D I G A N

B A Y

9

SCALE

| 0 | 1 | 2 | 3 | 4 | 5 miles |

| 0 | 1 | 2 | 3 | 4 | 5 kilometres |

8

SN

7

Llansant
Llar

A487

Aberarth
B4577

Aberaeron

Monachty

Llyswen

Cilc

6

New Quay
Llanina
Gilfachrheda
Llwyncelyn

Maen-y-groes
B4342
Oakford

Cross
Inn
Llanarth
Nanternis
A487
B4342
Dihewyd
B4339

Ynys-Lochtyn
Caerwedros
Mydroilyn

Llwyndafydd
A486

Llangranog
Synod Inn

Morfa
Pontgarreg
Ffynonddewi
311
B4338
Gorsgoch

Penbryn
B4334
Plwmp

B4321
324

Cardigan Island
Pentregat
Bwlchyfadfa

Parcllyn
Aberporth
Sarnau
Brynhoffnant

Gwbert-on-Sea
Verwig
Traethsaith
Talgarreg

5

Blaenannerch
Tan-y-groes
Capel Cynon
B4459

A487
Glynarthen
Cwrt-newydd

Penparc
Tremain
Blaenporth
Bettws Evan
Rhydlewis
B4334
Ffostrasol
Pontshaen
Cwmsychpant

Cardigan
Hawen
Penrhiwpal
Drefa

St Dogmaels
Beulah
Brongest
Tre-groes
Rhydowen
Llanwenog

Moylgrove
Bridgend
Clangoednior
Ponthirwaun
Troedyraur
Maeslyn
Croe
Pren-gwyn
Lla

Monington
A487
Llechryd
Llandygwydd
Llangynllo
A475
Rhyddlan

Pen-y-bryn
2
31
3
4
5

Pembrokeshire
Coast Path
B4546
B4548
A484
B4570
B4333
B4451

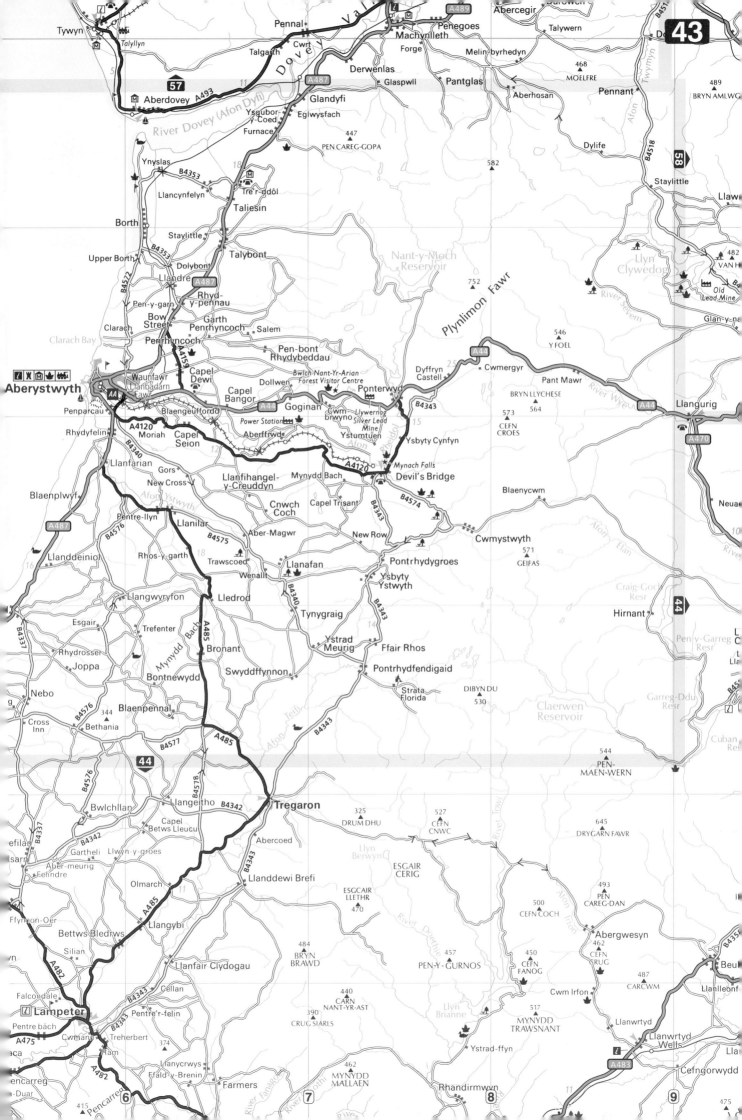

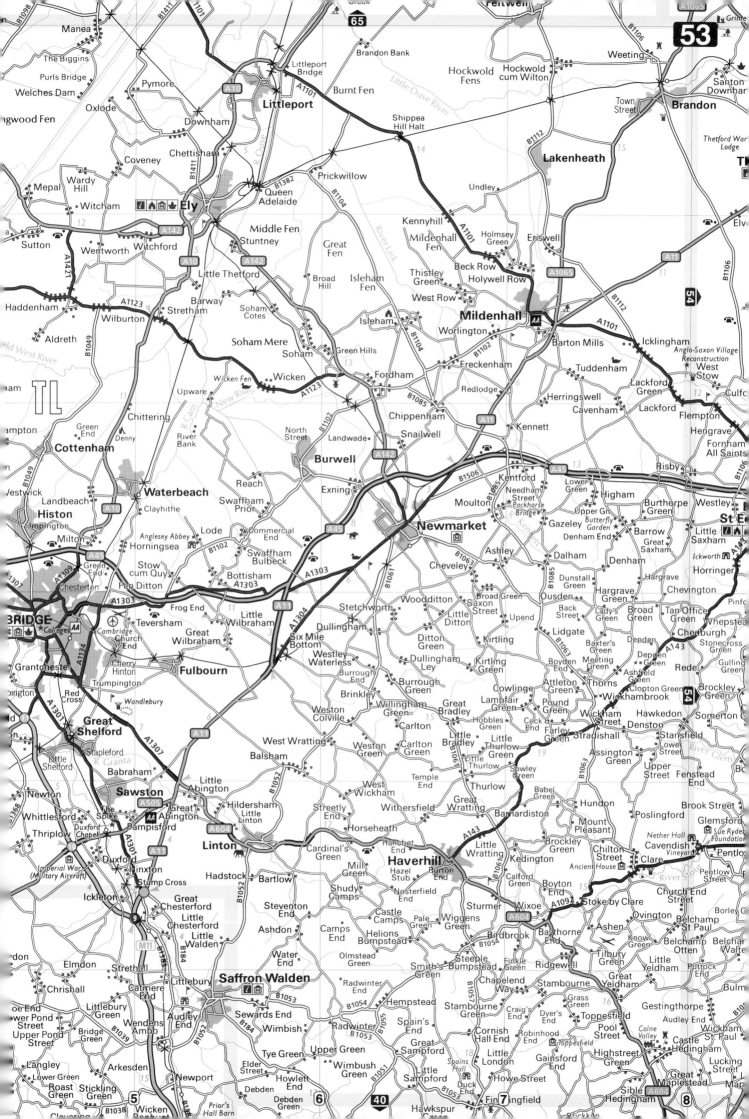

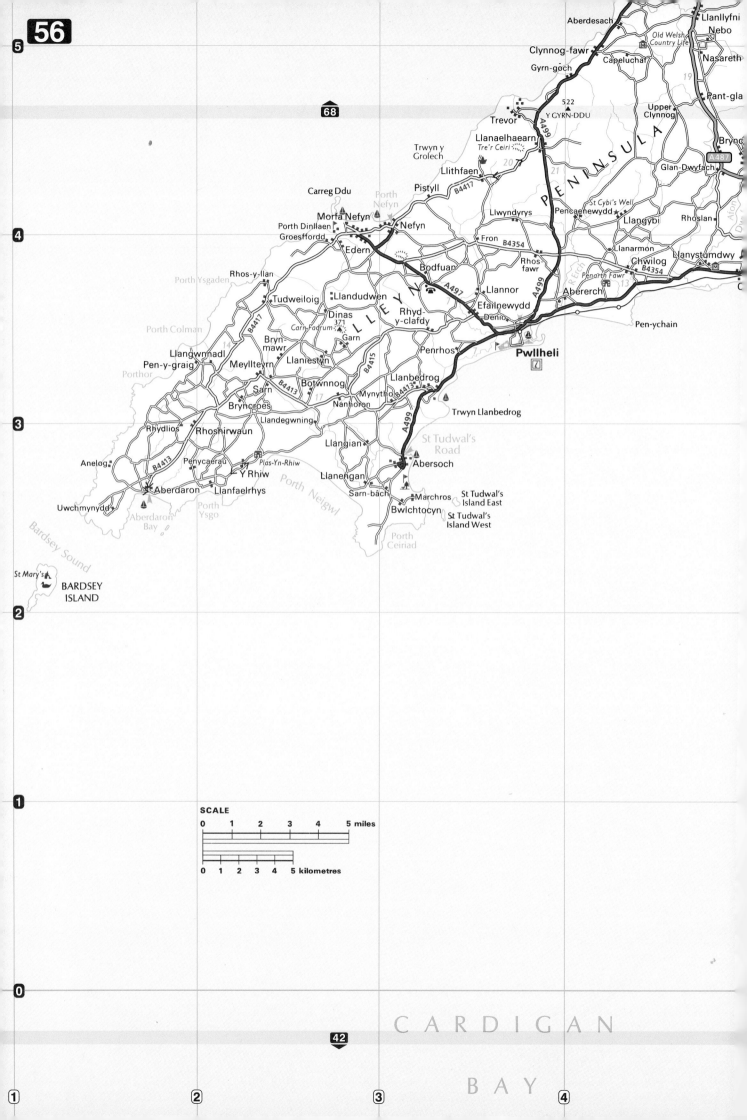

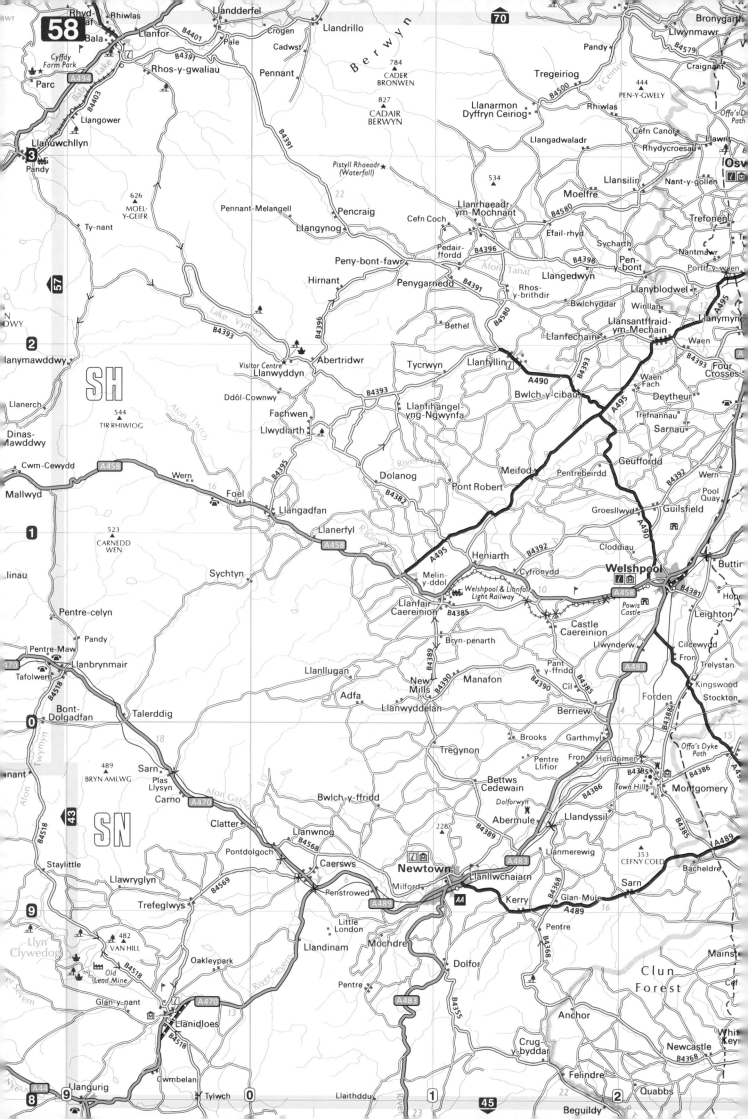

SCALE

0 1 2 3 4 5 miles

0 1 2 3 4 5 kilometres

East Runton
Cromer
Overstrand
Sidestrand
Trimingham
A148
B1436
Felbrigg
A140
Crossdale Street
Northrepps
Gimingham
A149
Southrepps
Mundesley
Lower Street
Thorpe Market
Trunch
Knapton
Paston
B1159
Bacton
Bradfield
Suffield
Antingham
Edingthorpe
Walcott
Colby
Swafield
B1150
Pollard Street
North Walsham
Edingthorpe Green
Witton
Ridlington
Happisburgh
Banningham
Spa Common
Ridlington Street
Whimpwell Green
Tungate
Felmingham
Meeting House Hill
Crostwight
Happisburgh Common
B1145
Honing
Hempstead
Tuttington
Skeyton Corner
Westwick
Bengates
Briggate
East Ruston
Ingham
Lessingham
Ingham Corner
Waxham
A140
Burgh next Aylsham
Skeyton
A149
Worstead
Dilham
Stalham
B1151
Stalham Green
Calthorpe Street
Sea Palling
B1159
Brampton
Swanton Abbot
Frankfort
Smallburgh
Low Street
Hickling
Horsey Corner
Buxton
Scottow
Sloley
Tunstead
A149
Sutton
Hickling Green
Horsey
Stratton Strawless
Sco Ruston
Pennygate
Wood Street
Hickling Heath
Hill Common
Lamas
Little Hautbois
Market Street
Beeston Hall
Barton Turf
Catfield Common
Horsey Windpump
B1159
Oxnead
St James
Crowgate Street
Neatishead
Catfield
West Somerton
Waterloo
Barton Broad
Hickling Broad
Horstead
Coltishall
B1354
Threehammer Common
Irstead
Sharp Green
Potter Heigham
Winterton-on-Sea
Hainford
Belaugh
Hoveton
Ludham
B1152
East Somerton
Frettenham
Wroxham
Johnson's Street
Bastwick
Martham
Cess
Hemsby
Hemsby Hole
Helena
A1062
Upper Street
Horning
Thurne
Repps
A149
Newport
Scratby
Newton St Faith
Crostwick
Upper Street
Broadland Conservation Centre
Woodbastwick
Thurne
B1152
Rollesby
Ormesby St Michael
California
A140
River Ant
River Thurne
Ranworth
Clippesby
Burgh St Margaret
Spixworth
Rackheath
Salhouse
Pilson Green
Cargate Green
Billockby
Filby
Ormesby St Margaret
Thrigby
Mautby
Caister-on-Sea
Horsham St Faith
Panxworth
South Walsham
Upton
A1064
Stokesby
West End
New Rackheath
B1140
Town Green
Acle
Runham
West Caister
Thorpe End
Little Plumstead
Great Plumstead
Burlingham Green
North Burlingham
Sprowston
Hemblington
Damgate
Runham
A47
Catton
Witton
Lingwood
Moulton St Mary
Tunstall
Great Yarmouth
New Lakenham
Thorpe St Andrew
A47
Blofield
Beighton
Halvergate
Southtown
Norwich
Postwick
Strumpshaw
South Burlingham
River Yare
Trowse Newton
Brundall
Buckenham
Southwood
Freethorpe
Burgh Castle
Kirby Bedon
Surlingham
Hassingham
Wickhampton
Berney Arms
Bradwell
Gorleston on Sea
Caister St Edmund
Bramerton
Rockland St Mary
Cantley
Freethorpe Common
Elm Grove
A140
Arminghall
Framingham Pigot
Claxton
Limpenhoe
Witton Green
Belton
Hobland Hall
Dunston
Hellington
Ashby St Mary
Carleton St Peter
Langley Street
Pettitts Crafts
Framingham Earl
Yelverton
Upper Stoke
Alpington
Mill Common
Hardley Street
Reedham
Fritton
A12
Hopton on Sea
Stoke Holy Cross
East Poringland
Thurton
Nogdam End
Lower Thurlton
St Olaves
Lound
A143
Browston Gn
Bergh Apton
Chedgrave
Norton Subcourse
Thorpe
Herringfleet
Hawe's Green
Shotesham
Howe
Brooke
Mundham
Loddon
Thurlton
Haddiscoe
Somerleyton
Blundeston
Corton
Saxlingham Thorpe
Stubbs Green
High Gn
Seething
Hales
Ravingham
B1074
Pleasurewood Hills
Saxlingham Nethergate
Saxlingham Green
Kirstead Green
Thwaite St Mary
Maypole Green
Toft Monks
Wheatacre
Gunton
TM
Hempnall
Hales Hall
A146
B1140
Bull's Green
Oulton
Upper Tasburgh
Road Green
B1135
Woodton
Kirby Cane
Stockton
Aldeby
Burgh St Peter
Oulton Broad
Stratton St Michael
Hempnall Green
Hedenham
Ellingham
A143
LOWESTOFT
Fritton
Lundy Green
Topcroft
Topcroft Street
B1332
Kirby Row
Broome
Geldeston
Gillingham
Kirkley
Morningthorpe
Shelton Green
Ditchingham
Upgate Street
Shipmeadow
Worlingham
Pakefield
Shelton
Bungay
Wainford
B1062
A146
Barnby
Carlton Colville
River Waveney
Mettingham
55 3 4 5 55

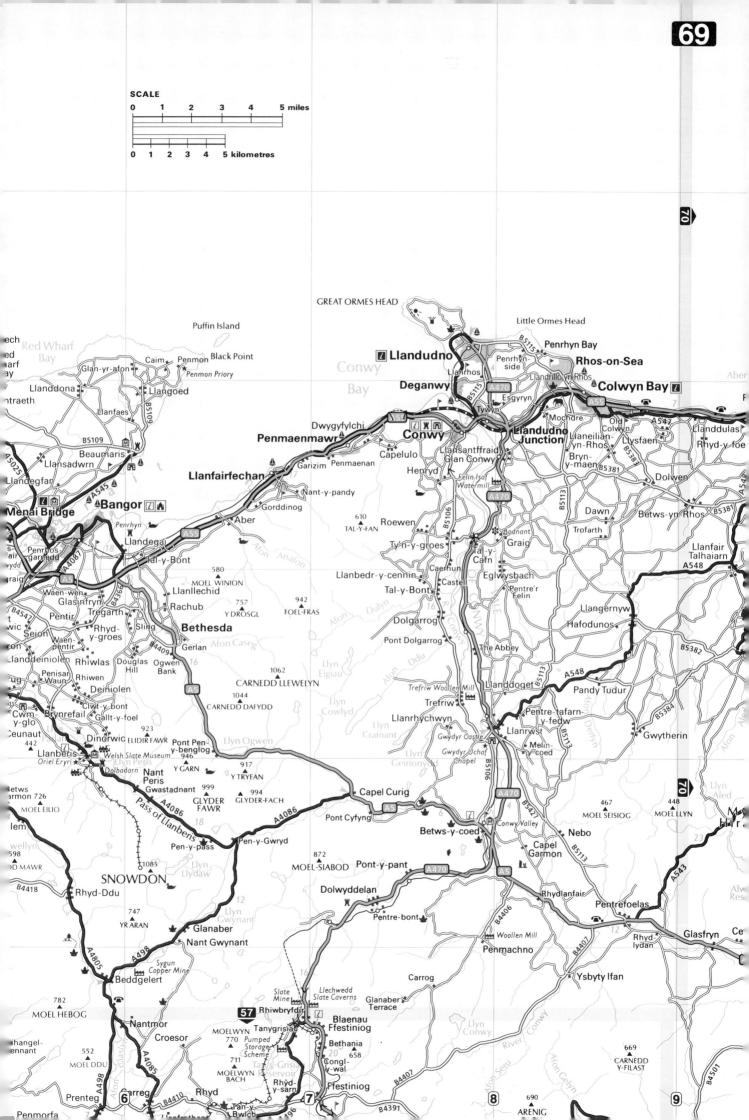

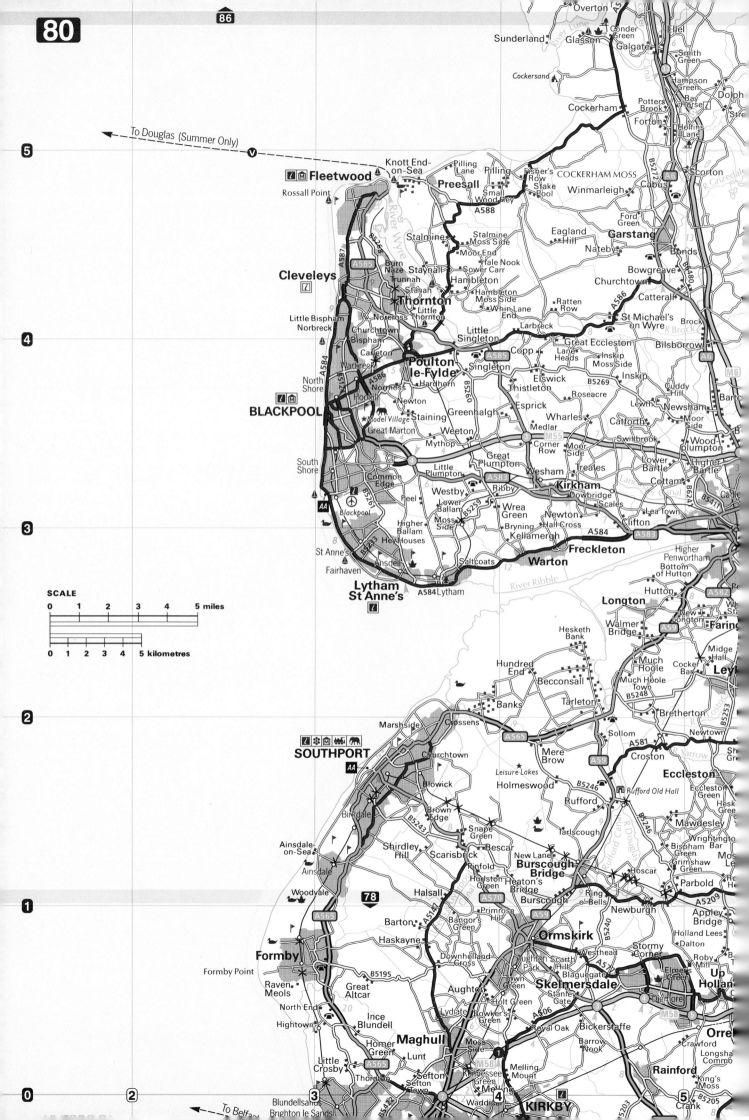

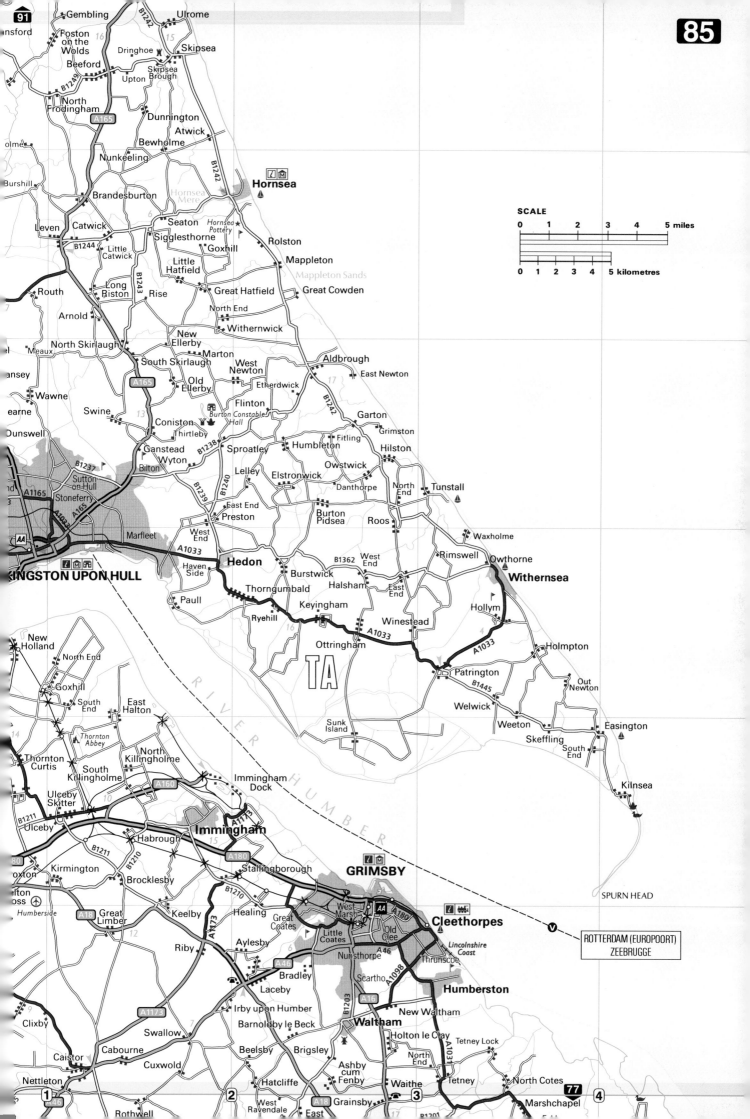

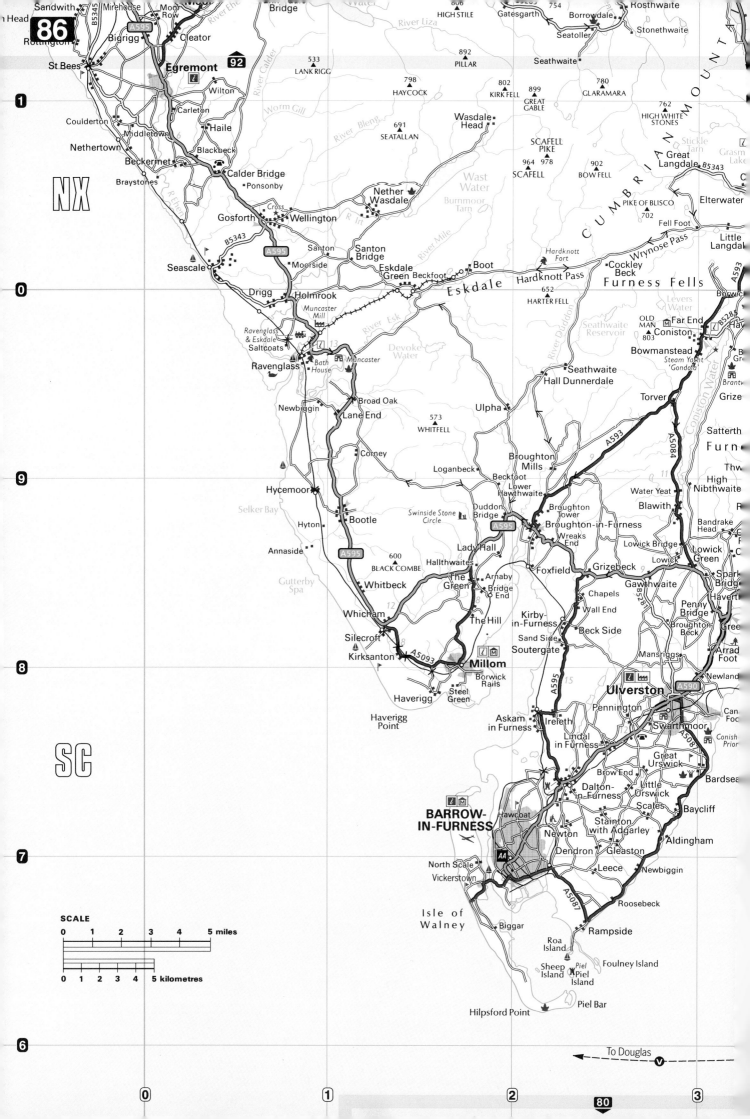

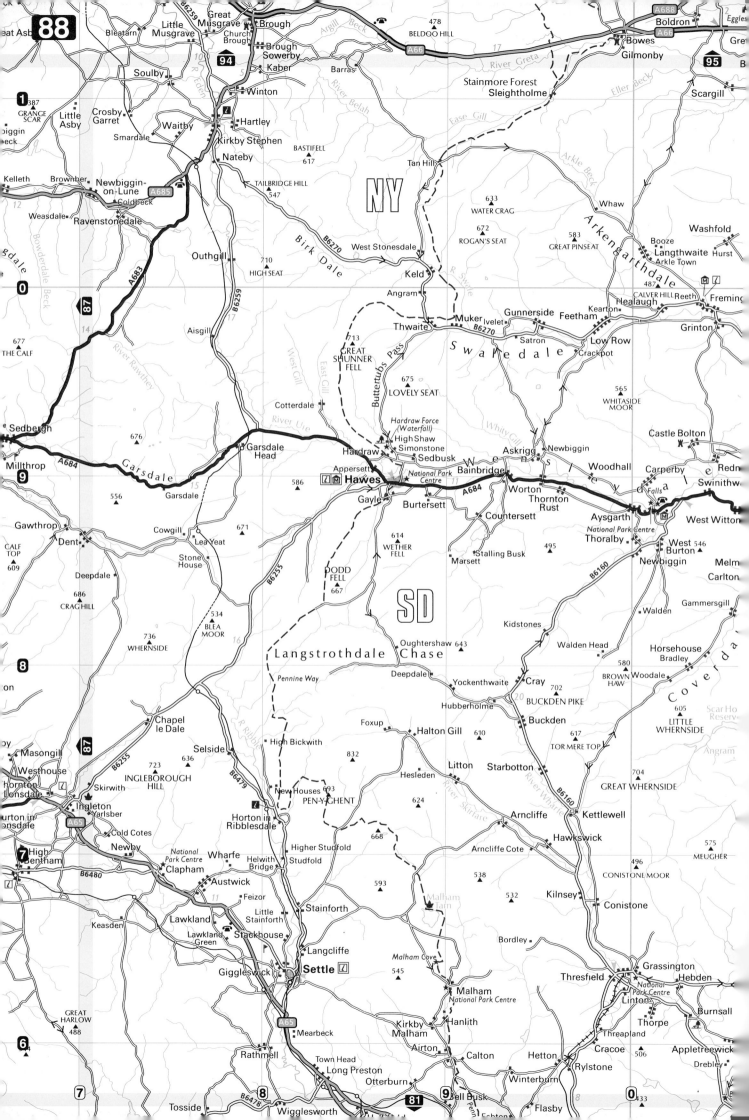

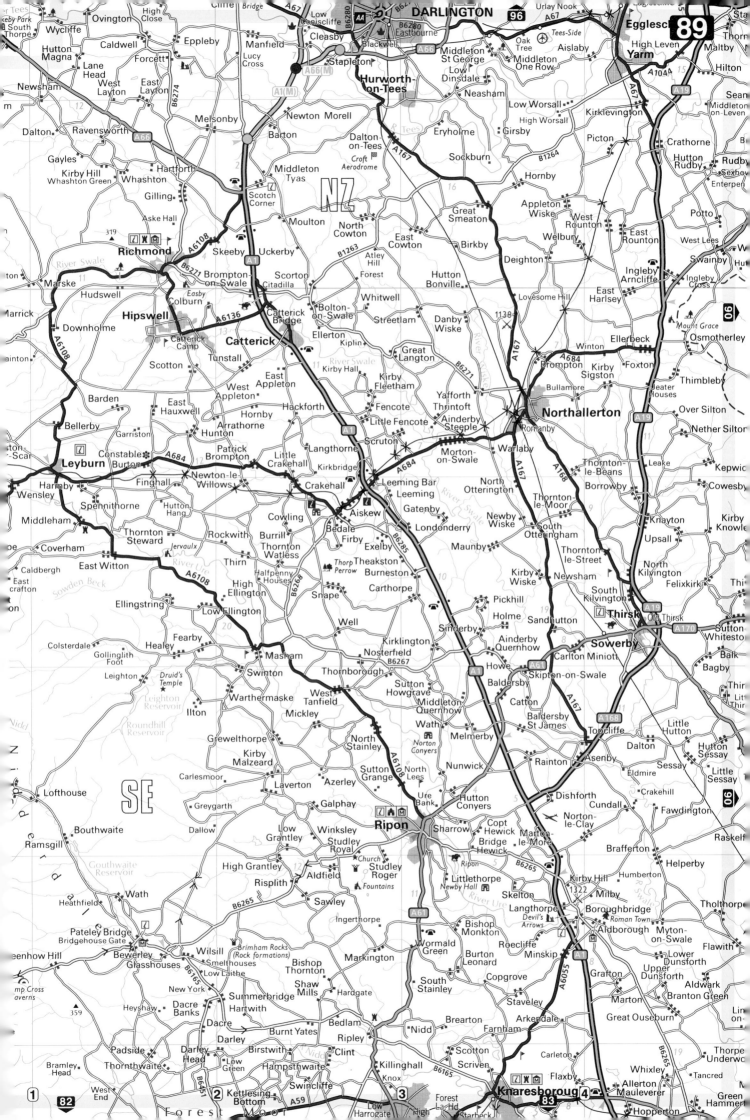

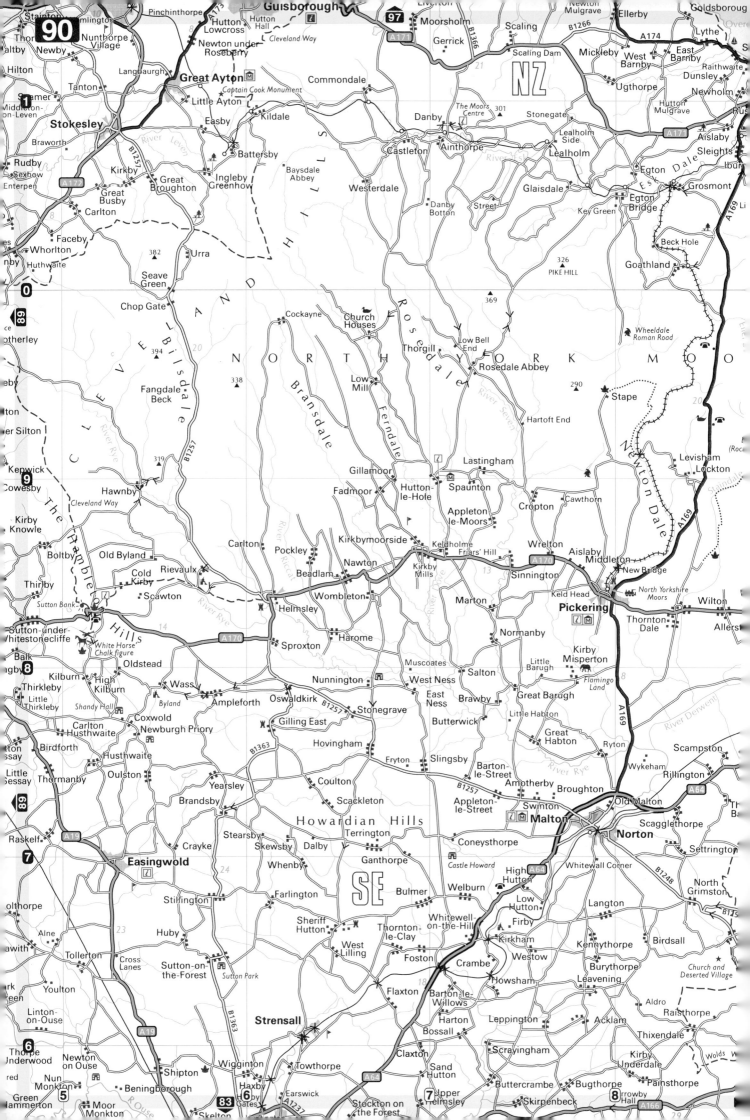

⚓ **Whitby** ⓘ ⛺ Ⓜ

Saltwick Bay

Stainsacre
Sneaton
parnby · High Hawsker
Low
Hawsker
neatonthorpe · Raw
Ness Point or
North Cheek
Robin Hood's Bay

Robin Hood's Bay

Fylingthorpe

Old Peak or
South Cheek

Ravenscar

A171

Staintondale

Hayburn Wyke
Cloughton
Newlands

Cloughton Wyke

Cloughton
Burniston
Cromer Point

Cleveland Way

R. Derwent
Silpho
Broxa
ckley
Hackness
Suffield
Scalby
A165
Langdale
End
Wrench Green
Everley
Newby

Falsgrave

Scarborough
ⓘ ⛺ Ⓜ 🐘 ⛲

A170

River Derwent
Sea Cut
Oliver's Mount

Bee Dale
East
Ayton
AA
A165
West
Ayton
Osgodby
Sawdon
Hutton
Buscel
Irton
Cayton Bay

TA

bberston
Ruston
Wykeham
Seamer
B1261
High Killerby
The Wyke

A170
Brompton
Cayton
Lebberston
Filey Brigg

nainton
s
Gristhorpe
Filey ⓘ

A64
R. Hertford
Folkton
Muston

Willerby
Staxton
Flixton
West
Flotmanby
Filey Bay

A1039

A64
Sherburn
Ganton
Hunmanby
A165

East Heslerton
Potter
Brompton
Reighton

West
Heslerton
Fordon
Speeton

gham
B1249
B1229
Buckton

Foxholes
Wold
Newton
Burton
Fleming
Thornwick Bay
Bempton

Butterwick
Grindale
Selwicks Bay
FLAMBOROUGH
HEAD

Weaverthorpe
Thwing
B1255
Flamborough

Helperthorpe
Octon
Boynton
Sewerby

West
Lutton
East Lutton
B1253
BRIDLINGTON

Kirby
Grindalythe
Low
thorpe
Langtoft
Rudston
Monolith
Bessingby
Hilderthorpe
Bridlington ⓘ Ⓜ
BAY

Sledmere
Cottam
Carnaby
Haisthorpe

B1251
B1252
Kilham
Burton
Agnes
Carnaby
Thornholme

B1249
*Norman
Manor House*
Fraisthorpe

thorpe
Ruston Parva
Harpham

A166
Garton-on-
the-Wolds
A166
Lowthorpe
Nafferton
Gransmoor

Wetwang
Elmswell
**Great
Driffield**
Little
Kelk
Great
Kelk
Lisset
Barmston

Little
Driffield
①
Gembling
85
B1242
Ulrome
②

Wansford
Foston

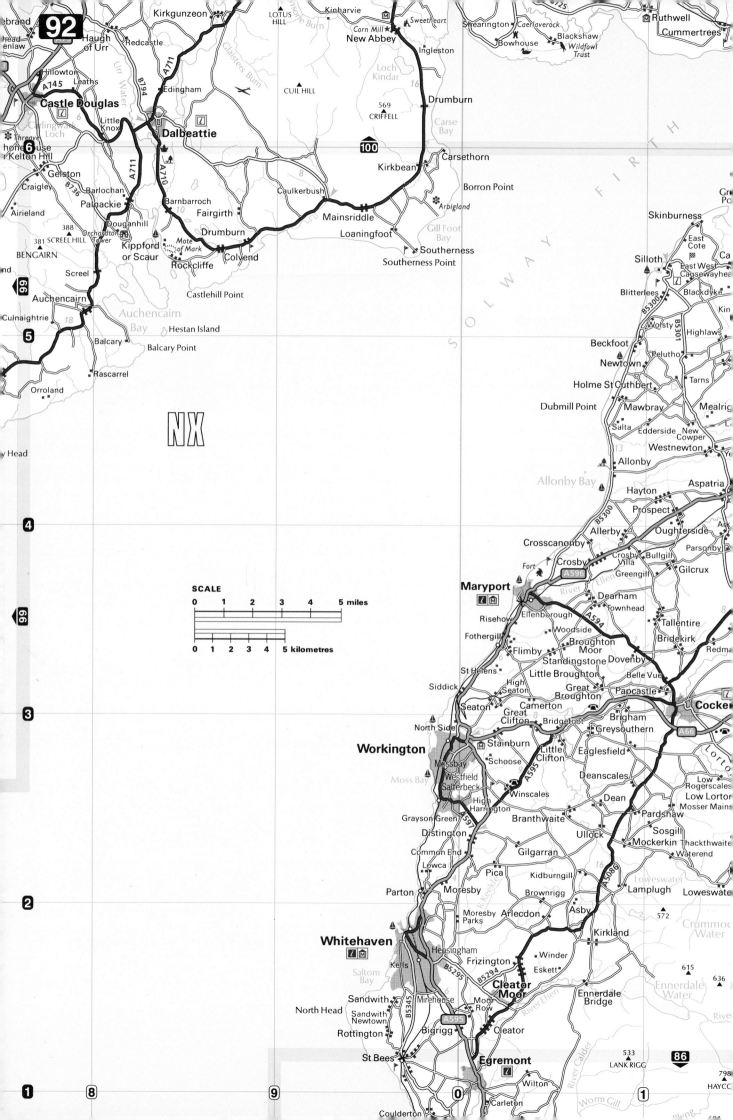

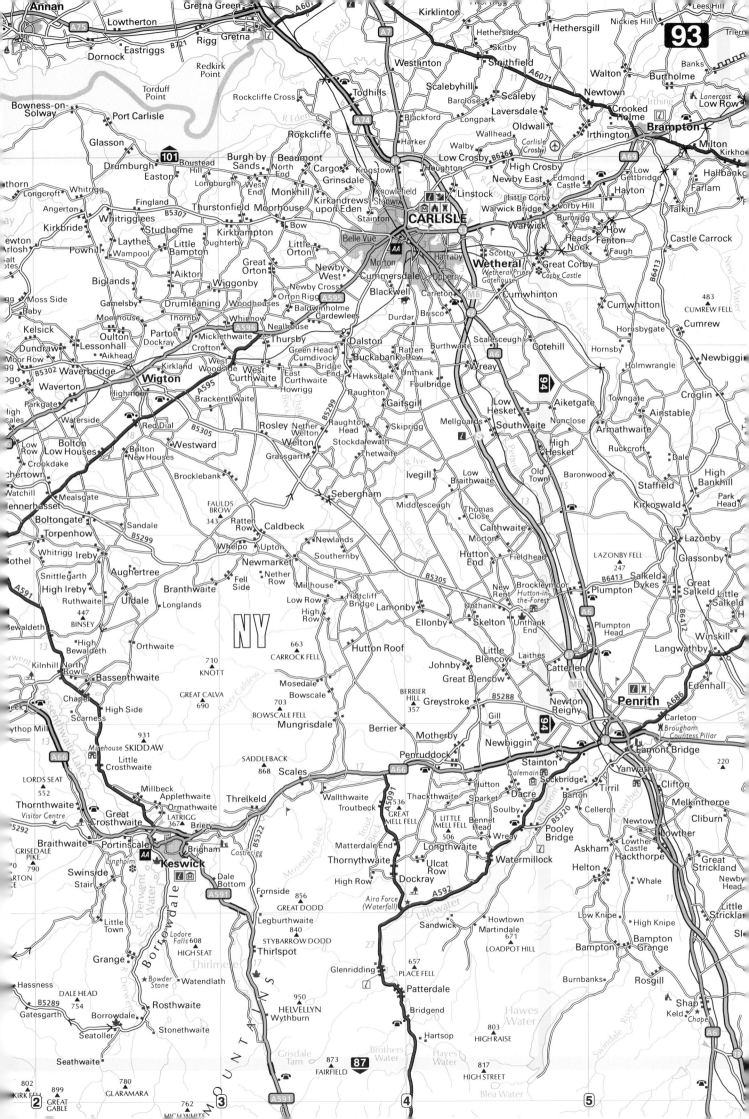

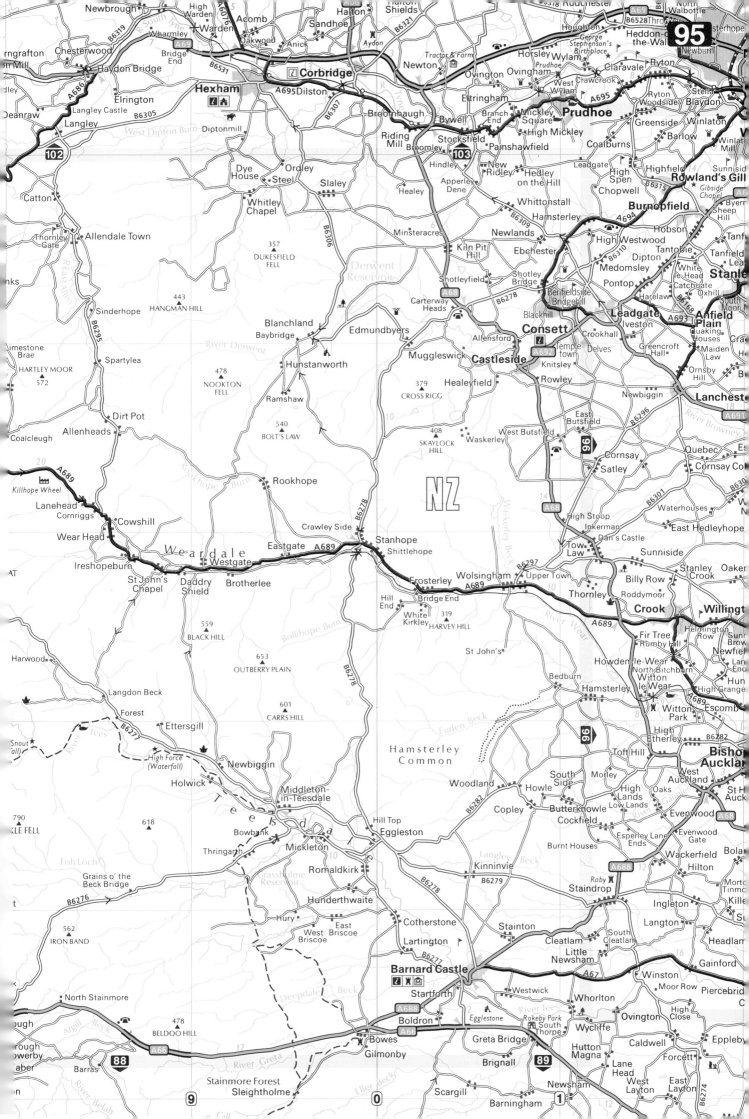

GOTEBORG
Summer Only

ESBJERG
Summer Only

SCALE

| 0 | 1 | 2 | 3 | 4 | 5 miles |

| 0 | 1 | 2 | 3 | 4 | 5 kilometres |

NZ

ton
ery

rlee

Blackhall Colliery
Blackhall Rocks

Monk
Heden

Hart
Station

Hart

High
Throston

wick

HARTLEPOOL

Hartlepool Bay

Dalton
Piercy

Brierton

Seaton Carew

Greatham

Graythorpe

Tees Bay

Newton
Bewley

illingham

Cowpen
Bewley

Haverton Hill

Port
Clarence

Warrenby

Coatham

Redcar

River Tees

Toll

South
Bank

Grangetown

Kirkleatham

Lazenby

Yearby

Marske-by-the-Sea

Saltburn-by-the-Sea

New
Brotton

Hummersea Scar

North
Ormesby

Lackenby

Wilton

Upleatham

New Marske

Brotton

Skinningrove

Street
Houses

Boulby

MIDDLESBROUGH

Eston

Dunsdale

Skelton

Carlin
How

Loftus

Staithes

Acklam

Ormesby

Normanby

Tocketts

New
Skelton

North
Skelton

Kilton

Kilton
Thorpe

Liverton
Mines

Easington

Dalehouse

Port Mulgrave

Hinderwell

Marton

Boosbeck

Lingdale

Roxby

Runswick
Bay

Stainton

Hemlington

Pinchinthorpe

Guisborough

Margrove
Park

Stanghow

Liverton

Handale

Borrowby

Newton
Mulgrave

Runswick

Goldsbo

Hutton
Lowcross

Hutton
Hall

90

Moorsholm

Scaling

llerby

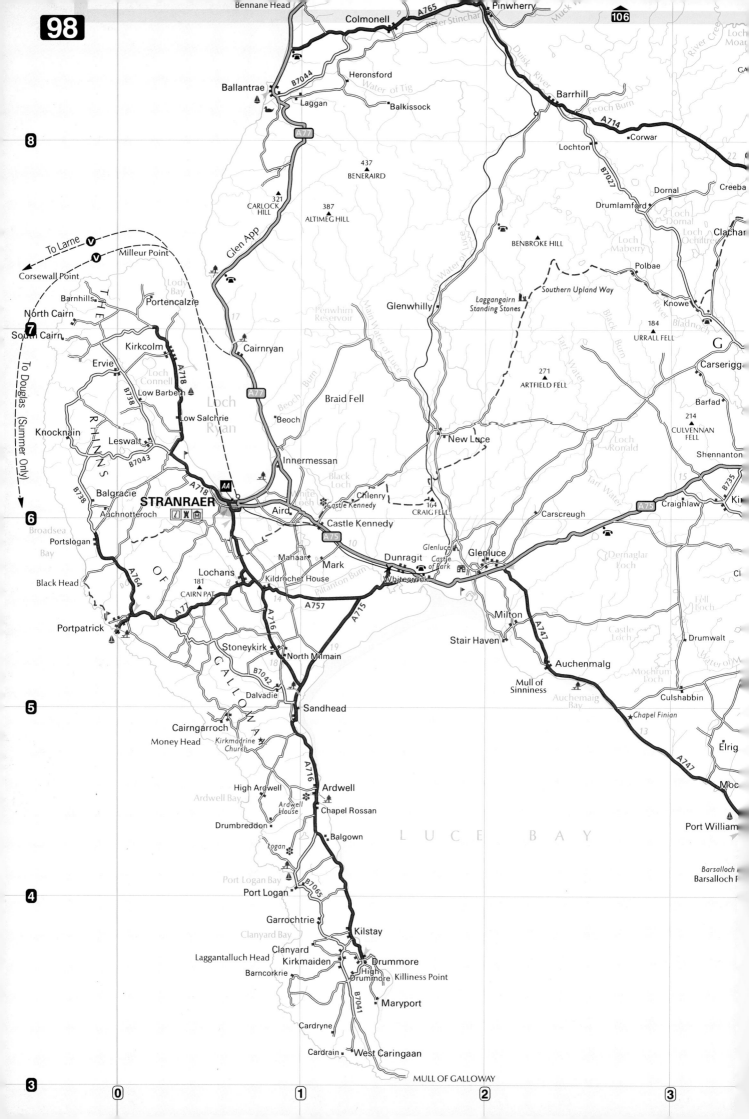

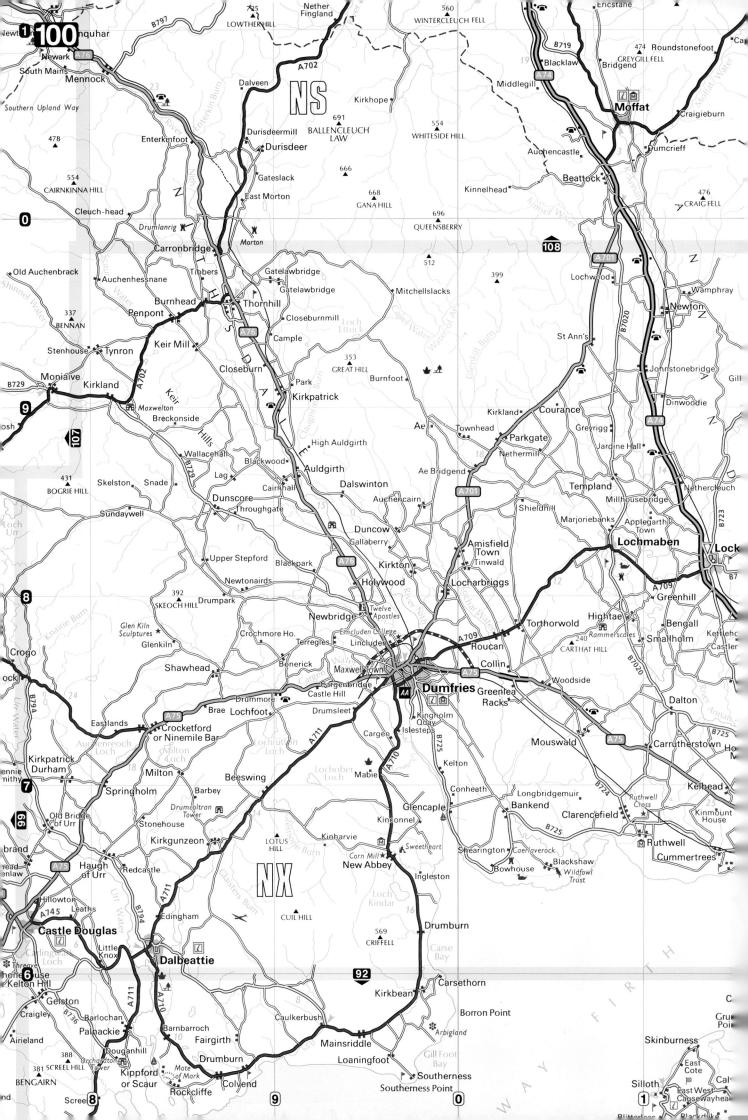

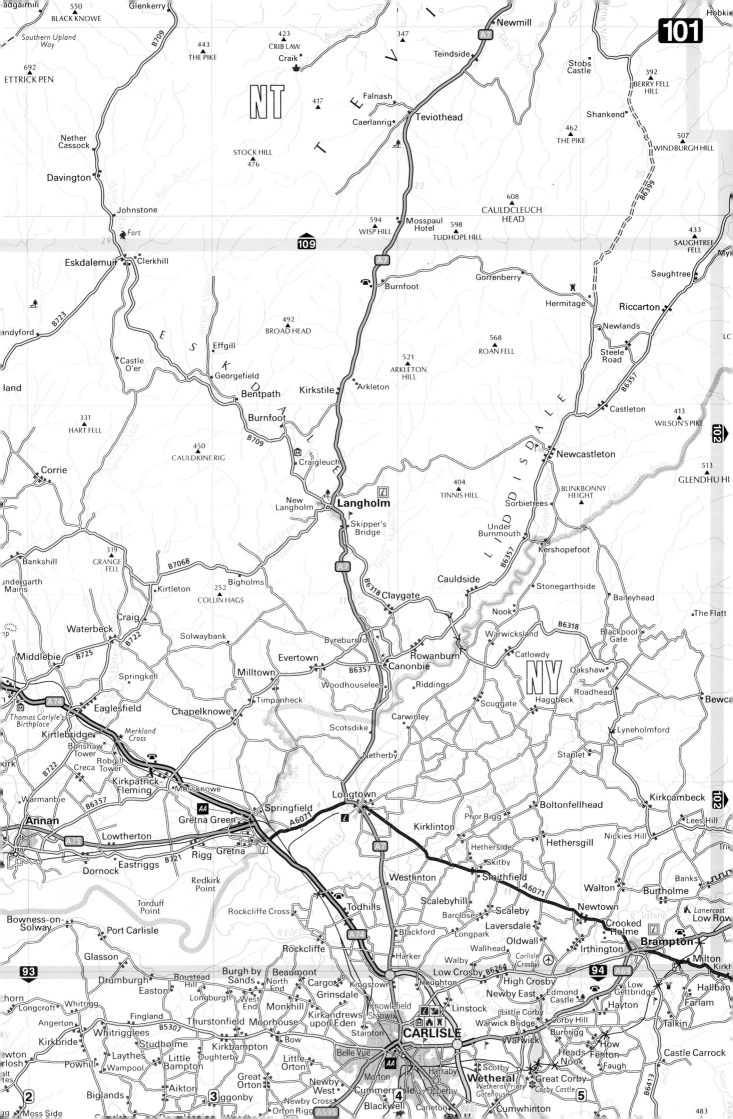

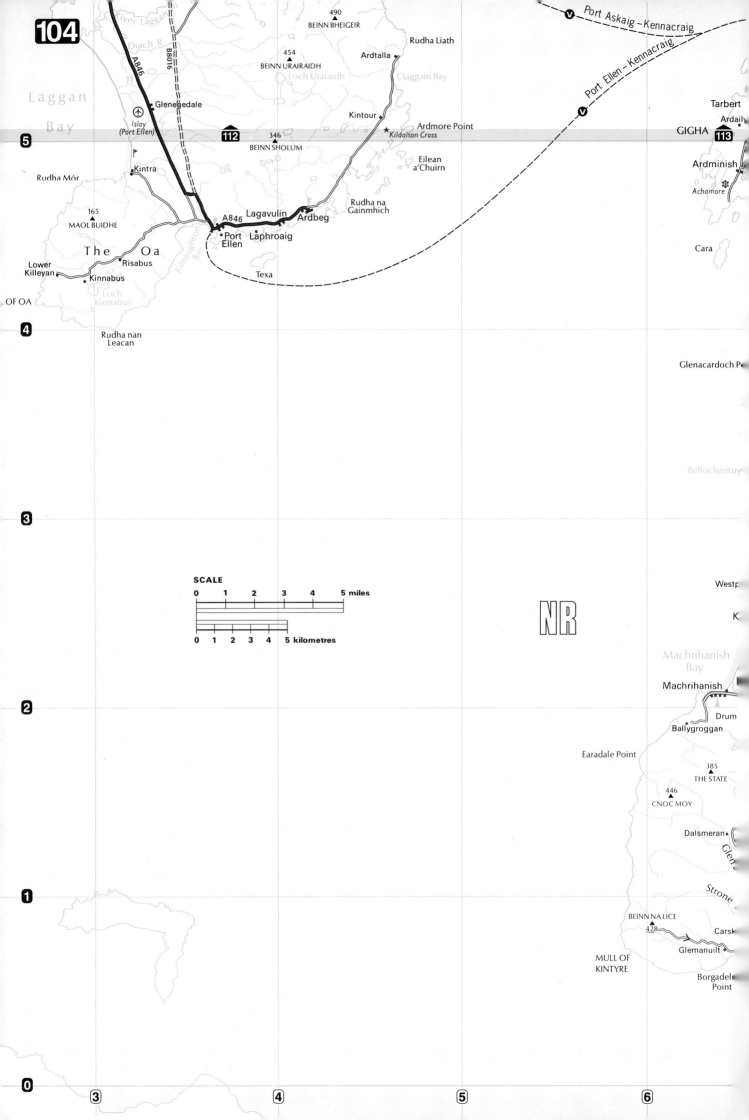

River Laggan

490
BEINN BHEIGEIR

Port Askaig – Kennacraig

Rudha Liath

Ardtalla

Claggain Bay

454
BEINN URAIRAIDH

Loch Uraraidh

Duich R.

B8016

A846

Laggan
Bay

Port Ellen – Kennacraig

Glenegedale

11

Islay
(Port Ellen)

112

346
BEINN SHOLUM

Kintour

Ardmore Point

Kildalton Cross

Eilean
a'Chuirn

Tarbert

Ardaily

GIGHA

113

Ardminish

Achamore

5

Rudha Mòr

Kintra

165
MAOL BUIDHE

The Oa

A846

Lagavulin

Ardbeg

Rudha na
Gainmhich

Cara

Kilnaughton Bay

Port
Ellen

Laphroaig

Lower
Killeyan

Risabus

Kinnabus

Loch
Kinnabus

Texa

OF OA

4

Rudha nan
Leacan

Glenacardoch P

Bellochantuy

3

SCALE

0 1 2 3 4 5 miles

0 1 2 3 4 5 kilometres

NR

Westp

K

Machrihanish
Bay

Machrihanish

2

Drum

Ballygroggan

Earadale Point

385
THE STATE

446
CNOC MOY

Dalsmeran

Glen

Strone

1

BEINN NA LICE

Carsk

428

Glemanuilt

MULL OF
KINTYRE

Borgadel
Point

0

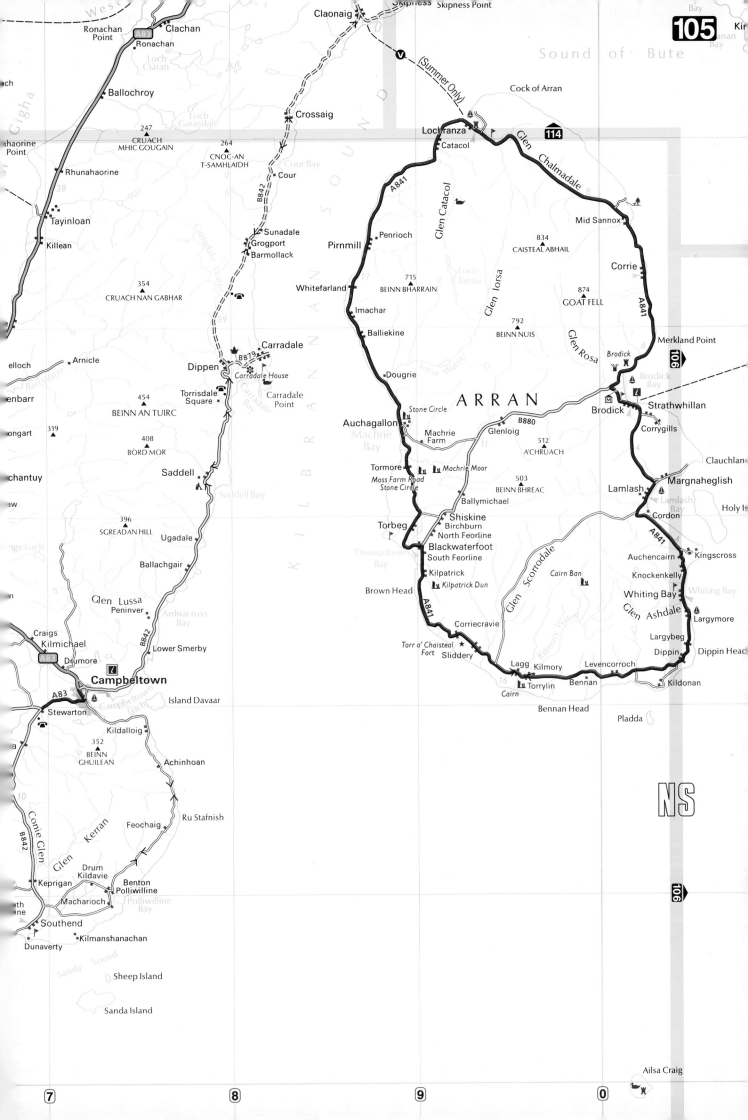

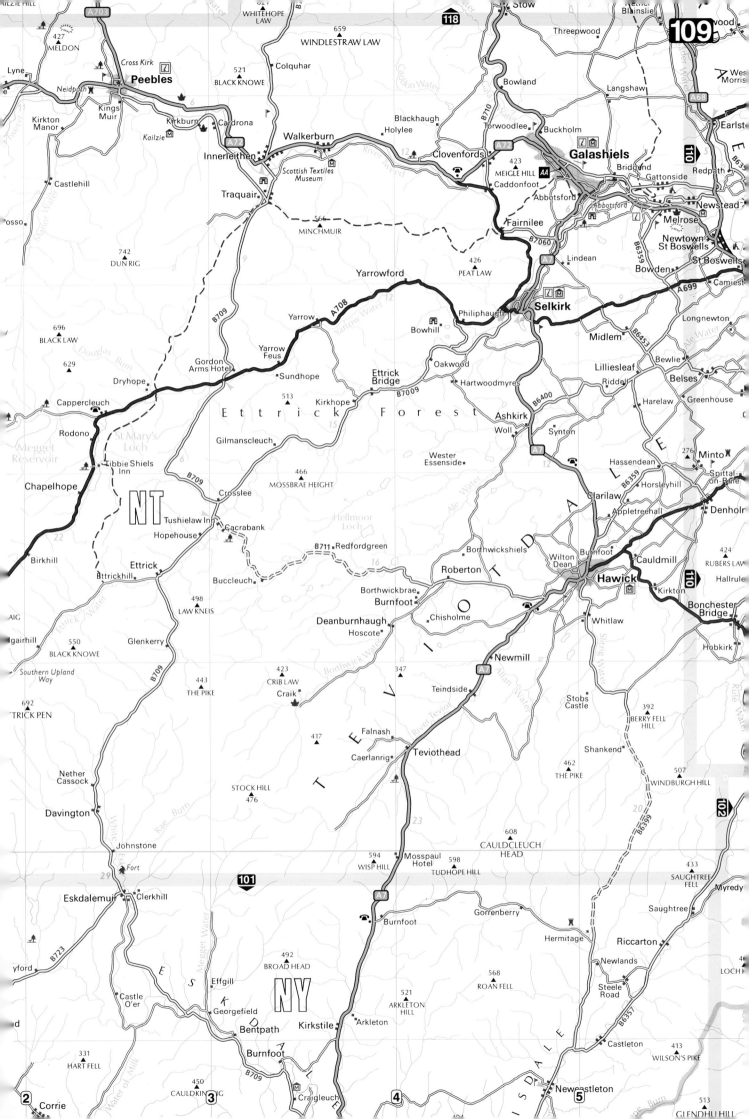

Barn
1333
6705
B6461
Barracks
Town Ramparts
Berwick-upon-Tweed
Tweedmouth
t Ord
Spittal
A698
A1167
B119
Huds Head

rton
Unthank
ornton
Scremerston
West Allerdean
Cheswick
Ancroft
A1
Goswick
Haggerston
B6525
Berrington
Beal

CAUSEWAY
FLOODED
AT HIGH TIDE
HOLY ISLAND

Bowsden
B6353
Kyloe
Lowick
East Kyloe
Fenwick
Buckton
Smeafield
Holburn
Detchant
Middleton
St Cuthbert's Cave
North Hazelrigg

Holy Island
Lindisfarne Priory
Lindisfarne
Castle Point
Guile Point
Fenham

Elwick
Ross
Low Middleton
Budle
Waren Mill
B1341
B1340
Bamburgh
Glororum
New Shoreston
Burton
Bradford
Elford

FARNE ISLANDS
Staple Sound
Inner Sound

the Lady
erford Hall
Nesbit
Doddington
South Hazelrigg
Belford
B6349
Easington
Outchester
B1342
Spindlestone

the Lady
West Horton
East Horton
Bellshill
Warenton
B6348
Adderstone
Warenford
Lucker
Newham
North Sunderland
Seahouses
Beadnell

bleton
Wooler
B6525
B6348
West Weetwood
Chatton

Newstead
Chathill
Ellingham
Preston
Brunton
Swinhoe
Beadnell Bay
High Newton by-the-Sea

Earle
Haugh Head
Newtown
Liburn Tower
Chillingham
Ros Castle
Hepbu
CATERAN HILL
267
North Charlton
Doxford
Christon Bank
Embleton
Embleton Bay
Dunstan Steads
Dunstanburgh

North Middleton
South Middleton
Ilderton
Roseden
Roddham
A697
New Bewick
Old Bewick
Harehope
Ditchburn
South Charlton
Falloden
Rock
B6347
Dunstan
Craster

567
MOOR HILL
Brandon
Wooperton
Eglingham
Beanley
B6346
Shipley
Rennington
Stamford
Howick Hall
B1339
Cullernose Point
Howick

side
Ingram
Branton
Fawdon
Powburn
East Bolton
Titlington
Broxfield
Littlehoughton
B1340
Longhoughton
Boulmer

334
COCHRANE PIKE
Glanton
Glanton Pike
Shawdon Hill
Bolton
Broome Park
Abberwick
Alnwick
Denwick
Hawkhill
Lesbury
Seaton Point

Prendwick
Great Ryle
Whittingham
Little Ryle
Thrunton
Lemmington Hall
B6341
Bilton
Alnmouth
Alnmouth Bay

Alnham
Yetlington
Callaly
Edlingham
A1
Bilton Banks
High Buston
Birling
Warkworth

law
Scrainwood
Netherton
A697
260
GRANTLEES HILL
Newton-on-the-Moor
Shilbottle
Low Buston
Hermitage
Amble

arradon
High Trewhitt
Lorbottle
Cartington
103
Forest
Swarland Estate
Guyzance
Gloster Hill
Coquet Island

harperton
Warton
Snitter
B6341
Swarland
North End
Felton
East Thirston
South Broomhill
Togston
Hauxley
Radcliffe

Flotterton
Rothbury
Cragside
Longframlington
Acklington
B6345
Broomhill
B1339

Caistron
Thropton
Great Tosson
Newtown
Whitton
Pauperhaugh
Red Row
East Chevington
Chevington Drift

Bickerton
Swindon
0
TOSSON HILL
11
Brinkburn
B6344
1
Eshott
2
West
Druridge
3
A1068

SCALE
0 1 2 3 4 5 miles
0 1 2 3 4 5 kilometres

NU

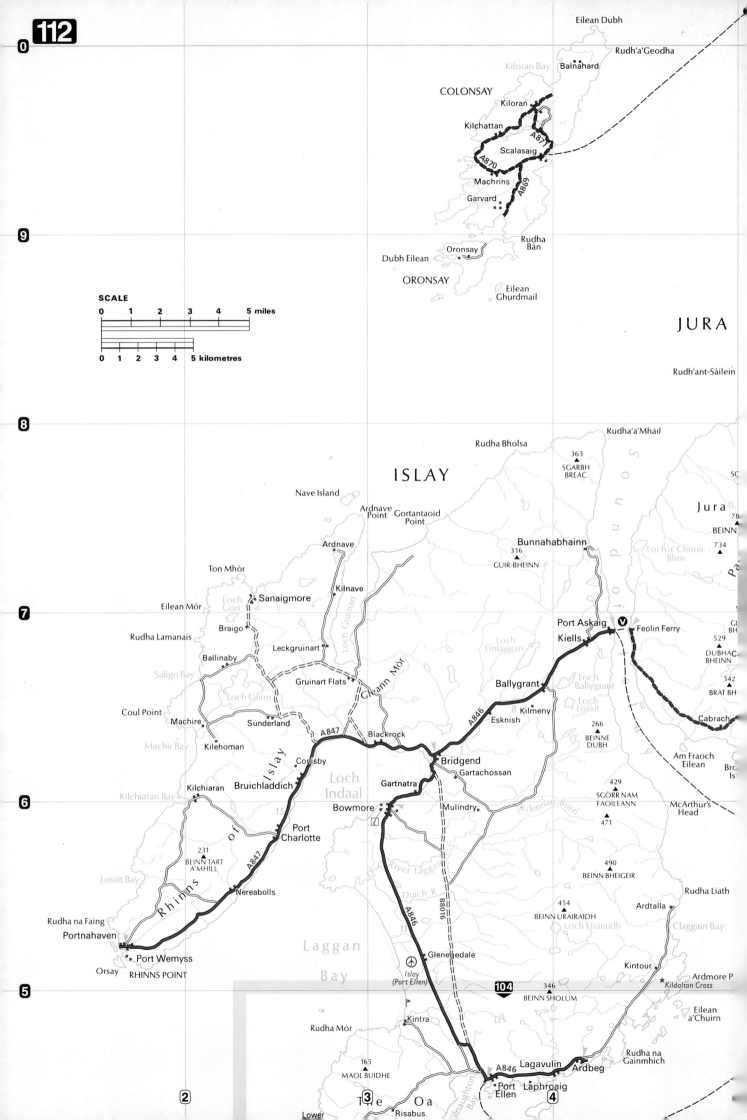

0

9

8

7

6

5

SCALE

0 1 2 3 4 5 miles

0 1 2 3 4 5 kilometres

COLONSAY

Eilean Dubh

Rudh'a'Geodha

Kiloran Bay

Balnahard

Kiloran

Kilchattan

A871

Scalasaig

A870

A869

Machrins

Garvard

Rudha Bàn

Dubh Eilean

Oronsay

ORONSAY

Eilean Ghurdmail

JURA

Rudh'ant-Sàilein

Rudha'a'Mhàil

Rudha Bholsa

363

SGARBH BREAC

ISLAY

J u r a

78

BEINN

Nave Island

Ardnave Point

Gortantaoid Point

Bunnahabhainn

316

GUIR-BHEINN

734

Loch a' Chnuic Bhric

P a

Ardnave

Kilnave

Ton Mhòr

Loch Gorm

Sanaigmore

Port Askaig

Kiells

Feolin Ferry

529

GL BH

Eilean Mòr

Braigo

Loch Gruinart

Ballygrant

Loch Finlaggan

Loch Ballygrant

Loch Lossit

DUBHAC BHEINN

Rudha Lamanais

Leckgruinart

Gleann Mòr

A846

Kilmeny

Esknish

266

BEINNE DUBH

342

BRAT BH

Ballinaby

Gruinart Flats

Saligo Bay

Loch Gorm

Coul Point

Machire

Sunderland

A847

Blackrock

Bridgend

Gartachossan

Am Fraoch Eilean

Br Is

Machir Bay

Kilchoman

Comsby

Gartnatra

429

SGÒRR NAM FAOILEANN

McArthur's Head

Bruichladdich

Loch Indaal

Bowmore

Mulindry

Kilchiaran

471

Kilchiaran Bay

Kilchiaran

R h i n n s   o f   I s l a y

Port Charlotte

231

BEINN TART A'MHILL

A847

River Laggan

Duich R.

490

BEINN BHEIGEIR

Rudha Liath

Lossit Bay

Nereabolls

A846

B8016

454

BEINN URAIRAIDH

Loch Uraraidh

Ardtalla

Claggain Bay

Rudha na Faing

Portnahaven

L a g g a n

Glenegedale

Islay (Port Ellen)

Kintour

Ardmore P

Orsay

Port Wemyss

RHINNS POINT

B a y

346

BEINN SHOLUM

104

Kildalton Cross

Eilean a'Chuirn

Rudha Mòr

Kintra

Rudha na Gainmhich

165

MAOL BUIDHE

A846

Lagavulin

Ardbeg

Port Ellen

Laphroaig

T h e   O a

Lower

Risabus

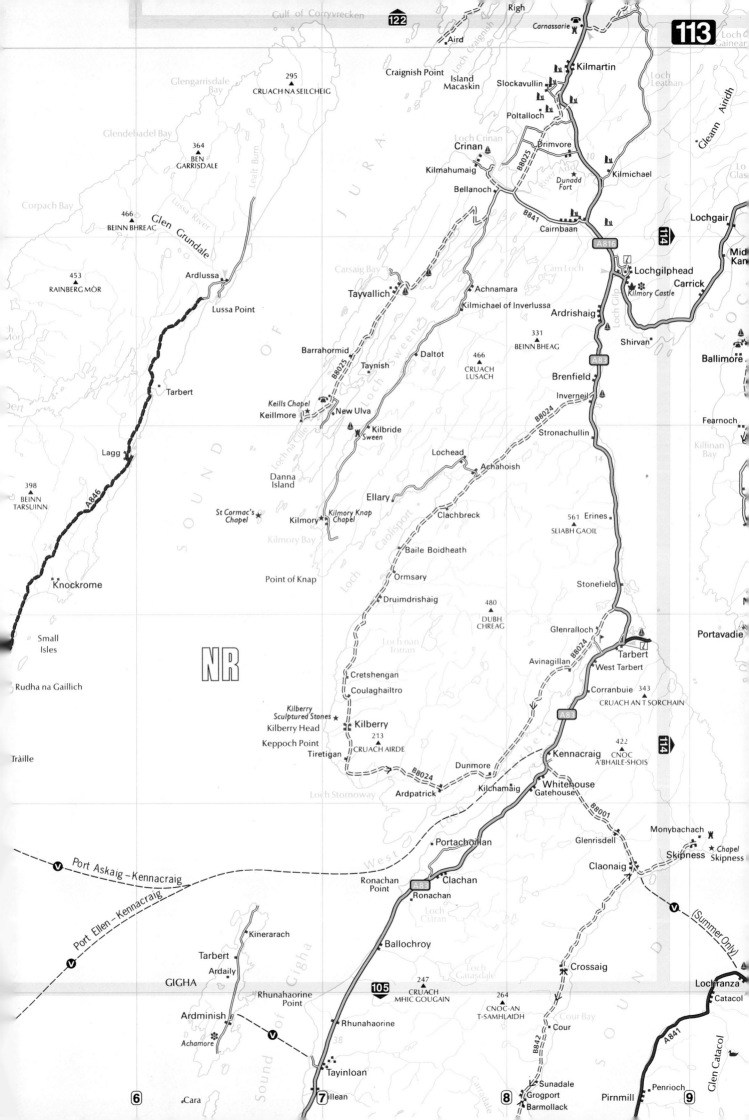

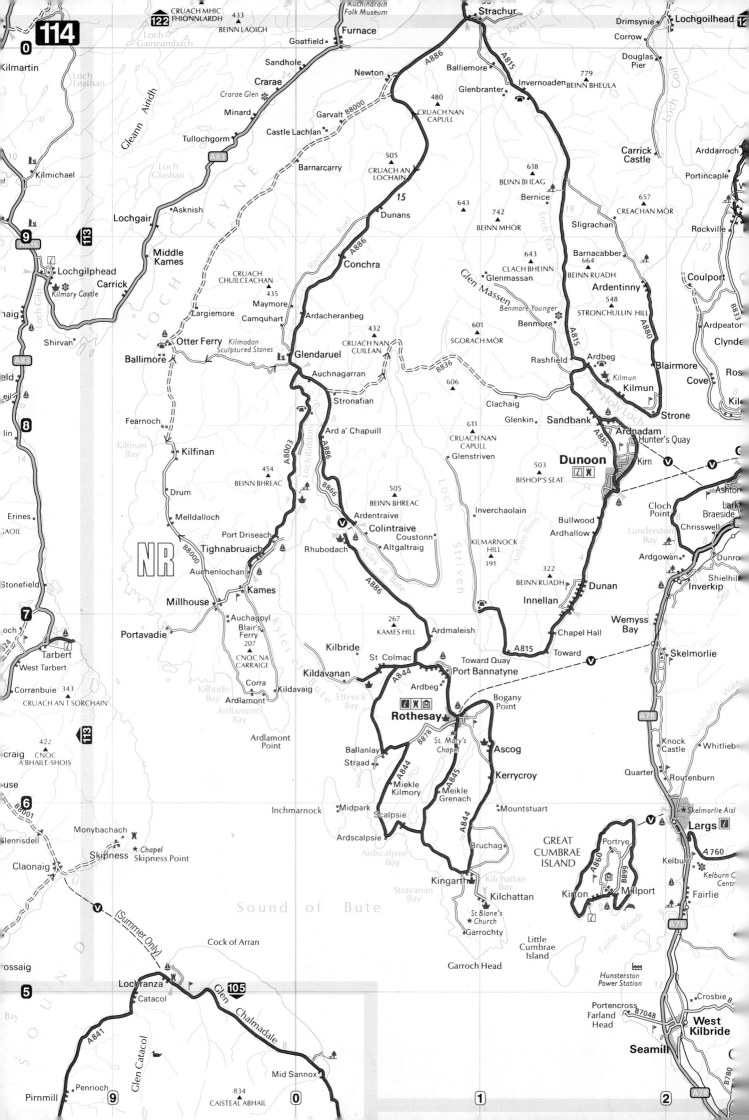

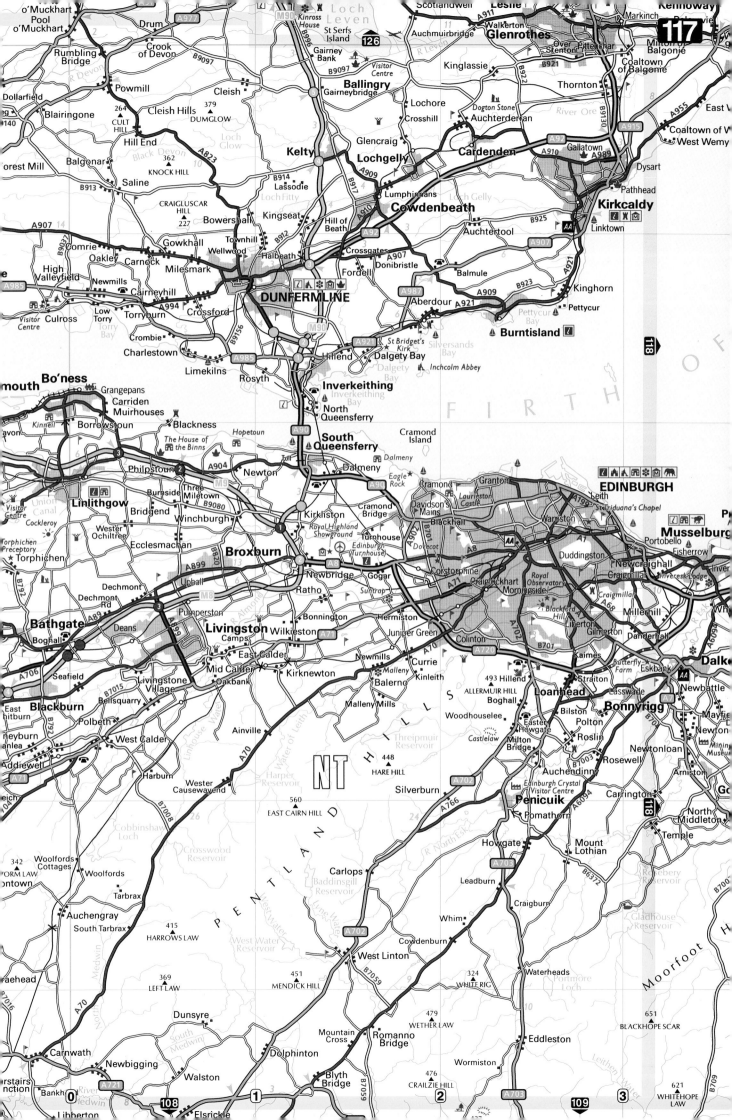

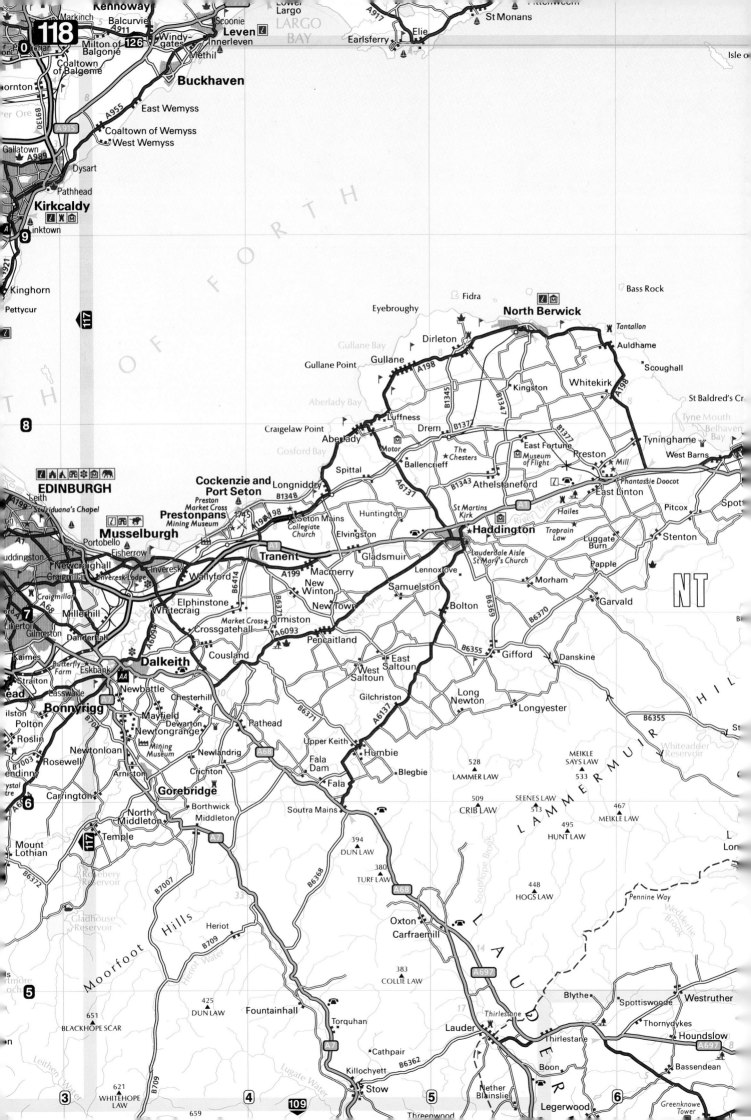

NU

SCALE

0 1 2 3 4 5 miles

0 1 2 3 4 5 kilometres

...ar

...oxburn
1650
Barns Ness
East Barns
Chapel Point
Skateraw
Thorntonloch
Crownhill
Innerwick
319
COCKLAW HILL
Dunglass
Collegiate Church
Reed Point
Pease Bay
Siccar Point
Fast Castle Head
Oldhamstocks
Cockburnspath
ST ABB'S HEAD
196
BROWN RIG
A1107
A1
Ecclaw
Southern Upland Way
Northfield
St Abbs
391
HEART LAW
Grantshouse
Coldingham
Coldingham Bay
Eye Water
Butterdean
21
Houndwood
22
Quixwood
Heugh Head
Cairncross
Eyemouth
262
HORSELEY HILL
B6438
Reston
A1
Abbey St Bathans
A6112
14
Auchencrow
Ayton
Burnmouth
Edin's Hall Broch
...tchester
325
COCKBURN LAW
Marygold
Ellemford
...ERMI...
B6355
Lintlaw
B6437
B6355
Lamberton
Marshall Meadows Bay
Primrosehill
Preston
East Blanerne
Chirnside
B6365
Cumledge
Edrom
Church
15
Edington
Foulden
...GTON
...LAW
Chirnsidebridge
Broadhaugh
Whiteadder Water
Tithe Barn
1333
A1
A6105
Manderston
Allanton
Hutton
Crumstane
Barracks
Town Ramparts
Gavinton
Duns
Blackadder Water
Blackadder
B6460
Sunwick
Paxton
B6461
Berwick-upon-Tweed
B6456
Sinclair's Hill
Whitsome
Hilton
Fishwick
Tweedmouth
...9
...GTON
...T LAW
Polwarth
Nisbet Hill
13
East Ord
Spittal
Fogo
B6461
Loanend
A698
Huds Head
110
A6105
Horncliffe
111
A6112
Horndean
Murton
Unthank
6
Forgorig
Ladykirk
Thornton
Scremerston
Greenlaw
Charterhall
B6437
B6470
Norham
West Allerdean
Cheswick
Swinton
Upsettlington
Shoreswood
Simprim
Ladykirk Ho.
Grindon
Ancroft
0
A1
Göswick
11
River Tweed
Shellacres
Felkington
B6354
Haggerston
8
9
Leitholm
10

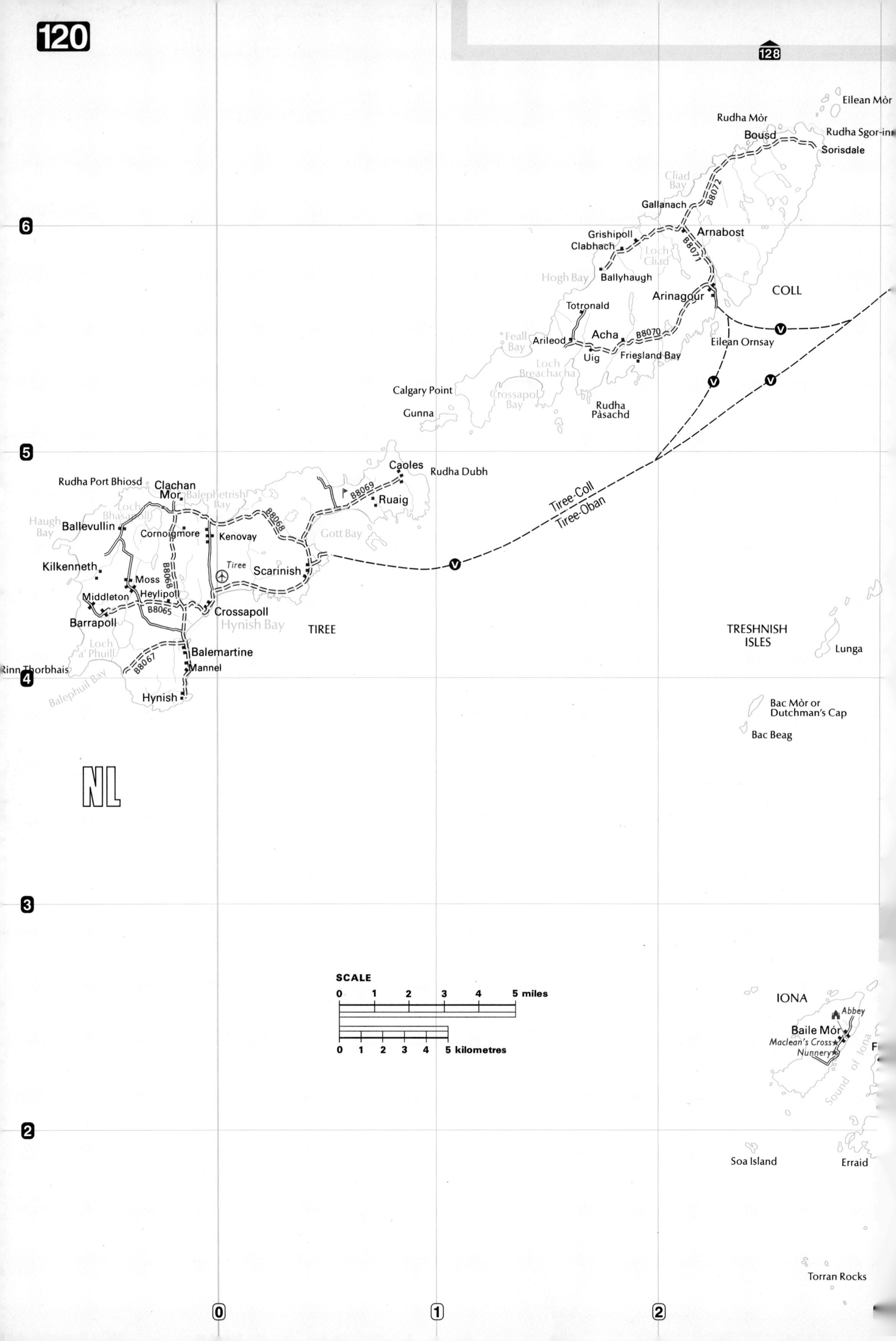

128

Eilean Mòr

Rudha Mòr

Rudha Sgor-in

Bousd

Sorisdale

Cliad Bay

6

Gallanach

B8072

Grishipoll

Clabhach

Arnabost

Totronald

B8071

Loch Cliad

COLL

Hogh Bay

Ballyhaugh

Arinagour

Feall Bay

Arileod

Acha

B8070

Loch Breachacha

Uig

Friesland Bay

Eilean Ornsay

V

Calgary Point

Crossapol Bay

Gunna

Rudha Pàsachd

5

Caoles

Rudha Dubh

Rudha Port Bhiosd

Clachan Mor

Balephetrish Bay

B8069

Ruaig

Tiree-Coll

Tiree-Oban

Loch Bhasapoll

Haugh Bay

Ballevullin

Cornaigmore

B8068

Kenovay

Gott Bay

V

Kilkenneth

Tiree

B8068

Scarinish

Moss

Heylipoll

Middleton

B8065

Crossapoll

TIREE

TRESHNISH ISLES

Barrapoll

Hynish Bay

Lunga

Loch a' Phuill

Balemartine

Rinn Thorbhais

B8067

Mannel

Bac Mòr or Dutchman's Cap

4

Balephuil Bay

Hynish

Bac Beag

NL

3

SCALE

| 0 | 1 | 2 | 3 | 4 | 5 miles |

| 0 | 1 | 2 | 3 | 4 | 5 kilometres |

IONA

Abbey

Baile Mór

Maclean's Cross

Nunnery

2

Soa Island

Erraid

Torran Rocks

0

1

2

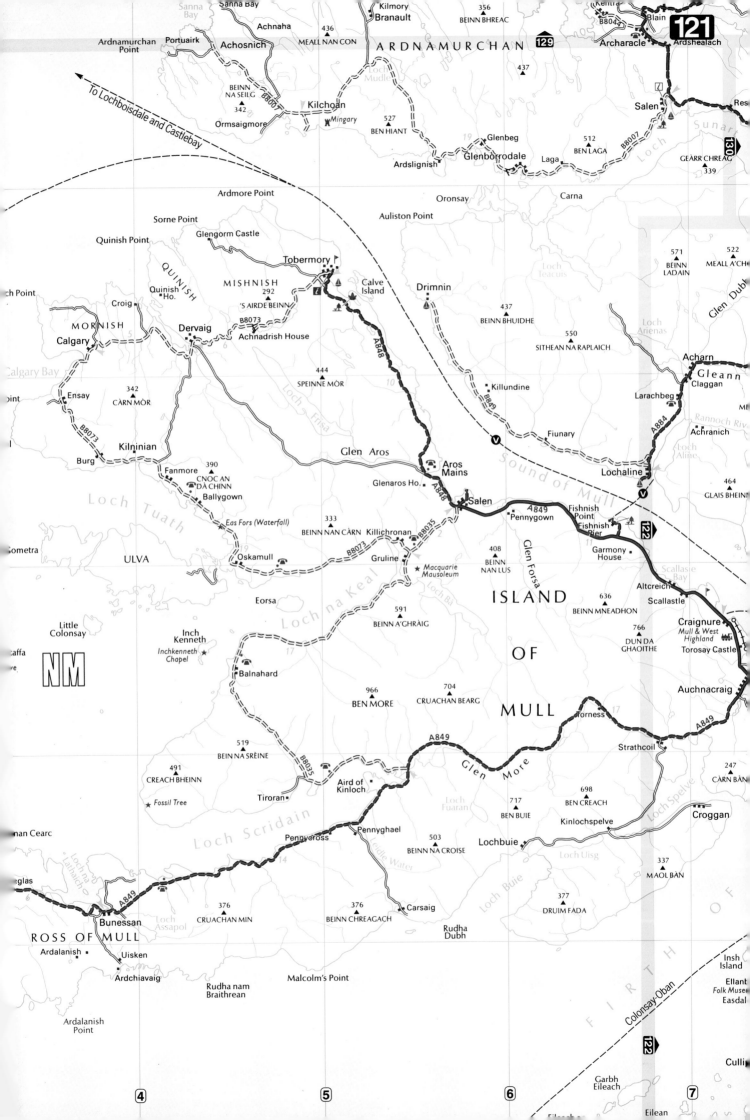

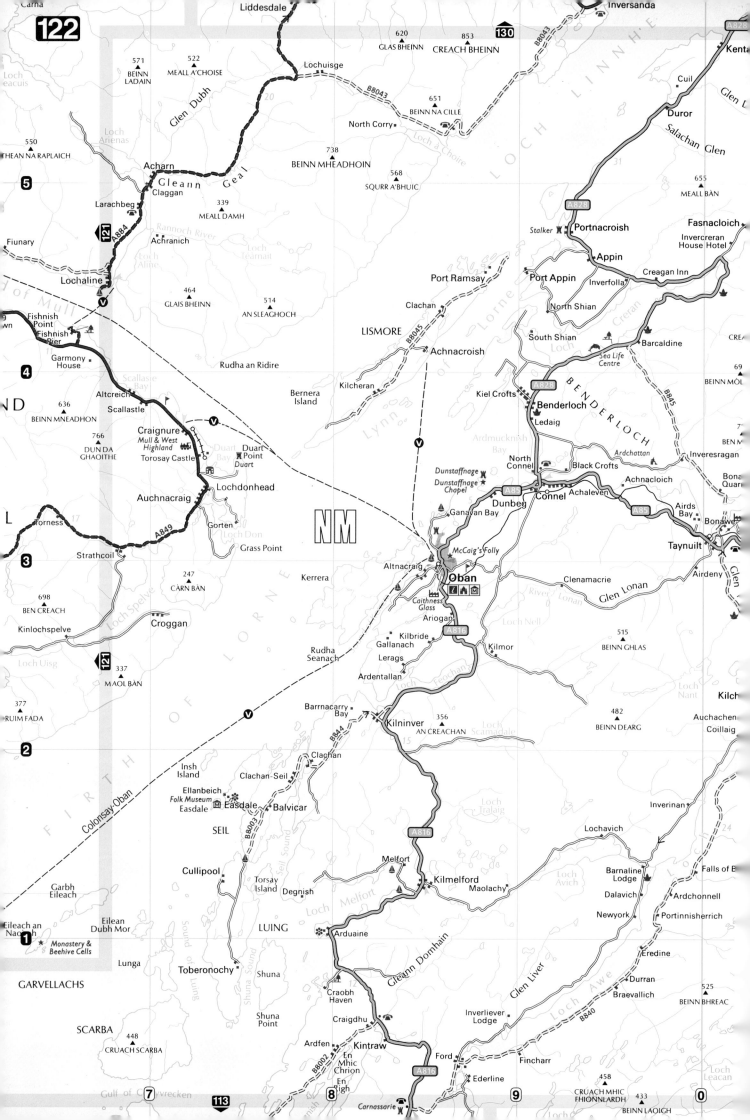

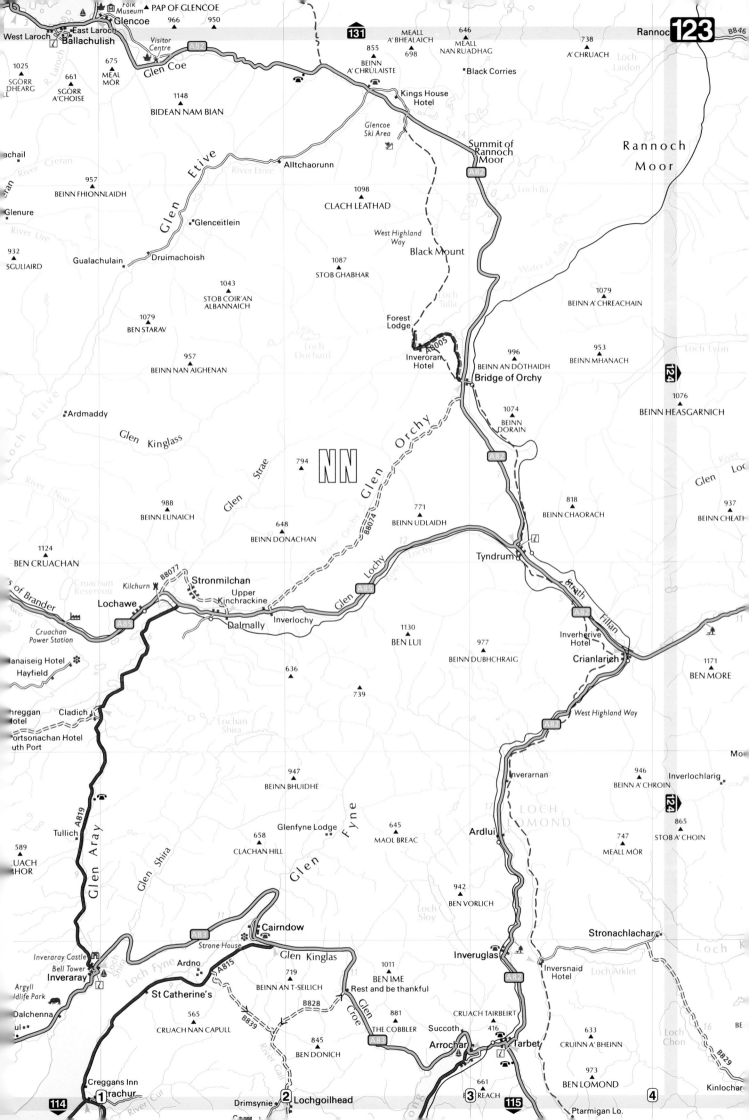

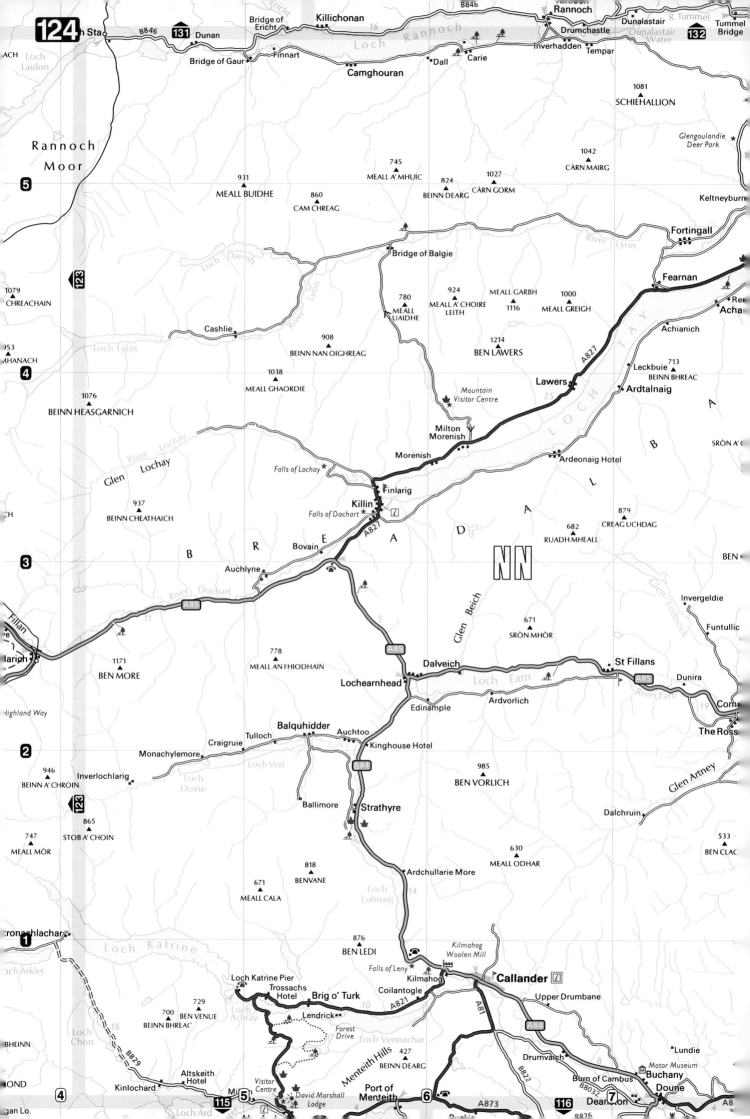

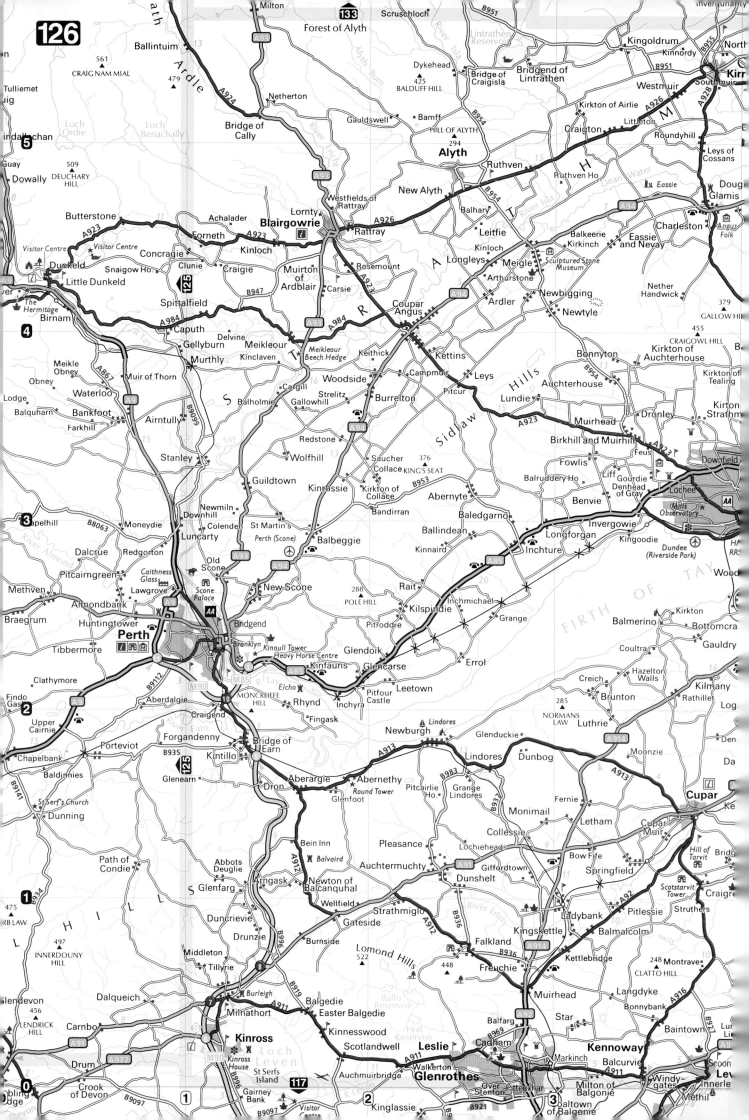

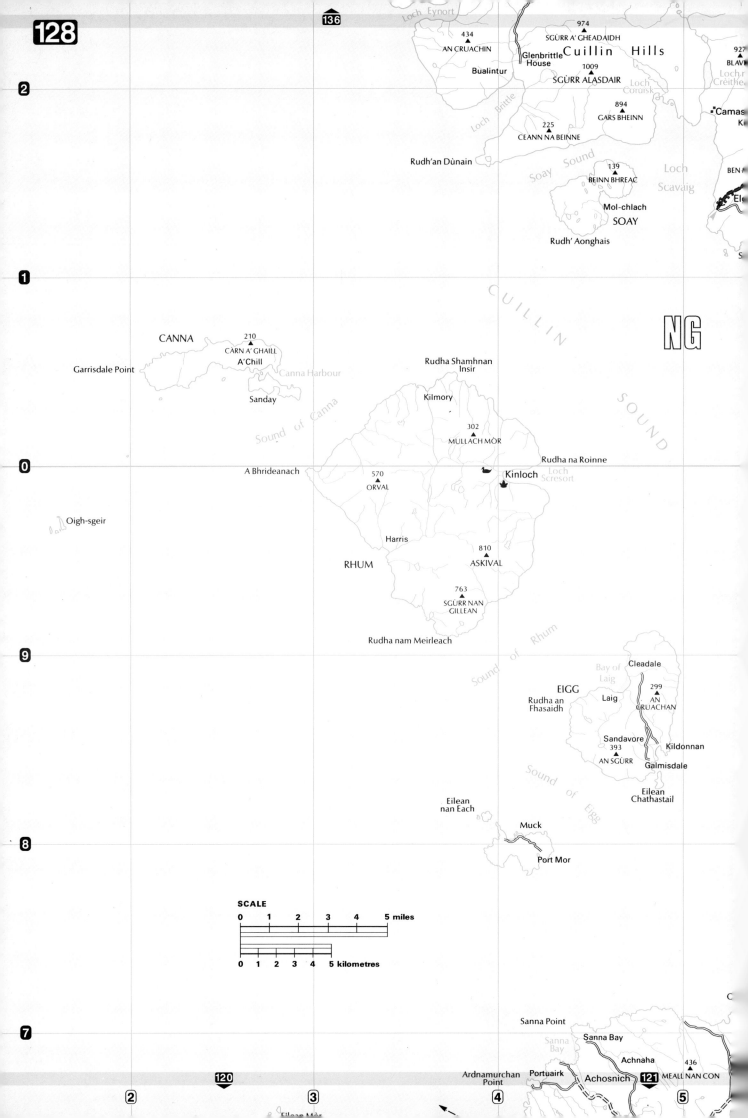

2

1

0

9

8

7

SGÙRR A' GHEADAIDH

974

434
AN CRUACHIN

Glenbrittle
House

Cuillin Hills

Bualintur

1009
SGÙRR ALASDAIR

Loch

927
BLAV

Camas
K

Loch
Corùisk

894
GARS BHEINN

225
CEANN NA BEINNE

Rudh'an Dùnain

Soay Sound

139
BEINN BHREAC

Loch
Scavaig

BEN

El

Mol-chlach

SOAY

Rudh' Aonghais

CUILLIN

NG

CANNA

210
CÀRN A' GHAILL
A'Chill

Garrisdale Point

Canna Harbour

Rudha Shamhnan
Insir

Kilmory

SOUND

Sanday

Sound of Canna

302
MULLACH MÒR

A Bhrideanach

Oigh-sgeir

570
ORVAL

Rudha na Roinne

Kinloch

Loch
Scresort

Harris

810
ASKIVAL

RHUM

763
SGÙRR NAN
GILLEAN

Rudha nam Meirleach

Sound of Rhum

Bay of
Laig

Cleadale

EIGG

Laig

299
AN
CRUACHAN

Rudha an
Fhasaidh

Sandavore

393
AN SGÙRR

Kildonnan

Galmisdale

Eilean
nan Each

Muck

Sound of Eigg

Eilean
Chathastail

Port Mor

SCALE

0   1   2   3   4   5 miles

0 1 2 3 4   5 kilometres

Sanna Point

Sanna Bay

Sanna
Bay

Achnaha

436
MEALL NAN CON

Ardnamurchan
Point

Portuairk

Achosnich

121

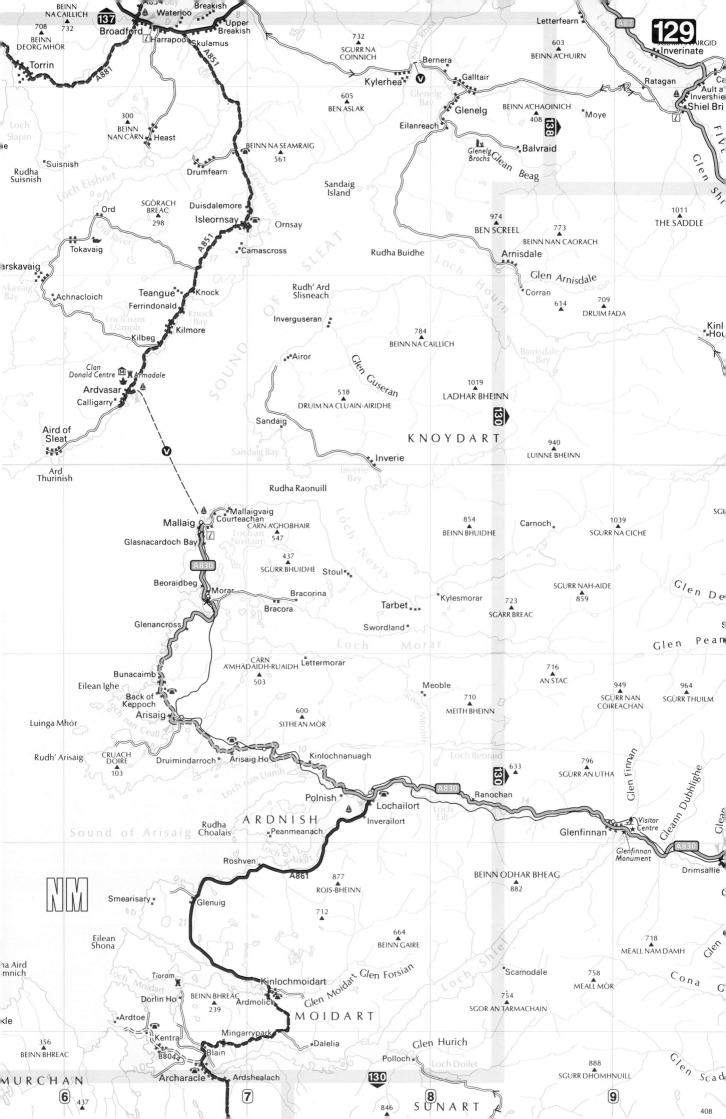

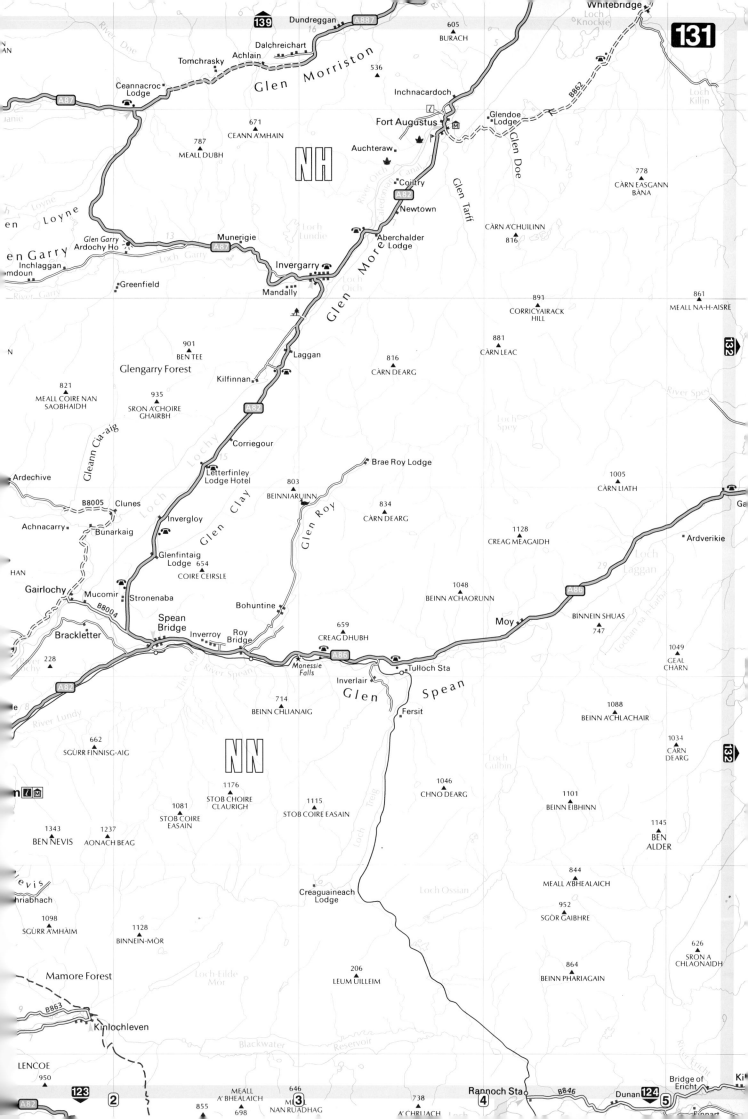

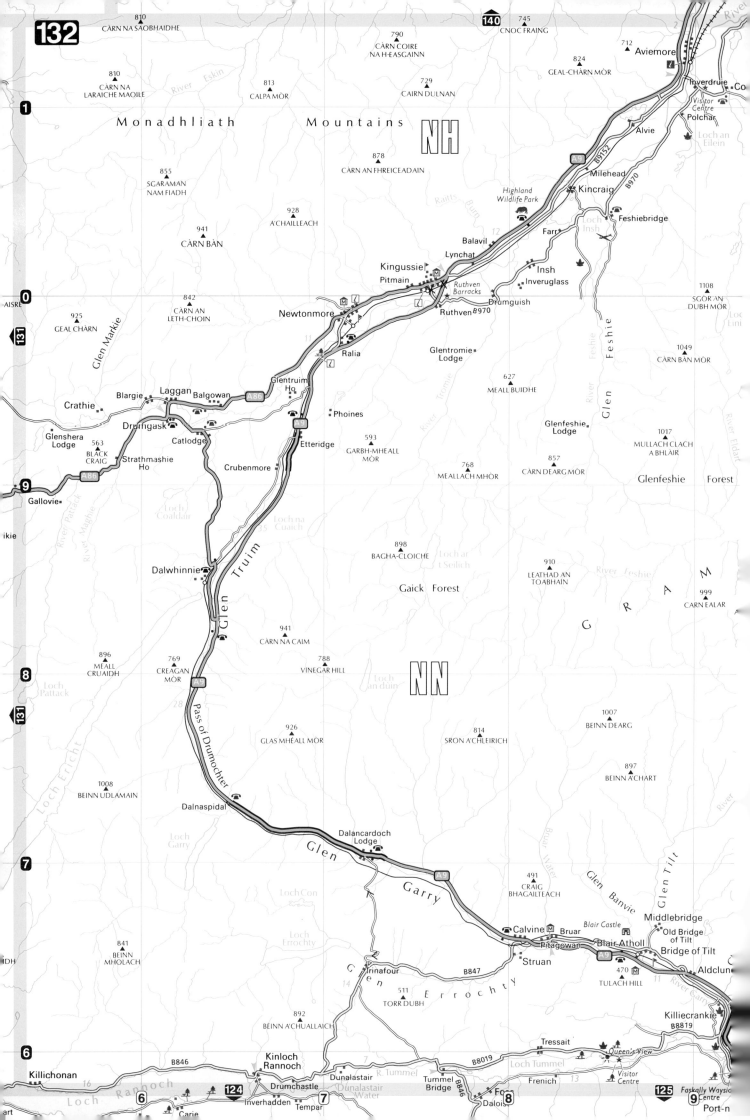

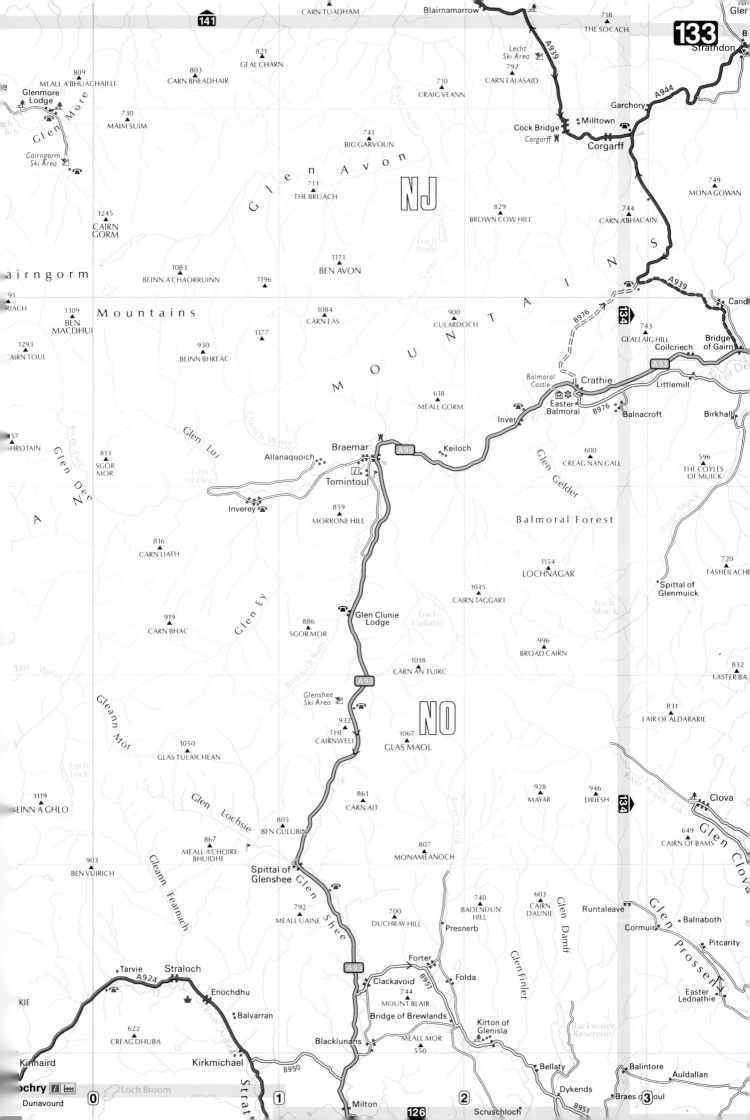

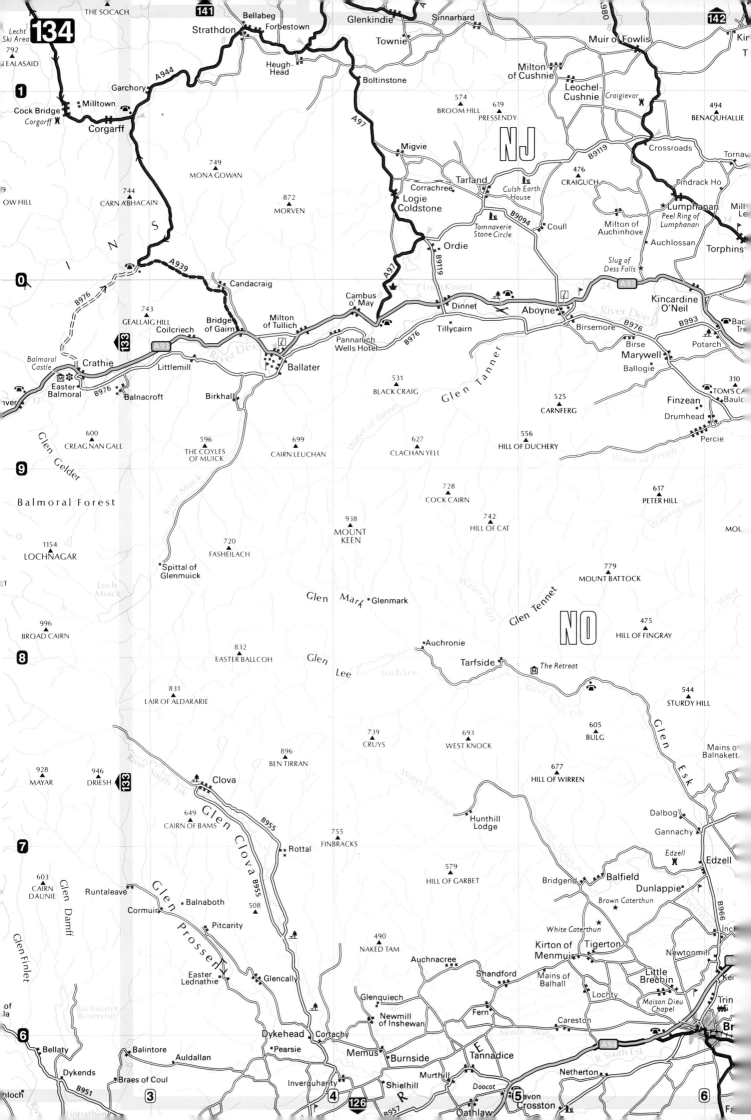

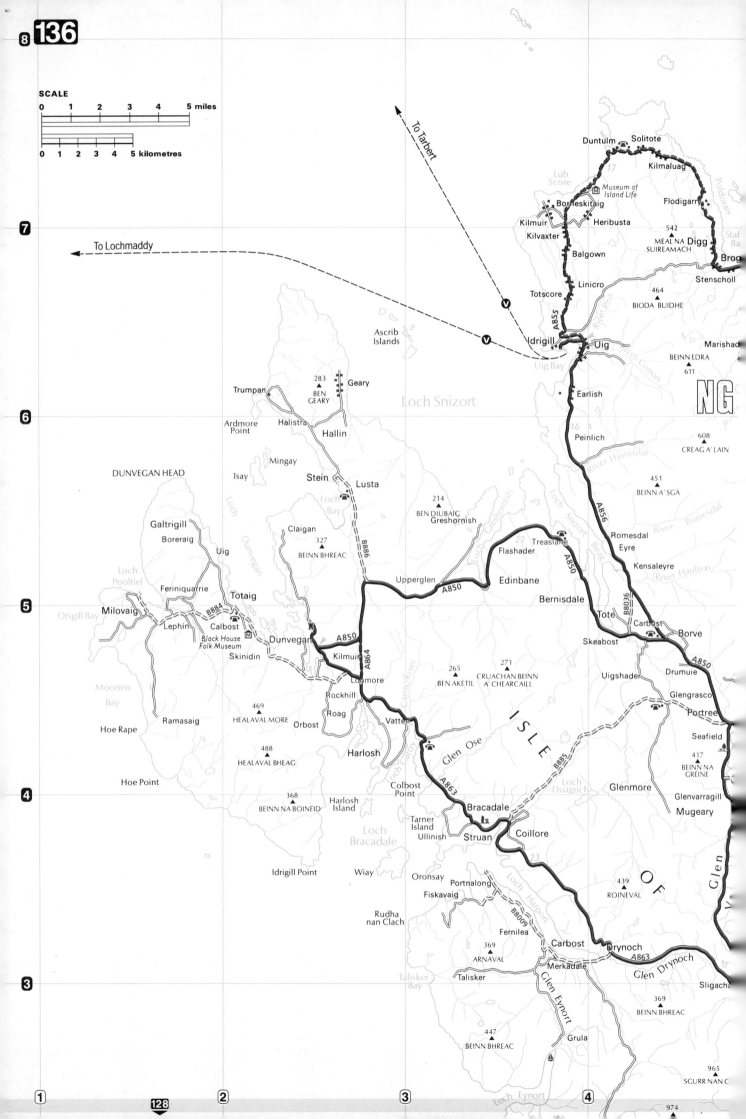

North Erradale
B8021
Big Sand
Longa Island
Strath
Smithstown
Gairloch
Loch
Gairloch
Port
Henderson
144
Badachro
Opinan
South Erradale
Red Point

Londubb
Poolewe
MEALL NA
137
A832
Auchtercairn
Heritage
Museum
Eilean
Horrisdale
Charlestown
MEALL AN DOIREIN
421
B8056
Loch
Mar
Tal

Kilt Rock Waterfall
Ellishader
Valtos
Rudha nam
Brathairean
Tote

ISLAND
OF
RONA

Loch a' Bhraige

Rudha na Fearn
Fearnmore
Loch
Diabaig
Fearnbeg
Arinacrinachd
Cuaig
Kenmore
Kalnalkill
Lonbain
AN GARBH-MHEALL
492
CRÒIC-BHEINN
493

Loch
Torridon
Craig River
BEINN BHREAC
619
138
BEINN ALLIGIN
985
Lower Diabaig
Alligin Shuas
Inveralligin
Torridon Ho
Ardheslaig
Loch
Shieldaig
Shieldaig
Island
Shieldaig
A896
Glenshieldaig
Forest
BEINN DAMH
902
Loch
Damh
LIATH
Torr
To
Annat
Upper Loch Torridon
10
MA

Eilean
Tigh

Eilean
Fladday
Umachan
Manish Point
Loch
Arnish
Torran
Arnish
Brochel

ISLAND
OF
RAASAY

DÙN
CAAN
444
Rudha
na' Leac

SOUND OF RAASAY

INNER SOUND

River Applecross

Loch
Lundie

Applecross
Bay
Applecross
Milton
Camusteel
Camusterrach
Culduie
Toscaig

BEINN BHAN
895
SGURR
A CHAORACHAIN
774
Bealach-Na-Ba

River Toscaig

SGURR A GHARAIDH
730
Loch
Coultrie
14
Kirkton
Ardarroch
Lochcarron
Slumbay
Achintraid
BAD A CHREAMHA
394
Ardaneaskan
Strome
Ardnarf
Ardnā
Sallach
A8

NAVAIG
amastianavaig
Ollach
Tianavaig
Bay
Upper
Ollach
ailor
The
aes
orran
Sconser
73
MAIG

Oskaig
Clachan
310
BEINN NA LEAC
Inverarish
Eyre Point
Suisnish
Point
V

SCALPAY

Loch Ainort
17

564
GLAS BHEINN
MHÒR

Longay
67

396
MULLACH NA
CARN

Dunan
Luib

A850

Corry
A854
Broadford
Bay
Waterloo

BEINN
NA CAILLICH
708
732

Eilean
Meadhonach
Eilean
Mòr
CROWLIN
ISLANDS

Caolas Mor

Caolas Scalpay

Pabay
27

Lower
Breakish
Upper
Breakish

6

7

Loch Kishorn
Kishorn
Island
Ardaneaskan
Loch Carron
Plockton
Port-an-Eorna
Drumbuie
Erbusaig
Badicaul
Kyle of Lochalsh
Kyleakin
V

Achmore
Stromeferry
Duirinish
BEINN RAIMH
447
138
Lochalsh House
& Garden
Balmacara
Auchtertyre
A87
Kirkton
Loch Alsh

8

Conchra
Nostie
Ardelve
Eilean Donan
Dornie
Carndu
Letterfearn
Buno
Keppo
9

15
A8

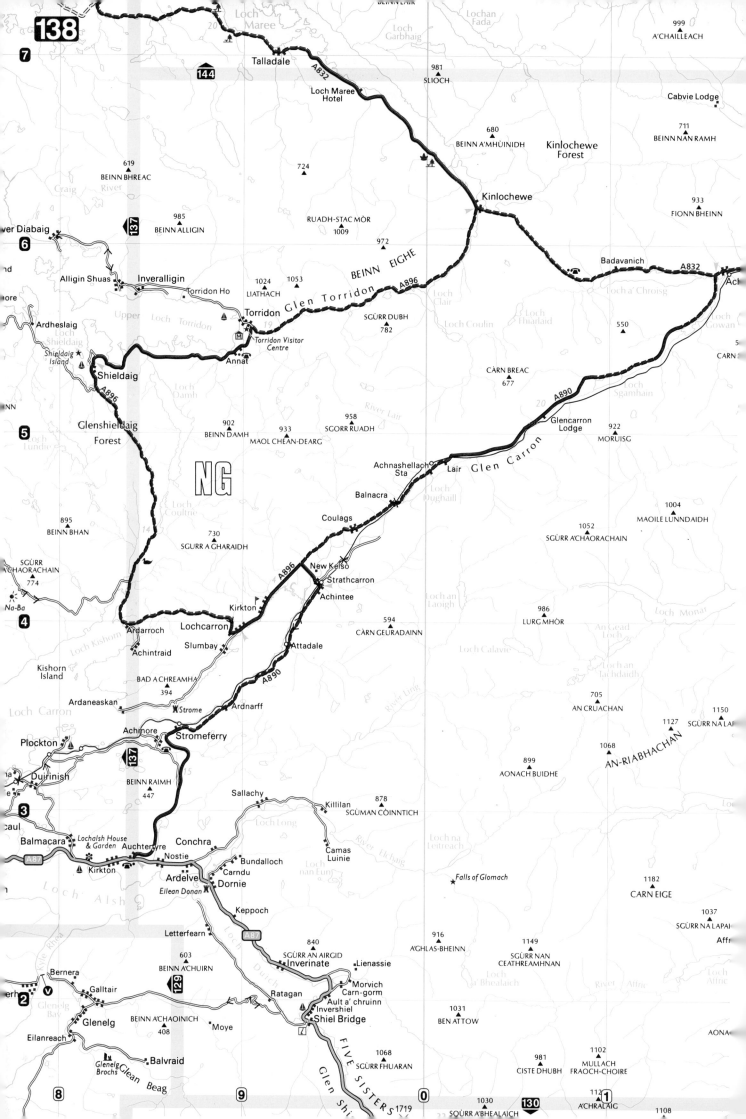

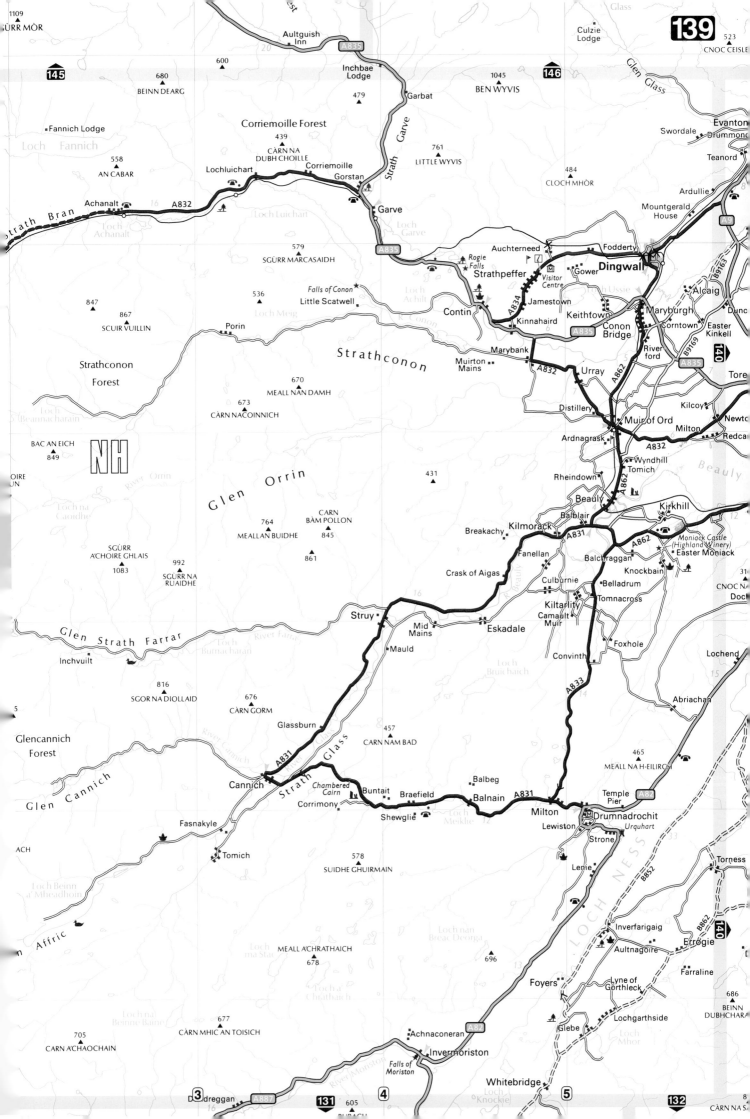

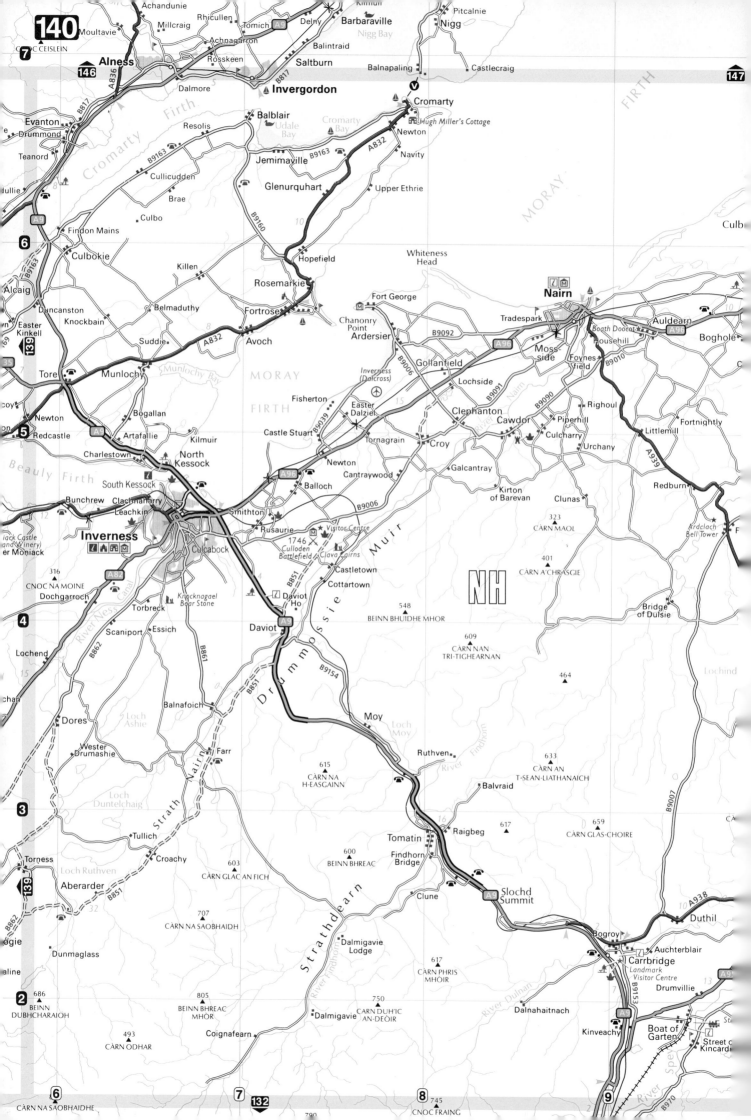

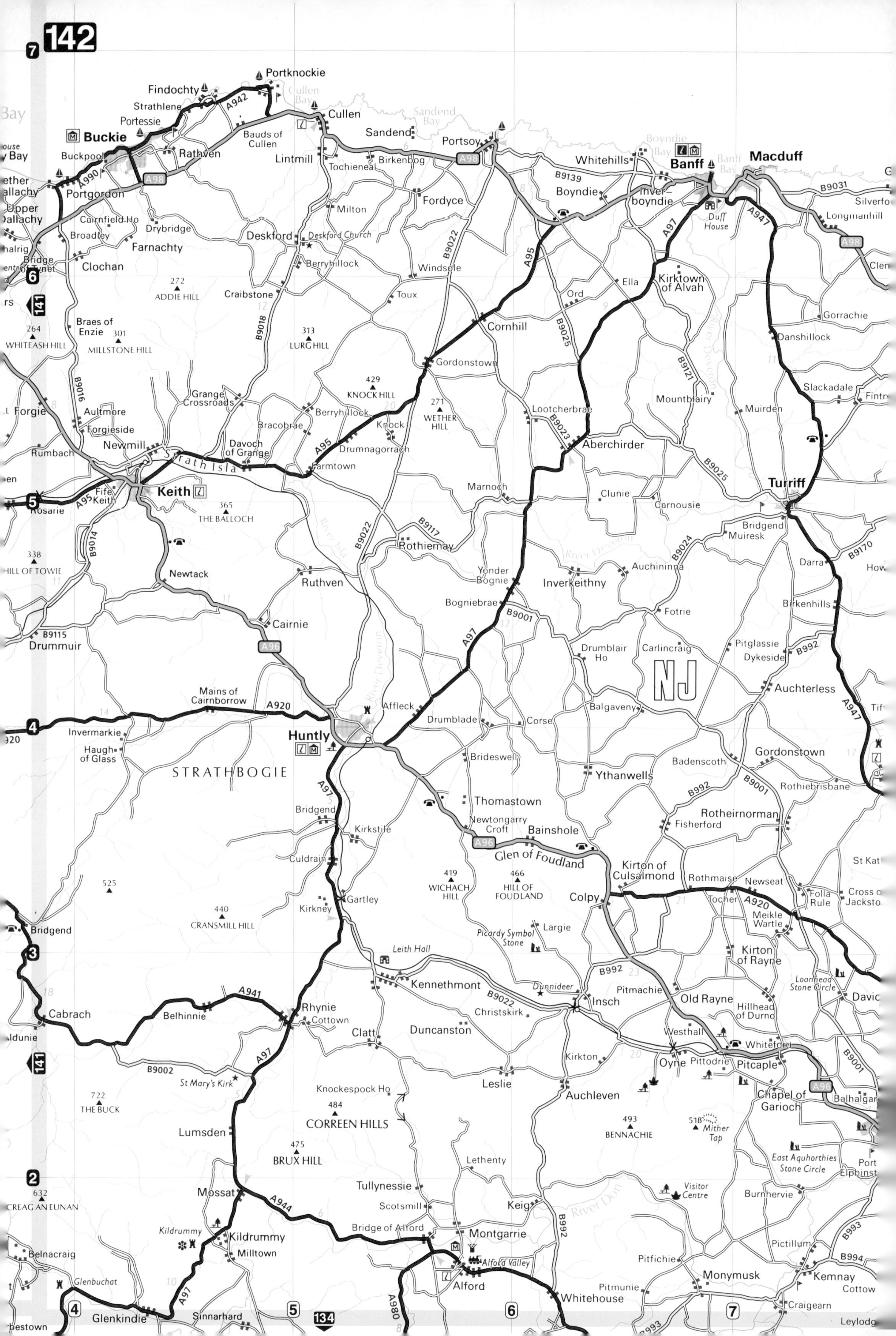

Portknockie
Findochty
Strathlene
Portessie
Buckie
Buckpool
Portgordon
Cairnfield Ho
Broadley
Drybridge
Farnachty
Clochan
ADDIE HILL 272
Braes of Enzie
WHITEASH HILL 264
MILLSTONE HILL 301
Craibstone
Forgie
Aultmore
Forgieside
Rumbach
Newmill
Strathisla
Keith
Fife Keith
Rosarie
HILL OF TOWIE 338
Newtack
THE BALLOCH 365
Drummuir
Ruthven
Cairnie
Mains of Cairnborrow
Invermarkie
Haugh of Glass
STRATHBOGIE
Bridgend
Cabrach
Belhinnie
CREAG AN EUNAN 632
THE BUCK 722
Lumsden
Kildrummy
Kildrummy Milltown
Belnacraig
Glenbuchat
Glenkindie
Sinnarhard

Rathven
Bauds of Cullen
Cullen
Lintmill
Sandend
Tochieneag
Birkenbog
Milton
Deskford
Deskford Church
Berryhillock
Windsole
Toux
Fordyce
LURG HILL 313
Cornhill
Gordonstown
KNOCK HILL 429
Grange Crossroads
Berryhillock
Bracobrae
Davoch of Grange
Knock
WETHER HILL 271
Drumnagorrach
Farmtown
Marnoch
Rothiemay
B9117
Yonder Bognie
Bogniebrae
Affleck
Drumblade
Corse
Bridgend
Kirkstile
Culdrain
Gartley
Kirkney
CRANSMILL HILL 440
WICHACH HILL 419
HILL OF FOUNDLAND 466
Glen of Foundland
Bainshole
Newtongarry Croft
Thomastown
Brideswell
Ythanwells
Colpy
Leith Hall
Picardy Symbol Stone
Largie
Kennethmont
Christskirk
Duncanston
Clatt
Rhynie
Cottown
St Mary's Kirk
B9002
Knockespock Ho
BRUX HILL 475
CORREEN HILLS
Mossat
Tullynessie
Scotsmill
Leslie
Kirkton
Auchleven
Lethenty
BENNACHIE 493
Bridge of Alford
Montgarrie
Alford Valley
Alford
Whitehouse

Portsoy
Whitehills
Boyndie
Inverboyndie
Banff
Macduff
Duff House
B9139
B9031
Silverfo
Longmanhill
Kirktown of Alvah
Ord
Ella
Gorrachie
Danshillock
Slackadale
Fintr
Lootcherbrae
Mountblairy
Muirden
Aberchirder
Clunie
Carnousie
Turriff
Bridgend Muiresk
Auchininna
Inverkeithny
Darra
Birkenhills
Drumblair Ho
Carlincraig
Pitglassie
Dykeside
NJ
Balgaveny
Auchterless
Badenscoth
Gordonstown
Rotheirnorman
Fisherford
Rothiebrisbane
Kirton of Culsalmond
Rothmaise
Newseat
St Kat
Cross o Jacksto
Tocher
Meikle Wartle
Folla Rule
Dunnideer
Insch
Pitmachie
Old Rayne
Kirton of Rayne
Loanhead Stone Circle
Davic
Westhall
Hillhead of Durno
Oyne
Pittodrie
Pitcaple
Whiteford
Chapel of Garioch
Balhalgar
Mither Tap 518
East Aquhorthies Stone Circle
Port Elphinst
Burnhervie
Monymusk
Pitfichie
Pitmunie
Keig
Kemnay
Cottow
Craigearn
Leyloda

A942 A98 A990 A96 A920 A941 A97 A944 A980 A95 A947 A98

Troup Head
Cullykhan Bay
Crovie 21
Pennan
B9031
Protstonhill
New Aberdour
Netherbrae
BRACKLAMORE HILL 221
New Byth
B9027
Bonnykelly
armond
Oldwhat
nestown
Balthangie 13

Rosehearty
Pittulie
Sandhaven
Kinnairds Head
Fraserburgh
Craigiefold
Peathill
Percyhorner
Pitblae
Kirktown
Fraserburgh Bay
Cairnbulg
Coburby
Mid Ardlaw
Inverallochy
B9032
Memsie
St Combs
Boyndlie
A92
B9033
A98
Newburgh
Rathen
Lonmay
Crimonmogate
Old Rattray
Rattray Head
234 WAUGHTON HILL
A981
A952
Crimond
Blackhill
B9030
Strichen
New Pitsligo
New Leeds
Longhill
St Fergus
B9093
Denhead
Leys
Backfolds
Rora
A981
Fetterangus
A952
A950
Feddrate
Deer Abbey
Dunshillock
Mintlaw
River Ugie
Maud
B9106
Old Deer
Inverugie
Buchanhaven
Peterhead
New Deer
B9029
Visitor Centre
Longside
A950
Blackhill of Clackriach
A948
Drymuir
Bulwark
Stuartfield
Inverquhomery
Peterhead Bay
Maryhill
Slacks of Cairnbanno
Nethermuir
Millbreck
Nether Kinmundy
Hillhead of Cocklaw
Burnhaven
Millbrex
Clola
B9170
Knaven
B9030
Kinnadie
Little Dens
Blackhill
Boddam
Buchan Ness
Kirkton
Auchnagatt
Cairnorrie
Inkhorn
Kinknockie
Stirling
Lendrum Terrace
Cottown
Brownhill
Blackhill
NK
Coldwells
B9005
Haddo
Coldwells
Muirtack
Hatton
Auchiries
Bullers of Buchan
Methlick
Arthrath
A92
North Haven
B9005
Ythan
14
Cruden Bay
Barthol Chapel
Haddo
Birness
Bogbrae
Port Errol
Chapel Hill
Bay of Cruden
Earlsford
Auchedly
A948
The Skares
Wedderlairs
Medieval Tomb
Ythsie
Kinharrachie
Artrochie
A975
Tulloch
Tarves
Auchmacoy
Kirktown of Slains
Craigdam
Tolquhon
Ellon
Esslemont
Kirkton of Logie Buchan
Collieston
B999
um
A920
Pitmedden
B9000
Carnbrogie
Udny Green
Housieside
rktown
Bourtie
A947
Whiterashes
Woodland
Pettymuk
Cultercullen
A92
Newburgh
Foveran
Nether Crimond
Tillygreig
B979
Stralocil
Delfrigs
B993
Reisque
New Machar
Causeyend
inmuck urch
B979
Whitecairns
Belhelvie
Balmedie
B977
Kinmundy
Hatton of Fintray
Dyce Symbol Stones
ParkHill
B997
Potterton
135
9
Overton
B997
Blackdog
Dyce
Aberdeen

To Stromness
To Lerwick

SCALE

0   1   2   3   4   5 miles

0 1 2 3 4 5 kilometres

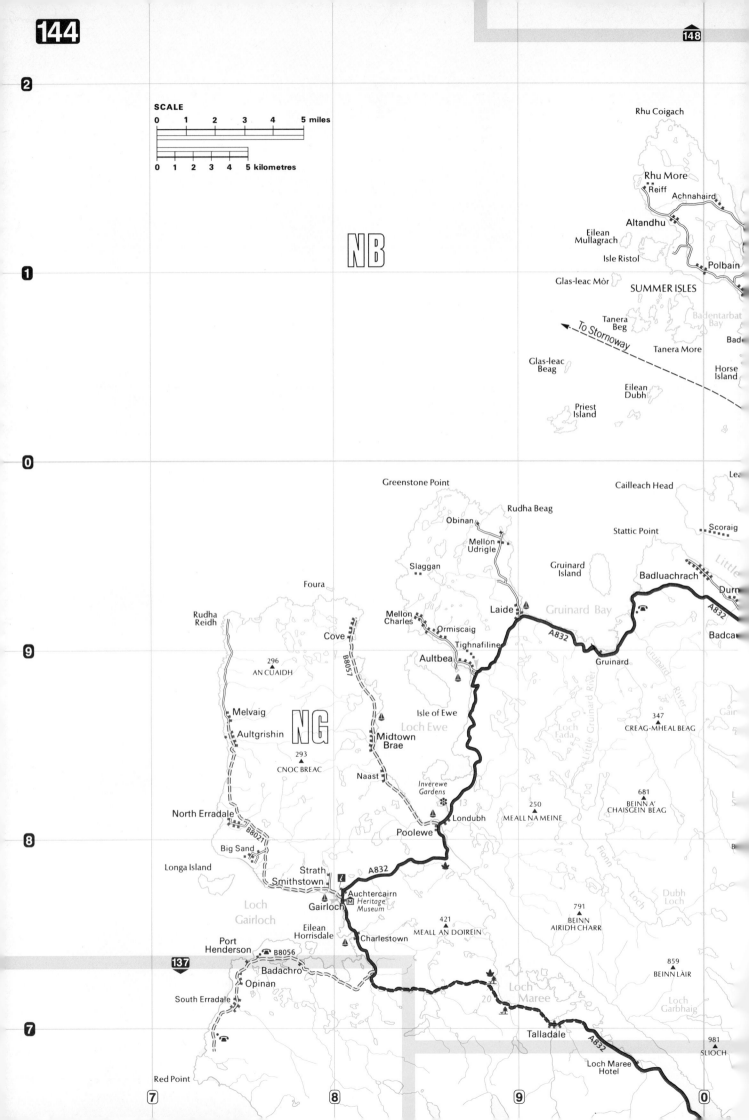

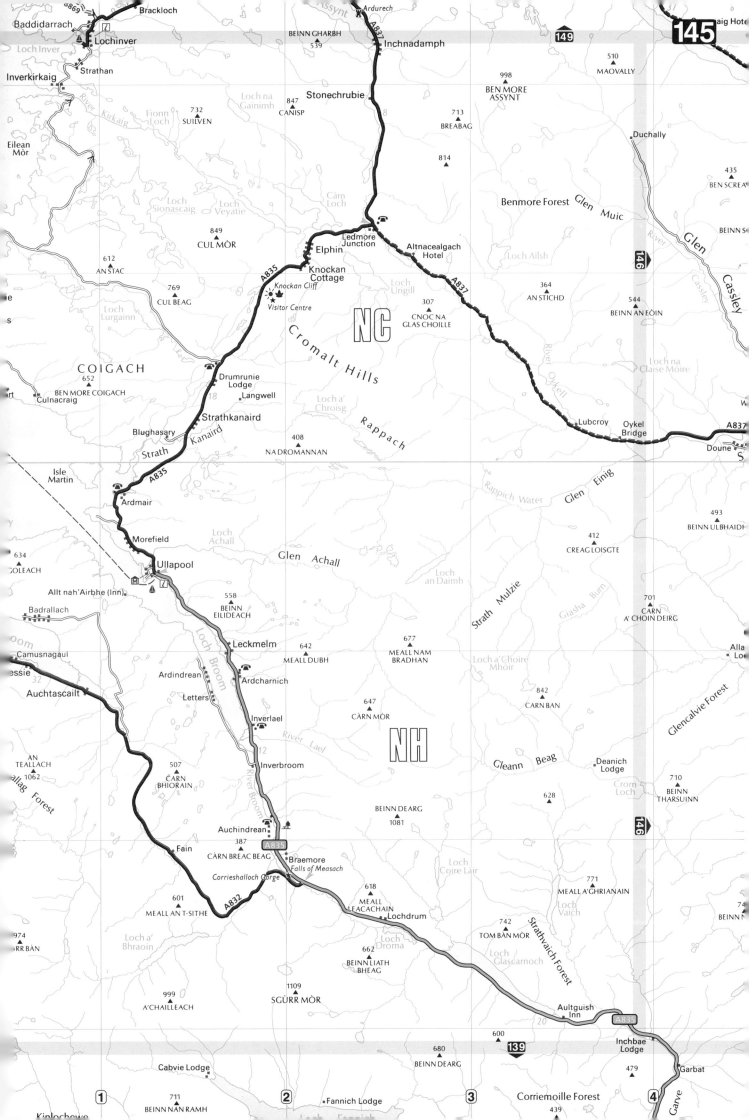

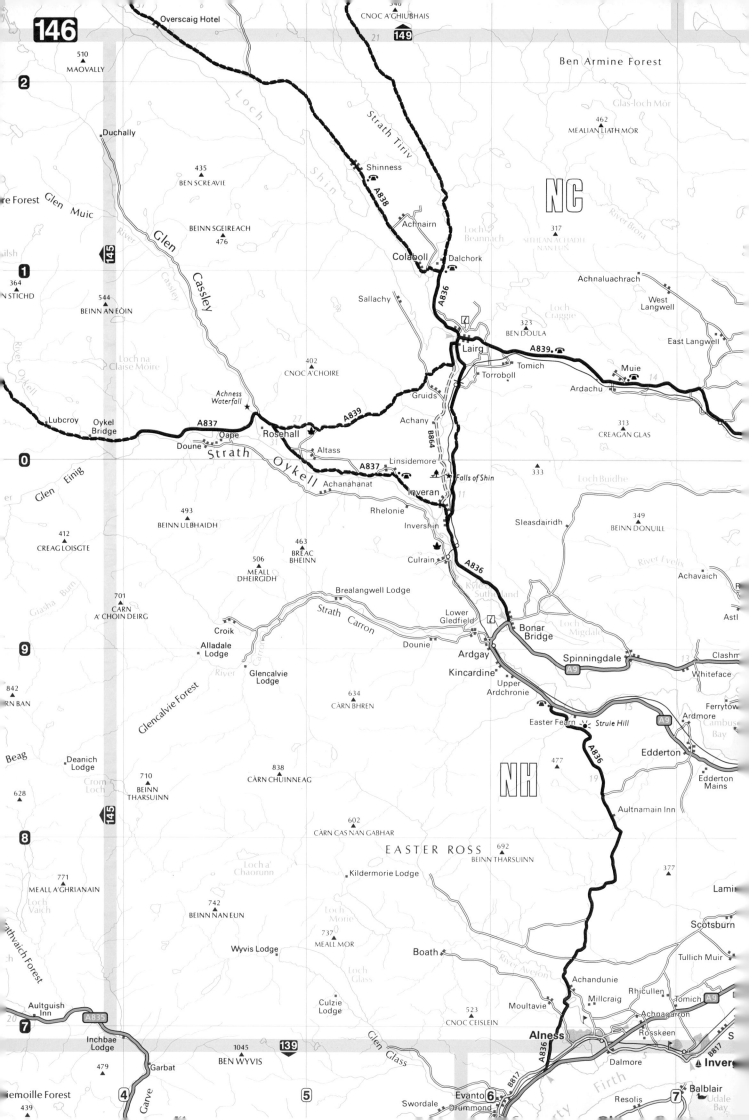

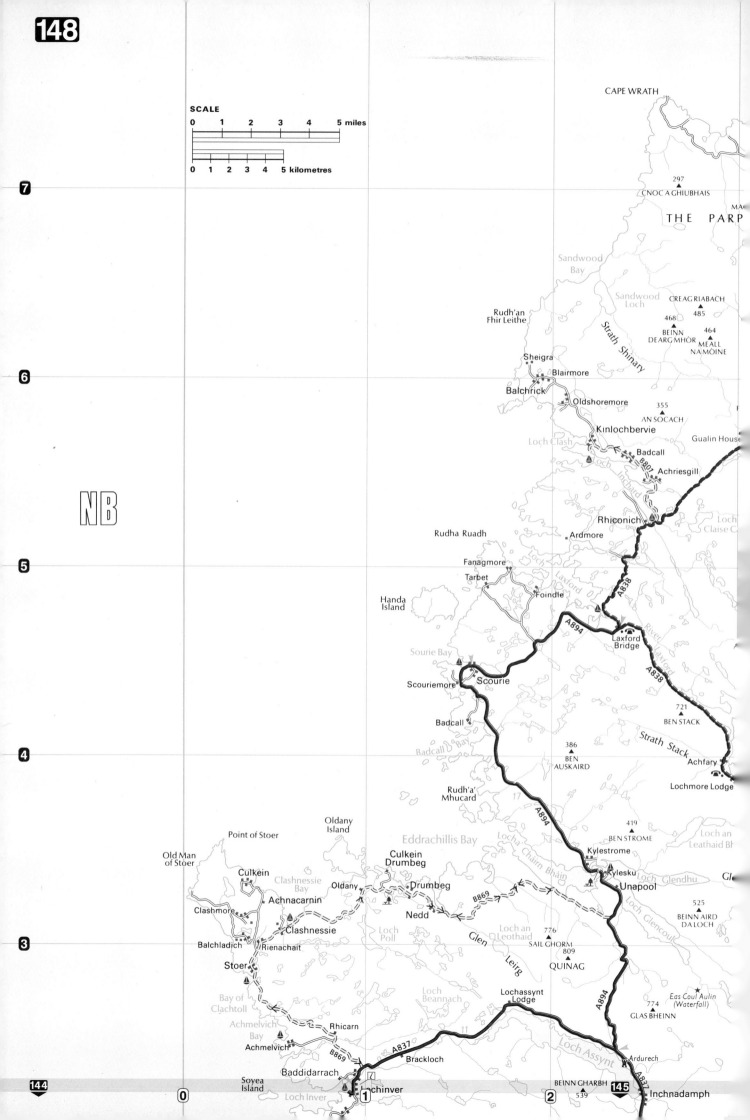

SCALE

0 1 2 3 4 5 miles

0 1 2 3 4 5 kilometres

NB

CAPE WRATH

THE PARP

297
CNOC A GHIUBHAIS

MA

Sandwood
Bay

Sandwood
Loch

CREAG RIABACH

468   485

BEINN
DEARG MHÒR

464
MEALL
NA MÒINE

Strath Shinary

Rudh'an
Fhir Leithe

Sheigra

Blairmore

Balchrick

Oldshoremore

355
AN SOCACH

Kinlochbervie

Gualin House

Loch Clash

Badcall

B801

Achriesgill

Rhiconich

Loch
Claise C

Rudha Ruadh

Ardmore

Loch Inchard

Loch Laxford

Fanagmore

Tarbet

Foindle

A838

River Laxford

Handa
Island

A894

Laxford
Bridge

A838

Sourie Bay

Scouriemore

Scourie

721
BEN STACK

Strath Stack

Badcall

386
BEN
AUSKAIRD

Achfary

Lochmore Lodge

Badcall Bay

Rudh'a'
Mhucard

17

A894

419
BEN STROME

Loch an
Leathaid Bh

Oldany
Island

Point of Stoer

Eddrachillis Bay

Locha Chàirn Bhàin

Kylestrome

Kylesku

Loch Glendhu

Gle

Old Man
of Stoer

Culkein

Clashnessie
Bay

Oldany

Culkein
Drumbeg

Drumbeg

B869

Unapool

525
BEINN AIRD
DA LOCH

Achnacarnin

Clashmore

Clashnessie

Nedd

Loch
Poll

Glen
Leirg

Loch an
Leothaid

776
SAIL GHORM

Loch Glencoul

Balchladich

Rienachait

Stoer

809
QUINAG

774
GLAS BHEINN

Eas Coul Aulin
(Waterfall)

Bay of
Clachtoll

Loch
Beannach

Lochassynt
Lodge

A894

Achmelvich
Bay

Rhicarn

11

Achmelvich

B869

Brackloch

A837

Loch Assynt

Ardurech

A837

144

Baddidarrach

Soyea
Island

Lochinver

Loch Inver

0

BEINN GHARBH

539

145

Inchnadamph

2

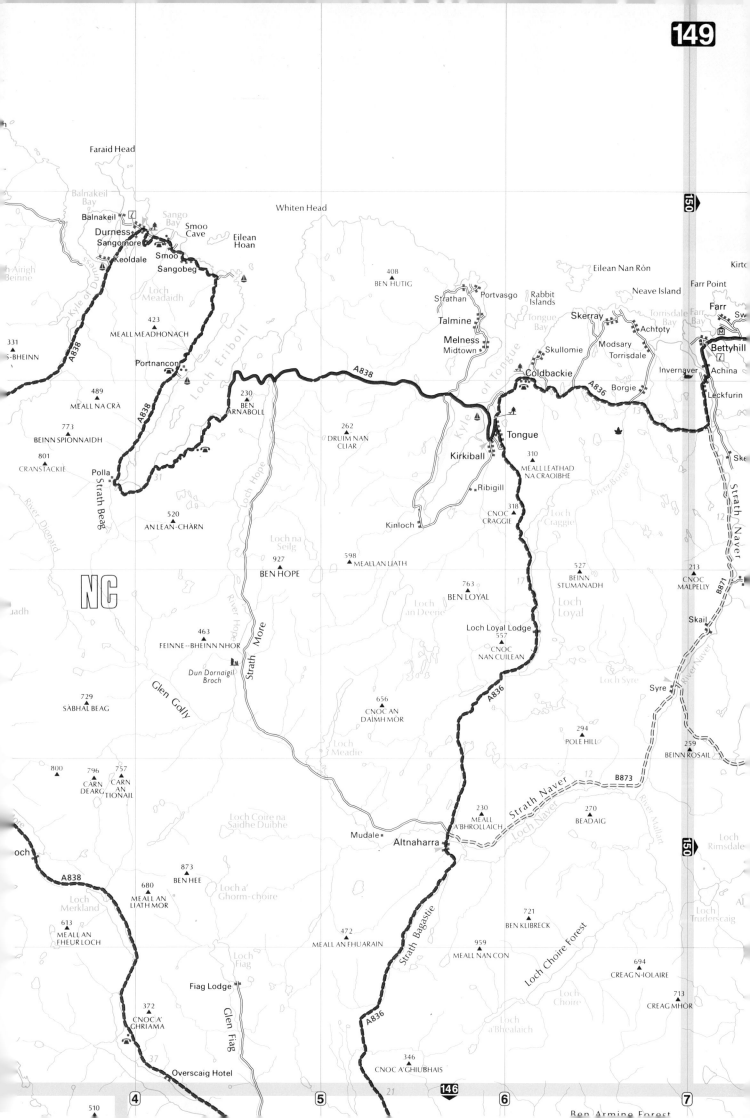

150

Faraid Head

Whiten Head

Balnakeil Bay

Balnakeil
Durness
Sangomore
Keoldale
Smoo
Sangobeg
Sango Bay
Smoo Cave
Eilean Hoan

Loch Meadaidh

h Airigh Beinne

331 S-BHEINN

A838

423 MEALL MEADHONACH

Portnancon

489 MEALL NA CRÀ

773 BEINN SPIONNAIDH

801 CRANSTACKIE

Polla
Strath Beag

Loch Eriboll

230 BEN ARNABOLL

A838

River Dionard

262 DRUIM NAN CLIAR

408 BEN HUTIG

Strathan
Talmine
Melness
Midtown

Portvasgo

Rabbit Islands

Eilean Nan Ròn

Neave Island

Farr Point

Farr

Sw

Torrisdale Bay Farr Bay

Skerray
Achtoty
Modsary
Torrisdale

Skullomie

Coldbackie

Bettyhill
Achina
Invernaver
Leckfurin

A836
Borgie

Tongue

Kirkiball

Ske

Kyle of Tongue

310 MEALL LEATHAD NA CRAOIBHE

River Borgie

NC

520 AN LEAN-CHÀRN

Loch na Seilg

927 BEN HOPE

463 FEINNE--BHEINN NHOR

Dun Dornaigil Broch

729 SÀBHAL BEAG

Glen Golly

Strath More

River Hope

Loch Hope

598 MEALLAN LIATH

Ribigill

Kinloch

318 CNOC CRAGGIE

527 BEINN STUMANADH

Loch Craggie

213 CNOC MALPELLY

B871

Strath Naver

763 BEN LOYAL

Loch an Deeire

Loch Loyal

Loch Loyal Lodge

557 CNOC NAN CUILEAN

Skail

Syre

Loch Syre

River Naver

656 CNOC AN DAIMH MÒR

A836

294 POLE HILL

259 BEINN ROSAIL

Loch Meadie

800

796 CARN DEARG

757 CARN AN TIONAIL

Loch Coire na Saidhe Duibhe

Mudale

Altnaharra

230 MEALL A'BHROLLAICH

Strath Naver

Loch Naver

270 BEADAIG

River Mallart

B873

150

Loch Rimsdale

och

A838

Loch Merkland

680 MEALL AN LIATH MOR

873 BEN HEE

Loch a' Ghorm-chóire

721 BEN KLIBRECK

Loch Choire Forest

Loch Truderscaig

Al

613 MEALL AN FHEUR LOCH

472 MEALL AN FHUARAIN

Strath Bagastie

959 MEALL NAN CON

694 CREAG N-IOLAIRE

Loch Choire

713 CREAG MHÒR

Fiag Lodge

372 CNOC A' GHRIAMA

Glen Fiag

37

A836

Loch a'Bhealaich

Overscaig Hotel

346 CNOC A'GHIUBHAIS

510

21

146

Ben Arming Forest

4   5   6   7

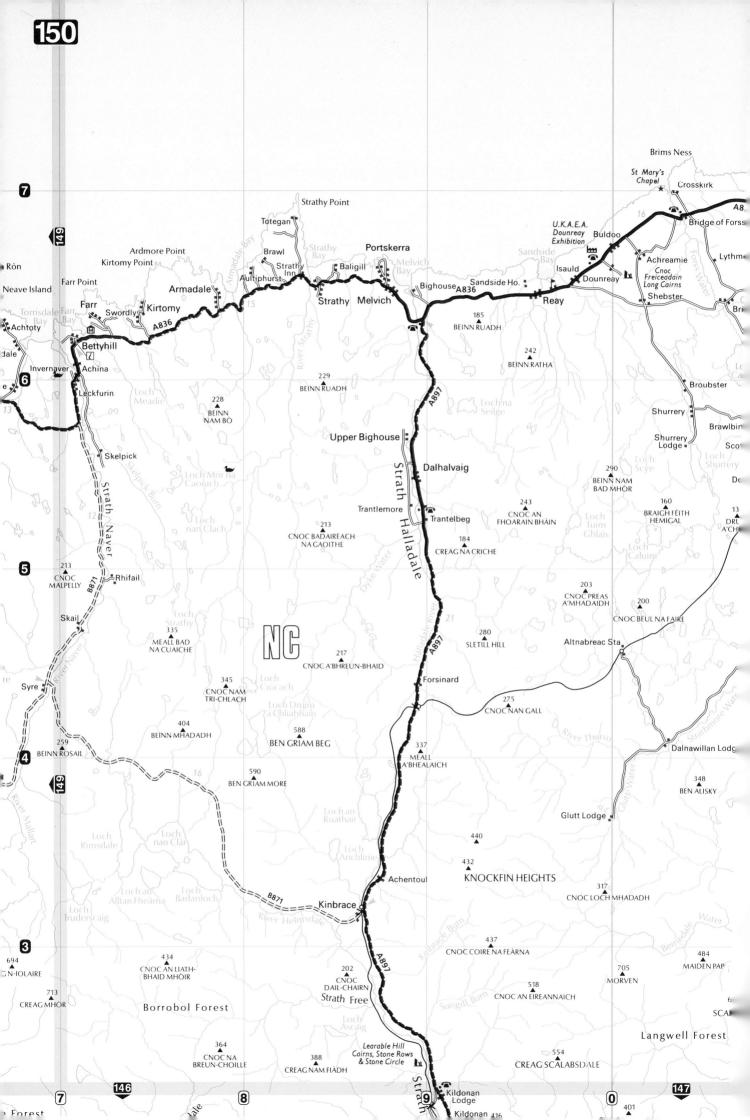

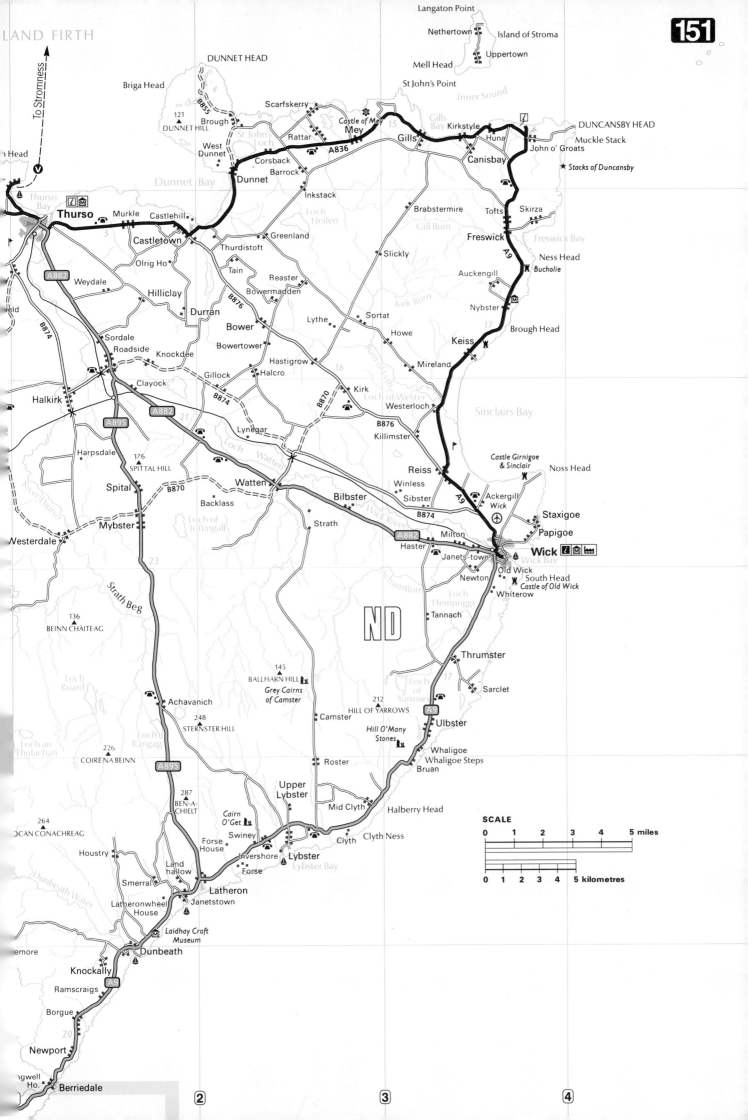

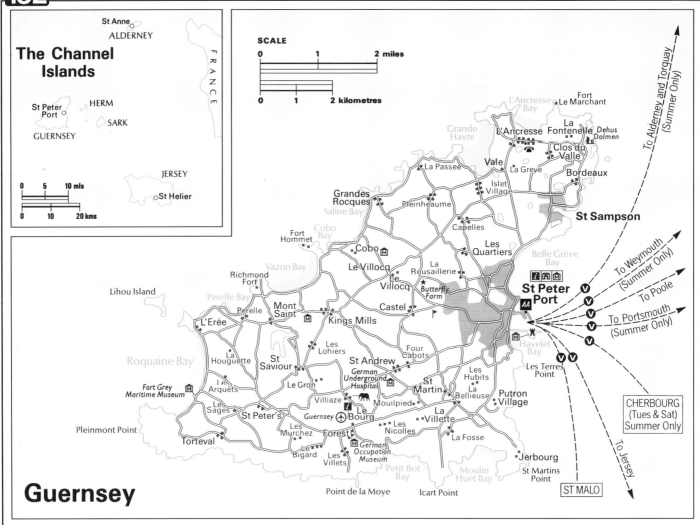

The Channel Islands

St Anne
ALDERNEY

St Peter
Port
GUERNSEY

HERM
SARK

JERSEY

St Helier

SCALE

0   5   10 mis

0   10   20 kms

Guernsey

SCALE

0   1   2 miles

0   1   2 kilometres

FRANCE

L'Ancresse
Bay

Grande
Havre

La Passee

Fort
Le Marchant

L'Ancresse La
Fontenelle Dehus
Dolmen

Vale Clos du
Valle

La Grève
Bordeaux

Islet
Village

St Sampson

Grandes
Rocques

Pléinheaume

Capelles

Les
Quartiers

Belle Grève
Bay

Saline Bay

Fort
Hommet

Cobo
Bay

Cobo

Le Villocq

La
Rousaillerie

Butterfly
Farm

St Peter
Port

AA

Vazon Bay

Le
Villocq

Castel

Havelet
Bay

Lihou Island

Richmond
Fort

Perelle

Perelle Bay

Mont
Saint

Kings Mills

Four
Cabots

Les Terres
Point

L'Erée

Roquaine Bay

La
Houguette

St
Saviour

Les
Lohiers

St Andrew

German
Underground
Hospital

St
Martin

Les
Hubits

La
Bellieuse

Putron
Village

To Alderney and Torquay
(Summer Only)

To Weymouth
(Summer Only)

To Poole

To Portsmouth
(Summer Only)

CHERBOURG
(Tues & Sat)
Summer Only

Fort Grey
Maritime Museum

Les
Arquêts

Le Gron

Villiaze

Mouilpied

Les
Sages

St Peter's

Les
Murchez

Forest

Le
Bourg

Guernsey

La
Villette

Les
Nicolles

La Fosse

To Jersey

Pleinmont Point

Torteval

Le
Bigard

Les
Villets

German
Occupation
Museum

Jerbourg

St Martins
Point

ST MALO

Point de la Moye

Petit Bot
Bay

Icart Point

Moulin
Huet Bay

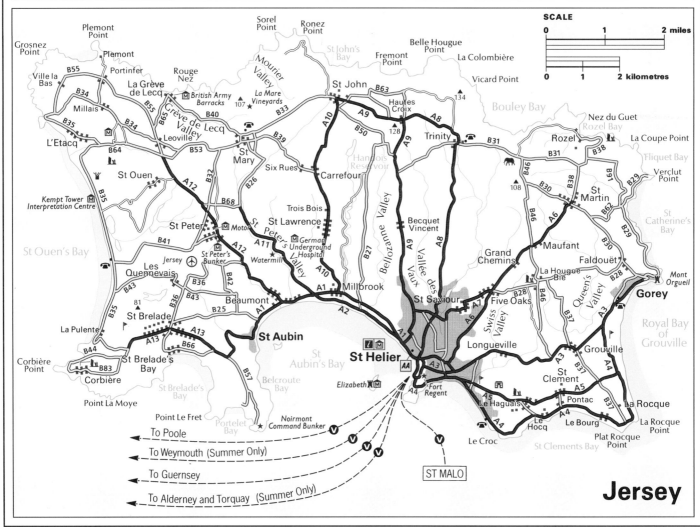

Jersey

SCALE

0   1   2 miles

0   1   2 kilometres

Grosnez
Point

Plemont
Point

Sorel
Point

Ronez
Point

Belle Hougue
Point

Ville la Bas

B55

Plemont

Portinfer

Mourier
Valley

Fremont
Point

La Colombière

Vicard Point

Bouley Bay

Nez du Guet
Rozel Bay

B34

La Grève
de Lecq

Rouge
Nez

St John's
Bay

St John

B63

Hautes
Croix

A8

Rozel

La Coupe Point

Millais

B35

B34

B65

Grève de Lecq
Valley

British Army
Barracks
107

La Mare
Vineyards

B33

A10

A9

128

Trinity

B31

B38

Fliquet
Bay

L'Etacq

B64

B53

Leoville

St
Mary

B39

B50

A9

108

B30

St Martin

B52

Verclut
Point

St Ouen

A12

B32

Six Rues

B26

Carrefour

B46

A6

Maufant

B38

B28

St
Catherine's
Bay

Kempt Tower
Interpretation Centre

B35

B68

Trois Bois

St Lawrence

Becquet
Vincent

Grand
Chemins

Faldouët

Mont
Orgueil

St Ouen's Bay

St Peter

Motor

German
Underground
Hospital

A8

Jersey

B41

St Peter's
Bunker

A12

A11

Watermill

A10

St Saviour

A7

Five Oaks

B28

La Hougue
Bie

B37

B30

Gorey

Les
Quennevais

B43

B36

B42

Millbrook

A1

Longueville

Queen's Valley

A3

Royal Bay
of
Grouville

81

Beaumont

B25

A7

A1

Grouville

St Brelade

La Pulente

B44

A13

B66

St Aubin

St
Aubin's Bay

St Helier

AA

Fort
Regent

St
Clement

A5

La Rocque

Corbière
Point

B83

St Brelade's
Bay

Corbière

B57

Belcroute
Bay

Elizabeth

A4

Le Haguais

Pontac

Le Bourg

B37

La Rocque
Point

Point La Moye

St Brelade's
Bay

Noirmont
Command Bunker

Le
Hocq

A4

Plat Rocque
Point

Point Le Fret

Portelet
Bay

To Poole

To Weymouth (Summer Only)

To Guernsey

To Alderney and Torquay (Summer Only)

ST MALO

Le Croc

St Clements Bay

Isle of Man

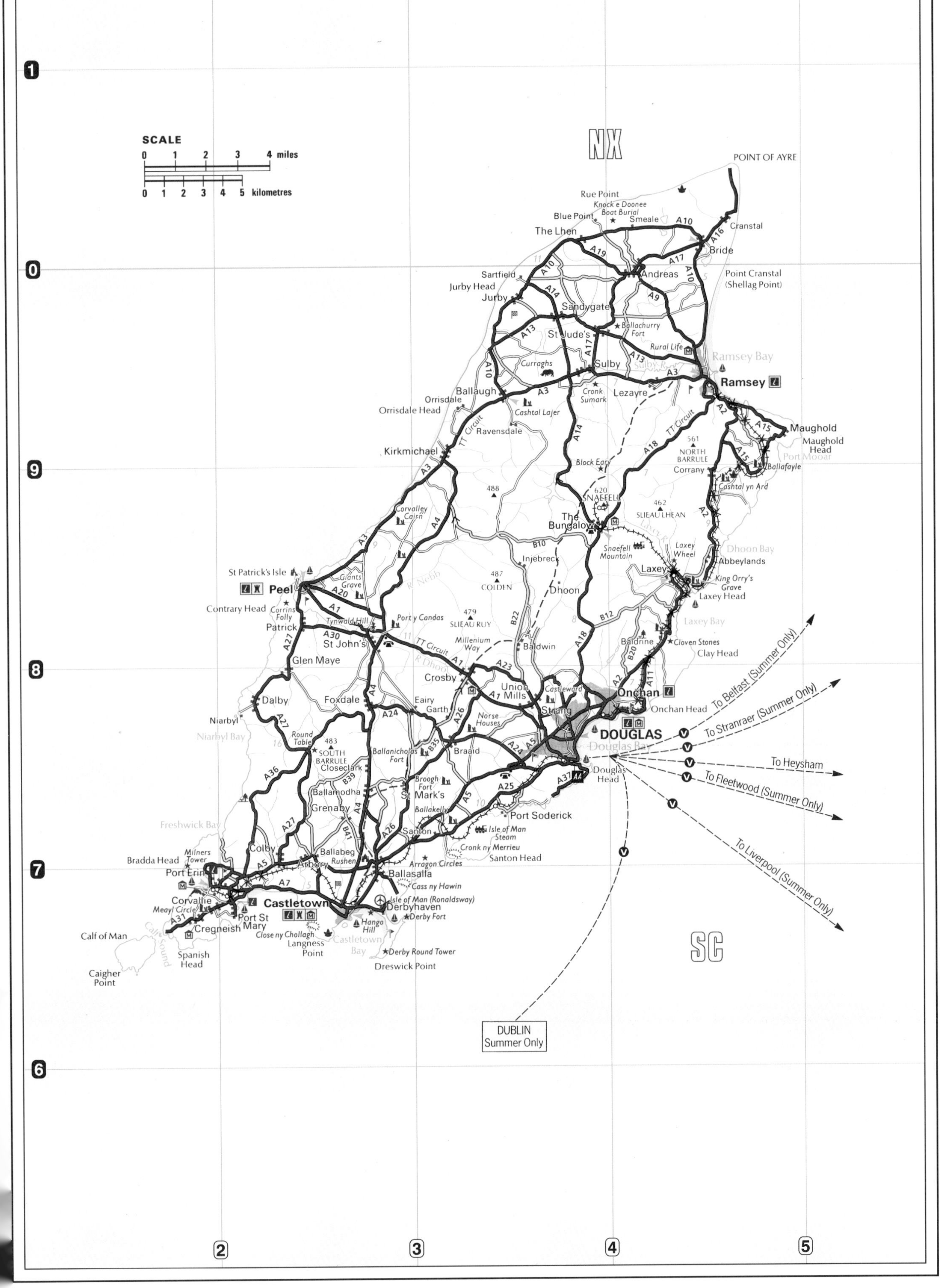

NX

SCALE

0 1 2 3 4 miles

0 1 2 3 4 5 kilometres

POINT OF AYRE

Rue Point
Knock e Doonee
Boat Burial
Blue Point ★ Smeale A10 Cranstal
The Lhen A16
A19 Bride
A17
Sartfield A10 Andreas Point Cranstal
Jurby Head A14 A10 (Shellag Point)
Jurby A9
Sandygate
St Jude's ★Ballachurry
A13 Fort
Curraghs Rural Life
A13 Sulby A3 Ramsey Bay
Ballaugh Lezayre Ramsey
Orrisdale A3 Cronk A2
Orrisdale Head Sumark Maughold
Cashtal Lajer A14 561 Maughold
TT Circuit Ravensdale NORTH Head
A18 BARRULE Ballafayle
Kirkmichael A10 Block Earl Corrany A15 Port Mooar
★ Cashtal yn Ard
488 620
SNAEFELL A2
Corvalley 462
Cairn The SLIEAU LHEAN
A4 Bungalow Dhoon Bay
A3 B10 Snaefell Laxey
Injebreck Mountain Wheel Abbeylands
St Patrick's Isle 487 King Orry's
Giants COLDEN Grave
Peel Grave B12 Dhoon Laxey Head
A20 Port y Candas Laxey Bay
Contrary Head Corrins 479 B22
Folly SLIEAU RUY A18 Baldrine
Patrick Tynwald Hill TT Circuit Cloven Stones
A1 A1 Millenium B20 Clay Head
A30 Way Baldwin
St John's A23 A2
Glen Maye Crosby Castleward To Belfast (Summer Only)
Union A1 Onchan
Dalby Foxdale Eairy A26 Mills Strang Onchan Head To Stranraer (Summer Only)
Niarbyl A27 Garth Norse A2 A5 DOUGLAS To Heysham
Niarbyl Bay Round Houses Braaid Douglas Bay To Fleetwood (Summer Only)
Table 483 B35 Douglas
SOUTH A5 Head
A36 BARRULE Ballanicholas A25 A31 A4 To Liverpool (Summer Only)
Closeclark Fort Brough
B39 Fort
Ballamodha St Mark's
Grenaby A4 Ballakelly
A27 Santon Port Soderick
A26 Isle of Man
Milners Arragon Circles Steam
Bradda Head Tower Colby Ballabeg Cronk ny Merriu Santon Head
Port Erin A5 Arbory Rushen Cass ny Hawin
A7 Ballasalla DUBLIN
Corvalhe A31 Castletown Derbyhaven Summer Only
Meayl Circle Port St ★Derby Fort
Calf of Man Cregneish Mary Hango
Close ny Chollagh Hill Castletown
Spanish Langness Bay
Head Point Dreswick Point ★Derby Round Tower
Caigher
Point SC

Freshwick Bay

Outer Hebrides

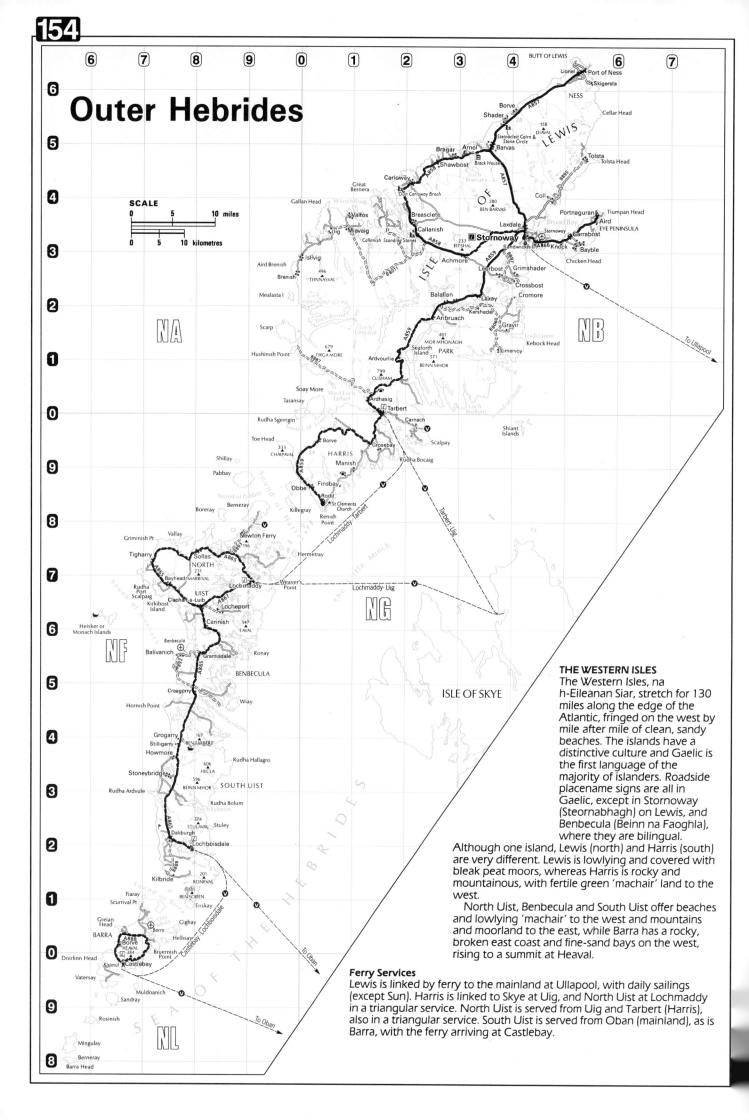

SCALE

0   5   10 miles

0   5   10 kilometres

BUTT OF LEWIS
Lionel • Port of Ness
Skigersta
NESS
Borve
Shader   A857
28
DIAVAL   158   Cellar Head
Steinacleit Cairn &
Stone Circle
Bragar   Arnol   Barvas   Black House   Tolsta Head
Shawbost   Tolsta
Carloway   A856
Dun Carloway Broch
LEWIS
Great
Bernera   Coll
Gallan Head   BEN BARVAS
280   Portnaguran   Tiumpan Head
Valtos   Breasclete   Laxdale   Aird   EYE PENINSULA
Uig   Miavaig   Callanish   Stornoway   Garrabost
Callanish Standing Stones   Stornoway
Islivig   Achmore   A859   Knock   Bayble
Aird Brenish   233   Sandwickhill   Chicken Head
Brenish   EITSHAL   Leurbost   Grimshader
496   Crossbost   Cromore
TEINNASVAL   Balallan   Laxay
Mealasta I   Kershader
Scarp   Aribruach   Gravir
679   401   Kebock Head
Hushinish Point   TIRGA MORE   MOR MHONADH
Ardvourlie   Seaforth   PARK
Island   571   Limervoy
799   BEINN MHOR
CLISHAM   Kebock Head
Soay More   Ardhasig
Taransay   Tarbert   Carnach   Shiant
Islands
Rudha Sgeirigin   West Loch
Tarbert
Toe Head   Borve   Grosebay   Scalpay
333   HARRIS   Rudha Bocaig
CHAIPAVAL   Manish
Shillay   Obbe   Finsbay
Pabbay   Rodil   St Clements
Church
Killegray   Renish
Boreray   Point
Berneray
Sound of Pabbay   Newton Ferry
Griminish Pt   Vallay   196
Tigharry   Sollas   Hermetray
NORTH   Weaver's
Bayhead   231   Point
Rudha   MARRIVAL   Lochmaddy
Port   UIST
Scalpaig   Clachan-a-Luib   Lochmaddy-Uig
Kirkibost   Locheport   Weaver's
Island   Carinish   Point
Heisker or   347   NG
Monach Islands   EAVAL
NF   Benbecula
Balivanich   Ronay
Gramsdale
BENBECULA
Creagorry   Wiay   ISLE OF SKYE
Hornish Point
Grogarry   167
Stilligarry   BEN TARBERT
Howmore
606
Stoneybridge   HECLA
596   SOUTH UIST
Rudha Ardvule   BEINN MHOR
374
Rudha Bolum   STULAVAL   Stuley
Dalburgh
Lochboisdale
Kilbride   RONEVAL
201
Fiaray   BEN SCRIEN
Scurrival Pt   Eriskay
185
Greian   Gighay
Head   Barra   Hellisay
BARRA   Borve
HEAVAL   Castlebay Lochboisdale
384
Doirlinn Head   Kisimul   Castlebay   To Oban
Vatersay
Muldoanich   To Oban
Sandray
Rosinish   NL
Mingulay
Berneray
Barra Head

THE WESTERN ISLES

The Western Isles, na h-Eileanan Siar, stretch for 130 miles along the edge of the Atlantic, fringed on the west by mile after mile of clean, sandy beaches. The islands have a distinctive culture and Gaelic is the first language of the majority of islanders. Roadside placename signs are all in Gaelic, except in Stornoway (Steornabhagh) on Lewis, and Benbecula (Beinn na Faoghla), where they are bilingual.

Although one island, Lewis (north) and Harris (south) are very different. Lewis is lowlying and covered with bleak peat moors, whereas Harris is rocky and mountainous, with fertile green 'machair' land to the west.

North Uist, Benbecula and South Uist offer beaches and lowlying 'machair' to the west and mountains and moorland to the east, while Barra has a rocky, broken east coast and fine-sand bays on the west, rising to a summit at Heaval.

Ferry Services

Lewis is linked by ferry to the mainland at Ullapool, with daily sailings (except Sun). Harris is linked to Skye at Uig, and North Uist at Lochmaddy in a triangular service. North Uist is served from Uig and Tarbert (Harris), also in a triangular service. South Uist is served from Oban (mainland), as is Barra, with the ferry arriving at Castlebay.

To Ullapool

SEA OF THE HEBRIDES

The Little Minch

Sound of Barra

Scottish Islands

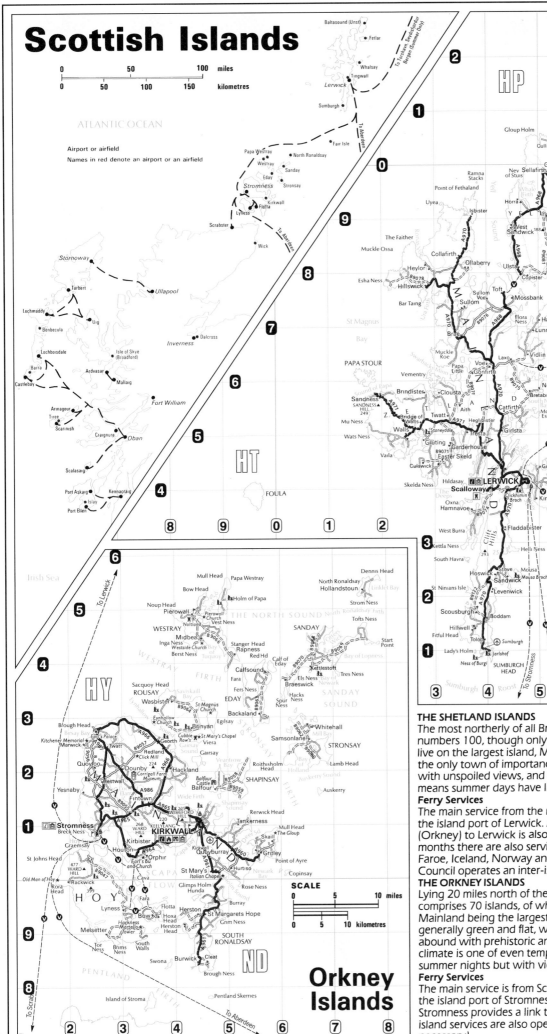

Airport or airfield
Names in red denote an airport or an airfield

Shetland Islands

Orkney Islands

THE SHETLAND ISLANDS
The most northerly of all Britain's islands, this group numbers 100, though only 15 are inhabited. Most people live on the largest island, Mainland, on which Lerwick is the only town of importance. The scenery is magnificent, with unspoiled views, and the islands' northerly position means summer days have little or no darkness.

Ferry Services
The main service from the mainland is from Aberdeen to the island port of Lerwick. A service from Stromness (Orkney) to Lerwick is also available. During the summer months there are also services linking Shetland with Faroe, Iceland, Norway and Denmark. Shetland Islands Council operates an inter-island service.

THE ORKNEY ISLANDS
Lying 20 miles north of the Scottish mainland, Orkney comprises 70 islands, of which 18 are inhabited, Mainland being the largest. Apart from Hoy, Orkney is generally green and flat, with few trees. The islands abound with prehistoric antiquities and rare bird life. The climate is one of even temperatures and 'twilight' summer nights but with violent winds at times.

Ferry Services
The main service is from Scrabster on Caithness coast to the island port of Stromness. A service from Aberdeen to Stromness provides a link to Shetland at Lerwick. Inter-island services are also operated (advance reservations necessary).

Ireland

LEGEND

M1	Motorway
N17	National Primary Route ⎫
N54	National Secondary Route ⎬ Republic of Ireland
R182	Regional Road ⎭
A4	Primary Route ⎫
A21	A Road ⎬ Northern Ireland
B75	B Road ⎭

Distance in miles between symbols

International Boundary

Frontier Posts

Scale: 16 miles to 1 inch (approx)

```
0        10        20        30
├────────┼────────┼────────┤  miles
├──────┼──────┼──────┼──────┤  kilometres
0     10     20     30     40
```

Aran Island

G

Gweeba

Rossan Point
Malin More
Glencolumbkille
Folk Museum
Glencolumbkille
(Gleann Cholm
Cille)
1972 An Char
SLIEVE LEAGUE
Carrick
Kilcar
(Cill Charthaigh)
Killy

St John's Poin

F

Donegal

Inishmurray

R279

Grange
1722
Lissadell
House
BEN

Erris Head
Broad
Haven
Downpatrick Head
Ballycastle
R314
Killala
Bay
R297
Easky
Dromore
West
Strandhill
Rosses Point
Sligo Bay
R29

Belmullet
(Béal an Mhuirhead)
R314
R314
Killala
Enniscrone
N59
32
N59
Colloony

Bunnahowen
Carrowmore
Lough
R315
N59
Bunnyconnellan
N17
R299

Inishkea
R313
Bangor Erris
N59
Crossmolina
Ballina
OX MTS
R294
Ballyr

Duvillaun More
Blacksod Bay
2369
R312
Lough Cillin
2646
NEPHIN
R310
Connaught
Regional Airport
Tobercurry
R296
R293

2204
SLIEVE MORE
Keel
R315
Foxford
N57
Curry
Charlestown
Carracastle
R284

Achill Head
R319
R317
R312
Lough Cullin
N58
N57
Swinford
N5
Ballaghade

Achill Island
Lough
Feeagh
R311
Turlough
N5
Kilkelly
R320
R325

N59
Newport
Castlebar
R321
Kiltimagh
R322
R293
Frenchpark

Clare
Clew Bay
N60
N60
R324
N17
R291
R325
Loughglinn

Westport
R335
Ballyhean
Balla
Knock
R323
Castlerea

Louisburgh
CROAGH PATRICK
2510
Westport Zoo
R330
N84
Ballyhaunis
N60
Ballinlough

Inishturk
Caher
R335
Claremorris
R327
R383
Bal

Inishbofin
Partry
R331
Ballindine
R328
R327
R360
R364

Inishark
2239
Ballinrobe
Lough
Mask
Kilmaine
R362
Glenamado
Creg

Cruagh
Leenene
R344
R330
Neale
R345
Shrule
R382
Dunmore
N17
Cla

Letterfrack
2395
Clonbur
(An Fhairche)
R347
R334
Tuam
R364
R356
Ba

Clifden
N59
Cornamona
R333
R322
Mount
Bellew
Ca

Ballyconneely
R341
R342
R340
Headford
N84
N83
R347
Monivea
R339
Ahascra

Slyne Head
Roundstone
R340
Oughterard
N63
R359

Croagnakeela
Glinsk
Glinsce
R336
N59
Galway
N17
N64
Athenry
R348
R350

Gorumna
Island
Kilkieran
(Cill Ciaráin)
Spiddal
(An Spidéal)
Oranmore
N18
Craughwell
N6

Rock
Inishmore
North Sound
Clarinbridge
Kilcolgan
R347
Loughrea
N65

D

E

1

2

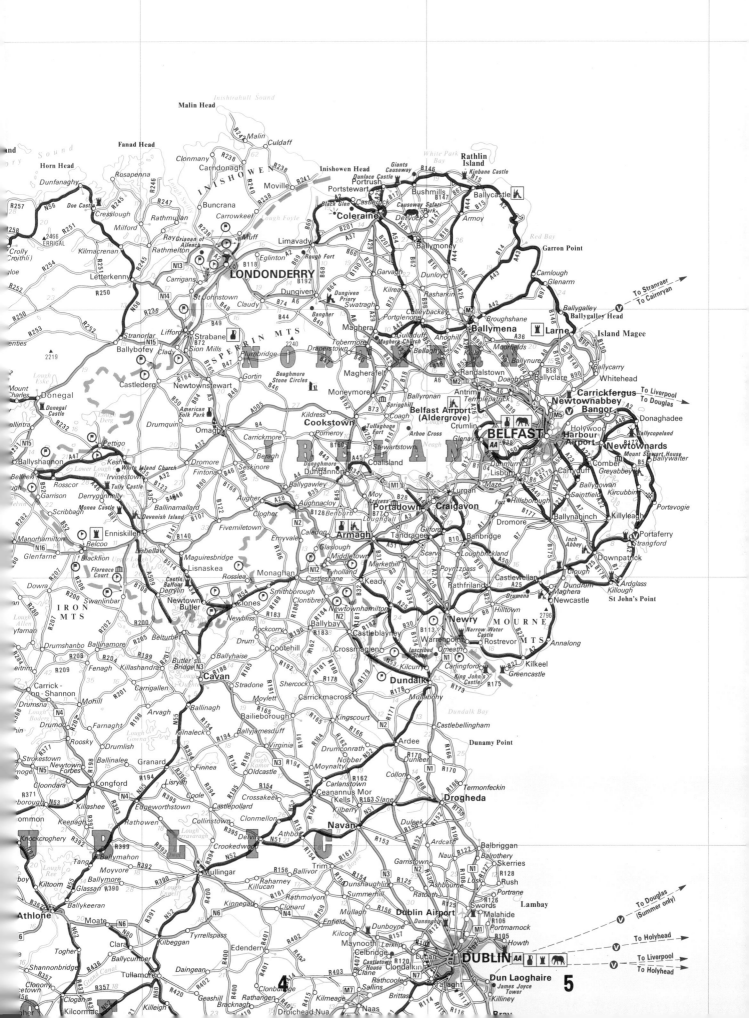

INDEX To Ireland

The map for Ireland employs an arbitrary system of grid reference. Each entry is identified by the page number, and is followed by a letter on the left-hand side of the map and by a number at the top or the bottom. The entry can be located in the square where the lettered and numbered sections converge, e.g., Londonderry is to be found in the square marked by the dissecting blue lines of G4.

London

Inner London

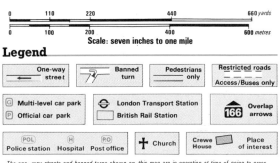

0	110	220	440	660 *yards*
0	100	200	400	600 *metres*

Scale: seven inches to one mile

Legend

One-way street · Banned turn · Pedestrians only · Restricted roads Access/Buses only

Ⓖ Multi-level car park · Ⓟ Official car park · ⊖ London Transport Station · British Rail Station · Overlap arrows 166

POL Police station · Ⓗ Hospital · P.O Post office · ✝ Church · Crewe House · Place of interest

The one-way streets and banned turns shown on this map are in operation at time of going to press. Some of these are experimental and liable to change. Only the more important banned turns are shown, some of which operate between 7am and 7pm only, and these are sign-posted accordingly. No waiting or unilateral waiting restrictions apply to many streets. All such restrictions are indicated by official signs.

Key to Map Pages

163	164-65	166-67
Paddington · Marylebone	Kings Cross · Bloomsbury · Soho	Clerkenwell · Spitalfields · Holborn · City
Bayswater	Mayfair	Thames · Southwark
168-69	**170-71**	**172**
Brompton · Kensington · Belgravia · Chelsea	Westminster · River · Lambeth · Kennington	Bermondsey · Walworth

Theatreland

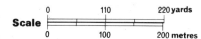

0	110	220 **yards**
0	100	200 **metres**

Scale

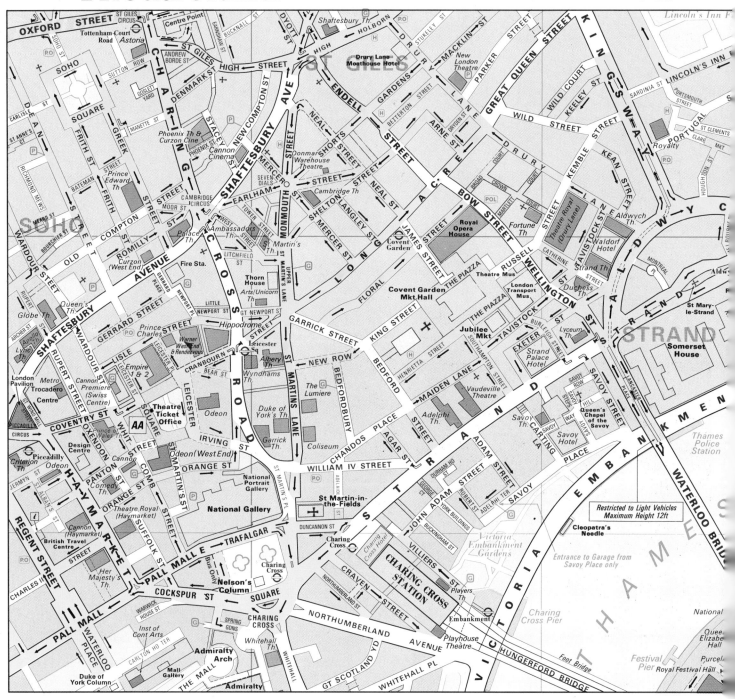

INDEX To Inner London Maps

This map employs an arbitrary system of grid reference. Pages are identified by numbers and divided into twelve squares. Each square contains a black letter; all references give the page number first, followed by the letter of the square in which a particular street can be found. Reference for Exhibition Road is *168*E, meaning that the relevant map is on page *168* and that the street appears in the square designated E.

174

Key to Town Plans

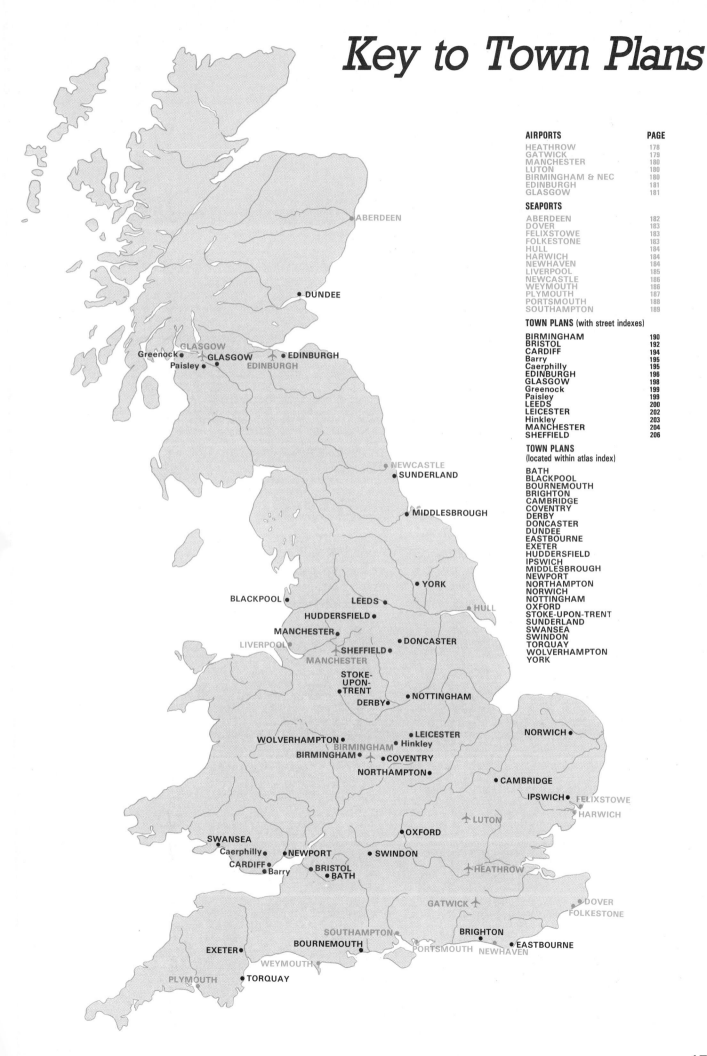

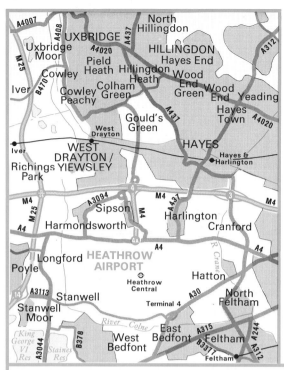

Airports and Seaports

Most people who leave Britain by air or sea use the airports and seaports detailed in these pages. The maps indicate the approach roads into each complex with information on parking and telephone numbers through which details on costs and other travel information can be obtained. The hotels listed are AA-appointed, and the garages have been selected because they provide adequate long term parking facilities.

HEATHROW AIRPORT Tel: 01-759 4321 (Airport Information)

Heathrow, one of the world's busiest international airports, lies sixteen miles west of London. The airport is situated on the Piccadilly Underground line at Heathrow Central station. It is also served by local bus and long distance coach services. For short-term parking, multi-storey car parks are sited at each of the passenger terminals Tel: 01-745 7160 (terminals 1, 2, 3) & 01-759 4931 (terminal 4). Charges for the long-term car parks on the northern perimeter road are designed to encourage their use for a stay in excess of four hours. A free coach takes passengers to and from the terminals. Commercial garages offering long-term parking facilities within easy reach of the airport include: Airways Garage Ltd. Tel: 01-759 9661/4; Quo-Vadis Airport Parking Tel:

01-759 2778; Cranford Parking Tel: 01-759 9661; Flyaway Car Storage Tel: 01-759 1567 or 2020; Kenning Car Hire Tel: 01-759 9701; and National Car Parks Tel: 01-759 9878. Car Hire: Avis Rent-A-Car Tel: 01-897 9321; Budget Rent-A-Car Tel: 01-759 2216; Godfrey Davis Europcar Tel: 01-897 0811/5; Guy Salmon Tel: 01-897 0541; Hertz Rent-A-Car Tel: 01-897 3347; and Kenning Car Hire Tel: 01-759 9701. The 4-star hotels in the area are The Excelsior Tel: 01-759 6611; the Heathrow Penta Tel: 01-897 6363; the Holiday Inn Tel: (0895) 445555 and the Sheraton-Heathrow Tel: 01-759 2424. The 3-star hotels are the Berkeley Arms Tel: 01-897 2121; the Ariel Tel: 01-759 2552; the Post House Tel: 01-759 2323; and the Skyway Tel: 01-759 6311.

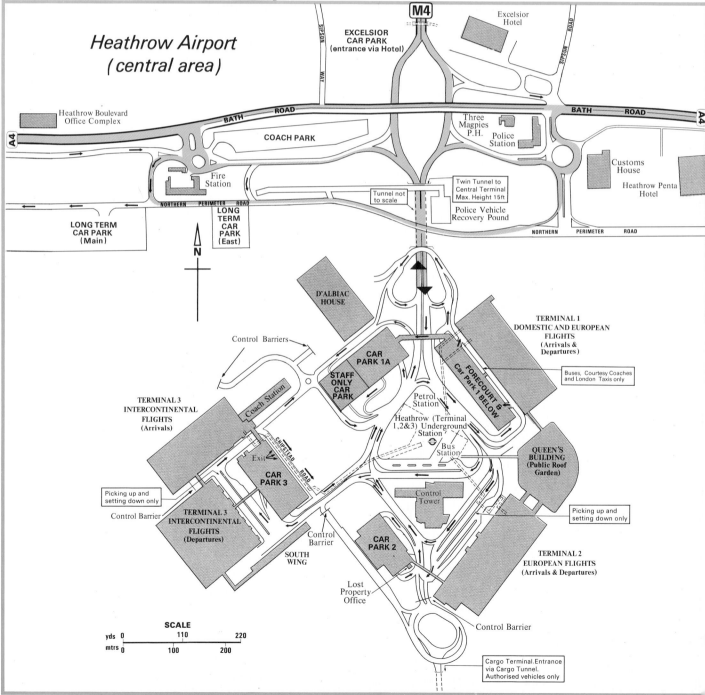

Heathrow Airport (central area)

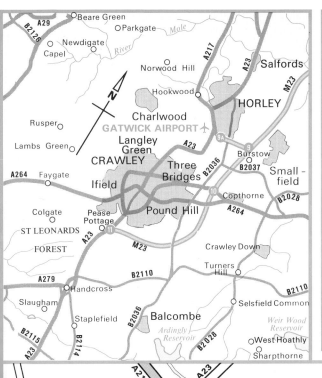

GATWICK AIRPORT Tel: (0293) 28822 or 01-668 4211. London's second airport is served by regular bus and coach services. There is direct covered access by escalator and lift to the South Terminal concourse from the adjacent airport railway station where fast 15-minute frequency services link London (Victoria) with Gatwick 24 hours a day. Parking: ample multi-storey and open-air car parking is available. Tel: Gatwick (0293) 28822 or 01-668 4211. South Terminal ext 2395, North Terminal ext 2747 for information.

MANCHESTER AIRPORT Tel: 061-489 3000. Situated nine miles south of the city, Manchester Airport provides regular scheduled services for many of the leading airlines. A spacious concourse, restaurants and parking facilities are available for passengers. For parking inquiries Tel: 061-489 3723 or 061-489 3000 ext 4635 or 2021.

LUTON AIRPORT Tel: (0582) 405100. Used mainly for package holiday tour operators, the airport has ample open-air car parking. Covered garage space is available from Central Car Storage Tel: (0582) 26189 or (0582) 20957 for a booking form. Allow five weeks.

BIRMINGHAM AIRPORT Tel: 021-767 5511. A three-storey terminal building gives access from the first floor to the Maglev transit system which offers a 90 second shuttle service to Birmingham International Railway Station. Multi-storey parking for 800 cars, and surface parking is available Tel: 021-767 7861.

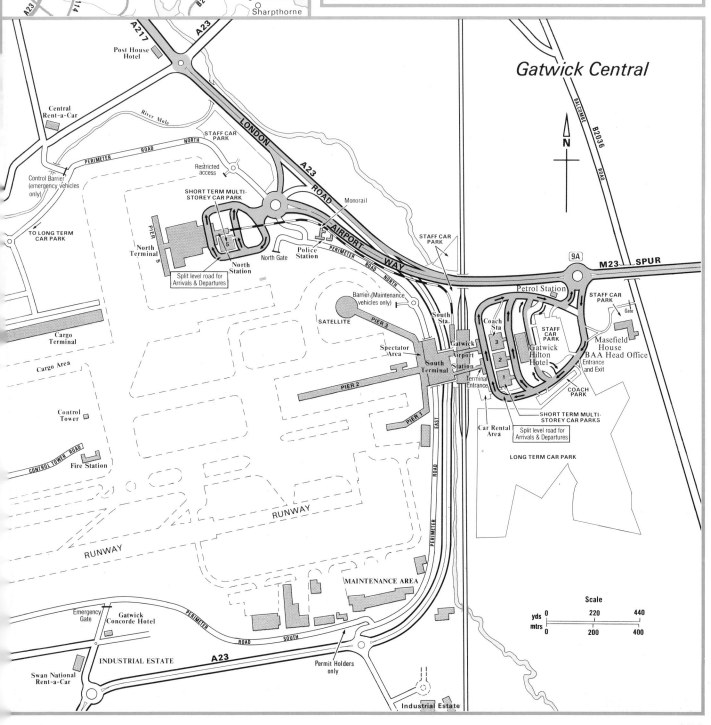

Gatwick Central

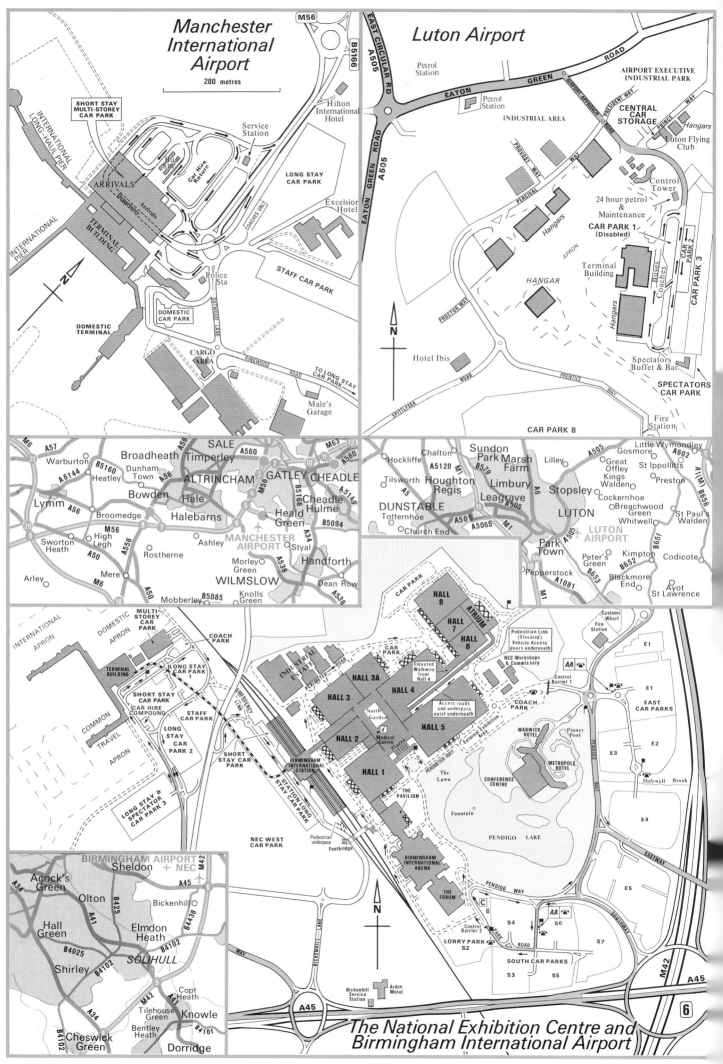

Manchester International Airport

200 metres

SHORT STAY MULTI-STOREY CAR PARK

INTERNATIONAL LONG-HAUL PIER

M56

B5166

Hilton International Hotel

Service Station

Bus Stn

Car Hire Return

ARRIVALS

Departures

Arrivals

LONG STAY CAR PARK

Excelsior Hotel

INTERNATIONAL PIER

TERMINAL BUILDING

N

COACHES ONLY

Police Sta

STAFF CAR PARK

DOMESTIC CAR PARK

DOMESTIC TERMINAL

CARGO AREA

OUTWOOD LANE

RINGWOOD ROAD

TO LONG STAY CAR PARK

Male's Garage

Luton Airport

EAST CIRCULAR RD

A505

EATON GREEN ROAD

Petrol Station

AIRPORT EXECUTIVE INDUSTRIAL PARK

AIRPORT APPROACH

PRESIDENT WAY

PRINCE WAY

CENTRAL CAR STORAGE

Hangars

Luton Flying Club

Petrol Station

INDUSTRIAL AREA

EATON GREEN ROAD

PROVOST WAY

PERCIVAL

Hangars

Control Tower

24 hour petrol & Maintenance

CAR PARK 1 (Disabled)

CAR PARK 2

CAR PARK 3

APRON

Terminal Building

Buses Coaches

PROCTOR WAY

HANGAR

Hangars

Hotel Ibis

SPITTLESEA ROAD

PRENTICE WAY

Spectators Buffet & Bar

SPECTATORS CAR PARK

CAR PARK 8

Fire Station

M6 21 A57 A56 SALE 9 M63 12

Warburton B5160 Broadheath Timperley A560 A560

Dunham Town A56 GATLEY CHEADLE

A6144 Heatley ALTRINCHAM M56

Lymm A56 Bowden Hale Cheadle Hulme B5166

Broomedge Halebarns A5149 B5094

20 M56 Heald Green

9 High Legh Ashley MANCHESTER AIRPORT Styal A34

Sworton Heath A556 Rostherne Morley Green A536 Handforth

Arley Mere M6 WILMSLOW Dean Row

A50 Mobberley B5085 Knolls Green A538

18

Hockliffe Chalton Sundon Park Marsh Farm Lilley Little Wymondley Gosmore A602

A5120 M1 Great Offley St Ippollitts A505

Tilsworth Houghton Regis B579 Limbury A6 Kings Walden Preston A1(M)

A5 DUNSTABLE Leagrave A505 Stopsley Cockernhoe B656

Totternhoe Church End A505 LUTON Breachwood Green St Paul's Walden

A5065 M1 Whitwell B651

Park Town LUTON AIRPORT

10A Peter's Green Kimpton Codicote

Pepperstock A1081 B652 Blackmore End Ayot St Lawrence

B663 M1

The National Exhibition Centre and Birmingham International Airport

INTERNATIONAL APRON

DOMESTIC APRON

MULTI-STOREY CAR PARK

COACH PARK

TERMINAL BUILDING

LONG STAY PARK 1

SHORT STAY CAR PARK

CAR HIRE COMPOUND

STAFF CAR PARK

LONG STAY CAR PARK 2

COMMON TRAVEL APRON

SHORT STAY CAR PARK

LONG STAY & SPECTATOR CAR PARK 3

EMERGENCY LINK

PERIMETER ROAD

INDUSTRIAL ESTATE

HALL 8

HALL 7

ATRIUM

HALL 6

Pedestrian Link (Elevated) Vehicle Access doors underneath

NEC Workshops & Commissary

CAR PARK

HALL 3A

Elevated Walkway from Hall 4

HALL 3 HALL 4

Access roads and underpass exist underneath

COACH PARK

Control Barrier 1

HALL 2

North Garden

HALL 5

Medical Centre

Piazza

External Exhibition Area

WARWICK HOTEL

Pinney Pool

HALL 1

BIRMINGHAM INTERNATIONAL STATION

The Lawn

CONFERENCE CENTRE

METROPOLE HOTEL

STATION LONG STAY CAR PARK

THE PAVILION

Fountain

PENDIGO LAKE

Holywell Brook

NEC WEST CAR PARK

Pedestrian underpass

Footbridge

BIRMINGHAM INTERNATIONAL ARENA

PENDIGO WAY

Customs Wharf

Fire Station

AA

E1

EAST CAR PARKS

E1

E2

E3

E4

PENDIGO WAY

SOUTHWAY

E5

N

THE FORUM

C

AA

S4 S6

Control Barrier 2

LORRY PARK S2

PARK ROAD

S7

SOUTH CAR PARKS

S3 S5

BICKENHILL LANE

Bickenhill Service Station

Arden Motel

A45

M42

A45

6

BIRMINGHAM AIRPORT + NEC

M42

Sheldon A45

Acock's Green

A34 Olton B425 Bickenhill

Hall Green A41 Elmdon Heath B4438

B4025 B4102

Shirley B4102 SOLIHULL

M42 Copt Heath A41

A34 Tilehouse Green Knowle

Cheswick Green Bentley Heath B4101

B4102 Dorridge

180

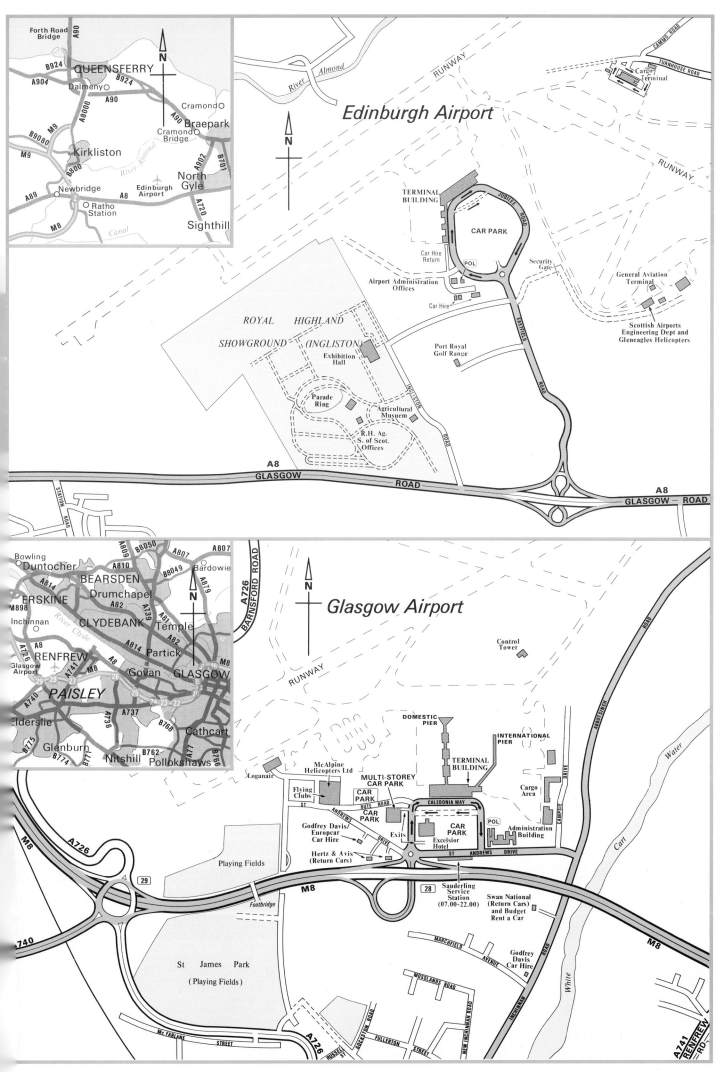

Edinburgh Airport

Forth Road Bridge
QUEENSFERRY
Dalmeny
Cramond
Braepark
Cramond Bridge
Kirkliston
North Gyle
Newbridge
Edinburgh Airport
Ratho Station
Sighthill
Canal

River Almond
River Almond
RUNWAY
RUNWAY
CAMMO ROAD
TURNHOUSE ROAD
Cargo Terminal

TERMINAL BUILDING
CAR PARK
JUBILEE ROAD
Car Hire Return
POL
Security Gate
Airport Administration Offices
Car Hire
EASTFIELD ROAD
General Aviation Terminal
Scottish Airports Engineering Dept and Gleneagles Helicopters

ROYAL HIGHLAND SHOWGROUND (INGLISTON)
Exhibition Hall
Port Royal Golf Range
Parade Ring
Agricultural Museum
INGLISTON ROAD
R.H. Ag. S. of Scot. Offices

A8
GLASGOW ROAD
A8
GLASGOW ROAD

Glasgow Airport

Bowling
Duntocher
BEARSDEN
Drumchapel
ERSKINE
Inchinnan
CLYDEBANK
Temple
RENFREW
Partick
Glasgow Airport
Govan
GLASGOW
PAISLEY
Elderslie
Cathcart
Glenburn
Nitshill
Pollokshaws
River Clyde

BARNSFORD ROAD
Control Tower
RUNWAY
ABBOTSINCH ROAD
White Cart Water

DOMESTIC PIER
INTERNATIONAL PIER
TERMINAL BUILDING
Cargo Area
McAlpine Helicopters Ltd
Loganair
MULTI-STOREY CAR PARK
Flying Clubs
CAR PARK
BUTE ROAD
CALEDONIA WAY
CAMPSIE DRIVE
CAR PARK
ST ANDREWS DRIVE
Godfrey Davis/ Europcar Car Hire
CAR PARK
POL
Administration Building
Exits
Excelsior Hotel
Hertz & Avis (Return Cars)
ST ANDREWS DRIVE
Sauderling Service Station (07.00-22.00)
Swan National (Return Cars) and Budget Rent a Car
Playing Fields
Footbridge
M8
A726
St James Park (Playing Fields)
MARCHFIELD AVENUE
MOSSLANDS ROAD
Godfrey Davis Car Hire
NEW INCHINNAN ROAD
McFarlane Street
ROCKSTON ROAD
FULLERTON STREET
Russell St
A726
A740
A741 RENFREW RD

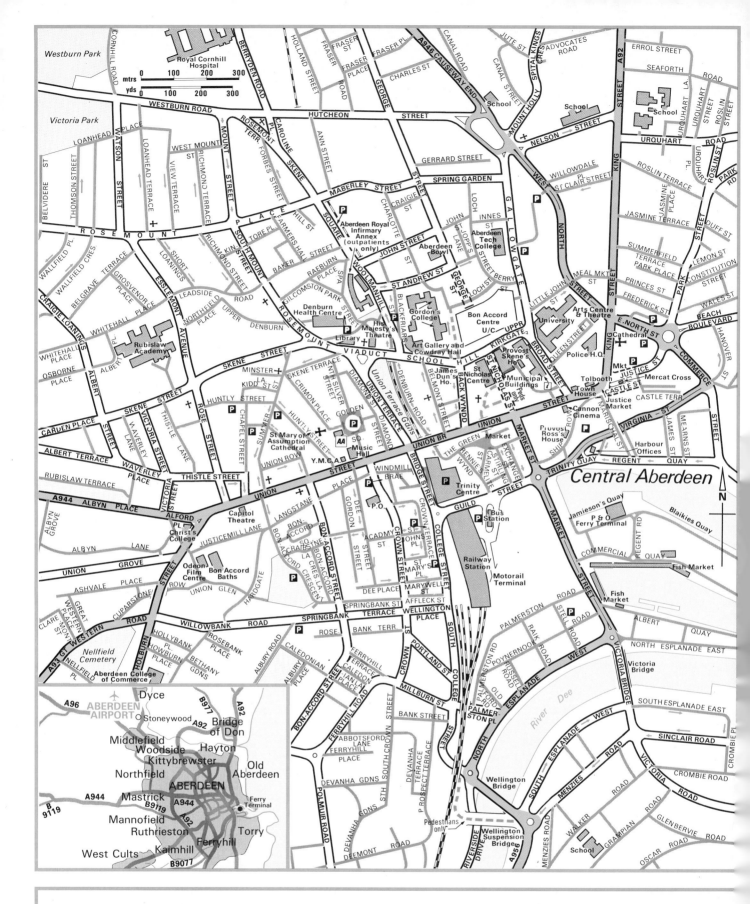

Central Aberdeen

EDINBURGH AIRPORT Tel: 031-333 1000
A regular coach service operates between Edinburgh (Waverley Bridge) and the airport seven miles away. The service also links with Glasgow and Glasgow Airport. The airport has parking for 1,400 vehicles, all open air, Tel: 031-344 3197. The information desk is located on the main concourse. Tel: 031-333 1000 or 031-344 3136. There are several top class hotels within easy reach of the airport, and car hire facilities are provided by Avis Tel: 031-333 1866, Europcar Tel: 031-333 2588, Hertz Tel: 031-333 1019 and Swan National Tel: 031-333 1922.

GLASGOW AIRPORT Tel: 041-887 1111
Situated eight miles west of Glasgow, the airport is linked with Central Glasgow and Edinburgh by regular coach services. Nearly 2,000 parking spaces are available, some under cover. Tel: 041-889 2751. The information desk is located on the first floor Tel: 041-887 1111 ext 4552. There is one 4-star hotel within easy reach of the airport, as well as four 3-star and one 2-star hotel. Car hire is available, from among others, Avis Tel: 041-887 2261, Hertz Tel: 041-887 2451, Europcar Tel: 041-887 0414 and Swan National Tel: 041-887 7915.

ABERDEEN AIRPORT AND HELIPORT Tel: (0224) 722331
Situated seven miles north-west of Aberdeen, the airport has its main access from the A96 which also serves for the West Heliport. Coach services operate between Aberdeen City Centre and the Main Terminal/West Heliport. Bus services from Aberdeen pass the entrance to East heliport. There is open air parking for 900 vehicles. Tel: (0224) 722331, extension 5142. At the Heliport there is open air parking for 300 vehicles. The information desk is in the check-in area, Tel: (0224) 722331 extension 5312. There are three 4-star hotels in the airport area and car hire is available through Avis. Tel: (0224) 722282, Europcar Tel: (0224) 723404, Hertz Tel: (0224) 722373, Budget Rent-a-Car Tel: (0224) 725067.

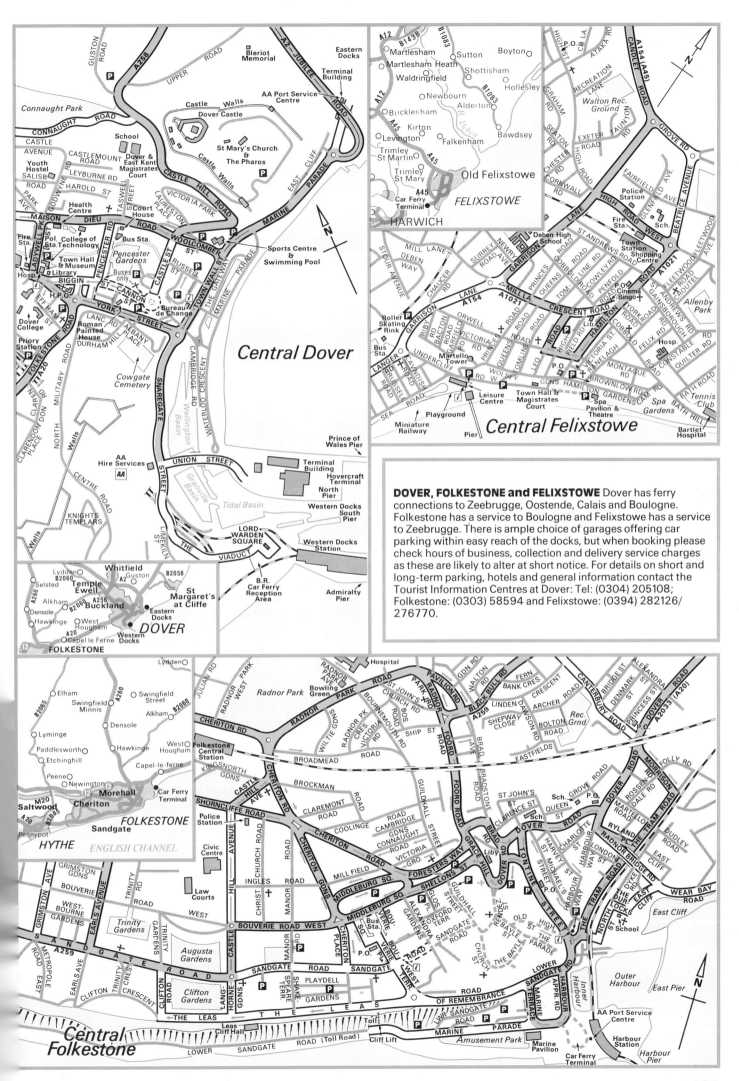

DOVER, FOLKESTONE and FELIXSTOWE Dover has ferry connections to Zeebrugge, Oostende, Calais and Boulogne. Folkestone has a service to Boulogne and Felixstowe has a service to Zeebrugge. There is ample choice of garages offering car parking within easy reach of the docks, but when booking please check hours of business, collection and delivery service charges as these are likely to alter at short notice. For details on short and long-term parking, hotels and general information contact the Tourist Information Centres at Dover: Tel: (0304) 205108; Folkestone: (0303) 58594 and Felixstowe: (0394) 282126/276770.

Central Dover

Central Felixstowe

DOVER

FOLKESTONE

HYTHE

ENGLISH CHANNEL

Central Folkestone

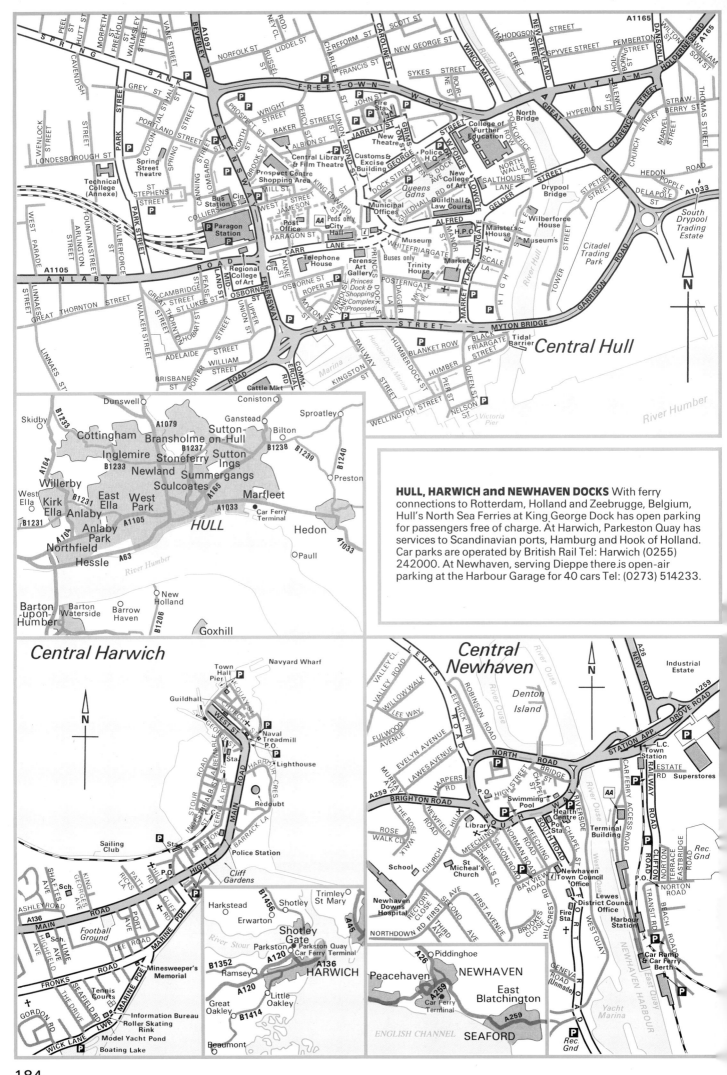

Central Hull

HULL, HARWICH and NEWHAVEN DOCKS With ferry connections to Rotterdam, Holland and Zeebrugge, Belgium, Hull's North Sea Ferries at King George Dock has open parking for passengers free of charge. At Harwich, Parkeston Quay has services to Scandinavian ports, Hamburg and Hook of Holland. Car parks are operated by British Rail Tel: Harwich (0255) 242000. At Newhaven, serving Dieppe there is open-air parking at the Harbour Garage for 40 cars Tel: (0273) 514233.

Central Harwich

Central Newhaven

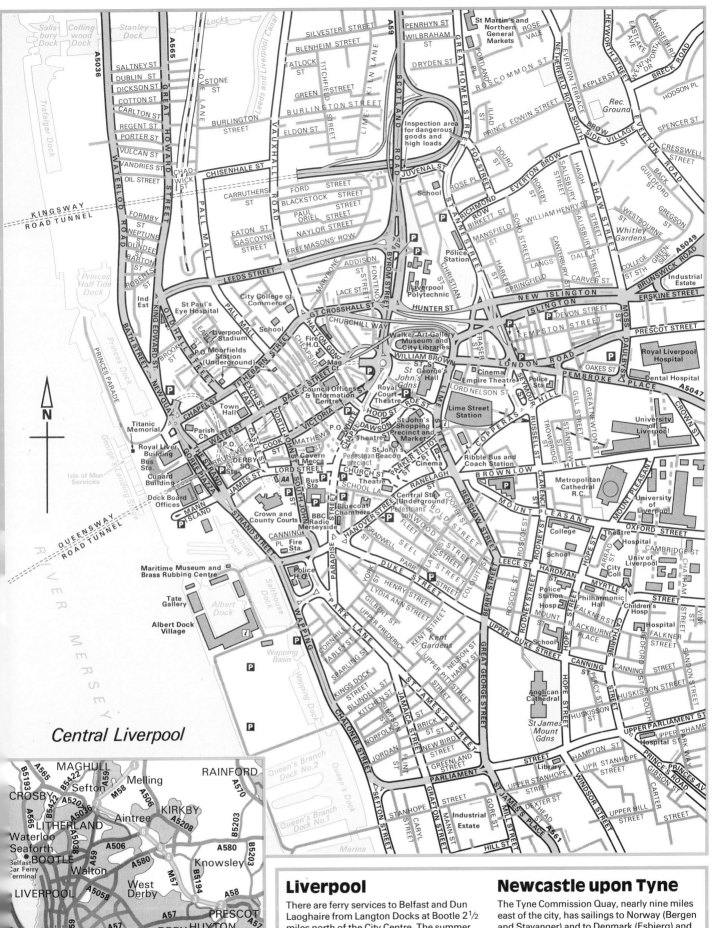

Central Liverpool

Liverpool

There are ferry services to Belfast and Dun Laoghaire from Langton Docks at Bootle 2½ miles north of the City Centre. The summer service to the Isle of Man leaves from Pier Head in Liverpool. Free open air parking for 70 cars is available close to Langton Dock for travellers to Ireland. For travellers to the Isle of Man numerous public car parks and a garage are available in the city centre close to Pier Head, contact Mersey Docks & Harbour Co for details, Tel: 051-200 2020. There are two 4-star, two 3-star and two 2-star hotels in Liverpool.

Newcastle upon Tyne

The Tyne Commission Quay, nearly nine miles east of the city, has sailings to Norway (Bergen and Stavanger) and to Denmark (Esbjerg) and to Sweden (Göteborg). Garage accommodation is normally available near the quay, but covered parking is scarce, particularly during the summer. Advance booking is necessary. Send applications to E J Turnbull & Son Ltd, Albion Road, North Shields, Tel: 091-257 1201 who have a collection and delivery service. Accommodation is available in 3-star hotels at Tynemouth or Wallsend. Other hotels are in Whitley Bay.

Weymouth

Weymouth, which handles sailings to Cherbourg and the Channel Islands, provides garage facilities at Channel Ferry Car Parks, Tel: (0305) 783408. Open parking available for 600 cars. Collection and delivery service from the ferry terminal is free. Caravan Transit Service Tel: (0305) 783408 provides parking for caravanners arriving in Weymouth a day prior to shipping and on their return. Weymouth has seven 2-star hotels and one 1-star.

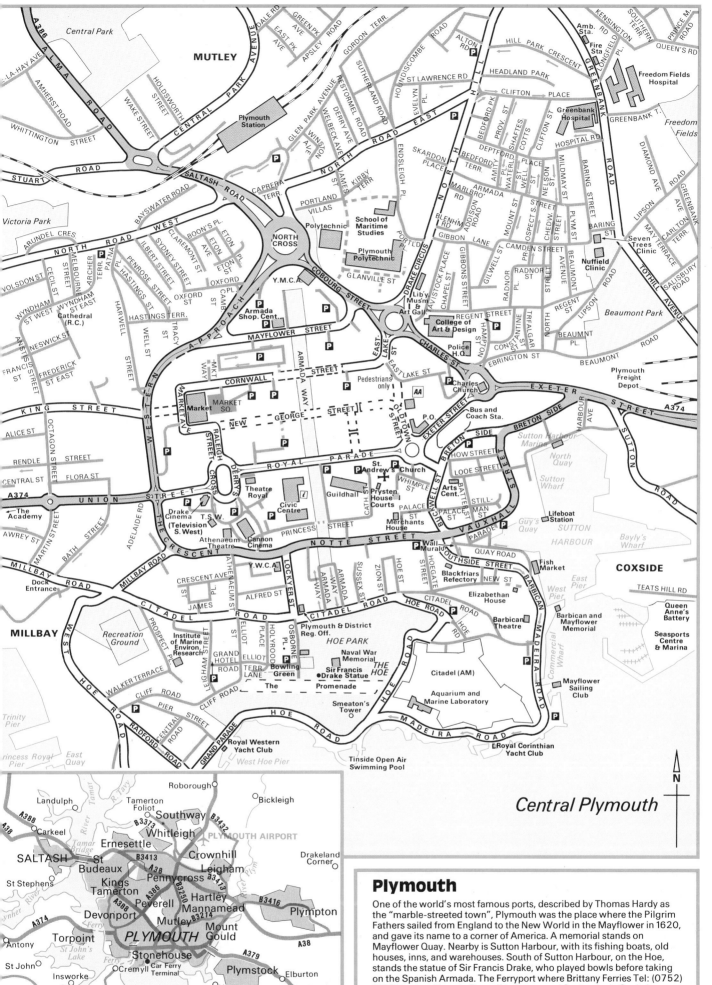

Plymouth

One of the world's most famous ports, described by Thomas Hardy as the "marble-streeted town", Plymouth was the place where the Pilgrim Fathers sailed from England to the New World in the Mayflower in 1620, and gave its name to a corner of America. A memorial stands on Mayflower Quay. Nearby is Sutton Harbour, with its fishing boats, old houses, inns, and warehouses. South of Sutton Harbour, on the Hoe, stands the statue of Sir Francis Drake, who played bowls before taking on the Spanish Armada. The Ferryport where Brittany Ferries Tel: (0752) 21321 have sailings to Roscoff in France and Santander in Spain has parking facilities within easy reach of the quayside. Garage parking facilities are available at Turnbull's Garage Tel: (0752) 667111, covered parking for six cars is one mile from the quay. There is also a collection and delivery service. Two 4-star, four 3-star, three 2-star and three 1-star hotels are near the Ferryport.

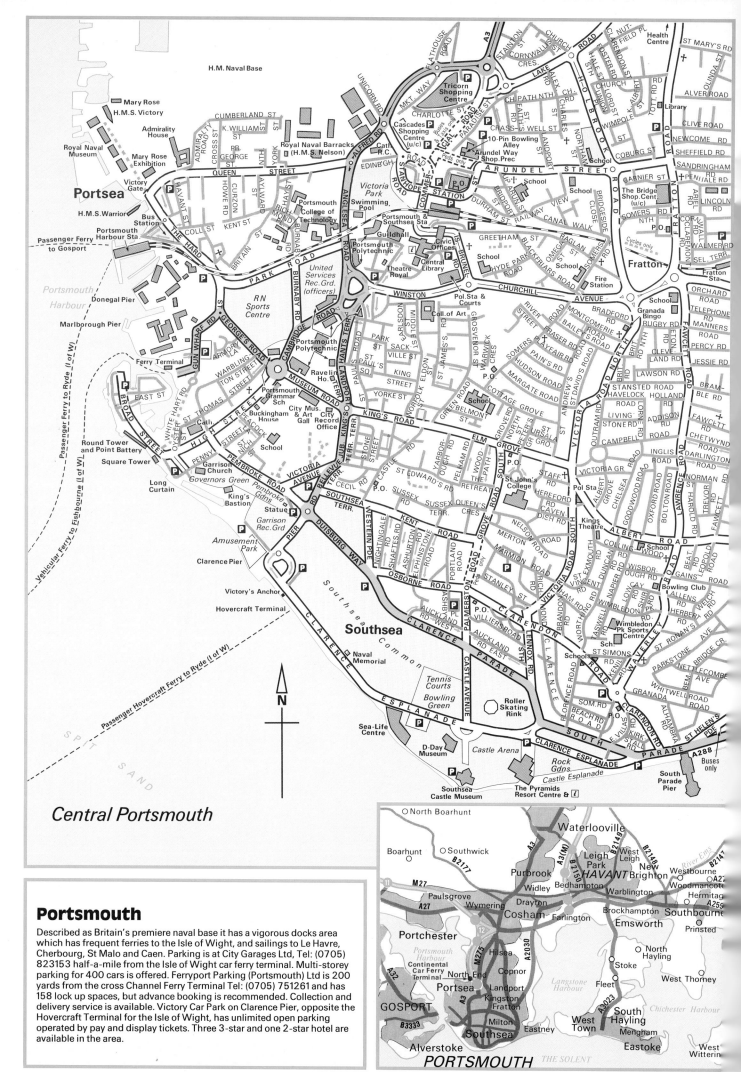

Central Portsmouth

Portsmouth

Described as Britain's premiere naval base it has a vigorous docks area which has frequent ferries to the Isle of Wight, and sailings to Le Havre, Cherbourg, St Malo and Caen. Parking is at City Garages Ltd, Tel: (0705) 823153 half-a-mile from the Isle of Wight car ferry terminal. Multi-storey parking for 400 cars is offered. Ferryport Parking (Portsmouth) Ltd is 200 yards from the cross Channel Ferry Terminal Tel: (0705) 751261 and has 158 lock up spaces, but advance booking is recommended. Collection and delivery service is available. Victory Car Park on Clarence Pier, opposite the Hovercraft Terminal for the Isle of Wight, has unlimited open parking operated by pay and display tickets. Three 3-star and one 2-star hotel are available in the area.

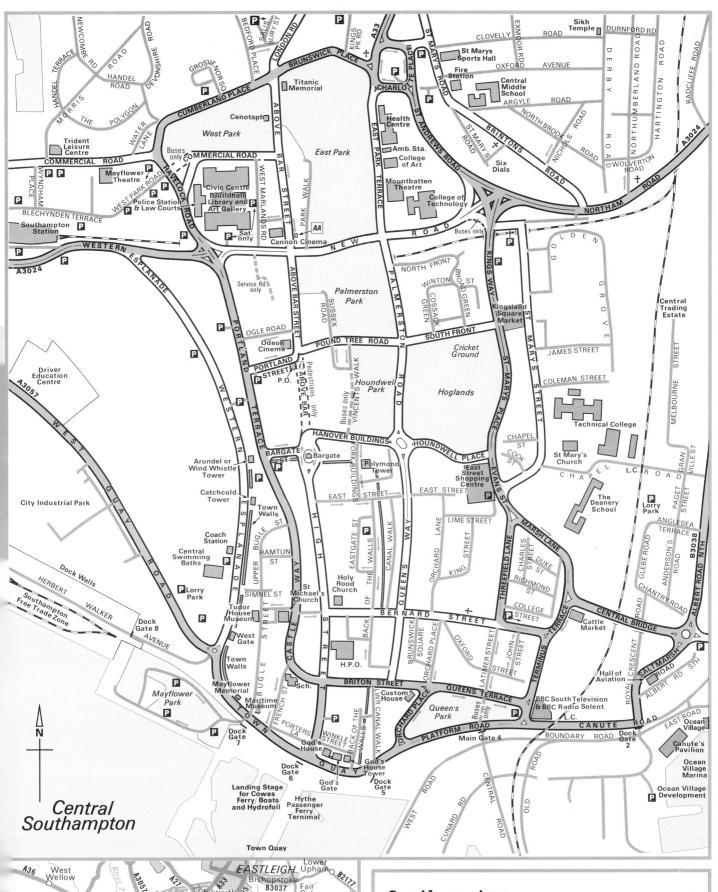

Central Southampton

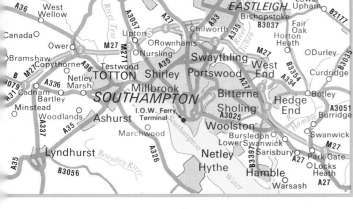

Southampton

Southampton was the major port for transatlantic sailings from 1911, when it took over from Liverpool. The great ocean liners are no longer crowding the dock area, but the cruise liners QE2 and Canberra still dominate the docks skyline when they berth. The British Transport Docks Board runs the dock traffic and accommodates Andrews (Shipside Services) Ltd, garage at 10 Gate Western Docks, Tel: (0703) 228001/2/3 where covered or fenced compound parking is available for 1600 vehicles. It is open for all departures and arrivals. A collection and delivery service is provided. There are several multi-storey car parks in the city centre area. There are a number of AA-appointed hotels within a mile or so of the dock area, and these include four 3-star and one 2-star hotel.

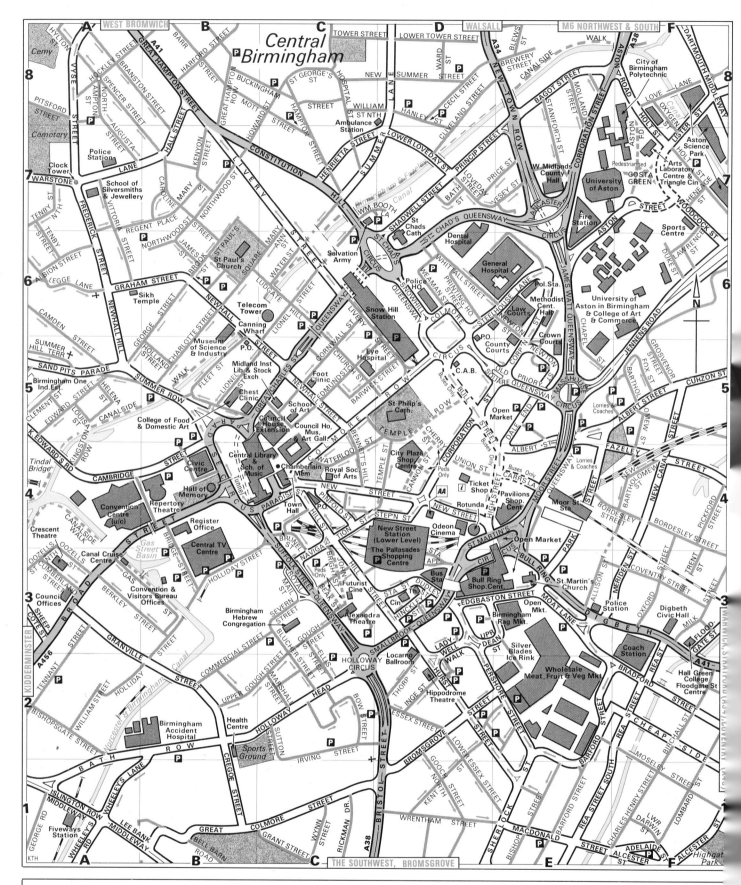

Birmingham

It is very difficult to visualise Birmingham as it was before it began the growth which eventually made it the second-largest city in England. When the Romans were in Britain it was little more than a staging post on Icknield Street. Throughout medieval times it was a sleepy agricultural centre in the middle of a heavily-forested region. Timbered houses clustered together round a green that was

eventually to be called the Bull Ring. But by the 16th century, although still a tiny and unimportant village by today's standards, it had begun to gain a reputation as a manufacturing centre. Tens of thousands of sword blades were made here during the Civil War. Throughout the 18th century more and more land was built on. In 1770 the Birmingham Canal was completed, making trade very much easier and increasing the town's development dramatically. All of that pales into near

insignificance compared with what happened in the 19th century. Birmingham was not represented in Parliament until 1832 and had no town council until 1838. Yet by 1889 it had already been made a city, and after only another 20 years it had become the second largest city in England. Many of Birmingham's most imposing public buildings date from the 19th century, when the city was growing so rapidly. Surprisingly, the city has more miles of waterway than Venice.

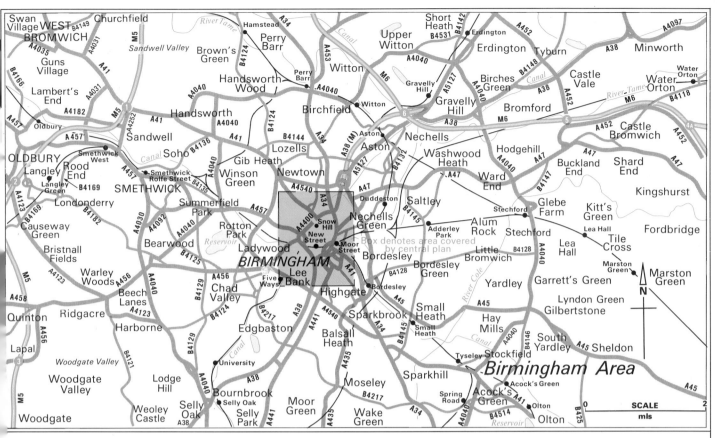

Key to Town Plan and Area Plan

Town Plan

AA Recommended roads	
Restricted roads	
Other roads	
Buildings of interest	Station ▣
One Way Streets	←
Car Parks	🅿
Parks and open spaces	
Churches	+

Area Plan

A roads	
B roads	
Locations	Meer End ○
Urban area	☐

Street Index with Grid Reference

Birmingham

Adelaide Street	F1
Albert Street	E4-E5-F5
Albion Street	A6
Alcester Street	F1
Allison Street	E3
Aston Road	F8-E8-F8-F7
Aston Street	E6-E7-F7
Augusta Street	A7-A8
Bagot Street	E8
Barford Street	E1-E2-F2
Barr Street	B8
Bartholomew Street	F4-F5
Barwick Street	C5-D5
Bath Row	A1-A2-B2
Bath Street	D7
Beak Street	C3
Bell Barn Road	B1
Bennett's Hill	C4-C5
Berkley Street	A3-B3
Birchall Street	F1-F2
Bishop Street	E1
Bishopsgate Street	A2
Blews Street	E8
Blucher Street	C2-C3
Bordesley Street	E4-F4-F3
Bow Street	C2
Bradford Street	E3-E2-F2
Branston Street	A8-B8-B7
Brewery Street	E8
Bridge Street	B3-B4
Bristol Street	C1-D1-D2-C2
Broad Street	A2-A3-A4-B4
Bromsgrove Street	D1-D2-E2
Brook Street	B6
Brunel Street	C3-C4
Buckingham Street	B8-C8
Bull Ring	E3
Bull Street	D5-E5-E4

Cambridge Street	A4-B4-B5
Camden Street	A5-A6
Cannon Street	D4
Caroline Street	B6-B7
Carrs Lane	E4
Cecil Street	D8
Chapel Street	E5-E6
Charles Henry Street	F1
Charlotte Street	B5-B6
Cheapside	F1-F2
Cherry Street	D4-D5
Church Street	C6-C5-D5
Clement Street	A5
Cliveland Street	D7-D8-E8
Colmore Circus	D5-D6
Colmore Row	C4-C5-D5
Commercial Street	B2-B3-C3
Constitution Hill	B7-C7
Cornwall Street	C5-C6
Corporation Street	D4-D5-E5-E6-E7-E8-F8
Coventry Street	E3-F3
Cregoe Street	B1-B2
Cumberland Street	A3
Curzon Street	F5
Dale End	E4-E5
Dartmouth Middleway	F7-F8
Digbeth	E3-F3
Dudley Street	D3
Duke Street	F6
Edgbaston Street	D3-E3
Edmund Street	C5-D5
Edward Street	A5
Ellis Street	C2-C3
Essex Street	D2
Fazeley Street	E5-E4-F4
Fleet Street	B5
Floodgate Street	F3
Fox Street	F5
Frederick Street	A6-A7
Gas Street	A3-B3
George Road	A1
George Street	A5-B5-B6
Gooch Street North	D1-D2
Gosta Green	F7
Gough Street	C3
Graham Street	A6-B6
Grant Street	C1
Granville Street	A3-A2-B2
Great Charles St Queensway	B5-C5-C6
Great Colmore Street	B1-C1-D1
Great Hampton Row	B8
Great Hampton Street	A8-B8
Grosvenor Street	F5-F6
Hall Street	B7-B8
Hampton Street	C7-C8
Harford Street	B8
Hanley Street	D7-D8
Helena Street	A5
Heneage Street	F7
Henrietta Street	C7-D7
High Street	D4-E4
Hill Street	C4-C3-D3
Hinckley Street	D3
Hockley Street	A8-B8
Holland Street	B5
Holliday Street	A2-B2-B3-C3-C4
Holloway Circus	C2-C3-D3-D2
Holloway Head	B2-C2
Holt Street	F7-F8
Hospital Street	C7-C8
Howard Street	B7-C7-C8
Hurst Street	D3-D2-E2-E1

Hylton Street	A8
Inge Street	D2
Irving Street	C2-D2
Islington Row Middleway	A1
James Street	B6
James Watt Queensway	E5-E6
Jennens Road	E5-F5-F6
John Bright Street	C3-C4
Kent Street	D1-D2
Kenyon Street	B7
King Edward's Road	A4-A5
Kingston Row	A4
Ladywell Walk	D2-D3
Lancaster Circus	E6-E7
Lawrence Street	F6-F7
Lee Bank Middleway	A1-B1
Legge Lane	A6
Lionel Street	B5-C5-C6
Lister Street	F7-F8
Livery Street	B7-C7-C6-D6-D5
Lombard Street	F1-F2
Louisa Street	A5
Love Lane	F8
Loveday Street	D7
Lower Darwin Street	F1
Lower Essex Street	D2-D1-E1
Lower Loveday Street	D7
Lower Tower Street	D8
Ludgate Hill	B6-C6
Macdonald Street	E1-F1
Marshall Street	C2
Mary Street	B7
Mary Ann Street	C6-C7
Masshouse Circus	E5
Meriden Street	E3-F3
Milk Street	F3
Moat Lane	E3
Molland Street	E8
Moor Street Queensway	E4-E5
Moseley Street	E2-F2-F1
Mott Street	B8-C8-C7
Navigation Street	C3-C4
New Street	C4-D4
New Bartholomew Street	F4
New Canal Street	F4-F5
Newhall Hill	A5-A6
Newhall Street	B6-B5-C5
New Summer Street	C8-B8
Newton Street	E5
New Town Row	D8-E8-E7
Northampton Street	A8
Northwood Street	B6-B7
Old Square	D5-E5
Oozells Street	A3-A4
Oozells Street North	A3-A4
Oxford Street	F3-F4
Oxygen Street	F7-F8
Paradise Circus	B4-B5
Paradise Street	C4
Park Street	E3-E4
Pershore Street	D3-D2-E2
Pickford Street	F4
Pinfold Street	C4
Pitsford Street	A8
Price Street	D7-E7
Princip Street	D7-E7-E8
Printing House Street	D6
Priory Queensway	E5
Rea Street	E2-F2-F3
Rea Street South	E1-F1-F2
Regent Place	A7-B7
Rickman Drive	C1

Royal Mail Street	C3
St Chad's Circus	C7-C6-D6
St Chad's Queensway	D6-D7-E7
St George's Street	C8
St Martin's Circus	D3-D4-E4-E3
St Paul's Square	B7-B6-C6
Sand Pits Parade	A5
Severn Street	C3
Shadwell Street	D6-D7
Sheepcote Street	A3
Sherlock Street	D1-E1-E2
Smallbrook Queensway	C3-D3
Snow Hill Queensway	D6
Spencer Street	A8-A7-B7
Staniforth Street	E7-E8
Station Approach	D3
Station Street	D3
Steelhouse Lane	D6-E6
Stephenson Street	C4-D4
Suffolk Street Queensway	B4-C4-C3
Summer Hill Terrace	A5
Summer Row	A5-B5
Summer Lane	C7-D7-D8
Sutton Street	C2
Temple Row	C5-D5
Temple Street	D4-D5
Tenby Street	A6-A7
Tenby Street North	A7
Tennant Street	A2-A3
Thorp Street	D2-D3
Tower Street	C8-D8
Trent Street	F3-F4
Union Street	D4
Upper Dean Street	D3-E3
Upper Gough Street	B2-C2-C3
Vesey Street	D7-E7
Vittoria Street	A6-A7
Vyse Street	A7-A8
Ward Street	D8
Warstone Lane	A7-B7
Water Street	C6
Waterloo Street	C4-C5-D5
Weaman Street	D6
Wheeley's Lane	A1-B1-B2
Wheeley's Road	A1
Whittall Street	D6-E6
William Booth Lane	C7-D7
William Street	A2
William Street North	C8-D8
Woodcock Street	F6-F7
Wrentham Street	D1-E1
Wynn Street	C1

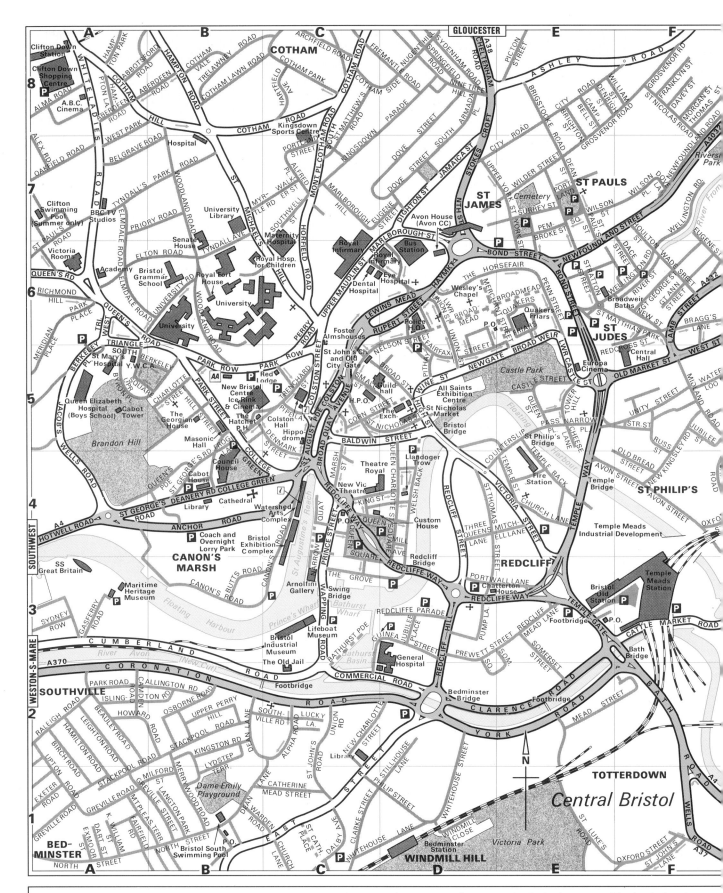

Bristol

One of Britain's most historic seaports, Bristol retains many of its visible links with the past, despite terrible damage inflicted during bombing raids in World War II. Most imposing is the cathedral, founded as an abbey church in 1140. Perhaps even more famous than the cathedral is the Church of St Mary Redcliffe. Ranking among the finest churches in the country, it owes much of

its splendour to 14th- and 15th-century merchants who bestowed huge sums of money on it.

The merchant families brought wealth to the whole of Bristol, and their trading links with the world are continued in today's modern aerospace and technological industries. Much of the best of Bristol can be seen in the area of the Floating Harbour – an arm of the Avon. Several of the old warehouses have been converted into museums, galleries and exhibition centres. Among them are

genuinely picturesque old pubs, the best-known of which is the Llandoger Trow. It is a timbered 17th-century house, the finest of its kind in Bristol. Further up the same street – King Street – is the Theatre Royal, built in 1766 and the oldest theatre in the country. In Corn Street, the heart of the business area, is a magnificent 18th-century corn exchange. In front of it are the four pillars known as the 'nails', on which merchants used to make cash transactions, hence 'to pay on the nail'.

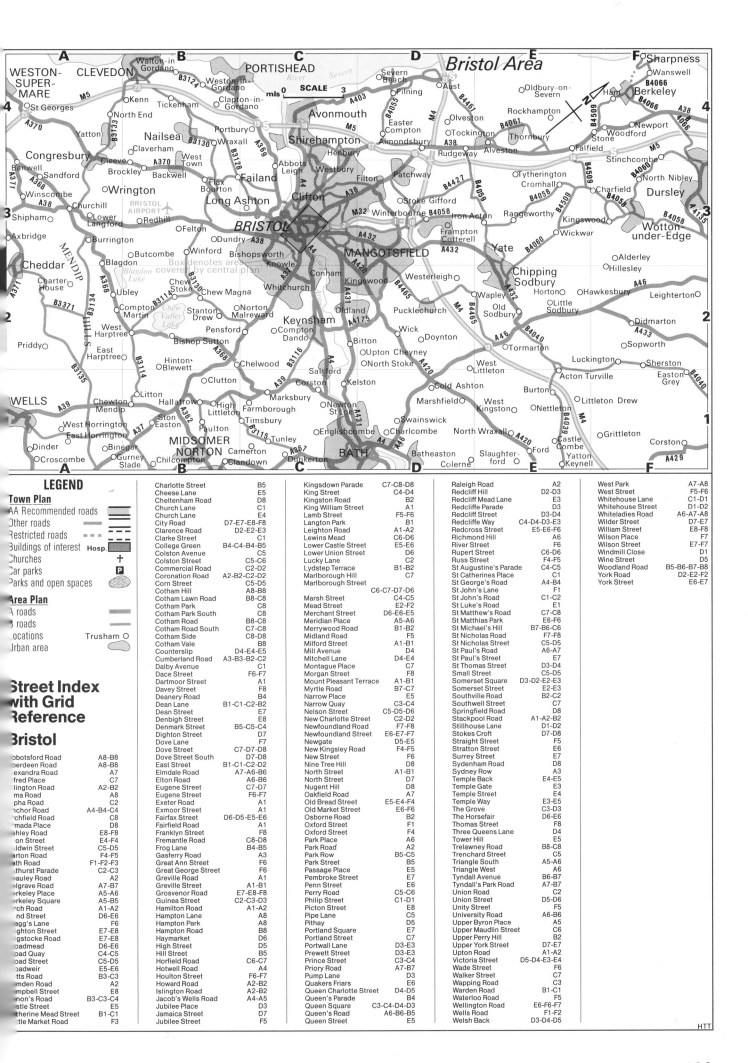

Bristol Area

LEGEND

Town Plan
- AA Recommended roads
- Other roads
- Restricted roads
- Buildings of interest — Hosp.
- Churches +
- Car parks P
- Parks and open spaces

Area Plan
- A roads
- B roads
- Locations — Trusham ○
- Urban area

Street Index with Grid Reference

Bristol

193

HTT

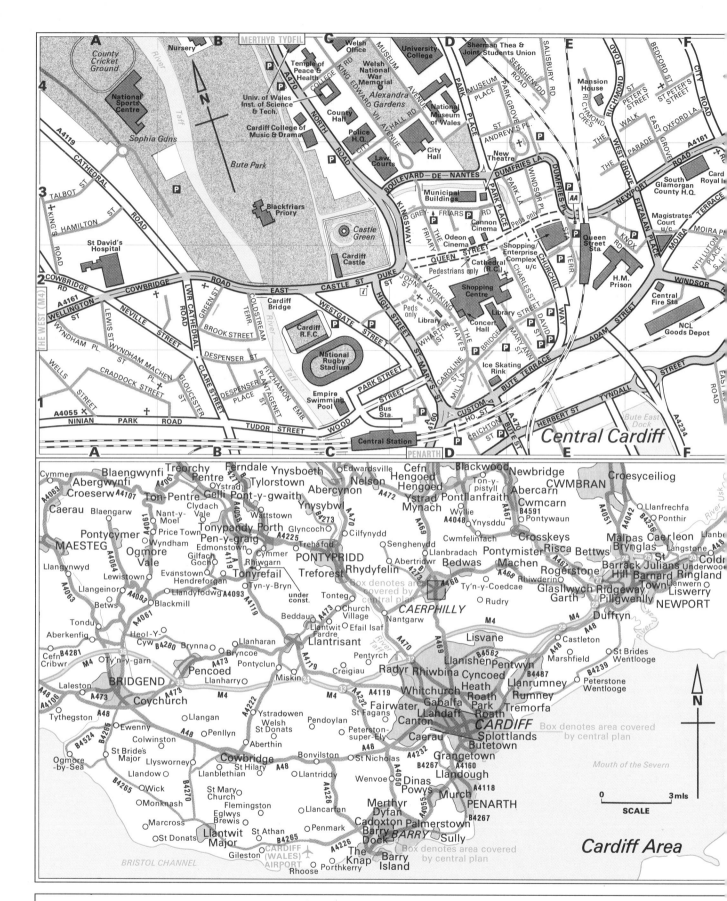

Cardiff

Strategically important to both the Romans and the Normans, Cardiff slipped from prominence in medieval times and remained a quiet market town in a remote area until it was transformed – almost overnight – by the effects of the Industrial Revolution. The valleys of South Wales were a principal source of iron and coal – raw materials which helped to change the shape and course of

the 19th-century world. Cardiff became a teeming export centre; by the end of the 19th century it was the largest coal-exporting city in the world.

Close to the castle – an exciting place with features from Roman times to the 19th century – is the city's civic centre – a fine concourse of buildings dating largely from the early part of the 20th century. Among them is the National Museum of Wales – a superb collection of art and antiquities from Wales and around the world.

Barry has sandy beaches, landscaped garden and parks, entertainment arcades and funfairs. Li Cardiff it grew as a result of the demand for coal and steel, but now its dock complex is involved in the petrochemical and oil industries.

Caerphilly is famous for two things – a castle and cheese. The cheese is no longer made here, but the 13th-century castle, slighted by Cromwell, still looms above its moat. No castle in Britain – except Windsor – is larger.

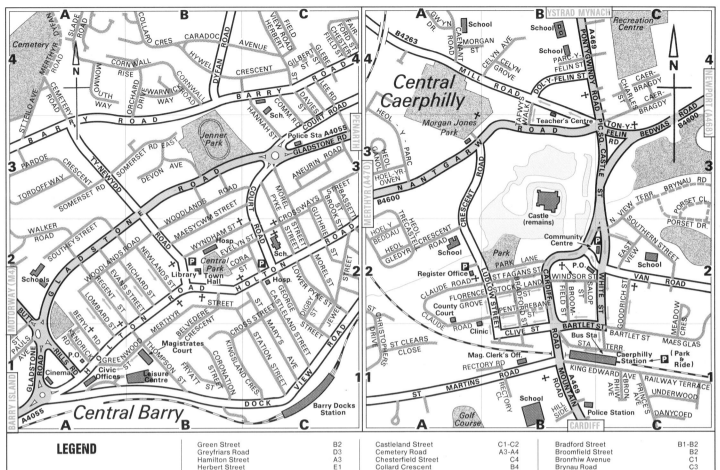

LEGEND

Town Plan

AA recommended route	
Restricted roads	
Other roads	
Buildings of interest	Cinema ▣
Car parks	P
Parks and open spaces	◭
One way streets	⌐

Area Plan

A roads	
B roads	
Locations	Glyncoch ○
Urban area	◯

Street Index with Grid Reference

Cardiff

Adam Street	E1-E2-F2
Bedford Street	F4
Boulevard de Nantes	C3-D3
Bridge Street	D1-D2-E2
Brook Street	B2
Bute Street	D1-E1
Bute Terrace	D1-E1
Caroline Street	D1
Castle Street	C2
Cathedral Street	A4-A3-B3-B2-A2
Charles Street	D2-E2
Churchill Way	E2-E3
City Hall Road	C3-C4-D4
City Road	F4
Clare Street	B1
Coldstream Terrace	B2
College Road	C4
Cowbridge Road	A2
Cowbridge Road East	A2-B2-C2
Craddock Street	A1-B1
Crichton Street	D1
Customhouse Street	D1
David Street	E2
Despenser Place	B1
Despenser Street	B1
Duke Street	C2-D2
Dumfries Lane	D3-E3
Dumfries Place	E3
East Grove	F4-F3
East Moor Road	F1
Fitzalan Place	F3-F2
Fitzhamon Embankment	B1-C1
Glossop Road	F3
Gloucester Street	B1

Green Street	B2
Greyfriars Road	D3
Hamilton Street	A3
Herbert Street	E1
High Street	C2-D2
King Edward VII Avenue	C4-D4-D3-C3
King's Road	A2-A3
Kingsway	C3-D3-D2
Knox Road	E3-F3-F2
Lewis Street	A2
Lower Cathedral Road	B1-B2
Machen Place	A1-B1
Mary Ann Street	E1-E2
Mill Lane	D1
Moira Place	F3
Moira Terrace	F2-F3
Museum Avenue	C4-D4
Museum Place	D4
Neville Street	A2-B2-B1
Newport Road	E3-F3-F4
Ninian Park Road	A1-B1
North Luton Place	F2-F3
North Road	B4-C4-C3
Oxford Lane	F4
Park Grove	D4-E4
Park Lane	D3-E3
Park Place	D4-D3-E3
Park Street	C1-D1
Plantagenet Street	B1-C1
Queen Street	D2-D3
Richmond Crescent	E4
Richmond Road	E4
St Andrew's Place	D4-E4
St John Street	D2
St Mary's Street	D1-D2
St Peter's Street	E4-F4
Salisbury Road	E4
Senghenydd Road	D4-E4
South Luton Place	F2-F3
Station Terrace	E2-E3
The Friary	D2-D3
The Hayes	D1-D2
The Parade	E3-F3-F4
The Walk	E3-E4-F4
Talbot Street	A3
Tudor Street	B1-C1
Tyndall Street	E1-F1
Wellington Street	A2
Wells Street	A1
Westgate Street	C2-D2-D1
West Grove	E4-E3-F3
Wharton Street	D2
Windsor Place	E3
Windsor Road	F2
Wood Street	C1-D1
Working Street	D1
Wyndham Place	A2
Wyndham Street	A1-A2

Barry

Aneurin Road	C3
Barry Road	A3-A4-B3-B4-C4
Bassett Street	C2-C3
Belvedere Crescent	B1-B2
Beryl Road	A1-A2
Brook Street	C2-C3
Buttrills Road	A1-A2
Caradoc Avenue	B4-C4

Castleland Street	C1-C2
Cemetery Road	A3-A4
Chesterfield Street	C4
Collard Crescent	B4
Commercial Road	C3-C4
Cora Street	B2-C2
Cornwall Rise	A3-A4
Cornwall Road	B4
Coronation Street	B1
Cross Street	B1-C1-C2
Crossways Street	C2-C3
Court Road	C2-C3-C4
Davies Street	C3-C4
Devon Avenue	B3
Digby Street	C2
Dock View Road	B1-C1-C2
Dyfan Road	B4
Evans Street	A2-B2
Evelyn Street	B2-C2
Fairford Street	C4
Field View Road	C4
Fryatt Street	B1
George Street	C1-C2
Gilbert Street	C4
Gladstone Road	A1-A2-B2-B3-C3
Glebe Street	C4
Greenwood Street	A1-B1
Guthrie Street	C3-C2
Hannah Street	C4-C3
Herbert Street	C4
Holton Road	A1-B1-B2-C2
Hywell Crescent	B4-C4
Jewel Street	C1-C2
Kendrick Road	A1
Kingsland Crescent	B1-C1
Lee Road	C4
Lombard Street	A1-A2
Lower Pyke Street	C2
Maesycwm Street	B2-B3-C3
Merthyr Dyfan Road	A4
Merthyr Street	B1-B2-C2
Monmouth Way	A4
Morel Street	C2-C3
Newlands Street	B2
Orchard Drive	B3-B4
Pardoe Crescent	A3
Pyke Street	C3-C2
Regent Street	A2-B2
Richard Street	A2-B2
St Mary's Avenue	C1-C2
St Pauls Avenue	A1
St Teilo Avenue	A3-A4
Slade Road	A4
Somerset Road	A3
Somerset Road East	A3-B3
Southey Street	A2-A3
Station Street	C1
Thompson Street	B1
Tordoff Way	A3
Ty-Newydd Road	A3-B3-B2
Walker Road	A2
Warwick Way	B4
Woodlands Road	A2-B2-B3-C3
Wyndham Street	B2-C2

Caerphilly

Bartlet Street	B2-B1-C1
Bedwas Road	C3-C4

Bradford Street	B1-B2
Broomfield Street	B2
Bronrhiw Avenue	C1
Brynau Road	C3
Caenant Road	A4
Caer Bragdy	C4
Cardiff Road	B1-B2
Castle Street	C3
Celyn Avenue	B4
Celyn Grove	B4
Charles Street	C4
Claude Road	A1-A2-B2
Clive Street	B1-B2
Crescent Rod	A2-A3-B3
Danycoed	C1
Dol-y-Felen Street	B4
East View	C2
Florence Grove	A2-B2
Goodrich Street	C1-C2
Gwyn Drive	A4
Heol Ganol	A3
Heol Gledyr	A2
Heol Trecastell	A2-A3
Hillside	B1
Heol y Beddau	A2
Heol-yr-Owen	A3
King Edward Avenue	B1-C1
Ludlow Street	A2-B2-B1
Maes Glas	C1
Meadow Crescent	C1-C2
Mill Road	A4-B4-B3
Morgan Street	A4-B4
Mountain Road	B1
Nantgarw Road	A3-B3
North View Terrace	C2-C3
Parc-y-Felin Street	B4
Park Lane	B2
Pentrebone Street	B2
Piccadilly Square	C3
Pontygwindy Road	B4-C4
Porset Close	C3
Porset Drive	C2-C3
Prince's Avenue	C1
Railway Terrace	C1
Rectory Road	A1-B1
Rectory Close	B1
St Christopher's Drive	A1-A2
St Clears Close	A1
St Fagans Street	B2
St Martins Road	A1-B1
Salop Street	B2
Southern Street	C2-C3
Station Terrace	B1-C1
Stockland Street	B2
Tafwy Walk	B3-B4
Ton-y-Felin Road	C3
Underwood	C1
Van Road	C2
White Street	C2
Windsor Street	B2

LTH

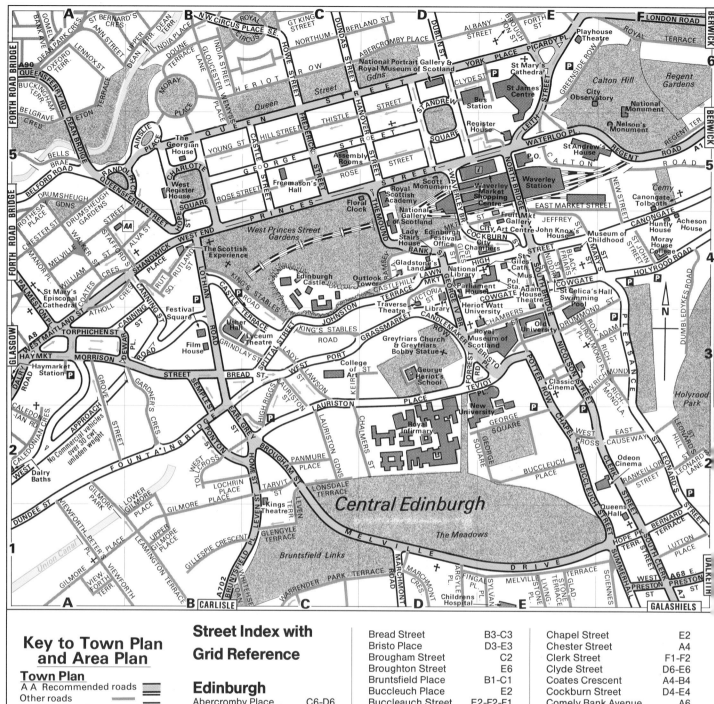

Key to Town Plan and Area Plan

Town Plan
A A Recommended roads
Other roads
Restricted roads
Buildings of intrest — Gallery
Car Parks — P
Parks and open spaces
A A Service Centre — AA
Churches — ✝

Area Plan
A roads
B roads
Locations — Newcraighall ○
Urban area

Street Index with Grid Reference

Edinburgh

Abercromby Place	C6-D6
Adam Street	F3
Ainslie Place	B5
Albany Street	D6-E6
Alva Street	A4-B4
Ann Street	A6
Argyle Place	D1
Athol Crescent	A3-A4-B4
Bank Street	D4
Belford Road	A5
Belgrave Crescent	A5
Bells Brae	A5
Bernard Terrace	F1
Blackfriars Street	E4
Bread Street	B3-C3
Bristo Place	D3-E3
Brougham Street	C2
Broughton Street	E6
Bruntsfield Place	B1-C1
Buccleuch Place	E2
Buccleauch Street	E2-F2-F1
Buckingham Terrace	A5-A6
Caledonian Crescent	A2
Caledonian Road	A2
Calton Road	E5-F5
Candlemaker Row	D3
Canning Street	A3-B3-B4
Canongate	E4-F4-F5
Castle Hill	D4
Castle Street	C5
Castle Terrace	B4-B3-C3
Chalmers Street	C2-D2
Chambers Street	D3-E3
Charlotte Square	B4-B5
Chapel Street	E2
Chester Street	A4
Clerk Street	F1-F2
Clyde Street	D6-E6
Coates Crescent	A4-B4
Cockburn Street	D4-E4
Comely Bank Avenue	A6
Cowgate	D4-E4-F4
Dalry Road	A3
Dean Bridge	A5
Dean Park Crescent	A6
Dean Terrace	B6
Dewar Place	A3-B3
Doune Terrace	B6
Drummond Street	E3-F3-F4
Drumsheugh Gardens	A4-A5
Dublin Street	D6
Dumbiedykes Road	F3-F4
Dundas Street	C6
Dundee Street	A1-A2

Edinburgh

Scotland's ancient capital, dubbed the "Athens of the North", is one of the most splendid cities in the whole of Europe. Its buildings, its history and its cultural life give it an international importance which is celebrated every year in its world-famous festival. The whole city is overshadowed by the craggy castle which seems to grow out of the rock itself. There has been a fortress here since the 7th

century and most of the great figures of Scottish history have been associated with it. The old town grew up around the base of Castle Rock within the boundaries of the defensive King's Wall and, unable to spread outwards, grew upwards in a maze of tenements. However, during the 18th century new prosperity from the shipping trade resulted in the building of the New Town and the regular, spacious layout of the Georgian development makes a striking contrast with the old

hotch-potch of streets. Princes Street is the main east-west thoroughfare with excellent shops on one side and Princes Street Gardens with their famous floral clock on the south side.

As befits such a splendid capital city there are numerous museums and art galleries packed with priceless treasures. Among these are the famous picture gallery in 16th-century Holyroodhouse, the present Royal Palace, and the fascinating and unusual Museum of Childhood.

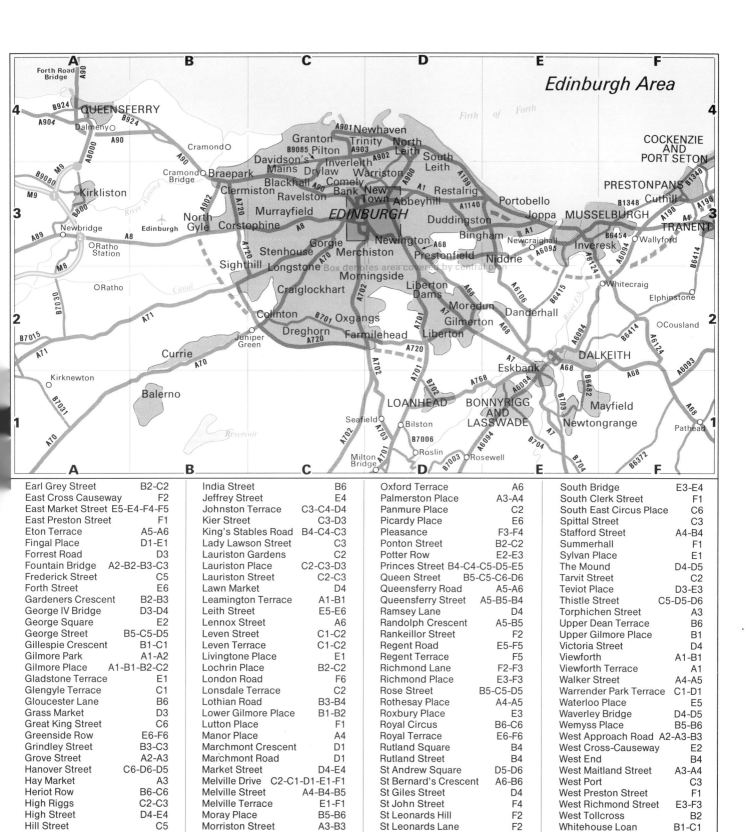

Edinburgh Area

EDINBURGH
Holyrood Palace orginated as a guest house for the Abbey of Holyrood in the 16th century, but most of the present building was built for Charles II. Mary Queen of Scots was one of its most famous inhabitants.

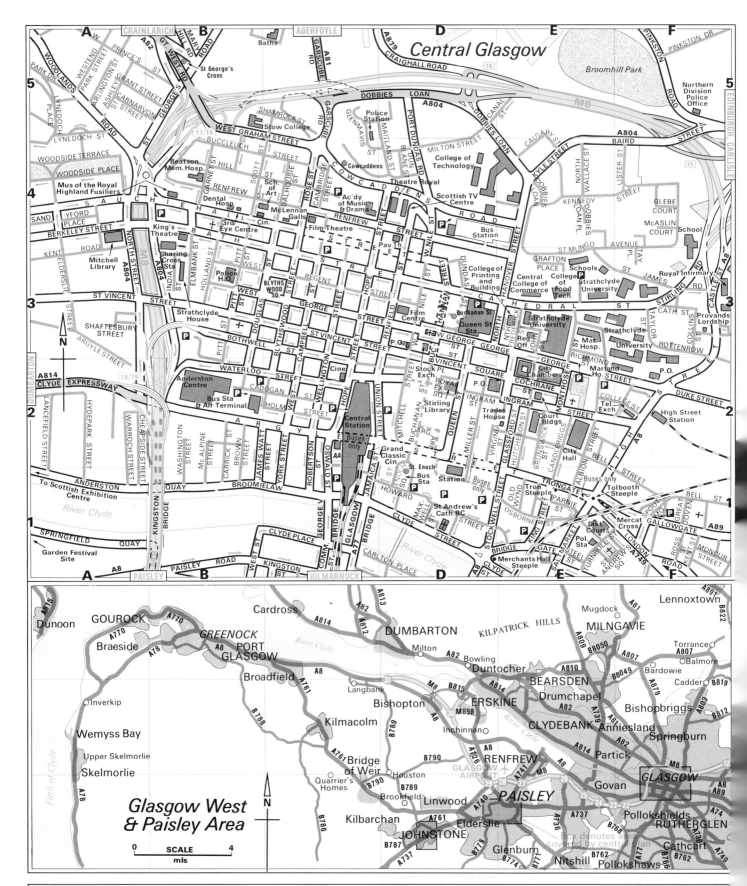

Glasgow

Although much of Glasgow is distinctly Victorian in character, its roots go back very many centuries. Best link with the past is the cathedral; founded in the 6th century, it has features from many succeeding centuries, including an exceptional 13th-century crypt. Nearby is Provand's Lordship, the city's oldest house. It dates from 1471 and is now a museum. Two much larger museums are to be found a little out of the centre – the Art Gallery and Museum contains one of the finest collections of paintings in Britain, while the Hunterian Museum, attached to the University, covers geology, archaeology, ethnography and more general subjects. On Glasgow Green is People's Palace – a museum of city life. Most imposing of the Victorian buildings are the City Chambers and City Hall which was built in 1841 as a concert hall but now houses the Scottish National Orchestra.

Paisley is famous for the lovely fabric pattern to which it gives its name. It was taken from fabrics brought from the Near East in the early 19th century, and its manufacture, along with the production of thread, is still important. Coats Observatory is one of the best-equipped in the country.

Johnstone grew rapidly as a planned industrial town in the 19th century, but suffered from the effects of the Industrial Revolution. Today, engineering is the main industry.

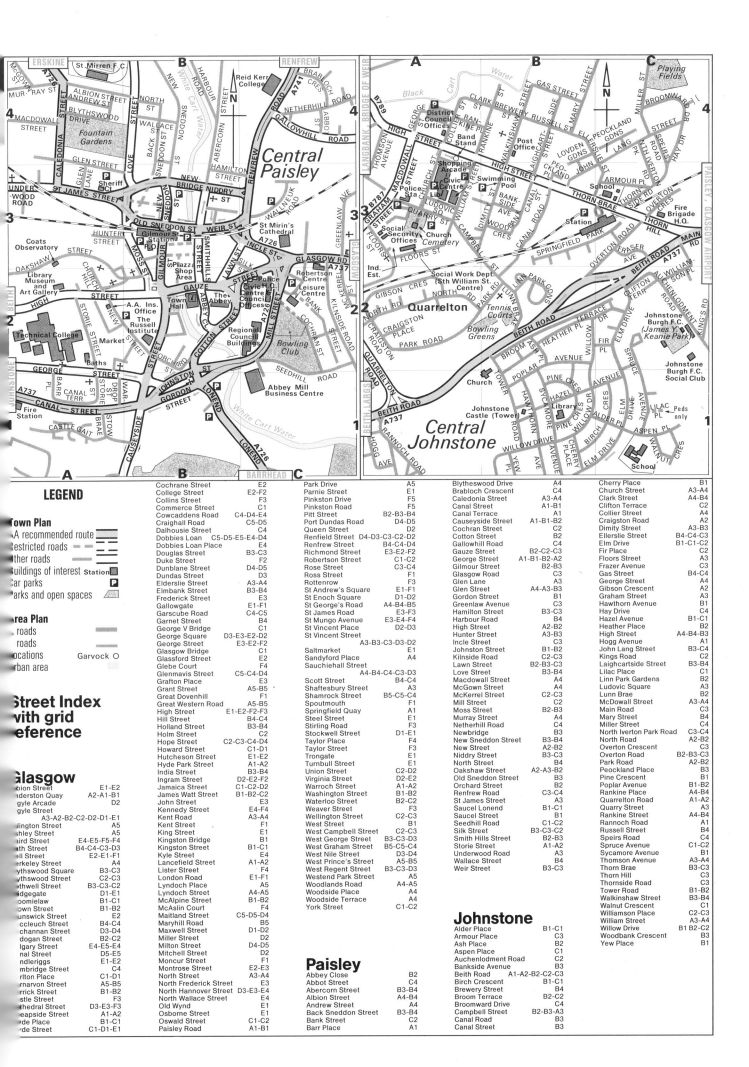

LEGEND

Town Plan

- A recommended route
- Restricted roads
- Other roads
- Buildings of interest — Station
- Car parks — P
- Parks and open spaces

Area Plan

- roads
- roads
- locations — Garvock O
- urban area

Street Index with grid reference

Glasgow

Albion Street	E1-E2
Anderston Quay	A2-A1-B1
Argyle Arcade	D2
Argyle Street	A3-A2-B2-C2-D2-D1-E1
Arlington Street	A5
Ashley Street	A5
Baird Street	E4-E5-F5-F4
Bath Street	B4-C4-C3-D3
Bell Street	E2-E1-F1
Berkeley Street	A4
Blythswood Square	B3-C3
Blythswood Street	C2-C3
Bothwell Street	B3-C3-C2
Bridgegate	D1-E1
Broomielaw	B1-C1
Brown Street	B1-B2
Brunswick Street	E2
Buccleuch Street	B4-C4
Buchannan Street	D3-D4
Cadogan Street	B2-C2
Calgary Street	E4-E5-E4
Canal Street	D5-E5
Candleriggs	E1-E2
Cambridge Street	C4
Carlton Place	C1-D1
Carnarvon Street	A5-B5
Carrick Street	B1-B2
Castle Street	F3
Cathedral Street	D3-E3-F3
Cheapside Street	A1-A2
Clyde Place	B1-C1
Clyde Street	C1-D1-E1
Cochrane Street	E2
College Street	E2-F2
Collins Street	F3
Commerce Street	C1
Cowcaddens Road	C4-D4-E4
Craighall Road	C5-D5
Dalhousie Street	C4
Dobbies Loan	C5-D5-E5-E4-D4
Dobbies Loan Place	E4
Douglas Street	B3-C3
Duke Street	F2
Dunblane Street	D4-D5
Dundas Street	D3
Elderslie Street	A3-A4
Elmbank Street	B3-B4
Frederick Street	E3
Gallowgate	E1-F1
Garnet Street	B4
Garscube Road	C4-C5
George V Bridge	C1
George Square	D3-E3-E2-D2
George Street	E3-E2-F2
Glasgow Bridge	C1
Glassford Street	E2
Glebe Court	F4
Glenmavis Street	C5-C4-D4
Grafton Place	E3
Grant Street	A5-B5
Great Dovenhill	F1
Great Western Road	A5-B5
High Street	E1-E2-F2-F3
Hill Street	B4-C4
Holland Street	B3-B4
Holm Street	C2
Hope Street	C2-C3-C4-D4
Howard Street	C1-D1
Hutcheson Street	E1-E2
Hyde Park Street	A1-A2
India Street	B3-B4
Ingram Street	D2-E2-F2
Jamaica Street	C1-C2-D2
James Watt Street	B1-B2-C2
John Street	E3
Kennedy Street	E4-F4
Kent Road	A3-A4
Kent Street	F1
King Street	E1
Kingston Bridge	B1
Kingston Street	B1-C1
Kyle Street	E4
Lancefield Street	A1-A2
Lister Street	F4
London Road	E1-F1
Lyndoch Place	A5
Lyndoch Street	A4-A5
McAlpine Street	B1-B2
McAslin Court	F4
Maitland Street	C5-D5-D4
Maryhill Road	B5
Maxwell Street	D1-D2
Miller Street	D2
Milton Street	D4-D5
Mitchell Street	D2
Moncur Street	F1
Montrose Street	E2-E3
North Street	A3-A4
North Frederick Street	E3
North Hannover Street	D3-E3-E4
North Wallace Street	E4
Old Wynd	E1
Osborne Street	E1
Oswald Street	C1-C2
Paisley Road	A1-B1
Park Drive	A5
Parnie Street	E1
Pinkston Drive	F5
Pinkston Road	F5
Pitt Street	B2-B3-B4
Port Dundas Road	D4-D5
Queen Street	D2
Renfield Street	D4-D3-C3-C2-D2
Renfrew Street	B4-C4-D4
Richmond Street	E3-E2-F2
Robertson Street	C1-C2
Rose Street	C3-C4
Ross Street	F1
Rottenrow	F3
St Andrew's Square	E1-F1
St Enoch Square	D1-D2
St George's Road	A4-B4-B5
St James Road	E3-F3
St Mungo Avenue	E3-E4-F4
St Vincent Place	D2-D3
St Vincent Street	A3-B3-C3-D3-D2
Saltmarket	E1
Sandyford Place	A4
Sauchiehall Street	A4-B4-C4-C3-D3
Scott Street	B4-C4
Shaftesbury Street	A3
Shamrock Street	B5-C5-C4
Spoutmouth	F1
Springfield Quay	A1
Steel Street	E1
Stirling Road	F3
Stockwell Street	D1-E1
Taylor Place	F4
Taylor Street	F3
Trongate	E1
Turnbull Street	E1
Union Street	C2-D2
Virginia Street	D2-E2
Warroch Street	A1-A2
Washington Street	B1-B2
Waterloo Street	B2-C2
Weaver Street	F3
Wellington Street	C2-C3
West Street	B1
West Campbell Street	B3-C3-D3
West George Street	B3-C3-D3
West Graham Street	B5-C5-C4
West Nile Street	D3-D4
West Prince's Street	A5-B5
West Regent Street	B3-C3-D3
Westend Park Street	A5
Woodlands Road	A4-A5
Woodside Place	A4
Woodside Terrace	A4
York Street	C1-C2

Paisley

Abbey Close	B2
Abbot Street	C4
Abercorn Street	B3-B4
Albion Street	A4-B4
Andrew Street	A4
Back Sneddon Street	B3-B4
Bank Street	C2
Barr Place	A1
Blythswood Drive	A4
Brabloch Crescent	C4
Caledonia Street	A3-A4
Canal Street	A1-B1
Canal Terrace	A1
Causeyside Street	A1-B1-B2
Cochran Street	C2
Cotton Street	B2
Gallowhill Road	C4
Gauze Street	B2-C2-C3
George Street	A1-B1-B2-A2
Gilmour Street	B2-B3
Glasgow Road	C3
Glen Lane	A3
Glen Street	A4-A3-B3
Gordon Street	B1
Greenlaw Avenue	C3
Hamilton Street	B3-C3
Harbour Road	B4
High Street	A2-B2
Hunter Street	A3-B3
Incle Street	C3
Johnston Street	B1-B2
Kilnside Road	C2-C3
Lawn Street	B2-B3-C3
Love Street	B3-B4
Macdowall Street	A4
McGown Street	A4
McKerrel Street	C2-C3
Mill Street	C2
Moss Street	B2-B3
Murray Street	A4
Netherhill Road	C4
Newbridge	B3
New Sneddon Street	B3-B4
New Street	A2-B2
Niddry Street	B3-C3
North Street	B4
Oakshaw Street	A2-A3-B2
Old Sneddon Street	B3
Orchard Street	B2
Renfrew Road	C3-C4
St James Street	A3
Saucel Lonend	B1-C1
Saucel Street	B1
Seedhill Road	C1-C2
Silk Street	B3-C3-C2
Smith Hills Street	B2-B3
Storie Street	A1-A2
Underwood Road	A3
Wallace Street	B4
Weir Street	B3-C3

Johnstone

Alder Place	B1-C1
Armour Place	C3
Ash Place	B2
Aspen Place	C1
Auchenlodment Road	C2
Bankside Avenue	B3
Beith Road	A1-A2-B2-C2-C3
Birch Crescent	B1-C1
Brewery Street	B4
Broom Terrace	B2-C2
Broomward Drive	C4
Campbell Street	B2-B3-A3
Canal Road	B3
Canal Street	B3
Cherry Place	B1
Church Street	A3-A4
Clark Street	A4-B4
Clifton Terrace	C2
Collier Street	A4
Craigston Road	A2
Dimity Street	A3-B3
Ellerslie Street	B4-C4-C3
Elm Drive	B1-C1-C2
Fir Place	C2
Floors Street	A3
Frazer Avenue	C3
Gas Street	B4-C4
George Street	A4
Gibson Crescent	A2
Graham Street	A3
Hawthorn Avenue	B1
Hay Drive	C4
Hazel Avenue	B1-C1
Heather Place	B2
High Street	A4-B4-B3-B2
Hogg Avenue	A1
John Lang Street	B3-B4
Kings Road	C2
Laighcartside Street	B3-B4
Lilac Place	C1
Linn Park Gardens	B2
Ludovic Square	A3
Lunn Brae	B2
McDowall Street	A3-A4
Main Road	C3
Mary Street	B4
Miller Street	C4
North Iverton Park Road	C3-C4
North Road	A2-B2
Overton Crescent	A2
Overton Road	B2-B3-C3
Park Road	A2-B2
Peockland Place	B3
Pine Crescent	B1
Poplar Avenue	B1-B2
Rankine Place	A4-B4
Quarrelton Road	A1-A2
Quarry Street	A3
Rankine Street	A4-B4
Rannoch Road	A1
Russell Street	B4
Speirs Road	C4
Spruce Avenue	C1-C2
Sycamore Avenue	B1
Thomson Avenue	A3-A4
Thorn Brae	B3-C3
Thorn Hill	C3
Thornside Road	C3
Tower Road	B1-B2
Walkinshaw Street	B3-B4
Walnut Crescent	C1
Williamson Place	C2-C3
William Street	A3-A4
Willow Drive	B1 B2-C2
Woodbank Crescent	B3
Yew Place	B1

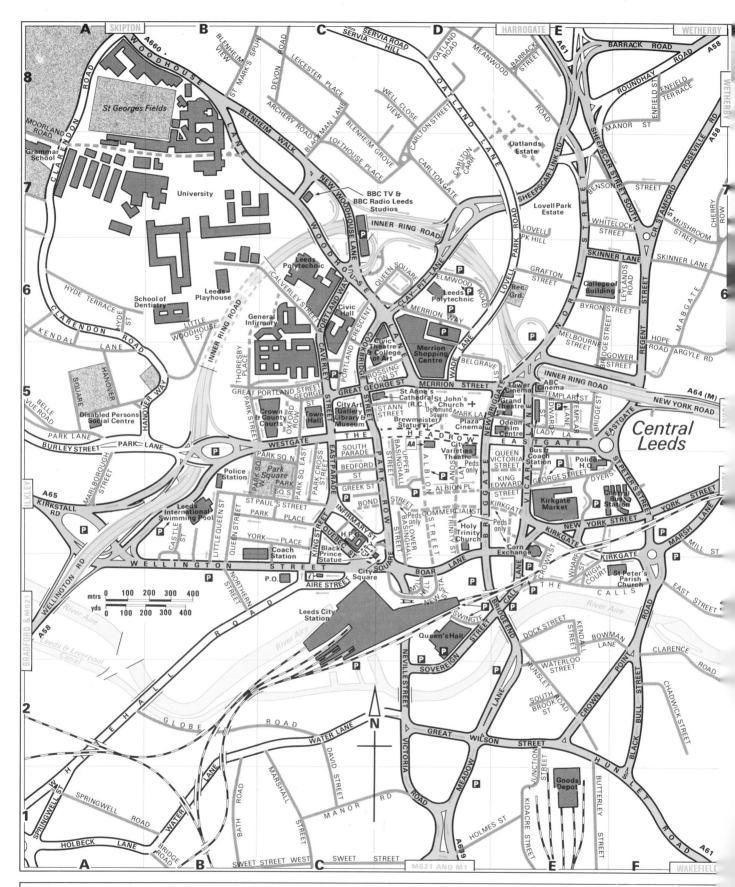

Leeds

In the centre of Leeds is its town hall – a monumental piece of architecture with a 225ft clock-tower. It was opened by Queen Victoria in 1858, and has been a kind of mascot for the city ever since. It exudes civic pride; such buildings could only have been created in the heyday of Victorian prosperity and confidence. Leeds' staple industry has always been the wool trade, but it only became a boom town towards the end of the 18th century, when textile mills were introduced. Today, the wool trade and ready-made clothing (Mr Hepworth and Mr Burton began their work here) are still important, though industries like paper, leather, furniture and electrical equipment are prominent.

Across Calverley Street from the town hall is the City Art Gallery, Library and Museum. Its collections include sculpture by Henry Moore, who was a student at Leeds School of Art. Nearby is the Headrow, Leeds' foremost shopping thoroughfare. On it is the City Varieties Theatre, venue for many years of the famous television programme 'The Good Old Days'. Off the Headrow are several shopping arcades, of which Leeds has many handsome examples. Leeds has a good number of interesting churches; perhaps the finest is St John's, unusual in that it dates from 1634, a time when few churches were built.

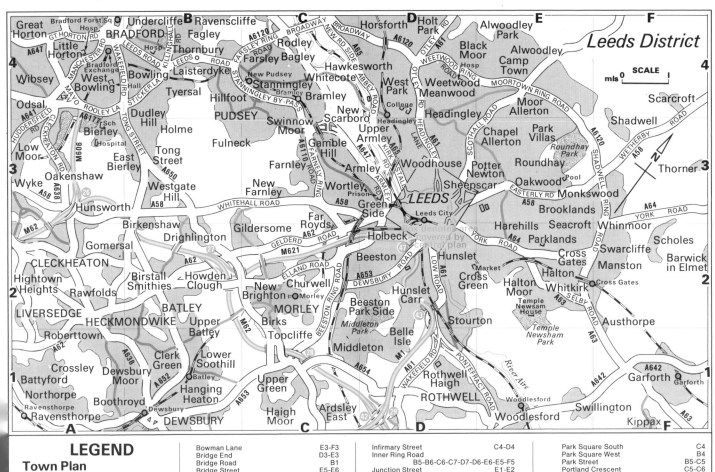

Leeds District

SCALE
mls 0 | 1

LEGEND

Town Plan
AA Recommended roads	
Other roads	
Restricted roads	
Buildings of interset	Museum
AA Centre	AA
Parks and open spaces	
Car Parks	P
Churches	†
One way streets	

District Plan
A roads	
B roads	
Stations	Kirkgate O
Urban area	
Buildings of interest	Hospital

Street Index with Grid Reference

Leeds

LEEDS
Offices now occupy the handsome twin-towered Civic Hall which stands in Calverley Street in front of the new buildings of Leeds Polytechnic. This area of the city – the commercial centre – has been extensively redeveloped

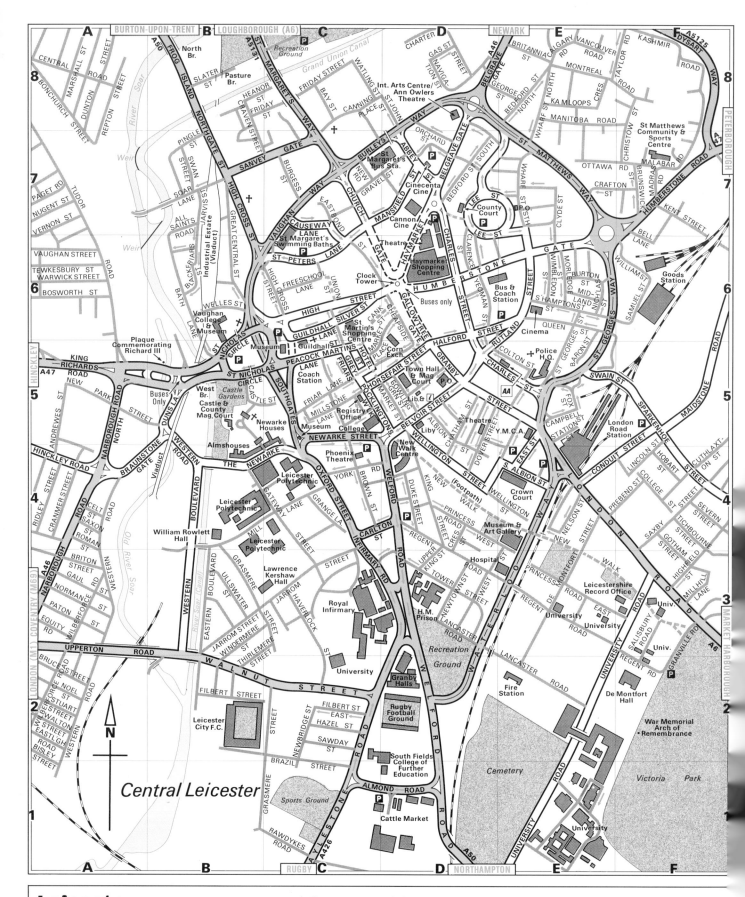

Leicester

A regional capital in Roman times, Leicester has retained many buildings from its eventful and distinguished past. Today the city is a thriving modern place, a centre for industry and commerce, serving much of the Midlands. Among the most outstanding monuments from the past is the Jewry Wall, a great bastion of Roman masonry. Close by are remains of the Roman baths and

several other contemporary buildings. Attached is a museum covering all periods from prehistoric times to 1500. Numerous other museums include the Wygston's House Museum of Costume, with displays covering the period 1769 to 1924; Newarke House, with collections showing changing social conditions in Leicester through four hundred years; and Leicestershire Museum and Art Gallery, with collections of drawings, paintings, ceramics, geology and natural history.

The medieval Guildhall has many features of interest, including a great hall, library and police cells. Leicester's castle, although remodelled in the 17th century, retains a 12th-century great hall. The Church of St Mary de Castro, across the road from the castle, has features going back at least as far as Norman times; while St Nicholas's Church is even older, with Roman and Saxon foundations. St Martin's Cathedral dates mainly from the 13th to 15th centuries and has a notable Bishop's throne.

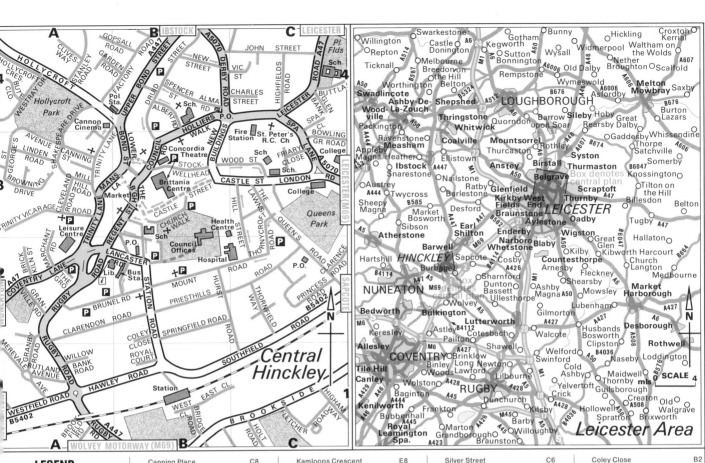

Central Hinckley

Leicester Area

Leicester (M69)

SCALE mls 0 4

WOLVEY MOTORWAY (M69)

LEGEND

own Plan
- A Recommended route
- estricted roads
- ther roads
- uildings of interest
- ar parks   P
- arks and open spaces

rea Plan
- roads
- roads
- locations   Creaton○
- rban area

Street Index with Grid Reference

eicester

bey Street	D7
ion Street	D4-D5
Saints Road	B7
mond Road	C1-D1
drewes Street	A4-A5
lestone Road	C1-C2
ron Street	E5-E6
th Lane	B5-B6
y Street	C8
dford Street North	E8
dford Street South	D7
grave Gate	D7-D8-E8
l Lane	F6-F7
voir Street	D5
sley Street	A1-A2
ckfriars Street	B6
nchurch Street	A7-A8
sworth Street	A6
wling Green Street	D5
aunstone Gate	A4-B4-B5
azil Street	C1-C2
annia Street	E8
ton Street	A3
own Street	C4
ice Street	A2
nswick Street	F7
rgess Street	C7
rleys Way	C7-D7-D8
rton Street	E6
gary Road	E8
mpbell Street	E5
nk Street	C6-D6

Canning Place	C8
Carlton Street	C4-D4
Castle Street	B5-C5
Celt Street	A4
Central Road	A8
Charles Street	D7-D6-D5-E5
Charter Street	D8
Chatham Street	D4-D5
Cheapside	D5-D6
Christow Street	F7-F8
Church Gate	C7-C6-D6
Clarence Street	D6-D7
Clyde Street	E6-E7
College Street	F4
Colton Street	D5-E5
Conduit Street	E4-F4-F5
Crafton Street	E7-F7
Cranmer Street	A4
Craven Street	B7-B8
Crescent Street	D4
Cuthlaxton Street	F4-F5
De Montfort Street	E3-E4
Dover Street	D4-D5
Duke Street	D4
Duns Lane	B5
Dunton Street	A8
Dysart Way	F7-F8
East Bond Street	C6-C7-D6
East Street	E4-E5
Eastern Boulevard	B3-B4
Eastleigh Road	A2
Equity Road	A3
Filbert Street	B2-C2
Filbert Street East	C2
Fox Street	E5
Freeschool Lane	C6
Friar Lane	C5
Friday Street	B8-C8
Frog Island	B8
Gallowtree Gate	D6
Gas Street	D8
Gateway Street	B4-C4-C3
Gaul Street	A3
George Street	D8-E8
Gotham Street	F3-F4
Granby Street	D5-E5
Grange Lane	C4
Granville Road	F2-F3
Grasmere Street	B4-B3-C3-C2-C1-B1
Gravel Street	C7-D7
Great Central Street	B6-B7
Greyfriars	C5
Guildhall Lane	C6
Halford Street	D5-D6-E6
Haverlock Street	C2-C3
Haymarket	D6-D7
Hazel Street	C2
Heanor Street	B8-C8
High Cross Street	B7-B6-C6
Highfield Street	F3
High Street	C6-D6
Hinckley Road	A4
Hobart Street	F4
Horsefair Street	C5-D5
Hotel Street	C5
Humberstone Gate	D6-E6
Humberstone Road	F7
Infirmary Road	C4-C3-D3
Jarrom Street	B3-C3
Jarvis Street	B7

Kamloops Crescent	E8
Kashmir Road	F8
Kent Street	F7
King Richards Road	A5
King Street	D4-D5
Lancaster Road	D3-E3-E2
Lee Street	D6-D7-E7
Lincoln Street	F4-F5
London Road	E5-E4-F4-F3
Madras Road	F7
Maidstone Road	F5-F6
Malabar Road	F7
Manitoba Road	E8-F8
Mansfield Street	C7-D7
Market Place	C5-C6-D6
Market Street	D5
Marshall Street	A8
Midland Street	E6
Mill Hill Lane	F3
Mill Lane	B4-C4
Millstone Lane	C5
Morledge Street	E6
Montreal Road	E8-F8
Narborough Road	A3-A4
Narborough Road North	A4-A5
Navigation Street	D8
Nelson Street	E4
Newarke Street	C5
Newbridge Street	C2
New Park Street	A5-B5
New Road	C7
Newtown Street	D3
New Walk	D4-E4-E3-F3
Nicholas Street	E6
Noel Street	A2
Northgate Street	B7-B8
Norman Street	A3
Nugent Street	A7
Orchard Street	D7-D8
Ottawa Road	E7-F7
Oxford Street	C4
Paget Road	A7
Paton Street	A3
Peacock Lane	C5
Pingle Street	B7
Pocklingtons Walk	C5-D5
Prebend Street	E4-F4
Princess Road East	E3-F3
Princess Road West	D4-E4
Queen Street	E6
Rawdykes Road	B1-C1
Regent Road	D4-D3-E3-F3-F2
Repton Street	A7-A8
Ridley Street	A4
Roman Street	A4
Rutland Street	D5-E5-E6
St George Street	E5-E6
St George's Way	E6-F6
St John Street	D8
St Margaret's Way	B8-C8-C7
St Martins	C5
St Mathews Way	E7
St Nicholas Circle	B6-B5-C5
St Peters Lane	C6
Salisbury Road	F2-F3
Samuel Stuart	F6
Sanvey Gate	B7-C7
Sawday Street	C2
Saxby Street	F4
Saxon Street	A4
Severn Street	F4

Silver Street	C6
Slater Street	B8
Soar Lane	B7
South Albion Street	E4
Southampton Street	E6
Southgates	C5
Sparkenhoe Street	F4-F5
Station Street	E5
Stuart Street	A2
Swain Street	E5-F5
Swan Street	B7
The Newarke	B4-C4
Taylor Road	E8-F8
Tewkesbury Street	A6
Thirlemere Street	B2-B3-C3
Tichbourne Street	F3-F4
Tower Street	D3
Tudor Road	A5-A6-A7-A8
Ullswater Street	B3
Union Street	C6
University Road	E1-E2-E3-F3
Upper King Street	D3-D4
Upperton Road	A3-B3-B2
Vancouver Road	E8
Vaughan Way	C6-C7
Vaughan Street	A6
Vernon Street	A6-A7
Walnut Street	B3-B2-C2
Walton Street	A2
Warwick Street	A6
Waterloo Way	D2-D3-E3-E4
Watling Street	C8
Welford Road	D1-D2-D3-D4
Welles Street	B6
Wellington Street	D4-E4-D5
Western Boulevard	B3-B4
Western Road	A1-A2-A3-A4-B4-B5
West Street	D3-E3-E4
Wharf Street North	E7-E8
Wharf Street South	E7
Wilberforce Road	A2-A3
William Street	F6
Wimbledon Street	E6
Windermere Street	B2-B3-C3
Yeoman Street	D6
York Road	C5

Hinckley

Albert Road	B4
Alma Road	B4
Bowling Green Road	C3
Brick Kiln Street	A2
Bridge Road	B1
Brookfield Road	A1
Brookside	B1-C1
Browning Drive	A3
Brunel Road	A2-B2
Bute Close	A4
Butt Lane	C4
Canning Street	A3
Castle Street	B3-C3
Charles Street	C4
Church Walk	B3
Clarence Road	C4
Clarendon Road	A2-B2
Cleveland Road	A3
Clivesway	A4

Coley Close	B2
Council Road	B3
Coventry Lane	A2
Derby Road	B4
Druid Street	B3-B4
East Close	B1-C1
Factory Road	A4-B4
Fletcher Road	C1
Friary Close	C3
Garden Road	A4-B4
Glen Road	B4
Gopsall Road	B4
Granby Road	A1-A2
Granville Road	A2
Hawley Road	A1-B1
Higham Way	C1
Highfields Road	C4
Hill Street	C2-C3
Holliers Walk	B3-B4
Hollycroft	A4
Hollycroft Crescent	A4
Holt Road	C1
Hurst Road	B2-C1-C2
John Street	B4
Lancaster Road	A2-B2
Leicester Road	C4
Linden Road	A3
London Road	C3
Lower Bond Street	B3-B4
Mansion Lane	A3-B3
Marchant Road	A2-A3
Merevale Avenue	A1
Mill Hill Road	A3
Mount Road	B2-C2
New Buildings	B3-B4
New Street	B4
Priesthills Road	B2-C2
Princess Road	C2
Queens Road	C2
Regent Street	A2-B2-A3-A3
Royal Court	B1
Rugby Road	A2-A1-B1
Rutland Avenue	A1
St George's Avenue	A3-A4
Shakespeare Drive	A3-A4
Southfield Road	B1-C1-C2
Spa Close	C4
Spa Lane	C3-C4
Spencer Street	B4
Springfield Road	B2
Stanley Road	A4
Station Road	B1-B2
Stockwellhead	B3
The Borough	B3
The Grove	A2
The Lawns	C3
Thornfield Way	C2
Thornycroft Road	C2-C3
Trinity Lane	A2-A3-A4-B4
Trinity Vicarage Road	A3
Upper Bond Street	B4
Victoria Road	C4
West Close	B1
Westray Drive	A4
Westfield Road	A1
Willow Bank Road	A1
Wood Street	B3-C3

LLTT

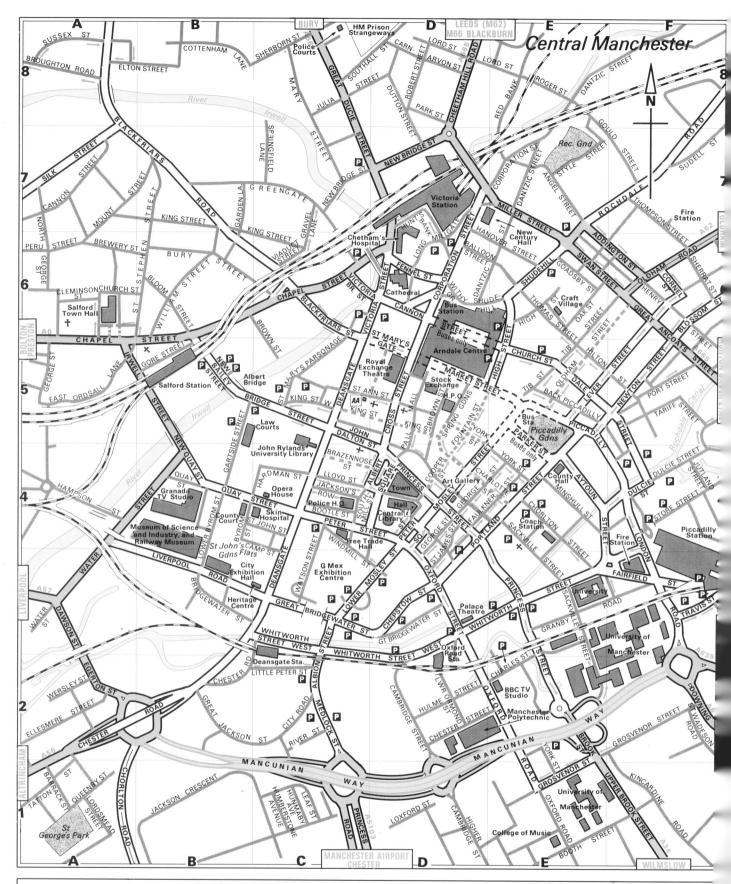

Manchester

The gigantic conurbation called Greater Manchester covers a staggering 60 square miles, reinforcing Manchester's claim to be Britain's second city. Commerce and industry are vital aspects of the city's character, but it is also an important cultural centre – the Halle Orchestra has its home at the Free Trade Hall (a venue for many concerts besides classical music), there are several theatres, a library (the John Rylands) which houses one of the most important collections of books in the world, and a number of museums and galleries, including the Whitworth Gallery with its lovely watercolours.

Like many great cities it suffered badly during the bombing raids of World War II, but some older buildings remain, including the town hall, a huge building designed in Gothic style by Alfred Waterhouse and opened in 1877. Manchester Cathedral dates mainly from the 15th century and is noted for its fine tower and outstanding carved woodwork. Nearby is Chetham's Hospital, also 15th-century and now housing a music school. Much new development has taken place, and more is planned. Shopping precincts cater for the vast population, and huge hotels have provided service up to international standards. On the edge of the city is the Belle Vue centre, a large entertainments complex including concert and exhibition facilities and a speedway stadium.

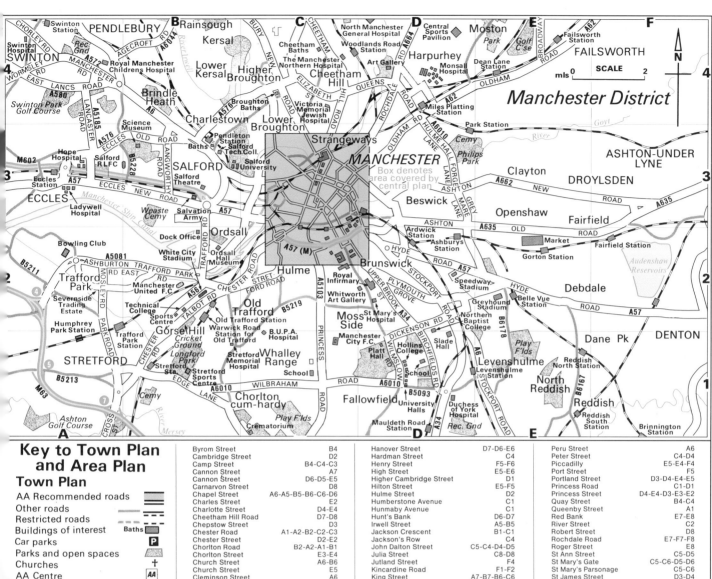

Manchester District

SCALE
mls 0 ——— 2

Box denotes area covered by central plan

Key to Town Plan and Area Plan

Town Plan

AA Recommended roads
Other roads
Restricted roads
Buildings of interest — Baths
Car parks — P
Parks and open spaces
Churches — +
AA Centre — AA
One Way Streets — ←

District Plan

A roads
B roads

STREET INDEX
-with grid reference

Manchester

Street	Grid
Addington Street	E7-E6-F6
Albert Square	C4-D4
Albion Street	C2-C3
Angel Street	E7
Aytoun Street	E4-F4-F3-E3
Back Piccadilly	E5-F5-F4
Balloon Street	D6-E6
Barrack Street	A1
Blackfriars Road	A8-A7-B7-B6-C6
Blackfriars Street	C5-C6
Bloom Street	B6
Blossom Street	F6
Booth Street	E1-F1
Bootle Street	C4
Brazennose Street	C4-D4
Brewery Street	A6-B6
Bridge Street	B5-C5
Bridgewater Street	B3
Brook Street	E2
Broughton Road	A8
Brown Street	B6-C6-C5
Brown Street	D4-D5
Bury Street	B6-C6
Byrom Street	B4
Cambridge Street	D2
Camp Street	B4-C4-C3
Cannon Street	A7
Cannon Street	D6-D5-E5
Carnarvon Street	D8
Chapel Street	A6-A5-B5-B6-C6-D6
Charles Street	E2
Charlotte Street	D4-E4
Cheetham Hill Road	D7-D8
Chepstow Street	D3
Chester Road	A1-A2-B2-C2-C3
Chester Street	D2-E2
Chorlton Road	B2-A2-A1-B1
Chorlton Street	E3-E4
Church Street	A6-B6
Church Street	E5
City Road	C2
Cleminson Street	A6
Cooper Street	D4
Cornel Street	F6
Corporation Street	D6-D7-E7
Cottenham Lane	B8
Cross Street	D4-D5-D6
Dale Street	E5-F5-F4
Dantzic Street	D6-E6-E7-E8-F8
Dawson Street	A3
Deansgate	C3-C4-C5
Downing Street	F2
Dulcie Street	F4
Dutton Street	D7-D8
East Ordsall Lane	A5
Egerton Street	A2
Ellesmere Street	A2
Elton Street	A8-B8
Fairfield Street	F3
Faulkner Street	D4-E4
Fennel Street	D6
Fountain Street	D4-D5
Garden Lane	B6-B7
Gartside Street	B4-B5
George Street	A5
George Street	D3-D4-E4
Goadsby Street	E6
Gore Street	B5
Gould Street	E8-E7-F7
Granby Road	E3-F3
Gravel Lane	C6-C7
Great Ancoats Street	F5-F6
Great Bridgewater Street	C3-D3
Great Ducie Street	C8-C7-D7
Great Jackson Street	B2-C2
Greengate	B7-C7
Grosvenor Street	E1-E2-F2
Hampson Street	A4

Street	Grid
Hanover Street	D7-D6-E6
Hardman Street	C4
Henry Street	F5-F6
High Street	E5-E6
Higher Cambridge Street	D1
Hilton Street	E5-F5
Hulme Street	D2
Humberstone Avenue	C1
Hunmaby Avenue	C1
Hunt's Bank	D6-D7
Irwell Street	A5-B5
Jackson Crescent	B1-C1
Jackson's Row	C4
John Dalton Street	C5-C4-D4-D5
Julia Street	C8-D8
Jutland Street	F4
Kincardine Road	F1-F2
King Street	A7-B7-B6-C6
King Street	C5-D5
King St West	C5
Leaf Street	C1
Lever Street	E5-F5-F6
Little Peter Street	B2-C2
Liverpool Road	A4-A3-B4-B3-C3
Lloyd Street	C4
London Road	F3-F4
Long Millgate	D6-D7
Lord Street	D8-E8
Lordsmead Street	A1
Lower Byrom Street	B3-B4
Lower Mosley Street	C3-D3-D4
Lower Ormond Street	D2
Loxford Street	D1
Mancunian Way	B2-B1-C2-C1-D1-D2-E2-F2
Market Street	D5-E5
Mary Street	C7-C8
Medlock Street	C2
Miller Street	D7-E7-E6
Minshull Street	E4
Mosley Street	D4-D5-E4-E5
Mount Street	A6-A7-B7
Newton Street	F5
New Bailey Street	B5
New Bridge Street	C7-D7
North George Street	A6-A7
New Quay Street	B4-B5
Oak Street	E6
Oldham Road	F6-F7
Oldham Street	E5-E6-F6
Oxford Road	D2-E2-E1
Oxford Street	D4-D3-D2
Pall Mall	D4-D5
Park Street	D8
Parker Street	E4-E5

Street	Grid
Peru Street	A6
Peter Street	C4-D4
Piccadilly	E5-E4-F4
Port Street	F5
Portland Street	D3-D4-E4-E5
Princess Road	F5
Princess Street	D4-E4-D3-E3-E2
Quay Street	B4-C4
Queenby Street	A1
Red Bank	E7-E8
River Street	C2
Robert Street	D8
Rochdale Road	E7-F7-F8
Roger Street	E8
St Ann Street	D5
St Mary's Gate	C5-C6-D5-D6
St Mary's Parsonage	C5-C6
St James Street	D3-D4
St John Street	B4-C4
St Peter Square	D4
St Stephen Street	A6-B6-B7
Sackville Street	E2-E3-E4
Sherrat Street	F6
Sherborn Street	B8-C8
Shudehill	D6-E6
Silk Street	A7
Southall Street	C8-D8
Southmill Street	C4
Spring Gardens	D4-D5
Springfield Lane	C7-C8
Store Street	F4
Style Street	E7-E8
Sudell Street	F7-F8
Sussex Street	A8
Swan Street	E6-F6
Tatton Street	A1
Tariff Street	F5
Thomas Street	E5-E6
Thompson Street	F6-F7
Tib Street	E5-E6-F6
Travis Street	F3
Upper Brook Street	E2-E1-F1
Viaduct Street	C6
Victoria Bridge Street	C6-D6
Victoria Street	C6-D6
Wadeson Road	F2
Water Street	A3-A4-B4
Watson Street	C3-C4
Wersley Street	A2
Whitworth Street	D3-E3
Whitworth Street West	B3-C3-C2-D2-D3
William Street	B6
Windmill Street	C4-C3-D3
Withy Green	D6
York Street	D5-D4-E4

MANCHESTER
The Barton Swing Bridge carries the Bridgewater Canal over the Manchester Ship Canal, which links Manchester with the sea nearly 40 miles away. Completed in 1894, the canal is navigable by vessels up to 15,000 tons.

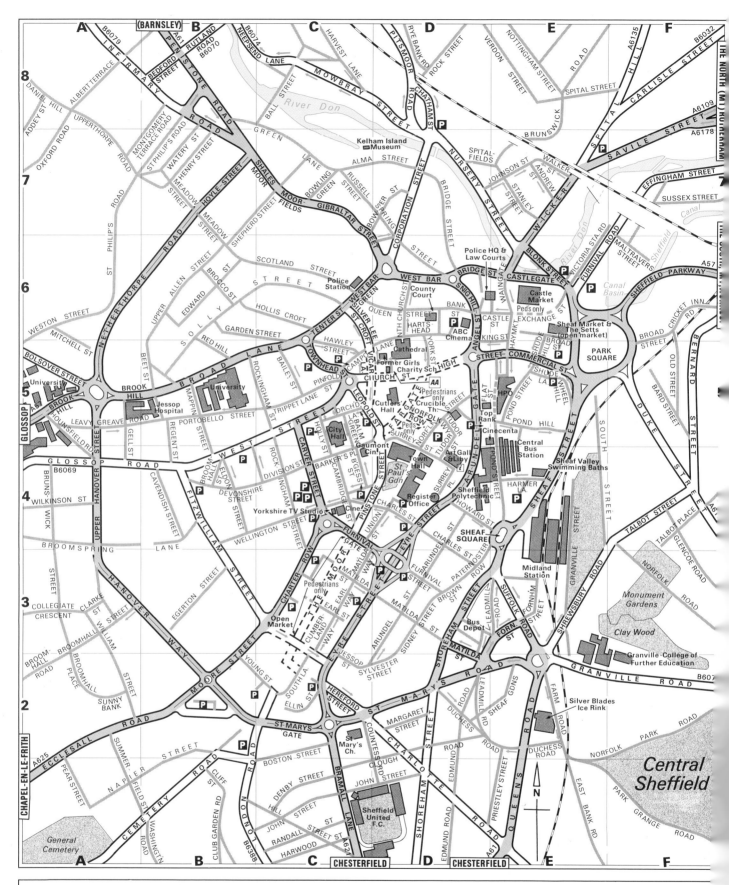

Sheffield

Cutlery – which has made the name of Sheffield famous throughout the world – has been manufactured here since at least as early as the time of Chaucer. The god of blacksmiths, Vulcan, is the symbol of the city's industry, and he crowns the town hall, which was opened in 1897 by Queen Victoria. At the centre of the industry, however, is Cutlers' Hall, the headquarters of the Company of Cutlers. This society was founded in 1624 and has the right to grant trade marks to articles of a sufficiently high standard. In the hall is the company's collection of silver, with examples of craftsmanship dating back every year to 1773. A really large collection of cutlery is kept in the city museum. Steel production, a vital component of the industry, was greatly improved when the crucible process was invented here in 1740. At Abbeydale Industrial Hamlet, 3½ miles south-west of the city centre, is a complete restored site open as a museum and showing 18th-century methods of steel production. Sheffield's centre, transformed since World War II, is one of the finest and most modern in Europe. There are no soot-grimed industrial eyesores here, for the city has stringent pollution controls and its buildings are carefully planned and set within excellent landscaping projects. Many parks are set in and around the city and the Pennines are within easy reach.

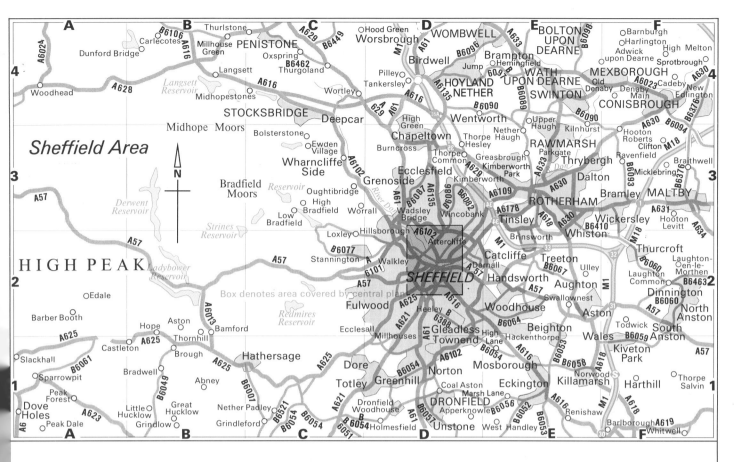

LEGEND

Town Plan

AA Recommended roads
Other roads
Restricted roads
Buildings of interest
AA Centre
Car Parks
Parks and open spaces

Area Plan

A roads
B roads
Locations   Oakworth ○
Urban area

Street Index with grid reference

Sheffield

Addey Street	A7-A8
Albert Terrace	A8
Alma Street	C7 D7
Andrew Street	E7
Angel Street	D5-D6
Arundel Gate	D4-D5
Arundel Street	C2-D2-D3-D4
Bailey Street	C5
Ball Street	C8
Balm Green	C4-C5
Bank Street	D6
Bard Street	F5
Barker's Pool	C4-C5-D5
Bedford Street	B8
Beet Street	B5
Bernard Street	F4-F5-F6
Blonk Street	E6
Bolsover Street	A5
Boston Street	C1-C2
Bower Street	C7-D7
Bowling Green	C7
Bramall Lane	C1-C2
Bridge Street	D7-D6-E6
Broad Lane	B5-C5-C6
Broad Street	E6-F5-F6
Brocco Street	B6
Brook Hill	A5-B5
Broomhall Place	A2
Broomhall Road	A2
Broomhall Street	A2-A3-B4
Broomspring Lane	A4-B4
Brown Street	D3
Brunswick Street	A3-A4
Brunswick Road	E7-E8
Burgess Street	C4
Cambridge Street	C4
Campo Lane	C5-D5-D6
Carlisle Street	F8
Carver Street	C4-C5
Castle Street	D6-E6
Castlegate	E6
Cavendish Street	B4
Cemetery Road	A1-B1-B2
Charles Street	D3-D4
Charlotte Road	C2-D2-D1-E1
Charter Row	C3-C4
Chatham Street	D7-D8
Church Street	C5-D5
Clarke Street	A3
Cliff Street	B1
Clough Road	C1-D1-D2
Club Garden Road	B1
Collegiate Crescent	A3
Commercial Street	E5
Corporation Street	D6-D7
Countess Road	C2-D2-D1
Cricket Inn Road	F6
Cumberland Way	C3
Daniel Hill	A8
Denby Street	C1
Devonshire Street	B4-C4
Division Street	C4
Duchess Road	D2-E2
Duke Street	F4-F5
Earl Street	C3
Earl Way	C3
East Bank Road	E1-E2
Ecclesall Road	A1-A2-B2
Edmund Road	D1-D2
Edward Street	B6
Effingham Street	F7
Egerton Street	B3
Eldon Street	B4
Ellin Street	C2
Eyre Street	C2-C3-D3-D4
Exchange Street	E6
Fargate	D5
Farm Road	E2
Fitzwilliam Street	B4-B3-C3
Flat Street	E5
Fornham Street	E3
Furnival Gate	C3-C4-D3-D4
Furnival Road	E6-F6-F7
Furnival Street	D3
Garden Street	B6-C6-C5
Gell Street	A4-A5
Gibraltar Street	C7-C6-D6
Glencoe Road	F3-F4
Glossop Road	A4-B4
Granville Road	E2-F2
Granville Street	E3-E4
Green Lane	B8-C8-C7
Hanover Way	A3-B3-B2
Harmer Lane	E4
Hartshead	D6
Harwood Street	C1
Harvest Lane	C8

Hawley Street	C5
Haymarket	E5-E6
Henry Street	B7
Hereford Street	C2
High Street	D5-E5
Hill Street	B1-C1
Hollis Croft	B6-C6
Holly Street	C4-C5
Hounsfield Road	A4-A5
Howard Street	D4-E4
Hoyle Street	B7
Infirmary Road	A8-B8 B7
Jessop Street	C2
John Street	C1-D1
Johnson Street	D7-E7
King Street	D5-E5-E6
Leadmill Road	D2-D3-E3
Leavy Greave Road	A5-B5
Lee Croft	C5-C6
Leopold Street	C5-D5
London Road	C1-B1-B2-C2
Maltravers Street	F6
Mappin Street	B4-B5
Margaret Street	D2
Matilda Street	C3-D3-D2
Matilda Way	C3
Meadow Street	B6-B7
Mitchell Street	A5-A6
Montgomery Terrace Road	A7-B7-B8
Moorfields	C7
Moore Street	B2-B3-C3
Mowbray Street	C8-D8-D7
Napier Street	A1-B1-B2
Neepsend Lane	B8-C8
Netherthorpe Road	A5-A6-B6-B7
Norfolk Park Road	E1-E2-F2
Norfolk Road	F3-F4
Norfolk Row	D5
Norfolk Street	D4-D5
North Church Street	D6
Nottingham Street	E8
Nursery Street	D7-E7-E6
Old Street	F5-F6
Orchard Lane	C5
Oxford Road	A7-A8
Park Grange Road	E1-F1
Park Square	E5-E6-F6-F5
Paternoster Row	D3-D4-E4
Pear Street	A1
Penistone Road	B7-B8
Pinfold Street	C5
Pinstone Street	C4-D4-D5
Pitsmoor Road	D8
Pond Hill	E5
Pond Street	E4-E5
Portobello Street	B5-C5
Priestley Street	D1-E1-E2
Queen Street	C6-D6
Queen's Road	E1-E2
Randall Street	C1
Red Hill	B5-B6
Regent Street	B4-B5
Rock Street	D8
Rockingham Street	B5-C5-C4
Russell Street	C7

Rutland Road	B8
Rye Bank Road	D8
St Mary's Gate	C2
St Mary's Road	C2-D2-E2
St Philip's Road	A6-A7-B7-B8
Savile Street	E7-F7-F8
Scotland Street	B6-C6
Shales Moor	B7-C7
Sheaf Gardens	D2-E2
Sheaf Street	E4-E5
Sheffield Parkway	F6
Shepherd Street	B6-B7-C7
Shoreham Street	D1-D2-D3-E3
Shrewsbury Road	E3-E4-F3-F4
Shude Lane	E5
Shude Hill	E5-E6
Sidney Street	D3
Silver Street	C6
Snig Hill	D6
Solly Street	B5-B6-C6
South Lane	C2
South Street	E4-E5
Spital Hill	E7-E8-F8
Spital Street	E8-F8
Spitalfields	D7-E7
Spring Street	D6-D7
Stanley Street	E7
Suffolk Road	E3
Summerfield Street	A2-A1-B1
Sunny Bank	A2
Surrey Place	D4
Surrey Street	D4-D5
Sussex Street	F7
Sylvester Street	C2-D2
Talbot Place	F4
Talbot Street	F4
Tenter Street	C6
The Moor	C3-C4
Townhead Street	C5
Trippet Lane	C5
Tudor Street	D4-D5
Tudor Way	D5
Union Street	C4-D4
Upper Allen Street	B6
Upper Hanover Street	A3-A4-A5
Upperthorpe Road	A7-A8
Verdon Street	D8-E8
Vicar Lane	C5-D5
Victoria Station Road	E6-E7-F7
Waingate	E6
Walker Street	E7
Washington Road	B1
Watery Street	B7-B8
Wellington Street	B4-C4
West Bar	D6
West Bar Green	C6-D6
West Street	B4-B5-C5
Weston Street	A5-A6
Wheel Hill	E6-E7
Wicker	E6
Wilkinson Street	A4
William Street	A2-A3
York Street	D5-D6
Young Street	B2-C2

INDEX
TO
ATLAS

This index contains over 32,000 entries.
All towns and large villages are included, as are locally important settlements.

To locate a place in the atlas, first look up the name of the town or village required in the index. Turn to the page number indicated in *italic* type, and find the location using the last four numbers. Taking Hythe *Kent* .... **29** TR1634 as our example, take the first **bold** figure of the reference, 1, which refers to the number along the bottom of the page. The second figure, 6, tells you the distance to move in tenths to the right of this numbered line. A vertical line through this point is the first half of the reference. The third, **bold** figure, 3, refers to the number on the lefthand side of the page. Finally, the fourth figure, 4, indicates the distance to move in tenths above this numbered line. A horizontal line drawn through this point to intersect with the first line gives the precise location of the place in question. (For an explanation of the double letters, ie TR, in the reference, see the national grid page.)

Street plans of towns included within the index on the pages shown:

A'Chill Amber Row

A'Chill *Highld* **128** NG2705
Ab Kettleby *Leics* **63** SK7223
Ab Lench *H & W* **47** SP0152
Abbas Combe *Somset* **22** ST7022
Abberley *H & W* **47** SO7568
Abberley Common *H & W* **47** SO7467
Abberton *Essex* **41** TM0019
Abberton *H & W* **47** SO9953
Abberwick *Nthumb* **111** NU1313
Abbess Roding *Essex* **40** TL5711
Abbey *Devon* **9** ST1410
Abbey Cowpe *Cumb* **92** NY1550
Abbey Dore *H & W* **46** SO3830
Abbey Gate *Devon* **10** SY2996
Abbey Green *Staffs* **72** SJ9757
Abbey Hill *Somset* **9** ST1717
Abbey St. Bathans *Border* **119** NT7661
Abbey Town *Cumb* **93** NY1750
Abbey Village *Lancs* **81** SD6422
Abbey Wood *Gt Lon* **27** TQ4779
Abbeycwmhir *Powys* **45** SO0571
Abbeydale *S York* **74** SK3282
Abbeylands *IOM* **153** SC4585
Abbeystead *Lancs* **81** SD5654
Abbot's Chair *Derbys* **74** SK0290
Abbot's Salford *Warwks* **48** SP0650
Abbotrule *Border* **110** NT6113
Abbots Bickington *Devon* **18** SS3813
Abbots Bromley *Staffs* **73** SK0824
Abbots Deuglie *Tays* **126** NO1111
Abbots Langley *Herts* **26** TL0902
Abbots Leigh *Avon* **34** ST5474
Abbots Morton *H & W* **48** SP0255
Abbots Ripton *Cambs* **52** TL2377
Abbots Worthy *Hants* **24** SU4932
Abbotsford *Border* **109** NT5034
Abbotsham *Devon* **18** SS4226
Abbotskerswell *Devon* **7** SX8569
Abbotsleigh *Devon* **7** SX8048
Abbotsley *Cambs* **52** TL2256
Abbotstone *Hants* **24** SU5634
Abbotswood *Hants* **23** SU3623
Abbott Street *Dorset* **11** ST9800
Abbotts Ann *Hants* **23** SU3243
Abbottsbury *Dorset* **10** SY5785
Abcott *Shrops* **46** SO3978
Abdon *Shrops* **59** SO5786
Abenhall *Gloucs* **35** SO6717
Aber *Gwynd* **69** SH6572
Aber Clydach *Powys* **33** SO1021
Aber-arad *Dyfed* **31** SN3140
Aber-banc *Dyfed* **31** SN3541
Aber-giar *Dyfed* **44** SN5040
Aber-Magwr *Dyfed* **43** SN6673
Aber-meurig *Dyfed* **44** SN5656
Aber-nant *M Glam* **33** SO0103
Aberaeron *Dyfed* **42** SN4562
Aberaman *M Glam* **33** SO0101
Aberangell *Powys* **57** SH8410
Aberarder *Highld* **140** NH6235
Aberargie *Tays* **126** NO1615
Aberarth *Dyfed* **42** SN4763
Aberavon *W Glam* **32** SS7589
Aberbargoed *M Glam* **33** SO1500
Aberbargoed *M Glam* **33** ST1699
Aberbeeg *Gwent* **33** SO2102
Abercairny *Tays* **108** NS9122
Abercanaid *M Glam* **33** SO0503
Abercarn *Gwent* **33** ST2195
Abercastle *Dyfed* **30** SM8533
Abercegir *Powys* **57** SH8001
Aberchader Lodge *Highld* **131** NH3403
Aberchirder *Gramp* **142** NJ6252
Abercraf *Powys* **33** SN8213
Abercregan *W Glam* **33** SS8496
Abercrombie *Fife* **127** NO5102
Abercwmboi *M Glam* **33** ST0299
Abercych *Dyfed* **31** SN2441
Abercynon *M Glam* **33** ST0794
Aberdalgie *Tays* **125** NO0720
Aberdare *Powys* **33** SO0002
Aberdaron *Gwynd* **56** SH1726
Aberdeen *Gramp* **135** NJ9306
Aberdesach *Gwynd* **68** SH4251
Aberdour *Fife* **117** NT1985
Aberdovey *Gwynd* **43** SN6196
Aberdulais *W Glam* **32** SS7799
Aberedw *Powys* **45** SO0847
Abereiddy *Dyfed* **30** SM7931
Abererch *Gwynd* **56** SH3936
Aberfan *M Glam* **33** SO0700
Aberfeldy *Tays* **125** NN8549
Aberffraw *Gwynd* **68** SH3568
Aberffrwd *Dyfed* **43** SN6879
Aberford *W York* **83** SE4336
Aberfoyle *Cent* **115** NN5200
Abergarw *M Glam* **33** SS9184
Abergarwed *W Glam* **33** SN8102
Abergavenny *Gwent* **34** SO2914
Abergele *Clwyd* **70** SH9477
Abergorlech *Dyfed* **44** SN5833
Abergwesyn *Powys* **45** SN8552
Abergwili *Dyfed* **31** SN4320
Abergwydel *Powys* **57** SH7902
Abergwynfi *W Glam* **33** SS8995
Abergynolwyn *Gwynd* **57** SH6707
Aberhosan *Powys* **43** SN8197
Aberkenfig *M Glam* **33** SS8984
Aberlady *Loth* **118** NT4679
Aberlemno *Tays* **127** NO5255
Aberllefenni *Gwynd* **57** SH7609
Aberllynfi *Powys* **45** SO1737
Aberlour *Gramp* **141** NJ2642
Abermorddu *Clwyd* **71** SJ3056
Abermule *Powys* **58** SO1594
Abernant *Dyfed* **31** SN3423
Abernethy *Tays* **126** NO1916
Abernyte *Tays* **126** NO2531
Aberporth *Dyfed* **42** SN2651
Abersoch *Gwynd* **56** SH3128
Abersychan *Gwent* **34** SO2604
Aberthin *S Glam* **33** ST0075
Abertillery *Gwent* **33** SO2104
Abertridwr *M Glam* **33** ST1289
Abertridwr *Powys* **58** SJ0319
Abertysswg *M Glam* **33** SO1305
Aberuthven *Tays* **125** NN9815
Aberyscir *Powys* **45** SN9929
Aberystwyth *Dyfed* **43** SN5881
Abingdon *Oxon* **37** SU4997
Abinger *Surrey* **14** TQ1145
Abinger Hammer *Surrey* **14** TQ0947
Abington *Nhants* **50** SP7860
Abington *Strath* **108** NS9323
Abington Pigotts *Cambs* **39** TL3044
Ablington *Gloucs* **36** SP1007
Ablington *Wilts* **23** SU1645
Abney *Derbys* **74** SK1980
Above Church *Staffs* **73** SK0150
Aboyne *Gramp* **134** NO5298
Abram *Gt Man* **78** SD6001
Abriachan *Highld* **139** NH5535
Abridge *Essex* **27** TQ4696
Abson *Avon* **35** ST7074
Abthorpe *Nhants* **49** SP6446
Aby *Lincs* **77** TF4078
Acaster Malbis *N York* **83** SE5845
Acaster Selby *N York* **83** SE5741
Accott *Devon* **19** SS6432
Accrington *Lancs* **81** SD7628
Accurach *Strath* **123** NN1120
Acha *Strath* **120** NM1854
Achalader *Tays* **126** NO1245
Achaleven *Strath* **122** NM9233
Achanalt *Highld* **139** NH2561
Achanamara *Strath* **113** NR7887
Achandunie *Highld* **146** NH6472
Achanoish *Strath* **113** NR7877
Achany *Highld* **146** NC5602
Acharn *Tays* **124** NN7543
Achavanich *Highld* **151** ND1842
Achduart *Highld* **145** NC0403
Achentoul *Highld* **150** NC8733
Achfary *Highld* **148** NC2939
Achianich *Tays* **124** NN7242
Achiltibuie *Highld* **144** NC0208
Achina *Highld* **150** NC7060
Achintee *Highld* **138** NG9441
Achintoan *Strath* **105** NR7516
Achintraid *Highld* **138** NG8438
Achlain *Highld* **131** NH3712
Achlyness *Highld* **148** NC2452
Achmelvich *Highld* **148** NC0524
Achmore *Cent* **124** NN5832
Achmore *Highld* **138** NG8533
Achmore *W Isls* **154** NB3029
Achnacarnin *Highld* **148** NC0332
Achnacarry *Highld* **131** NN1787
Achnacloich *Highld* **129** NG5908
Achnacloich *Strath* **122** NM9534
Achnaconeran *Highld* **139** NH4118
Achnacroish *Strath* **122** NM8541
Achnadrish House *Strath* **121** NM4652
Achnafauld *Tays* **125** NN8736
Achnagarron *Highld* **146** NH6870
Achnaha *Highld* **128** NM4668
Achnahaird *Highld* **144** NC0110
Achnahanat *Highld* **146** NH5198
Achnairn *Highld* **146** NC5512
Achnalea *Highld* **130** NM8561
Achnaluachrach *Highld* **146** NC6709
Achnasheen *Highld* **138** NH1658
Achnashellach Station *Highld* **138** NH0047
Achnastank *Gramp* **141** NJ2733
Achosnich *Highld* **121** NM4467
Achranich *Highld* **122** NM7047
Achreamie *Highld* **150** ND0166
Achriabhach *Highld* **131** NN1468
Achriesgill *Highld* **148** NC2554
Achtoty *Highld* **149** NC6762
Achurch *Nhants* **51** TL0282
Achvaich *Highld* **146** NH7194
Ackenthwaite *Cumb* **87** SD5082
Ackergill *Highld* **151** ND3553
Acklam *Cleve* **97** NZ4817
Acklam *N York* **90** SE7861
Ackleton *Shrops* **60** SO7798
Acklington *Nthumb* **103** NU2302
Ackton *W York* **83** SE4121
Ackworth Moor Top *W York* **83** SE4316
Acle *Norfk* **67** TG4010
Acock's Green *W Mids* **61** SP1283
Acol *Kent* **29** TR3067
Acomb *N York* **83** SE5751
Acomb *Nthumb* **102** NY9366
Acombe *Somset* **9** ST1913
Aconbury *H & W* **46** SO5133
Acre *Lancs* **81** SD7924
Acrefair *Clwyd* **70** SJ2843
Acresford *Derbys* **61** SK2913
Acton *Ches* **71** SJ6352
Acton *Dorset* **11** SY9878
Acton *Gt Lon* **26** TQ2080
Acton *H & W* **47** SO8467
Acton *Shrops* **59** SO3185
Acton *Staffs* **72** SJ8241
Acton *Suffk* **54** TL8945
Acton Beauchamp *H & W* **47** SO6750
Acton Bridge *Ches* **71** SJ6075
Acton Burnell *Shrops* **59** SJ5302
Acton Green *H & W* **47** SO6950
Acton Park *Clwyd* **71** SJ3451
Acton Pigott *Shrops* **59** SJ5402
Acton Round *Shrops* **59** SO6395
Acton Scott *Shrops* **59** SO4589
Acton Trussell *Staffs* **72** SJ9317
Acton Turville *Avon* **35** ST8080
Adbaston *Staffs* **72** SJ7628
Adber *Dorset* **21** ST5920
Adbolton *Notts* **62** SK5938
Adderbury *Oxon* **49** SP4735
Adderley *Shrops* **72** SJ6640
Adderstone *Nthumb* **111** NU1330
Addiewell *Loth* **117** NS9962
Addingham *W York* **82** SE0749
Addington *Bucks* **49** SP7428
Addington *Gt Lon* **27** TQ3763
Addington *Kent* **28** TQ6559
Addiscombe *Gt Lon* **27** TQ3366
Addlestone *Surrey* **26** TQ0565
Addlestonemore *Surrey* **26** TQ0565
Addlethorpe *Lincs* **77** TF5469
Adeney *Shrops* **72** SJ7018
Adeyfield *Herts* **38** TL0708
Adfa *Powys* **58** SJ0601
Adforton *H & W* **46** SO4071
Adisham *Kent* **29** TR2253
Adlestrop *Gloucs* **48** SP2426
Adlingfleet *Humb* **84** SE8421
Adlington *Ches* **79** SJ9180
Adlington *Lancs* **81** SD6013
Admaston *Shrops* **59** SJ6313
Admaston *Staffs* **73** SK0423
Admington *Warwks* **48** SP2045
Adsborough *Somset* **20** ST2729
Adscombe *Somset* **20** ST1838
Adstock *Bucks* **49** SP7330
Adstone *Nhants* **49** SP5951
Adswood *Gt Man* **79** SJ8888
Adversane *W Susx* **14** TQ0723
Adwalton *W York* **82** SE2228
Adwell *Oxon* **37** SU6999
Adwick le Street *S York* **83** SE5308
Adwick upon Dearne *S York* **83** SE4601
AE Bridgend *D & G* **100** NY0186
Ae *D & G* **100** NX9889
Affeton Barton *Devon* **19** SS7513
Affetside *Gt Man* **81** SD7513
Affleck *Gramp* **142** NJ5540
Affleck *Gramp* **142** NJ5540
Affpuddle *Dorset* **11** SY8093
Affric Lodge *Highld* **138** NH1823
Afon-wen *Clwyd* **70** SJ1371
Afton *Devon* **7** SX8462
Afton *IOW* **12** SZ3486
Afton Bridgend *Strath* **107** NS6213
Agglethorpe *N York* **89** SE0886
Aigburth *Mersyd* **78** SJ3886
Aike *Humb* **84** TA0445
Aiketgate *Cumb* **94** NY4846
Aikhead *Cumb* **93** NY2349
Aikton *Cumb* **93** NY2753
Ailby *Lincs* **77** TF4476
Ailey *H & W* **46** SO3348
Ailsworth *Cambs* **64** TL1198
Ainderby *N York* **89** SE3480
Ainderby Quernhow *N York* **89** SE3480
Ainderby Steeple *N York* **89** SE3392
Aingers Green *Essex* **41** TM1120
Ainsdale *Mersyd* **80** SD3112
Ainsdale-on-Sea *Mersyd* **80** SD3012
Ainstable *Cumb* **94** NY5246
Ainsworth *Gt Man* **79** SD7610
Ainthorpe *N York* **90** NZ7007
Aintree *Mersyd* **78** SJ3898
Aird *D & G* **98** NX0960
Aird *W Isls* **154** NB5635
Aird *Strath* **113** NM7600
Aird of Kinloch *Strath* **121** NM5228
Aird of Sleat *Highld* **129** NG5900
Airdeny *Strath* **122** NM9929
Airdrie *Strath* **116** NS7665
Airdriehill *Strath* **116** NS7867
Airds Bay *Strath* **122** NM9932
Airds of Kells *D & G* **99** NX6770
Airieland *D & G* **99** NX7556
Airmyn *Humb* **84** SE7224
Airntully *Tays* **125** NO0935
Airor *Highld* **129** NG7205
Airth *Cent* **116** NS8987
Airton *N York* **88** SD9059
Aisby *Lincs* **76** SK8792
Aisby *Lincs* **64** TF0138
Aisgill *Cumb* **88** SD7797
Aish *Devon* **7** SX6960
Aish *Devon* **7** SX8458
Aiskew *N York* **89** SE2788
Aislaby *Cleve* **89** NZ4012
Aislaby *N York* **90** NZ8508
Aislaby *N York* **90** SE7785
Aisthorpe *Lincs* **76** SK9480
Aisthorpe *Lincs* **76** SK9480
Aith *Shet* **155** HU3455
Akeld *Nthumb* **111** NT9529
Akeley *Bucks* **49** SP7037
Akenham *Suffk* **54** TM1449
Albaston *Devon* **6** SX4270
Alberbury *Shrops* **59** SJ3614
Albert Street *Clwyd* **70** SJ2660
Albourne *W Susx* **15** TQ2616
Albourne Green *W Susx* **15** TQ2616
Albrighton *Shrops* **59** SJ4918
Albrighton *Shrops* **60** SJ8104
Alburgh *Norfk* **55** TM2687
Albury *Herts* **39** TL4324
Albury *Oxon* **37** SP6505
Albury *Surrey* **14** TQ0547
Albury End *Herts* **39** TL4223
Albury Heath *Surrey* **14** TQ0646
Alby Hill *Norfk* **67** TG1934
Alcaig *Highld* **139** NH5657
Alcaston *Shrops* **59** SO4687
Alcester *Warwks* **48** SP0857
Alcester Lane End *W Mids* **61** SP0780
Alciston *E Susx* **16** TQ5005
Alcombe *Wilts* **35** ST8069
Alconbury *Cambs* **52** TL1876
Alconbury Weston *Cambs* **52** TL1777
Aldborough *N York* **89** SE4066
Aldborough *Norfk* **66** TG1834
Aldbourne *Wilts* **36** SU2675
Aldbrough *Humb* **85** TA2438
Aldbury *Herts* **38** SP9612
Aldcliffe *Cumb* **87** SD4660
Aldclune *Tays* **132** NN8964
Aldeburgh *Suffk* **55** TM4656
Aldeby *Norfk* **67** TM4593
Aldenham *Herts* **26** TQ1498
Alder Moor *Staffs* **73** SK2227
Alderbury *Wilts* **23** SU1827
Aldercar *Derbys* **62** SK4447
Alderford *Norfk* **66** TG1218
Alderholt *Dorset* **12** SU1212
Alderley *Gloucs* **35** ST7690
Alderley Edge *Ches* **79** SJ8478
Aldermans Green *W Mids* **61** SP3583
Aldermaston *Berks* **24** SU5965
Alderminster *Warwks* **48** SP2248
Aldershot *Hants* **25** SU8650
Alderton *Gloucs* **47** SP0033
Alderton *Nhants* **49** SP7346
Alderton *Shrops* **59** SJ4924
Alderton *Suffk* **55** TM3441
Alderton *Wilts* **35** ST8482
Alderwasley *Derbys* **74** SK3153
Aldfield *N York* **89** SE2669
Aldford *Ches* **71** SJ4159
Aldgate *Leics* **63** SK9804
Aldham *Essex* **40** TL9126
Aldham *Suffk* **54** TM0545
Aldingbourne *W Susx* **14** SU9205
Aldingham *Cumb* **86** SD2870
Aldington *H & W* **48** SP0644
Aldington *Kent* **29** TR0736
Aldington Corner *Kent* **28** TR0536
Aldivalloch *Gramp* **141** NJ3536
Aldochlay *Strath* **115** NS3591
Aldon *Shrops* **46** SO4379
Aldoth *Cumb* **92** NY1448
Aldreth *Cambs* **53** TL4473
Aldridge *W Mids* **61** SK0500
Aldringham *Suffk* **55** TM4461
Aldro *N York* **90** SE8162
Aldsworth *Gloucs* **36** SP1510
Aldsworth *W Susx* **14** SU7608
Aldunie *Gramp* **141** NJ3626
Aldwark *Derbys* **74** SK2257
Aldwark *N York* **89** SE4663
Aldwick *W Susx* **14** SZ9199
Aldwincle *Nhants* **51** TL0081
Aldworth *Berks* **37** SU5579
Alexandria *Strath* **115** NS3980
Aley *Somset* **20** ST1837
Alfardisworthy *Devon* **18** SS2911
Alfington *Devon* **9** SY1197
Alfold *Surrey* **14** TQ0334
Alfold Bars *W Susx* **14** TQ0333
Alford *Gramp* **142** NJ5715
Alford *Lincs* **77** TF4575
Alford *Somset* **21** ST6032
Alford Crossways *Surrey* **14** TQ0435
Alfreton *Derbys* **74** SK4155
Alfrick *H & W* **47** SO7453
Alfrick Pound *H & W* **47** SO7352
Alfriston *E Susx* **16** TQ5103
Algarkirk *Lincs* **64** TF2935
Alhampton *Somset* **21** ST6234
Alkborough *Humb* **84** SE8821
Alkerton *Gloucs* **35** SO7705
Alkerton *Oxon* **48** SP3743
Alkham *Kent* **29** TR2542
Alkington *Shrops* **71** SJ5339
Alkmonton *Derbys* **73** SK1838
All Cannings *Wilts* **36** SU0771
All Saints South Elmham *Suffk* **55** TM3482
All Stretton *Shrops* **59** SO4695
Alladale Lodge *Highld* **146** NH4489
Allaleigh *Devon* **7** SX8053
Allanaquoich *Gramp* **133** NO1291
Allanbank *Strath* **116** NS8458
Allanton *Border* **119** NT8654
Allanton *Strath* **116** NS7454
Allanton *Strath* **116** NS8457
Allardice *Gramp* **135** NO8173
Allardice *Gramp* **135** NO8173
Allaston *Gloucs* **35** SO6304
Allbrook *Hants* **13** SU4521
Allen's Green *Herts* **39** TL4516
Allendale Town *Nthumb* **95** NY8455
Allenheads *Nthumb* **95** NY8645
Allensford *Dur* **95** NZ0749
Allensmore *H & W* **46** SO4635
Allenton *Derbys* **62** SK3732
Aller *Devon* **19** SS7625
Aller *Somset* **21** ST4029
Allerby *Cumb* **92** NY0839
Allercombe *Devon* **9** SY0494
Allerford *Somset* **20** SS9047
Allerston *N York* **90** SE8782
Allerthorpe *Humb* **84** SE7847
Allerton *Mersyd* **78** SJ3987
Allerton *W York* **82** SE1234
Allerton Bywater *W York* **83** SE4127
Allerton Mauleverer *N York* **89** SE4158
Allesley *W Mids* **61** SP2980
Allestree *Derbys* **62** SK3439
Allet Common *Cnwll* **3** SW7948
Allexton *Leics* **51** SK8100
Allgreave *Ches* **72** SJ9767
Allhallows *Kent* **28** TQ8377
Allhallows-on-Sea *Kent* **40** TQ8478
Alligin Shuas *Highld* **137** NG8358
Allimore Green *Staffs* **72** SJ8519
Allington *Dorset* **10** SY4693
Allington *Kent* **28** TQ7557
Allington *Lincs* **63** SK8540
Allington *Wilts* **35** ST8975
Allington *Wilts* **23** SU0663
Allington *Wilts* **23** SU2039
Allithwaite *Cumb* **87** SD3876
Allen End *Warwks* **61** SP1696
Alloa *Cent* **116** NS8893
Allonby *Cumb* **92** NY0843
Alloway *Strath* **106** NS3318
Allowenshay *Somset* **10** ST3913
Allscott *Shrops* **60** SO7396
Allscott *Shrops* **59** SJ6113
Allt Na h'Airbhe (Inn *Highld* **145** NH1193
Alltami *Clwyd* **70** SJ2665
Alltchaorunn *Highld* **123** NN1951
Alltmawr *Powys* **45** SO0746
Alltwalis *Dyfed* **31** SN4431
Alltwen *W Glam* **32** SN7303
Alltyblaca *Dyfed* **44** SN5245
Allweston *Dorset* **11** ST6614
Allwood Green *Suffk* **54** TM0472
Almeley *H & W* **46** SO3351
Almeley Wooton *H & W* **46** SO3352
Almer *Dorset* **11** SY9098
Almholme *S York* **83** SE5808
Almington *Staffs* **72** SJ7034
Alminstone Cross *Devon* **18** SS3420
Almodington *W Susx* **14** SZ8297
Almondbank *Tays* **125** NO0625
Almondbury *W York* **82** SE1615
Almondsbury *Avon* **34** ST6083
Alne *N York* **90** SE4965
Alnesbourn Priory *Suffk* **55** TM1940
Alness *Highld* **146** NH6599
Alnham *Nthumb* **111** NT9810
Alnmouth *Nthumb* **111** NU2410
Alnwick *Nthumb* **111** NU1813
Alperton *Gt Lon* **26** TQ1884
Alphamstone *Essex* **54** TL8835
Alpheton *Suffk* **54** TL8850
Alphington *Devon* **9** SX9090
Alpington *Norfk* **67** TG2901
Alport *Derbys* **74** SK2264
Alpraham *Ches* **71** SJ5859
Alresford *Essex* **41** TM0721
Alrewas *Staffs* **73** SK1715
Alsager *Ches* **72** SJ7955
Alsagers Bank *Staffs* **72** SJ8048
Alshot *Somset* **20** ST1936
Alsop en le Dale *Derbys* **73** SK1655
Alston *Devon* **10** ST3002
Alston Sutton *Somset* **21** ST4151
Alstone *Gloucs* **47** SO9832
Alstone *Somset* **21** ST3147
Alstone Green *Staffs* **72** SJ8618
Alstonefield *Staffs* **73** SK1355
Alswear *Devon* **19** SS7222
Alt *Gt Man* **79** SD9403
Altandhu *Highld* **144** NB9812
Altarnun *Cnwll* **5** SX2281
Altass *Highld* **146** NC5000
Altcreich *Strath* **122** NM6939
Altgaltraig *Strath* **114** NS0473
Altham *Lancs* **81** SD7733
Althorne *Essex* **40** TQ9199
Althorpe *Humb* **84** SE8309
Altnabreac Station *Highld* **150** ND0045
Altnacealgach Hotel *Highld* **145** NC2810
Altnacraig *Strath* **122** NM8429
Altnaharra *Highld* **149** NC5635
Altofts *W York* **83** SE3723
Alton *Derbys* **74** SK3664
Alton *Hants* **24** SU7139
Alton *Staffs* **73** SK0742
Alton *Wilts* **23** SU1546
Alton Barnes *Wilts* **23** SU1062
Alton Pancras *Dorset* **11** ST6902
Alton Priors *Wilts* **23** SU1062
Altrincham *Gt Man* **79** SJ7687
Alva *Cent* **116** NS8897
Alvanley *Ches* **71** SJ4974
Alvaston *Derbys* **62** SK3833
Alvechurch *H & W* **61** SP0372
Alvecote *Warwks* **61** SK2404
Alvediston *Wilts* **22** ST9723
Alveley *Shrops* **60** SO7684
Alverdiscott *Devon* **19** SS5225
Alverstoke *Hants* **13** SZ6098
Alverstone *IOW* **13** SZ5785
Alverthorpe *W York* **82** SE3121
Alverton *Notts* **63** SK7942
Alves *Gramp* **141** NJ1362
Alvescot *Oxon* **36** SP2704
Alveston *Avon* **35** ST6388
Alveston *Warwks* **48** SP2256
Alvie *Highld* **132** NH8609
Alvingham *Lincs* **77** TF3691
Alvington *Gloucs* **34** SO6000
Alwalton *Cambs* **64** TL1396
Alwinton *Nthumb* **110** NT9106
Alwoodley *W York* **82** SE2840
Alwoodley Gates *W York* **82** SE3140
Alyth *Tays* **126** NO2448
Amber Hill *Lincs* **76** TF2346
Amber Row *Derbys* **74** SK3856

211

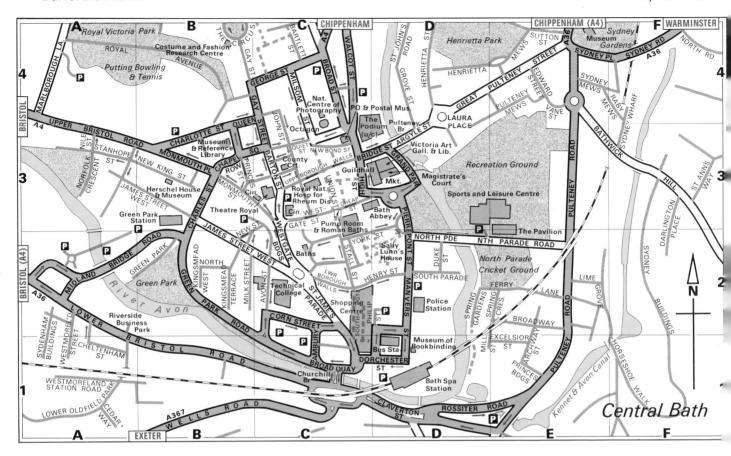

Central Bath

Baythorpe End
Birchgrove

Baythorne End Essex 53 TL7242
Bayton H & W 60 SO6973
Bayton Common H & W 60 SO7172
Bayworth Oxon 37 SP4901
Beach Avon 35 ST7070
Beachampton Bucks 49 SP7736
Beachamwell Norfk 65 TF7505
Beachborough Kent 29 TR1638
Beachley Gloucs 34 ST5491
Beacon Devon 9 ST1705
Beacon End Essex 40 TL9524
Beacon Hill E Susx 16 TQ5030
Beacon Hill Kent 17 TQ8232
Beacon Hill Notts 75 SK8153
Beacon Hill Surrey 14 SU8736
Beacon's Bottom Bucks 37 SU7895
Beaconsfield Bucks 26 SU9490
Beacontree Gt Lon 27 TQ4786
Beadlam N York 90 SE6584
Beadlow Beds 38 TL1038
Beadnell Nthumb 111 NU2229
Beaford Devon 19 SS5515
Beal N York 83 SE5325
Beal Nthumb 111 NU0642
Bealbury M Glam 5 SX3766
Bealsmill Cnwll 5 SX3677
Beam Hill Staffs 73 SK2326
Beamhurst Staffs 73 SK0536
Beaminster Dorset 10 ST4801
Beamish Dur 96 NZ2253
Beamsley N York 82 SE0752
Bean Kent 27 TQ5872
Beanacre Wilts 22 ST9066
Beanley Nthumb 111 NU0818
Beara Charter Barton Devon 19 SS5238
Beardon Devon 5 SX5184
Beardwood Lancs 81 SD6629
Beare Devon 9 SS9800
Beare Green Surrey 15 TQ1742
Bearley Warwks 48 SP1860
Bearley Cross Warwks 48 SP1761
Bearpark Dur 96 NZ2343
Bearsbridge Nthumb 94 NY7857
Bearsden Strath 115 NS5372
Bearstead Kent 28 TQ8055
Bearstone Shrops 72 SJ7239
Bearwood W Mids 60 SP0286
Beatley Heath Herts 27 TQ2599
Beattock D & G 108 NT0702
Beauchamp Roding Essex 40 TL5809
Beauchief S York 74 SK3381
Beaudesert Warwks 48 SP1565
Beaufort Gwent 33 SO1611
Beaulieu Hants 12 SU3802
Beauly Highld 139 NH5246
Beaumaris Gwynd 69 SH6076
Beaumont Cumb 93 NY3459
Beaumont Essex 41 TM1625
Beaumont Jersey 152 JS0000
Beaumont Hill Dur 96 NZ2918
Beausale Warwks 61 SP2470
Beauworth Hants 25 SU7960
Beauworth Hants 13 SU5726
Beaver Kent 28 TR0040
Beaver Green Kent 28 TR0041
Beaworthy Devon 18 SX4699
Beazley End Essex 40 TL7429
Bebington Mersyd 78 SJ3383
Bebside Nthumb 103 NZ2781
Beccles Suffk 55 TM4290
Becconsall Lancs 80 SD4523
Beck Foot Cumb 87 SD6196
Beck Hole N York 90 NZ8102
Beck Row Suffk 53 TL6977
Beck Side Cumb 86 SD2382
Beckbury Shrops 60 SJ7601
Beckenham Gt Lon 27 TQ3769
Beckering Lincs 76 TF1180
Beckermet Cumb 86 NY0206
Beckett End Norfk 65 TL7798
Beckfoot Cumb 86 SD1989
Beckfoot Cumb 92 NY0949
Beckfoot Cumb 86 NY1600
Beckford H & W 47 SO9735
Beckhampton Wilts 23 SU0868
Beckingham Lincs 76 SK8753
Beckingham Notts 75 SK7889
Beckington Somset 22 ST7951
Beckjay Shrops 46 SO3977
Beckley E Susx 17 TQ8523
Beckley Hants 12 SZ2297
Beckley Oxon 37 SP5611
Becks W York 82 SE0345
Beckside Cumb 87 SD6187
Beckton Gt Lon 27 TQ4381
Beckwithshaw N York 82 SE2653
Becquet Vincent Jersey 152 JS0000
Bedale N York 89 SE2687
Bedburn Dur 95 NZ0931
Bedchester Dorset 11 ST8517
Beddau M Glam 33 ST0585
Beddgelert Gwynd 69 SH5848
Beddingham E Susx 16 TQ4407
Beddington Gt Lon 27 TQ3065
Beddington Corner Gt Lon 27 TQ2866
Bedfield Suffk 55 TM2266
Bedfield Little Green Suffk 55 TM2365
Bedford Beds 38 TL0449
Bedgebury Cross Kent 17 TQ7134
Bedham W Susx 14 TQ0122
Bedhampton Hants 13 SU6906
Bedingfield Suffk 54 TM1768
Bedingfield Green Suffk 54 TM1866
Bedingfield Street Suffk 54 TM1767
Bedlam N York 89 SE2661
Bedlam Lane Kent 28 TQ8845
Bedlington T & W 103 NZ2581
Bedlinog M Glam 33 SO0901
Bedminster Avon 34 ST5771
Bedminster Down Avon 34 ST5770
Bedmond Herts 38 TL0903
Bednall Staffs 72 SJ9517
Bedrule Border 110 NT6017
Bedstone Shrops 46 SO3776
Bedwas M Glam 33 ST1789
Bedwellty Gwent 33 SO1600
Bedworth Warwks 61 SP3687
Bedworth Woodlands Warwks 61 SP3487
Beeby Leics 63 SK6608
Beech Hants 24 SU6938
Beech Staffs 72 SJ8538
Beech Hill Berks 24 SU6964
Beechingstoke Wilts 23 SU0859
Beedon Berks 37 SU4877
Beedon Hill Berks 37 SU4877
Beeford Humb 85 TA1253
Beeley Derbys 74 SK2667
Beelsby Humb 85 TA2001
Beenham Berks 24 SU5868
Beer Devon 9 SY2289
Beer Somset 21 ST4031
Beer Hackett Dorset 10 ST5911
Beercrocombe Somset 21 ST3220
Beesands Devon 7 SX8140
Beesby Lincs 77 TF4680
Beeson Devon 7 SX8140
Beeston Beds 52 TL1648
Beeston Ches 71 SJ5458
Beeston Norfk 66 TF9015
Beeston Notts 62 SK5336
Beeston W York 82 SE2930
Beeston Regis Norfk 66 TG1742
Beeswing D & G 100 NX8969
Beetham Cumb 87 SD4979
Beetham Somset 10 ST2712
Beetley Norfk 66 TF9718
Began S Glam 34 ST2283
Begbroke Oxon 37 SP4613
Begdale Cambs 65 TF4506
Begelly Dyfed 31 SN1107
Beggar's Bush Powys 46 SO2664
Beggarinton Hill W York 82 SE2824
Beguildy Powys 45 SO1979
Beighton Norfk 67 TG3808
Beighton S York 75 SK4483
Beighton Hill Derbys 73 SK2951
Bein Inn Tays 126 NO1613
Beith Strath 115 NS3553
Bekesbourne Kent 29 TR1955
Bekesbourne Hill Kent 29 TR1856
Belaugh Norfk 67 TG2818
Belbroughton H & W 60 SO9277
Belchalwell Dorset 11 ST7909
Belchalwell Street Dorset 11 ST7908
Belchamp Otten Essex 54 TL8041
Belchamp St. Paul Essex 53 TL7942
Belchamp Walter Essex 54 TL8240
Belchford Lincs 77 TF2975
Belford Nthumb 111 NU1034
Belgrave Leics 62 SK5906
Belhelvie Gramp 143 NJ9417
Belhinnie Gramp 142 NJ4627
Bell Bar Herts 39 TL2505
Bell Busk N York 81 SD9056
Bell End H & W 60 SO9477
Bell Heath H & W 60 SO9577
Bell Hill Hants 13 SU7424
Bell o' th'Hill Ches 71 SJ5245
Bellabeg Gramp 134 NJ3513
Belladrum Highld 139 NH5142
Bellanoch Strath 113 NR7992
Bellasize Humb 84 SE8227
Bellaty Tays 133 NO2359
Belle Vue Cumb 93 NY3756
Belle Vue Cumb 92 NY1232
Belle Vue W York 83 SE3419
Belleau Lincs 77 TF4078
Bellerby N York 89 SE1192
Bellever Devon 8 SX6577
Bellfield Strath 108 NS8234
Bellfield Strath 108 NS9620
Bellimoor H & W 46 SO3840
Bellingdon Bucks 38 SP9405
Bellingham Nthumb 102 NY8383
Belloch Strath 104 NR3738
Bellochantuy Strath 104 NR6632
Bellows Cross Dorset 12 SU0613
Bells Cross Suffk 54 TM1552
Bells Yew Green E Susx 16 TQ6035
Bellshill Nthumb 111 NU1230
Bellside Strath 116 NS8058
Bellsmyre Strath 115 NS4076
Bellsquarry Loth 117 NT0465
Belluton Avon 21 ST6164
Belmaduthy Highld 140 NH6456
Belmesthorpe Leics 64 TF0410
Belmont Gt Lon 27 TQ2562
Belmont Lancs 81 SD6715
Belmont Shet 155 HP5600
Belmont Strath 106 NS3520
Belnacraig Gramp 141 NJ3716
Belowda Cnwll 4 SW9661
Belper Derbys 62 SK3447
Belper Lane End Derbys 74 SK3349
Belph Notts 90 SE5475
Belsay Nthumb 103 NZ0978
Belsay Castle Nthumb 103 NZ0878
Belses Border 110 NT5725
Belsford Devon 7 SX7659
Belsize Herts 26 TL0301
Belstead Suffk 54 TM1241
Belstone Devon 8 SX6193
Belstone Corner Devon 8 SX6298
Belthorn Lancs 81 SD7124
Beltinge Kent 29 TR1967
Beltingham Nthumb 102 NY7863
Beltoft Humb 84 SE8006
Belton Humb 84 SE7806
Belton Leics 62 SK4420
Belton Leics 63 SK8101
Belton Lincs 63 SK9339
Belton Norfk 67 TG4802
Beltring Kent 28 TQ6747
Belvedere Gt Lon 27 TQ4978
Belvoir Leics 63 SK8133
Bembridge IOW 13 SZ6488
Bemersley Green Staffs 72 SJ8854
Bemersyde Border 110 NT5933
Bemerton Wilts 23 SU1230
Bempton Humb 91 TA1972
Ben Rhydding W York 82 SE1448
Benacre Suffk 55 TM5184
Benbuie D & G 107 NX7196
Benderloch Strath 122 NM9038
Benenden Kent 17 TQ8033
Benfield D & G 99 NX3764
Benfieldside Dur 95 NZ0952
Bengall D & G 100 NY1178
Bengates Norfk 67 TG3027
Bengeworth H & W 48 SP0443
Benhall Green Suffk 55 TM3961
Benhall Street Suffk 55 TM3561
Benholm Gramp 135 NO8069
Beningborough N York 90 SE5257
Benington Herts 39 TL2923
Benington Lincs 77 TF3946
Benllech Gwynd 68 SH5182
Benmore Cent 124 NN4125
Benmore Strath 114 NS1385
Bennacott Cnwll 5 SX2992
Bennan Strath 105 NR9921
Bennet Head Cumb 93 NY4423
Bennetland Humb 84 SE8228
Bennett End Bucks 37 SU7897
Bennington Sea End Lincs 65 TF4145
Benniworth Lincs 76 TF2081
Benny Cnwll 4 SX1192
Benover Kent 28 TQ7048
Benson Oxon 37 SU6291
Bentfield Green Essex 39 TL5025
Benthall Shrops 60 SJ6602
Bentham Gloucs 35 SO9116
Benthoul Gramp 135 NJ8003
Bentlawn Shrops 59 SJ3301
Bentley Hants 25 SU7844
Bentley Humb 84 TA0135
Bentley S York 83 SE5605
Bentley Suffk 54 TM1238
Bentley Warwks 61 SP2895
Bentley Heath W Mids 61 SP1676
Bentley Rise S York 83 SE5605
Benton Devon 19 SS6536
Benton Polliwilline Strath 105 NR7310
Bentpath D & G 101 NY3190
Bentwichen Devon 19 SS7334
Bentworth Hants 24 SU6640
Benvie Tays 126 NO3231
Benville Dorset 10 ST5403
Benwick Cambs 52 TL3490
Beoch D & G 98 NX0865
Beoley H & W 48 SP0669
Beoraidbeg Highld 129 NM6793
Bepton W Susx 14 SU8518
Berden Essex 39 TL4629
Bere Alston Devon 6 SX4466
Bere Ferrers Devon 6 SX4563
Bere Regis Dorset 11 SY8494
Berea Dyfed 30 SM7930
Berepper Cnwll 2 SW6522
Bergh Apton Norfk 67 TG3000
Berhill Somset 21 ST4435
Berinsfield Oxon 37 SU5696
Berkeley Gloucs 35 ST6899
Berkeley Heath Gloucs 35 ST6999
Berkeley Road Gloucs 35 ST7299
Berkhamsted Herts 38 SP9907
Berkley Somset 22 ST8049
Berkswell W Mids 61 SP2479
Bermondsey Gt Lon 27 TQ3479
Bernera Highld 129 NG8021
Bernice Strath 114 NS1391
Bernisdale Highld 136 NG4050
Berrick Prior Oxon 37 SU6294
Berrick Salome Oxon 37 SU6293
Berriedale Highld 147 ND1222
Berrier Cumb 93 NY3929
Berrier Cumb 93 NY3929
Berriew Powys 58 SJ1801
Berrington H & W 46 SO5767
Berrington Nthumb 111 NU0043
Berrington Shrops 59 SJ5207
Berrington Green H & W 46 SO5866
Berrow Somset 20 ST2952
Berry Brow W York 82 SE1514
Berry Cross Devon 18 SS4714
Berry Down Cross Devon 19 SS5743
Berry Head Devon 7 SX9456
Berry Hill Dyfed 30 SN0640
Berry Hill Gloucs 34 SO5712
Berry Pomeroy Devon 7 SX8261
Berry's Green Gt Lon 27 TQ4358
Berryhillock Gramp 142 NJ5054
Berryhillock Gramp 142 NJ5060
Berryhillock Gramp 142 NJ5054
Berrynarbor Devon 19 SS5546
Bersham Clwyd 71 SJ3048
Berthengam Temp 70 SJ1179
Berwick E Susx 16 TQ5105
Berwick Bassett Wilts 36 SU0973
Berwick Hill Nthumb 103 NZ1775
Berwick St. James Wilts 23 SU0739
Berwick St. John Wilts 22 ST9421
Berwick St. Leonard Wilts 22 ST9233
Berwick-upon-Tweed Nthumb 119 NT9953
Bescaby Leics 63 SK8126
Bescar Cumb 80 SD3913
Besford H & W 47 SO9145
Besford Shrops 59 SJ5525
Besom Hill Gt Man 79 SD9508
Bessacarr S York 83 SE6101
Bessels Leigh Oxon 37 SP4501
Besses O' Th' Barn Gt Man 79 SD8005
Bessingby Humb 91 TA1565
Bessingham Norfk 66 TG1636
Bestbeech Hill E Susx 16 TQ6131
Besthorpe Norfk 66 TM0595
Besthorpe Notts 75 SK8264
Beswick Humb 84 TA0148
Betchcott Shrops 59 SO4399
Betchworth Surrey 26 TQ2150
Bethania Dyfed 43 SN5763
Bethania Gwynd 57 SH7044
Bethel Gwynd 70 SH9839
Bethel Gwynd 68 SH3970
Bethel Gwynd 68 SH5265
Bethel Powys 58 SJ1021
Bethersden Kent 28 TQ9240
Bethesda Dyfed 31 SN0918
Bethesda Gwynd 69 SH6266
Bethlehem Dyfed 44 SN6825
Bethnal Green Gt Lon 27 TQ3482
Betley Staffs 72 SJ7548
Betsham Kent 27 TQ6071
Betteshanger Kent 29 TR3152
Bettiscombe Dorset 10 SY3999
Bettiscombe Dorset 10 SY3999
Bettisfield Clwyd 59 SJ4635
Betton Shrops 72 SJ6937
Betton Strange Shrops 59 SJ5109
Bettws Gwent 34 ST2990
Bettws Bledrws Dyfed 44 SN5952
Bettws Cedewain Powys 58 SO1296
Bettws Evan Dyfed 42 SN3047
Bettws Gwerfil Goch Clwyd 70 SJ0346
Bettws Malpas Somset 34 ST3090
Bettws-Newydd Gwent 34 SO3606
Bettyhill Highld 150 NC7061
Betws Dyfed 32 SN6311
Betws M Glam 33 SS9086
Betws Garmon Gwynd 69 SH5357
Betws-y-coed Gwynd 69 SH7956
Betws-yn-Rhos Clwyd 69 SH9073
Beulah Dyfed 42 SN2846
Beulah Powys 45 SN9251
Bevendean E Susx 15 TQ3406
Bevercotes Notts 75 SK6972
Beverley Humb 84 TA0339
Beverston Gloucs 35 ST8693
Bevington Gloucs 35 ST6596
Bewaldeth Cumb 93 NY2034
Bewcastle Cumb 101 NY5674
Bewdley H & W 60 SO7875
Bewerley N York 89 SE1564
Bewholme Humb 85 TA1649
Bewlbridge Kent 16 TQ6834
Bewlie Border 109 NT5626
Bexhill E Susx 17 TQ7407
Bexley Gt Lon 27 TQ4973
Bexley Heath Gt Lon 27 TQ4875
Bexleyhill W Susx 14 SU9125
Bexwell Norfk 65 TF6303
Beyton Suffk 54 TL9363
Beyton Green Suffk 54 TL9363
Bibstone Avon 35 ST6991
Bibury Gloucs 36 SP1106
Bicester Oxon 37 SP5822
Bickenhill W Mids 61 SP1882
Bicker Lincs 64 TF2237
Bicker Bar Lincs 64 TF2438
Bicker Gauntlet Lincs 64 TF2139
Bickershaw Gt Man 79 SD6201
Bickerstaffe Lancs 78 SD4404
Bickerton Ches 71 SJ5052
Bickerton Devon 7 SX8139
Bickerton N York 83 SE4450
Bickerton Nthumb 103 NT9900
Bickford Staffs 60 SJ8814
Bickington Devon 19 SS5332
Bickington Devon 7 SX7972
Bickleigh Devon 9 SS9407
Bickleigh Devon 6 SX5262
Bickleton Devon 19 SS5031
Bickley Ches 71 SJ5448
Bickley Gt Lon 27 TQ4268
Bickley N York 91 SE9191
Bickley Moss Ches 71 SJ5449
Bicknacre Essex 40 TL7802
Bicknoller Somset 20 ST1039
Bicknor Kent 28 TQ8658
Bickton H & W 47 SO6371
Bickton Hants 12 SU1412
Bicton H & W 46 SO4764
Bicton Shrops 59 SJ4415
Bicton Shrops 59 SO2983
Bidborough Kent 16 TQ5643
Bidden Hants 24 SU7049
Biddenden Kent 28 TQ8538
Biddenden Green Kent 28 TQ8842
Biddenham Beds 38 TL0250
Biddestone Wilts 35 ST8673
Biddisham Somset 21 ST3853
Biddlesden Bucks 49 SP6340
Biddlestone Nthumb 111 NT9508
Biddulph Staffs 72 SJ8857
Biddulph Moor Staffs 72 SJ9058
Bideford Devon 18 SS4426
Bidford-on-Avon Warwks 48 SP1052
Bidston Mersyd 78 SJ2890
Bielby Humb 84 SE7843
Bieldside Gramp 135 NJ8702
Bierley IOW 13 SZ5178
Bierton Bucks 38 SP8315
Big Balcraig D & G 99 NX3843
Big Corlae D & G 107 NX6697
Big Sand Highld 144 NG7579
Bigbury Devon 7 SX6646
Bigbury-on-Sea Devon 7 SX6544
Bigby Lincs 84 TA0507
Biggar Cumb 86 SD1966
Biggar Strath 108 NT0437
Biggin Derbys 74 SK1559
Biggin Derbys 73 SK2549
Biggin N York 83 SE5434
Biggin Hill Gt Lon 27 TQ4159
Biggleswade Beds 39 TL1944
Bigholms D & G 101 NY3181
Bighouse Highld 150 NC8964
Bighton Hants 24 SU6134
Biglands Cumb 93 NY2553
Bignor W Susx 14 SU9814
Bigrigg Cumb 92 NY0013
Bilborough Notts 62 SK5241
Bilbrook Somset 20 ST0341
Bilbrook Staffs 60 SJ8703
Bilbrough N York 83 SE5246
Bilbster Highld 151 ND2853
Bildershaw Dur 96 NZ2024
Bildeston Suffk 54 TL9949
Bildeston Suffk 54 TL9949
Bill Street Kent 28 TQ7370
Billacott Cnwll 5 SX2691
Billericay Essex 40 TQ6794
Billesdon Leics 63 SK7202
Billesley Warwks 48 SP1456
Billingborough Lincs 64 TF1134
Billinge Mersyd 78 SD5200
Billingford Norfk 66 TG0120
Billingford Norfk 54 TM1678
Billingham Cleve 97 NZ4624
Billinghay Lincs 76 TF1554
Billingley S York 83 SE4304
Billingshurst W Susx 14 TQ0825
Billingsley Shrops 60 SO7085
Billington Beds 38 SP9422
Billington Lancs 81 SD7235
Billington Staffs 72 SJ8820
Billockby Norfk 67 TG4313
Billy Row Dur 96 NZ1637
Bilsborrow Lancs 80 SD5139
Bilsby Lincs 77 TF4776
Bilsham W Susx 14 SU9702
Bilsington Kent 17 TR0434
Bilsthorpe Notts 75 SK6460
Bilsthorpe Manor Notts 75 SK6560
Bilston Loth 117 NT2664
Bilston W Mids 60 SO9596
Bilstone Leics 62 SK3605
Bilting Kent 28 TR0549
Bilton Humb 85 TA1532
Bilton N York 83 SE4749
Bilton N York 83 SE4749
Bilton Nthumb 111 NU2211
Bilton Warwks 50 SP4873
Bilton Banks Nthumb 111 NU2010
Binbrook Lincs 76 TF2093
Binchester Blocks Dur 96 NZ2231
Bincombe Dorset 11 SY6884
Bindal Highld 147 NH9284
Binegar Somset 21 ST6149
Bines Green W Susx 15 TQ1817
Binfield Berks 25 SU8471
Binfield Heath Oxon 37 SU7477
Bingfield Nthumb 102 NY9772
Bingham Notts 63 SK7039
Bingham's Melcombe Dorset 11 ST7701
Bingley W York 82 SE1039
Bings Shrops 59 SJ5318
Binham Norfk 66 TF9839
Binley Hants 24 SU4153
Binley W Mids 61 SP3778
Binnegar Dorset 11 SY8887
Binniehill Cent 116 NS8572
Binns Farm Gramp 141 NJ3164
Binscombe Surrey 25 SU9746
Binsey Oxon 37 SP4907
Binstead Hants 25 SU7741
Binstead IOW 13 SZ5792
Binsted W Susx 14 SU9806
Binton Warwks 48 SP1454
Bintree Norfk 66 TG0123
Binweston Shrops 59 SJ3004
Birch Essex 40 TL9420
Birch Gt Man 79 SD8507
Birch Close Dorset 11 ST8803
Birch Cross Staffs 73 SK1230
Birch Green Essex 40 TL9418
Birch Green Herts 39 TL2911
Birch Heath Ches 71 SJ5461
Birch Hill Ches 71 SJ5273
Birch Vale Derbys 74 SK0286
Bircham Newton Norfk 65 TF7734
Bircham Tofts Norfk 65 TF7732
Birchanger Essex 39 TL5122
Birchencliffe W York 82 SE1218
Bircher H & W 46 SO4765
Bircher H & W 46 SO4765
Birchfield W Mids 61 SP0690
Birchgrove E Susx 15 TQ4029
Birchgrove S Glam 33 ST1679
Birchgrove W Glam 32 SS7098

Birchington
Blandford St Mary

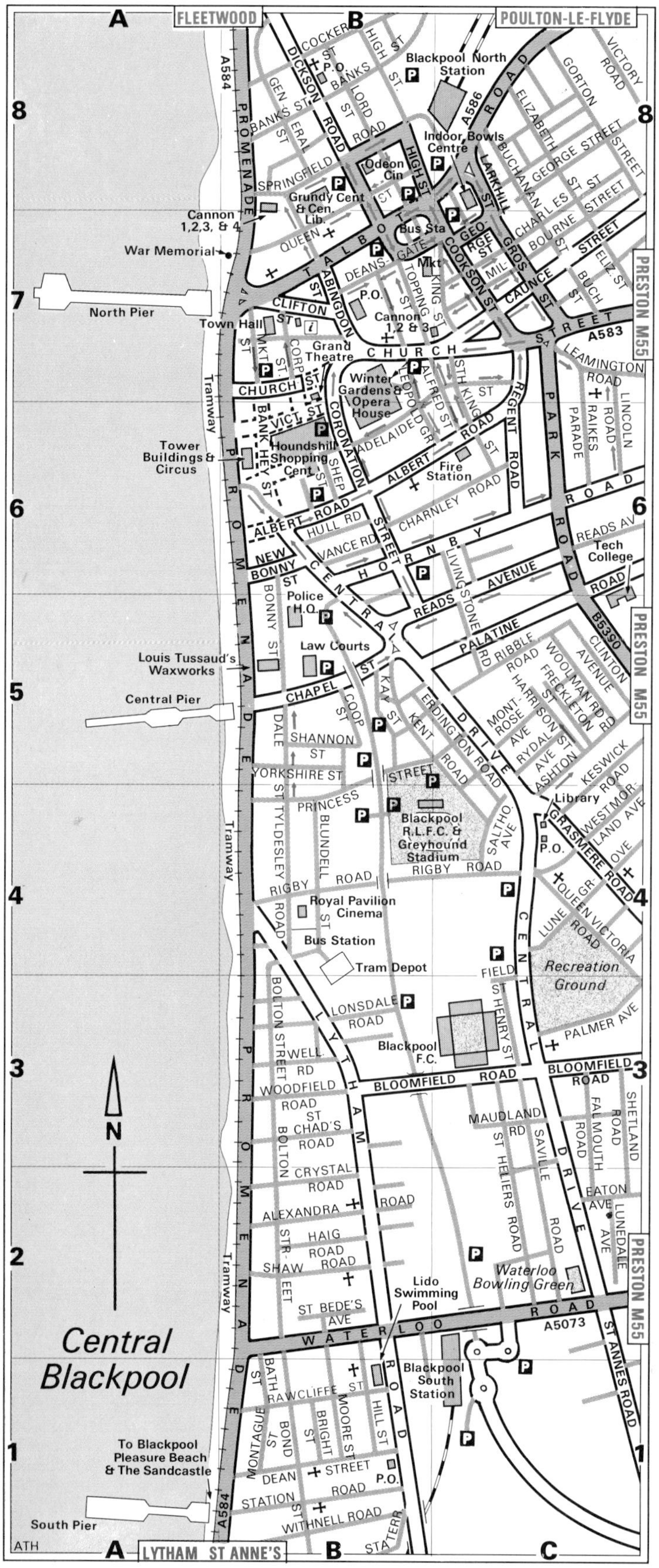
FLEETWOOD
POULTON-LE-FLYDE
PRESTON M55
LYTHAM ST ANNE'S
Central Blackpool
Blackpool North Station
Indoor Bowls Centre
Odeon Cin
Grundy Cent & Cen. Lib.
Cannon 1,2,3, & 4
War Memorial
North Pier
Town Hall
Bus Sta
Mkt
Cannon 1,2 & 3
Grand Theatre
Winter Gardens & Opera House
Tower Buildings & Circus
Houndshill Shopping Cent
Fire Station
Tech College
Police H.Q.
Law Courts
Louis Tussaud's Waxworks
Central Pier
Library
P.O.
Blackpool R.L.F.C. & Greyhound Stadium
Royal Pavilion Cinema
Bus Station
Tram Depot
Recreation Ground
Blackpool F.C.
Lido Swimming Pool
Waterloo Bowling Green
Blackpool South Station
To Blackpool Pleasure Beach & The Sandcastle
South Pier
Tramway
PROMENADE
TALBOT ROAD
CHURCH STREET
CENTRAL DRIVE
PARK ROAD
LYTHAM ROAD
BLOOMFIELD ROAD
WATERLOO ROAD
A584
A586
A583
B5390
A5073
N

Birchington *Kent* 29 TR3069
Birchley Heath *Warwks* 61 SP2994
Birchmoor Green *Beds* 38 SP9434
Birchover *Derbys* 74 SK2462
Birchwood *Somset* 9 ST2414
Birchyfield *H & W* 47 SO6453
Bircotes *Notts* 75 SK6391
Bird End *W Mids* 60 SP0194
Bird Street *Suffk* 54 TM0052
Birdbrook *Essex* 53 TL7041
Birdforth *N York* 90 SE4875
Birdham *W Susx* 14 SU8200
Birdingbury *Warwks* 50 SP4368
Birdlip *Gloucs* 35 SO9214
Birdoswald *Cumb* 102 NY6166
Birds Edge *W York* 74 SE2000
Birds Green *Essex* 40 TL5809
Birdsall *N York* 90 SE8165
Birdsgreen *Shrops* 60 SO7785
Birdsmoorgate *Dorset* 10 ST3900
Birdston *Strath* 116 NS6575
Birdwell *S York* 83 SE3401
Birdwood *Gloucs* 35 SO7318
Birgham *Border* 110 NT7939
Birichin *Highld* 147 NH7592
Birkacre *Lancs* 81 SD5715
Birkby *N York* 89 NZ3202
Birkdale *Mersyd* 80 SD3215
Birkenbog *Gramp* 142 NJ5365
Birkenbog *Gramp* 142 NJ5365
Birkenhead *Mersyd* 78 SJ3288
Birkenhills *Gramp* 142 NJ7445
Birkenshaw *W York* 82 SE2028
Birkenshaw *W York* 82 SE2028
Birkhall *Gramp* 134 NO3493
Birkhill *D & G* 109 NT2015
Birkhill & Muirhill *Tays* 126 NO3343
Birkholme *Lincs* 63 SK9723
Birkin *N York* 83 SE5226
Birks *W York* 82 SE2626
Birkshaw *Nthumb* 102 NY7765
Birley *H & W* 46 SO4553
Birley Carr *S York* 74 SK3391
Birling *Kent* 28 TQ6860
Birling *Nthumb* 111 NU2406
Birling Gap *E Susx* 16 TV5596
Birlingham *H & W* 47 SO9343
Birmingham *W Mids* 61 SP0787
Birnam *Tays* 125 NO0341
Birness *Gramp* 143 NJ9933
Birse *Gramp* 134 NO5596
Birsemore *Gramp* 134 NO5297
Birstall *Leics* 62 SK5909
Birstall *W York* 82 SE2325
Birstall Smithies *W York* 82 SE2226
Birstwith *N York* 89 SE2359
Birstwith *N York* 89 SE2359
Birthorpe *Lincs* 64 TF1033
Birtley *H & W* 46 SO3669
Birtley *Nthumb* 102 NY8778
Birtley *T & W* 96 NZ2756
Birts Street *H & W* 47 SO7836
Bisbrooke *Leics* 51 SP8899
Biscathorpe *Lincs* 76 TF2284
Biscovey *Cnwll* 3 SX0553
Bish Mill *Devon* 19 SS7425
Bisham *Berks* 26 SU8485
Bishampton *H & W* 47 SO9851
Bishop Auckland *Dur* 96 NZ2029
Bishop Burton *Humb* 84 SE9839
Bishop Middleham *Dur* 96 NZ3231
Bishop Monkton *N York* 89 SE3366
Bishop Norton *Lincs* 76 SK9892
Bishop Sutton *Avon* 21 ST5859
Bishop Thornton *N York* 89 SE2663
Bishop Wilton *Humb* 84 SE7955
Bishop's Castle *Shrops* 59 SO3288
Bishop's Cleeve *Gloucs* 47 SO9527
Bishop's Frome *H & W* 47 SO6648
Bishop's Green *Essex* 40 TL6217
Bishop's Green *Hants* 24 SU5062
Bishop's Itchington *Warwks* 48 SP3857
Bishop's Norton *Gloucs* 47 SO8424
Bishop's Nympton *Devon* 19 SS7523
Bishop's Offley *Staffs* 72 SJ7829
Bishop's Stortford *Herts* 39 TL4821
Bishop's Sutton *Hants* 24 SU6031
Bishop's Tachbrook *Warwks* 48 SP3161
Bishop's Tawton *Devon* 19 SS5630
Bishop's Waltham *Hants* 13 SU5517
Bishop's Wood *Staffs* 60 SJ8309
Bishop's Caundle *Dorset* 11 ST6913
Bishopbridge *Lincs* 76 TF0391
Bishopbriggs *Strath* 116 NS6070
Bishopmill *Gramp* 141 NJ2164
Bishops Cannings *Wilts* 23 SU0364
Bishops Gate *Surrey* 25 SU9871
Bishops Hull *Somset* 20 ST2024
Bishops Lydeard *Somset* 20 ST1729
Bishopsbourne *Kent* 29 TR1852
Bishopsteignton *Devon* 7 SX9173
Bishopstoke *Hants* 13 SU4619
Bishopston *W Glam* 32 SS5889
Bishopston *Warwks* 48 SP1956
Bishopstone *Bucks* 38 SP8010
Bishopstone *E Susx* 16 TQ4701
Bishopstone *H & W* 46 SO4143
Bishopstone *Kent* 26 TQ2068
Bishopstone *Wilts* 23 SU0625
Bishopstone *Wilts* 36 SU2483
Bishopstrow *Wilts* 22 ST8943
Bishopswood *Somset* 10 ST2612
Bishopsworth *Avon* 21 ST5768
Bishopthorpe *N York* 83 SE5947
Bishopton *Dur* 96 NZ3621
Bishopton *Strath* 115 NS4371
Bishton *Gwent* 34 ST3887
Bishton *Staffs* 73 SK0220
Bisley *Gloucs* 35 SO9005
Bisley *Surrey* 25 SU9559
Bisley Camp *Surrey* 25 SU9357
Bispham *Lancs* 80 SD3140
Bispham Green *Lancs* 80 SD4813
Bissoe *Cnwll* 3 SW7741
Bisterne *Hants* 12 SU1401
Bitchet Green *Kent* 27 TQ5654
Bitchfield *Lincs* 63 SK9828
Bittadon *Devon* 19 SS5042
Bittaford *Devon* 7 SX6657
Bittering *Norfk* 66 TF9317
Bitterlees *Cumb* 92 NY1252
Bitterley *Shrops* 46 SO5677
Bitterne *Hants* 13 SU4513
Bitteswell *Leics* 50 SP5385
Bitton *Avon* 35 ST6869
Bix *Oxon* 37 SU7285
Blaby *Leics* 50 SP5697
Black Bourton *Oxon* 36 SP2804
Black Callerton *T & W* 103 NZ1769
Black Car *Norfk* 66 TM0995
Black Corner *W Susx* 15 TQ2939
Black Corries *Highld* 123 NN2956
Black Crofts *Strath* 122 NM9234
Black Cross *Cnwll* 4 SW9160
Black Dog *Devon* 19 SS8009
Black Heddon *Nthumb* 103 NZ0776
Black Lane *Gt Man* 79 SD7708
Black Lane Ends *Lancs* 81 SD9243
Black Moor *W York* 82 SE2939
Black Notley *Essex* 40 TL7621
Black Street *Suffk* 55 TM5186
Black Tar *Dyfed* 30 SM9909
Black Torrington *Devon* 18 SS4605
Black Torrington *Devon* 18 SS4605
Blackadder *Border* 119 NT8452
Blackawton *Devon* 7 SX8050
Blackback *Cumb* 86 NY0207
Blackbank *Warwks* 61 SP3586
Blackborough *Devon* 9 ST0909
Blackborough End *Norfk* 65 TF6614
Blackboys *E Susx* 16 TQ5220
Blackbrook *Derbys* 62 SK3347
Blackbrook *Staffs* 72 SJ7639
Blackbrook *Surrey* 15 TQ1846
Blackburn *Gramp* 135 NJ8212
Blackburn *Lancs* 81 SD6827
Blackburn *Loth* 117 NS9865
Blackcraig *Strath* 107 NS6308
Blackden Heath *Ches* 79 SJ7871
Blackdog *Gramp* 143 NJ9514
Blackdown *Devon* 5 SX5079
Blackdown *Dorset* 10 ST3903
Blackdyke *Cumb* 92 NY1452
Blackenhall Heath *W Mids* 60 SK0001
Blacker *S York* 83 SE3309
Blacker Hill *S York* 83 SE3602
Blackfield *Hants* 13 SU4402
Blackford *Cumb* 101 NY3962
Blackford *Somset* 21 ST4147
Blackford *Somset* 21 ST6526
Blackford *Tays* 125 NN8908
Blackford Bridge *Gt Man* 79 SD8007
Blackfordby *Leics* 62 SK3318
Blackgang *IOW* 13 SZ4876
Blackhall Colliery *Dur* 97 NZ4539
Blackhaugh *Border* 109 NT4238
Blackheath *Essex* 38 TL0022
Blackheath *Gt Lon* 27 TQ3876
Blackheath *Suffk* 55 TM4275
Blackheath *Surrey* 14 TQ0346
Blackheath *W Mids* 60 SO9786
Blackhill *Dur* 95 NZ0852
Blackhill *Gramp* 143 NK0039
Blackhill *Gramp* 143 NK0755
Blackhill of Clackriach *Gramp* 143 NJ9236
Blackhorse *Devon* 9 SX9893
Blackhorse Hill *E Susx* 17 TQ7714
Blackjack *Lincs* 64 TF2639
Blackland *Somset* 19 SS8336
Blackland *Wilts* 22 SU0168
Blacklaw *D & G* 108 NT0408
Blackley *Gt Man* 79 SD8502
Blacklunans *Tays* 133 NO1560
Blackmarstone *H & W* 46 SO5038
Blackmill *M Glam* 33 SS9386
Blackmoor *Avon* 21 ST4661
Blackmoor *Hants* 14 SU7833
Blackmoor Gate *Devon* 19 SS6443
Blackmoorfoot *W York* 82 SE0913
Blackmore *Essex* 40 TL6002
Blackmore End *Essex* 40 TL7430
Blackmore End *Herts* 39 TL1716
Blackness *Loth* 117 NT0579
Blacknest *Berks* 25 SU9568
Blacknest *Hants* 25 SU7941
Blacko *Lancs* 81 SD8541
Blackpark *D & G* 100 NX9181
Blackpill *W Glam* 32 SS6190
Blackpool *Devon* 7 SX8547
Blackpool *Lancs* 80 SD3036
Blackpool Gate *Cumb* 101 NY5378
Blackridge *Loth* 116 NS8967
Blackrock *Cnwll* 2 SW6635
Blackrock *Gwent* 34 ST5188
Blackrock *Gwent* 33 SO2112
Blackrock *Strath* 112 NR3063
Blackrod *Gt Man* 81 SD6111
Blacks Boat *Gramp* 141 NJ1838
Blackshaw *D & G* 100 NY0465
Blackshaw Head *W York* 82 SD9527
Blacksmith's Green *Suffk* 54 TM1465
Blacksnape *Lancs* 81 SD7121
Blackstone *W Susx* 15 TQ2416
Blackthorn *Oxon* 37 SP6219
Blackthorpe *Suffk* 54 TL9063
Blacktoft *Humb* 84 SE8324
Blacktop *Gramp* 135 NJ8604
Blackwall *Derbys* 73 SK2548
Blackwater *Cnwll* 3 SW7346
Blackwater *Hants* 25 SU8559
Blackwater *IOW* 13 SZ5086
Blackwater *Somset* 10 ST2615
Blackwaterfoot *Strath* 105 NR9028
Blackwell *Cumb* 93 NY4053
Blackwell *Derbys* 74 SK1272
Blackwell *Derbys* 75 SK4458
Blackwell *Dur* 89 NZ2713
Blackwell *H & W* 60 SO9972
Blackwell *Warwks* 48 SP2443
Blackwellsend Green *Gloucs* 47 SO7825
Blackwood *D & G* 100 NX9087
Blackwood *Gwent* 33 ST1797
Blackwood *Strath* 116 NS7844
Blackwood Hill *Staffs* 72 SJ9255
Blacon *Ches* 71 SJ3868
Bladbean *Kent* 29 TR1847
Bladnoch *D & G* 99 NX4254
Bladon *Oxon* 37 SP4414
Bladon *Somset* 21 ST4220
Blaen Dyryn *Powys* 45 SN9336
Blaen-y-Coed *Dyfed* 31 SN3427
Blaen-y-cwm *Gwent* 33 SO1311
Blaen-y-cwm *M Glam* 33 SS9298
Blaenannerch *Dyfed* 42 SN2449
Blaenau Ffestiniog *Gwynd* 57 SH7045
Blaenavon *Gwent* 34 SO2509
Blaenawey *Gwent* 34 SO2919
Blaenffos *Dyfed* 31 SN1937
Blaengarw *M Glam* 33 SS9092
Blaengeuffardd *Dyfed* 43 SN6379
Blaengwrach *W Glam* 33 SN8605
Blaengwynfi *W Glam* 33 SS8996
Blaenllechau *M Glam* 33 ST0097
Blaenpennal *Dyfed* 43 SN6264
Blaenplwyf *Dyfed* 43 SN5775
Blaenporth *Dyfed* 42 SN2648
Blaenrhondda *M Glam* 33 SS9299
Blaenwaun *Dyfed* 31 SN2327
Blaenycwm *Dyfed* 43 SN8275
Blagdon *Avon* 21 ST5059
Blagdon *Devon* 7 SX8561
Blagdon *Somset* 9 ST2117
Blagdon Hill *Somset* 9 ST2117
Blagill *Cumb* 94 NY7347
Blaguegate *Lancs* 78 SD4506
Blaich *Highld* 130 NN0476
Blain *Highld* 129 NM6769
Blaina *Gwent* 33 SO2008
Blair Atholl *Tays* 132 NN8765
Blair Drummond *Cent* 116 NS7399
Blairgowrie *Tays* 126 NO1745
Blairingone *Fife* 117 NS9896
Blairlogie *Cent* 116 NS8396
Blairmore *Highld* 148 NC1960
Blairmore *Strath* 114 NS1983
Blairnamarrow *Gramp* 141 NJ2015
Blairs Ferry *Strath* 114 NR9869
Blaisdon *Gloucs* 35 SO7017
Blake End *Essex* 40 TL7023
Blakebrook *H & W* 60 SO8177
Blakedown *H & W* 60 SO8878
Blakeley Lane *Staffs* 72 SJ9747
Blakemere *Ches* 71 SJ5571
Blakemere *H & W* 46 SO3640
Blakemore *Devon* 7 SX7759
Blakeney *Gloucs* 35 SO6707
Blakeney *Norfk* 66 TG0243
Blakenhall *Ches* 72 SJ7247
Blakenhall *W Mids* 60 SO9197
Blakeshall *H & W* 60 SO8381
Blakesley *Nhants* 49 SP6250
Blanchland *Nthumb* 95 NY9650
Bland Hill *N York* 82 SE2053
Blandford Camp *Dorset* 11 ST9108
Blandford Forum *Dorset* 11 ST8806
Blandford St. Mary *Dorset* 11 ST8805

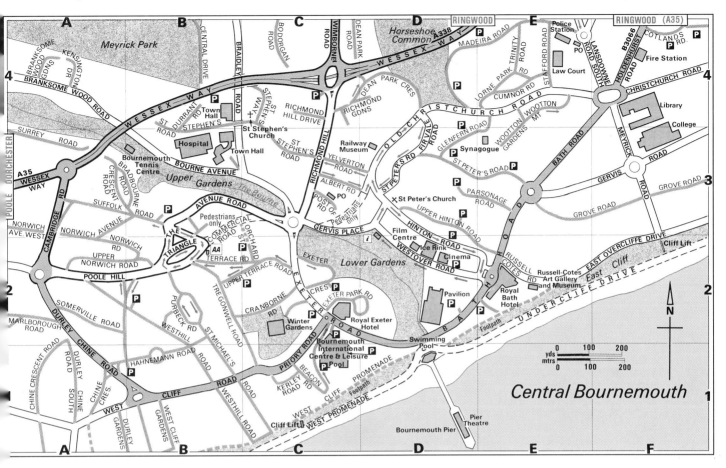

Central Bournemouth

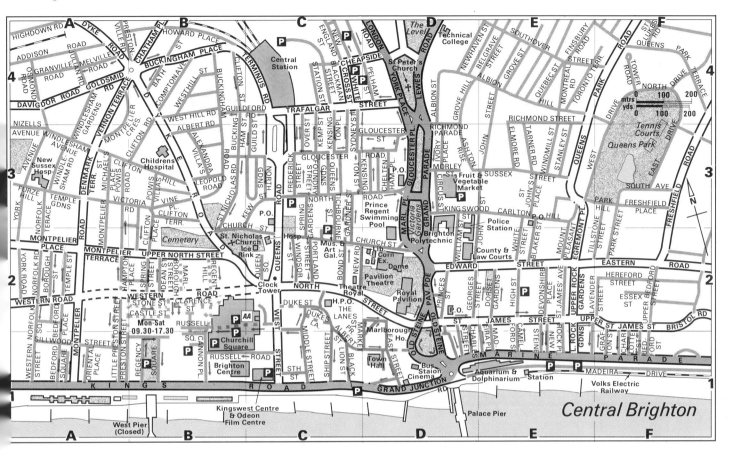

Central Brighton

Bromley Burton

Bromley *Shrops* 60 SO7395
Bromley *W Mids* 60 SO9088
Bromley Common *Gt Lon* 27 TQ4266
Bromley Cross *Essex* 41 TM0627
Bromlow *Shrops* 59 SJ3201
Brompton *Kent* 28 TQ7668
Brompton *Kent* 28 TQ7668
Brompton *N York* 89 SE3796
Brompton *N York* 91 SE9482
Brompton *Shrops* 59 SJ5408
Brompton Ralph *Somset* 20 ST0832
Brompton Regis *Somset* 20 SS9531
Brompton-on-Swale *N York* 89 SE2199
Bromsash *H & W* 47 SO6523
Bromsberrow *Gloucs* 47 SO7434
Bromsberrow Heath *Gloucs* 47 SO7332
Bromsgrove *H & W* 60 SO9570
Bromstead Heath *Staffs* 72 SJ7917
Bromyard *H & W* 47 SO6554
Bromyard Downs *H & W* 47 SO6655
Bronaber *Gwynd* 57 SH7132
Bronant *Dyfed* 43 SN6467
Broncroft *Shrops* 59 SO5486
Brongest *Dyfed* 42 SN3245
Bronington *Clwyd* 71 SJ4839
Bronllys *Powys* 45 SO1434
Bronwydd Arms *Dyfed* 31 SN4124
Bronygarth *Shrops* 58 SJ2637
Brook *Dyfed* 31 SN2609
Brook *Hants* 12 SU2713
Brook *Hants* 23 SU3428
Brook *Hants* 12 SU2713
Brook *IOW* 13 SZ3983
Brook *Kent* 29 TR0644
Brook *Surrey* 25 SU9338
Brook *Surrey* 14 TQ0646
Brook End *Beds* 51 TL0763
Brook End *Beds* 52 TL1547
Brook End *Bucks* 38 SP9144
Brook End *Cambs* 61 SP0773
Brook End *Staffs* 61 SK0714
Brook Hill *Hants* 12 SU2714
Brook Hill *Hants* 12 SU2714
Brook Street *Essex* 27 TQ5792
Brook Street *Kent* 17 TQ9334
Brook Street *Suffk* 54 TL8348
Brook Street *W Susx* 15 TQ3026
Brooke *Leics* 63 SK8405
Brooke *Norfk* 67 TM2999
Brookfield *Strath* 115 NS4164
Brookhampton *Oxon* 37 SU6098
Brookhampton *Somset* 21 ST6327
Brookhouse *Lancs* 87 SD5464
Brookhouse *S York* 75 SK5188
Brookhouse Green *Ches* 72 SJ8161
Brookhouses *Derbys* 74 SK0389
Brookland *Kent* 17 TQ9926
Brooklands *Gt Man* 79 SJ7890
Brookmans Park *Herts* 39 TL2404
Brooks *Powys* 58 SO1499
Brooks End *Kent* 27 TQ2967
Brooks Green *W Susx* 14 TQ1225
Brooksby *Leics* 63 SK6716
Brookthorpe *Gloucs* 35 SO8312
Brookville *Norfk* 65 TL7396
Brookwood *Surrey* 25 SU9557
Broom *Beds* 39 TL1742
Broom *S York* 75 SK4491
Broom *Warwks* 48 SP0953
Broom Green *Norfk* 66 TF9924
Broom Hill *Dorset* 12 SU0302
Broom Hill *H & W* 60 SO9275
Broom Hill *Notts* 75 SK5448
Broom Hill *S York* 83 SE4102
Broom of Dalreoch *Tays* 125 NO0017
Broom Street *Kent* 28 TR0462
Broom's Green *H & W* 47 SO7133
Broome *H & W* 60 SO9078
Broome *Norfk* 67 TM3591
Broome *Shrops* 59 SO3981
Broome Park *Nthumb* 111 NU1012
Broomedge *Ches* 79 SJ6985
Broomer's Corner *W Susx* 14 TQ1221
Broomershill *W Susx* 14 TQ0619
Broomfield *Essex* 40 TL7011
Broomfield *Kent* 28 TQ8352
Broomfield *Kent* 29 TR1966
Broomfield *Somset* 20 ST2221
Broomfields *Shrops* 59 SJ4217
Broomfleet *Humb* 84 SE8727
Broomhall *Surrey* 25 SU9566
Broomhaugh *Nthumb* 103 NZ0261
Broomhill *Highld* 141 NH9922
Broomhill *Nthumb* 103 NU2401
Broomhill Green *Ches* 71 SJ6247
Broomley *Nthumb* 103 NZ0360
Broomsthorpe *Norfk* 66 TF8428
Brora *Highld* 147 NC9104
Broseley *Shrops* 60 SJ6701
Brotherhouse Bar *Lincs* 64 TF2614
Brotherlee *Dur* 95 NY9237
Brotherstone *Border* 110 NT6145
Brothertoft *Lincs* 77 TF2746
Brothertoft *Lincs* 77 TF2746
Brotherton *N York* 83 SE4825
Brotton *Cleve* 97 NZ6819
Broubster *Highld* 150 ND0359
Brough *Cumb* 95 NY7914
Brough *Derbys* 74 SK1882
Brough *Highld* 151 ND2273
Brough *Humb* 84 SE9326
Brough *Notts* 76 SK8458
Brough *Shet* 155 HU5564
Brough Lodge *Shet* 155 HU5892
Brough Sowerby *Cumb* 95 NY7912
Broughall *Shrops* 71 SJ5741
Broughton *Border* 108 NT1136
Broughton *Bucks* 38 SP8939
Broughton *Bucks* 38 SP8413
Broughton *Cambs* 52 TL2877
Broughton *Clwyd* 71 SJ3363
Broughton *Gt Man* 79 SD8201
Broughton *Hants* 23 SU3132
Broughton *Humb* 84 SE9508
Broughton *Lancs* 80 SD5234
Broughton *N York* 82 SD9451
Broughton *N York* 90 SE7673
Broughton *Nhants* 51 SP8375
Broughton *Oxon* 49 SP4238
Broughton *S Glam* 33 SS9271
Broughton *Staffs* 72 SJ7634
Broughton Astley *Leics* 50 SP5292
Broughton Beck *Cumb* 86 SD2882
Broughton Gifford *Wilts* 22 ST8763
Broughton Green *H & W* 47 SO9561
Broughton Hackett *H & W* 47 SO9254
Broughton in Furness *Cumb* 86 SD2187
Broughton Mains *D & G* 99 NX4545
Broughton Mills *Cumb* 86 SD2290
Broughton Moor *Cumb* 92 NY0533
Broughton Poggs *Oxon* 36 SP2303
Broughton Tower *Cumb* 101 NY2188
Broughty Ferry *Tays* 127 NO4630
Browy-of-the-Hill *Norfk* 65 TF6819
Brown Candover *Hants* 24 SU5739
Brown Edge *Lancs* 80 SD3614
Brown Edge *Staffs* 72 SJ9053
Brown Heath *Ches* 71 SJ4564
Brown Lees *Staffs* 72 SJ8756
Brown Street *Suffk* 54 TM0664
Brown's Green *W Mids* 61 SP0491
Brownber *Cumb* 87 NY7005
Brownheath *Shrops* 59 SJ4629
Brownhill *Gramp* 143 NJ8640
Brownhills *Fife* 127 NO5215
Brownhills *W Mids* 61 SK0405
Browninghill Green *Hants* 24 SU5859
Brownlow Heath *Ches* 72 SJ8360
Brownmuir *Gramp* 135 NO7377
Brownrigg *Cumb* 92 NY0420
Brownrigg *Cumb* 92 NY1652
Brownsham *Devon* 18 SS2826
Brownsover *Warwks* 50 SP5177
Brownston *Devon* 7 SX6952
Brownstone *Devon* 7 SX9051
Browston Green *Norfk* 67 TG4901
Brox *Surrey* 26 TQ0263
Broxa *N York* 91 SE9491
Broxbourne *Herts* 39 TL3607
Broxburn *Loth* 117 NT0872
Broxburn *Loth* 119 NT6977
Broxfield *Nthumb* 111 NU2016
Broxted *Essex* 40 TL5727
Broxton *Ches* 71 SJ4854
Broxwood *H & W* 46 SO3654
Broyle Side *E Susx* 16 TQ4513
Bruan *Highld* 151 ND3139
Bruar *Tays* 132 NN8266
Brucefield *Highld* 147 NH9386
Brucefield *Highld* 147 NH9386
Bruchag *Strath* 114 NS1157
Brue *W Isls* 154 NB3349
Bruera *Ches* 71 SJ4360
Bruern Abbey *Oxon* 36 SP2620
Bruernish *W Isls* 154 NF7102
Bruisyard *Suffk* 55 TM3266
Bruisyard Street *Suffk* 55 TM3365
Brumby *Humb* 84 SE8009
Brund *Staffs* 74 SK1061
Brundall *Norfk* 67 TG3208
Brundish *Suffk* 55 TM2669
Brundish Street *Suffk* 55 TM2671
Brunnian *Cnwll* 2 SW5036
Bruno *Derbys* 74 SK1061
Brunslow *Shrops* 59 SO3684
Bruntcliffe *W York* 82 SE2526
Brunthwaite *W York* 82 SE0546
Bruntingthorpe *Leics* 50 SP6090
Brunton *Fife* 126 NO3220
Brunton *Nthumb* 111 NU2024
Brunton *Wilts* 23 SU2456
Brushford *Somset* 20 SS9225
Brushford Barton *Devon* 8 SS6707
Bruton *Somset* 22 ST6834
Bryan's Green *H & W* 47 SO8868
Bryanston *Dorset* 11 ST8706
Bryant's Bottom *Bucks* 26 SU8599
Brydekirk *D & G* 101 NY1870
Brymbo *Clwyd* 71 SJ2953
Brympton *Somset* 10 ST5115
Bryn *Ches* 71 SJ6072
Bryn *Gt Man* 78 SD5600
Bryn *Shrops* 59 SO2985
Bryn *W Glam* 33 SS8192
Bryn Du *Gwynd* 68 SH3472
Bryn Gates *Lancs* 78 SD5901
Bryn Golau *M Glam* 33 ST0088
Bryn Saith Marchog *Clwyd* 70 SJ0750
Bryn-bwbach *Gwynd* 57 SH6236
Bryn-coch *W Glam* 32 SS7499
Bryn-Eden *Gwynd* 57 SH7129
Bryn-henllan *Dyfed* 30 SN0139
Bryn-Mawr *Gwynd* 56 SH2433
Bryn-newydd *Clwyd* 70 SJ1842
Bryn-penarth *Powys* 58 SJ1004
Bryn-y-bal *Clwyd* 70 SJ2564
Bryn-y-maen *Clwyd* 69 SH8376
Bryn-yr-Eos *Clwyd* 70 SJ2840
Brynamman *Dyfed* 32 SN7114
Brynberian *Dyfed* 31 SN1035
Brynbryddan *W Glam* 32 SS7792
Bryncae *M Glam* 33 SS9982
Bryncethin *M Glam* 33 SS9083
Bryncir *Gwynd* 56 SH4641
Bryncroes *Gwynd* 56 SH2231
Bryncrug *Gwynd* 57 SH6003
Bryneglwys *Clwyd* 70 SJ1447
Brynfields *Clwyd* 71 SJ3044
Brynford *Clwyd* 70 SJ1774
Bryngwran *Gwynd* 68 SH3477
Bryngwyn *Gwent* 34 SO3809
Bryngwyn *Powys* 45 SO1849
Brynhoffnant *Dyfed* 42 SN3351
Bryning *Lancs* 80 SD4030
Brynithel *Gwent* 33 SO2101
Brynmawr *Gwent* 33 SO1911
Brynmenyn *M Glam* 33 SS9085
Brynmill *W Glam* 32 SS6392
Brynna *M Glam* 33 SS9883
Brynrefail *Gwynd* 68 SH4786
Brynrefail *Gwynd* 69 SH5662
Brynsadler *M Glam* 33 ST0280
Brynsiencyn *Gwynd* 68 SH4867
Brynteg *Gwynd* 68 SH4982
Bualintur *Highld* 128 NG4010
Buarth-draw *Clwyd* 70 SJ1779
Bubbenhall *Warwks* 61 SP3672
Bubwith *Humb* 84 SE7136
Buccleuch *Border* 109 NT3214
Buchanan Smithy *Cent* 115 NS4689
Buchanhaven *Gramp* 143 NK1247
Buchanty *Tays* 125 NN9328
Buchany *Cent* 124 NN7102
Buchlyvie *Cent* 115 NS5793
Buchtrig *Border* 110 NT7714
Buck's Cross *Devon* 18 SS3523
Buck's Mills *Devon* 18 SS3523
Buckabank *Cumb* 93 NY3649
Buckden *Cambs* 52 TL1967
Buckden *N York* 88 SD9477
Buckenham *Norfk* 67 TG3506
Buckerell *Devon* 9 ST1200
Buckfast *Devon* 7 SX7367
Buckfastleigh *Devon* 7 SX7366
Buckhaven *Fife* 118 NT3598
Buckholm *Border* 109 NT4738
Buckholt *Gwent* 34 SO5016
Buckhorn Weston *Dorset* 22 ST7524
Buckhurst Hill *Essex* 27 TQ4194
Buckie *Gramp* 142 NJ4265
Buckingham *Bucks* 49 SP6933
Buckland *Bucks* 38 SP8812
Buckland *Devon* 7 SX6743
Buckland *Gloucs* 48 SP0836
Buckland *Hants* 12 SZ3196
Buckland *Herts* 39 TL3533
Buckland *Kent* 29 TR3042
Buckland *Oxon* 36 SU3497
Buckland *Surrey* 26 TQ2250
Buckland Brewer *Devon* 18 SS4120
Buckland Common *Bucks* 38 SP9307
Buckland Dinham *Somset* 22 ST7550
Buckland Filleigh *Devon* 18 SS4608
Buckland in the Moor *Devon* 7 SX7273
Buckland Monachorum *Devon* 6 SX4868
Buckland Newton *Dorset* 11 ST6905
Buckland Ripers *Dorset* 11 SY6482
Buckland St. Mary *Somset* 10 ST2713
Buckland-Tout-Saints *Devon* 7 SX7546
Bucklebury *Berks* 24 SU5570
Bucklerheads *Tays* 127 NO4636
Bucklers Hard *Hants* 13 SU4000
Bucklesham *Suffk* 55 TM2442
Buckley *Clwyd* 70 SJ2864
Buckley Green *Warwks* 48 SP1667
Buckley Mountain *Clwyd* 70 SJ2865
Bucklow Hill *Ches* 79 SJ7383
Buckminster *Leics* 63 SK8722
Bucknall *Lincs* 76 TF1668
Bucknall *Staffs* 72 SJ9047
Bucknell *Oxon* 49 SP5626
Bucknell *Shrops* 46 SO3574
Buckpool *Gramp* 142 NJ4265
Bucks Green *W Susx* 14 TQ0732
Bucks Hill *Herts* 26 TL0500
Bucks Horn Oak *Hants* 25 SU8041
Bucksburn *Gramp* 135 NJ8909
Buckshead *Cnwll* 3 SW8346
Buckton *H & W* 46 SO3873
Buckton *Humb* 91 TA1872
Buckton *Nthumb* 111 NU0838
Buckworth *Cambs* 52 TL1476
Budbrooke *Warwks* 48 SP2665
Budby *Notts* 75 SK6169
Budd's Titson *Cnwll* 18 SS2401
Buddileigh *Staffs* 72 SJ7449
Buddon *Tays* 127 NO5232
Bude *Cnwll* 18 SS2006
Budge's Shop *Cnwll* 5 SX3259
Budlake *Devon* 9 SS9700
Budle *Nthumb* 111 NU1535
Budleigh Salterton *Devon* 9 SY0682
Budlett's Common *E Susx* 16 TQ4723
Budock Water *Cnwll* 3 SW7832
Buerton *Ches* 72 SJ6843
Bugbrooke *Nhants* 49 SP6757
Bugford *Devon* 7 SX8350
Buglawton *Ches* 72 SJ8763
Bugle *Cnwll* 4 SX0158
Bugley *Dorset* 22 ST7824
Bugthorpe *Humb* 90 SE7757
Buildwas *Shrops* 59 SJ6304
Builth Road *Powys* 45 SO0353
Builth Wells *Powys* 45 SO0350
Bulbourne *Herts* 38 SP9313
Bulbridge *Wilts* 23 SU0930
Bulby *Lincs* 64 TF0526
Buldoo *Highld* 150 ND0067
Bulford *Wilts* 23 SU1643
Bulford Barracks *Wilts* 23 SU1843
Bulkeley *Ches* 71 SJ5254
Bulkington *Warwks* 61 SP3986
Bulkington *Wilts* 22 ST9458
Bulkworthy *Devon* 18 SS3914
Bull Bay *Gwynd* 68 SH4294
Bull's Green *Herts* 39 TL2717
Bull's Green *Norfk* 67 TM4194
Bullamore *N York* 89 SE3994
Bullbridge *Derbys* 74 SK3552
Bullbrook *Berks* 25 SU8869
Bullen's Green *Herts* 39 TL2105
Bulley *Gloucs* 35 SO7619
Bullgill *Cumb* 92 NY0938
Bullinghope *H & W* 46 SO5136
Bullington *Hants* 24 SU4541
Bullington *Lincs* 76 TF0977
Bullington End *Bucks* 38 SP8144
Bullockstone *Kent* 29 TR1665
Bullwood *Strath* 114 NS1675
Bulmer *Essex* 54 TL8440
Bulmer *N York* 90 SE6967
Bulmer Tye *Essex* 54 TL8439
Bulphan *Essex* 40 TQ6386
Bulstone *Devon* 9 SY1789
Bulstrode *Herts* 38 TL0303
Bulstrode Park *Bucks* 26 SU9888
Bulterley Heath *Staffs* 72 SJ7450
Bulverhythe *E Susx* 17 TQ7708
Bulwark *Gramp* 143 NJ9345
Bulwell *Notts* 62 SK5345
Bulwick *Nhants* 51 SP9694
Bumble's Green *Essex* 39 TL4004
Bunacaimb *Highld* 129 NM6588
Bunarkaig *Highld* 131 NN1888
Bunbury *Ches* 71 SJ5658
Bunbury Heath *Ches* 71 SJ5558
Bunchrew *Highld* 140 NH6246
Buncton *W Susx* 15 TQ1413
Bundalloch *Highld* 138 NG8927
Bunessan *Strath* 121 NM3821
Bungay *Suffk* 55 TM3389
Bunker's Hill *Lincs* 77 TF2653
Bunnahabhainn *Strath* 112 NR4173
Bunny *Notts* 62 SK5829
Buntait *Highld* 139 NH4030
Buntingford *Herts* 39 TL3629
Bunwell *Norfk* 66 TM1292
Bunwell Street *Norfk* 66 TM1194
Bupton *Derbys* 73 SK2237
Burbage *Derbys* 74 SK0472
Burbage *Leics* 50 SP4492
Burbage *Wilts* 23 SU2261
Burcher *H & W* 46 SO3360
Burchett's Green *Berks* 37 SU8381
Burchett's Green *E Susx* 16 TQ6631
Burcombe *Wilts* 23 SU0630
Burcot *H & W* 60 SO9871
Burcot *Oxon* 37 SU5595
Burcote *Shrops* 60 SO7494
Burcott *Bucks* 38 SP8415
Burcott *Bucks* 38 SP8723
Burdale *N York* 90 SE8762
Bures *Suffk* 54 TL9034
Burford *H & W* 46 SO5868
Burford *Oxon* 36 SP2411
Burg *Strath* 121 NM3845
Burgates *Hants* 24 SU7728
Burge End *Herts* 38 TL1432
Burgess Hill *W Susx* 15 TQ3118
Burgh *Suffk* 55 TM2351
Burgh by Sands *Cumb* 93 NY3259
Burgh Castle *Norfk* 67 TG4805
Burgh Heath *Surrey* 26 TQ2457
Burgh Hill *E Susx* 17 TQ7227
Burgh Le Marsh *Lincs* 77 TF4965
Burgh next Aylsham *Norfk* 67 TG2125
Burgh on Bain *Lincs* 76 TF2186
Burgh St. Margaret *Norfk* 67 TG4413
Burgh St. Peter *Norfk* 67 TM4693
Burghclere *Hants* 24 SU4761
Burghead *Gramp* 141 NJ1168
Burghfield *Berks* 24 SU6668
Burghfield Common *Berks* 24 SU6566
Burghill *H & W* 46 SO4744
Burghill *H & W* 46 SO4844
Burghwallis *S York* 83 SE5312
Burham *Kent* 28 TQ7262
Buriton *Hants* 13 SU7320
Burland *Ches* 71 SJ6153
Burlawn *Cnwll* 4 SW9970
Burleigh *Berks* 25 SU9069
Burleigh *Gloucs* 35 SO8601
Burlescombe *Devon* 9 ST0716
Burleston *Dorset* 11 SY7794
Burlestone *Devon* 7 SX8248
Burley *Hants* 12 SU2103
Burley *Leics* 63 SK8810
Burley *Shrops* 59 SO4881
Burley Gate *H & W* 46 SO5947
Burley in Wharfedale *W York* 82 SE1646
Burley Lawn *Hants* 12 SU2103
Burley Street *Hants* 12 SU2004
Burley Wood Head *W York* 82 SE1544
Burleydam *Ches* 71 SJ6042
Burlingham Green *Norfk* 67 TG3611
Burlingjobb *Powys* 46 SO2558
Burlington *Shrops* 60 SJ7611
Burlton *Shrops* 59 SJ4526
Burmarsh *Kent* 17 TR1032
Burmington *Warwks* 48 SP2638
Burn *N York* 83 SE5928
Burn Cross *S York* 74 SK3495
Burn Naze *Lancs* 80 SD3443
Burn of Cambus *Cent* 124 NN7103
Burnage *Gt Man* 79 SJ8692
Burnaston *Derbys* 73 SK2832
Burnbanks *Cumb* 94 NY5016
Burnbrae *Strath* 116 NS8759
Burnby *Humb* 84 SE8346
Burndell *W Susx* 14 SU9802
Burnden *Gt Man* 79 SD7207
Burnedge *Gt Man* 79 SD9110
Burneside *Cumb* 87 SD5095
Burneston *N York* 89 SE3084
Burnett *Avon* 22 ST6665
Burnfoot *Border* 109 NT5116
Burnfoot *Border* 109 NT4113
Burnfoot *D & G* 101 NY3896
Burnfoot *D & G* 101 NY3388
Burnfoot *D & G* 100 NX9791
Burnfoot *Tays* 125 NN9904
Burnham *Bucks* 26 SU9382
Burnham *Humb* 84 TA0517
Burnham Beeches *Bucks* 26 SU9585
Burnham Deepdale *Norfk* 66 TF8044
Burnham Green *Herts* 39 TL2616
Burnham Market *Norfk* 66 TF8342
Burnham Norton *Norfk* 66 TF8243
Burnham Overy *Norfk* 66 TF8442
Burnham Thorpe *Norfk* 66 TF8541
Burnham-on-Crouch *Essex* 40 TQ9496
Burnham-on-Sea *Somset* 20 ST3049
Burnhaven *Gramp* 143 NK1244
Burnhead *D & G* 100 NX8695
Burnhervie *Gramp* 142 NJ7319
Burnhill Green *Staffs* 60 SJ7800
Burnhope *Dur* 96 NZ1948
Burnhouse *Strath* 115 NS3850
Burniston *N York* 91 TA0193
Burnley *Lancs* 81 SD8432
Burnmouth *Border* 119 NT9560
Burnopfield *Dur* 96 NZ1756
Burnrigg *Cumb* 94 NY4856
Burnsall *N York* 88 SE0361
Burnside *Fife* 117 NT0575
Burnside *Fife* 126 NO1608
Burnside *Gramp* 142 NJ1669
Burnside *Tays* 134 NO4259
Burnside *Tays* 127 NO5050
Burnside of Duntrune *Tays* 127 NO4434
Burnt Heath *Essex* 41 TM0628
Burnt Hill *Berks* 24 SU5774
Burnt Houses *Dur* 96 NZ1223
Burnt Oak *E Susx* 16 TQ5126
Burnt Yates *N York* 89 SE2461
Burntcommon *Surrey* 26 TQ0354
Burntheath *Derbys* 73 SK2431
Burnthouse *Cnwll* 3 SW7636
Burntisland *Fife* 117 NT2385
Burntwood *Staffs* 61 SK0608
Burntwood Green *Staffs* 61 SK0708
Burnville *Devon* 5 SX4982
Burnworthy *Somset* 9 ST1915
Burpham *Surrey* 26 TQ0151
Burpham *W Susx* 14 TQ0408
Burradon *Nthumb* 111 NT9806
Burradon *T & W* 103 NZ2772
Burrafirth *Shet* 155 HP6113
Burras *Cnwll* 2 SW6734
Burraton *Cnwll* 5 SX4167
Burraton *Devon* 6 SX6152
Burravoe *Shet* 155 HU5279
Burrells *Cumb* 94 NY6718
Burrelton *Tays* 126 NO2037
Burridge *Devon* 10 ST3106
Burridge *Hants* 13 SU5110
Burrill *N York* 89 SE2386
Burringham *Humb* 84 SE8309
Burrington *Avon* 21 ST4759
Burrington *Devon* 19 SS6316
Burrington *H & W* 46 SO4472
Burrough End *Cambs* 53 TL6256
Burrough Green *Cambs* 53 TL6355
Burrough on the Hill *Leics* 63 SK7510
Burrow *Somset* 20 SS9342
Burrow Bridge *Somset* 21 ST3530
Burrowhill *Surrey* 25 SU9763
Burrows Cross *Surrey* 14 TQ0846
Burry *W Glam* 32 SS4596
Burry Port *Dyfed* 32 SN4400
Burrygreen *W Glam* 32 SS4591
Burscough *Lancs* 78 SD4310
Burscough Bridge *Lancs* 80 SD4412
Bursea *Humb* 84 SE8033
Burshill *Humb* 85 TA0948
Bursledon *Hants* 13 SU4809
Burslem *Staffs* 72 SJ8749
Burstall *Suffk* 54 TM1044
Burstock *Dorset* 10 ST4202
Burston *Devon* 8 SS7102
Burston *Norfk* 54 TM1383
Burston *Staffs* 72 SJ9330
Burstow *Surrey* 15 TQ3141
Burstwick *Humb* 85 TA2228
Burtersett *N York* 88 SD8959
Burtersett *N York* 88 SD8989
Burtholme *Cumb* 101 NY5463
Burthorpe Green *Suffk* 53 TL7764
Burthwaite *Cumb* 93 NY4149
Burthy *Cnwll* 3 SW9155
Burtle Hill *Somset* 21 ST3943
Burtoft *Lincs* 64 TF2635
Burton *Ches* 71 SJ3174
Burton *Ches* 71 SJ5063
Burton *Cumb* 87 SD5276
Burton *Dorset* 11 SY6892
Burton *Dorset* 12 SZ1794
Burton *Dyfed* 30 SM9805
Burton *Lincs* 76 SK9574
Burton *Nthumb* 111 NU1833

C

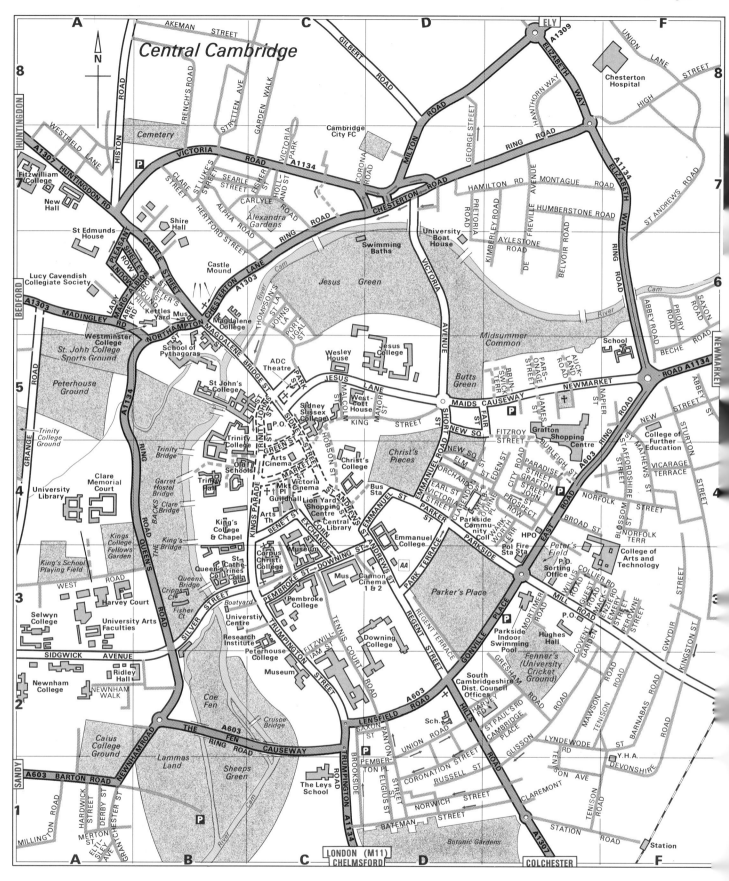

Carrington Chesterfield

Carrington Loth 117 NT3160
Carrington Moss Gt Man 79 SJ7592
Carrismerry Cnwll 4 SX0158
Carrog Clwyd 70 SJ1143
Carrog Gwynd 69 SH7648
Carron Cent 116 NS8882
Carron Gramp 141 NJ2241
Carron Highld 141 NJ1234
Carron Bridge Cent 116 NS7483
Carronbridge D & G 100 NX8698
Carronshore Cent 116 NS8983
Carrow Hill Gwent 34 ST4390
Carruth House Strath 115 NS3566
Carrutherstown D & G 100 NY1071
Carrville Dur 96 NZ3243
Carrycoats Hall Nthumb 102 NY9279
Carsaig Strath 121 NM5421
Carscreugh D & G 98 NX2260
Carse Gray Tays 127 NO4553
Carseriggen D & G 98 NX3167
Carsethorn D & G 92 NX9959
Carshalton Gt Lon 27 TQ2764
Carsie Tays 126 NO1742
Carsington Derbys 73 SK2553
Carskiey Strath 104 NR6508
Carsluith D & G 99 NX4854
Carsphairn D & G 107 NX5693
Carstairs Strath 116 NS9346
Carstairs Junction Strath 117 NS9545
Carswell Marsh Oxon 36 SU3298
Carter Bar Border 110 NT6907
Carter's Clay Hants 23 SU3024
Carters Green Essex 39 TL5111
Carterton Oxon 36 SP2706
Carterway Heads Nthumb 95 NZ0552
Carthew Cnwll 3 SX0056
Carthorpe N York 89 SE3083
Cartington Nthumb 103 NU0204
Cartland Strath 116 NS8646
Cartledge Derbys 74 SK3477
Cartmel Cumb 87 SD3778
Cartmel Fell Cumb 87 SD4188
Carway Dyfed 32 SN4606
Carwinley Cumb 101 NY4073
Cashe's Green Gloucs 35 SO8305
Cashlie Tays 124 NN4942
Cashmoor Dorset 11 ST9813
Cassington Oxon 37 SP4511
Cassop Colliery Dur 96 NZ3438
Castel Guern 152 GN0000
Castell Gwynd 69 SH7669
Castell-y-bwch Gwent 34 ST2792
Castellau M Glam 33 ST0687
Casterton Cumb 87 SD6279
Casterton Lancs 87 SD6279
Castle Cnwll 4 SX0958
Castle Gwynd 69 SH7669
Castle Acre Norfk 66 TF8115
Castle Ashby Nhants 51 SP8659
Castle Bolton N York 88 SE0391
Castle Bromwich W Mids 61 SP1489
Castle Bytham Lincs 63 SK9818
Castle Caereinion Powys 58 SJ1605
Castle Camps Cambs 53 TL6242
Castle Carrock Cumb 94 NY5455
Castle Cary Somset 21 ST6332
Castle Combe Wilts 35 ST8477
Castle Donington Leics 62 SK4427
Castle Douglas D & G 99 NX7662
Castle Eaton Wilts 36 SU1495
Castle Eden Dur 96 NZ4338
Castle End Cambs 64 TF1208
Castle Frome H & W 47 SO6645
Castle Gate Cnwll 2 SW4934
Castle Green Cumb 87 SD5391
Castle Green Surrey 25 SU9761
Castle Gresley Derbys 73 SK2717
Castle Hedingham Essex 53 TL7835
Castle Hill Kent 28 TQ6942
Castle Hill Suffk 54 TM1446
Castle Howard N York 90 SE7069
Castle Inn Cumb 93 NY2233
Castle Kennedy D & G 98 NX1059
Castle Lachlan Strath 114 NS0195
Castle Morris Dyfed 30 SM9031
Castle O'er D & G 101 NY2492
Castle Pulverbatch Shrops 59 SJ4202
Castle Rising Norfk 65 TF6624
Castle Street W York 82 SD9524
Castle Stuart Highld 140 NH7349
Castlebay W Isls 154 NL6698
Castlebythe Dyfed 30 SN0229
Castlecary Strath 116 NS7878
Castlecraig Highld 147 NH8269
Castlecroft W Mids 60 SO8797
Castleford W York 83 SE4225
Castlehill Border 109 NT2135
Castlehill Highld 151 ND1968
Castlehill Strath 116 NS8452
Castlemartin Dyfed 30 SR9198
Castlemilk D & G 100 NY1577
Castlemorton H & W 47 SO7937
Castleside Dur 95 NZ0748
Castlethorpe Bucks 38 SP7944
Castlethorpe Humb 84 SE9807
Castleton Border 101 NY5190
Castleton Derbys 74 SK1582
Castleton Gt Man 79 SD8810
Castleton Gwent 34 ST2583
Castleton N York 90 NZ6808
Castleton Strath 113 NR8884
Castletown Dorset 11 SY6874
Castletown Highld 151 ND1967
Castletown Highld 140 NH7442
Castletown IOM 153 SC2667
Castletown T & W 96 NZ3558
Castley N York 82 SE2645
Caston Norfk 66 TL9597
Castor Cambs 64 TL1298
Cat & Fiddle Inn Derbys 79 SK0072
Cat's Ash Gwent 34 ST3790
Catacol Strath 105 NR9149
Catbrain Avon 34 ST5780
Catbrook Gwent 34 SO5102
Catch Clwyd 70 SJ2070
Catchall Cnwll 2 SW4328
Catchem's Corner W Mids 61 SP2576
Catchgate Dur 96 NZ1652
Catcliffe S York 74 SK4288
Catcomb Wilts 35 SU0076
Catcott Somset 21 ST3939
Catcott Burtle Somset 21 ST4043
Caterham Surrey 27 TQ3455
Catfield Norfk 67 TG3821
Catfield Common Norfk 67 TG4021
Catfirth Shet 155 HU4354
Catford Gt Lon 27 TQ3772
Catforth Lancs 80 SD4735
Cath Pair Border 118 NT4646
Cathcart Strath 115 NS5860
Cathedine Powys 45 SO1425
Catherine de-Barnes Heath W Mids 61 SP1780
Catherine Slack W York 82 SE0928
Catherington Hants 13 SU6914
Catherston Leweston Dorset 10 SY3694
Catherton Shrops 47 SO6578
Catisfield Hants 13 SU5406
Catley Lane Head Gt Man 81 SD8715
Catley Southfield H & W 47 SO6844
Catlodge Highld 132 NN6392
Catlow Lancs 81 SD8836
Catlowdy Cumb 101 NY4677
Catmere End Essex 39 TL4939
Catmore Berks 37 SU4580
Caton Lancs 87 SD5364
Caton Green Lancs 87 SD5564
Cator Court Devon 8 SX6877
Catrine Strath 107 NS5225
Catsfield E Susx 17 TQ7213
Catsfield Stream E Susx 17 TQ7113
Catsham Somset 21 ST5534
Catshill H & W 60 SO9673
Catstree Shrops 60 SO7496
Catsyke W York 83 SE4324
Cattadale Strath 105 NR6710
Cattal N York 83 SE4454
Cattawade Suffk 41 TM1033
Catterall Lancs 80 SD5042
Catteralslane Shrops 71 SJ5640
Catterick N York 89 SE2397
Catterick Bridge N York 89 SE2299
Catterick Camp N York 89 SE1897
Catterlen Cumb 94 NY4833
Catterton N York 83 SE5145
Catteshall Surrey 25 SU9844
Catthorpe Leics 50 SP5578
Cattishall Suffk 54 TL8865
Cattistock Dorset 10 SY5999
Catton Cumb 95 NY8257
Catton N York 89 SE3678
Catton Norfk 67 TG2312
Catwick Humb 85 TA1245
Catworth Cambs 51 TL0873
Caudle Green Gloucs 35 SO9410
Caulcott Beds 38 TL0042
Caulcott Oxon 49 SP5024
Cauldcots Tays 127 NO6547
Cauldhame Cent 116 NS6493
Cauldmill Border 109 NT5315
Cauldon Staffs 73 SK0749
Cauldon Lowe Staffs 73 SK0747
Cauldside D & G 101 NY4480
Cauldwell Derbys 73 SK2517
Caulkerbush D & G 92 NX9357
Caundle Marsh Dorset 11 ST6713
Caunsall H & W 60 SO8581
Caunton Notts 75 SK7460
Causeway Hants 13 SU7422
Causeway End Cumb 87 SD4885
Causeway End D & G 99 NX4260
Causeway End Essex 40 TL6819
Causewayend Strath 108 NT0336
Causewayhead Cent 116 NS8095
Causey Park Nthumb 103 NZ1794
Causeyend Gramp 143 NJ9419
Caute Devon 18 SS4310
Cautley Cumb 87 SD6994
Cavendish Suffk 54 TL8046
Cavenham Suffk 53 TL7669
Caversfield Oxon 49 SP5825
Caversham Berks 24 SU7274
Caverswall Staffs 72 SJ9542
Caverton Mill Border 110 NT7425
Cavil Humb 84 SE7630
Cawdor Highld 140 NH8450
Cawkwell Lincs 77 TF2879
Cawood N York 83 SE5737
Cawsand Cnwll 6 SX4350
Cawston Norfk 66 TG1323
Cawston Warwks 50 SP4773
Cawthorn N York 90 SE7788
Cawthorne S York 82 SE2807
Caxton Cambs 52 TL3058
Caxton End Cambs 52 TL2759
Caxton End Cambs 52 TL3157
Caxton Gibbet Cambs 52 TL2960
Caynham Shrops 46 SO5573
Caythorpe Lincs 76 SK9348
Caythorpe Notts 63 SK6845
Cayton N York 91 TA0583
Ceannacroc Lodge Highld 131 NH3211
Ceciliford Gwent 34 SO5003
Cefn Gwent 34 ST2788
Cefn Berain Clwyd 70 SH9969
Cefn Byrle Powys 33 SN8311
Cefn Canel Clwyd 58 SJ2331
Cefn Coch Powys 58 SJ1026
Cefn Cribwr M Glam 33 SS8582
Cefn Cross M Glam 33 SS8682
Cefn Mably M Glam 34 ST2284
Cefn-brith Clwyd 70 SH9350
Cefn-bryn-brain Dyfed 32 SN7413
Cefn-coed-y-cymmer M Glam 33 SO0308
Cefn-ddwysarn Gwynd 70 SH9638
Cefn-Einion Shrops 58 SO2886
Cefn-mawr Clwyd 70 SJ2842
Cefn-y-bedd Clwyd 71 SJ3156
Cefn-y-pant Dyfed 31 SN1925
Cefneithin Dyfed 32 SN5514
Cefngorwydd Powys 45 SN9045
Cefnpennar M Glam 33 SO0300
Ceint Gwynd 68 SH4875
Cellan Dyfed 44 SN6149
Cellarhead Staffs 72 SJ9547
Cellerton Cumb 94 NY4925
Celynen Gwent 33 ST2195
Cemaes Gwynd 68 SH3793
Cemmaes Powys 57 SH8406
Cemmaes Road Powys 57 SH8104
Cenarth Dyfed 31 SN2641
Cennin Gwynd 56 SH4645
Cerbyd Dyfed 30 SM8227
Ceres Fife 126 NO4011
Cerne Abbas Dorset 11 ST6601
Cerney Wick Gloucs 36 SU0796
Cerrigceinwen Gwynd 68 SH4274
Cerrigydrudion Clwyd 70 SH9548
Cess Norfk 67 TG4417
Ceunant Gwynd 69 SH5361
Chaceley Gloucs 47 SO8530
Chacewater Cnwll 3 SW7444
Chackmore Bucks 49 SP6835
Chacombe Nhants 49 SP4943
Chadbury H & W 47 SP0146
Chadderton Gt Man 79 SD9204
Chadderton Fold Gt Man 79 SD9006
Chaddesden Derbys 62 SK3737
Chaddesley Corbett H & W 60 SO8973
Chaddlehanger Devon 5 SX4678
Chaddleworth Berks 36 SU4177
Chadlington Oxon 36 SP3222
Chadshunt Warwks 48 SP3552
Chadwell Leics 63 SK7824
Chadwell Shrops 60 SJ7814
Chadwell End Beds 51 TL0865
Chadwell Heath Gt Lon 27 TQ4888
Chadwell St. Mary Essex 40 TQ6478
Chadwick H & W 47 SO8369
Chadwick End W Mids 61 SP2073
Chadwick Green Mersyd 78 SJ5299
Chaffcombe Somset 10 ST3510
Chagford Devon 8 SX7087
Chailey E Susx 15 TQ3919
Chainbridge Cambs 65 TL4299
Chainhurst Kent 28 TQ7248
Chalbury Common Dorset 12 SU0206
Chaldon Surrey 27 TQ3055
Chaldon Herring or East C Dorset 11 SY7983
Chale IOW 13 SZ4877
Chale Green IOW 13 SZ4879
Chalfont Common Bucks 26 TQ0092
Chalfont St. Giles Bucks 26 SU9893
Chalfont St. Peter Bucks 26 TQ0090
Chalford Gloucs 35 SO8902
Chalford Oxon 37 SP7101
Chalford Wilts 22 ST8750
Chalgrove Beds 38 TL0127
Chalgrove Oxon 37 SU6396
Chalk Kent 28 TQ6773
Chalk End Essex 40 TL6310
Chalkhouse Green Berks 37 SU7178
Chalkway Somset 10 ST3707
Chalkwell Kent 28 TQ8963
Challaborough Devon 7 SX6545
Challacombe Devon 19 SS6941
Challoch D & G 99 NX3867
Challock Lees Kent 28 TR0050
Chalmington Dorset 10 ST5901
Chalton Beds 52 TL1450
Chalton Beds 38 TL0326
Chalton Hants 13 SU7316
Chalvey Berks 26 SU9679
Chalvington E Susx 16 TQ5109
Chambers Green Kent 28 TQ9243
Chandler's Cross Herts 26 TQ0698
Chandler's Ford Hants 13 SU4320
Chanler's Cross H & W 47 SO7738
Channel's Green Beds 51 TL1057
Chantry Somset 22 ST7146
Chantry Suffk 54 TM1443
Chapel Cumb 93 NY2231
Chapel Fife 117 NT2593
Chapel Allerton Somset 21 ST4050
Chapel Allerton W York 82 SE3037
Chapel Amble Cnwll 4 SW9975
Chapel Brampton Nhants 50 SP7266
Chapel Chorlton Staffs 72 SJ8137
Chapel Cross E Susx 16 TQ6120
Chapel End Beds 38 TL0542
Chapel End Beds 51 TL1057
Chapel End Cambs 52 TL1282
Chapel End Warwks 61 SP3393
Chapel Field Gt Man 79 SD7906
Chapel Green Warwks 49 SP4660
Chapel Green Warwks 61 SP2785
Chapel Haddlesey N York 83 SE5826
Chapel Hall Strath 114 NS1368
Chapel Hill Gramp 143 NK0635
Chapel Hill Gwent 34 SO5300
Chapel Hill Lincs 76 TF2054
Chapel Hill N York 83 SE3346
Chapel Lawn Shrops 46 SO3176
Chapel Le Dale N York 88 SD7377
Chapel Leigh Somset 20 ST1222
Chapel Milton Derbys 74 SK0581
Chapel of Garioch Gramp 142 NJ7124
Chapel Rossan D & G 98 NX1044
Chapel Row Berks 24 SU5669
Chapel Row E Susx 16 TQ6312
Chapel Row Essex 40 TL7900
Chapel St. Leonards Lincs 77 TF5572
Chapel Stile Cumb 86 NY3205
Chapel Town Cnwll 3 SW8855
Chapel-en-le-Frith Derbys 74 SK0580
Chapelbridge Cambs 64 TL2993
Chapelend Way Essex 53 TL7139
Chapelgate Lincs 65 TF4124
Chapelhall Strath 116 NS7862
Chapelhill Tays 125 NO0030
Chapelhope Border 109 NT2308
Chapelknowe D & G 101 NY3173
Chapelknowe D & G 101 NY3173
Chapelton Devon 19 SS5826
Chapelton Strath 116 NS6848
Chapelton Tays 127 NO6247
Chapeltown Gramp 141 NJ2320
Chapeltown Lancs 81 SD7315
Chapeltown S York 74 SK3596
Chapmans Well Devon 5 SX3592
Chapmanslade Wilts 22 ST8247
Chapmore End Herts 39 TL3216
Chappel Essex 40 TL8928
Charaton M Glam 5 SX3169
Chard Somset 10 ST3208
Chard Junction Somset 10 ST3404
Chardleigh Green Somset 10 ST3110
Chardleigh Green Somset 10 ST3110
Chardleigh Green Somset 10 ST3110
Chardstock Devon 10 ST3004
Charfield Avon 35 ST7292
Chargrove Gloucs 35 SO9219
Charing Kent 28 TQ9549
Charing Heath Kent 28 TQ9249
Charing Hill Kent 28 TQ9550
Charingworth Gloucs 48 SP1939
Charlbury Oxon 36 SP3519
Charlcombe Avon 22 ST7467
Charlcutt Wilts 35 ST9875
Charlecote Warwks 48 SP2656
Charles Devon 19 SS6832
Charles Tye Suffk 54 TM0252
Charleshill Surrey 25 SU8944
Charleston Tays 126 NO3845
Charlestown Cnwll 3 SX0351
Charlestown Derbys 74 SK0392
Charlestown Dorset 11 SY6579
Charlestown Fife 117 NT0683
Charlestown Gramp 135 NJ9300
Charlestown Gt Man 79 SD8100
Charlestown Highld 144 NG8174
Charlestown Highld 140 NH6448
Charlestown Lincs 63 SK9844
Charlestown W York 82 SE1538
Charlestown W York 82 SD9726
Charlesworth Derbys 79 SK0093
Charlinch Somset 20 ST2338
Charlton Gt Lon 27 TQ4277
Charlton H & W 60 SO8371
Charlton H & W 47 SP0045
Charlton Hants 23 SU3547
Charlton Herts 39 TL1728
Charlton Nhants 49 SP5236
Charlton Nthumb 102 NY8184
Charlton Oxon 36 SU4088
Charlton Shrops 59 SJ5911
Charlton Somset 20 ST2827
Charlton Somset 21 ST6242
Charlton W Susx 14 SU8812
Charlton Wilts 22 ST9021
Charlton Wilts 35 ST9688
Charlton Wilts 23 SU1155
Charlton Wilts 23 SU1723
Charlton Abbots Gloucs 48 SP0324
Charlton Adam Somset 21 ST5328
Charlton Hill Shrops 59 SJ5807
Charlton Horethorne Somset 22 ST6623
Charlton Kings Gloucs 35 SO9620
Charlton Mackrell Somset 21 ST5228
Charlton Marshall Dorset 11 ST8903
Charlton Musgrove Somset 22 ST7229
Charlton on the Hill Dorset 11 ST8903
Charlton-on-Otmoor Oxon 37 SP5616
Charlwood Hants 24 SU6731
Charlwood Surrey 15 TQ2441
Charminster Dorset 11 SY6792
Charmouth Dorset 10 SY3693
Charndon Bucks 49 SP6724
Charney Bassett Oxon 36 SU3894
Charnock Green Lancs 81 SD5516
Charnock Richard Lancs 81 SD5515
Charsfield Suffk 55 TM2556
Chart Corner Kent 28 TQ7950
Chart Hill Kent 28 TQ7949
Chart Sutton Kent 28 TQ8049
Charter Alley Hants 24 SU5957
Charterhall Border 110 NT7647
Charterhouse Somset 21 ST4955
Chartershall Cent 116 NS7990
Charterville Allotments Oxon 36 SP3110
Chartham Kent 29 TR1054
Chartham Hatch Kent 29 TR1056
Charton Surrey 26 TQ0869
Chartridge Bucks 38 SP9303
Chartway Street Kent 28 TQ8350
Charwelton Nhants 49 SP5355
Chase Terrace Staffs 61 SK0409
Chasetown Staffs 61 SK0408
Chastleton Oxon 48 SP2429
Chasty Devon 18 SS3330
Chatburn Lancs 81 SD7644
Chatcull Staffs 72 SJ7934
Chatham Gwent 33 ST2189
Chatham Kent 28 TQ7567
Chatham Green Essex 40 TL7115
Chathill Nthumb 111 NU1827
Chatley H & W 47 SO8561
Chattenden Kent 28 TQ7572
Chatter End Essex 39 TL4725
Chatteris Cambs 52 TL3985
Chatterton Lancs 81 SD7918
Chattisham Suffk 54 TM0942
Chatto Border 110 NT7717
Chatton Nthumb 111 NU0528
Chawleigh Devon 19 SS7112
Chawley Oxon 37 SP4604
Chawston Beds 52 TL1556
Chawton Hants 24 SU7037
Chaxhill Gloucs 35 SO7414
Chazey Heath Oxon 37 SU6977
Cheadle Gt Man 79 SJ8688
Cheadle Staffs 73 SK0043
Cheadle Heath Gt Man 79 SJ8789
Cheadle Hulme Gt Man 79 SJ8786
Cheam Gt Lon 27 TQ2563
Cheapside Berks 25 SU9469
Chearsley Bucks 37 SP7110
Chebsey Staffs 72 SJ8528
Checkendon Oxon 37 SU6683
Checkley Ches 72 SJ7346
Checkley Staffs 73 SK0237
Checkley Green Ches 72 SJ7245
Chedburgh Suffk 53 TL7957
Cheddar Somset 21 ST4553
Cheddington Bucks 38 SP9217
Cheddleton Staffs 72 SJ9752
Cheddleton Heath Staffs 72 SJ9853
Cheddon Fitzpaine Somset 20 ST2327
Chedglow Wilts 35 ST9492
Chedgrave Norfk 67 TM3699
Chedington Dorset 10 ST4805
Chediston Suffk 55 TM3577
Chediston Green Suffk 55 TM3578
Chedworth Gloucs 36 SP0511
Chedzoy Somset 21 ST3337
Cheesden Gt Man 81 SD8216
Cheeseman's Green Kent 28 TR0238
Cheetham Hill Gt Man 79 SD8301
Cheetwood Gt Man 79 SJ8399
Cheldon Devon 19 SS7313
Chelford Ches 79 SJ8174
Chellaston Derbys 62 SK3730
Chellington Beds 51 SP9555
Chelmarsh Shrops 60 SO7288
Chelmondiston Suffk 55 TM2037
Chelmorton Derbys 74 SK1169
Chelmsford Essex 40 TL7007
Chelmsley Wood W Mids 61 SP1886
Chelsea Gt Lon 27 TQ2778
Chelsfield Gt Lon 27 TQ4864
Chelsham Surrey 27 TQ3758
Chelston Somset 20 ST1720
Chelsworth Suffk 54 TL9748
Cheltenham Gloucs 35 SO9422
Chelveston Nhants 51 SP9969
Chelvey Avon 21 ST4668
Chelwood Avon 21 ST6361
Chelwood Common E Susx 15 TQ4128
Chelwood Gate E Susx 15 TQ4130
Chelworth Wilts 35 ST9694
Chelworth Lower Green Wilts 36 SU0892
Chelworth Upper Green Wilts 36 SU0892
Cheney Longville Shrops 59 SO4284
Chenies Bucks 26 TQ0198
Chepstow Gwent 34 ST5393
Chequerbent Gt Man 79 SD6706
Chequers Corner Norfk 65 TF4908
Cherhill Wilts 36 SU0370
Cherington Gloucs 35 ST9098
Cherington Warwks 48 SP2936
Cheriton Devon 19 SS7346
Cheriton Devon 9 ST1001
Cheriton Devon 19 SS7346
Cheriton Hants 24 SU5828
Cheriton Kent 29 TR2037
Cheriton W Glam 32 SS4593
Cheriton Bishop Devon 8 SX7793
Cheriton Fitzpaine Devon 9 SS8606
Cheriton or Stackpole Eli Dyfed 30 SR9997
Cherrington Shrops 72 SJ6619
Cherry Burton Humb 84 SE9842
Cherry Hinton Cambs 53 TL4856
Cherry Orchard H & W 47 SO8553
Cherry Willingham Lincs 76 TF0372
Chertsey Surrey 26 TQ0466
Cheselbourne Dorset 11 SY7699
Chesham Bucks 26 SP9601
Chesham Gt Man 81 SD8012
Chesham Bois Bucks 26 SU9699
Cheshunt Herts 27 TL3502
Chesley Kent 28 TQ8563
Cheslyn Hay Staffs 60 SJ9707
Chessetts Wood Warwks 61 SP1873
Chessington Surrey 26 TQ1863
Chester Ches 71 SJ4066
Chester Moor Dur 96 NZ2649
Chester-le-Street T & W 96 NZ2751
Chesterblade Somset 22 ST6641
Chesterfield Derbys 74 SK3871

Chesterfield Clunie

Chesterfield Staffs 61 SK1005
Chesterhill Loth 118 NT3765
Chesters Border 110 NT6022
Chesters Border 110 NT6210
Chesterton Cambs 64 TL1295
Chesterton Cambs 53 TL4660
Chesterton Gloucs 35 SP0200
Chesterton Oxon 37 SP5621
Chesterton Shrops 60 SO7897
Chesterton Staffs 72 SJ8349
Chesterton Green Warwks 48 SP3558
Chesterwood Nthumb 102 NY8365
Chestfield Kent 29 TR1365
Chestnut Street Kent 28 TQ8862
Cheston Devon 7 SX6758
Cheswardine Shrops 72 SJ7130
Cheswell Shrops 72 SJ7116
Cheswick Nthumb 111 NU0346
Cheswick Green W Mids 61 SP1376
Chetnole Dorset 10 ST6008
Chettiscombe Devon 9 SS9614
Chettiscombe Devon 9 SS9614
Chettisham Cambs 53 TL5483
Chettle Dorset 11 ST9513
Chetton Shrops 60 SO6690
Chetwode Bucks 49 SP6429
Chetwynd Shrops 72 SJ7321
Chetwynd Aston Shrops 72 SJ7517
Cheveley Cambs 53 TL6861
Chevening Kent 27 TQ4857
Cheverton IOW 13 SZ4584
Chevington Suffk 53 TL7860
Chevington Drift Nthumb 103 NZ2598
Chevithorne Devon 9 SS9715
Chew Magna Avon 21 ST5763
Chew Moor Gt Man 79 SD6607
Chew Stoke Avon 21 ST5561
Chewton Keynsham Avon 21 ST6566
Chewton Mendip Somset 21 ST5952
Chichacott Devon 8 SX6296
Chicheley Bucks 38 SP9046
Chichester W Susx 14 SU8604
Chickerell Dorset 11 SY6480
Chickering Suffk 55 TM2176
Chicklade Wilts 22 ST9134
Chickward H & W 46 SO2853
Chidden Hants 13 SU6517
Chiddingfold Surrey 14 SU9635
Chiddingly E Susx 16 TQ5414
Chiddingstone Kent 16 TQ5045
Chiddingstone Causeway Kent 16 TQ5146
Chideock Dorset 10 SY4292
Chidgley Somset 20 ST0436
Chidham W Susx 14 SU7903
Chidswell W York 82 SE2623
Chieveley Berks 24 SU4773
Chignall Smealy Essex 40 TL6611
Chignall St. James Essex 40 TL6610
Chigwell Essex 27 TQ4494
Chigwell Row Essex 27 TQ4693
Chilbolton Hants 23 SU3939
Chilcomb Hants 24 SU5028
Chilcombe Dorset 10 SY5291
Chilcompton Somset 21 ST6452
Chilcote Leics 61 SK2811
Child Okeford Dorset 11 ST8312
Child's Ercall Shrops 72 SJ6625
Childer Thornton Ches 71 SJ3677
Childrey Oxon 36 SU3687
Childswickham H & W 48 SP0738
Childwall Mersyd 78 SJ4189
Childwick Bury Herts 38 TL1410
Childwick Green Herts 38 TL1410
Chilfrome Dorset 10 SY5898
Chilgrove W Susx 14 SU8314
Chilham Kent 29 TR0653
Chilhampton Wilts 23 SU0933
Chilla Devon 18 SS4402
Chillaton Devon 5 SX4382
Chillenden Kent 29 TR2653
Chillerton IOW 13 SZ4984
Chillesford Suffk 55 TM3852
Chillingham Nthumb 111 NU0525
Chillington Devon 7 SX7942
Chillington Somset 10 ST3811
Chilmark Wilts 22 ST9632
Chilmington Green Kent 28 TQ9740
Chilson Oxon 36 SP3119
Chilsworthy Cnwll 5 SX4172
Chilsworthy Devon 18 SS3206
Chiltern Green Beds 38 TL1319
Chilthorne Domer Somset 21 ST5219
Chiltington E Susx 15 TQ3815
Chilton Bucks 37 SP6811
Chilton Devon 9 SS8604
Chilton Kent 29 TR2743
Chilton Oxon 37 SU4885
Chilton Suffk 54 TL8942
Chilton Candover Hants 24 SU5940
Chilton Cantelo Somset 21 ST5621
Chilton Foliat Wilts 36 SU3170
Chilton Polden Somset 21 ST3739
Chilton Street Suffk 53 TL7547
Chilton Trinity Somset 20 ST2939
Chilwell Notts 62 SK5135
Chilworth Hants 13 SU4118
Chilworth Surrey 14 TQ0247
Chimney Oxon 36 SP3501
Chineham Hants 24 SU6554
Chingford Gt Lon 27 TQ3894
Chinley Derbys 74 SK0482
Chinnor Oxon 37 SP7501
Chipchase Castle Nthumb 102 NY8775
Chipnall Shrops 72 SJ7231
Chippenham Bucks 26 SU9480
Chippenham Cambs 53 TL6669
Chippenham Wilts 35 ST9273
Chipperfield Herts 26 TL0401
Chipping Herts 39 TL3532
Chipping Lancs 81 SD6243
Chipping Campden Gloucs 48 SP1539
Chipping Hill Essex 40 TL8215
Chipping Norton Oxon 48 SP3127
Chipping Ongar Essex 39 TL5503
Chipping Sodbury Avon 35 ST7281
Chipping Warden Nhants 49 SP4948
Chipstable Somset 20 ST0427
Chipstead Kent 27 TQ5056
Chipstead Surrey 27 TQ2757
Chirbury Shrops 58 SO2698
Chirk Clwyd 71 SJ2938
Chirnside Border 119 NT8756
Chirnsidebridge Border 119 NT8556
Chirton Wilts 23 SU0757
Chisbury Wilts 23 SU2766
Chiselborough Somset 10 ST4614
Chiseldon Wilts 36 SU1879
Chisholme Border 109 NT4112
Chislehampton Oxon 37 SU5999
Chislehurst Gt Lon 27 TQ4470
Chislet Kent 29 TR2264
Chisley W York 82 SE0028
Chiswellgreen Herts 38 TL1304
Chiswick Gt Lon 26 TQ2078
Chiswick End Cambs 52 TL3745
Chisworth Derbys 79 SJ9991
Chisworth Derbys 79 SJ9991
Chitcombe E Susx 17 TQ8120
Chithurst W Susx 14 SU8423
Chittering Cambs 53 TL4969
Chitterne Wilts 22 ST9843
Chittlehamholt Devon 19 SS6421
Chittlehampton Devon 19 SS6325
Chittlehampton Devon 19 SS6511
Chittoe Wilts 22 ST9566
Chivelstone Devon 7 SX7838
Chivelstone Devon 7 SX7838
Chivenor Devon 19 SS5034
Chlenry D & G 98 NX1261
Chobham Surrey 25 SU9762
Cholderton Wilts 23 SU2242
Cholesbury Bucks 38 SP9307
Chollerford Nthumb 102 NY9170
Chollerton Nthumb 102 NY9372
Cholsey Oxon 37 SU5886
Cholstrey H & W 46 SO4659
Chop Gate N York 90 SE5699
Choppington T & W 103 NZ2484
Chopwell T & W 95 NZ1158
Chorley Ches 71 SJ5751
Chorley Lancs 81 SD5817
Chorley Shrops 60 SO6983
Chorley Staffs 61 SK0711
Chorleywood Herts 26 TQ0396
Chorleywood West Herts 26 TQ0296
Chorlton Ches 72 SJ7250
Chorlton Lane Ches 71 SJ4548
Chorlton-cum-Hardy Gt Man 79 SJ8193
Choulton Shrops 59 SO3788
Chowley Ches 71 SJ4756
Chrishall Essex 39 TL4439
Chrisswell Strath 114 NS2274
Christchurch Cambs 65 TL4996
Christchurch Dorset 12 SZ1593
Christchurch Gloucs 34 SO5713
Christchurch Gwent 34 ST3489
Christian Malford Wilts 35 ST9678
Christleton Ches 71 SJ4465
Christmas Common Oxon 37 SU7193
Christon Avon 21 ST3956
Christon Bank Nthumb 111 NU2123
Christow Devon 8 SX8385
Christskirk Gramp 142 NJ6027
Christskirk Gramp 142 NJ6027
Chuck Hatch E Susx 16 TQ4733
Chudleigh Devon 9 SX8679
Chudleigh Knighton Devon 8 SX8477
Chulmleigh Devon 19 SS6814
Chunal Derbys 74 SK0391
Church Lancs 81 SD7429
Church Ashton Shrops 72 SJ7317
Church Brampton Nhants 50 SP7165
Church Brough Cumb 95 NY7913
Church Broughton Derbys 73 SK2033
Church Crookham Hants 25 SU8152
Church Eaton Staffs 72 SJ8417
Church End Beds 38 SP9921
Church End Beds 38 SP9832
Church End Beds 38 TL0334
Church End Beds 51 TL0458
Church End Beds 51 TL1059
Church End Beds 39 TL1937
Church End Cambs 52 TL3278
Church End Cambs 52 TL2083
Church End Cambs 51 TL0973
Church End Cambs 65 TF3909
Church End Cambs 53 TL4857
Church End Essex 40 TL7416
Church End Essex 40 TL7228
Church End Essex 40 TL6323
Church End Gt Lon 26 TQ2490
Church End Hants 24 SU6756
Church End Herts 39 TL4422
Church End Herts 39 TL2630
Church End Herts 38 TL1011
Church End Lincs 64 TF2234
Church End Lincs 77 TF4195
Church End Warwks 61 SP2892
Church End Warwks 61 SP2491
Church End Street Essex 53 TL7943
Church Enstone Oxon 48 SP3725
Church Fenton N York 83 SE5136
Church Green Devon 9 SY1796
Church Gresley Derbys 73 SK2918
Church Hanborough Oxon 36 SP4212
Church Hill Ches 72 SJ6465
Church Hill Staffs 60 SK0012
Church Houses N York 90 SE6697
Church Knowle Dorset 11 SY9481
Church Laneham Notts 75 SK8176
Church Langton Leics 50 SP7293
Church Lawford Warwks 50 SP4576
Church Lawton Staffs 72 SJ8255
Church Leigh Staffs 73 SK0235
Church Lench H & W 48 SP0251
Church Mayfield Staffs 73 SK1544
Church Minshull Ches 72 SJ6660
Church Norton W Susx 14 SZ8695
Church Preen Shrops 59 SO5498
Church Pulverbatch Shrops 59 SJ4303
Church Stoke Powys 58 SO2694
Church Stowe Nhants 49 SP6357
Church Street Kent 28 TQ7174
Church Street Suffk 55 TM4883
Church Stretton Shrops 59 SO4593
Church Town Humb 84 SE7806
Church Village M Glam 33 ST0886
Church Warsop Notts 75 SK5668
Church Wilne Derbys 62 SK4431
Churcham Gloucs 35 SO7618
Churchbridge Staffs 60 SJ9808
Churchdown Gloucs 35 SO8819
Churchend Essex 41 TR0093
Churchfield W Mids 60 SP0092
Churchgate Herts 27 TL3402
Churchgate Street Essex 39 TL4811
Churchill Avon 21 ST4359
Churchill Devon 10 ST2901
Churchill Devon 19 SS5940
Churchill H & W 60 SO8879
Churchill H & W 47 SO9253
Churchill Oxon 48 SP2824
Churchill Green Avon 21 ST4360
Churchingford Devon 9 ST2112
Churchover Warwks 50 SP5180
Churchstanton Somset 9 ST1914
Churchstow Devon 7 SX7145
Churchthorpe Lincs 77 TF3297
Churchtown Cumb 93 NY3742
Churchtown Derbys 74 SK2663
Churchtown Devon 19 SS6744
Churchtown IOM 153 SC4294
Churchtown Lancs 80 SD3240
Churchtown Lancs 80 SD4843
Churchtown Mersyd 80 SD3618
Churnsike Lodge Nthumb 102 NY6777
Churston Ferrers Devon 7 SX9056
Churt Surrey 25 SU8538
Churton Ches 71 SJ4156
Churwell W York 82 SE2729
Chute Lodge Wilts 23 SU3151
Chwilog Gwynd 56 SH4338
Chyandour Cnwll 2 SW4731
Chyanvounder Cnwll 2 SW6522
Chyeowling Cnwll 3 SW7941
Chyvarloe Cnwll 2 SW6523
Cil Powys 58 SJ1701
Cilcain Clwyd 70 SJ1765
Cilcennin Dyfed 44 SN5160
Cilcewydd Powys 58 SJ2304
Cilfrew W Glam 32 SN7700
Cilfynydd M Glam 33 ST0892
Cilgerran Dyfed 31 SN1943
Cilgwyn Dyfed 44 SN7429
Ciliau-Aeron Dyfed 44 SN5058
Cilmaengwyn W Glam 32 SN7406
Cilmery Powys 45 SO0051
Cilrhedyn Dyfed 31 SN2835
Cilsan Dyfed 32 SN5922
Ciltalgarth Gwynd 57 SH8840
Cilycwm Dyfed 44 SN7540
Cimla W Glam 32 SS7696
Cinder Hill W Mids 60 SO9294
Cinderford Gloucs 35 SO6513
Cirencester Gloucs 35 SP0201
Citadilla N York 89 NZ2200
City S Glam 33 SS9878
City Dulas Gwynd 68 SH4687
Clabhach Strath 120 NM1858
Clachaig Strath 114 NS1181
Clachan Highld 137 NG5436
Clachan S Glam 113 NR7656
Clachan Strath 122 NM7819
Clachan Strath 122 NM8543
Clachan Strath 123 NN1812
Clachan W Isls 154 NF7746
Clachan W Isls 154 NF8163
Clachan Mor Strath 120 NL9847
Clachan-Seil Strath 122 NM7718
Clachaneasy D & G 98 NX3575
Clachbreck Strath 113 NR7675
Clachnaharry Highld 140 NH6446
Clachtoll Highld 145 NC0427
Clackavoid Tays 133 NO1463
Clackmannan Cent 116 NS9191
Clackmarass Gramp 141 NJ2458
Clacton-on-Sea Essex 41 TM1715
Cladich Strath 123 NN0921
Cladswell H & W 48 SP0458
Claggan Highld 122 NM6949
Claigan Highld 136 NG2354
Clandown Avon 22 ST6955
Clanfield Hants 13 SU6916
Clanfield Oxon 36 SP2801
Clannaborough Devon 8 SS7402
Clanville Hants 23 SU3148
Clanville Somset 21 ST6232
Clanyard D & G 98 NX1037
Claonaig Strath 113 NR8656
Clap Hill Kent 28 TR0537
Clapgate Dorset 11 SU0102
Clapgate Herts 39 TL4424
Clapham Beds 38 TL0352
Clapham Devon 9 SX8987
Clapham Gt Lon 27 TQ2875
Clapham N York 88 SD7469
Clapham W Susx 14 TQ0906
Clapham Folly Beds 38 TL0252
Clappersgate Cumb 87 NY3603
Clapton Somset 22 ST6852
Clapton Somset 10 ST4106
Clapton Somset 21 ST6453
Clapton-in-Gordano Avon 34 ST4773
Clapton-on-the-Hill Gloucs 36 SP1617
Clapworthy Devon 19 SS6724
Clarach Dyfed 43 SN6084
Claravale T & W 103 NZ1365
Clarbeston Dyfed 30 SN0421
Clarbeston Road Dyfed 30 SN0121
Clarborough Notts 75 SK7383
Clare Suffk 53 TL7745
Clarebrand D & G 99 NX7666
Claredon Park Leics 62 SK6002
Clarencefield D & G 100 NY0968
Clarewood Nthumb 103 NZ0169
Clarilaw Border 109 NT5218
Clark's Green Surrey 15 TQ1739
Clarken Green Hants 24 SU5631
Clarkston Strath 115 NS5757
Clashmore Highld 148 NC0331
Clashmore Highld 146 NH7489
Clashnessie Highld 148 NC0530
Clashnoir Gramp 141 NJ2222
Clathy Tays 108 NS9920
Clathymore Tays 125 NO0121
Clatt Gramp 142 NJ5326
Clatter Powys 58 SN9994
Clatterford End Essex 40 TL6113
Clatworthy Somset 20 ST0530
Claughton Lancs 80 SD5342
Claughton Lancs 87 SD5666
Claughton Mersyd 78 SJ3088
Clavelshay Somset 20 ST2531
Claverdon Warwks 48 SP1965
Claverham Avon 21 ST4566
Clavering Essex 39 TL4731
Claverley Shrops 60 SO7993
Claverton Avon 22 ST7864
Claverton Down Avon 22 ST7763
Clawdd-coch S Glam 33 ST0577
Clawdd-newydd Clwyd 70 SJ0852
Clawthorpe Cumb 87 SD5377
Clawton Devon 18 SX3599
Claxby Lincs 76 TF1194
Claxby Lincs 77 TF4571
Claxton N York 90 SE6959
Claxton Norfk 67 TG3303
Clay Common Suffk 55 TM4781
Clay Coton Nhants 50 SP5977
Clay Cross Derbys 74 SK3963
Clay End Herts 39 TL3024
Claybrooke Magna Leics 50 SP4988
Claydon Oxon 49 SP4549
Claydon Suffk 54 TM1349
Claygate D & G 101 NY3979
Claygate Kent 28 TQ7144
Claygate Surrey 26 TQ1563
Claygate Cross Kent 27 TQ6155
Clayhanger Devon 20 ST0222
Clayhanger W Mids 61 SK0404
Clayhidon Devon 9 ST1615
Clayhill E Susx 17 TQ8323
Clayhill Hants 12 SU3007
Clayhithe Cambs 53 TL5064
Clayock Highld 151 ND1659
Claypits Gloucs 35 SO7606
Claypole Lincs 76 SK8449
Claythorpe Lincs 77 TF4178
Clayton S York 83 SE4507
Clayton W Susx 15 TQ2914
Clayton W York 82 SE1131
Clayton Green Lancs 81 SD5723
Clayton West W York 82 SE2511
Clayton-le-Moors Lancs 81 SD7530
Clayton-le-Woods Lancs 81 SD5622
Clayworth Notts 75 SK7288
Cleadale Highld 128 NM4789
Cleadon T & W 96 NZ3862
Clearbrook Devon 6 SX5265
Clearwell Gloucs 34 SO5608
Clearwell Meend Gloucs 34 SO5808
Cleasby N York 89 NZ2412
Cleat Ork 155 ND4584
Cleatlam Dur 95 NZ1118
Cleator Cumb 92 NY0123
Cleator Moor Cumb 92 NY0125
Cleckheaton W York 82 SE1825
Clee St. Margaret Shrops 59 SO5684
Cleedownton Shrops 59 SO5880
Cleehill Shrops 46 SO5975
Cleekhimin Strath 116 NS7658
Cleestanton Shrops 46 SO5779
Cleethorpes Humb 85 TA3008
Cleeton St. Mary Shrops 46 SO6178
Cleeve Avon 21 ST4666
Cleeve Oxon 37 SU6081
Cleeve Hill Gloucs 47 SO9827
Cleeve Prior H & W 48 SP0849
Clehonger H & W 46 SO4637
Cleish Tays 117 NT0998
Cleland Strath 116 NS7958
Clement Street Kent 27 TQ5671
Clement's End Beds 38 TL0214
Clenamacrie Strath 122 NM9228
Clench Common Wilts 23 SU1765
Clenchwarton Norfk 65 TF5920
Clent H & W 60 SO9279
Clenterty Gramp 142 NJ7760
Cleobury Mortimer Shrops 60 SO6775
Cleobury North Shrops 59 SO6287
Cleongart Strath 105 NR6734
Clephanton Highld 140 NH8150
Cleuch Head Border 110 NT5910
Cleuch-head D & G 108 NS8200
Clevancy Wilts 36 SU0575
Clevedon Avon 34 ST4071
Cleveleys Lancs 80 SD3143
Clevelode H & W 47 SO8347
Cleverton Wilts 35 ST9785
Clewer Somset 21 ST4351
Cley next the Sea Norfk 66 TG0444
Cliburn Cumb 94 NY5724
Cliddesden Hants 24 SU6349
Cliff Warwks 61 SP2198
Cliff End E Susx 17 TQ8813
Cliffe Dur 96 NZ2015
Cliffe Kent 28 TQ7376
Cliffe Lancs 81 SD7333
Cliffe N York 83 SE6631
Cliffe Woods Kent 28 TQ7373
Clifford H & W 46 SO2445
Clifford W York 83 SE4244
Clifford Chambers Warwks 48 SP1952
Clifford's Mesne Gloucs 47 SO7023
Cliffsend Kent 29 TR3464
Clifton Avon 34 ST5774
Clifton Beds 39 TL1639
Clifton Cumb 94 NY5326
Clifton Derbys 73 SK1644
Clifton Gt Man 79 SD7703
Clifton H & W 47 SO8446
Clifton Lancs 80 SD4630
Clifton N York 83 SE5953
Clifton Notts 62 SK5434
Clifton Nthumb 103 NZ2082
Clifton Oxon 49 SP4931
Clifton S York 75 SK5196
Clifton W York 82 SE1948
Clifton W York 82 SE1622
Clifton Campville Staffs 61 SK2510
Clifton Hampden Oxon 37 SU5495
Clifton Reynes Bucks 38 SP9051
Clifton upon Dunsmore Warwks 50 SP5376
Clifton upon Teme H & W 47 SO7161
Cliftonville Kent 29 TR3771
Climping W Susx 14 TQ0002
Clink Somset 22 ST7848
Clint N York 89 SE2559
Clint Green Norfk 66 TG0211
Clinterty Gramp 135 NJ8311
Clintmains Border 110 NT6132
Clipiau Gwynd 57 SH8410
Clippesby Norfk 67 TG4214
Clipsham Leics 63 SK9616
Clipston Nhants 50 SP7181
Clipston Notts 63 SK6333
Clipstone Beds 38 SP9426
Clipstone Notts 75 SK6064
Clitheroe Lancs 81 SD7441
Clive Shrops 59 SJ5124
Cloatley Wilts 35 ST9890
Clocaenog Clwyd 70 SJ0854
Cloch Mhor Highld 139 NH5063
Clochan Gramp 142 NJ4060
Clochtow Tays 127 NO4852
Clock Face Mersyd 78 SJ5291
Cloddiau Powys 58 SJ2009
Clodock H & W 46 SO3227
Cloford Somset 22 ST7244
Clola Gramp 143 NK0043
Clophill Beds 38 TL0838
Clopton Nhants 51 TL0680
Clopton Suffk 55 TM2253
Clopton Corner Suffk 55 TM2254
Clopton Green Suffk 54 TL9759
Clopton Green Suffk 53 TL7655
Clos du Valle Guern 152 GN0000
Close Clark IOM 153 SC2775
Closeburn D & G 100 NX8992
Closeburnmill D & G 100 NX9094
Closworth Somset 10 ST5610
Clothall Herts 39 TL2731
Clotton Ches 71 SJ5264
Cloudesley Bush Warwks 50 SP4686
Clough Gt Man 79 SD9408
Clough Foot W York 81 SD9123
Clough Head Staffs 72 SJ9864
Clough Head W York 82 SE0518
Cloughton N York 91 TA0094
Cloughton Newlands N York 91 TA0096
Clousta Shet 155 HU3157
Clova Tays 134 NO3273
Clovelly Devon 18 SS3124
Clovelly Cross Devon 18 SS3123
Clovenfords Border 109 NT4536
Clovulin Highld 130 NN0063
Clow Bridge Lancs 81 SD8228
Clowne Derbys 75 SK4875
Clows Top H & W 60 SO7171
Cloy Clwyd 71 SJ3943
Cluanie Inn Highld 130 NH0711
Cluanie Lodge Highld 130 NH0910
Clubworthy Cnwll 5 SX2792
Clugston D & G 98 NX3557
Clun Shrops 59 SO3081
Clunas Highld 140 NH8846
Clunbury Shrops 59 SO3780
Clune Highld 140 NH7925
Clunes Highld 131 NN2088
Clungunford Shrops 46 SO4078
Clunie Gramp 142 NJ6450

Clunie Corriegour

Clunie *Tays*	**126**	NO1043
Clunton *Shrops*	**59**	SO3381
Clutton *Avon*	**21**	ST6159
Clutton *Ches*	**71**	SJ4654
Clutton Hill *Avon*	**21**	ST6359
Clwt-y-bont *Gwynd*	**69**	SH5763
Clydach *Gwent*	**34**	SO2213
Clydach *W Glam*	**32**	SN6801
Clydach Vale *M Glam*	**33**	SS9792
Clydebank *Strath*	**115**	NS5069
Clydey *Dyfed*	**31**	SN2535
Clyffe Pypard *Wilts*	**36**	SU0776
Clynder *Strath*	**114**	NS2484
Clynderwen *Dyfed*	**31**	SN1219
Clyne *W Glam*	**32**	SN8000
Clynelish *Highld*	**147**	NC8905
Clynnog-fawr *Gwynd*	**68**	SH4149
Clyro *Powys*	**45**	SO2143
Clyst Honiton *Devon*	**9**	SX9893
Clyst Hydon *Devon*	**9**	ST0301
Clyst St. George *Devon*	**9**	SX9888
Clyst St. Lawrence *Devon*	**9**	ST0200
Clyst St. Mary *Devon*	**9**	SX9790
Clyth *Highld*	**151**	ND2836
Cnwch Coch *Dyfed*	**43**	SN6775
Coad's Green *Cnwll*	**5**	SX2976
Coal Aston *Derbys*	**74**	SK3679
Coal Pool *W Mids*	**60**	SK0100
Coal Street *Suffk*	**55**	TM2371
Coalbrookdale *Shrops*	**60**	SJ6603
Coalbrookvale *Gwent*	**33**	SO1909
Coalburn *Strath*	**108**	NS8134
Coalburns *T & W*	**96**	NZ1261
Coalcleugh *Nthumb*	**95**	NY8045
Coaley *Gloucs*	**35**	SO7701
Coalfel *Cumb*	**94**	NY5959
Coalhill *Essex*	**40**	TQ7598
Coalmoor *Shrops*	**60**	SJ6607
Coalpit Heath *Avon*	**35**	ST6781
Coalport *Shrops*	**60**	SJ6902
Coalsnaughton *Cent*	**116**	NS9295
Coaltown of Balgonie *Fife*	**117**	NT3099
Coaltown of Wemyss *Fife*	**118**	NT3295
Coalville *Leics*	**62**	SK4214
Coanwood *Nthumb*	**94**	NY6759
Coat *Somset*	**21**	ST4520
Coatbridge *Strath*	**116**	NS7365
Coatdyke *Strath*	**116**	NS7465
Coate *Wilts*	**23**	SU0461
Coate *Wilts*	**36**	SU1783
Coates *Cambs*	**64**	TL3097
Coates *Gloucs*	**35**	SO9700
Coates *Lincs*	**75**	SK8181
Coates *Lincs*	**76**	SK9083
Coates *W Susx*	**14**	SU9917
Coatham *Cleve*	**97**	NZ5925
Coatham Mundeville *Dur*	**96**	NZ2820
Cobbaton *Devon*	**19**	SS6126
Cobberley *Gloucs*	**35**	SO9616
Cobhall Common *H & W*	**46**	SO4535
Cobham *Kent*	**28**	TQ6768
Cobham *Surrey*	**26**	TQ1060
Coblers Green *Essex*	**40**	TL6819
Cobley *Dorset*	**12**	SU0220
Cobnash *H & W*	**46**	SO4560
Cobo *Guern*	**152**	GN0000
Cobridge *Staffs*	**72**	SJ8748
Coburby *Gramp*	**143**	NJ9164
Cock Alley *Derbys*	**74**	SK4170
Cock Bank *Clwyd*	**71**	SJ3545
Cock Bridge *Gramp*	**133**	NJ2508
Cock Clarks *Essex*	**40**	TL8103
Cock End *Suffk*	**53**	TL7253
Cock Green *Essex*	**40**	TL6920
Cock Marling *E Susx*	**17**	TQ8719
Cock Street *Kent*	**28**	TQ7850
Cockayne *N York*	**90**	SE6298
Cockayne Hatley *Beds*	**52**	TL2549
Cockburnspath *Border*	**119**	NT7770
Cockenzie and Port Seton *Loth*	**118**	NT4075
Cocker Bar *Lancs*	**80**	SD5022
Cocker Brook *Lancs*	**81**	SD7425
Cockerdale *W York*	**82**	SE2329
Cockerham *Lancs*	**80**	SD4651
Cockermouth *Cumb*	**92**	NY1230
Cockernhoe Green *Herts*	**38**	TL1223
Cockett *W Glam*	**32**	SS6394
Cockfield *Dur*	**96**	NZ1224
Cockfield *Suffk*	**54**	TL9054
Cockfosters *Gt Lon*	**27**	TQ2796
Cocking *W Susx*	**14**	SU8717
Cocking Causeway *W Susx*	**14**	SU8819
Cockington *Devon*	**7**	SX8964
Cocklake *Somset*	**21**	ST4349
Cockley Beck *Cumb*	**86**	NY2501
Cockley Cley *Norfk*	**66**	TF7904
Cockpole Green *Berks*	**37**	SU7981
Cocks *Cnwll*	**3**	SW7652
Cockshutford *Shrops*	**59**	SO5885
Cockshutt *Shrops*	**59**	SJ4328
Cockthorpe *Norfk*	**66**	TF9842
Cockwells *Cnwll*	**2**	SW5234
Cockwood *Devon*	**9**	SX9780
Cockwood *Somset*	**20**	ST2223
Cockyard *Derbys*	**74**	SK0480
Cockyard *H & W*	**46**	SO4133
Coddenham *Suffk*	**54**	TM1354
Coddington *Ches*	**71**	SJ4555
Coddington *H & W*	**47**	SO7142
Coddington *Notts*	**76**	SK8354
Codford St. Mary *Wilts*	**22**	ST9739
Codford St. Peter *Wilts*	**22**	ST9640
Codicote *Herts*	**39**	TL2118
Codmore Hill *W Susx*	**14**	TQ0520
Codnor *Derbys*	**74**	SK4149
Codrington *Avon*	**35**	ST7278
Codsall *Staffs*	**60**	SJ8603
Codsall Wood *Staffs*	**60**	SJ8405
Coed Morgan *Gwent*	**34**	SO3511
Coed Talon *Clwyd*	**70**	SJ2658
Coed Ystumgwern *Gwynd*	**57**	SH5824
Coed-y-caerau *Gwent*	**34**	ST3891
Coed-y-paen *Gwent*	**34**	ST3398
Coed-yr-ynys *Powys*	**33**	SO1520
Coedana *Gwynd*	**68**	SH4381
Coedely *M Glam*	**33**	ST0285
Coedkernew *Gwent*	**34**	ST2783
Coedpoeth *Clwyd*	**70**	SJ2850
Coedway *Powys*	**59**	SJ3315
Coelbren *Powys*	**33**	SN8511
Coffinswell *Devon*	**7**	SX8868
Coffle End *Beds*	**51**	TL0059
Cofnpennar *Gwent*	**34**	SO3006
Cofton Hackett *H & W*	**60**	SP0075
Cogan *S Glam*	**33**	ST1772
Cogenhoe *Nhants*	**51**	SP8260
Cogges *Oxon*	**36**	SP3609
Coggeshall *Essex*	**40**	TL8522
Coggin's Mill *E Susx*	**16**	TQ5927
Coignafearn *Highld*	**140**	NH7017
Coilacriech *Gramp*	**134**	NO3296
Coilantogle *Cent*	**124**	NN5907
Coillaig *Strath*	**122**	NN0120
Coillore *Highld*	**136**	NG3538
Coiltry *Highld*	**131**	NH3506
Coity *M Glam*	**33**	SS9281
Colaboll *Highld*	**146**	NC5610
Colan *Cnwll*	**4**	SW8661
Colaton Raleigh *Devon*	**9**	SY0787
Colbone *Somset*	**19**	SS8448
Colburn *N York*	**89**	SE1999
Colbury *Hants*	**12**	SU3410
Colby *Cumb*	**94**	NY6620
Colby *IOM*	**153**	SC2370
Colby *Norfk*	**67**	TG2231
Colchester *Essex*	**41**	TL9925
Cold Ash *Berks*	**24**	SU5169
Cold Ashby *Nhants*	**50**	SP6576
Cold Ashton *Avon*	**35**	ST7472
Cold Aston *Gloucs*	**36**	SP1219
Cold Blow *Dyfed*	**31**	SN1212
Cold Brayfield *Bucks*	**38**	SP9252
Cold Cotes *N York*	**88**	SD7171
Cold Green *H & W*	**47**	SO6842
Cold Hanworth *Lincs*	**76**	TF0383
Cold Harbour *Herts*	**38**	TL1415
Cold Harbour *Oxon*	**37**	SU6379
Cold Harbour *Wilts*	**22**	ST8646
Cold Hatton *Shrops*	**59**	SJ6121
Cold Hatton Heath *Shrops*	**59**	SJ6321
Cold Hesledon *Dur*	**96**	NZ4146
Cold Hiendly *W York*	**83**	SE3714
Cold Higham *Nhants*	**49**	SP6653
Cold Kirby *N York*	**90**	SE5384
Cold Newton *Leics*	**63**	SK7106
Cold Northcott *Cnwll*	**5**	SX2086
Cold Norton *Essex*	**40**	TL8500
Cold Overton *Leics*	**63**	SK8110
Cold Weston *Shrops*	**59**	SO5583
Coldbackie *Highld*	**149**	NC6160
Coldbeck *Cumb*	**88**	NY7104
Coldblow *Gt Lon*	**27**	TQ5073
Coldean *E Susx*	**15**	TQ3308
Coldeast *Devon*	**7**	SX8274
Colden *W York*	**82**	SD9628
Colden Common *Hants*	**13**	SU4822
Coldfair Green *Suffk*	**55**	TM4361
Coldham *Cambs*	**65**	TF4302
Coldharbour *Cnwll*	**3**	SW7548
Coldharbour *Devon*	**9**	ST0612
Coldharbour *Gloucs*	**34**	SO5503
Coldharbour *Surrey*	**26**	TQ0360
Coldharbour *Surrey*	**15**	TQ1443
Coldingham *Border*	**119**	NT9065
Coldmeece *Staffs*	**72**	SJ8532
Coldred *Kent*	**29**	TR2747
Coldridge *Devon*	**8**	SS6907
Coldstone *Kent*	**27**	TQ2961
Coldstream *Border*	**110**	NT8439
Coldwaltham *W Susx*	**14**	TQ0216
Coldwell *H & W*	**46**	SO4235
Coldwells *Gramp*	**143**	NJ9538
Coldwells *Gramp*	**143**	NK1039
Cole *Somset*	**22**	ST6633
Cole End *Warwks*	**61**	SP1989
Cole Green *Herts*	**39**	TL4330
Cole Green *Herts*	**39**	TL2911
Cole Henley *Hants*	**24**	SU4751
Cole's Cross *Devon*	**7**	SX7747
Colebatch *Shrops*	**59**	SO3187
Colebrook *Devon*	**6**	SX5457
Colebrook *Devon*	**9**	ST0006
Colebrooke *Devon*	**8**	SX7799
Coleby *Humb*	**84**	SE8919
Coleby *Lincs*	**76**	SK9760
Coleford *Devon*	**8**	SS7701
Coleford *Gloucs*	**34**	SO5710
Coleford *Somset*	**22**	ST6848
Coleford Water *Somset*	**20**	ST1234
Colegate End *Norfk*	**55**	TM1988
Colehill *Dorset*	**12**	SU0300
Coleman Green *Herts*	**39**	TL1812
Coleman's Hatch *E Susx*	**16**	TQ4533
Colemere *Shrops*	**59**	SJ4232
Colemore *Hants*	**24**	SU7030
Colemore Green *Shrops*	**60**	SO7097
Colenden *Tays*	**126**	NO1029
Coleorton *Leics*	**62**	SK3917
Colerne *Wilts*	**35**	ST8171
Coles Cross *Dorset*	**10**	ST3902
Coles Green *Suffk*	**54**	TM1041
Colesbourne *Gloucs*	**35**	SP0013
Colesden *Beds*	**52**	TL1255
Coleshill *Bucks*	**26**	SU9495
Coleshill *Oxon*	**36**	SU2393
Coleshill *Warwks*	**61**	SP2089
Colestocks *Devon*	**9**	ST0900
Coleton *Devon*	**7**	SX9051
Coley *Avon*	**21**	ST5855
Colgate *W Susx*	**15**	TQ2332
Colgrain *Strath*	**115**	NS3280
Colinsburgh *Fife*	**127**	NO4703
Colinton *Loth*	**117**	NT2268
Colintraive *Strath*	**114**	NS0374
Colkirk *Norfk*	**66**	TF9126
Coll *W Isls*	**154**	NB4539
Collace *Tays*	**126**	NO2032
Collafirth *Shet*	**155**	HU3482
Collation *Devon*	**7**	SX7338
Collaton *Devon*	**7**	SX7952
Collaton St. Mary *Devon*	**7**	SX8660
College Green *Somset*	**21**	ST5736
College of Roseisle *Gramp*	**141**	NJ1466
College Town *Berks*	**25**	SU8560
Collessie *Fife*	**126**	NO2813
Colleton Mills *Devon*	**19**	SS6615
Collier Row *Gt Lon*	**27**	TQ4991
Collier Street *Kent*	**28**	TQ7145
Collier's End *Herts*	**39**	TL3720
Collier's Green *Kent*	**17**	TQ7822
Colliers Green *Kent*	**28**	TQ7439
Colliery Row *T & W*	**96**	NZ3349
Collieston *Gramp*	**143**	NK0328
Collin *D & G*	**100**	NY0276
Collingbourne Ducis *Wilts*	**23**	SU2453
Collingbourne Kingston *Wilts*	**23**	SU2355
Collingham *Notts*	**75**	SK8261
Collingham *W York*	**83**	SE3845
Collington *H & W*	**47**	SO6460
Collingtree *Nhants*	**49**	SP7555
Collins Green *Ches*	**78**	SJ5694
Colliston *Tays*	**127**	NO6045
Colliton *Devon*	**9**	ST0804
Collyweston *Nhants*	**63**	SK9902
Colmonell *Strath*	**98**	NX1485
Colmworth *Beds*	**51**	TL1058
Coln Rogers *Gloucs*	**36**	SP0809
Coln St. Aldwyns *Gloucs*	**36**	SP1405
Coln St. Dennis *Gloucs*	**36**	SP0811
Colnbrook *Gt Lon*	**26**	TQ0277
Colne *Cambs*	**52**	TL3776
Colne *Lancs*	**81**	SD8940
Colne Bridge *W York*	**82**	SE1720
Colne Edge *Lancs*	**81**	SD8841
Colne Engaine *Essex*	**40**	TL8530
Colney *Norfk*	**66**	TG1807
Colney Heath *Herts*	**39**	TL2005
Colney Street *Herts*	**26**	TL1502
Colpy *Gramp*	**142**	NJ6432
Colquhar *Border*	**109**	NT3341
Colquite *Cnwll*	**4**	SX0570
Colscott *Devon*	**18**	SS3614
Colsterdale *N York*	**89**	SE1381
Colsterworth *Lincs*	**63**	SK9324
Colston Bassett *Notts*	**63**	SK7033
Colt Hill *Hants*	**24**	SU7451
Colt's Hill *Kent*	**16**	TQ6443
Coltfield *Gramp*	**141**	NJ1163
Coltishall *Norfk*	**67**	TG2619
Colton *Cumb*	**86**	SD3186
Colton *N York*	**83**	SE5444
Colton *Norfk*	**66**	TG1009
Colton *Staffs*	**73**	SK0520
Colton *W York*	**83**	SE3732
Columbjohn *Devon*	**9**	SX9699
Colva *Powys*	**45**	SO1952
Colvend *D & G*	**92**	NX8654
Colwall Green *H & W*	**47**	SO7441
Colwall Stone *H & W*	**47**	SO7542
Colwell *Nthumb*	**102**	NY9575
Colwich *Staffs*	**73**	SK0121
Colwick *Notts*	**62**	SK6140
Colwinston *S Glam*	**33**	SS9375
Colworth *W Susx*	**14**	SU9102
Colwyn Bay *Clwyd*	**69**	SH8479
Colyford *Devon*	**9**	SY2492
Colyton *Devon*	**9**	SY2493
Combe *Berks*	**23**	SU3760
Combe *Devon*	**7**	SX9173
Combe *Devon*	**7**	SX8448
Combe *Devon*	**7**	SX7138
Combe *H & W*	**46**	SO3463
Combe *Oxon*	**36**	SP4116
Combe Almer *Dorset*	**11**	SY9497
Combe Common *Surrey*	**14**	SU9436
Combe Fishacre *Devon*	**7**	SX8465
Combe Florey *Somset*	**20**	ST1531
Combe Hay *Avon*	**22**	ST7359
Combe Martin *Devon*	**19**	SS5846
Combe Moor *H & W*	**46**	SO3663
Combe Raleigh *Devon*	**9**	ST1502
Combe St. Nicholas *Somset*	**10**	ST3011
Combebow *Devon*	**5**	SX4888
Combeinteignhead *Devon*	**7**	SX9071
Comberbach *Ches*	**79**	SJ6477
Comberford *Staffs*	**61**	SK1907
Comberton *Cambs*	**52**	TL3856
Comberton *H & W*	**46**	SO4968
Combridge *Staffs*	**73**	SK0937
Combrook *Warwks*	**48**	SP3051
Combs *Derbys*	**74**	SK0478
Combs *Suffk*	**54**	TM0456
Combs Ford *Suffk*	**54**	TM0557
Combwich *Somset*	**20**	ST2542
Comedivock *Cumb*	**93**	NY3449
Comers *Gramp*	**135**	NJ6707
Comhampton *H & W*	**47**	SO8366
Commercial *Dyfed*	**31**	SN1416
Commercial End *Cambs*	**53**	TL5563
Commins Coch *Powys*	**57**	SH8403
Common Edge *Lancs*	**80**	SD3232
Common End *Cumb*	**92**	NY0022
Common Moor *Cnwll*	**5**	SX2469
Common Platt *Wilts*	**36**	SU1186
Common Side *Derbys*	**74**	SK3375
Common The *Wilts*	**23**	SU2432
Commondale *N York*	**90**	NZ6610
Commonside *Ches*	**71**	SJ5573
Commonside *Derbys*	**73**	SK2441
Commonwood *Clwyd*	**71**	SJ3753
Commonwood *Shrops*	**59**	SJ4828
Compass *Somset*	**20**	ST2934
Compstall *Gt Man*	**79**	SJ9690
Compstonend *D & G*	**99**	NX6652
Compton *Berks*	**37**	SU5280
Compton *Devon*	**7**	SX8664
Compton *Hants*	**23**	SU3529
Compton *Hants*	**13**	SU4625
Compton *Staffs*	**60**	SO8285
Compton *Surrey*	**25**	SU9547
Compton *W Susx*	**14**	SU7714
Compton *Wilts*	**23**	SU1352
Compton Abbas *Dorset*	**22**	ST8718
Compton Abdale *Gloucs*	**36**	SP0516
Compton Bassett *Wilts*	**36**	SU0372
Compton Beauchamp *Oxon*	**36**	SU2886
Compton Bishop *Somset*	**21**	ST3955
Compton Chamberlayne *Wilts*	**23**	SU0229
Compton Dando *Avon*	**21**	ST6464
Compton Dundon *Somset*	**21**	ST4933
Compton Durville *Somset*	**10**	ST4117
Compton Greenfield *Avon*	**34**	ST5682
Compton Martin *Avon*	**21**	ST5456
Compton Pauncefoot *Somset*	**21**	ST6425
Compton Valence *Dorset*	**10**	SY5993
Compton Verney *Warwks*	**48**	SP3152
Comrie *Fife*	**117**	NT0289
Comrie *Tays*	**124**	NN7722
Conaglen House *Highld*	**130**	NN0268
Conchra *Highld*	**138**	NG8828
Conchra *Strath*	**114**	NS0288
Concraigie *Tays*	**126**	NO1044
Conderton *H & W*	**47**	SO9637
Condicote *Gloucs*	**48**	SP1528
Condorrat *Strath*	**116**	NS7373
Condover *Shrops*	**59**	SJ4906
Coney Hill *Gloucs*	**35**	SO8516
Coney Weston *Suffk*	**54**	TL9578
Coneyhurst Common *W Susx*	**14**	TQ1024
Coneysthorpe *N York*	**90**	SE7171
Conford *Hants*	**14**	SU8233
Congdon's Shop *Cnwll*	**5**	SX2778
Congerstone *Leics*	**62**	SK3605
Congham *Norfk*	**65**	TF7123
Conghurst *Kent*	**17**	TQ7628
Congl-y-wal *Gwynd*	**57**	SH7044
Congleton *Ches*	**72**	SJ8563
Congresbury *Avon*	**21**	ST4363
Congreve *Staffs*	**60**	SJ8914
Conicavel *Gramp*	**140**	NH9853
Conichan *Tays*	**125**	NN8432
Coningsby *Lincs*	**76**	TF2258
Conington *Cambs*	**52**	TL1885
Conington *Cambs*	**52**	TL3266
Conisbrough *S York*	**75**	SK5098
Conisby *Strath*	**112**	NR2661
Conisholme *Lincs*	**77**	TF3995
Coniston *Cumb*	**86**	SD3097
Coniston *Humb*	**85**	TA1535
Coniston Cold *N York*	**81**	SD9054
Conistone *N York*	**88**	SD9867
Connah's Quay *Clwyd*	**71**	SJ2969
Connel *Strath*	**122**	NM9133
Connel Park *Strath*	**107**	NS6012
Connor Downs *Cnwll*	**2**	SW5939
Conon Bridge *Highld*	**139**	NH5455
Cononley *N York*	**82**	SD9847
Consall *Staffs*	**72**	SJ9748
Consett *Dur*	**95**	NZ1150
Constable Burton *N York*	**89**	SE1690
Constable Lee *Lancs*	**81**	SD8123
Constantine *Cnwll*	**3**	SW7329
Contin *Highld*	**139**	NH4556
Convinth *Highld*	**139**	NH5138
Conwy *Gwynd*	**69**	SH7777
Conyer *Kent*	**28**	TQ9664
Conyer's Green *Suffk*	**54**	TL8867
Cooden *E Susx*	**17**	TQ7107
Coodham *Strath*	**106**	NS3932
Cooil *IOM*	**153**	SC3475
Cook's Green *Essex*	**41**	TM1819
Cookbury *Devon*	**18**	SS4005
Cookbury Wick *Devon*	**18**	SS3805
Cookham *Berks*	**26**	SU8985
Cookham Dean *Berks*	**26**	SU8685
Cookham Rise *Berks*	**26**	SU8885
Cookhill *Warwks*	**48**	SP0558
Cookley *H & W*	**60**	SO8480
Cookley *Suffk*	**55**	TM3475
Cookley Green *Oxon*	**37**	SU6990
Cookney *Gramp*	**135**	NO8693
Cooks Green *Suffk*	**54**	TL9853
Cooksbridge *E Susx*	**15**	TQ4013
Cooksey Green *H & W*	**47**	SO9069
Cookshill *Staffs*	**72**	SJ9443
Cooksland *Cnwll*	**4**	SX0867
Cooksmill Green *Essex*	**40**	TL6306
Cookson Green *Ches*	**71**	SJ5774
Cookson's Green *Dur*	**96**	NZ2933
Coolham *W Susx*	**14**	TQ1222
Cooling *Kent*	**28**	TQ7575
Cooling Street *Kent*	**28**	TQ7474
Coombe *Cnwll*	**2**	SW6242
Coombe *Cnwll*	**3**	SW8340
Coombe *Cnwll*	**3**	SW9551
Coombe *Devon*	**20**	SS9725
Coombe *Devon*	**8**	SX8384
Coombe *Devon*	**9**	SY1092
Coombe *Gloucs*	**35**	ST7693
Coombe *Hants*	**13**	SU6620
Coombe *Wilts*	**23**	SU1550
Coombe Bissett *Wilts*	**23**	SU1026
Coombe Cellars *Devon*	**7**	SX9072
Coombe Cross *Hants*	**13**	SU6621
Coombe End *Somset*	**20**	ST0329
Coombe Hill *Gloucs*	**47**	SO8827
Coombe Keynes *Dorset*	**11**	SY8484
Coombe Pafford *Devon*	**7**	SX9267
Coombe Street *Somset*	**22**	ST7531
Coombes *W Susx*	**15**	TQ1908
Coombeswood *W Mids*	**60**	SO9685
Cooper Street *Kent*	**29**	TR3060
Cooper Turning *Gt Man*	**79**	SD6308
Cooper's Corner *Kent*	**16**	TQ4849
Cooperhill *Gramp*	**141**	NH9953
Coopers Green *E Susx*	**16**	TQ4723
Coopersale Common *Essex*	**27**	TL4702
Coopersale Street *Essex*	**27**	TL4701
Cootham *W Susx*	**14**	TQ0714
Cop Street *Kent*	**27**	TQ2960
Copdock *Suffk*	**54**	TM1242
Copetown *W York*	**83**	SE3923
Copford Green *Essex*	**40**	TL9222
Copgrove *N York*	**89**	SE3463
Copister *Shet*	**155**	HU4878
Cople *Beds*	**38**	TL1048
Copley *Dur*	**95**	NZ0825
Copley *Gt Man*	**79**	SJ9798
Copley *W York*	**82**	SE0822
Coplow Dale *Derbys*	**74**	SK1679
Copmanthorpe *N York*	**83**	SE5646
Copmere End *Staffs*	**72**	SJ8029
Copp *Lancs*	**80**	SD4239
Coppathorne *Cnwll*	**18**	SS2000
Coppenhall *Staffs*	**72**	SJ9019
Coppenhall Moss *Ches*	**72**	SJ7058
Copperhouse *Cnwll*	**2**	SW5738
Coppers Green *Herts*	**39**	TL1909
Coppicegate *Shrops*	**60**	SO7380
Coppingford *Cambs*	**52**	TL1680
Coppins Corner *Kent*	**28**	TQ9448
Copplestone *Devon*	**8**	SS7702
Coppull *Lancs*	**81**	SD5614
Coppull Moor *Lancs*	**81**	SD5512
Copsale *W Susx*	**15**	TQ1724
Copster Green *Lancs*	**81**	SD6733
Copston Magna *Warwks*	**50**	SP4588
Copt Heath *W Mids*	**61**	SP1778
Copt Hewick *N York*	**89**	SE3471
Copthall Green *Essex*	**27**	TL4200
Copthorne *Cnwll*	**5**	SX2692
Copthorne *W Susx*	**15**	TQ3139
Copy's Green *Norfk*	**66**	TF9439
Copythorne *Hants*	**12**	SU3014
Coram Street *Suffk*	**54**	TM0042
Corbets Tay *Gt Lon*	**27**	TQ5685
Corbiere *Jersey*	**152**	JS0000
Corbridge *Nthumb*	**103**	NY9964
Corby *Nhants*	**51**	SP8988
Corby Glen *Lincs*	**63**	SK9925
Corby Hill *Cumb*	**94**	NY4857
Cordon *Strath*	**105**	NS0230
Cordwell Unthank *Derbys*	**74**	SK2076
Coreley *Shrops*	**47**	SO6273
Cores End *Bucks*	**26**	SU9087
Corfe *Somset*	**20**	ST2319
Corfe Castle *Dorset*	**11**	SY9681
Corfe Mullen *Dorset*	**11**	SY9798
Corfton *Shrops*	**59**	SO4985
Corgarff *Gramp*	**133**	NJ2708
Corhampton *Hants*	**13**	SU6120
Corks Pond *Kent*	**28**	TQ6540
Corley *Warwks*	**61**	SP3085
Corley Ash *Warwks*	**61**	SP2986
Corley Moor *Warwks*	**61**	SP2885
Cormuir *Tays*	**134**	NO3066
Cornabus *Strath*	**104**	NR3346
Cornard Tye *Suffk*	**54**	TL9041
Corndon *Devon*	**8**	SX6885
Cornelly *M Glam*	**33**	SS8281
Corner Row *Lancs*	**80**	SD4134
Corney *Cumb*	**86**	SD1191
Cornforth *Dur*	**96**	NZ3134
Cornheath *D & G*	**100**	NX9969
Cornhill *Gramp*	**142**	NJ5858
Cornhill-on-Tweed *Nthumb*	**110**	NT8639
Cornholme *W York*	**81**	SD9126
Cornish Hall End *Essex*	**53**	TL6836
Cornoigmore *Strath*	**120**	NL9846
Cornriggs *Dur*	**95**	NY8441
Cornsay *Dur*	**96**	NZ1443
Cornsay Colliery *Dur*	**96**	NZ1643
Corntown *Highld*	**139**	NH5556
Corntown *M Glam*	**33**	SS9177
Cornwell *Oxon*	**48**	SP2727
Cornwood *Devon*	**6**	SX6059
Cornworthy *Devon*	**7**	SX8255
Corpach *Highld*	**130**	NN0976
Corpusty *Norfk*	**66**	TG1130
Corra *Strath*	**114**	NR9765
Corrachree *Gramp*	**134**	NJ4604
Corran *Cnwll*	**3**	SW9946
Corran *Highld*	**130**	NG8509
Corran *Highld*	**130**	NN0263
Corranbuie *Strath*	**113**	NR8465
Corrany *IOM*	**153**	SC4589
Corrie *D & G*	**101**	NY2086
Corrie *Strath*	**105**	NS0242
Corriecravie *Strath*	**105**	NR9223
Corriegour *Highld*	**131**	NN2692

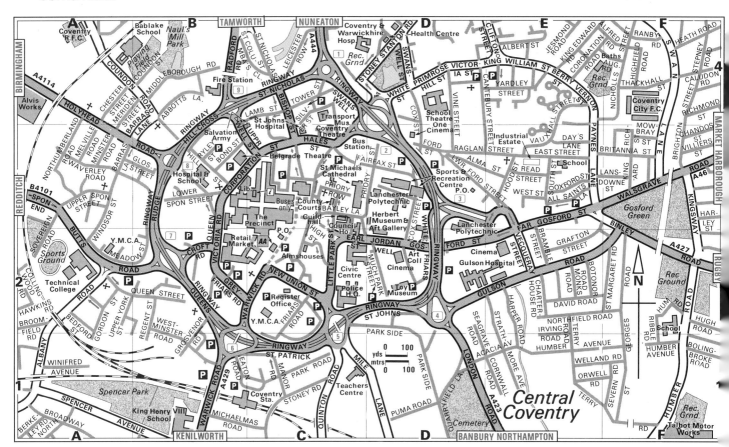

Crambe Cwmfelin Boeth

Crambe N York	90	SE7364
Cramlington Nthumb	103	NZ2676
Cramond Loth	117	NT1976
Cramond Bridge Loth	117	NT1775
Cranage Ches	79	SJ7568
Cranberry Staffs	72	SJ8235
Cranborne Dorset	12	SU0513
Cranbrook Devon	8	SX7488
Cranbrook Kent	28	TQ7736
Cranbrook Common Kent	28	TQ7838
Crane Moor S York	82	SE3001
Crane's Corner Norfk	66	TF9113
Cranfield Beds	38	SP9542
Cranford Devon	18	SS3421
Cranford Gt Lon	26	TQ1077
Cranford St. Andrew Nhants	51	SP9277
Cranford St. John Nhants	51	SP9276
Cranham Gloucs	35	SO8913
Cranham Gt Lon	27	TQ5786
Cranhill Warwks	48	SP1253
Crank Mersyd	78	SJ5099
Cranleigh Surrey	14	TQ0639
Cranmer Green Suffk	54	TM0271
Cranmore IOW	13	SZ3990
Cranmore Somset	22	ST6843
Cranoe Leics	50	SP7695
Cransford Suffk	55	TM3164
Cranshaws Border	118	NT6861
Cranstal IOM	153	NX4602
Cranswick Humb	84	TA0252
Crantock Cnwll	4	SW7960
Cranwell Lincs	76	TF0349
Cranwich Norfk	65	TL7795
Cranworth Norfk	66	TF9804
Crapstone Devon	6	SX5067
Crarae Strath	114	NR9897
Crask of Aigas Highld	139	NH4642
Craster Nthumb	111	NU2520
Craswall H & W	46	SO2735
Crateford Staffs	60	SJ9009
Cratfield Suffk	55	TM3175
Crathes Gramp	135	NO7596
Crathie Gramp	133	NO2695
Crathie Highld	132	NN5794
Crathorne N York	89	NZ4407
Craven Arms Shrops	59	SO4382
Crawcrook T & W	103	NZ1363
Crawford Lancs	78	SD5003
Crawford Strath	108	NS9520
Crawfordjohn Strath	108	NS8824
Crawick D & G	107	NS7811
Crawley Hants	24	SU4234
Crawley Oxon	36	SP3412
Crawley W Susx	15	TQ2636
Crawley Down W Susx	15	TQ3437
Crawleyside Dur	95	NY9840
Crawshawbooth Lancs	81	SD8125
Crawton Gramp	135	NO8779
Cray N York	88	SD9479
Cray's Pond Oxon	37	SU6380
Crayford Gt Lon	27	TQ5175
Crayke N York	90	SE5670
Craymere Beck Norfk	66	TG0631
Crays Hill Essex	40	TQ7192
Craythorne Staffs	73	SK2426
Craze Lowman Devon	9	SS9814
Creacombe Devon	19	SS8119
Creagan Inn Strath	122	NM9744
Creagorry W Isls	154	NF7948
Creaguaineach Lodge Highld	131	NN3068
Creamore Bank Shrops	59	SJ5130
Creaton Nhants	50	SP7071
Creca D & G	101	NY2270
Credenhill H & W	46	SO4543
Crediton Devon	8	SS8300
Creebank D & G	98	NX3477
Creech Heathfield Somset	20	ST2827
Creech St. Michael Somset	20	ST2725
Creed Cnwll	3	SW9347
Creedy Park Devon	8	SS8302
Creekmouth Gt Lon	27	TQ4581
Creeting St. Mary Suffk	54	TM0956
Creeton Lincs	64	TF0120
Creetown D & G	99	NX4758
Creggans Hotel Strath	123	NN0902
Cregneish IOM	153	SC1967
Cregrina Powys	45	SO1252
Creich Fife	126	NO3221
Creigiau M Glam	33	ST0781
Crelly Cnwll	2	SW6732
Cremyll Cnwll	6	SX4553
Cressage Shrops	59	SJ5904
Cressbrook Derbys	74	SK1673
Cresselly Dyfed	30	SN0606
Cressex Bucks	37	SU8392
Cressing Essex	40	TL7920
Cresswell Dyfed	30	SN0506
Cresswell Nthumb	103	NZ2993
Cresswell Staffs	72	SJ9739
Creswell Derbys	75	SK5274
Creswell Green Staffs	61	SK0710
Cretingham Suffk	55	TM2260
Cretshengan Strath	113	NR7166
Crew Green Powys	59	SJ3215
Crewe Ches	71	SJ4253
Crewe Ches	72	SJ7055
Crewe Green Ches	72	SJ7255
Crewkerne Somset	10	ST4409
Crews Hill H & W	35	SO6722
Crews Hill Station Herts	27	TL3100
Crewton Derbys	62	SK3733
Crianlarich Strath	123	NN3825
Cribb's Causeway Avon	34	ST5780
Cribyn Dyfed	44	SN5251
Criccieth Gwynd	56	SH4938
Crich Derbys	74	SK3554
Crich Carr Derbys	74	SK3354
Crich Common Derbys	74	SK3553
Crichton Loth	118	NT3862
Crick Gwent	34	ST4890
Crick Nhants	50	SP5972
Crickadarn Powys	45	SO0942
Cricket St. Thomas Somset	10	ST3708
Crickheath Shrops	59	SJ2923
Crickhowell Powys	33	SO2118
Cricklade Wilts	36	SU0993
Cricklewood Gt Lon	26	TQ2385
Cridling Stubbs N York	83	SE5221
Crieff Tays	125	NN8621
Criggan Cnwll	4	SX0160
Criggion Powys	59	SJ2915
Crigglestone W York	82	SE3116
Crimble Gt Man	81	SD8611
Crimesthorpe S York	74	SK3690
Crimond Gramp	143	NK0556
Crimonmogate Gramp	143	NK0358
Crimplesham Norfk	65	TF6503
Crimscote Warwks	48	SP2347
Crinan Strath	113	NR7894
Crindledyke Strath	116	NS8356
Cringleford Norfk	67	TG1905
Cringles N York	82	SE0448
Crinow Dyfed	31	SN1214
Cripp's Corner E Susx	17	TQ7721
Cripplesease Cnwll	2	SW5036
Cripplestyle Dorset	12	SU0912
Crizeley H & W	46	SO4432
Croachy Highld	140	NH6527
Croanford Cnwll	4	SX0371
Croasdale Cumb	92	NY0917
Crochmare House D & G	100	NX8977
Crock Street Somset	10	ST3213
Crockenhill Kent	27	TQ5067
Crocker End Oxon	37	SU7086
Crocker's Ash H & W	34	SO5316
Crockerhill W Susx	14	SU9207
Crockernwell Devon	8	SX7592
Crockerton Wilts	22	ST8642
Crockey Hill N York	83	SE6246
Crockham Hill Kent	27	TQ4450
Crockhurst Street Kent	16	TQ6235
Crockleford Heath Essex	41	TM0426
Croes-lan Dyfed	42	SN3844
Croes-y-mwyalch Gwent	34	ST3092
Croes-y-pant Gwent	34	SO3104
Croeserw W Glam	33	SS8795
Croesgoch Dyfed	30	SM8330
Croesor Gwynd	57	SH6344
Croesyceiliog Dyfed	31	SN4016
Croesyceiliog Gwent	34	ST3096
Croesywaun Gwynd	68	SH5159
Croft Ches	79	SJ6393
Croft Devon	5	SX5296
Croft Leics	50	SP5195
Croft Lincs	77	TF5162
Croft Michael Cnwll	2	SW6637
Croftamie Cent	115	NS4786
Crofton Cumb	93	NY3050
Crofton Devon	9	SX9680
Crofton W York	83	SE3717
Crofton Wilts	23	SU2562
Crofts Gramp	141	NJ2850
Crofts of Dipple Gramp	141	NJ3258
Crofts of Savoch Gramp	143	NK0460
Crofty W Glam	32	SS5295
Crogen Gwynd	58	SJ0036
Croggan Strath	122	NM7027
Croglin Cumb	94	NY5747
Crogo D & G	99	NX7576
Croick Highld	146	NH4591
Croig Strath	121	NM3953
Cromarty Highld	140	NH7867
Crombie Fife	117	NT0584
Cromdale Highld	141	NJ0728
Cromer Herts	52	TL2980
Cromer Herts	39	TL2928
Cromer Norfk	67	TG2242
Cromford Derbys	73	SK2956
Cromhall Avon	35	ST6990
Cromhall Common Avon	35	ST6989
Cromore W Isls	154	NB4021
Crompton Fold Gt Man	79	SD9409
Cromwell Notts	75	SK7761
Cronberry Strath	107	NS6022
Crondall Hants	25	SU7948
Cronk The IOM	153	SC3495
Cronk-y-Voddy IOM	153	SC3086
Cronton Mersyd	78	SJ4988
Crook Cumb	87	SD4695
Crook Dur	96	NZ1635
Crook of Devon Tays	117	NO0300
Crookdake Cumb	93	NY1943
Crooke Gt Man	78	SD5507
Crooked End Gloucs	35	SO6217
Crooked Holme Cumb	101	NY5162
Crooked Soley Wilts	34	ST3172
Crookedholm Strath	107	NS4537
Crookes S York	74	SK3288
Crookhall Dur	95	NZ1150
Crookham Berks	24	SU5364
Crookham Nthumb	110	NT9138
Crookham Village Hants	25	SU7952
Crooklands Cumb	87	SD5383
Cropper Derbys	73	SK2335
Cropredy Oxon	49	SP4646
Cropston Leics	62	SK5511
Cropthorne H & W	47	SO9944
Cropton N York	90	SE7589
Cropwell Bishop Notts	63	SK6835
Cropwell Butler Notts	63	SK6837
Crosbie Strath	114	NS2149
Crosby Cumb	92	NY0738
Crosby Humb	84	SE8912
Crosby IOM	153	SC3279
Crosby Mersyd	78	SJ3198
Crosby Garrett Cumb	88	NY7309
Crosby Ravensworth Cumb	94	NY6214
Crosby Villa Cumb	92	NY0939
Croscombe Somset	21	ST5844
Crosemere Shrops	59	SJ4329
Cross Somset	21	ST4154
Cross Ash Gwent	34	SO4019
Cross Bush W Susx	14	TQ0306
Cross Coombe Cnwll	3	SW7351
Cross End Beds	51	TL0658
Cross End Essex	54	TL8634
Cross Flatts W York	82	SE1040
Cross Gates W York	83	SE3534
Cross Green Devon	5	SX3888
Cross Green Devon	5	SX3888
Cross Green Staffs	60	SJ9105
Cross Green Suffk	54	TL8353
Cross Green Suffk	54	TL8955
Cross Green Suffk	54	TL9953
Cross Hands Dyfed	31	SN0712
Cross Hands Dyfed	32	SN5612
Cross Hill Derbys	74	SK4148
Cross Hills N York	82	SE0145
Cross Houses Shrops	60	SO6991
Cross Houses Shrops	59	SJ5307
Cross Inn Dyfed	42	SN3957
Cross Inn Dyfed	43	SN5463
Cross Inn Dyfed	44	SN7725
Cross Inn M Glam	33	ST0583
Cross in Hand E Susx	16	TQ5521
Cross Keys Wilts	35	ST8771
Cross Lane IOW	13	SZ5090
Cross Lane Head Shrops	60	SO7095
Cross Lanes Clwyd	71	SJ3746
Cross Lanes Cnwll	2	SW6921
Cross Lanes Cnwll	3	SW7642
Cross Lanes N York	90	SE5264
Cross Oak Powys	45	SO1023
Cross o' th' hands Derbys	73	SK2846
Cross of Jackston Gramp	142	NJ7432
Cross Roads Devon	5	SX4586
Cross Roads Powys	45	SN9756
Cross Street Suffk	54	TM1876
Cross Town Ches	79	SJ7578
Cross Ways Dorset	11	SY7688
Cross-at-Hand Kent	28	TQ7846
Crossaig Strath	113	NR8351
Crossapoll Strath	120	NL9943
Crossbost Highld	999	NB3924
Crosscanonby Cumb	92	NY0739
Crossdale Street Norfk	67	TG2239
Crossens Mersyd	80	SD3720
Crossford Fife	117	NT0786
Crossford Strath	116	NS8246
Crossgate Lincs	64	TF2426
Crossgate M Glam	5	SX3488
Crossgate Staffs	72	SJ9437
Crossgatehall Loth	118	NT3669
Crossgates Fife	117	NT1488
Crossgates Powys	45	SO0865
Crossgates Strath	115	NS3744
Crossgill Lancs	87	SD5563
Crosshands Dyfed	31	SN1923
Crosshands Strath	107	NS4830
Crosshill Fife	117	NT1796
Crosshill Strath	106	NS3206
Crosshouse Strath	106	NS3938
Crosskeys Gwent	34	ST2292
Crosskeys Strath	115	NS3385
Crosskirk Highld	150	ND0369
Crossland Edge W York	82	SE1212
Crossland Hill W York	82	SE1114
Crosslands Cumb	101	NY3489
Crosslanes Shrops	59	SJ3218
Crosslee Border	109	NT3018
Crosslee Strath	115	NS4066
Crossley W York	82	SE2021
Crossmichael D & G	99	NX7367
Crosspost W Susx	15	TQ2522
Crossroads Gramp	134	NJ5607
Crossroads Gramp	135	NO7594
Crossroads Gramp	134	NJ5607
Crosston Tays	127	NO5256
Crossway Dyfed	31	SN1542
Crossway Gwent	34	SO4419
Crossway Powys	45	SO0558
Crossway Green Gwent	34	ST5294
Crossway Green H & W	47	SO8368
Crosswell Dyfed	31	SN1236
Crosthwaite Cumb	87	SD4391
Croston Lancs	80	SD4918
Crostwick Norfk	67	TG2515
Crostwight Norfk	67	TG3429
Crouch Kent	28	TR0458
Crouch End Gt Lon	27	TQ3088
Crouch Hill Dorset	11	ST7010
Croucheston Wilts	23	SU0625
Crough House Green Kent	16	TQ4346
Croughton Nhants	49	SP5433
Crovie Gramp	143	NJ8065
Crow Hants	12	SU1603
Crow Edge S York	82	SE1804
Crow End Cambs	52	TL3257
Crow Hill H & W	47	SO6326
Crow Street Essex	27	TQ5796
Crow's Green Essex	40	TL6926
Crow's Nest Cnwll	5	SX2669
Crowan Cnwll	2	SW6434
Crowborough E Susx	16	TQ5131
Crowborough Town E Susx	16	TQ5031
Crowcombe Somset	20	ST1336
Crowden Derbys	74	SK0699
Crowden Devon	18	SX4999
Crowdhill Hants	13	SU4920
Crowdicote Derbys	74	SK1065
Crowdleham Kent	27	TQ5658
Crowell Oxon	37	SU7499
Crowfield Nhants	49	SP6141
Crowfield Suffk	54	TM1557
Crowfield Green Suffk	54	TM1458
Crowgate Street Norfk	67	TG3121
Crowhill Loth	119	NT7374
Crowhole Derbys	74	SK3375
Crowhurst E Susx	17	TQ7512
Crowhurst Surrey	15	TQ3847
Crowhurst Lane End Surrey	15	TQ3847
Crowland Lincs	64	TF2410
Crowland Suffk	54	TM0170
Crowlas Cnwll	2	SW5133
Crowle H & W	47	SO9256
Crowle Humb	84	SE7712
Crowle Green H & W	47	SO9256
Crowmarsh Gifford Oxon	37	SU6189
Crown Corner Suffk	55	TM2570
Crownhill Devon	6	SX4857
Crownpits Surrey	25	SU9743
Crownthorpe Norfk	66	TG0803
Crowntown Cnwll	2	SW6331
Crows-an-Wra Cnwll	2	SW3927
Crowshill Norfk	66	TF9406
Crowsnest Shrops	59	SJ3701
Crowthorne Berks	25	SU8464
Crowton Ches	71	SJ5774
Croxall Staffs	61	SK1913
Croxby Lincs	76	TF1898
Croxdale Dur	96	NZ2636
Croxden Staffs	73	SK0639
Croxley Green Herts	26	TQ0795
Croxton Cambs	52	TL2460
Croxton Humb	85	TA0912
Croxton Norfk	66	TF9831
Croxton Norfk	54	TL8786
Croxton Staffs	72	SJ7832
Croxton Green Ches	71	SJ5552
Croxton Kerrial Leics	63	SK8329
Croxtonbank Staffs	72	SJ7832
Croy Highld	140	NH7949
Croy Strath	116	NS7275
Croyde Devon	18	SS4439
Croyde Bay Devon	18	SS4339
Croydon Cambs	52	TL3149
Croydon Gt Lon	27	TQ3265
Crubenmore Highld	132	NN6790
Cruckmeole Shrops	59	SJ4309
Cruckton Shrops	59	SJ4310
Cruden Bay Gramp	143	NK0836
Crudgington Shrops	59	SJ6318
Crudwell Wilts	35	ST9592
Crug Powys	45	SO1972
Crug-y-byddar Powys	58	SO1682
Crugmeer Cnwll	4	SW9076
Crugybar Dyfed	44	SN6537
Crulivig W Isls	154	NB1733
Crumlin Gwent	33	ST2198
Crumplehorn Cnwll	5	SX2051
Crumpsall Gt Man	79	SD8402
Crumstane Border	119	NT8053
Crundale Dyfed	30	SM9718
Crundale Kent	29	TR0749
Crunwear Dyfed	31	SN1810
Cruwys Morchard Devon	19	SS8712
Crux Easton Hants	24	SU4256
Cruxton Dorset	10	SY6096
Crwbin Dyfed	32	SN4713
Cryers Hill Bucks	26	SU8797
Crymmych Dyfed	31	SN1833
Crynant W Glam	32	SN7904
Crystal Palace Gt Lon	27	TQ3371
Cuaig Highld	137	NG7057
Cubbington Warwks	48	SP3468
Cubert Cnwll	4	SW7857
Cubley S York	82	SE2401
Cublington Bucks	38	SP8422
Cublington H & W	46	SO3938
Cuckfield W Susx	15	TQ3025
Cucklington Somset	22	ST7527
Cuckney Notts	75	SK5671
Cuckold's Green Kent	28	TQ8276
Cuckoo Bridge Lincs	64	TF2020
Cuckoo's Corner Hants	24	SU7441
Cuckoo's Nest Ches	71	SJ3860
Cuddesdon Oxon	37	SP5903
Cuddington Bucks	37	SP7311
Cuddington Ches	71	SJ5971
Cuddington Heath Ches	71	SJ4747
Cuddy Hill Lancs	80	SD4937
Cudham Gt Lon	27	TQ4459
Cudliptown Devon	5	SX5279
Cudworth S York	83	SE3808
Cudworth Somset	10	ST3810
Cudworth Common S York	83	SE4007
Cuerden Green Lancs	80	SD5425
Cuerdley Cross Ches	78	SJ5487
Cufaude Hants	24	SU6557
Cuffley Herts	39	TL3003
Culbo Highld	140	NH6461
Culbokie Highld	140	NH6059
Culburnie Highld	139	NH4941
Culcabock Highld	140	NH6844
Culcharry Highld	140	NH8650
Culcheth Ches	79	SJ6694
Culdrain Gramp	142	NJ5134
Culduie Highld	137	NG7140
Culford Suffk	54	TL8370
Culgaith Cumb	94	NY6029
Culham Oxon	37	SU5095
Culinlongart Strath	104	NR6511
Culkein Highld	148	NC0333
Culkein Drumbeg Highld	148	NC1133
Culkerton Gloucs	35	ST9395
Cullen Gramp	142	NJ5167
Cullercoats T & W	103	NZ3671
Cullerlie Gramp	135	NJ7603
Cullicudden Highld	140	NH6463
Cullingworth W York	82	SE0636
Cullipool Strath	122	NM7313
Cullivoe Shet	155	HP5402
Cullompton Devon	9	ST0207
Culm Davy Devon	9	ST1215
Culmalzie D & G	99	NX3752
Culmington Shrops	59	SO4982
Culmstock Devon	9	ST1013
Culnacraig Highld	145	NC0603
Culnaightrie D & G	92	NX7750
Culnaknock Highld	137	NG5263
Culpho Suffk	55	TM2149
Culrain Highld	146	NH5794
Culross Fife	117	NS9886
Culroy Strath	106	NS3114
Culscadden D & G	99	NX4748
Culshabbin D & G	98	NX3050
Culswick Shet	155	HU2745
Cultercullen Gramp	143	NJ9223
Cults D & G	99	NX4643
Cults Gramp	135	NJ8903
Culverlane Devon	7	SX7460
Culverstone Green Kent	27	TQ6362
Culverthorpe Lincs	64	TF0240
Culworth Nhants	49	SP5446
Culzie Lodge Highld	146	NH5171
Cum brwyno Dyfed	43	SN7180
Cumbernauld Strath	116	NS7674
Cumberworth Lincs	77	TF5073
Cumergyr Dyfed	43	SN7982
Cuminestown Gramp	143	NJ8050
Cummersdale Cumb	93	NY3953
Cummertrees D & G	100	NY1366
Cummingston Gramp	141	NJ1368
Cumnor Oxon	37	SP4504
Cumrew Cumb	94	NY5450
Cumwhinton Cumb	93	NY4552
Cumwhitton Cumb	89	NY5052
Cundall N York	89	SE4272
Cunninghamhead Strath	106	NS3741
Cupar Fife	126	NO3714
Cupar Muir Fife	126	NO3613
Cupernham Hants	23	SU3622
Curbar Derbys	74	SK2574
Curbridge Hants	13	SU5211
Curbridge Oxon	36	SP3208
Curdridge Hants	13	SU5313
Curdworth Warwks	61	SP1892
Curland Somset	10	ST2716
Currarie Strath	106	NX1691
Curridge Berks	24	SU4972
Currie Loth	117	NT1867
Curry Mallet Somset	21	ST3221
Curry Rivel Somset	21	ST3824
Curt Gwynd	57	SN6899
Curteis Corner Kent	28	TQ8539
Curtisden Green Kent	28	TQ7440
Curtisknowle Devon	7	SX7353
Cury Cnwll	2	SW6721
Cusgarne Cnwll	3	SW7540
Cushuish Somset	20	ST1930
Cusop H & W	46	SO2441
Cutcloy D & G	99	NX4534
Cutcombe Somset	20	SS9239
Cutgate Gt Man	81	SD8614
Cuthill Highld	147	NH7587
Cutiau Gwynd	57	SH6317
Cutler's Green Essex	40	TL5930
Cutmadoc Cnwll	4	SX0963
Cutmere M Glam	5	SX3260
Cutnall Green H & W	47	SO8868
Cutsdean Gloucs	48	SP0831
Cutthorpe Derbys	74	SK3473
Cuxham Oxon	37	SU6695
Cuxton Kent	28	TQ7066
Cuxton Kent	28	TQ7066
Cuxwold Lincs	85	TA1701
Cwm Clwyd	70	SJ0677
Cwm Gwent	33	SO1805
Cwm W Glam	32	SS6895
Cwm Capel Dyfed	32	SN4502
Cwm Irfon Powys	45	SN8549
Cwm Morgan Dyfed	31	SN2935
Cwm-bach Dyfed	32	SN4801
Cwm-Cewydd Gwynd	57	SH8713
Cwm-Crownon Powy's	33	SO1419
Cwm-celyn Gwent	33	SO2008
Cwm-Llinau Powys	57	SH8408
Cwm-y-glo Gwynd	69	SH5562
Cwmafan W Glam	32	SS7791
Cwmaman M Glam	33	ST0099
Cwmann Dyfed	44	SN5847
Cwmavon Gwent	34	SO2706
Cwmbach Dyfed	31	SN2526
Cwmbach M Glam	33	SO0201
Cwmbach Powys	45	SO1639
Cwmbach Llechrhyd Powys	45	SO0254
Cwmbelan Powys	58	SN9481
Cwmbran Gwent	34	ST2994
Cwmcarn Gwent	34	ST2293
Cwmcarvan Gwent	34	SO4707
Cwmcoy Dyfed	31	SN2942
Cwmdare M Glam	33	SN9803
Cwmdu Dyfed	44	SN6330
Cwmdu Powys	45	SO1823
Cwmdu W Glam	32	SS6494
Cwmduad Dyfed	31	SN3731
Cwmdwr Dyfed	44	SN7132
Cwmfelin M Glam	33	SO0901
Cwmfelin M Glam	33	SS8689
Cwmfelin Boeth Dyfed	31	SN1919

Cwmfelin Mynach Doley

Cwmfelin Mynach *Dyfed* **31** SN2324
Cwmfelinfach *Gwent* **33** ST1891
Cwmffrwd *Dyfed* **31** SN4217
Cwmgiedd *Powys* **32** SN7911
Cwmgorse *W Glam* **32** SN7010
Cwmgwili *Dyfed* **32** SN5710
Cwmgwrach *W Glam* **33** SN8604
Cwmhiraeth *Dyfed* **31** SN3438
Cwmisfael *Dyfed* **32** SN4915
Cwmllynfell *Dyfed* **32** SN7412
Cwmparc *M Glam* **33** SS9495
Cwmpengraig *Dyfed* **31** SN3436
Cwmpennar *M Glam* **33** SO0400
Cwmrhos *Powys* **31** SN1824
Cwmrhydyceirw *W Glam* **32** SS6699
Cwmsychpant *Dyfed* **44** SN4746
Cwmtillery *Gwent* **33** SO2105
Cwmyoy *Gwent* **46** SO2923
Cwmystwyth *Dyfed* **32** SN7874
Cwn-y-glo *Dyfed* **32** SN5513
Cwrt-newydd *Dyfed* **44** SN4847
Cwrt-y-gollen *Powys* **34** SO2317
Cyffylliog *Clwyd* **70** SJ0557
Cyfronydd *Powys* **58** SJ1408
Cylibebyll *W Glam* **32** SN7404
Cymmer *M Glam* **33** ST0290
Cymmer *W Glam* **33** SS8696
Cynghardy *Dyfed* **44** SN8040
Cynheidre *Dyfed* **32** SN4907
Cynonville *W Glam* **33** SS8395
Cynwyd *Clwyd* **70** SJ0541
Cynwyl Elfed *Dyfed* **31** SN3727

D

Daccombe *Devon* **7** SX9068
Dacre *Cumb* **93** NY4526
Dacre *N York* **89** SE1960
Dacre Banks *N York* **89** SE1962
Daddry Shield *Dur* **95** NY8937
Dadford *Bucks* **49** SP6638
Dadlington *Leics* **61** SP4098
Dafen *Dyfed* **32** SN5201
Daffy Green *Norfk* **66** TF9609
Dagenham *Gt Lon* **27** TQ5084
Daglingworth *Gloucs* **35** SO9905
Dagnall *Bucks* **38** SP9916
Dagworth *Suffk* **54** TM0361
Dailly *Strath* **106** NS2701
Dainton *Devon* **7** SX8466
Dairsie *Fife* **126** NO4117
Daisy Hill *Gt Man* **79** SD6504
Daisy Hill *W York* **82** SE2728
Dalavich *Strath* **122** NM9612
Dalbeattie *D & G* **100** NX8361
Dalbeg *W Isls* **154** NB2345
Dalblair *Strath* **107** NS6419
Dalbog *Tays* **134** NO5871
Dalbury *Derbys* **73** SK2634
Dalby *IOM* **153** SC2178
Dalby *Lincs* **77** TF4169
Dalby *N York* **90** SE6370
Dalcapon *Tays* **125** NN9754
Dalchalm *Highld* **147** NC9105
Dalchenna *Strath* **123** NN0706
Dalchork *Highld* **146** NC5710
Dalchreichart *Highld* **131** NH2912
Dalchruin *Tays* **124** NN7116
Dalcrue *Tays* **125** NO0417
Dalderby *Lincs* **77** TF2465
Dalditch *Devon* **4** SX0483
Dale *Cumb* **94** NY5443
Dale *Derbys* **62** SK4338
Dale *Dyfed* **30** SM8005
Dale End *Derbys* **74** SK2161
Dale End *N York* **82** SD9646
DaleHead *Cumb* **93** NY4316
Dale Hill *E Susx* **16** TQ7030
Dalebottom *Cumb* **93** NY2921
Dalehouse *N York* **97** NZ7717
Dalelia *Highld* **129** NM7369
Dalgarven *Strath* **115** NS2846
Dalgety Bay *Fife* **117** NT1683
Dalgig *Strath* **107** NS5513
Dalginross *Tays* **124** NN7721
Dalguise *Tays* **125** NN9947
Dalhalvaig *Highld* **150** NC8954
Dalham *Suffk* **53** TL7261
Daliburgh *W Isls* **154** NF7421
Dalkeith *Loth* **118** NT3367
Dall *Tays* **124** NN5956
Dallas *Gramp* **141** NJ1252
Dalleagles *Strath* **107** NS5610
Dallinghoo *Suffk* **55** TM2655
Dallington *E Susx* **16** TQ6519
Dallow *N York* **89** SE1971
Dalmally *Strath* **123** NN1527
Dalmarnoch *Tays* **117** NS9945
Dalmary *Cent* **115** NS5195
Dalmellington *Strath* **107** NS4706
Dalmeny *Loth* **117** NT1477
Dalmigavie *Highld* **140** NH7319
Dalmigavie Lodge *Highld* **140** NH7523
Dalmore *Highld* **140** NH6668
Dalnacardoch Lodge *Tays* **132** NN7270
Dalnaspidal *Tays* **132** NN6473
Dalnawillan Lodge *Highld* **150** ND0240
Daloist *Tays* **124** NN7857
Dalqueich *Tays* **125** NO0704
Dalquhairn *Strath* **106** NX3296
Dalreavoch Lodge *Highld* **147** NC7508
Dalry *Strath* **115** NS2949
Dalrymple *Strath* **106** NS3514
Dalserf *Strath* **116** NS7950
Dalsmeran *Strath* **104** NR6413
Dalston *Cumb* **93** NY3650
Dalston *Gt Lon* **27** TQ3384
Dalswinton *D & G* **100** NX9385
Dalton *Cumb* **87** SD5476
Dalton *D & G* **100** NY1173
Dalton *Lancs* **78** SD4908
Dalton *N York* **89** NZ1108
Dalton *N York* **89** SE4376
Dalton *Nthumb* **103** NZ1172
Dalton *S York* **75** SK4594
Dalton in Furness *Cumb* **86** SD2273
Dalton Magna *S York* **75** SK4693
Dalton Parva *S York* **75** SK4593
Dalton Piercy *Cleve* **97** NZ4631
Dalton-le-Dale *Dur* **96** NZ4047
Dalton-on-Tees *N York* **89** NZ2907
Daltot *Strath* **113** NR7583
Dalvadie *D & G* **98** NX0851
Dalveich *Cent* **124** NN6124
Dalwhinnie *Highld* **132** NN6385
Dalwood *Devon* **9** ST2400
Dam Green *Norfk* **54** TM0485
Damask Green *Herts* **39** TL2529
Damerham *Hants* **12** SU1015
Damgate *Norfk* **67** TG4009
Dan's Castle *Dur* **95** NZ1149
Dan-y-Parc *Powys* **34** SO2217
Danaway *Kent* **28** TQ8663
Danbury *Essex* **40** TL7805
Danby *N York* **90** NZ7008
Danby Bottom *N York* **90** NZ6904
Danby Wiske *N York* **89** SE3398
Dandaleith *Gramp* **141** NJ2845
Danderhall *Loth* **117** NT3069
Dane End *Herts* **39** TL3321
Dane Hills *Leics* **62** SK5605
Dane Street *Kent* **28** TR0552
Danebridge *Ches* **72** SJ9665
Danegate *E Susx* **16** TQ5634
Danehill *E Susx* **15** TQ4027
Danemoor Green *Norfk* **66** TG0505
Danesford *Shrops* **60** SO7391
Danesmoor *Derbys* **74** SK4263
Daniel's Water *Kent* **28** TQ9541
Danshillack *Gramp* **142** NJ7157
Danskine *Loth* **118** NT5667
Danthorpe *Humb* **85** TA2732
Danzey Green *Warwks* **48** SP1269
Dapple Heath *Staffs* **73** SK0425
Darass Hall *T & W* **103** NZ1570
Darby Green *Hants* **25** SU8360
Darcy Lever *Gt Man* **79** SD7308
Daren-felen *Gwent* **34** SO2212
Darenth *Kent* **27** TQ5571
Daresbury *Ches* **78** SJ5882
Darfield *S York* **83** SE4104
Dargate *Kent* **29** TR0761
Darite *Cnwll* **5** SX2569
Darland *Clwyd* **71** SJ3757
Darland *Kent* **28** TQ7964
Darlaston *Staffs* **72** SJ8835
Darlaston *W Mids* **60** SO9796
Darlaston Green *W Mids* **60** SO9797
Darley *N York* **89** SE2059
Darley Abbey *Derbys* **62** SK3538
Darley Bridge *Derbys* **74** SK2661
Darley Dale *Derbys* **74** SK2663
Darley Green *Warwks* **61** SP1874
Darley Head *N York* **89** SE1959
Darleyhall *Herts* **38** TL1422
Darlingscott *Warwks* **48** SP2342
Darlington *Dur* **89** NZ2914
Darliston *Shrops* **59** SJ5833
Darlton *Notts* **75** SK7773
Darnford *Staffs* **61** SK1308
Darowen *Powys* **57** SH8301
Darra *Gramp* **142** NJ7447
Darracott *Devon* **18** SS2317
Darracott *Devon* **18** SS4739
Darrington *W York* **83** SE4919
Darsham *Suffk* **55** TM4170
Dartford *Kent* **27** TQ5474
Dartington *Devon* **7** SX7862
Dartmeet *Devon* **7** SX6773
Dartmouth *Devon* **7** SX8751
Darton *S York* **82** SE3110
Darvel *Strath* **107** NS5637
Darwell Hole *E Susx* **16** TQ6919
Darwen *Lancs* **81** SD6922
Datchet *Berks* **26** SU9877
Datchworth *Herts* **39** TL2619
Datchworth Green *Herts* **39** TL2618
Daubhill *Gt Man* **79** SD7007
Dauntsey *Wilts* **35** ST9782
Dauntsey Green *Wilts* **35** ST9982
Dava *Highld* **141** NJ0138
Davenham *Ches* **79** SJ6571
Davenport *Gt Man* **79** SJ9088
Davenport Green *Ches* **79** SJ8379
Davenport Green *Gt Man* **79** SJ8086
Daventry *Nhants* **49** SP5762
David Street *Kent* **27** TQ6466
Davidson's Mains *Loth* **117** NT2175
Davidstow *Cnwll* **4** SX1587
Davington *D & G* **109** NT2302
Davington Hill *Kent* **28** TR0161
Daviot *Gramp* **142** NJ7528
Daviot *Highld* **140** NH7239
Daviot House *Highld* **140** NH7240
Davis Street *Berks* **25** SU7872
Davis's Town *E Susx* **16** TQ5217
Davoch of Grange *Gramp* **142** NJ4851
Daw End *W Mids* **61** SK0300
Daw's House *Cnwll* **5** SX3182
Dawesgreen *Surrey* **15** TQ2147
Dawley *Shrops* **60** SJ6807
Dawlish *Devon* **9** SX9676
Dawlish Warren *Devon* **9** SX9778
Dawn *Clwyd* **69** SH8672
Daws Green *Somset* **20** ST2021
Daws Heath *Essex* **40** TQ8188
Dawsmere *Lincs* **65** TF4430
Day Green *Ches* **72** SJ7757
Daybrook *Notts* **62** SK5745
Dayhills *Staffs* **72** SJ9532
Dayhouse Bank *H & W* **60** SO9678
Daylesford *Gloucs* **48** SP2425
Ddol *Clwyd* **70** SJ1471
Ddol-Cownwy *Powys* **58** SJ0117
Deal *Kent* **29** TR3752
Dean *Cumb* **92** NY0725
Dean *Devon* **19** SS6245
Dean *Devon* **19** SS7048
Dean *Devon* **7** SX7364
Dean *Dorset* **11** ST9715
Dean *Hants* **24** SU4431
Dean *Hants* **13** SU5619
Dean *Lancs* **81** SD8526
Dean *Oxon* **36** SP3422
Dean *Somset* **22** ST6743
Dean Bottom *Kent* **27** TQ5868
Dean Court *Oxon* **37** SP4705
Dean Cross *Devon* **19** SS5042
Dean End *Dorset* **11** ST9617
Dean Head *S York* **74** SE2500
Dean Prior *Devon* **7** SX7363
Dean Row *Ches* **79** SJ8781
Dean Street *Kent* **28** TQ7451
Deanburnhaugh *Border* **109** NT3912
Deancombe *Devon* **7** SX7264
Deane *Gt Man* **79** SD6907
Deane *Hants* **24** SU5450
Deanhead *W York* **82** SE0415
Deanich Lodge *Highld* **145** NH3683
Deanland *Dorset* **22** ST9918
Deanlane End *W Susx* **13** SU7412
Deanraw *Nthumb* **102** NY8162
Deanscale *Cumb* **92** NY0926
Deanshanger *Nhants* **49** SP7639
Deanshaugh *Gramp* **141** NJ3550
Deanston *Cent* **116** NN7101
Dearnley *Gt Man* **81** SD9215
Debach *Suffk* **55** TM2454
Debden *Essex* **39** TL5533
Debden Cross *Essex* **40** TL5731
Debden Green *Essex* **40** TL5732
Debden Green *Essex* **27** TQ4398
Debenham *Suffk* **54** TM1763
Deblin's Green *H & W* **47** SO8149
Dechmont *Loth* **117** NT0470
Dechmont Road *Loth* **117** NT0269
Deddington *Oxon* **49** SP4631
Dedham *Essex* **41** TM0533
Dedham Heath *Essex* **41** TM0531
Dedworth *Berks* **26** SU9476
Deebank *Gramp* **135** NO6994
Deebank *Gramp* **135** NO6994
Deene *Nhants* **51** SP9492
Deenethorpe *Nhants* **51** SP9591
Deepcar *S York* **74** SK2897
Deepcut *Surrey* **25** SU9057
Deepdale *Cumb* **88** SD7284
Deepdale *N York* **88** SD8989
Deeping Gate *Lincs* **64** TF1509
Deeping St. James *Lincs* **64** TF1609
Deeping St. Nicholas *Lincs* **64** TF2115
Deerhurst *Gloucs* **47** SO8729
Deerhurst Walton *Gloucs* **47** SO8828
Deerton Street *Kent* **28** TQ9762
Defford *H & W* **47** SO9143
Defynnog *Powys* **45** SN9227
Deganwy *Gwynd* **69** SH7779
Degnish *Strath* **122** NM7812
Deighton *N York* **89** NZ3801
Deighton *N York* **83** SE6244
Deighton *W York* **82** SE1519
Deiniolen *Gwynd* **69** SH5863
Delabole *Cnwll* **4** SX0683
Delamere *Ches* **71** SJ5668
Delfrigs *Gramp* **143** NJ9620
Dell Quay *W Susx* **14** SU8302
Delley *Devon* **19** SS5424
Delliefure *Highld* **141** NJ0731
Delly End *Oxon* **36** SP3513
Delmonden Green *Kent* **17** TQ7330
Delnashaugh Hotel *Gramp* **141** NJ1835
Delnato *Gramp* **141** NJ1517
Delny *Highld* **146** NH7372
Delph *Gt Man* **82** SD9807
Delves *Dur* **95** NZ1149
Delvine *Tays* **126** NO1240
Dembleby *Lincs* **64** TF0437
Demelza *Cnwll* **4** SW9763
Denaby *S York* **75** SK4899
Denaby Main *S York* **75** SK4999
Denbies *Surrey* **26** TQ1450
Denbigh *Clwyd* **70** SJ0566
Denbrae *Fife* **126** NO3818
Denbury *Devon* **7** SX8268
Denby *Derbys* **62** SK3946
Denby Bottles *Derbys* **62** SK3846
Denby Dale *W York* **82** SE2208
Denchworth *Oxon* **36** SU3891
Dendron *Cumb* **86** SD2470
Denel End *Beds* **38** TL0335
Denfield *Strath* **108** NS9517
Denford *Nhants* **51** SP9976
Dengie *Essex* **41** TL9802
Denham *Bucks* **26** TQ0487
Denham *Suffk* **53** TL7561
Denham *Suffk* **55** TM1974
Denham End *Suffk* **53** TL7663
Denham Green *Bucks* **26** TQ0388
Denham Green *Suffk* **55** TM1974
Denhead *Fife* **127** NO4613
Denhead *Gramp* **143** NJ9952
Denhead of Gray *Tays* **126** NO3531
Denholm *Border* **110** NT5718
Denholme *W York* **82** SE0734
Denholme Clough *W York* **82** SE0732
Denio *Gwynd* **56** SH3635
Denmead *Hants* **13** SU6512
Denmore *Gramp* **135** NJ9411
Denne Park *W Susx* **15** TQ1628
Dennington *Suffk* **55** TM2867
Dennis Park *W Mids* **60** SO9585
Denny *Cent* **116** NS8082
Dennyloanhead *Cent* **116** NS8180
Denshaw *Gt Man* **82** SD9710
Denside *Gramp* **135** NO8095
Densole *Kent* **29** TR2141
Denston *Suffk* **53** TL7652
Denstone *Staffs* **73** SK0940
Denstroude *Kent* **29** TR1061
Dent *Cumb* **87** SD7087
Dent-de-Lion *Kent* **29** TR3269
Denton *Cambs* **52** TL1487
Denton *Dur* **96** NZ2118
Denton *E Susx* **16** TQ4502
Denton *Gt Man* **79** SJ9295
Denton *Kent* **28** TQ6673
Denton *Kent* **29** TR2147
Denton *Lincs* **63** SK8632
Denton *N York* **82** SE1448
Denton *Nhants* **51** SP8358
Denton *Norfk* **55** TM2888
Denton *Oxon* **37** SP5902
Denver *Norfk* **65** TF6101
Denwick *Nthumb* **111** NU2014
Deopham *Norfk* **66** TG0500
Deopham Green *Norfk* **66** TM0499
Depden *Suffk* **53** TL7857
Depden Green *Suffk* **53** TL7756
Deptford *Gt Lon* **27** TQ3777
Deptford *Wilts* **22** SU0038
Derby *Derbys* **62** SK3536
Derbyhaven *IOM* **153** SC2867
Derculich *Tays* **125** NN8852
Deri *M Glam* **33** SO1201
Derril *Devon* **18** SS3003
Derringstone *Kent* **29** TR2049
Derrington *Staffs* **72** SJ8922
Derriton *Devon* **18** SS3303
Derry Hill *Wilts* **35** ST9670
Derrythorpe *Humb* **84** SE8208
Dersingham *Norfk* **65** TF6830
Dervaig *Strath* **121** NM4352
Derwen *Clwyd* **70** SJ0750
Derwenlas *Powys* **57** SN7298
Desborough *Nhants* **51** SP8083
Desford *Leics* **62** SK4703
Deskford *Gramp* **142** NJ5061
Deskford *Gramp* **142** NJ5061
Detchant *Nthumb* **111** NU0836
Detling *Kent* **28** TQ7958
Deuxhill *Shrops* **60** SO6987
Devauden *Gwent* **34** ST4898
Devil's Bridge *Dyfed* **43** SN7477
Deviock *M Glam* **5** SX3155
Devitts Green *Warwks* **61** SP2790
Devizes *Wilts* **22** SU0061
Devonport *Devon* **6** SX4554
Devonside *Cent* **116** NS9296
Devoran *Cnwll* **3** SW7939
Dewarton *Loth* **118** NT3763
Dewlish *Dorset* **11** SY7798
Dewsbury *W York* **82** SE2422
Dewsbury Moor *W York* **82** SE2321
Deytheur *Powys* **58** SJ2417
Dhoon *IOM* **153** SC3784
Dhoor *IOM* **153** SC4396
Dhowin *IOM* **153** NX4101
Dial *Avon* **21** ST5367
Dial Green *W Susx* **14** SU9227
Dial Post *W Susx* **15** TQ1519
Dibberford *Dorset* **10** ST4504
Dibden *Hants* **13** SU4108
Dibden Purlieu *Hants* **13** SU4106
Dickens Heath *W Mids* **61** SP1076
Dickleburgh *Norfk* **54** TM1682
Didbrook *Gloucs* **48** SP0531
Didcot *Oxon* **37** SU5190
Diddington *Cambs* **52** TL1965
Diddlebury *Shrops* **59** SO5085
Didley *H & W* **46** SO4532
Didling *W Susx* **14** SU8318
Didmarton *Gloucs* **35** ST8287
Didsbury *Gt Man* **79** SJ8392
Didworthy *Devon* **7** SX6862
Digby *Lincs* **76** TF0854
Digg *Highld* **136** NG4669
Diggle *Gt Man* **82** SE0008
Digmore *Lancs* **78** SD4805
Digswell *Herts* **39** TL2415
Digswell Water *Herts* **39** TL2414
Dihewyd *Dyfed* **44** SN4855
Dilham *Norfk* **67** TG3325
Dilhorne *Staffs* **72** SJ9743
Dillington *Cambs* **52** TL1365
Dilston *Nthumb* **102** NY9763
Dilton *Wilts* **22** ST8548
Dilton Marsh *Wilts* **22** ST8449
Dilwyn *H & W* **46** SO4154
Dimma *Cnwll* **5** SX1997
Dimple *Gt Man* **81** SD7015
Dinas *Cnwll* **4** SW9174
Dinas *Dyfed* **31** SN2730
Dinas *Dyfed* **30** SN0139
Dinas *Gwynd* **56** SH2736
Dinas *M Glam* **33** ST0091
Dinas Dinlle *Gwynd* **68** SH4356
Dinas Powis *S Glam* **33** ST1571
Dinas-Mawddwy *Gwynd* **57** SH8615
Dinder *Somset* **21** ST5744
Dinedor *H & W* **46** SO5336
Dingestow *Gwent* **34** SO4510
Dinghurst *Avon* **21** ST4459
Dingle *Mersyd* **78** SJ3687
Dingleden *Kent* **17** TQ8131
Dingley *Nhants* **50** SP7787
Dingwall *Highld* **139** NH5458
Dinham *Gwent* **34** ST4792
Dinmael *Clwyd* **70** SJ0044
Dinnet *Gramp* **134** NO4598
Dinnington *S York* **75** SK5386
Dinnington *Somset* **10** ST4012
Dinnington *T & W* **103** NZ2073
Dinorwic *Gwynd* **69** SH5961
Dinton *Bucks* **37** SP7611
Dinton *Wilts* **22** SU0131
Dinwoodie *D & G* **100** NY1090
Dinworthy *Devon* **18** SS3015
Dipford *Somset* **20** ST2022
Dipley *Hants* **24** SU7457
Dippen *Strath* **105** NR7937
Dippenhall *Surrey* **25** SU8146
Dippermill *Devon* **18** SS4406
Dippertown *Devon* **5** SX4385
Dippin *Strath* **105** NS0422
Dipple *Gramp* **141** NJ3258
Dipple *Strath* **106** NS2002
Diptford *Devon* **7** SX7256
Dipton *Dur* **96** NZ1554
Diptonmill *Nthumb* **102** NY9361
Dirleton *Loth* **118** NT5184
Dirt Pot *Nthumb* **95** NY8546
Discoed *Powys* **46** SO2764
Diseworth *Leics* **62** SK4524
Dishforth *N York* **89** SE3873
Disley *Ches* **79** SJ9784
Diss *Norfk* **54** TM1180
Disserth *Powys* **45** SO0358
Distington *Cumb* **92** NY0023
Ditchampton *Wilts* **23** SU0831
Ditchburn *Nthumb* **111** NU1320
Ditcheat *Somset* **21** ST6236
Ditchingham *Norfk* **67** TM3391
Ditchley *Oxon* **36** SP3820
Ditchling *E Susx* **15** TQ3215
Ditherington *Shrops* **59** SJ5014
Ditteridge *Wilts* **35** ST8169
Dittisham *Devon* **6** SX5370
Dittisham *Devon* **7** SX8654
Ditton *Ches* **78** SJ4986
Ditton *Kent* **28** TQ7158
Ditton Green *Cambs* **53** TL6558
Ditton Priors *Shrops* **59** SO6089
Dixton *Gloucs* **47** SO9830
Dixton *Gwent* **34** SO5113
Dizzard *Cnwll* **4** SX1698
Dobcross *Gt Man* **82** SD9906
Dobroyd Castle *W York* **81** SD9323
Dobwalls *Cnwll* **5** SX2165
Doccombe *Devon* **8** SX7786
Dochgarroch *Highld* **140** NH6241
Docker *Lancs* **87** SD5774
Docking *Norfk* **65** TF7636
Docklow *H & W* **46** SO5557
Dockray *Cumb* **93** NY2649
Dockray *Cumb* **93** NY3921
Dod's Leigh *Staffs* **73** SK0134
Dodbrooke *Devon* **7** SX7444
Dodd's Green *Ches* **71** SJ6043
Doddinghurst *Essex* **27** TQ5999
Doddington *Cambs* **52** TL4090
Doddington *Kent* **28** TQ9357
Doddington *Lincs* **76** SK9070
Doddington *Nthumb* **111** NT9932
Doddington *Shrops* **46** SO6176
Doddiscombsleigh *Devon* **8** SX8586
Doddshill *Norfk* **65** TF6930
Doddy Cross *M Glam* **5** SX3062
Dodford *H & W* **60** SO9373
Dodford *Nhants* **49** SP6160
Dodington *Avon* **35** ST7580
Dodington *Somset* **20** ST1740
Dodleston *Ches* **71** SJ3661
Dodscott *Devon* **19** SS5419
Dodside *Strath* **115** NS5053
Dodworth *S York* **82** SE3105
Dodworth Bottom *S York* **83** SE3205
Dodworth Green *S York* **82** SE3103
Doe Bank *W Mids* **61** SP1197
Doe Lea *Derbys* **75** SK4566
Dog Village *Devon* **9** SX9896
Dogdyke *Lincs* **76** TF2055
Dogley Lane *W York* **82** SE1914
Dogmersfield *Hants* **25** SU7852
Dogridge *Wilts* **36** SU0787
Dogsthorpe *Cambs* **64** TF1901
Dol-for *Powys* **57** SH8106
Dol-gran *Dyfed* **31** SN4334
Dolanog *Powys* **58** SJ0612
Dolau *Powys* **45** SO1367
Dolbenmaen *Gwynd* **56** SH5043
Dolcombe *Devon* **8** SX7786
Doley *Shrops* **72** SJ7429

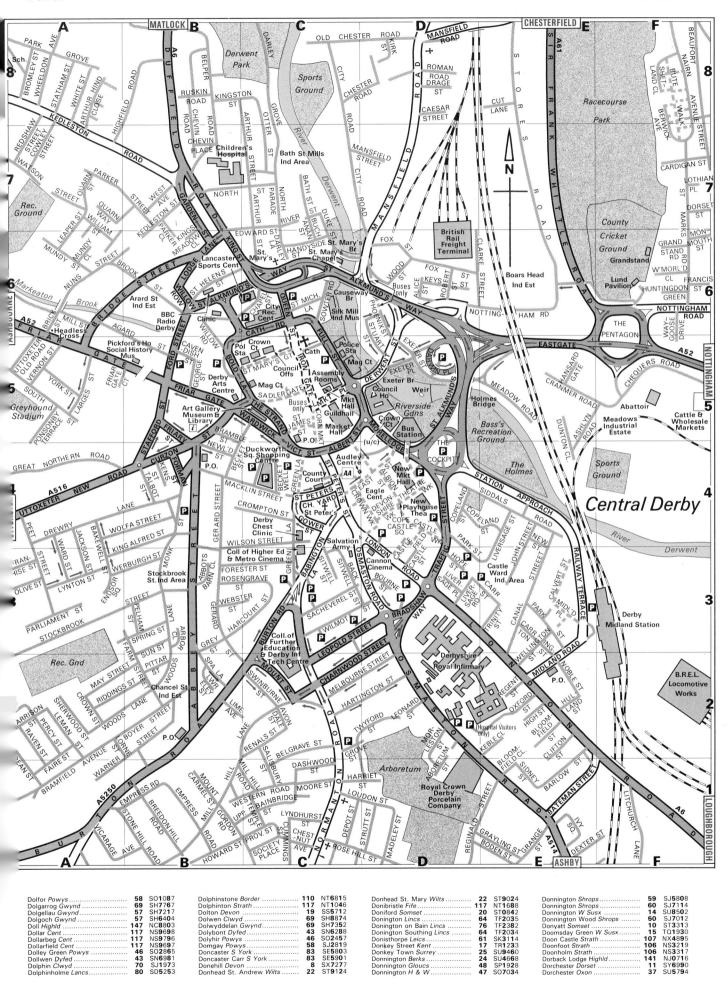

Central Derby

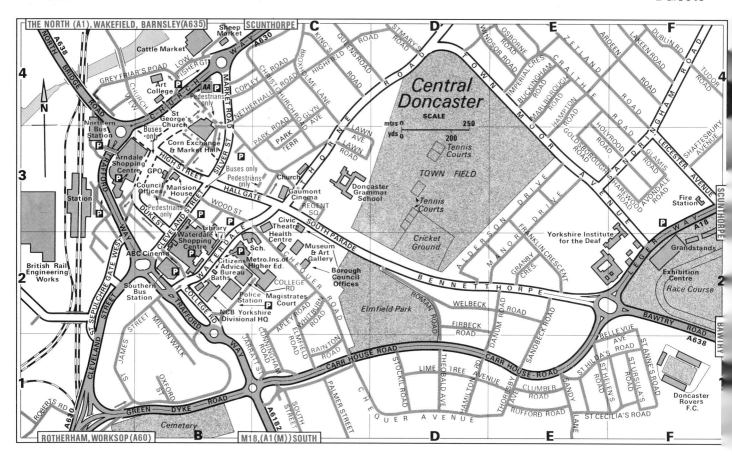

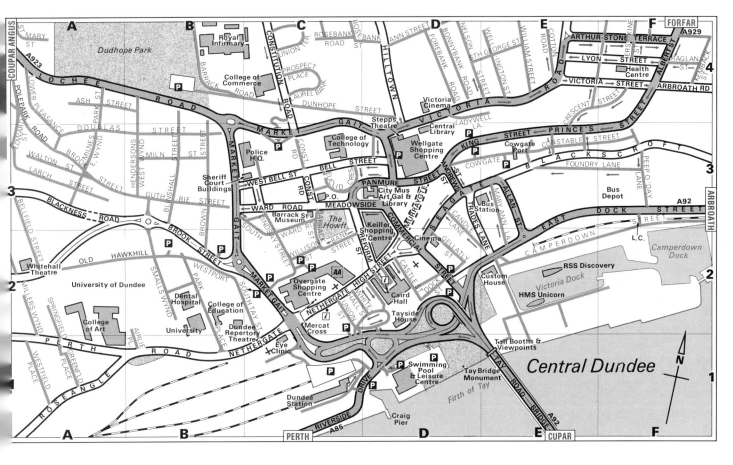

E

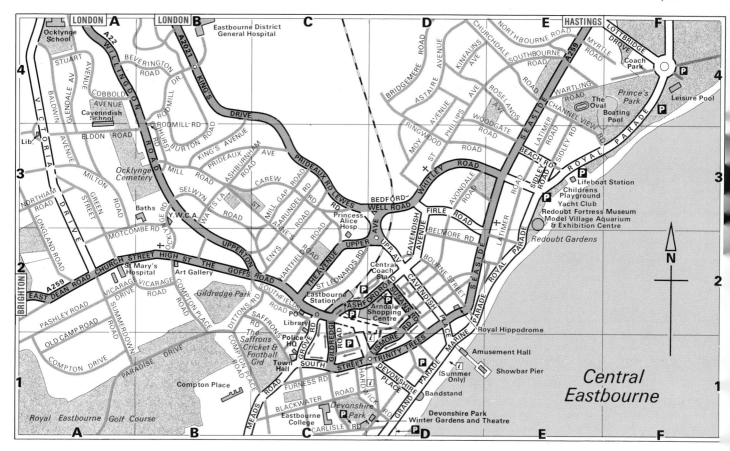

Central Eastbourne

Easthampton Ewyas Harold

Easthampton *H & W* 46 SO4063
Easthope *Shrops* 59 SO5695
Easthorpe *Essex* 40 TL9121
Easthorpe *Notts* 75 SK7053
Eastington *Devon* 19 SS7409
Eastington *Gloucs* 36 SP1213
Eastlands *D & G* 100 NX8172
Eastleach Martin *Gloucs* 36 SP2005
Eastleach Turville *Gloucs* 36 SP1905
Eastleigh *Devon* 18 SS4827
Eastleigh *Hants* 13 SU4519
Eastling *Kent* 28 TQ9656
Eastly End *Surrey* 26 TQ0368
Eastmoor *Norfk* 65 TF7303
Eastney *Hants* 13 SZ6698
Eastnor *H & W* 47 SO7337
Eastoft *Humb* 84 SE8016
Easton *Berks* 24 SU4271
Easton *Cambs* 52 TL1371
Easton *Cumb* 93 NY2759
Easton *Devon* 8 SX7288
Easton *Dorset* 11 SY6871
Easton *Hants* 24 SU5132
Easton *IOW* 12 SZ3486
Easton *Lincs* 63 SK9326
Easton *Norfk* 66 TG1310
Easton *Somset* 21 ST5147
Easton *Suffk* 55 TM2858
Easton *Wilts* 35 ST8970
Easton Grey *Wilts* 35 ST8787
Easton Maudit *Nhants* 51 SP8858
Easton on the Hill *Nhants* 64 TF0104
Easton Royal *Wilts* 23 SU2060
Easton-in-Gordano *Avon* 34 ST5175
Eastpeek *Devon* 5 SX3494
Eastrea *Cambs* 64 TL2997
Eastriggs *D & G* 101 NY2465
Eastrington *Humb* 84 SE7929
Eastrop *Wilts* 36 SU2092
Eastry *Kent* 29 TR3055
Eastshaw *W Susx* 14 SU8724
Eastville *Lincs* 77 TF4056
Eastwell *Leics* 63 SK7728
Eastwick *Herts* 39 TL4311
Eastwood *Essex* 40 TQ8688
Eastwood *Notts* 62 SK4646
Eastwood *W York* 82 SD9727
Eastwood *Cambs* 65 TL4293
Eathorpe *Warwks* 48 SP3969
Eaton *Ches* 71 SJ5763
Eaton *Ches* 72 SJ8765
Eaton *Leics* 63 SK7928
Eaton *Norfk* 67 TG2006
Eaton *Notts* 75 SK7077
Eaton *Oxon* 37 SP4403
Eaton *Shrops* 59 SO3789
Eaton *Shrops* 59 SO5090
Eaton Bishop *H & W* 46 SO4439
Eaton Bray *Beds* 38 SP9620
Eaton Constantine *Shrops* 59 SJ5906
Eaton Ford *Beds* 52 TL1759
Eaton Green *Beds* 38 SP9621
Eaton Hastings *Oxon* 36 SU2698
Eaton Mascott *Shrops* 59 SJ5305
Eaton Socon *Beds* 52 TL1659
Eaton upon Tern *Shrops* 72 SJ6523
Eaves Brow *Ches* 79 SJ6493
Eaves Green *W Mids* 61 SP2682
Ebberston *N York* 91 SE8982
Ebbesborne Wake *Wilts* 22 ST9824
Ebbw Vale *Gwent* 33 SO1609
Ebbw Vale *Gwent* 33 ST2094
Ebchester *Dur* 95 NZ1055
Ebdon *Avon* 21 ST3664
Ebford *Devon* 9 SX9887
Ebley *Gloucs* 35 SO8205
Ebnal *Ches* 71 SJ4948
Ebnall *H & W* 46 SO4758
Ebrington *Gloucs* 48 SP1840
Ebsworthy Town *Devon* 5 SX5090
Ebworth Turbary *Humb* 84 SE7604
Ecchinswell *Hants* 24 SU5059
Ecclaw *Loth* 119 NT7568
Ecclefechan *D & G* 101 NY1974
Eccles *Border* 110 NT7641
Eccles *Gt Man* 79 SJ7798
Eccles *Kent* 28 TQ7360
Eccles Green *H & W* 46 SO3748
Eccles Road *Norfk* 54 TM0190
Ecclesfield *S York* 74 SK3393
Ecclesgreig *Gramp* 135 NO7365
Eccleshall *S York* 74 SK3184
Eccleshall *Staffs* 72 SJ8329
Eccleshill *W York* 82 SE1736
Ecclesmachan *Loth* 117 NT0673
Eccleston *Ches* 71 SJ4162
Eccleston *Lancs* 80 SD5217
Eccleston *Mersyd* 78 SJ4895
Eccleston Green *Lancs* 80 SD5216
Echt *Gramp* 135 NJ7405
Eckford *Border* 110 NT7026
Eckington *Derbys* 74 SK4279
Eckington *H & W* 47 SO9241
Ecton *Nhants* 51 SP8263
Ecton *Staffs* 74 SK0958
Edale *Derbys* 74 SK1285
Edburton *W Susx* 15 TQ2311
Edderside *Cumb* 92 NY1045
Edderton *Highld* 146 NH7084
Edderton Mains *Highld* 146 NH7183
Eddington *Kent* 29 TR1767
Eddleston *Border* 117 NT2447
Eddlewood *Strath* 116 NS7153
Eden Mount *Cumb* 87 SD4078
Edenbridge *Kent* 16 TQ4446
Edenfield *Lancs* 81 SD8019
Edenhall *Cumb* 94 NY5632
Edenham *Lincs* 64 TF0621
Edensor *Derbys* 74 SK2469
Edentaggart *Strath* 115 NS3293
Edenthorpe *S York* 83 SE6206
Ederline *Strath* 122 NM8702
Edern *Gwynd* 56 SH2739
Edgarley *Somset* 21 ST5138
Edgbaston *W Mids* 61 SP0684
Edgcombe *Cnwll* 3 SW7233
Edgcott *Bucks* 37 SP6722
Edgcott *Devon* 19 SS8438
Edge *Gloucs* 35 SO8409
Edge *Shrops* 59 SJ3909
Edge End *Gloucs* 34 SO5913
Edge Green *Ches* 71 SJ4851
Edgebolton *Shrops* 59 SJ5721
Edgefield *Norfk* 66 TG0934
Edgefield Green *Norfk* 66 TG0934
Edgefold *Gt Man* 79 SD7005
Edgerley *Shrops* 59 SJ3518
Edgertown *W York* 82 SE1218
Edgeside *Lancs* 81 SD8322
Edgetown *W York* 82 SE1217
Edgeworth *Gloucs* 35 SO9406
Edgeworthy *Devon* 19 SS8413
Edgiock *H & W* 48 SP0461
Edgmond *Shrops* 72 SJ7119
Edgmond Marsh *Shrops* 72 SJ7120
Edgton *Shrops* 59 SO3886
Edgware *Gt Lon* 26 TQ1991
Edgworth *Lancs* 81 SD7416
Edial *Staffs* 61 SK0708
Edinample *Cent* 124 NN6022
Edinbane *Highld* 136 NG3451
Edinburgh *Loth* 117 NT2573
Edingale *Staffs* 61 SK2112
Edingham *D & G* 100 NX8363
Edingley *Notts* 75 SK6655
Edingthorpe *Norfk* 67 TG3132
Edingthorpe Green *Norfk* 67 TG3131
Edington *Border* 119 NT8956
Edington *Nthumb* 103 NZ1582
Edington *Somset* 21 ST3940
Edington *Wilts* 22 ST9252
Edington Burtle *Somset* 21 ST3943
Edingworth *Somset* 21 ST3553
Edith Weston *Leics* 63 SK9205
Edithmead *Somset* 21 ST3249
Edlesborough *Bucks* 38 SP9719
Edlingham *Nthumb* 111 NU1109
Edlington *Lincs* 76 TF2371
Edmond Castle *Cumb* 94 NY4958
Edmondsham *Dorset* 12 SU0611
Edmondsley *Dur* 96 NZ2349
Edmondthorpe *Leics* 63 SK8517
Edmonton *Cnwll* 4 SW9672
Edmonton *Gt Lon* 27 TQ3492
Edmundbyers *Dur* 95 NZ0150
Ednam *Border* 110 NT7337
Ednaston *Derbys* 73 SK2341
Edradynate *Tays* 125 NN8851
Edrom *Border* 119 NT8255
Edstaston *Shrops* 59 SJ5131
Edstone *Warwks* 48 SP1962
Edvin Loach *H & W* 47 SO6658
Edwalton *Notts* 62 SK5935
Edwardstone *Suffk* 54 TL9442
Edwardsville *M Glam* 33 ST0896
Edwinsford *Dyfed* 44 SN6334
Edwinstowe *Notts* 75 SK6266
Edworth *Beds* 39 TL2241
Edwyn Ralph *H & W* 47 SO6457
Edzell *Tays* 134 NO5968
Efail Isaf *M Glam* 33 ST0884
Efail-fach *W Glam* 32 SS7895
Efail-rhyd *Clwyd* 58 SJ1626
Efailnewydd *Gwynd* 56 SH3536
Efailwen *Dyfed* 31 SN1325
Efenechtyd *Clwyd* 70 SJ1155
Effgill *D & G* 101 NY3092
Effingham *Surrey* 26 TQ1253
Efflinch *Staffs* 73 SK1917
Efford *Devon* 9 SS8901
Egbury *Hants* 24 SU4452
Egerton *Gt Man* 81 SD7014
Egerton *Kent* 28 TQ9047
Eggesford *Devon* 19 SS6810
Eggington *Beds* 38 SP9525
Egginton *Derbys* 73 SK2628
Egglescliffe *Cleve* 89 NZ4113
Eggleston *Dur* 95 NY9923
Egham *Surrey* 26 TQ0171
Egham Wick *Surrey* 25 SU9870
Eginswell *Devon* 7 SX8865
Egleton *Leics* 63 SK8707
Eglingham *Nthumb* 111 NU1019
Egloshayle *Cnwll* 4 SX0072
Egloskerry *Cnwll* 5 SX2786
Eglwys Cross *Clwyd* 71 SJ4741
Eglwys-Brewis *S Glam* 20 ST0069
Eglwysbach *Gwynd* 69 SH8070
Eglwysfach *Dyfed* 43 SN6896
Eglwyswrw *Dyfed* 31 SN1438
Egmanton *Notts* 75 SK7368
Egremont *Cumb* 86 NY0110
Egremont *Mersyd* 78 SJ3192
Egton *N York* 90 NZ8006
Egton Bridge *N York* 90 NZ8005
Eight Ash Green *Essex* 40 TL9425
Eight and Forty *Humb* 84 SE8529
Eilanreach *Highld* 129 NG8017
Elan Village *Powys* 45 SN9364
Elberton *Avon* 34 ST6088
Elbridge *W Susx* 14 SU9102
Elburton *Devon* 6 SX5353
Elcombe *Wilts* 36 SU1280
Elcot *Berks* 36 SU3969
Elder Street *Essex* 53 TL5734
Eldernell *Cambs* 64 TL3298
Eldersfield *H & W* 47 SO7931
Elderslie *Strath* 115 NS4463
Eldmire *N York* 89 SE4274
Eldon *Dur* 96 NZ2328
Eldroth *N York* 88 SD7665
Eldwick *W York* 82 SE1240
Elfhill *Gramp* 135 NO8085
Elfhill *Gramp* 135 NO8085
Elford *Nthumb* 111 NU1831
Elford *Staffs* 61 SK1810
Elgin *Gramp* 141 NJ2162
Elgol *Highld* 128 NG5214
Elham *Kent* 29 TR1744
Elie *Fife* 118 NO4900
Elilaw *Nthumb* 111 NT9708
Elim *Gwynd* 68 SH3584
Eling *Hants* 12 SU3612
Elishader *Highld* 137 NG5065
Elishaw *Nthumb* 102 NY8595
Elkesley *Notts* 75 SK6875
Elkstone *Gloucs* 35 SO9612
Ella *Gramp* 142 NJ6459
Ella *Gramp* 142 NJ6459
Ellanbeich *Strath* 122 NM7417
Elland *W York* 82 SE1020
Elland Lower Edge *W York* 82 SE1121
Ellary *Strath* 113 NR7476
Ellastone *Staffs* 73 SK1143
Ellel *Lancs* 80 SD4856
Ellemford *Border* 119 NT7260
Ellen's Green *Surrey* 14 TQ0935
Ellenborough *Cumb* 92 NY0535
Ellenhall *Staffs* 72 SJ8426
Ellerbeck *N York* 89 SE4396
Ellerby *N York* 90 NZ7914
Ellerdine Heath *Shrops* 59 SJ6122
Ellerhayes *Devon* 9 SS9702
Elleric *Strath* 122 NN0348
Ellerker *Humb* 84 SE9229
Ellers *N York* 82 SE0043
Ellerton *Humb* 84 SE7039
Ellerton *N York* 89 SE2497
Ellerton *Shrops* 72 SJ7126
Ellesborough *Bucks* 38 SP8306
Ellesmere *Shrops* 59 SJ3934
Ellesmere Port *Ches* 71 SJ4076
Ellicombe *Somset* 20 SS9844
Ellingham *Hants* 12 SU1408
Ellingham *Norfk* 67 TM3592
Ellingham *Nthumb* 111 NU1725
Ellingstring *N York* 89 SE1783
Ellington *Cambs* 52 TL1671
Ellington *Nthumb* 103 NZ2791
Ellington *Nthumb* 103 NZ2791
Ellington Thorpe *Cambs* 52 TL1670
Elliots Green *Somset* 22 ST7945
Ellisfield *Hants* 24 SU6346
Ellistown *Leics* 62 SK4311
Ellon *Gramp* 143 NJ9530
Ellon Brook *Gt Man* 79 SD7201
Ellonby *Cumb* 93 NY4235
Ellough *Suffk* 55 TM4486
Elloughton *Humb* 84 SE9428
Ellwood *Gloucs* 34 SO5908
Elm *Cambs* 65 TF4707
Elm Green *Essex* 40 TL7705
Elm Grove *Norfk* 67 TG4803
Elm Park *Gt Lon* 27 TQ5385
Elmbridge *H & W* 47 SO9068
Elmdon *Essex* 39 TL4639
Elmdon *W Mids* 61 SP1783
Elmdon Heath *W Mids* 61 SP1680
Elmer *W Susx* 14 SU9800
Elmer's Green *Lancs* 78 SD5006
Elmers End *Gt Lon* 27 TQ3668
Elmesthorpe *Leics* 50 SP4696
Elmhurst *Staffs* 61 SK1112
Elmley Castle *H & W* 47 SO9841
Elmley Lovett *H & W* 47 SO8769
Elmore *Gloucs* 35 SO7815
Elmore Back *Gloucs* 35 SO7616
Elms Green *H & W* 47 SO7266
Elmscott *Devon* 18 SS2321
Elmsett *Suffk* 54 TM0546
Elmstead Heath *Essex* 41 TM0622
Elmstead Market *Essex* 41 TM0624
Elmstead Row *Essex* 41 TM0622
Elmsted Court *Kent* 29 TR1144
Elmstone *Kent* 29 TR2660
Elmstone Hardwicke *Gloucs* 47 SO9226
Elmswell *Humb* 91 SE9958
Elmswell *Suffk* 54 TL9964
Elmton *Derbys* 75 SK5073
Elphin *Highld* 145 NC2111
Elphinstone *Loth* 118 NT3970
Elrick *Gramp* 135 NJ8206
Elrig *D & G* 98 NX3247
Elrington *Nthumb* 102 NY8663
Elsdon *H & W* 46 SO3154
Elsdon *Nthumb* 102 NY9393
Elsecar *S York* 74 SK3899
Elsenham *Essex* 39 TL5326
Elsfield *Oxon* 37 SP5310
Elsham *Humb* 84 TA0312
Elsick House *Gramp* 135 NO8894
Elsick House *Gramp* 135 NO8894
Elsing *Norfk* 66 TG0517
Elslack *N York* 81 SD9349
Elson *Hants* 13 SU6001
Elson *Shrops* 59 SJ3735
Elsrickle *Strath* 108 NT0643
Elstead *Surrey* 25 SU9043
Elsted *W Susx* 14 SU8119
Elstob *Dur* 96 NZ3323
Elston *Lancs* 81 SD5932
Elston *Notts* 63 SK7647
Elston *Wilts* 23 SU0644
Elstone *Devon* 19 SS6716
Elstow *Beds* 38 TL0547
Elstree *Herts* 26 TQ1895
Elstree *Herts* 26 TQ1895
Elstronwick *Humb* 85 TA2232
Elswick *Lancs* 80 SD4238
Elswick *T & W* 103 NZ2263
Elsworth *Cambs* 52 TL3163
Elterwater *Cumb* 86 NY3204
Eltham *Gt Lon* 27 TQ4274
Eltisley *Cambs* 52 TL2759
Elton *Cambs* 51 TL0893
Elton *Ches* 71 SJ4575
Elton *Cleve* 96 NZ4017
Elton *Derbys* 74 SK2261
Elton *Gloucs* 35 SO7014
Elton *Gt Man* 81 SD7811
Elton *H & W* 46 SO4570
Elton *Notts* 63 SK7638
Elton Green *Ches* 71 SJ4575
Eltringham *Nthumb* 103 NZ0762
Elvaston *Derbys* 62 SK4132
Elveden *Suffk* 54 TL8280
Elvetham Hall *Hants* 25 SU7856
Elvingston *Loth* 118 NT4674
Elvington *Kent* 29 TR2750
Elvington *N York* 83 SE6947
Elwell *Devon* 19 SS6613
Elwick *Cleve* 97 NZ4532
Elwick *Nthumb* 111 NU1137
Elworth *Ches* 72 SJ7361
Elworthy *Somset* 20 ST0835
Ely *Cambs* 53 TL5480
Ely *S Glam* 33 ST1476
Emberton *Bucks* 38 SP8849
Embleton *Cumb* 92 NY1639
Embleton *Dur* 96 NZ4129
Embleton *Nthumb* 111 NU2322
Embo *Highld* 147 NH8192
Embo Street *Highld* 147 NH8091
Emborough *Somset* 21 ST6151
Embsay *N York* 82 SE0053
Emery Down *Hants* 12 SU2808
Emery Down *Hants* 12 SU2808
Emley *W York* 82 SE2413
Emley Moor *W York* 82 SE2313
Emmbrook *Berks* 25 SU8069
Emmer Green *Berks* 37 SU7276
Emmett Carr *Derbys* 75 SK4477
Emmington *Oxon* 37 SP7402
Emneth *Cambs* 65 TF4807
Emneth Hungate *Norfk* 65 TF5107
Empingham *Leics* 63 SK9508
Empshott *Hants* 24 SU7531
Empshott Green *Hants* 24 SU7431
Emsworth *Hants* 13 SU7405
Enaclete *W Isls* 154 NB1228
Enborne *Berks* 24 SU4365
Enborne Row *Hants* 24 SU4463
Enchmarsh *Shrops* 59 SO5096
Encombe *Dorset* 11 SY9478
End Moor *Cumb* 87 SD5484
Enderby *Leics* 50 SP5399
Endon *Staffs* 72 SJ9253
Endon Bank *Staffs* 72 SJ9253
Enfield *Gt Lon* 27 TQ3597
Enfield Lock *Gt Lon* 27 TQ3698
Enfield Wash *Gt Lon* 27 TQ3598
Enford *Wilts* 23 SU1351
Engine Common *Avon* 35 ST6984
England's Gate *H & W* 46 SO5451
Englefield *Berks* 24 SU6272
Englefield Green *Surrey* 25 SU9971
Englesea-brook *Ches* 72 SJ7551
English Bicknor *Gloucs* 34 SO5815
English Frankton *Shrops* 59 SJ4529
Englishcombe *Avon* 22 ST7162
Engollan *Cnwll* 4 SW8670
Enham-Alamein *Hants* 23 SU3649
Enmore *Somset* 20 ST2335
Enmore Green *Dorset* 22 ST8523
Ennerdale Bridge *Cumb* 92 NY0615
Enniscaven *Cnwll* 4 SW9659
Enochdhu *Tays* 133 NO0662
Ensay *Strath* 121 NM3648
Ensbury *Dorset* 12 SZ0896
Ensdon *Shrops* 59 SJ4016
Ensis *Devon* 19 SS5626
Enson *Staffs* 72 SJ9428
Enstone *Oxon* 48 SP3724
Enterkinfoot *D & G* 108 NS8504
Enterpen *N York* 89 NZ4605
Enville *Staffs* 60 SO8286
Enys *Cnwll* 3 SW7936
Epney *Gloucs* 35 SO7611
Epperstone *Notts* 75 SK6548
Epping *Essex* 27 TL4602
Epping Green *Essex* 39 TL4305
Epping Green *Herts* 39 TL2906
Epping Upland *Essex* 39 TL4404
Eppleby *N York* 89 NZ1713
Eppleworth *Humb* 84 TA0131
Epsom *Surrey* 26 TQ2160
Epwell *Oxon* 48 SP3540
Epworth *Humb* 84 SE7803
Erbistock *Clwyd* 71 SJ3541
Erbusaig *Highld* 137 NG7629
Erdington *W Mids* 61 SP1191
Ericstane *D & G* 108 NT0711
Eridge Green *E Susx* 16 TQ5535
Eridge Station *E Susx* 16 TQ5434
Erines *Strath* 113 NR8575
Erisey *Cnwll* 2 SW7117
Eriswell *Suffk* 53 TL7278
Erith *Gt Lon* 27 TQ5177
Erlestoke *Wilts* 22 ST9853
Ermington *Devon* 6 SX6353
Erpingham *Norfk* 67 TG1931
Erriottwood *Kent* 28 TQ9359
Errogie *Highld* 139 NH5622
Errol *Tays* 126 NO2422
Ersary *W Isls* 154 NF7100
Erskine *Strath* 115 NS4771
Ervie *D & G* 98 NX0067
Erwarton *Suffk* 55 TM2234
Erwood *Powys* 45 SO1042
Eryholme *N York* 89 NZ3208
Eryrys *Clwyd* 70 SJ2057
Escalls *Cnwll* 2 SW3627
Escomb *Dur* 96 NZ1830
Escott *Somset* 20 ST0937
Escrick *N York* 83 SE6242
Esgair *Dyfed* 31 SN3729
Esgair *Dyfed* 43 SN5868
Esgairgeiliog *Powys* 57 SH7606
Esgyryn *Gwynd* 69 SH8078
Esh *Dur* 96 NZ1944
Esh Winning *Dur* 96 NZ1942
Esher *Surrey* 26 TQ1364
Esholt *W York* 82 SE1840
Eshott *Nthumb* 103 NZ2097
Eshton *N York* 81 SD9356
Eskadale *Highld* 139 NH4539
Eskbank *Loth* 118 NT3266
Eskdale Green *Cumb* 86 NY1400
Eskdalemuir *D & G* 101 NY2597
Eskett *Cumb* 92 NY0516
Eskham *Lincs* 77 TF3698
Eskholme *S York* 83 SE6317
Esknish *Strath* 112 NR3664
Esperley Lane Ends *Dur* 96 NZ1324
Esprick *Lancs* 80 SD4036
Essendine *Leics* 64 TF0412
Essendon *Herts* 39 TL2708
Essich *Highld* 140 NH6439
Essington *Staffs* 60 SJ9603
Esslemont *Gramp* 143 NJ9239
Esthorpe *Lincs* 64 TF0623
Eston *Cleve* 97 NZ5519
Etal *Nthumb* 110 NT9339
Etchilhampton *Wilts* 23 SU0460
Etching Green *E Susx* 16 TQ5022
Etchingham *E Susx* 17 TQ7126
Etchinghill *Kent* 29 TR1639
Etchinghill *Staffs* 73 SK0218
Etherdwick *Humb* 85 TA2337
Etling Green *Norfk* 66 TG0113
Etloe *Gloucs* 35 SO6705
Eton *Berks* 26 SU9678
Eton Wick *Berks* 26 SU9478
Etruria *Staffs* 72 SJ8647
Etteridge *Highld* 132 NN6892
Ettersgill *Dur* 95 NY8829
Ettiley Heath *Ches* 72 SJ7360
Ettingshall *W Mids* 60 SO9396
Ettington *Warwks* 48 SP2649
Etton *Cambs* 64 TF1306
Etton *Humb* 84 SE9743
Etton *Humb* 84 SE9743
Ettrick *Border* 109 NT2714
Ettrick Bridge *Border* 109 NT3824
Ettrick Hill *Border* 109 NT2514
Etwall *Derbys* 73 SK2631
Eudon George *Shrops* 60 SO6889
Euston *Suffk* 54 TL8979
Euximoor Drove *Cambs* 65 TL4798
Euxton *Lancs* 81 SD5519
Evancoyd *Powys* 46 SO2663
Evanton *Highld* 140 NH6066
Evedon *Lincs* 76 TF0947
Evelith *Shrops* 60 SJ7405
Evelix *Highld* 147 NH7790
Evenjobb *Powys* 46 SO2662
Evenley *Oxon* 49 SP5834
Evenlode *Gloucs* 48 SP2229
Evenwood *Dur* 96 NZ1525
Evenwood Gate *Dur* 96 NZ1624
Evercreech *Somset* 21 ST6438
Everingham *Humb* 84 SE8042
Everleigh *Wilts* 23 SU1953
Everley *N York* 91 SE9788
Eversfield *Devon* 5 SX4792
Eversholt *Beds* 38 SP9833
Evershot *Dorset* 10 ST5704
Eversley *Hants* 25 SU7762
Eversley Cross *Hants* 25 SU7961
Everthorpe *Humb* 84 SE9031
Everton *Beds* 52 TL2051
Everton *Hants* 12 SZ2993
Everton *Mersyd* 78 SJ3491
Everton *Notts* 75 SK6891
Evertown *D & G* 101 NY3576
Evesbatch *H & W* 47 SO6848
Evesham *H & W* 48 SP0343
Evington *Leics* 62 SK6203
Ewden Village *S York* 74 SK2796
Ewdness *Shrops* 60 SO7398
Ewell *Surrey* 26 TQ2262
Ewell Minnis *Kent* 29 TR2643
Ewelme *Oxon* 37 SU6491
Ewen *Gloucs* 35 SU0097
Ewenny *M Glam* 33 SS9077
Ewerby *Lincs* 76 TF1247
Ewerby Thorpe *Lincs* 76 TF1347
Ewesley *Nthumb* 103 NZ0592
Ewhurst *E Susx* 17 TQ7924
Ewhurst *Surrey* 14 TQ0940
Ewhurst Green *Surrey* 14 TQ0939
Ewloe *Clwyd* 71 SJ3066
Ewloe Green *Clwyd* 71 SJ2966
Ewood *Lancs* 81 SD6725
Ewood Bridge *Lancs* 81 SD7920
Eworthy *Devon* 5 SX4494
Ewshot *Hants* 25 SU8149
Ewyas Harold *H & W* 46 SO3828

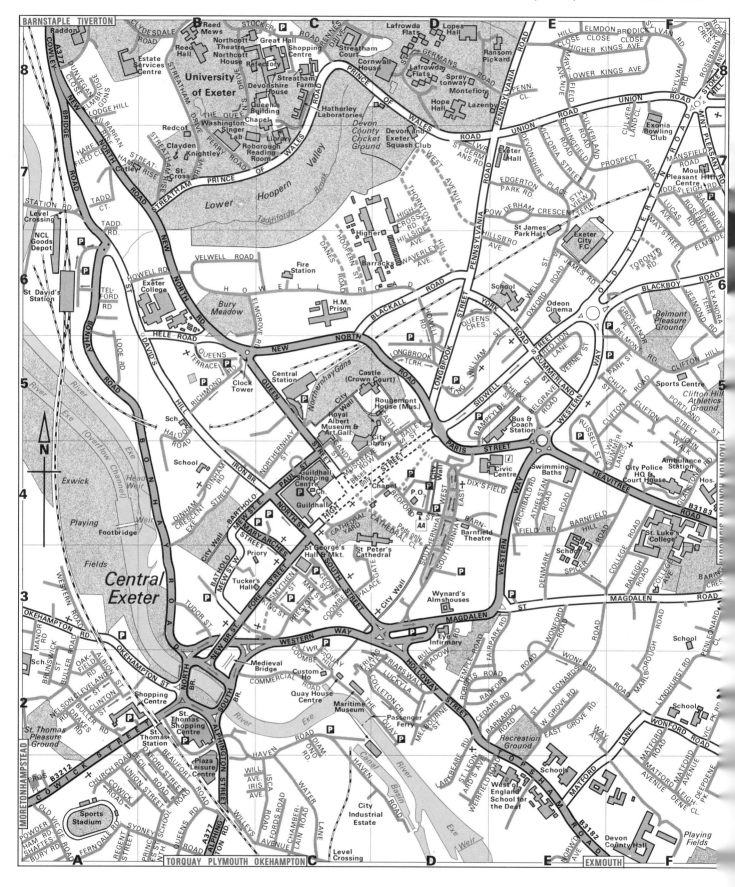

Faccombe Ford

F

Faccombe *Hants* 23 SU3958
Faceby *N York* 90 NZ4902
Fachwen *Powys* 58 SJ0316
Facit *Lancs* 81 SD8819
Fackley *Notts* 75 SK4761
Faddiley *Ches* 71 SJ5852
Fadmoor *N York* 90 SE6789
Failand *Avon* 34 ST5171
Failford *Strath* 107 NS4626
Failsworth *Gt Man* 79 SD8901
Fain *Highld* 145 NH1379
Fair Oak *Hants* 13 SU4918
Fair Oak Green *Hants* 24 SU6660
Fairbourne *Gwynd* 57 SH6113
Fairburn *N York* 83 SE4727
Fairfield *Derbys* 74 SK0674
Fairfield *H & W* 60 SO9475
Fairfield *Kent* 17 TQ9626
Fairford *Gloucs* 36 SP1501
Fairford Park *Gloucs* 36 SP1501
Fairgirth *D & G* 92 NX8756
Fairhaven *Lancs* 80 SD3228
Fairlie *Strath* 114 NS2154
Fairlight *E Susx* 17 TQ8511
Fairmile *Devon* 9 SY0997
Fairmile *Surrey* 26 TQ1161
Fairnilee *Border* 109 NT4532
Fairoak *Staffs* 72 SJ7632
Fairseat *Kent* 27 TQ6261
Fairstead *Essex* 40 TL7616
Fairwarp *E Susx* 16 TQ4626
Fairwater *S Glam* 33 ST1477
Fairy Cross *Devon* 18 SS4024
Fakenham *Norfk* 66 TF9229
Fakenham Magna *Suffk* 54 TL9076
Fala *Loth* 118 NT4461
Fala Dam *Loth* 118 NT4361
Falcondale *Dyfed* 44 SN5649
Falcut *Nhants* 49 SP5942
Faldingworth *Lincs* 76 TF0684
Faldouet *Jersey* 152 JS0000
Falfield *Gloucs* 35 ST6893
Falkenham *Suffk* 55 TM2939
Falkirk *Cent* 116 NS8880
Falkland *Fife* 126 NO2507
Fallgate *Derbys* 74 SK3561
Fallin *Cent* 116 NS8391
Falloden *Nthumb* 111 NU1922
Fallowfield *Gt Man* 79 SJ8594
Fallowfield *Nthumb* 102 NY9268
Falls of Blarghour *Strath* 122 NM9913
Falmer *E Susx* 15 TQ3509
Falmouth *Cnwll* 3 SW8032
Falnash *Border* 109 NT3906
Falsgrave *N York* 91 TA0287
Falstone *Nthumb* 102 NY7287
Fambridge Station *Essex* 40 TQ8698
Fanagmore *Highld* 148 NC1750
Fancott *Beds* 38 TL0127
Fanellan *Highld* 139 NH4842
Fangdale Beck *N York* 90 SE5694
Fangfoss *Humb* 84 SE7653
Fanmore *Strath* 121 NM4144
Fannich Lodge *Highld* 139 NH2266
Fans *Border* 110 NT6140
Far Bletchley *Bucks* 38 SP8533
Far Cotton *Nhants* 49 SP7459
Far End *Cumb* 101 NY3098
Far Forest *H & W* 60 SO7274
Far Green *Gloucs* 35 SO7700
Far Moor *Gt Man* 78 SD5204
Far Oakridge *Gloucs* 35 SO9203
Far Sawrey *Cumb* 87 SD3795
Far Thorpe *Lincs* 77 TF2673
Farcet *Cambs* 64 TL2094
Farden *Shrops* 46 SO5775
Fareham *Hants* 13 SU5806
Farewell *Staffs* 61 SK0811
Farforth *Lincs* 77 TF3178
Faringdon *Oxon* 36 SU2895
Farington *Lancs* 80 SD5325
Farkhill *Tays* 125 NO0435
Farlam *Cumb* 94 NY5558
Farleigh *Avon* 21 ST4969
Farleigh *Devon* 7 SX7553
Farleigh *Surrey* 27 TQ3760
Farleigh Hungerford *Somset* 22 ST7957
Farleigh Wallop *Hants* 24 SU6246
Farlesthorpe *Lincs* 77 TF4774
Farleton *Cumb* 87 SD5380
Farleton *Lancs* 87 SD5767
Farley *Derbys* 74 SK2962
Farley *Staffs* 73 SK0644
Farley *Wilts* 23 SU2229
Farley Green *Suffk* 53 TL7353
Farley Green *Surrey* 14 TQ0545
Farley Hill *Berks* 24 SU7564
Farleys End *Gloucs* 35 SO7615
Farlington *N York* 90 SE6167
Farlow *Shrops* 59 SO6380
Farm Town *Leics* 62 SK3916
Farmborough *Avon* 21 ST6560
Farmbridge End *Essex* 40 TL6211
Farmcote *Gloucs* 48 SP0629
Farmcote *Shrops* 60 SO7892
Farmers *Dyfed* 44 SN6444
Farmington *Gloucs* 36 SP1315
Farmoor *Oxon* 37 SP4506
Farms Common *Cnwll* 2 SW6734
Farmtown *Gramp* 142 NJ5051
Farnachty *Gramp* 142 NJ4261
Farnah Green *Derbys* 62 SK3347
Farnborough *Berks* 36 SU4381
Farnborough *Gt Lon* 27 TQ4564
Farnborough *Hants* 25 SU8753
Farnborough *Warwks* 49 SP4349
Farnborough *Warwks* 49 SP4349
Farnborough Park *Hants* 25 SU8755
Farnborough Street *Hants* 25 SU8556
Farncombe *Surrey* 25 SU9745
Farndish *Beds* 51 SP9263
Farndon *Ches* 71 SJ4154
Farndon *Notts* 75 SK7651
Farnell *Tays* 127 NO6255
Farnham *Dorset* 11 ST9514
Farnham *Essex* 39 TL4724
Farnham *N York* 89 SE3460
Farnham *Suffk* 55 TM3660
Farnham *Surrey* 25 SU8446
Farnham Common *Bucks* 26 SU9585
Farnham Green *Essex* 39 TL4625
Farnham Royal *Bucks* 26 SU9583
Farningham *Kent* 27 TQ5467
Farnley *N York* 82 SE2147
Farnley *W York* 82 SE2533
Farnley Tyas *W York* 82 SE1612
Farnsfield *Notts* 75 SK6456
Farnworth *Ches* 78 SJ5187
Farnworth *Gt Man* 79 SD7306
Farnworth *Gt Man* 79 SD7306
Farr *Highld* 150 NC7163
Farr *Highld* 140 NH6833
Farr *Highld* 132 NH8203
Farraline *Highld* 139 NH5621
Farringdon *Devon* 9 SY0191
Farrington Gurney *Avon* 21 ST6255
Farsley *W York* 82 SE2135
Farther Howegreen *Essex* 40 TL8401
Farthing Green *Kent* 28 TQ8146
Farthing Street *Gt Lon* 27 TQ4262
Farthinghoe *Nhants* 49 SP5339
Farthingloe *Kent* 29 TR2940
Farthingstone *Nhants* 49 SP6154
Fartown *W York* 82 SE1518
Fartown *W York* 82 SE2232
Farway *Devon* 9 SY1895
Fasnacloich *Strath* 122 NN0247
Fasnakyle *Highld* 139 NH3128
Fasque *Gramp* 135 NO6575
Fassfern *Highld* 130 NN0278
Fatfield *T & W* 96 NZ2954
Faugh *Cumb* 94 NY5154
Fauld *Staffs* 73 SK1728
Faulkbourne *Essex* 40 TL7917
Faulkland *Somset* 22 ST7354
Fauls *Shrops* 59 SJ5932
Faversham *Kent* 28 TR0161
Fawdington *N York* 89 SE4372
Fawdon *Nthumb* 111 NU0315
Fawfieldhead *Staffs* 74 SK0763
Fawkham Green *Kent* 27 TQ5865
Fawler *Oxon* 36 SP3717
Fawley *Berks* 36 SU3981
Fawley *Bucks* 37 SU7586
Fawley *Hants* 13 SU4503
Fawley Chapel *H & W* 46 SO5829
Fawnog *Clwyd* 70 SJ2466
Fawsley *Nhants* 49 SP5656
Faxfleet *Humb* 84 SE8624
Faygate *W Susx* 15 TQ2134
Fazakerley *Mersyd* 78 SJ3797
Fazeley *Staffs* 61 SK2001
Fearby *N York* 89 SE1981
Fearn *Highld* 147 NH8378
Fearnan *Tays* 124 NN7244
Fearnbeg *Highld* 137 NG7359
Fearnhead *Ches* 79 SJ6390
Fearnmore *Highld* 137 NG7260
Fearnoch *Strath* 114 NR9279
Featherstone *Staffs* 60 SJ9305
Featherstone *W York* 83 SE4221
Feckenham *H & W* 47 SP0162
Fedderate *Gramp* 143 NJ8949
Feering *Essex* 40 TL8720
Feetham *N York* 88 SD9898
Feindside *Border* 109 NT4408
Feizor *N York* 88 SD7867
Felbridge *Surrey* 15 TQ3739
Felbrigg *Norfk* 67 TG2039
Felcourt *Surrey* 15 TQ3841
Felday *Surrey* 14 TQ1144
Felden *Herts* 38 TL0404
Felin Fach *Dyfed* 44 SN5255
Felin Gwm Uchaf *Dyfed* 31 SN4034
Felin-gwm Uchaf *Dyfed* 44 SN5024
Felin-newydd *Powys* 45 SO1135
Felindre *Dyfed* 32 SN5521
Felindre *Dyfed* 44 SN5555
Felindre *Dyfed* 44 SN7027
Felindre *Powys* 31 SN1723
Felindre *Powys* 58 SO1681
Felinfach *Powys* 45 SO0933
Felinfoel *Dyfed* 32 SN5202
Felingem Isaf *Dyfed* 44 SN5023
Felixkirk *N York* 89 SE4684
Felixstowe *Suffk* 55 TM3035
Felixstoweferry *Suffk* 55 TM3237
Felkington *Nthumb* 110 NT9444
Felkirk *W York* 83 SE3812
Fell Foot *Cumb* 86 NY2903
Fell Lane *W York* 82 SE0440
Fell Side *Cumb* 93 NY3037
Felling *T & W* 96 NZ2761
Felmersham *Beds* 51 SP9957
Felmingham *Norfk* 67 TG2529
Felpham *W Susx* 14 SZ9599
Felsham *Suffk* 54 TL9457
Felsted *Essex* 40 TL6720
Feltham *Gt Lon* 26 TQ1073
Felthamhill *Gt Lon* 26 TQ0971
Felthorpe *Norfk* 66 TG1618
Felton *Avon* 21 ST5265
Felton *H & W* 46 SO5748
Felton *Nthumb* 103 NU1800
Felton Butler *Shrops* 59 SJ3917
Feltwell *Norfk* 53 TL7190
Fen Ditton *Cambs* 53 TL4860
Fen Drayton *Cambs* 52 TL3368
Fen End *Lincs* 64 TF2420
Fen End *W Mids* 61 SP2274
Fen Street *Norfk* 66 TL9895
Fen Street *Suffk* 54 TM1862
Fenay Bridge *W York* 82 SE1815
Fence *Lancs* 81 SD8237
Fence *S York* 75 SK4485
Fencehouses *T & W* 96 NZ3249
Fencote *N York* 89 SE2893
Fencott *Oxon* 37 SP5716
Fendike Corner *Lincs* 77 TF4560
Fenham *Nthumb* 103 NU0800
Fenham *T & W* 103 NZ2264
Feniscliffe *Lancs* 81 SD6526
Feniscowles *Lancs* 81 SD6425
Feniton *Devon* 9 SY1199
Fenn Green *Shrops* 60 SO7783
Fenn Street *Kent* 28 TQ7975
Fenny Bentley *Derbys* 73 SK1750
Fenny Bridges *Devon* 9 SY1198
Fenny Compton *Warwks* 49 SP4151
Fenny Drayton *Leics* 61 SP3597
Fenny Stratford *Bucks* 38 SP8834
Fenrother *Nthumb* 103 NZ1792
Fenstanton *Cambs* 52 TL3168
Fenstead End *Suffk* 54 TL8050
Fenton *Cambs* 52 TL3279
Fenton *Lincs* 76 SK8476
Fenton *Lincs* 76 SK8751
Fenton *Notts* 75 SK7984
Fenton *Staffs* 72 SJ8944
Fenton Town *Nthumb* 111 NT9734
Fenwick *Nthumb* 111 NU0640
Fenwick *Nthumb* 103 NZ0572
Fenwick *S York* 83 SE5916
Fenwick *Strath* 107 NS4643
Feochaig *Strath* 105 NR7613
Feock *Cnwll* 3 SW8238
Feolin Ferry *Strath* 112 NR4469
Feriniquarrie *Highld* 136 NG1750
Fern *Tays* 134 NO4861
Ferndale *M Glam* 33 SS9996
Ferndown *Dorset* 12 SU0700
Ferness *Highld* 140 NH9645
Fernham *Oxon* 36 SU2991
Fernhill Heath *H & W* 47 SO8659
Fernhurst *W Susx* 14 SU8928
Fernie *Fife* 126 NO3115
Ferniegair *Strath* 116 NS7354
Fernilea *Highld* 136 NG3732
Fernilee *Derbys* 79 SK0178
Ferny Common *H & W* 46 SO3651
Ferriby Sluice *Humb* 84 SE9720
Ferrindonald *Highld* 129 NG6608
Ferring *W Susx* 14 TQ0902
Ferry Point *Highld* 146 NH7385
Ferrybridge *W York* 83 SE4824
Ferryden *Tays* 127 NO7156
Ferryhill *Dur* 96 NZ2932
Ferryside *Dyfed* 31 SN3610
Ferrytown *Highld* 146 NH7387
Fersfield *Norfk* 54 TM0683
Fersit *Highld* 131 NN3577
Fetcham *Surrey* 26 TQ1455
Fetterangus *Gramp* 143 NJ9850
Fettercairn *Gramp* 135 NO6573
Feus *Tays* 126 NO3533
Fewcott *Oxon* 49 SP5328
Fewston *N York* 82 SE1954
Ffair Rhos *Dyfed* 43 SN7368
Ffairfach *Dyfed* 32 SN6220
Ffawyddog *Powys* 33 SO2018
Ffestiniog *Gwynd* 57 SH7042
Ffordd-Las *Clwyd* 70 SJ1264
Fforest *Dyfed* 32 SN5804
Fforest *Gwent* 34 SO2820
Fforest Fach *W Glam* 32 SS6295
Fforest Goch *W Glam* 32 SN7401
Ffostrasol *Dyfed* 42 SN3747
Ffridd Uchaf *Gwynd* 69 SH5751
Ffrith *Clwyd* 70 SJ2855
Ffrwdgrech *Powys* 45 SO0227
Ffynnon-Oer *Dyfed* 44 SN5353
Ffynnongroew *Clwyd* 70 SJ1381
Ffynonddewi *Dyfed* 42 SN3853
Fiag Lodge *Highld* 149 NC4528
Fickleshole *Surrey* 27 TQ3860
Fiddes *Gramp* 135 NO8080
Fiddington *Gloucs* 47 SO9231
Fiddington *Somset* 20 ST2140
Fiddleford *Dorset* 11 ST8013
Fiddlers Green *Cnwll* 3 SW8254
Fiddlers Hamlet *Essex* 27 TL4701
Field *Staffs* 73 SK0233
Field Broughton *Cumb* 87 SD3881
Field Dalling *Norfk* 66 TG0039
Field Head *Leics* 62 SK4909
Fieldhead *Cumb* 93 NY4539
Fife Keith *Gramp* 142 NJ4250
Fifehead Magdalen *Dorset* 22 ST7721
Fifehead Neville *Dorset* 11 ST7610
Fifehead St. Quinton *Dorset* 11 ST7710
Fifield *Berks* 26 SU9076
Fifield *Oxon* 36 SP2318
Fifield *Wilts* 23 SU1450
Figheldean *Wilts* 23 SU1547
Filands *Wilts* 35 ST9388
Filby *Norfk* 67 TG4613
Filey *N York* 91 TA1180
Filgrave *Bucks* 38 SP8648
Filkins *Oxon* 36 SP2304
Filleigh *Devon* 19 SS6628
Filleigh *Devon* 19 SS7410
Fillingham *Lincs* 76 SK9485
Fillongley *Warwks* 61 SP2887
Filmore Hill *Hants* 13 SU6627
Filton *Avon* 34 ST6079
Fimber *Humb* 91 SE8960
Finavon *Tays* 127 NO4956
Fincham *Norfk* 65 TF6806
Finchampstead *Berks* 25 SU7963
Fincharr *Strath* 122 NM9003
Finchdean *Hants* 13 SU7312
Finchingfield *Essex* 40 TL6832
Finchley *Gt Lon* 27 TQ2690
Find O' Gask *Tays* 125 NO0019
Findern *Derbys* 73 SK3030
Findhorn *Gramp* 141 NJ0463
Findhorn Bridge *Highld* 140 NH8027
Findochty *Gramp* 142 NJ4667
Findon *Gramp* 135 NO9397
Findon *W Susx* 14 TQ1208
Findon Mains *Highld* 140 NH6060
Findrack House *Gramp* 134 NJ6004
Finedon *Nhants* 51 SP9172
Fingal Street *Suffk* 55 TM2270
Fingask *Gramp* 142 NJ7827
Fingask *Tays* 126 NO1619
Fingest *Bucks* 37 SU7791
Finghall *N York* 89 SE1789
Fingland *Cumb* 93 NY2557
Fingland *D & G* 107 NS7517
Finglesham *Kent* 29 TR3353
Fingringhoe *Essex* 41 TM0320
Finkle Green *Essex* 53 TL7040
Finkle Street *S York* 74 SK3099
Finlarig *Cent* 124 NN5733
Finmere *Oxon* 49 SP6333
Finnart *Tays* 124 NN5157
Finningham *Suffk* 54 TM0669
Finningley *Notts* 75 SK6699
Finsbay *W Isls* 154 NG0786
Finstall *H & W* 60 SO9870
Finsthwaite *Cumb* 87 SD3687
Finstock *Oxon* 36 SP3616
Finstown *Ork* 155 HY3514
Fintry *Cent* 116 NS6186
Fintry *Gramp* 142 NJ7554
Finzean *Gramp* 134 NO5993
Finzean *Gramp* 134 NO5993
Fionnphort *Strath* 120 NM3023
Fir Tree *Dur* 96 NZ1434
Firbank *Cumb* 87 SD6293
Firbeck *S York* 75 SK5688
Firby *N York* 90 SE7466
Firby *N York* 89 SE2686
Firgrove *Gt Man* 81 SD9113
Firsby *Lincs* 77 TF4562
Fishbourne *IOW* 13 SZ5592
Fishbourne *W Susx* 14 SU8304
Fishburn *Dur* 96 NZ3632
Fishcross *Cent* 116 NS8995
Fisher *W Susx* 14 SU8700
Fisher's Pond *Hants* 13 SU4820
Fisher's Row *Lancs* 80 SD4148
Fisherford *Gramp* 142 NJ6735
Fisherrow *Loth* 118 NT3472
Fisherstreet *W Susx* 14 SU9531
Fisherton *Highld* 140 NH7451
Fisherton *Strath* 106 NS2717
Fisherton de la Mere *Wilts* 22 ST9938
Fishery Estate *Berks* 26 SU8980
Fishguard *Dyfed* 30 SM9637
Fishinghurst *Kent* 28 TQ7537
Fishlake *S York* 83 SE6513
Fishleigh *Devon* 8 SS5405
Fishmere End *Lincs* 64 TF2837
Fishnish Pier *Strath* 121 NM6542
Fishpond Bottom *Dorset* 10 SY3698
Fishponds *Avon* 35 ST6375
Fishpool *Gt Man* 79 SD8009
Fishtoft *Lincs* 64 TF3642
Fishtoft Drove *Lincs* 77 TF3148
Fishtown of Usan *Tays* 127 NO7254
Fishwick *Border* 119 NT9151
Fishwick *Lancs* 81 SD5529
Fiskavaig *Highld* 136 NG3334
Fiskerton *Lincs* 76 TF0472
Fiskerton *Notts* 75 SK7351
Fitling *Humb* 85 TA2534
Fittleton *Wilts* 23 SU1449
Fittleworth *W Susx* 14 TQ0119
Fitton End *Cambs* 65 TF4313
Fitz *Shrops* 59 SJ4418
Fitzhead *Somset* 20 ST1228
Fitzroy *Somset* 20 ST1927
Fitzwilliam *W York* 83 SE4115
Fiunary *Highld* 121 NM6246
Five Acres *Gloucs* 34 SO5712
Five Ash Down *E Susx* 16 TQ4724
Five Ashes *E Susx* 16 TQ5525
Five Bells *Somset* 20 ST0642
Five Bridges *H & W* 47 SO6446
Five Lanes *Gwent* 34 ST4490
Five Oak Green *Kent* 16 TQ6445
Five Oaks *Jersey* 152 JS0000
Five Oaks *W Susx* 14 TQ0928
Five Roads *Dyfed* 32 SN4905
Five Wents *Kent* 28 TQ8050
Fivecrosses *Ches* 71 SJ5376
Fivehead *Somset* 21 ST3522
Fivelanes *Cnwll* 5 SX2280
Fiveways *Warwks* 61 SP2370
Flack's Green *Essex* 40 TL7614
Flackwell Heath *Bucks* 26 SU8990
Fladbury *H & W* 47 SO9946
Fladdabister *Shet* 155 HU4332
Flagg *Derbys* 74 SK1368
Flamborough *Humb* 91 TA2270
Flamstead *Herts* 38 TL0714
Flansham *W Susx* 14 SU9601
Flanshaw *W York* 82 SE3020
Flappit Spring *W York* 82 SE0536
Flasby *N York* 82 SD9456
Flash *Staffs* 74 SK0267
Flashader *Highld* 136 NG3453
Flatt *Strath* 116 NS6551
Flatt The *Cumb* 101 NY5678
Flaunden *Herts* 26 TL0100
Flawborough *Notts* 63 SK7842
Flawith *N York* 90 SE4865
Flax Bourton *Avon* 21 ST5069
Flaxby *N York* 89 SE3957
Flaxley *Gloucs* 35 SO6815
Flaxmere *Ches* 71 SJ5672
Flaxpool *Somset* 20 ST1435
Flaxton *N York* 90 SE6762
Fleckney *Leics* 50 SP6493
Flecknoe *Warwks* 49 SP5163
Fledborough *Notts* 75 SK8072
Fleet *Dorset* 10 SY6380
Fleet *Hants* 13 SU7201
Fleet *Hants* 25 SU8053
Fleet *Lincs* 65 TF3923
Fleet Hargate *Lincs* 65 TF3924
Fleetend *Hants* 13 SU5006
Fleetwood *Lancs* 80 SD3348
Flemingston *S Glam* 33 ST0170
Flemington *Strath* 116 NS6559
Flempton *Suffk* 54 TL8169
Fletcher Green *Kent* 16 TQ5349
Fletchersbridge *Cnwll* 4 SX1065
Fletchertown *Cumb* 93 NY2042
Fletching *E Susx* 16 TQ4223
Fleur-de-lis *M Glam* 58 SO1596
Flexbury *Cnwll* 18 SS2107
Flexford *Surrey* 25 SU9350
Flimby *Cumb* 92 NY0233
Flimwell *E Susx* 17 TQ7131
Flint *Clwyd* 70 SJ2472
Flint Mountain *Clwyd* 70 SJ2470
Flint's Green *W Mids* 61 SP2680
Flintham *Notts* 63 SK7445
Flinton *Humb* 85 TA2136
Flitcham *Norfk* 65 TF7326
Flitton *Beds* 38 TL0535
Flitwick *Beds* 38 TL0334
Flixborough *Humb* 84 SE8715
Flixborough Stather *Humb* 84 SE8614
Flixton *Gt Man* 79 SJ7494
Flixton *N York* 91 TA0479
Flixton *Suffk* 55 TM3186
Flockton *W York* 82 SE2314
Flockton Green *W York* 82 SE2514
Flodda *W Isls* 154 NF8455
Flodden *Nthumb* 110 NT9235
Flodigarry *Highld* 136 NG4671
Flookburgh *Cumb* 87 SD3675
Flordon *Norfk* 66 TM1897
Flore *Nhants* 49 SP6460
Flotterton *Nthumb* 103 NT9902
Flowers Green *E Susx* 16 TQ6311
Flowton *Suffk* 54 TM0847
Flushdyke *W York* 82 SE2821
Flushing *Cnwll* 3 SW8034
Fluxton *Devon* 9 SY0892
Flyford Flavell *H & W* 47 SO9854
Fobbing *Essex* 40 TQ7184
Fochabers *Gramp* 141 NJ3458
Fochriw *M Glam* 33 SO1005
Fockerby *Humb* 84 SE8519
Fodderty *Highld* 139 NH5159
Foddington *Somset* 21 ST5829
Foel *Powys* 58 SH9911
Foel y Dyffryn *M Glam* 33 SS8594
Foelgastell *Dyfed* 32 SN5415
Foffarty *Tays* 126 NO4145
Foggathorpe *Humb* 84 SE7537
Fogo *Border* 110 NT7749
Fogwatt *Gramp* 141 NJ2356
Foindle *Highld* 148 NC1948
Folda *Tays* 133 NO1963
Fole *Staffs* 73 SK0437
Foleshill *W Mids* 61 SP3582
Foliejon Park *Berks* 25 SU8974
Folke *Dorset* 11 ST6513
Folkestone *Kent* 29 TR2336
Folkingham *Lincs* 64 TF0733
Folkington *E Susx* 16 TQ5603
Folksworth *Cambs* 52 TL1489
Folkton *N York* 91 TA0579
Folla Rule *Gramp* 142 NJ7332
Follifoot *N York* 83 SE3452
Folly Gate *Devon* 8 SX5797
Folly Hill *Surrey* 25 SU8348
Fonmon *S Glam* 20 ST0467
Font-y-gary *S Glam* 20 ST0566
Fonthill Bishop *Wilts* 22 ST9332
Fonthill Gifford *Wilts* 22 ST9231
Fontmell Magna *Dorset* 11 ST8616
Fontmell Parva *Dorset* 11 ST8214
Fontwell *W Susx* 14 SU9507
Foolow *Derbys* 74 SK1976
Foord *Kent* 29 TR2236
Footbridge *Cumb* 93 NY4148
Foots Cray *Gt Lon* 27 TQ4770
Forbestown *Gramp* 134 NJ3613
Forcett *N York* 89 NZ1712
Ford *Bucks* 37 SP7709

G

Garton-on-the-Wolds Graims

Garton-on-the-Wolds *Humb* **91** SE9759
Gartsherrie *Strath* **116** NS7265
Gartymore *Highld* **147** ND0114
Garvald *Loth* **118** NT5870
Garvalt *Strath* **114** NS0296
Garvan *Highld* **130** NM9777
Garvard *Strath* **112** NR3691
Garve *Highld* **139** NH3961
Garvestone *Norfk* **66** TG0207
Garvock *Strath* **114** NS2570
Garway *H & W* **34** SO4522
Garway Common *H & W* **34** SO4622
Garway Hill *H & W* **46** SO4425
Garynahine *W Isls* **154** NB2331
Gasper *Wilts* **22** ST7533
Gass *Strath* **106** NS4105
Gastard *Wilts* **22** ST8868
Gasthorpe *Norfk* **54** TL9781
Gaston Green *Essex* **39** TL4917
Gatcombe *IOW* **13** SZ4885
Gate Burton *Lincs* **76** SK8382
Gate Helmsley *N York* **83** SE6855
Gatebeck *Cumb* **87** SD5485
Gateford *Notts* **75** SK5781
Gateforth *N York* **83** SE5628
Gatehead *Strath* **106** NS3936
Gatehouse *Nthumb* **102** NY7989
Gatehouse *Strath* **113** NR8160
Gatehouse of Fleet *D & G* **99** NX5956
Gatelawbridge *D & G* **100** NX9096
Gateley *Norfk* **66** TF9624
Gatenby *N York* **89** SE3287
Gates Heath *Ches* **71** SJ4760
Gatesgarth *Cumb* **93** NY1925
Gatesgarth *Cumb* **93** NY1915
Gateshaw *Border* **110** NT7722
Gateshead *T & W* **96** NZ2562
Gateside *Fife* **126** NO1809
Gateside *Strath* **115** NS4858
Gateside *Strath* **115** NS3653
Gateside *Tays* **127** NO4344
Gateslack *D & G* **108** NS8902
Gathurst *Gt Man* **78** SD5507
Gatley *Gt Man* **79** SJ8488
Gatton *Surrey* **27** TQ2752
Gattonside *Border* **109** NT5435
Gauldry *Fife* **126** NO3723
Gauldswell *Tays* **126** NO2151
Gaulkthorn *Lancs* **81** SD7526
Gaultree *Norfk* **65** TF4907
Gaunt's Common *Dorset* **12** SU0205
Gaunt's End *Essex* **39** TL5525
Gaunton's Bank *Ches* **71** SJ5647
Gautby *Lincs* **76** TF1772
Gavinton *Border* **119** NT7652
Gawber *S York* **83** SE3207
Gawcott *Bucks* **49** SP6831
Gawsworth *Ches* **79** SJ8969
Gawthorpe *W York* **82** SE2721
Gawthrop *Cumb* **87** SD6987
Gawthwaite *Cumb* **86** SD2784
Gay Bowers *Essex* **40** TL7904
Gay Street *W Susx* **14** TQ0820
Gaydon *Warwks* **48** SP3654
Gayhurst *Bucks* **38** SP8446
Gayle *N York* **88** SD8688
Gayles *N York* **89** NZ1207
Gayton *Mersyd* **78** SJ2780
Gayton *Nhants* **49** SP7054
Gayton *Norfk* **65** TF7219
Gayton *Staffs* **72** SJ9828
Gayton le Marsh *Lincs* **77** TF4284
Gayton Thorpe *Norfk* **65** TF7418
Gaywood *Norfk* **65** TF6320
Gazeley *Suffk* **53** TL7264
Gear *Cnwll* **3** SW7224
Geary *Highld* **136** NG2661
Gedding *Suffk* **54** TL9458
Geddinge *Kent* **29** TR2346
Geddington *Nhants* **51** SP8983
Gedintailor *Highld* **137** NG5235
Gedling *Notts* **62** SK6142
Gedney *Lincs* **65** TF4024
Gedney Broadgate *Lincs* **65** TF4022
Gedney Drove End *Lincs* **65** TF4629
Gedney Dyke *Lincs* **65** TF4126
Gedney Hill *Lincs* **64** TF3311
Gee Cross *Gt Man* **79** SJ9593
Geldeston *Norfk* **67** TM3991
Gelli *Gwent* **34** ST2793
Gelli *M Glam* **33** SS9794
Gelli Gynan *Clwyd* **70** SJ1854
Gellideg *M Glam* **33** SO0207
Gellifor *Clwyd* **70** SJ1262
Gelligaer *M Glam* **33** ST1397
Gelligroes *Gwent* **33** ST1794
Gelligron *W Glam* **32** SN7104
Gellilydan *Gwynd* **57** SH6839
Gellinudd *W Glam* **32** SN7304
Gellinudd *W Glam* **32** SN7303
Gelly *Dyfed* **31** SN0819
Gellyburn *Tays* **125** NO0939
Gellywen *Dyfed* **31** SN2723
Gelston *D & G* **92** NX7758
Gelston *Lincs* **63** SK9145
Gentleshaw *Staffs* **61** SK0511
George Green *Bucks* **26** TQ0081
George Nympton *Devon* **19** SS7023
Georgefield *D & G* **101** NY3091
Georgeham *Devon* **18** SS4639
Georgetown *Gwent* **33** SO1508
Georgia *Cnwll* **2** SW4836
Georth *Ork* **155** HY3626
Gerlan *Gwynd* **69** SH6366
Germansweek *Devon* **5** SX4394
Germoe *Cnwll* **2** SW5829
Gerrans *Cnwll* **3** SW8735
Gerrards Cross *Bucks* **26** TQ0088
Gerrick *Cleve* **90** NZ7012
Geshader *W Isls* **154** NB1131
Gestingthorpe *Essex* **54** TL8138
Geuffordd *Powys* **58** SJ2114
Geufron *Powys* **45** SN8968
Gib Hill *Ches* **79** SJ6478
Gibraltar *Lincs* **77** TF5558
Gibralter *Kent* **29** TR2038
Gibsmere *Notts* **75** SK7248
Giddeahall *Wilts* **35** ST8674
Giddy Green *Dorset* **11** SY8286
Gidea Park *Gt Lon* **27** TQ5290
Gidleigh *Devon* **8** SX6788
Gidleigh *Devon* **8** SX6788
Giffnock *Strath* **115** NS5658
Gifford *Loth* **118** NT5368
Giffordtown *Fife* **126** NO2811
Giggleswick *N York* **88** SD8163
Gilberdyke *Humb* **84** SE8329
Gilbert Street *Hants* **24** SU6532
Gilbert's Cross *Staffs* **60** SO8186
Gilbert's End *H & W* **47** SO8242
Gilchriston *Loth* **118** NT4865
Gilcrux *Cumb* **92** NY1138
Gildersome *W York* **82** SE2429
Gildingwells *S York* **75** SK5585
Gilesgate Moor *Dur* **96** NZ2943
Gileston *S Glam* **20** ST0167
Gilfach *M Glam* **33** ST1598
Gilfach *M Glam* **33** ST1598
Gilfach Goch *M Glam* **33** SS9890
Gilfachrheda *Dyfed* **42** SN4159
Gilgarran *Cumb* **92** NY0323
Gill *Cumb* **93** NY4429
Gill's Green *Kent* **17** TQ7532
Gillamore *N York* **90** SE6890
Gillesbie *D & G* **100** NY1691
Gilling *N York* **89** NZ1805
Gilling East *N York* **90** SE6176
Gillingham *Dorset* **22** ST8026
Gillingham *Kent* **28** TQ7768
Gillingham *Norfk* **67** TM4191
Gillock *Highld* **151** ND2159
Gillow Heath *Staffs* **72** SJ8858
Gills *Highld* **151** ND3272
Gilmanscleuch *Border* **109** NT3321
Gilmerton *Loth* **117** NT2968
Gilmerton *Tays* **125** NN8823
Gilmonby *Dur* **95** NY9912
Gilmorton *Leics* **50** SP5787
Gilsland *Nthumb* **102** NY6366
Gilson *Warwks* **61** SP1890
Gilstead *W York* **82** SE1131
Gilston *Herts* **39** TL4413
Gilwern *Gwent* **34** SO2414
Gimingham *Norfk* **67** TG2836
Ginclough *Ches* **79** SJ9576
Ginger Green *E Susx* **16** TQ6212
Gipping *Suffk* **54** TM0763
Gipsey Bridge *Lincs* **77** TF2849
Girdle Toll *Strath* **106** NS3440
Girlington *W York* **82** SE1334
Girlsta *Shet* **155** HU4250
Girsby *Cleve* **89** NZ3508
Girtford *Beds* **52** TL1649
Girthon *D & G* **99** NX6053
Girton *Cambs* **53** TL4262
Girton *Notts* **75** SK8266
Girvan *Strath* **106** NX1897
Gisburn *Lancs* **81** SD8248
Gisleham *Suffk* **55** TM5188
Gislingham *Suffk* **54** TM0771
Gissing *Norfk* **54** TM1485
Gittisham *Devon* **9** SY1398
Gladestry *Powys* **45** SO2355
Gladsmuir *Loth* **118** NT4573
Glais *W Glam* **32** SN7000
Glaisdale *N York* **90** NZ7705
Glamis *Tays* **126** NO3846
Glan-Duar *Dyfed* **44** SN5243
Glan-Mule *Powys* **58** SO1690
Glan-rhyd *W Glam* **32** SN7809
Glan-y-don *Clwyd* **70** SJ1679
Glan-y-llyn *M Glam* **33** ST1184
Glan-y-nant *Powys* **58** SN9384
Glan-yr-afon *Gwynd* **69** SH6080
Glan-yr-afon *Gwynd* **70** SH9140
Glan-yr-afon *Gwynd* **70** SJ0142
Glanaber *Gwynd* **69** SH6350
Glanaber Terrace *Gwynd* **69** SH7547
Glanafon *Dyfed* **30** SM9517
Glanaman *Dyfed* **32** SN6713
Glandford *Norfk* **66** TG0441
Glandwr *Dyfed* **31** SN1928
Glandyfi *Dyfed* **43** SN6996
Glangrwyne *Powys* **34** SO2416
Glanllynfi *M Glam* **33** SS8690
Glanrhyd *Dyfed* **31** SN1442
Glanton *Nthumb* **111** NU0714
Glanton Pike *Nthumb* **111** NU0514
Glanvilles Wootton *Dorset* **11** ST6708
Glapthorn *Nhants* **51** TL0290
Glapwell *Derbys* **75** SK4766
Glasbury *Powys* **45** SO1739
Glascoed *Clwyd* **70** SH9973
Glascoed *Gwent* **34** SO3201
Glascote *Staffs* **61** SK2203
Glascwm *Powys* **45** SO1552
Glasfryn *Clwyd* **70** SH9250
Glasgow *Strath* **115** NS5865
Glasinfryn *Gwynd* **69** SH5868
Glaslaw *Gramp* **135** NO8585
Glasnacardoch Bay *Highld* **129** NM6795
Glasnakille *Highld* **128** NG5313
Glaspwll *Powys* **43** SN7397
Glass Houghton *W York* **83** SE4324
Glassburn *Highld* **139** NH3634
Glassel *Gramp* **135** NO6599
Glassel *Gramp* **135** NO6599
Glassenbury *Kent* **28** TQ7536
Glasserton *D & G* **99** NX4237
Glassford *Strath* **116** NS7247
Glasshouse *Gloucs* **35** SO7021
Glasshouse Hill *Gloucs* **35** SO7020
Glasshouses *N York* **89** SE1764
Glasson *Cumb* **101** NY2560
Glasson *Lancs* **80** SD4456
Glassonby *Cumb* **94** NY5738
Glasterlaw *Tays* **127** NO5951
Glaston *Leics* **51** SK8900
Glastonbury *Somset* **21** ST4938
Glatton *Cambs* **52** TL1586
Glazebury *Ches* **79** SJ6797
Glazeley *Shrops* **60** SO7088
Gleadless Townend *Derbys* **74** SK3883
Gleadsmoss *Ches* **79** SJ8168
Gleaston *Cumb* **86** SD2570
Gledhow *W York* **82** SE3137
Gleding *Notts* **62** SK5132
Gledpark *D & G* **99** NX6250
Gledrid *Shrops* **59** SJ2936
Glehearn *Tays* **126** NO1016
Glemanault *Strath* **104** NR6407
Glemsford *Suffk* **54** TL8348
Glen *D & G* **99** NX5457
Glen Auldyn *IOM* **153** SC4393
Glen Clunie Lodge *Gramp* **133** NO1383
Glen Nevis House *Highld* **130** NN1272
Glen of Foudland *Gramp* **142** NJ6035
Glen of Foudland *Gramp* **142** NJ6035
Glen Parva *Leics* **50** SP5798
Glen Trool Lodge *D & G* **99** NX4080
Glen Village *Cent* **116** NS8878
Glen Vine *IOM* **153** SC3378
Glenancross *Highld* **129** NM6691
Glenaros House *Strath* **121** NM5544
Glenbarr *Strath* **105** NR6736
Glenbeg *Highld* **121** NM5862
Glenbervie *Gramp* **135** NO7680
Glenboig *Strath* **116** NS7269
Glenborrodale *Highld* **121** NM6061
Glenbranter *Strath* **114** NS1197
Glenbreck *Border* **108** NT0521
Glenbrittle House *Highld* **128** NG4121
Glenbuck *Strath* **107** NS7429
Glencally *Tays* **134** NO3562
Glencalvie Lodge *Highld* **146** NH4689
Glencaple *D & G* **100** NX9968
Glencarron Lodge *Highld* **138** NH0650
Glencarse *Tays* **126** NO1922
Glenceitlein *Highld* **123** NN1548
Glencoe *Highld* **130** NN1058
Glencothe *Border* **108** NT0829
Glencraig *Fife* **117** NT1894
Glencrosh *D & G* **107** NX7689
Glendaruel *Strath* **114** NR9983
Glendevon *Tays* **125** NN9904
Glendoe Lodge *Highld* **131** NH4009
Glendoik *Tays* **126** NO2022
Glenduckie *Fife* **126** NO2818
Gleneagles *Tays* **125** NN9209
Glenegedale *Strath* **112** NR3351
Glenelg *Highld* **129** NG8119
Glenerney *Gramp* **141** NJ0146
Glenfarg *Tays* **126** NO1310
Glenfeshie Lodge *Highld* **132** NN8493
Glenfield *Leics* **62** SK5306
Glenfinnan *Highld* **130** NM8980
Glenfinntaig Lodge *Highld* **131** NN2286
Glenfoot *Tays* **126** NO1815
Glenfyne Lodge *Strath* **123** NN2215
Glengarnock *Strath* **115** NS3252
Glengolly *Highld* **151** ND1065
Glengorm Castle *Strath* **121** NM4357
Glengrasco *Highld* **136** NG4444
Glenholm *Border* **108** NT1033
Glenhoul *D & G* **107** NX6187
Glenkerry *Border* **109** NT2711
Glenkiln *D & G* **100** NX8477
Glenkin *Strath* **114** NS1280
Glenkindie *Gramp* **142** NJ4314
Glenlee *D & G* **99** NX6080
Glenlochar *D & G* **99** NX7364
Glenloig *Strath* **105** NR9435
Glenluce *D & G* **98** NX1957
Glenmallan *Strath* **114** NS2595
Glenmark *Tays* **134** NO4283
Glenmassan *Strath* **114** NS1087
Glenmavis *Strath* **116** NS7467
Glenmaye *IOM* **153** SC2380
Glenmore *Highld* **136** NG4340
Glenmore *Strath* **122** NM8412
Glenmore Lodge *Highld* **133** NH9709
Glenmuirshaw *Strath* **107** NS6920
Glenquiech *Tays* **134** NO4266
Glenralloch *Strath* **113** NR8569
Glenridding *Cumb* **93** NY3817
Glenrisdell *Strath* **113** NR8658
Glenrothes *Fife* **117** NO2700
Glenshero Lodge *Highld* **132** NN5593
Glenstriven *Strath* **114** NS0878
Glentham *Lincs* **76** TF0090
Glentromie Lodge *Highld* **132** NN7897
Glentrool Village *D & G* **98** NX3578
Glentruim House *Highld* **132** NN6894
Glentworth *Lincs* **76** SK9488
Glenuig *Highld* **129** NM6676
Glenure *Strath* **123** NN0448
Glenurquhart *Highld* **140** NH7462
Glenvarragill *Highld* **136** NG4739
Glenwhilly *D & G* **98** NX1771
Glespin *Strath* **108** NS8128
Glewstone *H & W* **34** SO5521
Glinton *Cambs* **64** TF1505
Glooston *Leics* **50** SP7595
Glororum *Nthumb* **111** NU1633
Glossop *Derbys* **74** SK0493
Gloster Hill *Nthumb* **103** NU2504
Gloucester *Gloucs* **35** SO8318
Glover's Hill *Staffs* **73** SK0416
Glusburn *N York* **82** SE0344
Glutt Lodge *Highld* **150** ND0036
Gluvian *Cnwll* **4** SW9164
Glympton *Oxon* **36** SP4221
Glyn Ceiriog *Clwyd* **70** SJ2038
Glyn-Neath *W Glam* **33** SN8806
Glynarthen *Dyfed* **42** SN3148
Glyncoch *M Glam* **33** ST0792
Glyncorrwg *W Glam* **33** SS8799
Glynde *E Susx* **16** TQ4509
Glyndebourne *E Susx* **16** TQ4510
Glyndyfrdwy *Clwyd* **70** SJ1442
Glynn *Cnwll* **4** SX1165
Glynogwr *M Glam* **33** SS9585
Glyntaff *M Glam* **33** ST0889
Glyntawe *Powys* **33** SN8416
Glynteg *Dyfed* **31** SN3638
Gnosall *Staffs* **72** SJ8220
Gnosall Heath *Staffs* **72** SJ8220
Goadby *Leics* **50** SP7598
Goadby Marwood *Leics* **63** SK7826
Goat Lees *Kent* **28** TR0145
Goatacre *Wilts* **35** SU0176
Goatfield *Strath* **114** NN0100
Goatham Green *E Susx* **17** TQ8120
Goathill *Dorset* **11** ST6717
Goathland *N York* **90** NZ8301
Goathurst *Somset* **20** ST2534
Goathurst Common *Kent* **27** TQ4952
Gobowen *Shrops* **59** SJ3033
Godalming *Surrey* **25** SU9743
Godameavy *Devon* **6** SX5364
Goddard's Corner *Suffk* **55** TM2868
Goddard's Green *Kent* **17** TQ8134
Godford Cross *Devon* **9** ST1302
Godington *Bucks* **49** SP6427
Godley *Gt Man* **79** SJ9595
Godmanchester *Cambs* **52** TL2470
Godmanstone *Dorset* **11** SY6697
Godmersham *Kent* **28** TR0550
Godney *Somset* **21** ST4842
Godolphin Cross *Cnwll* **2** SW6031
Godre'r-graig *W Glam* **32** SN7506
Godshill *Hants* **12** SU1714
Godshill *IOW* **13** SZ5281
Godstone *Staffs* **73** SK0134
Godstone *Surrey* **27** TQ3551
Godstone Station *Surrey* **15** TQ3648
Godsworthy *Devon* **5** SX5277
Godwinscroft *Hants* **12** SZ1896
Goetre *Gwent* **34** SO3206
Goff's Oak *Herts* **39** TL3203
Gogar *Loth* **117** NT1672
Goginan *Dyfed* **43** SN6981
Golan *Gwynd* **57** SH5242
Golant *Cnwll* **3** SX1254
Golberdon *Cnwll* **5** SX3271
Golborne *Gt Man* **78** SJ6097
Golcar *W York* **82** SE0915
Gold Hill *Cambs* **65** TL5392
Gold Hill *Dorset* **11** ST8213
Goldcliff *Gwent* **34** ST3683
Golden Cross *E Susx* **16** TQ5312
Golden Green *Kent* **16** TQ6348
Golden Grove *Dyfed* **32** SN5919
Golden Hill *Dyfed* **30** SM9802
Golden Pot *Hants* **24** SU7043
Golden Valley *Derbys* **74** SK4251
Goldenhill *Staffs* **72** SJ8553
Golders Green *Gt Lon* **26** TQ2487
Goldfinch Bottom *Berks* **24** SU5063
Goldhanger *Essex* **40** TL9009
Golding *Shrops* **59** SJ5403
Goldington *Beds* **38** TL0750
Golds Green *W Mids* **60** SO9893
Goldsborough *N York* **90** NZ8314
Goldsborough *N York* **83** SE3856
Goldsithney *Cnwll* **2** SW5430
Goldstone *Shrops* **72** SJ7028
Goldsworth *Surrey* **25** SU9958
Goldthorpe *S York* **83** SE4604
Goldworthy *Devon* **18** SS3923
Golford *Kent* **28** TQ7936
Golford Green *Kent* **28** TQ7936
Gollanfield *Highld* **140** NH8053
Gollinglith Foot *N York* **89** SE1480
Golly *Clwyd* **71** SJ3358
Golsoncott *Somset* **20** ST0338
Golspie *Highld* **132** NH8300
Gomeldon *Wilts* **23** SU1936
Gomersal *W York* **82** SE2026
Gomshall *Surrey* **14** TQ0847
Gonachan *Cent* **116** NS6386
Gonalston *Notts* **63** SK6747
Gonerby Hill Foot *Lincs* **63** SK9037
Gonfirth *Shet* **155** HU3761
Good Easter *Essex* **40** TL6212
Gooderstone *Norfk* **65** TF7602
Goodleigh *Devon* **19** SS6034
Goodmanham *Humb* **84** SE8842
Goodnestone *Kent* **28** TR0461
Goodnestone *Kent* **29** TR2554
Goodrich *H & W* **34** SO5719
Goodrich Cross *H & W* **34** SO5619
Goodrington *Devon* **7** SX8958
Goodshaw *Lancs* **81** SD8125
Goodshaw Fold *Lancs* **81** SD8026
Goodstone *Devon* **7** SX7871
Goodwick *Dyfed* **30** SM9438
Goodworth Clatford *Hants* **23** SU3642
Goodyers End *Warwks* **61** SP3385
Goole *Humb* **84** SE7423
Goolefields *Humb* **84** SE7520
Goonbell *Cnwll* **3** SW7249
Goonhavern *Cnwll* **3** SW7853
Goonvrea *Cnwll* **2** SW7149
Goose Green *Avon* **35** ST6774
Goose Green *Essex* **41** TM1425
Goose Green *Essex* **41** TM1425
Goose Green *Gt Man* **78** SD5603
Goose Green *Kent* **28** TQ8437
Goose Green *Kent* **27** TQ6451
Goose Green *W Susx* **14** TQ1118
Goose Pool *H & W* **46** SO4636
Goosecruives *Gramp* **135** NO7583
Goosecruives *Gramp* **135** NO7583
Gooseford *Devon* **8** SX6892
Gooseham *Cnwll* **18** SS2316
Goosehill Green *H & W* **47** SO9361
Goosemoor *Somset* **20** SS9635
Goosetrey *Ches* **79** SJ7770
Goosey *Oxon* **36** SU3591
Goosnargh *Lancs* **81** SD5536
Gorddinog *Gwynd* **69** SH6773
Gordon *Border* **110** NT6443
Gordon Arms Hotel *Border* **109** NT3125
Gordonbush *Highld* **147** NC8409
Gordonstown *Gramp* **142** NJ5656
Gordonstown *Gramp* **142** NJ7138
Gore *Powys* **46** SO2658
Gore Pit *Essex* **40** TL8719
Gore Street *Kent* **27** TQ2765
Gorebridge *Loth* **118** NT3461
Gorefield *Cambs* **65** TF4112
Gores *Wilts* **23** SU1158
Gorey *Jersey* **152** JS0000
Goring *Oxon* **37** SU6080
Goring Heath *Oxon* **37** SU6579
Goring-by-Sea *W Susx* **14** TQ1102
Gorleston on Sea *Norfk* **67** TG5204
Gorrachie *Gramp* **142** NJ7358
Gorran Churchtown *Cnwll* **3** SW9942
Gorran Haven *Cnwll* **3** SX0141
Gorran High Lanes *Cnwll* **3** SW9843
Gorrenberry *Border* **109** NY4699
Gorrowby Hall *Humb* **90** SE7957
Gors *Dyfed* **43** SN6277
Gorse Hill *Wilts* **36** SU1586
Gorsedd *Clwyd* **70** SJ1576
Gorseinon *W Glam* **32** SS5998
Gorseybank *Derbys* **73** SK2953
Gorsgoch *Dyfed* **44** SN4850
Gorslas *Dyfed* **32** SN5713
Gorsley *Gloucs* **47** SO6925
Gorsley Common *Gloucs* **47** SO6225
Gorsley Green *Ches* **79** SJ8469
Gorst Hill *H & W* **60** SO7473
Gorstage *Ches* **71** SJ6172
Gorstan *Highld* **139** NH3863
Gorstello *Ches* **71** SJ3562
Gorsty Common *H & W* **46** SO4437
Gorsty Hill *Staffs* **73** SK1029
Gorten *Strath* **122** NM7432
Gorton *Gt Man* **79** SJ8896
Gosbeck *Suffk* **54** TM1555
Gosberton *Lincs* **64** TF2331
Gosberton Clough *Lincs* **64** TF1929
Gosfield *Essex* **40** TL7829
Gosford *Devon* **4** SX1197
Gosforth *Cumb* **86** NY0603
Gosforth *T & W* **103** NZ2467
Gosland Green *Ches* **71** SJ5758
Gosling Street *Somset* **21** ST5633
Gosmore *Herts* **39** TL1827
Gospel End *Staffs* **60** SO8993
Gospel Green *W Susx* **14** SU9331
Gosport *Hants* **13** SZ6199
Gossard Green *Beds* **38** SP9643
Goswick *Nthumb* **111** NU0645
Gotham *Notts* **62** SK5330
Gotherington *Gloucs* **47** SO9629
Gotton *Somset* **20** ST2428
Goudhurst *Kent* **28** TQ7237
Goulceby *Lincs* **77** TF2579
Gourdas *Gramp* **142** NJ7741
Gourdie *Tays* **126** NO3532
Gourdon *Gramp* **135** NO8271
Gourock *Strath* **114** NS2477
Govan *Strath* **115** NS5465
Goveton *Devon* **7** SX7546
Govilon *Gwent* **34** SO2614
Gowdall *Humb* **83** SE6122
Gower *Highld* **139** NH5058
Gowerton *W Glam* **32** SS5896
Gowkhall *Fife* **117** NT0589
Gowthorpe *Humb* **84** SE7654
Goxhill *Humb* **85** TA1021
Goxhill *Humb* **85** TA1844
Graby *Lincs* **64** TF0929
Grade *Cnwll* **2** SW7114
Gradeley Green *Ches* **71** SJ5851
Graffham *W Susx* **14** SU9217
Grafham *Cambs* **52** TL1669
Grafham *Surrey* **14** TQ0241
Grafton *H & W* **46** SO5761
Grafton *H & W* **46** SO4936
Grafton *H & W* **47** SO9837
Grafton *H & W* **46** SO5761
Grafton *N York* **89** SE4163
Grafton *Oxon* **36** SP2600
Grafton *Shrops* **59** SJ4319
Grafton Flyford *H & W* **47** SO9656
Grafton Regis *Nhants* **49** SP7546
Grafton Underwood *Nhants* **51** SP9280
Grafty Green *Kent* **28** TQ8748
Graianrhyd *Clwyd* **70** SJ2156
Graig *Clwyd* **70** SJ0872
Graig *Gwynd* **69** SH8071
Graig-fechan *Clwyd* **70** SJ1454
Grains *Kent* **28** TQ8876

Graims Bar Gussage St Michael

Grains Bar Gt Man 79 SD9608
Grains o'the Beck Bridge Dur 95 NY8621
Grainsby Lincs 77 TF2799
Grainthorpe Lincs 77 TF3896
Gramisdale W Isls 154 NF8155
Grampound Cnwll 3 SW9348
Grampound Road Cnwll 3 SW9150
Gramsdale W Isls 154 NF8255
Granborough Bucks 49 SP7625
Granby Notts 63 SK7536
Grand Chemins Jersey 152 JS0000
Grandborough Warwks 50 SP4967
Grandes Rocques Guern 152 GN0000
Grandtully Tays 125 NN9153
Grange Cumb 93 NY2517
Grange Kent 28 TQ7968
Grange Mersyd 78 SJ2286
Grange Tays 126 NO2625
Grange Crossroads Gramp 142 NJ4754
Grange Gate Dorset 11 SY9182
Grange Hall Gramp 141 NJ0660
Grange Hill Gt Lon 27 TQ4492
Grange Lindores Fife 126 NO2516
Grange Moor W York 82 SE2216
Grange Villa Dur 96 NZ2352
Grange-over-Sands Cumb 87 SD4077
Grangehall Strath 108 NS9642
Grangemill Derbys 74 SK2457
Grangemouth Cent 116 NS9282
Grangepans Cent 117 NT0181
Grangetown Cleve 97 NZ5420
Gransmoor Humb 91 TA1259
Gransmore Green Essex 40 TL6922
Granston Dyfed 30 SM8934
Grantchester Cambs 53 TL4355
Grantham Lincs 63 SK9135
Granton Fife 117 NT2277
Grantown-on-Spey Highld 141 NJ0328
Grantsfield H & W 46 SO5360
Grantshouse Border 119 NT8165
Grappenhall Ches 79 SJ6486
Grasby Lincs 85 TA0804
Grasmere Cumb 86 NY3307
Grass Green Essex 53 TL7338
Grasscroft Gt Man 82 SD9704
Grassendale Mersyd 78 SJ3985
Grassgartin Cumb 93 NY3444
Grassington N York 88 SE0063
Grassmoor Derbys 74 SK4067
Grassthorpe Notts 75 SK7967
Grateley Hants 23 SU2742
Gratwich Staffs 73 SK0231
Graveley Cambs 52 TL2564
Graveley Herts 39 TL2327
Gravelly Hill W Mids 61 SP1090
Gravelsbank Shrops 59 SJ3600
Graveney Kent 28 TR0562
Gravesend Kent 27 TQ6474
Gravir W Isls 154 NB3715
Grayingham Lincs 76 SK9396
Grayrigg Cumb 87 SD5796
Grays Essex 27 TQ6177
Grayshott Hants 14 SU8735
Grayswood Surrey 14 SU9134
Graythorpe Cleve 97 NZ5227
Grazeley Berks 24 SU6966
Grazies Hill Oxon 37 SU7980
Greasbrough S York 74 SK4195
Greasby Mersyd 78 SJ2587
Greasley Notts 62 SK4947
Great Abington Cambs 53 TL5348
Great Addington Nhants 51 SP9675
Great Alne Warwks 48 SP1259
Great Altcar Lancs 78 SD3306
Great Amwell Herts 39 TL3712
Great Asby Cumb 94 NY6713
Great Ashfield Suffk 54 TL9967
Great Ayton N York 90 NZ5510
Great Baddow Essex 40 TL7305
Great Badminton Avon 35 ST8082
Great Bardfield Essex 40 TL6730
Great Barford Beds 52 TL1352
Great Barr W Mids 61 SP0495
Great Barrington Gloucs 36 SP2013
Great Barrow Ches 71 SJ4768
Great Barton Suffk 54 TL8967
Great Barugh N York 90 SE7478
Great Bavington Nthumb 102 NY9880
Great Bealings Suffk 55 TM2349
Great Bedwyn Wilts 23 SU2764
Great Bentley Essex 41 TM1021
Great Billing Nhants 51 SP8162
Great Bircham Norfk 65 TF7732
Great Blakenham Suffk 54 TM1150
Great Bolas Shrops 72 SJ6421
Great Bookham Surrey 26 TQ1354
Great Bosullow Cnwll 2 SW4133
Great Bourton Oxon 49 SP4545
Great Bowden Leics 50 SP7488
Great Bradley Suffk 53 TL6753
Great Braxted Essex 40 TL8614
Great Bricett Suffk 54 TM0350
Great Brickhill Bucks 38 SP9030
Great Bridge W Mids 60 SO9792
Great Bridgeford Staffs 72 SJ8827
Great Brington Nhants 50 SP6665
Great Bromley Essex 41 TM0826
Great Broughton Cumb 92 NY0731
Great Broughton N York 90 NZ5405
Great Budworth Ches 79 SJ6677
Great Burdon Dur 96 NZ3116
Great Burstead Essex 40 TQ6892
Great Busby N York 90 NZ5205
Great Canfield Essex 40 TL5918
Great Carlton Lincs 77 TF4085
Great Casterton Leics 63 TF0009
Great Chart Kent 28 TQ9741
Great Chatfield Wilts 22 ST8663
Great Chatwell Staffs 60 SJ7914
Great Chell Staffs 72 SJ8752
Great Chesterford Essex 39 TL5042
Great Cheverell Wilts 22 ST9858
Great Chishill Cambs 39 TL4238
Great Clacton Essex 41 TM1716
Great Cliffe W York 82 SE3015
Great Clifton Cumb 92 NY0429
Great Coates Humb 85 TA2309
Great Comberton H & W 47 SO9542
Great Comp Kent 27 TQ6356
Great Corby Cumb 93 NY4754
Great Cornard Suffk 54 TL8840
Great Cowden Humb 85 TA2342
Great Coxwell Oxon 36 SU2693
Great Cransley Nhants 51 SP8376
Great Cressingham Norfk 66 TF8501
Great Crosthwaite Cumb 93 NY2624
Great Cubley Derbys 73 SK1638
Great Dalby Leics 63 SK7414
Great Doddington Nhants 51 SP8864
Great Doward H & W 34 SO5416
Great Driffield Humb 91 TA0257
Great Dunham Norfk 66 TF8714
Great Dunmow Essex 40 TL6222
Great Durnford Wilts 23 SU1338
Great Easton Essex 40 TL6025
Great Easton Leics 51 SP8493
Great Eccleston Lancs 80 SD4240
Great Ellingham Norfk 66 TM0196
Great Elm Somset 22 ST7449
Great Englebourne Devon 7 SX7756
Great Everdon Nhants 49 SP5957
Great Eversden Cambs 52 TL3653
Great Finborough Suffk 54 TM0158
Great Fransham Norfk 66 TF8913
Great Gaddesden Herts 38 TL0211
Great Gidding Cambs 52 TL1183
Great Givendale Humb 84 SE8153
Great Glemham Suffk 55 TM3361
Great Glen Leics 50 SP6597
Great Gonerby Lincs 63 SK8938
Great Gransden Cambs 52 TL2655
Great Green Cambs 39 TL2844
Great Green Norfk 55 TM2889
Great Green Suffk 54 TL9365
Great Green Suffk 54 TL9156
Great Habton N York 90 SE7576
Great Hale Lincs 64 TF1442
Great Hallingbury Essex 39 TL5119
Great Hanwood Shrops 59 SJ4409
Great Harrowden Nhants 51 SP8770
Great Harwood Lancs 81 SD7332
Great Haseley Oxon 37 SP6401
Great Hatfield Humb 85 TA1842
Great Haywood Staffs 73 SJ9922
Great Heck N York 83 SE5921
Great Henny Essex 54 TL8637
Great Hinton Wilts 22 ST9058
Great Hockham Norfk 66 TL9592
Great Holland Essex 41 TM2019
Great Horkesley Essex 41 TL9731
Great Hormead Herts 39 TL4030
Great Horton W York 82 SE1411
Great Horwood Bucks 49 SP7731
Great Houghton Nhants 50 SP7958
Great Houghton S York 83 SE4206
Great Hucklow Derbys 74 SK1777
Great Kelk Humb 91 TA1058
Great Kimble Bucks 38 SP8206
Great Kingshill Bucks 26 SU8797
Great Langdale Cumb 86 NY2906
Great Langton N York 89 SE2996
Great Leighs Essex 40 TL7217
Great Limber Lincs 85 TA1308
Great Linford Bucks 38 SP8542
Great Livermere Suffk 54 TL8871
Great Longstone Derbys 74 SK1971
Great Lumley T & W 96 NZ2949
Great Lyth Shrops 59 SJ4507
Great Malvern H & W 47 SO7845
Great Maplestead Essex 54 TL8134
Great Marton Lancs 80 SD3235
Great Massingham Norfk 66 TF7923
Great Melton Norfk 66 TG1206
Great Meols Mersyd 78 SJ2390
Great Milton Oxon 37 SP6202
Great Missenden Bucks 26 SP8901
Great Mitton Lancs 81 SD7138
Great Mongeham Kent 29 TR3551
Great Moulton Norfk 54 TM1690
Great Munden Herts 39 TL3524
Great Ness Shrops 59 SJ3919
Great Nurcott Somset 20 SS9036
Great Oak Gwent 34 SO3809
Great Oakley Essex 41 TM1927
Great Oakley Nhants 51 SP8686
Great Offley Herts 38 TL1427
Great Ormside Cumb 94 NY7017
Great Orton Cumb 93 NY3254
Great Ouseburn N York 89 SE4461
Great Oxendon Nhants 50 SP7383
Great Oxney Green Essex 40 TL6606
Great Pattenden Kent 28 TQ7345
Great Paxton Cambs 52 TL2063
Great Plumpton Lancs 80 SD3833
Great Plumstead Norfk 67 TG3010
Great Ponton Lincs 63 SK9230
Great Potheridge Devon 19 SS5114
Great Preston W York 83 SE4029
Great Purston Nhants 49 SP5139
Great Raveley Cambs 52 TL2581
Great Rissington Gloucs 36 SP1917
Great Rollright Oxon 48 SP3231
Great Rudbaxton Dyfed 30 SM9620
Great Ryburgh Norfk 66 TF9527
Great Ryle Nthumb 111 NU0212
Great Ryton Shrops 59 SJ4803
Great Saling Essex 40 TL7026
Great Salkeld Cumb 94 NY5436
Great Sampford Essex 53 TL6435
Great Sankey Ches 78 SJ5688
Great Saredon Staffs 60 SJ9508
Great Saughall Ches 71 SJ3669
Great Saxham Suffk 53 TL7862
Great Shefford Berks 36 SU3875
Great Shelford Cambs 53 TL4652
Great Smeaton N York 89 NZ3404
Great Snoring Norfk 66 TF9434
Great Somerford Wilts 35 ST9682
Great Soudley Shrops 72 SJ7229
Great Stainton Dur 96 NZ3322
Great Stambridge Essex 40 TQ8992
Great Staughton Cambs 52 TL1264
Great Steeping Lincs 77 TF4364
Great Stoke Avon 35 ST6280
Great Stonar Kent 29 TR3359
Great Strickland Cumb 94 NY5522
Great Stukeley Cambs 52 TL2274
Great Sturton Lincs 76 TF2176
Great Sutton Ches 71 SJ3775
Great Sutton Shrops 59 SO5183
Great Swinburne Nthumb 102 NY9375
Great Tew Oxon 48 SP3929
Great Tey Essex 40 TL8925
Great Torrington Devon 18 SS4919
Great Tosson Nthumb 103 NU0200
Great Totham Essex 40 TL8611
Great Totham Essex 40 TL8713
Great Tows Lincs 76 TF2290
Great Urswick Cumb 86 SD2674
Great Wakering Essex 40 TQ9487
Great Waldingfield Suffk 54 TL9144
Great Walsingham Norfk 66 TF9437
Great Waltham Essex 40 TL6913
Great Warley Essex 27 TQ5890
Great Washbourne Gloucs 47 SO9834
Great Weeke Devon 8 SX7187
Great Weldon Nhants 51 SP9289
Great Welnetham Suffk 54 TL8859
Great Wenham Suffk 54 TM0738
Great Whittington Nthumb 103 NZ0070
Great Wigborough Essex 41 TL9615
Great Wilbraham Cambs 53 TL5557
Great Wishford Wilts 23 SU0835
Great Witchingham Norfk 66 TG1020
Great Witcombe Gloucs 35 SO9114
Great Witley H & W 47 SO7566
Great Wolford Warwks 48 SP2534
Great Wratting Essex 53 TL6848
Great Wymondley Herts 39 TL2128
Great Wyrley Staffs 60 SJ9907
Great Wytheford Shrops 59 SJ5719
Great Yarmouth Norfk 67 TG5207
Great Yeldham Essex 53 TL7638
Greatfield Wilts 36 SU0785
Greatford Lincs 64 TF0811
Greatgate Staffs 73 SK0540
Greatham Cleve 97 NZ4927
Greatham Hants 14 SU7730
Greatham W Susx 14 TQ0415
Greatstone-on-Sea Kent 17 TR0822
Greatworth Nhants 49 SP5542
Grebby Lincs 77 TF4368
Green Bank Cumb 101 NY3780
Green Cross Surrey 14 SU8634
Green Down Somset 21 ST5753
Green End Beds 51 TL1063
Green End Beds 51 TL0864
Green End Beds 38 TL0147
Green End Beds 52 TL1252
Green End Cambs 53 TL4668
Green End Cambs 53 TL4861
Green End Cambs 52 TL2274
Green End Cambs 52 TL3856
Green End Herts 39 TL3333
Green End Herts 39 TL3122
Green End Herts 39 TL2630
Green End Warwks 61 SP2686
Green Hammerton N York 83 SE4656
Green Head Cumb 93 NY3649
Green Heath Staffs 60 SJ9913
Green Hill Nthumb 95 NY8647
Green Hill Wilts 36 SU0686
Green Hills Cambs 53 TL6072
Green Lane Devon 8 SX7877
Green Lane H & W 48 SP0665
Green Moor S York 74 SK2899
Green Oak Humb 84 SE8127
Green Ore Somset 21 ST5749
Green Quarter Cumb 87 NY4603
Green Street E Susx 17 TQ7611
Green Street Gloucs 35 SO8915
Green Street H & W 47 SO8749
Green Street Herts 39 TL4521
Green Street Herts 26 TQ1998
Green Street W Susx 15 TQ1522
Green Street Green Gt Lon 27 TQ4563
Green Street Green Kent 27 TQ5870
Green The Cumb 86 SD1784
Green Tye Herts 39 TL4418
Greenburn Loth 116 NS9360
Greencroft Norfk 66 TG0243
Greencroft Hall Dur 96 NZ1549
Greenend Oxon 36 SP3221
Greenfield Beds 38 TL0534
Greenfield Clwyd 70 SJ1977
Greenfield Gt Man 82 SD9904
Greenfield Highld 131 NH2000
Greenfield Oxon 37 SU7191
Greenfield Strath 114 NS2490
Greenford Gt Lon 26 TQ1482
Greengairs Strath 116 NS7870
Greengates W York 82 SE1937
Greenhalgh Lancs 80 SD4035
Greenham Berks 24 SU4865
Greenham Somset 20 ST0719
Greenhaugh Nthumb 102 NY7987
Greenhead Nthumb 102 NY6565
Greenhey Gt Man 79 SD7104
Greenhill Cent 116 NS8279
Greenhill D & G 100 NY1079
Greenhill H & W 47 SO7248
Greenhill Kent 29 TR1666
Greenhill S York 74 SK3481
Greenhill Strath 108 NS9333
Greenhillocks Derbys 74 SK4049
Greenhithe Kent 27 TQ5875
Greenholm Strath 107 NS5437
Greenholme Cumb 87 NY5905
Greenhouse Border 109 NT5624
Greenhow Hill N York 89 SE1164
Greenland Highld 151 ND2367
Greenland S York 74 SK3988
Greenlands Bucks 37 SU7785
Greenlaw Border 110 NT7146
Greenlea D & G 100 NY0375
Greenloaning Tays 125 NN8307
Greenmoor Hill Oxon 37 SU6481
Greenmount Gt Man 81 SD7714
Greenock Strath 115 NS2776
Greenodd Cumb 86 SD3182
Greens Norton Nhants 49 SP6649
Greensgate Norfk 66 TG1015
Greenside T & W 96 NZ1362
Greenside W York 82 SE1616
Greenstead Essex 41 TM0125
Greenstead Green Essex 40 TL8227
Greensted Essex 39 TL5303
Greenstreet Green Suffk 54 TM0450
Greenway Gloucs 47 SO7032
Greenway H & W 60 SO7470
Greenway S Glam 33 ST0574
Greenway Somset 21 ST3124
Greenwich Gt Lon 27 TQ3877
Greet Gloucs 48 SP0230
Greete Shrops 46 SO5771
Greetham Leics 63 SK9214
Greetham Lincs 77 TF3070
Greetland W York 82 SE0821
Gregson Lane Lancs 81 SD5926
Greinton Somset 21 ST4136
Grenaby IOM 153 SC2672
Grendon Nhants 51 SP8760
Grendon Warwks 61 SP2799
Grendon Green H & W 46 SO5957
Grendon Underwood Bucks 37 SP6820
Grenofen Devon 6 SX5671
Grenofen Devon 6 SX4971
Grenoside S York 74 SK3394
Gresford Clwyd 71 SJ3454
Gresham Norfk 66 TG1638
Greshornish Highld 136 NG3454
Gressenhall Norfk 66 TF9615
Gressenhall Green Norfk 66 TF9616
Gressingham Lancs 87 SD5769
Grestey Green Ches 72 SJ7054
Greta Bridge Dur 95 NZ0813
Gretna D & G 101 NY3167
Gretna Green D & G 101 NY3268
Gretton Gloucs 47 SP0030
Gretton Nhants 51 SP8994
Gretton Shrops 59 SO5195
Grewelthorpe N York 89 SE2376
Grey Friars Suffk 55 TM4770
Grey Green Humb 84 SE7807
Grey's Green Oxon 37 SU7183
Greygarth N York 89 SE1872
Greylake Somset 21 ST3833
Greyrigg D & G 100 NY0889
Greyson Green Cumb 92 NX9925
Greysouthen Cumb 92 NY0729
Greysouthern Cumb 92 NY0629
Greystoke Cumb 93 NY4330
Greystone Tays 127 NO5343
Greywell Hants 24 SU7151
Gribb Dorset 10 ST3703
Gribthorpe Humb 84 SE7635
Griff Warwks 61 SP3689
Griffithstown Gwent 34 ST2999
Griffydam Leics 62 SK4118
Griggall Cumb 87 SD4691
Griggs Green Hants 14 SU8231
Grimeford Village Lancs 81 SD6112
Grimethorpe S York 83 SE4109
Grimley H & W 47 SO8360
Grimmet Strath 106 NS3210
Grimoldby Lincs 77 TF3988
Grimpo Shrops 59 SJ3526
Grimsargh Lancs 81 SD5834
Grimsby Humb 85 TA2710
Grimscote Nhants 49 SP6553
Grimscott Cnwll 18 SS2607
Grimshader W Isls 154 NB4026
Grimshaw Lancs 81 SD7024
Grimshaw Green Lancs 80 SD4912
Grimsthorpe Lincs 64 TF0422
Grimston Humb 85 TA2735
Grimston Leics 63 SK6821
Grimston Norfk 65 TF7222
Grimston Hill Notts 75 SK6865
Grimstone Dorset 10 SY6393
Grimstone End Suffk 54 TL9368
Grinacombe Moor Devon 5 SX4191
Grindale Humb 91 TA1271
Grindle Shrops 60 SJ7503
Grindleford Derbys 74 SK2477
Grindleton Lancs 81 SD7545
Grindley Brook Shrops 71 SJ5242
Grindlow Derbys 74 SK1878
Grindon Cleve 96 NZ3925
Grindon Nthumb 110 NT9144
Grindon Staffs 73 SK0854
Grindonrigg Nthumb 110 NT9243
Gringley on the Hill Notts 75 SK7390
Grinsdale Cumb 93 NY3758
Grinshill Shrops 59 SJ5223
Grinton N York 88 SE0498
Grishipoll Strath 120 NM1959
Grisling Common E Susx 16 TQ4422
Gristhorpe N York 91 TA0881
Griston Norfk 66 TL9499
Gritley Ork 155 HY5604
Grittenham Wilts 36 SU0382
Grittleton Wilts 35 ST8580
Grizebeck Cumb 86 SD2384
Grizedale Cumb 86 SD3394
Groby Leics 62 SK5207
Groes Clwyd 70 SJ0064
Groes W Glam 32 SS7986
Groes-faen M Glam 33 ST0680
Groes-Wen M Glam 33 ST1286
Groesffordd Gwynd 56 SH2739
Groesffordd Marli Clwyd 70 SJ0073
Groeslon Gwynd 68 SH4755
Groeslon Gwynd 68 SH5260
Grogport Strath 105 NR8044
Gromford Suffk 55 TM3858
Gronant Clwyd 70 SJ0883
Groom's Hill H & W 47 SP0154
Groombridge E Susx 16 TQ5337
Grosebay W Isls 154 NG1592
Grosmont Gwent 46 SO4024
Grosmont N York 90 NZ8305
Grossington Gloucs 35 SO7302
Groton Suffk 54 TL9641
Grotton Gt Man 79 SD9604
Grouville Jersey 152 JS0000
Grove Bucks 38 SP9122
Grove Dorset 11 SY6972
Grove Dyfed 30 SM9900
Grove Kent 29 TR2362
Grove Notts 75 SK7379
Grove Oxon 36 SU4090
Grove Green Kent 28 TQ7856
Grove Park Gt Lon 27 TQ4072
Grove Vale W Mids 61 SP0394
Grovenhurst Kent 28 TQ7140
Grovesend Avon 35 ST6489
Grovesend W Glam 32 SN5900
Grubb Street Kent 27 TQ5869
Gruesllwyd Powys 58 SJ2111
Gruids Highld 146 NC5603
Gruinard Highld 144 NG9489
Gruinart Flats Strath 112 NR2866
Grula Highld 136 NG3826
Gruline Strath 121 NM5440
Grumbla Cnwll 2 SW4029
Grundisburgh Suffk 55 TM2251
Gruting Shet 155 HU2849
Gualachulain Highld 123 NN1145
Gualin House Highld 148 NC3056
Guanockgate Lincs 64 TF3710
Guardbridge Fife 127 NO4518
Guarlford H & W 47 SO8145
Guay Tays 125 NO0049
Guestling Green E Susx 17 TQ8513
Guestling Thorn E Susx 17 TQ8516
Guestwick Norfk 66 TG0627
Guide Lancs 81 SD7025
Guide Bridge Gt Man 70 SH9297
Guide Post T & W 103 NZ2585
Guilden Down Shrops 59 SO3083
Guilden Morden Cambs 39 TL2744
Guilden Sutton Ches 71 SJ4468
Guildford Surrey 25 SU9949
Guildstead Kent 28 TQ8262
Guildtown Tays 126 NO1331
Guilreehill Strath 106 NS3610
Guilsborough Nhants 50 SP6772
Guilsfield Powys 58 SJ2211
Guilton Kent 29 TR2858
Guineaford Devon 19 SS5537
Guisborough Cleve 97 NZ6115
Guiseley W York 82 SE1942
Guist Norfk 66 TF9925
Guiting Power Gloucs 48 SP0924
Gullane Loth 118 NT4882
Gulling Green Suffk 54 TL8356
Gulval Cnwll 2 SW4831
Gulworthy Devon 6 SX4572
Gumfreston Dyfed 31 SN1101
Gumley Leics 50 SP6890
Gummow's Shop Cnwll 4 SW8657
Gun Green Kent 17 TQ7731
Gun Hill E Susx 16 TQ5614
Gun Hill Warwks 61 SP2889
Gunby Humb 84 SE7135
Gunby Lincs 63 SK9121
Gunby Lincs 77 TF4667
Gundleton Hants 24 SU6133
Gunn Devon 19 SS6333
Gunnerside N York 88 SD9598
Gunnerton Nthumb 102 NY9074
Gunness Humb 84 SE8411
Gunnislake Devon 6 SX4371
Gunnista Shet 155 HU5043
Gunthorpe Cambs 64 TF1803
Gunthorpe Norfk 66 TG0134
Gunthorpe Notts 63 SK6844
Gunton Suffk 67 TM5395
Gunville IOW 13 SZ4889
Gupworthy Somset 20 SS9735
Gurnard IOW 13 SZ4795
Gurnett Ches 79 SJ9271
Gurney Slade Somset 21 ST6249
Gurnos W Glam 32 SN7709
Gushmere Kent 28 TR0457
Gussage All Saints Dorset 11 SU0010
Gussage St. Michael Dorset 11 ST9811

Guston Harwich

Guston *Kent* 29 TR3244
Gutcher *Shet* 155 HU5499
Guthrie *Tays* 127 NO5650
Guy's Marsh *Dorset* 22 ST8420
Guyhirn *Cambs* 65 TF4003
Guyhirn Gull *Cambs* 65 TF3903
Guyzance *Nthumb* 103 NU2104
Gwaenysgor *Clwyd* 70 SJ0780
Gwalchmai *Gwynd* 68 SH3876
Gwastadnant *Gwynd* 69 SH6157
Gwaun-Cae-Gurwen *W Glam* 32 SN7011
Gwbert-on-Sea *Dyfed* 42 SN1649
Gwealavellan *Cnwll* 2 SW5942
Gwealeath *Cnwll* 2 SW6922
Gweek *Cnwll* 2 SW7026
Gwehelog *Gwent* 34 SO3804
Gwenddwr *Powys* 45 SO0643
Gwendreath *Cnwll* 3 SW7216
Gwennap *Cnwll* 3 SW7340
Gwenter *Cnwll* 3 SW7417
Gwern-y-Steeple *S Glam* 33 ST0775
Gwernaffield *Clwyd* 70 SJ2065
Gwernesney *Gwent* 34 SO4101
Gwernogle *Dyfed* 44 SN5334
Gwernymynydd *Clwyd* 70 SJ2162
Gwersyllt *Clwyd* 71 SJ3153
Gwespyr *Clwyd* 70 SJ1183
Gwindra *Cnwll* 3 SW9552
Gwinear *Cnwll* 2 SW5937
Gwithian *Cnwll* 2 SW5841
Gwredog *Gwynd* 68 SH4086
Gwrhay *Gwent* 33 ST1899
Gwyddelwern *Clwyd* 70 SJ0746
Gwyddgrug *Dyfed* 44 SN4635
Gwynfryn *Clwyd* 70 SJ2552
Gwystre *Powys* 45 SO0665
Gwytherin *Clwyd* 69 SH8761
Gyfelia *Clwyd* 71 SJ3245
Gyrn-goch *Gwynd* 68 SH4048

H

Habberley *H & W* 60 SO8176
Habberley *Shrops* 59 SJ3903
Habergham *Lancs* 81 SD8033
Habertoft *Lincs* 77 TF5069
Habin *W Susx* 14 SU8022
Habrough *Humb* 85 TA1413
Haccombe *Devon* 7 SX8970
Hacconby *Lincs* 64 TF1025
Haceby *Lincs* 64 TF0236
Hacheston *Suffk* 55 TM3059
Hack Green *Ches* 72 SJ6448
Hackenthorpe *S York* 74 SK4183
Hackford *Norfk* 66 TG0502
Hackforth *N York* 89 SE2493
Hackland *Ork* 155 HY3920
Hackleton *Nhants* 51 SP8055
Hacklinge *Kent* 29 TR3454
Hackman's Gate *H & W* 60 SO8978
Hackness *N York* 91 SE9790
Hackness *Somset* 21 ST3345
Hackney *Gt Lon* 27 TQ3484
Hackthorn *Lincs* 76 SK9982
Hackthorpe *Cumb* 94 NY5323
Hacton *Gt Lon* 27 TQ5585
Hadden *Border* 110 NT7836
Haddenham *Bucks* 37 SP7308
Haddenham *Cambs* 53 TL4675
Haddington *Lincs* 76 SK9163
Haddington *Loth* 118 NT5173
Haddiscoe *Norfk* 67 TM4497
Haddo *Gramp* 143 NJ8337
Haddon *Cambs* 64 TL1392
Hade Edge *W York* 82 SE1404
Hademore *Staffs* 61 SK1708
Hadfield *Derbys* 74 SK0296
Hadham Cross *Herts* 39 TL4218
Hadham Ford *Herts* 39 TL4321
Hadleigh *Essex* 40 TQ8187
Hadleigh *Suffk* 54 TM0242
Hadleigh Heath *Suffk* 54 TL9941
Hadley *H & W* 47 SO8664
Hadley *Shrops* 60 SJ6712
Hadley End *Staffs* 73 SK1320
Hadley Wood *Gt Lon* 27 TQ2698
Hadlow *Kent* 27 TQ6350
Hadlow Down *E Susx* 16 TQ5324
Hadnall *Shrops* 59 SJ5220
Hadstock *Essex* 53 TL5644
Hadzor *H & W* 47 SO9162
Haffenden Quarter *Kent* 28 TQ8840
Hafod-y-bwch *Clwyd* 71 SJ3147
Hafod-y-coed *Gwent* 34 SO2200
Hafodunos *Clwyd* 69 SH8667
Hafodyrynys *Gwent* 34 ST2299
Hafodyrynys *Gwent* 34 ST2499
Haggate *Lancs* 81 SD8735
Haggbeck *Cumb* 101 NY4774
Haggerston *Nthumb* 111 NU0443
Haggington Hill *Devon* 19 SS5647
Haggs *Cent* 116 NS7979
Hagley *H & W* 46 SO5641
Hagley *H & W* 60 SO9181
Hagnaby *Lincs* 77 TF3462
Hagworthingham *Lincs* 77 TF3469
Haigh *Gt Man* 78 SD6009
Haighton Green *Lancs* 81 SD5634
Hail Weston *Cambs* 52 TL1662
Haile *Cumb* 86 NY0308
Hailes *Gloucs* 48 SP0430
Hailey *Herts* 39 TL3710
Hailey *Oxon* 37 SU6485
Hailsham *E Susx* 16 TQ5909
Hainault *Gt Lon* 27 TQ4591
Haine *Kent* 29 TR3566
Hainford *Norfk* 67 TG2318
Hainton *Lincs* 76 TF1784
Hainworth *W York* 82 SE0639
Haisthorpe *Humb* 91 TA1264
Hakin *Dyfed* 30 SM8905
Halam *Notts* 75 SK6754
Halbeath *Fife* 117 NT1289
Halberton *Devon* 9 ST0012
Halcro *Highld* 151 ND2360
Hale *Ches* 78 SJ4782
Hale *Cumb* 87 SD5078
Hale *Gt Man* 79 SJ7786
Hale *Hants* 12 SU1919
Hale *Somset* 22 ST7527
Hale *Surrey* 25 SU8448
Hale Bank *Ches* 78 SJ4884
Hale Green *E Susx* 16 TQ5514
Hale Nook *Lancs* 80 SD3944
Hale Street *Kent* 28 TQ6749
Halebarns *Gt Man* 79 SJ7985
Hales *Norfk* 67 TM3897
Hales *Staffs* 72 SJ7134
Hales Green *Derbys* 73 SK1841
Hales Place *Kent* 29 TR1459
Halesgate *Lincs* 64 TF3226
Halesowen *W Mids* 60 SO9683
Halesworth *Suffk* 55 TM3877
Halewood *Mersyd* 78 SJ4585
Halewood Green *Mersyd* 78 SJ4486
Half Penny *Cumb* 87 SD5387
Halford *Shrops* 59 SO4383
Halford *Warwks* 48 SP2545
Halford Blackpool *Devon* 7 SX8175
Halfpenny Green *Staffs* 60 SO8291
Halfpenny Houses *N York* 89 SE2284
Halfway *Berks* 24 SU4068
Halfway *Dyfed* 44 SN6430
Halfway *Powys* 44 SN8332
Halfway *S York* 75 SK4381
Halfway Bridge *W Susx* 14 SU9322
Halfway House *Shrops* 59 SJ3411
Halfway Houses *Kent* 28 TQ9372
Halifax *W York* 82 SE0925
Halistra *Highld* 136 NG2459
Halket *Strath* 115 NS4252
Halkirk *Highld* 151 ND1359
Halkyn *Clwyd* 70 SJ2171
Hall *Strath* 115 NS4154
Hall Cliffe *W York* 82 SE2918
Hall cross *Lancs* 80 SD4230
Hall Dunnerdale *Cumb* 86 SD2195
Hall End *Beds* 38 TL0737
Hall End *Beds* 38 TL0045
Hall End *W Mids* 60 SP0092
Hall Green *Ches* 72 SJ8356
Hall Green *W Mids* 61 SP1181
Hall's Green *Essex* 39 TL4108
Hall's Green *Herts* 39 TL2728
Hallam Fields *Derbys* 62 SK4739
Halland *E Susx* 16 TQ4916
Hallaton *Leics* 50 SP7896
Hallatrow *Avon* 21 ST6356
Hallbankgate *Cumb* 94 NY5859
Hallbeck *Cumb* 87 SD6288
Hallen *Avon* 34 ST5480
Hallfield Gate *Derbys* 74 SK3958
Hallgarth *Dur* 96 NZ3343
Hallin *Highld* 136 NG2558
Halling *Kent* 28 TQ7063
Hallington *Lincs* 77 TF3085
Hallington *Nthumb* 102 NY9875
Hallins *Derbys* 74 SK3371
Halliwell *Gt Man* 79 SD6910
Halloughton *Notts* 75 SK6951
Hallow *H & W* 47 SO8258
Hallow Heath *H & W* 47 SO8259
Hallrule *Border* 110 NT5914
Hallsands *Devon* 7 SX8138
Hallthwaites *Cumb* 86 SD1785
Halltoft End *Lincs* 64 TF3645
Hallworthy *Cnwll* 4 SX1887
Hallyne *Border* 109 NT1940
Halmer End *Staffs* 72 SJ7949
Halmond's Frome *H & W* 47 SO6647
Halmore *Gloucs* 35 SO6902
Halnaker *W Susx* 14 SU9008
Halsall *Lancs* 78 SD3710
Halse *Nhants* 49 SP5640
Halse *Somset* 20 ST1428
Halsetown *Cnwll* 2 SW5038
Halsham *Humb* 85 TA2627
Halsinger *Devon* 19 SS5138
Halstead *Essex* 40 TL8130
Halstead *Kent* 27 TQ4961
Halstead *Leics* 63 SK7505
Halstock *Dorset* 10 ST5308
Halsway *Somset* 20 ST1338
Haltham *Lincs* 77 TF2463
Halton *Bucks* 38 SP8710
Halton *Ches* 78 SJ5481
Halton *Clwyd* 71 SJ3039
Halton *Lancs* 87 SD5064
Halton *Nthumb* 103 NY9967
Halton *W York* 83 SE3533
Halton East *N York* 82 SE0454
Halton Fenside *Lincs* 77 TF4263
Halton Gill *N York* 88 SD8876
Halton Green *Lancs* 87 SD5165
Halton Holegate *Lincs* 77 TF4165
Halton Lea Gate *Nthumb* 94 NY6458
Halton Quay *M Glam* 5 SX4165
Halton Shields *Nthumb* 103 NZ0168
Halton West *N York* 81 SD8454
Haltwhistle *Nthumb* 102 NY7064
Halvergate *Norfk* 67 TG4207
Halwell *Devon* 7 SX7753
Halwill *Devon* 5 SX4392
Halwill *Devon* 18 SX4299
Halwill Junction *Devon* 18 SS4400
Ham *Devon* 9 ST2301
Ham *Gloucs* 35 ST6898
Ham *Gloucs* 35 SO9721
Ham *Gt Lon* 26 TQ1772
Ham *Kent* 29 TR3354
Ham *Somset* 20 ST2825
Ham *Somset* 22 ST6748
Ham *Wilts* 23 SU3262
Ham Common *Dorset* 22 ST8125
Ham Green *Avon* 34 ST5375
Ham Green *H & W* 47 SO7444
Ham Green *H & W* 47 SP0164
Ham Green *Kent* 17 TQ8926
Ham Green *Kent* 28 TQ8468
Ham Hill *Kent* 28 TQ6960
Ham Street *Somset* 21 ST5534
Hamble *Hants* 13 SU4806
Hambleden *Bucks* 37 SU7886
Hambledon *Hants* 13 SU6415
Hambledon *Surrey* 25 SU9638
Hambleton *Lancs* 80 SD3742
Hambleton *N York* 83 SE5430
Hambleton Moss Side *Lancs* 80 SD3842
Hambridge *Somset* 21 ST5936
Hambridge *Somset* 21 ST3921
Hambrook *Avon* 35 ST6378
Hambrook *W Susx* 14 SU7806
Hamels *Herts* 39 TL3724
Hameringham *Lincs* 77 TF3067
Hamerton *Cambs* 52 TL1379
Hamilton *Strath* 116 NS7255
Hamlet *Dorset* 10 ST5908
Hamlins *E Susx* 16 TQ5909
Hammerpot *W Susx* 14 TQ0705
Hammersmith *Gt Lon* 26 TQ2378
Hammerwich *Staffs* 61 SK0607
Hammerwood *E Susx* 16 TQ4339
Hammond Street *Herts* 39 TL3304
Hammoon *Dorset* 11 ST8114
Hamnavoe *Shet* 155 HU3735
Hamnavoe *Shet* 155 HU4971
Hampden Park *E Susx* 16 TQ6002
Hampden Row *Bucks* 26 SP8501
Hamperden End *Essex* 40 TL5730
Hampnett *Gloucs* 36 SP0915
Hampole *S York* 83 SE5010
Hampreston *Dorset* 12 SZ0598
Hampsfield *Cumb* 87 SD4080
Hampson Green *Lancs* 80 SD4954
Hampstead *Gt Lon* 27 TQ2685
Hampstead Norrey's *Berks* 37 SU5276
Hampsthwaite *N York* 89 SE2558
Hampt *M Glam* 5 SX3974
Hampton *Devon* 5 SX2696
Hampton *Gt Lon* 26 TQ1369
Hampton *H & W* 48 SP0243
Hampton *Kent* 29 TR1568
Hampton *Shrops* 60 SO7486
Hampton *Wilts* 36 SU1892
Hampton Bishop *H & W* 46 SO5537
Hampton Green *Ches* 71 SJ5149
Hampton Green *Ches* 71 SJ5149
Hampton Heath *Ches* 71 SJ4949
Hampton in Arden *W Mids* 61 SP2081
Hampton Loade *Shrops* 60 SO7486
Hampton Lovett *H & W* 47 SO8865
Hampton Lucy *Warwks* 48 SP2557
Hampton on the Hill *Warwks* 48 SP2564
Hampton Poyle *Oxon* 37 SP5015
Hampton Wick *Gt Lon* 26 TQ1769
Hamptworth *Wilts* 12 SU2419
Hamrow *Norfk* 66 TF9124
Hamsey *E Susx* 15 TQ4012
Hamsey Green *Gt Lon* 27 TQ3760
Hamstall Ridware *Staffs* 73 SK1019
Hamstead *IOW* 13 SZ4091
Hamstead *W Mids* 61 SP0592
Hamstead Marshall *Berks* 24 SU4165
Hamsterley *Dur* 95 NZ1131
Hamsterley *Dur* 95 NZ1156
Hamstreet *Kent* 17 TR0034
Hamwood *Avon* 21 ST3756
Hanbury *H & W* 47 SO9664
Hanbury *Staffs* 73 SK1727
Hanby *Lincs* 64 TF0231
Hanchet End *Suffk* 53 TL6446
Hanchurch *Staffs* 72 SJ8441
Hand and Pen *Devon* 9 SY0495
Hand Green *Ches* 71 SJ5460
Handale *Cleve* 97 NZ7215
Handbridge *Ches* 71 SJ4065
Handcross *W Susx* 15 TQ2629
Handforth *Ches* 79 SJ8583
Handley *Ches* 71 SJ4657
Handley *Derbys* 74 SK3761
Handley Green *Essex* 40 TL6601
Handsacre *Staffs* 73 SK0916
Handsworth *S York* 74 SK4186
Handsworth *W Mids* 61 SP0589
Handy Cross *Bucks* 26 SU8490
Hanford *Dorset* 11 ST8410
Hanford *Staffs* 72 SJ8642
Hanging Langford *Wilts* 23 SU0237
Hangleton *E Susx* 15 TQ2607
Hangleton *W Susx* 14 TQ0803
Hanham *Avon* 35 ST6372
Hankelow *Ches* 72 SJ6745
Hankerton *Wilts* 35 ST9690
Hankham *E Susx* 16 TQ6105
Hanley *Staffs* 72 SJ8847
Hanley Castle *H & W* 47 SO8342
Hanley Child *H & W* 47 SO6565
Hanley Swan *H & W* 47 SO8143
Hanley William *H & W* 47 SO6766
Hanlith *N York* 88 SD8960
Hanmer *Clwyd* 71 SJ4540
Hannaford *Devon* 19 SS6029
Hannah *Lincs* 77 TF4979
Hannington *Hants* 24 SU5455
Hannington *Nhants* 51 SP8170
Hannington *Wilts* 36 SU1793
Hannington Wick *Wilts* 36 SU1795
Hanscombe End *Beds* 38 TL1133
Hanslope *Bucks* 38 SP8046
Hanthorpe *Lincs* 64 TF0823
Hanwell *Gt Lon* 26 TQ1579
Hanwell *Oxon* 49 SP4343
Hanworth *Gt Lon* 26 TQ1271
Hanworth *Norfk* 67 TG1935
Happendon *Strath* 108 NS8533
Happisburgh *Norfk* 67 TG3831
Happisburgh Common *Norfk* 67 TG3729
Hapsford *Ches* 71 SJ4774
Hapton *Lancs* 81 SD7931
Hapton *Norfk* 66 TM1796
Harberton *Devon* 7 SX7758
Harbertonford *Devon* 7 SX7856
Harbledown *Kent* 29 TR1357
Harborne *W Mids* 60 SP0284
Harborough Magna *Warwks* 50 SP4778
Harborough Parva *Warwks* 50 SP4778
Harbottle *Nthumb* 102 NT9304
Harbours Hill *H & W* 47 SO9566
Harbridge *Hants* 12 SU1409
Harbridge Green *Hants* 12 SU1411
Harburn *Loth* 117 NT0462
Harbury *Warwks* 48 SP3760
Harby *Leics* 63 SK7431
Harby *Notts* 76 SK8770
Harcombe *Devon* 9 SX8881
Harcombe *Devon* 9 SY1590
Harcombe Bottom *Devon* 10 SY3395
Harden *W Mids* 60 SK0101
Harden *W York* 82 SE0838
Hardenhuish *Wilts* 35 ST9074
Hardgate *Gramp* 135 NJ7901
Hardgate *N York* 89 SE2662
Hardgate *Strath* 115 NS5073
Hardham *W Susx* 14 TQ0317
Hardhorn *Lancs* 80 SD3537
Hardingham *Norfk* 66 TG0403
Hardings Wood *Staffs* 72 SJ8254
Hardingstone *Nhants* 49 SP7657
Hardington *Somset* 22 ST7452
Hardington Mandeville *Somset* 10 ST5111
Hardington Marsh *Somset* 10 ST5009
Hardington Moor *Somset* 10 ST5212
Hardley *Hants* 13 SU4205
Hardley Street *Norfk* 67 TG3801
Hardmead *Bucks* 38 SP9347
Hardraw *N York* 88 SD8691
Hardsough *Lancs* 81 SD7920
Hardstoft *Derbys* 75 SK4463
Hardway *Hants* 13 SU6101
Hardway *Somset* 22 ST7134
Hardwick *Bucks* 38 SP8019
Hardwick *Cambs* 52 TL3758
Hardwick *Lincs* 76 SK8675
Hardwick *Nhants* 51 SP8469
Hardwick *Norfk* 55 TM2290
Hardwick *Oxon* 36 SP3706
Hardwick *Oxon* 49 SP5729
Hardwick *S York* 75 SK4885
Hardwick *W Mids* 61 SP0798
Hardwick Green *H & W* 47 SO8133
Hardwicke *Gloucs* 35 SO7912
Hardwicke *Gloucs* 47 SO9027
Hardy's Green *Essex* 40 TL9320
Hare Croft *W York* 82 SE0835
Hare Green *Essex* 41 TM1025
Hare Hatch *Berks* 37 SU8077
Hare Street *Essex* 27 TL5300
Hare Street *Essex* 39 TL4209
Hare Street *Herts* 39 TL3929
Harebeating *E Susx* 16 TQ5910
Hareby *Lincs* 77 TF3365
Harefield *Gt Lon* 26 TQ0590
Harehill *Derbys* 73 SK1735
Harehills *W York* 82 SE3135
Harehope *Nthumb* 111 NU0920
Harelaw *Border* 109 NT5323
Harelaw *Dur* 96 NZ1552
Hareplain *Kent* 28 TQ8140
Haresceugh *Cumb* 94 NY6043
Harescombe *Gloucs* 35 SO8310
Haresfield *Gloucs* 35 SO8110
Harestock *Hants* 24 SU4631
Harewood *W York* 83 SE3245
Harewood End *H & W* 46 SO5227
Harford *Devon* 6 SX6359
Hargate *Norfk* 66 TM1291
Hargatewall *Derbys* 74 SK1274
Hargrave *Ches* 71 SJ4862
Hargrave *Nhants* 51 TL0370
Hargrave *Suffk* 53 TL7760
Hargrave Green *Suffk* 53 TL7759
Harker *Cumb* 101 NY3960
Harkstead *Suffk* 54 TM1834
Harlaston *Staffs* 61 SK2110
Harlaxton *Lincs* 63 SK8832
Harle Syke *Lancs* 81 SD8635
Harlech *Gwynd* 57 SH5831
Harlescott *Shrops* 59 SJ5115
Harlesden *Gt Lon* 26 TQ2383
Harlesthorpe *Derbys* 75 SK4976
Harleston *Devon* 7 SX7945
Harleston *Norfk* 55 TM2483
Harleston *Suffk* 54 TM0160
Harlestone *Nhants* 49 SP7064
Harley *S York* 74 SK3698
Harley *Shrops* 59 SJ5901
Harleyholm *Strath* 108 NS9238
Harlington *Beds* 38 TL0330
Harlington *Gt Lon* 26 TQ0877
Harlington *S York* 83 SE4802
Harlosh *Highld* 136 NG2841
Harlow *Herts* 39 TL4711
Harlow Hill *Nthumb* 103 NZ0768
Harlthorpe *Humb* 84 SE7337
Harlton *Cambs* 52 TL3852
Harlyn Bay *Cnwll* 4 SW8775
Harman's Cross *Dorset* 11 SY9880
Harmby *N York* 89 SE1289
Harmer Green *Herts* 39 TL2515
Harmer Hill *Shrops* 59 SJ4822
Harmondsworth *Gt Lon* 26 TQ0577
Harmston *Lincs* 76 SK9762
Harnage *Shrops* 59 SJ5604
Harnham *Nthumb* 103 NZ0781
Harnhill *Gloucs* 36 SP0600
Harold Hill *Gt Lon* 27 TQ5392
Harold Wood *Gt Lon* 27 TQ5590
Haroldston West *Dyfed* 30 SM8615
Haroldswick *Shet* 155 HP6312
Harome *N York* 90 SE6481
Harpenden *Herts* 38 TL1314
Harpford *Devon* 9 SY0890
Harpham *Humb* 91 TA0961
Harpley *H & W* 47 SO6861
Harpley *Norfk* 65 TF7825
Harpole *Nhants* 49 SP6961
Harpsdale *Highld* 151 ND1355
Harpsden *Oxon* 37 SU7680
Harpswell *Lincs* 76 SK9389
Harpur Hill *Derbys* 74 SK0671
Harpurhey *Gt Man* 79 SD8501
Harraby *Cumb* 93 NY4154
Harracott *Devon* 19 SS5627
Harrapool *Highld* 129 NG6522
Harrietfield *Tays* 125 NN9829
Harrietsham *Kent* 28 TQ8652
Harringay *Gt Lon* 27 TQ3188
Harrington *Cumb* 92 NX9926
Harrington *H & W* 60 SO8774
Harrington *Lincs* 77 TF3671
Harrington *Nhants* 50 SP7780
Harringworth *Nhants* 51 SP9197
Harris *Highld* 134 NO3396
Harriseahead *Staffs* 72 SJ8656
Harriston *Cumb* 92 NY1641
Harrogate *N York* 82 SE3055
Harrold *Beds* 51 SP9456
Harrop Dale *Gt Man* 82 SE0008
Harrow *Gt Lon* 26 TQ1588
Harrow Green *Suffk* 54 TL8654
Harrow on the Hill *Gt Lon* 26 TQ1587
Harrow Weald *Gt Lon* 26 TQ1591
Harrowbarrow *Cnwll* 5 SX3969
Harrowden *Beds* 38 TL0646
Harrowgate Village *Dur* 96 NZ2917
Harsgeir *W Isls* 154 NB1040
Harston *Cambs* 53 TL4250
Harston *Leics* 63 SK8331
Harswell *Humb* 84 SE8240
Hart *Cleve* 97 NZ4734
Hart Station *Cleve* 97 NZ4836
Hartburn *Nthumb* 103 NZ0886
Hartest *Suffk* 54 TL8352
Hartfield *E Susx* 16 TQ4735
Hartford *Cambs* 52 TL2572
Hartford *Ches* 71 SJ6372
Hartford *Somset* 20 SS9629
Hartford End *Essex* 40 TL6817
Hartfordbridge *Hants* 25 SU7757
Hartforth *N York* 89 NZ1606
Harthill *Ches* 71 SJ4955
Harthill *Loth* 116 NS9064
Harthill *S York* 75 SK4980
Hartington *Derbys* 74 SK1260
Hartland *Devon* 18 SS2624
Hartland Quay *Devon* 18 SS2224
Hartlebury *H & W* 60 SO8471
Hartlepool *Cleve* 97 NZ5032
Hartley *Cumb* 88 NY7808
Hartley *Kent* 27 TQ6166
Hartley *Kent* 17 TQ7634
Hartley *Nthumb* 103 NZ3475
Hartley Green *Kent* 27 TQ6066
Hartley Green *Staffs* 72 SJ9729
Hartley Wespall *Hants* 24 SU6958
Hartley Wintney *Hants* 24 SU7656
Hartlip *Kent* 28 TQ8364
Hartoft End *N York* 90 SE7592
Harton *N York* 90 SE7061
Harton *Shrops* 59 SO4888
Harton *T & W* 103 NZ3765
Hartpury *Gloucs* 47 SO7924
Hartshead *W York* 82 SE1822
Hartshead Moor Side *W York* 82 SE1625
Hartshill *Staffs* 72 SJ8645
Hartshill *Warwks* 61 SP3294
Hartshorne *Derbys* 62 SK3221
Hartside *Nthumb* 111 NT9716
Hartsop *Cumb* 93 NY4013
Hartswell *Somset* 20 ST0826
Hartwell *Nhants* 38 SP7850
Hartwith *N York* 89 SE2161
Hartwood *Strath* 116 NS8459
Hartwood *Strath* 116 NS8459
Hartwood Myres *Border* 109 NT4324
Harvel *Kent* 28 TQ6563
Harvington *H & W* 48 SP0548
Harwell *Notts* 75 SK6891
Harwell *Oxon* 37 SU4989
Harwich *Essex* 41 TM2531

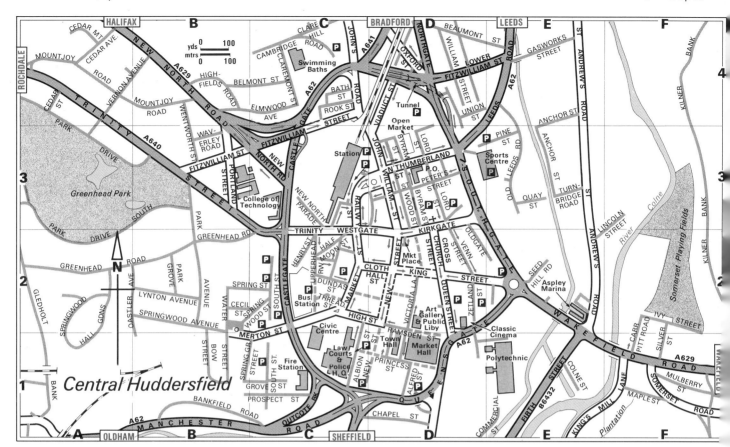

Central Huddersfield

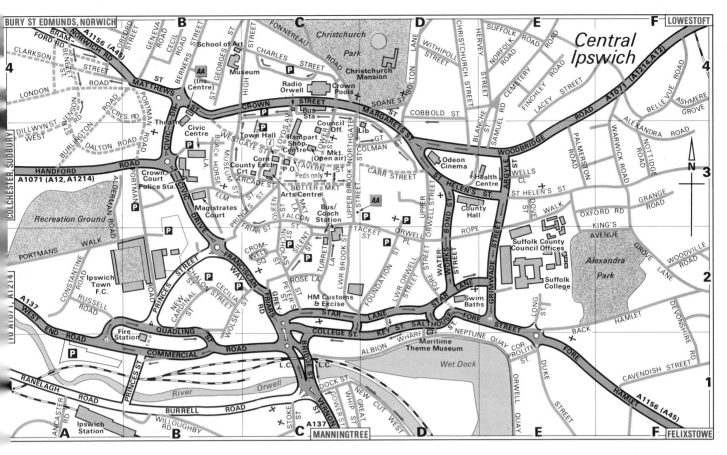

Central Ipswich

J

K

Kilbride Kneesall

Kilbride *W Isls* 154 NF7514
Kilburn *Derbys* 62 SK3845
Kilburn *Gt Lon* 26 TQ2483
Kilburn *N York* 90 SE5179
Kilby *Leics* 50 SP6295
Kilcadzow *Strath* 116 NS8848
Kilchamaig *Strath* 113 NR8060
Kilchattan *Strath* 112 NR3795
Kilchattan *Strath* 114 NS1054
Kilchenzie *Strath* 105 NR6724
Kilcheran *Strath* 122 NM8238
Kilchiaran *Strath* 112 NR2060
Kilchoan *Highld* 121 NM4964
Kilchrenan *Strath* 122 NN0322
Kilconquhar *Fife* 127 NO4802
Kilcot *Gloucs* 47 SO6925
Kilcoy *Highld* 139 NH5751
Kilcreggan *Strath* 114 NS2380
Kildale *N York* 90 NZ6009
Kildalloig *Strath* 105 NR7518
Kildary *Highld* 147 NH7674
Kildavanan *Strath* 114 NS0266
Kildermorie Lodge *Highld* 146 NH5277
Kildonan *Highld* 147 NC9120
Kildonan *Strath* 105 NS0321
Kildonan Lodge *Highld* 147 NC9022
Kildonnan *Highld* 128 NM4985
Kildrochet House *D & G* 98 NX0856
Kildrummy *Gramp* 142 NJ4617
Kildwick *N York* 82 SE0046
Kilehoman *Strath* 112 NR2163
Kilfinan *Strath* 114 NR9378
Kilfinnan *Highld* 131 NN2795
Kilgetty *Dyfed* 31 SN1207
Kilgrammie *Strath* 106 NS2502
Kilgwrrwg Common *Gwent* 34 ST4798
Kilham *Humb* 91 TA0664
Kilham *Nthumb* 110 NT8832
Kilkenneth *Strath* 120 NL9444
Kilkerran *Strath* 106 NS3003
Kilkhampton *Cnwll* 18 SS2511
Killamarsh *Derbys* 75 SK4580
Killay *W Glam* 32 SS6092
Killean *Strath* 105 NR6944
Killearn *Cent* 115 NS5286
Killen *Highld* 140 NH6758
Killerby *Dur* 96 NZ1919
Killerton *Devon* 9 SS9700
Killichonan *Tays* 132 NN5458
Killiechronan *Strath* 121 NM5441
Killiecrankie *Tays* 132 NN9162
Killilan *Highld* 138 NG9430
Killimster *Highld* 151 ND3156
Killin *Cent* 124 NN5733
Killinghall *N York* 89 SE2858
Killington *Cumb* 87 SD6188
Killington *Devon* 19 SS6646
Killingworth *T & W* 103 NZ2870
Killinochonoch *Strath* 113 NR8395
Killiow *Cnwll* 3 SW8042
Killivose *Cnwll* 3 SW8049
Killochyett *Border* 118 NT4545
Killocraw *Highld* 104 NR6530
Killundine *Highld* 121 NM5849
Kilmacolm *Strath* 115 NS3569
Kilmahog *Cent* 124 NN6108
Kilmahumaig *Strath* 113 NR7893
Kilmaluag *Highld* 136 NG4373
Kilmansharachan *Strath* 105 NR7107
Kilmany *Fife* 126 NO3821
Kilmarie *Highld* 129 NG5517
Kilmarnock *Strath* 107 NS4238
Kilmartin *Strath* 113 NR8398
Kilmaurs *Strath* 106 NS4141
Kilmelford *Strath* 122 NM8512
Kilmeny *Strath* 112 NR3865
Kilmersdon *Somset* 22 ST6952
Kilmeston *Hants* 13 SU5926
Kilmichael Glassary *Strath* 113 NR8593
Kilmichael of Inverlussa *Strath* 113 NR7786
Kilmington *Devon* 10 SY2798
Kilmington *Wilts* 22 ST7736
Kilmington Common *Wilts* 22 ST7736
Kilmington Street *Wilts* 22 ST7835
Kilmor *Strath* 122 NM8825
Kilmorack *Highld* 139 NH4944
Kilmore *Highld* 129 NG6507
Kilmory *Highld* 128 NG3603
Kilmory *Highld* 128 NM5369
Kilmory *Strath* 113 NR7075
Kilmuir *Highld* 136 NG2547
Kilmuir *Highld* 136 NG3770
Kilmuir *Highld* 140 NH6749
Kilmuir *Highld* 147 NH7573
Kilmun *Strath* 114 NS1781
Kiln Green *Berks* 37 SU8178
Kiln Pit Hill *Nthumb* 95 NZ0354
Kilnave *Strath* 112 NR2871
Kilndown *Kent* 16 TQ7035
Kilnhill *Cumb* 93 NY2132
Kilnhouses *Ches* 71 SJ6366
Kilnhurst *S York* 75 SK4597
Kilninian *Strath* 121 NM3946
Kilninver *Strath* 122 NM8221
Kilnsea *Humb* 85 TA4015
Kilnsey *N York* 88 SD9767
Kilnwick *Humb* 84 SE9949
Kilnwick Percy *Humb* 84 SE8249
Kiloran *Strath* 112 NR3996
Kilpeck *H & W* 46 SO4430
Kilpheder *W Isls* 154 NF7419
Kilphedir *Highld* 147 NC9818
Kilpin *Humb* 84 SE7726
Kilpin Pike *Humb* 84 SE7626
Kilrie *Ches* 79 SJ7478
Kilsby *Nhants* 50 SP5671
Kilspindie *Tays* 126 NO2125
Kilstay *D & G* 98 NX1238
Kilsyth *Strath* 116 NS7178
Kiltarlity *Highld* 139 NH5041
Kilton *Cleve* 97 NZ7018
Kilton *Somset* 20 ST1644
Kilton Thorpe *Cleve* 97 NZ6917
Kilvaxter *Highld* 136 NG3869
Kilve *Somset* 20 ST1443
Kilvington *Notts* 63 SK8042
Kilwinning *Strath* 106 NS2943
Kimberley *Norfk* 66 TG0704
Kimberley *Notts* 62 SK4944
Kimberworth *S York* 74 SK4092
Kimble Wick *Bucks* 38 SP8007
Kimblesworth *Dur* 96 NZ2547
Kimbolton *Cambs* 51 TL0967
Kimbolton *H & W* 46 SO5261
Kimcote *Leics* 50 SP5886
Kimmeridge *Dorset* 11 SY9179
Kimmerston *Nthumb* 111 NT9535
Kimpton *Hants* 23 SU2746
Kimpton *Hants* 23 SU2746
Kimpton *Herts* 39 TL1718
Kimworthy *Devon* 18 SS3012
Kinaird *Tays* 126 NO2428
Kinbrace *Highld* 150 NC8631
Kinbuck *Cent* 125 NN7905
Kincaple *Fife* 127 NO4618
Kincardine *Fife* 116 NS9387
Kincardine *Highld* 146 NH6089
Kincardine O'Neil *Tays* 134 NO5999
Kinclaven *Tays* 126 NO1538
Kincorth *Gramp* 135 NJ9403
Kincorth House *Gramp* 141 NJ0161
Kincraig *Highld* 132 NH8305
Kincraigie *Tays* 125 NN9849
Kindallachan *Tays* 125 NN9950
Kinerarach *Strath* 113 NR6653
Kineton *Gloucs* 48 SP0926
Kineton *Warwks* 48 SP3351
Kinfauns *Tays* 126 NO1622
King Sterndale *Derbys* 74 SK0972
King Street *Kent* 28 TQ6654
King's Acre *H & W* 46 SO4841
King's Bromley *Staffs* 73 SK1216
King's Cliffe *Nhants* 51 TL0097
King's Coughton *Warwks* 48 SP0859
King's Heath *W Mids* 61 SP0781
King's Hill *Warwks* 61 SP3274
King's Lynn *Norfk* 65 TF6220
King's Mills *Guern* 152 GN0000
King's Moss *Lancs* 78 SD5000
King's Newton *Derbys* 62 SK3926
King's Norton *Leics* 50 SK6800
King's Norton *W Mids* 61 SP0579
King's Nympton *Devon* 19 SS6819
King's Pyon *H & W* 46 SO4350
King's Somborne *Hants* 23 SU3631
King's Stag *Dorset* 11 ST7210
King's Stanley *Gloucs* 35 SO8103
King's Sutton *Oxon* 49 SP5036
King's Walden *Herts* 39 TL1623
Kingarth *Strath* 114 NS0956
Kingarvie *D & G* 100 NX9266
Kingcausie *Gramp* 135 NO8699
Kingcausie *Gramp* 135 NO8699
Kingcoed *Gwent* 34 SO4205
Kingerby *Lincs* 76 TF0593
Kingford *Devon* 18 SS2806
Kingham *Oxon* 48 SP2523
Kingholm Quay *D & G* 100 NX9773
Kinglassie *Loth* 117 NT2398
Kingoldrum *Tays* 126 NO3355
Kingoodie *Tays* 126 NO3329
Kings Bridge *W Glam* 32 SS5997
Kings Caple *H & W* 46 SO5528
Kings Hill *W Mids* 60 SO9896
Kings House Hotel *Highld* 123 NN2554
Kings Langley *Herts* 26 TL0702
Kings Meaburn *Cumb* 94 NY6121
Kings Muir *Border* 109 NT2539
Kings Newnham *Warwks* 50 SP4577
Kings Ripton *Cambs* 52 TL2576
Kings Weston *Avon* 34 ST5477
Kings Worthy *Hants* 24 SU4933
Kingsand *Cnwll* 6 SX4350
Kingsash *Bucks* 38 SP8805
Kingsbarns *Fife* 127 NO5912
Kingsbridge *Devon* 7 SX7344
Kingsbridge *Somset* 20 SS9837
Kingsbury *Gt Lon* 26 TQ1988
Kingsbury *Warwks* 61 SP2196
Kingsbury Episcopi *Somset* 21 ST4320
Kingsclere *Hants* 24 SU5258
Kingscote *Gloucs* 35 ST8196
Kingscott *Devon* 19 SS5318
Kingscross *Strath* 106 NS0528
Kingsdon *Somset* 21 ST5126
Kingsdown *Kent* 29 TR3748
Kingsdown *Wilts* 36 SU1688
Kingseat *Fife* 117 NT1290
Kingsey *Bucks* 37 SP7406
Kingsfold *W Susx* 15 TQ1636
Kingsford *H & W* 60 SO8281
Kingsford *Strath* 115 NS4447
Kingsgate *Kent* 29 TR3970
Kingshall Street *Suffk* 54 TL9161
Kingsheanton *Devon* 19 SS5537
Kingshouse *Cent* 124 NN5620
Kingshurst *W Mids* 61 SP1788
Kingside Hill *Cumb* 92 NY1651
Kingskerswell *Devon* 7 SX8767
Kingskettle *Fife* 126 NO3008
Kingsland *Dorset* 10 SY4597
Kingsland *H & W* 46 SO4461
Kingsley *Ches* 71 SJ5574
Kingsley *Hants* 25 SU7838
Kingsley *Staffs* 73 SK0147
Kingsley Green *W Susx* 14 SU8930
Kingsley Park *Nhants* 49 SP7762
Kingslow *Shrops* 60 SO7998
Kingsmead *Hants* 13 SU5813
Kingsmuir *Fife* 127 NO5308
Kingsmuir *Tays* 127 NO4849
Kingsnorth *Kent* 28 TR0039
Kingstanding *W Mids* 61 SP0794
Kingsteignton *Devon* 7 SX8773
Kingsthorne *H & W* 46 SO4931
Kingsthorpe *Nhants* 49 SP7563
Kingston *Cambs* 52 TL3455
Kingston *Devon* 4 SX0687
Kingston *Devon* 6 SX6347
Kingston *Dorset* 11 ST7509
Kingston *Dorset* 11 SY9579
Kingston *Gramp* 141 NJ3365
Kingston *Hants* 12 SU1401
Kingston *IOW* 13 SZ4781
Kingston *Kent* 29 TR1950
Kingston *Loth* 118 NT5482
Kingston *M Glam* 5 SX3676
Kingston *W Susx* 14 TQ0801
Kingston Bagpuize *Oxon* 36 SU4098
Kingston Blount *Oxon* 37 SU7399
Kingston by Sea *W Susx* 15 TQ2205
Kingston Deverill *Wilts* 22 ST8436
Kingston Lisle *Oxon* 36 SU3287
Kingston near Lewes *E Susx* 15 TQ3908
Kingston on Soar *Notts* 62 SK5027
Kingston Russell *Dorset* 10 SY5891
Kingston Seymour *Avon* 21 ST4066
Kingston St. Mary *Somset* 20 ST2229
Kingston Stert *Oxon* 37 SP7200
Kingston upon Hull *Humb* 85 TA0929
Kingston upon Thames *Gt Lon* 26 TQ1869
Kingstone *H & W* 46 SO4235
Kingstone *Oxon* 36 SU2685
Kingstone *Somset* 10 ST3713
Kingstone *Staffs* 73 SK0529
Kingstown *Cumb* 93 NY3959
Kingswear *Devon* 7 SX8851
Kingswells *Gramp* 135 NJ8606
Kingswells *Strath* 115 NS5047
Kingswinford *W Mids* 60 SO8888
Kingswood *Avon* 35 ST6473
Kingswood *Bucks* 37 SP6819
Kingswood *Gloucs* 35 ST7491
Kingswood *Kent* 28 TQ8350
Kingswood *Powys* 58 SJ2402
Kingswood *Somset* 20 ST1035
Kingswood *Surrey* 26 TQ2455
Kingswood *Warwks* 61 SP1971
Kingswood Brook *Warwks* 61 SP1970
Kingswood Common *H & W* 46 SO2954
Kingswood Common *Staffs* 60 SJ8302
Kingthorpe *Lincs* 76 TF1275
Kington *Avon* 34 ST6190
Kington *H & W* 47 SO9955
Kington *H & W* 46 SO2956
Kington Langley *Wilts* 35 ST9276
Kington Magna *Dorset* 22 ST7622
Kington St. Michael *Wilts* 35 ST9077
Kingussie *Highld* 132 NH7500
Kingweston *Somset* 21 ST5230
Kinharrachie *Gramp* 143 NJ9231
Kinkell Bridge *Tays* 125 NN9316
Kinknockie *Gramp* 143 NK0041
Kinleith *Loth* 117 NT1866
Kinlet *Shrops* 60 SO7280
Kinloch *Highld* 149 NC3434
Kinloch *Highld* 149 NC5552
Kinloch *Highld* 128 NM4099
Kinloch *Tays* 126 NO1544
Kinloch *Tays* 126 NO2644
Kinloch Hourn *Highld* 130 NG9407
Kinloch Rannoch *Tays* 132 NN6658
Kinlochard *Cent* 124 NN4502
Kinlochbervie *Highld* 148 NC2256
Kinlocheil *Highld* 130 NM9779
Kinlochewe *Highld* 138 NH0262
Kinlochleven *Highld* 131 NN1861
Kinlochmoidart *Highld* 129 NM7172
Kinlochnanuagh *Highld* 129 NM7384
Kinlochspelve *Strath* 121 NM6526
Kinloss *Gramp* 141 NJ0661
Kinmel Bay *Clwyd* 70 SH9880
Kinmount House *D & G* 100 NY1468
Kinmuck *Gramp* 143 NJ8119
Kinmundy *Gramp* 143 NJ8817
Kinnadie *Gramp* 143 NJ9743
Kinnahaird *Highld* 139 NH4755
Kinnaird *Tays* 117 NS9559
Kinnaird Castle *Tays* 134 NO6357
Kinneddar *Gramp* 141 NJ2269
Kinneff *Gramp* 135 NO8574
Kinnelhead *D & G* 108 NT0201
Kinnell *Tays* 127 NO6150
Kinnerley *Shrops* 59 SJ3321
Kinnersley *H & W* 46 SO3449
Kinnersley *H & W* 47 SO8743
Kinnerton *Powys* 46 SO2463
Kinnerton *Shrops* 59 SO3796
Kinnerton Green *Clwyd* 71 SJ3361
Kinnesswood *Tays* 126 NO1702
Kinninvie *Dur* 95 NZ0521
Kinnordy *Tays* 126 NO3655
Kinoulton *Notts* 63 SK6730
Kinross *Tays* 126 NO1202
Kinrossie *Tays* 126 NO1832
Kinsbourne *Herts* 38 TL1016
Kinsey Heath *Ches* 63 SK6642
Kinsham *H & W* 46 SO3665
Kinsham *H & W* 47 SO9335
Kinsley *W York* 83 SE4114
Kinson *Dorset* 12 SZ0696
Kintbury *Berks* 23 SU3866
Kintillo *Tays* 126 NO1317
Kinton *H & W* 46 SO4174
Kinton *Shrops* 59 SJ3619
Kintore *Gramp* 143 NJ7916
Kintour *Strath* 112 NR4551
Kintra *Strath* 120 NM3125
Kintradwell *Highld* 147 NC9208
Kintraw *Strath* 122 NM8204
Kinveachy *Highld* 140 NH9018
Kinver *Staffs* 60 SO8483
Kiplin *N York* 89 SE2796
Kippax *W York* 83 SE4130
Kippen *Cent* 116 NS6594
Kippford or Scaur *D & G* 92 NX8355
Kipping's Cross *Kent* 16 TQ6440
Kirbister *Ork* 155 HY3607
Kirby Bedon *Norfk* 67 TG2705
Kirby Bellars *Leics* 63 SK7117
Kirby Cane *Norfk* 67 TM3794
Kirby Corner *W Mids* 61 SP2976
Kirby Cross *Essex* 41 TM2121
Kirby Fields *Leics* 62 SK5303
Kirby Grindalythe *N York* 91 SE9067
Kirby Hill *N York* 89 NZ1306
Kirby Hill *N York* 89 SE3968
Kirby Knowle *N York* 89 SE4687
Kirby le Soken *Essex* 41 TM2122
Kirby Misperton *N York* 90 SE7779
Kirby Muxloe *Leics* 62 SK5104
Kirby Row *Norfk* 67 TM3792
Kirby Sigston *N York* 89 SE4194
Kirby Underdale *Humb* 90 SE8058
Kirby Wiske *N York* 89 SE3784
Kirdford *W Susx* 14 TQ0126
Kirivick *W Isls* 154 NB2041
Kirk *Highld* 151 ND2859
Kirk Bramwith *S York* 83 SE6111
Kirk Deighton *N York* 83 SE3950
Kirk Ella *Humb* 84 TA0229
Kirk Hallam *Derbys* 62 SK4540
Kirk Hammerton *N York* 83 SE4655
Kirk Haugh *Nthumb* 94 NY6950
Kirk Ireton *Derbys* 73 SK2650
Kirk Langley *Derbys* 73 SK2838
Kirk Merrington *Dur* 96 NZ2631
Kirk of Shotts *Strath* 116 NS8462
Kirk Sandall *S York* 83 SE6108
Kirk Smeaton *N York* 83 SE5116
Kirk Yetholm *Border* 110 NT8228
Kirkabister *Shet* 155 HU4938
Kirkandrews *D & G* 99 NX6048
Kirkandrews upon Eden *Cumb* 93 NY3558
Kirkbampton *Cumb* 93 NY3057
Kirkbean *D & G* 92 NX9859
Kirkbride *Cumb* 93 NY2356
Kirkbridge *N York* 89 SE2590
Kirkbuddo *Tays* 127 NO5043
Kirkburn *Border* 109 NT2938
Kirkburn *Humb* 84 SE9855
Kirkburton *W York* 82 SE1912
Kirkby *Lincs* 76 TF0692
Kirkby *Mersyd* 78 SJ4099
Kirkby *N York* 90 NZ5305
Kirkby Fleetham *N York* 89 SE2894
Kirkby Green *Lincs* 76 TF0857
Kirkby Hall *N York* 89 SE2795
Kirkby in Ashfield *Notts* 75 SK5056
Kirkby in Furness *Cumb* 101 NY2282
Kirkby Lonsdale *Cumb* 87 SD6178
Kirkby la Thorpe *Lincs* 76 TF0946
Kirkby Malham *N York* 88 SD8960
Kirkby Mallory *Leics* 50 SK4500
Kirkby Malzeard *N York* 89 SE2374
Kirkby Mills *N York* 90 SE7085
Kirkby Overblow *N York* 83 SE3249
Kirkby on Bain *Lincs* 77 TF2462
Kirkby Stephen *Cumb* 88 NY7708
Kirkby Thore *Cumb* 94 NY6325
Kirkby Underwood *Lincs* 64 TF0727
Kirkby Wharf *N York* 83 SE5041
Kirkby Woodhouse *Notts* 75 SK5055
Kirkbymoorside *N York* 90 SE6986
Kirkcaldy *Fife* 117 NT2892
Kirkcambeck *Cumb* 101 NY5368
Kirkchrist *D & G* 99 NX6751
Kirkcolm *D & G* 98 NX0268
Kirkconnel *D & G* 107 NS7312
Kirkconnel *D & G* 100 NX9868
Kirkconnell *D & G* 99 NX6760
Kirkcowan *D & G* 98 NX3260
Kirkcudbright *D & G* 99 NX6851
Kirkdale *Mersyd* 78 SJ3493
Kirkfieldbank *Strath* 108 NS8643
Kirkgunzeon *D & G* 100 NX8666
Kirkham *Lancs* 80 SD4232
Kirkham *N York* 90 SE7365
Kirkhamgate *W York* 82 SE2922
Kirkharle *Nthumb* 103 NZ0182
Kirkheaton *Nthumb* 103 NZ0177
Kirkheaton *W York* 82 SE1818
Kirkhill *Highld* 139 NH5545
Kirkhope *Border* 109 NT3723
Kirkhope *Strath* 108 NS9606
Kirkhouse *Cumb* 94 NY5659
Kirkhouse Green *S York* 83 SE6213
Kirkiboll *Highld* 149 NC5956
Kirkibost *Highld* 128 NG5418
Kirkibost *W Isls* 154 NB1835
Kirkinch *Tays* 126 NO3044
Kirkinner *D & G* 99 NX4251
Kirkintilloch *Strath* 116 NS6573
Kirkland *Cumb* 93 NY2648
Kirkland *Cumb* 92 NY0718
Kirkland *Cumb* 94 NY6432
Kirkland *D & G* 107 NS7214
Kirkland *D & G* 99 NX4356
Kirkland *D & G* 100 NY0389
Kirkland *D & G* 100 NX8190
Kirkland Guards *Cumb* 93 NY1840
Kirkleatham *Cleve* 97 NZ5921
Kirklevington *Cleve* 89 NZ4309
Kirkley *Suffk* 67 TM5391
Kirkleyditch *Ches* 79 SJ8778
Kirklington *N York* 89 SE3181
Kirklington *Notts* 75 SK6757
Kirklinton *Cumb* 101 NY4367
Kirkliston *Loth* 117 NT1274
Kirkmabreck *D & G* 99 NX4756
Kirkmaiden *D & G* 98 NX1236
Kirkmichael *IOM* 153 SC3190
Kirkmichael *Strath* 106 NS3408
Kirkmichael *Tays* 133 NO0759
Kirkmuirhill *Strath* 107 NS7842
Kirknewton *Fife* 117 NT1166
Kirknewton *Nthumb* 110 NT9330
Kirknewton *Nthumb* 110 NT9130
Kirkney *Gramp* 142 NJ5132
Kirkney *Gramp* 142 NJ5132
Kirkoswald *Cumb* 94 NY5541
Kirkoswald *Strath* 106 NS2407
Kirkpatrick Durham *D & G* 100 NX7870
Kirkpatrick-Fleming *D & G* 101 NY2770
Kirksanton *Cumb* 86 SD1380
Kirkstall *W York* 82 SE2635
Kirkstead *Lincs* 76 TF1762
Kirkstile *D & G* 101 NY3690
Kirkstile *Gramp* 142 NJ5235
Kirkstone Pass Inn *Cumb* 87 NY4108
Kirkstyle *Highld* 151 ND3472
Kirkthorpe *W York* 83 SE3621
Kirkton *Border* 109 NT5413
Kirkton *D & G* 100 NX9781
Kirkton *Fife* 126 NO3625
Kirkton *Gramp* 134 NJ6112
Kirkton *Gramp* 142 NJ6425
Kirkton *Gramp* 143 NJ8243
Kirkton *Highld* 137 NG8227
Kirkton *Highld* 138 NG9141
Kirkton *Strath* 114 NS1654
Kirkton *Tays* 125 NN9618
Kirkton Manor *Border* 109 NT2238
Kirkton of Airlie *Tays* 126 NO3151
Kirkton of Auchterhouse *Tays* 126 NO3438
Kirkton of Barevan *Highld* 140 NH8347
Kirkton of Collace *Tays* 126 NO1932
Kirkton of Craig *Tays* 127 NO6956
Kirkton of Durris *Gramp* 135 NO7796
Kirkton of Glenbuchat *Gramp* 141 NJ3715
Kirkton of Glenisla *Tays* 133 NO2160
Kirkton of Logie Buchan *Gramp* 143 NJ9829
Kirkton of Menmuir *Tays* 134 NO5364
Kirkton of Monikie *Tays* 127 NO5138
Kirkton of Rayne *Gramp* 142 NJ6930
Kirkton of Skene *Gramp* 135 NJ8007
Kirkton of Tealing *Tays* 126 NO4038
Kirktown *Gramp* 143 NJ9965
Kirktown of Alvah *Gramp* 142 NJ6760
Kirktown of Bourtie *Gramp* 143 NJ8025
Kirktown of Fetteresso *Gramp* 135 NO8486
Kirktown of Mortlach *Gramp* 141 NJ3138
Kirktown of Slains *Gramp* 143 NK0429
Kirkwall *Ork* 155 HY4410
Kirkwhelpington *Nthumb* 103 NY9984
Kirmington *Humb* 85 TA1011
Kirmond le Mire *Lincs* 76 TF1892
Kirn *Strath* 114 NS1878
Kirstead Green *Norfk* 67 TM2997
Kirtlebridge *D & G* 101 NY2372
Kirtleton *D & G* 101 NY2780
Kirtling *Cambs* 53 TL6857
Kirtling Green *Suffk* 53 TL6856
Kirtlington *Oxon* 37 SP4919
Kirtomy *Highld* 150 NC7463
Kirton *Lincs* 64 TF3038
Kirton *Notts* 75 SK6869
Kirton *Suffk* 55 TM2740
Kirton End *Lincs* 64 TF2840
Kirton Holme *Lincs* 64 TF2641
Kirton in Lindsey *Lincs* 76 SK9398
Kirton of Culsalmond *Gramp* 142 NJ6532
Kirton of Culsalmond *Gramp* 142 NJ6532
Kirton of Strathmartime *Tays* 126 NO3735
Kirtonhill *Strath* 115 NS3875
Kirwaugh *D & G* 99 NX4054
Kislingbury *Nhants* 49 SP6959
Kit Green *Gt Man* 78 SD5405
Kite Green *Warwks* 48 SP1666
Kites Hardwick *Warwks* 50 SP4768
Kitleigh *Cnwll* 18 SX2499
Kittisford *Somset* 20 ST0822
Kittle *W Glam* 32 SS5789
Kitts Green *W Mids* 61 SP1587
Kittybrewster *Gramp* 135 NJ9207
Kitwood *Hants* 24 SU6633
Kivernoll *H & W* 46 SO4632
Kiveton Park *S York* 75 SK4982
Knaith *Lincs* 75 SK8284
Knaith Park *Lincs* 76 SK8485
Knap Corner *Dorset* 22 ST8023
Knaphill *Surrey* 25 SU9658
Knaplock *Somset* 19 SS8633
Knapp *Somset* 20 ST3025
Knapp Hill *Hants* 13 SU4023
Knapthorpe *Notts* 75 SK7458
Knapton *N York* 83 SE5652
Knapton *N York* 90 SE8776
Knapton *Norfk* 67 TG3034
Knapton Green *H & W* 46 SO4452
Knapwell *Cambs* 52 TL3362
Knaresborough *N York* 89 SE3557
Knarsdale *Nthumb* 94 NY6754
Knaven *Gramp* 143 NJ8943
Knayton *N York* 89 SE4387
Knebworth *Herts* 39 TL2520
Knedlington *Humb* 84 SE7326
Kneesall *Notts* 75 SK7064

L

Lee

Little Singleton

Lee *Strath*	**121**	NM4022
Lee Brockhurst *Shrops*	**59**	SJ5427
Lee Chapel *Essex*	**40**	TQ6987
Lee Clump *Bucks*	**38**	SP9004
Lee Common *Bucks*	**38**	SP9303
Lee Green *Ches*	**72**	SJ6562
Lee Mill *Devon*	**6**	SX5855
Lee Moor *Devon*	**6**	SX5762
Lee Street *Surrey*	**15**	TQ2743
Lee-on-the-Solent *Hants*	**13**	SU5600
Leebotwood *Shrops*	**59**	SO4798
Leece *Cumb*	**86**	SD2469
Leedon *Beds*	**38**	SP9325
Leeds *Kent*	**28**	TQ8253
Leeds *W York*	**82**	SE3034
Leeds Beck *Lincs*	**76**	TF2065
Leedstown *Cnwll*	**2**	SW6034
Leek *Staffs*	**72**	SJ9856
Leek Wootton *Warwks*	**48**	SP2968
Leeming *N York*	**89**	SE2989
Leeming *W York*	**82**	SE0434
Leeming Bar *N York*	**89**	SE2889
Lees *Derbys*	**73**	SK2637
Lees *Gt Man*	**79**	SD9504
Lees *Gt Man*	**79**	SD9504
Lees *W York*	**82**	SE0437
Lees Green *Derbys*	**73**	SK2637
Lees Hill *Cumb*	**101**	NY5568
Leesthorpe *Leics*	**63**	SK7813
Leetown *Tays*	**126**	NO2121
Leftwich *Ches*	**79**	SJ6672
Legbourne *Lincs*	**77**	TF3684
Legburthwaite *Cumb*	**93**	NY3219
Legerwood *Border*	**110**	NT5843
Legsby *Lincs*	**76**	TF1385
Leicester *Leics*	**62**	SK5804
Leicester Forest East *Leics*	**62**	SK5303
Leigh *Devon*	**9**	SS9115
Leigh *Dorset*	**10**	ST6108
Leigh *Gloucs*	**47**	SO8626
Leigh *H & W*	**47**	SO7853
Leigh *Kent*	**16**	TQ5446
Leigh *Mersyd*	**79**	SJ6599
Leigh *Shrops*	**59**	SJ3303
Leigh *Surrey*	**15**	TQ2246
Leigh *Wilts*	**36**	SU0692
Leigh Beck *Essex*	**40**	TQ8183
Leigh Delamere *Wilts*	**35**	ST8879
Leigh Green *Kent*	**17**	TQ9033
Leigh Knoweglass *Strath*	**116**	NS6350
Leigh Sinton *H & W*	**47**	SO7750
Leigh upon Mendip *Somset*	**22**	ST6847
Leigh Woods *Avon*	**34**	ST5572
Leigh-on-Sea *Essex*	**40**	TQ8286
Leighland Chapel *Somset*	**20**	ST0336
Leighterton *Gloucs*	**35**	ST8290
Leighton *N York*	**89**	SE1679
Leighton *Powys*	**58**	SJ2406
Leighton *Shrops*	**59**	SJ6105
Leighton *Somset*	**22**	ST7043
Leighton Bromswold *Cambs*	**52**	TL1175
Leighton Buzzard *Beds*	**38**	SP9225
Leinthall Earls *H & W*	**46**	SO4467
Leinthall Starkes *H & W*	**46**	SO4369
Leintwardine *H & W*	**46**	SO4074
Leire *Leics*	**50**	SP5290
Leiston *Suffk*	**55**	TM4462
Leitfie *Tays*	**126**	NO2545
Leith *Loth*	**117**	NT2676
Leitholm *Border*	**110**	NT7944
Lelant *Cnwll*	**2**	SW5437
Lelley *Humb*	**85**	TA2032
Lem Hill *H & W*	**60**	SO7275
Lemmington Hall *Nthumb*	**111**	NU1211
Lempitlaw *Border*	**110**	NT7832
Lemreway *W Isls*	**154**	NB3711
Lemsford *Herts*	**39**	TL2212
Lenchwick *H & W*	**48**	SP0347
Lendalfoot *Strath*	**106**	NX1390
Lendrick *Cent*	**124**	NN5506
Lendrum Terrace *Gramp*	**143**	NK1141
Lenham *Kent*	**28**	TQ8952
Lenham Heath *Kent*	**28**	TQ9249
Lenie *Highld*	**139**	NH5126
Lennel *Border*	**110**	NT8540
Lennox Plunton *D & G*	**99**	NX6051
Lennoxlove *Loth*	**118**	NT5172
Lennoxtown *Strath*	**116**	NS6277
Lent *Bucks*	**26**	SU9381
Lenton *Lincs*	**64**	TF0230
Lenton *Notts*	**62**	SK5539
Lenwade *Norfk*	**66**	TG0918
Lenzie *Strath*	**116**	NS6572
Leochel-Cushnie *Gramp*	**134**	NJ5210
Leominster *H & W*	**46**	SO4958
Leonard Stanley *Gloucs*	**35**	SO8003
Leorin *Strath*	**104**	NR3548
Leoville *Jersey*	**152**	JS0000
Lepe *Hants*	**13**	SZ4598
Lephin *Highld*	**136**	NG1749
Lephinchapel *Strath*	**114**	NR9690
Lephinmore *Strath*	**114**	NR9892
Leppington *N York*	**90**	SE7661
Lepton *W York*	**82**	SE2015
Lerags *Strath*	**122**	NM8324
Lerryn *Cnwll*	**4**	SX1457
Lerwick *Shet*	**155**	HU4741
Les Arquets *Guern*	**152**	GN0000
Les Hubits *Guern*	**152**	GN0000
Les Lohiers *Guern*	**152**	GN0000
Les Murchez *Guern*	**152**	GN0000
Les Nicolles *Guern*	**152**	GN0000
Les Quartiers *Guern*	**152**	GN0000
Les Quennevais *Jersey*	**152**	JS0000
Les Sages *Guern*	**152**	GN0000
Les Villets *Guern*	**152**	GN0000
Lesbury *Nthumb*	**111**	NU2312
Leslie *Fife*	**126**	NO2501
Leslie *Gramp*	**142**	NJ5924
Lesmahagow *Strath*	**108**	NS8139
Lesnewth *Cnwll*	**4**	SX1390
Lessingham *Norfk*	**67**	TG3928
Lessonhall *Cumb*	**93**	NY2249
Lessonhall *Cumb*	**93**	NY2249
Lestowder *Cnwll*	**3**	SW7924
Leswalt *D & G*	**98**	NX0164
Letchmore Heath *Herts*	**26**	TQ1597
Letchworth *Herts*	**39**	TL2232
Letcombe Bassett *Oxon*	**36**	SU3785
Letcombe Regis *Oxon*	**36**	SU3786
Letham *Border*	**110**	NT6708
Letham *Fife*	**126**	NO3014
Letham *Tays*	**127**	NO5348
Letham Grange *Tays*	**127**	NO6345
Lethenty *Gramp*	**142**	NJ5820
Lethenty *Gramp*	**143**	NJ8140
Lethenty *Gramp*	**142**	NJ5820
Letheringham *Suffk*	**55**	TM2757
Letheringsett *Norfk*	**66**	TG0639
Lett's Green *Kent*	**27**	TQ4558
Lettaford *Devon*	**8**	SX7084
Letterfearn *Highld*	**138**	NG8823
Letterfinley Lodge Hotel *Highld*	**131**	NN2591
Lettermorar *Highld*	**129**	NM7389
Letters *Highld*	**145**	NH1687
Lettershaw *Strath*	**108**	NS8920
Letterston *Dyfed*	**30**	SM9429
Lettoch *Highld*	**141**	NJ0219
Lettoch *Highld*	**141**	NJ0932
Letton *H & W*	**46**	SO3346
Letton *H & W*	**46**	SO3770
Letty Green *Herts*	**39**	TL2810
Letwell *S York*	**75**	SK5587
Leuchars *Fife*	**127**	NO4521
Leurbost *W Isls*	**154**	NB3725
Levalsa Moor *Cnwll*	**3**	SX0049
Levedale *Staffs*	**72**	SJ9016
Level's Green *Essex*	**39**	TL4724
Leven *Fife*	**118**	NO3800
Leven *Humb*	**85**	TA1045
Levencorroch *Strath*	**105**	NS0021
Levens *Cumb*	**87**	SD4886
Levens Green *Herts*	**39**	TL3522
Levenshulme *Gt Man*	**79**	SJ8794
Levenwick *Shet*	**155**	HU4021
Leverburgh *W Isls*	**154**	NG0186
Leverington *Cambs*	**65**	TF4411
Leverstock Green *Herts*	**38**	TL0806
Leverton *Lincs*	**77**	TF3947
Levington *Suffk*	**55**	TM2339
Levisham *N York*	**90**	SE8390
Lew *Oxon*	**36**	SP3206
Lew Middleton *Nthumb*	**111**	NU1036
Lewannick *Cnwll*	**5**	SX2780
Lewdown *Devon*	**5**	SX4486
Lewes *E Susx*	**15**	TQ4110
Leweston *Dorset*	**10**	ST6312
Leweston *Dyfed*	**30**	SM9422
Lewis Wych *H & W*	**46**	SO3357
Lewisham *Gt Lon*	**27**	TQ3774
Lewiston *Highld*	**139**	NH5129
Lewknor *Oxon*	**37**	SU7197
Leworthy *Devon*	**19**	SS6738
Leworthy *Devon*	**18**	SS3201
Lewson Street *Kent*	**28**	TQ9661
Lewth *Lancs*	**80**	SD4836
Lewtrenchard *Devon*	**5**	SX4686
Lexden *Essex*	**41**	TL9625
Lexworthy *Somset*	**20**	ST2535
Ley *Cnwll*	**4**	SX1766
Leybourne *Kent*	**28**	TQ6858
Leyburn *N York*	**89**	SE1190
Leycett *Staffs*	**72**	SJ7946
Leygreen *Herts*	**39**	TL1624
Leyland *Lancs*	**80**	SD5422
Leyland Green *Mersyd*	**78**	SD5500
Leylodge *Gramp*	**135**	NJ7613
Leys *Gramp*	**143**	NK0052
Leys *Tays*	**126**	NO2537
Leys of Cossans *Tays*	**126**	NO3849
Leysdown-on-Sea *Kent*	**28**	TR0370
Leysmill *Tays*	**127**	NO6047
Leyton *Gt Lon*	**27**	TQ3886
Leytonstone *Gt Lon*	**27**	TQ3987
Lezant *Cnwll*	**5**	SX3379
Lezayre *IOM*	**153**	SC4294
Lezerea *Cnwll*	**2**	SW6833
Lhanbryde *Gramp*	**141**	NJ2761
Lhen The *IOM*	**153**	NX3801
LIttle Cheverell *Wilts*	**22**	ST9853
Libanus *Powys*	**45**	SN9925
Libberton *Strath*	**108**	NS9943
Liberton *Loth*	**117**	NT2769
Lichfield *Staffs*	**61**	SK1109
Lickey *H & W*	**60**	SO9975
Lickey End *H & W*	**60**	SO9772
Lickey Rock *H & W*	**60**	SO9774
Lickfold *W Susx*	**14**	SU9226
Liddaton Green *Devon*	**5**	SX4582
Liddesdale *Highld*	**130**	NM7759
Liddington *Wilts*	**36**	SU2081
Lidgate *Suffk*	**53**	TL7258
Lidget *S York*	**75**	SE6500
Lidgett *Notts*	**75**	SK6365
Lidham Hill *E Susx*	**17**	TQ8316
Lidlington *Beds*	**38**	SP9839
Lidsing *Kent*	**28**	TQ7862
Lienassie *Highld*	**138**	NG9621
Liff *Tays*	**126**	NO3332
Lifford *W Mids*	**61**	SP0580
Lifton *Devon*	**5**	SX3885
Liftondown *Devon*	**5**	SX3685
Lighthazles *W York*	**82**	SE0220
Lighthorne *Warwks*	**48**	SP3355
Lightwater *Surrey*	**25**	SU9362
Lightwood *Staffs*	**72**	SJ9241
Lightwood Green *Ches*	**63**	SK6342
Lightwood Green *Clwyd*	**71**	SJ3840
Lilbourne *Nhants*	**50**	SP5677
Lilburn Tower *Nthumb*	**111**	NU0224
Lilleshall *Shrops*	**72**	SJ7315
Lilley *Berks*	**37**	SU4479
Lilley *Herts*	**38**	TL1226
Lilliesleaf *Border*	**109**	NT5325
Lillingstone Dayrell *Bucks*	**49**	SP7039
Lillingstone Lovell *Bucks*	**49**	SP7140
Lillington *Dorset*	**10**	ST6212
Lilstock *Somset*	**20**	ST1644
Lilyhurst *Shrops*	**60**	SJ7413
Limbrick *Lancs*	**81**	SD6016
Limbury *Beds*	**38**	TL0724
Lime Street *H & W*	**47**	SO8130
Limebrook *H & W*	**46**	SO3766
Limefield *Gt Man*	**81**	SD8013
Limekilnburn *Strath*	**116**	NS7050
Limekilns *Fife*	**117**	NT0883
Limerigg *Cent*	**116**	NS8570
Limerstone *IOW*	**13**	SZ4482
Limestone Brae *Nthumb*	**95**	NY7949
Limington *Somset*	**21**	ST5422
Limmerhaugh *Strath*	**107**	NS6127
Limpenhoe *Norfk*	**67**	TG3903
Limpley Stoke *Wilts*	**22**	ST7760
Limpsfield *Surrey*	**27**	TQ4053
Linby *Notts*	**75**	SK5351
Linchmere *W Susx*	**14**	SU8731
Lincoln *Lincs*	**76**	SK9771
Lincomb *H & W*	**47**	SO8269
Lincombe *Devon*	**7**	SX7340
Lincombe *Devon*	**7**	SX7458
Lindal in Furness *Cumb*	**86**	SD2475
Lindale *Cumb*	**87**	SD4180
Lindean *Border*	**109**	NT4931
Lindfield *W Susx*	**15**	TQ3425
Lindford *Hants*	**14**	SU8036
Lindford Magna *Lincs*	**76**	TF1988
Lindley *W York*	**82**	SE1218
Lindley Green *N York*	**82**	SE2248
Lindores *Fife*	**126**	NO2617
Lindow End *Ches*	**79**	SJ8178
Lindridge *H & W*	**47**	SO6769
Lindsell *Essex*	**40**	TL6427
Lindsey *Suffk*	**54**	TL9745
Lindsey Tye *Suffk*	**54**	TL9845
Liney *Somset*	**21**	ST3535
Linford *Essex*	**40**	TQ6779
Linford *Hants*	**12**	SU1707
Ling Bob *W York*	**82**	SE0935
Lingague *IOM*	**153**	SC2172
Lingdale *Cleve*	**97**	NZ6716
Lingen *H & W*	**46**	SO3667
Lingfield *Surrey*	**15**	TQ3843
Lingfield Common *Surrey*	**15**	TQ3844
Lingley Green *Ches*	**78**	SJ5589
Lingwood *Norfk*	**67**	TG3608
Liniclett *W Isls*	**154**	NF7949
Linicro *Highld*	**136**	NG3967
Linkend *H & W*	**47**	SO8231
Linkenholt *Hants*	**23**	SU3658
Linkhill *Kent*	**17**	TQ8128
Linkinhorne *Cnwll*	**5**	SX3173
Linktown *Fife*	**117**	NT2890
Linkwood *Gramp*	**141**	NJ2361
Linley *Shrops*	**59**	SO3592
Linley Green *H & W*	**47**	SO6953
Linleygreen *Shrops*	**60**	SO6898
Linlithgow *Loth*	**117**	NS9977
Linnels Bridge *Nthumb*	**102**	NY9562
Linshiels *Nthumb*	**110**	NT8906
Linsidemore *Highld*	**146**	NH5499
Linslade *Beds*	**38**	SP9125
Linstead Parva *Suffk*	**55**	TM3377
Linstock *Cumb*	**93**	NY4258
Linthurst *H & W*	**60**	SO9972
Linthwaite *W York*	**82**	SE1014
Linthwaite *W York*	**82**	SE0913
Lintlaw *Border*	**119**	NT8258
Lintmill *Gramp*	**142**	NJ5165
Linton *Border*	**110**	NT7726
Linton *Cambs*	**53**	TL5646
Linton *Derbys*	**73**	SK2716
Linton *Gloucs*	**35**	SO7918
Linton *H & W*	**47**	SO6625
Linton *Kent*	**28**	TQ7550
Linton *N York*	**88**	SD9962
Linton *W York*	**83**	SE3846
Linton Heath *Derbys*	**73**	SK2816
Linton Hill *Gloucs*	**47**	SO6624
Linton-on-Ouse *N York*	**90**	SE4860
Linwood *Hants*	**12**	SU1809
Linwood *Lincs*	**76**	TF1186
Linwood *Strath*	**115**	NS4464
Lionel *W Isls*	**154**	NB5263
Lions Green *E Susx*	**16**	TQ5518
Liphook *Hants*	**14**	SU8431
Lipley *Shrops*	**72**	SJ7330
Liscard *Mersyd*	**78**	SJ2991
Liscombe *Devon*	**19**	SS8732
Liskeard *Cnwll*	**5**	SX2564
Liss *Hants*	**14**	SU7727
Liss Forest *Hants*	**14**	SU7829
Lissett *Humb*	**91**	TA1458
Lissington *Lincs*	**76**	TF1083
Liston *Essex*	**54**	TL8544
Lisvane *S Glam*	**33**	ST1983
Liswerry *Gwent*	**34**	ST3487
Litcham *Norfk*	**66**	TF8817
Litchard *M Glam*	**33**	SS9182
Litchborough *Nhants*	**49**	SP6354
Litchfield *Hants*	**24**	SU4653
Litherland *Mersyd*	**78**	SJ3397
Litlington *Cambs*	**39**	TL3142
Litlington *E Susx*	**16**	TQ5201
Little Abington *Cambs*	**53**	TL5349
Little Addington *Nhants*	**51**	SP9673
Little Airies *D & G*	**99**	NX4248
Little Almshoe *Herts*	**39**	TL2025
Little Alne *Warwks*	**48**	SP1461
Little Amwell *Herts*	**39**	TL3511
Little Asby *Cumb*	**87**	NY6909
Little Aston *Staffs*	**61**	SK0900
Little Atherfield *IOW*	**13**	SZ4680
Little Ayton *N York*	**90**	NZ5610
Little Baddow *Essex*	**40**	TL7708
Little Badminton *Avon*	**35**	ST8084
Little Bampton *Cumb*	**93**	NY2755
Little Bardfield *Essex*	**40**	TL6531
Little Barford *Beds*	**52**	TL1756
Little Barningham *Norfk*	**66**	TG1333
Little Barrington *Gloucs*	**36**	SP2012
Little Barrow *Ches*	**71**	SJ4770
Little Barugh *N York*	**90**	SE7579
Little Bavington *Nthumb*	**102**	NY9878
Little Bayton *Warwks*	**61**	SP3585
Little Bealings *Suffk*	**55**	TM2348
Little Bedwyn *Wilts*	**23**	SU2966
Little Bentley *Essex*	**41**	TM1125
Little Berkhamsted *Herts*	**39**	TL2907
Little Billing *Nhants*	**51**	SP8061
Little Billington *Beds*	**38**	SP9322
Little Birch *H & W*	**46**	SO5130
Little Bispham *Lancs*	**80**	SD3141
Little Blakenham *Suffk*	**54**	TM1049
Little Blencow *Cumb*	**93**	NY4532
Little Bloxwich *W Mids*	**60**	SK0003
Little Bognor *W Susx*	**14**	TQ0020
Little Bolehill *Derbys*	**73**	SK2954
Little Bookham *Surrey*	**26**	TQ1254
Little Bourton *Oxon*	**49**	SP4543
Little Bowden *Leics*	**50**	SP7487
Little Bradley *Suffk*	**53**	TL6852
Little Brampton *H & W*	**46**	SO3061
Little Brampton *Shrops*	**59**	SO3681
Little Braxted *Essex*	**40**	TL8314
Little Brechin *Tays*	**134**	NO5862
Little Brickhill *Bucks*	**38**	SP9032
Little Bridgeford *Staffs*	**72**	SJ8727
Little Brington *Nhants*	**49**	SP6663
Little Bromley *Essex*	**41**	TM0928
Little Budworth *Ches*	**71**	SJ6065
Little Burstead *Essex*	**40**	TQ6692
Little Bytham *Lincs*	**64**	TF0118
Little Carlton *Lincs*	**77**	TF3985
Little Carlton *Notts*	**75**	SK7757
Little Casterton *Leics*	**64**	TF0109
Little Catwick *Humb*	**85**	TA1444
Little Catworth *Cambs*	**51**	TL1072
Little Cawthorpe *Lincs*	**77**	TF3583
Little Chalfont *Bucks*	**26**	SU9997
Little Charlinch *Somset*	**20**	ST2437
Little Chart *Kent*	**28**	TQ9446
Little Chatfield *Wilts*	**22**	ST8563
Little Chesterford *Essex*	**39**	TL5141
Little Cheveney *Kent*	**28**	TQ7243
Little Chishill *Cambs*	**39**	TL4237
Little Clacton *Essex*	**41**	TM1618
Little Clanfield *Oxon*	**36**	SP2701
Little Clifton *Cumb*	**92**	NY0528
Little Coates *Humb*	**85**	TA2408
Little Comberton *H & W*	**47**	SO9643
Little Common *E Susx*	**17**	TQ7108
Little Comp *Kent*	**27**	TQ6357
Little Compton *Warwks*	**48**	SP2530
Little Corby *Cumb*	**93**	NY4757
Little Cornard *Suffk*	**54**	TL9039
Little Cowarne *H & W*	**46**	SO6051
Little Coxwell *Oxon*	**36**	SU2893
Little Crakehall *N York*	**89**	SE2490
Little Cransley *Nhants*	**51**	SP8376
Little Creaton *Nhants*	**50**	SP7171
Little Cressingham *Norfk*	**66**	TF8700
Little Crosby *Mersyd*	**78**	SD3201
Little Crosthwaite *Cumb*	**93**	NY2336
Little Cubley *Derbys*	**73**	SK1537
Little Dalby *Leics*	**63**	SK7714
Little Dens *Gramp*	**143**	NK0643
Little Dewchurch *H & W*	**46**	SO5231
Little Ditton *Cambs*	**53**	TL6658
Little Doward *H & W*	**34**	SO5416
Little Driffield *Humb*	**91**	TA0058
Little Dunham *Norfk*	**66**	TF8612
Little Dunkeld *Tays*	**125**	NO0342
Little Dunmow *Essex*	**40**	TL6521
Little Durnford *Wilts*	**23**	SU1234
Little Easton *Essex*	**40**	TL6023
Little Eaton *Derbys*	**62**	SK3641
Little Ellingham *Norfk*	**66**	TM0099
Little Elm *Somset*	**22**	ST7246
Little Everdon *Nhants*	**49**	SP5957
Little Eversden *Cambs*	**52**	TL3753
Little Faringdon *S York*	**36**	SP2201
Little Fencote *N York*	**89**	SE2793
Little Fenton *N York*	**83**	SE5135
Little Fransham *Norfk*	**66**	TF9011
Little Gaddesden *Herts*	**38**	SP9913
Little Garway *H & W*	**46**	SO4424
Little Gidding *Cambs*	**52**	TL1282
Little Glemham *Suffk*	**55**	TM3458
Little Gorsley *H & W*	**47**	SO6824
Little Gransden *Cambs*	**52**	TL2755
Little Green *Notts*	**63**	SK7243
Little Green *Somset*	**22**	ST7248
Little Grimsby *Lincs*	**77**	TF3291
Little Grindley *Notts*	**75**	SK7380
Little Habton *N York*	**90**	SE7477
Little Hadham *Herts*	**39**	TL4322
Little Hale *Lincs*	**64**	TF1441
Little Hallam *Derbys*	**62**	SK4640
Little Hallingbury *Essex*	**39**	TL5017
Little Hanford *Dorset*	**11**	ST8311
Little Harrowden *Nhants*	**51**	SP8771
Little Hartlip *Kent*	**28**	TQ8464
Little Haseley *Oxon*	**37**	SP6400
Little Hatfield *Humb*	**85**	TA1743
Little Hautbois *Norfk*	**67**	TG2521
Little Haven *Dyfed*	**30**	SM8513
Little Hay *Staffs*	**61**	SK1202
Little Haywood *Staffs*	**73**	SK0021
Little Heath *Berks*	**24**	SU6537
Little Heath *Staffs*	**72**	SJ9017
Little Heath *W Mids*	**61**	SP3482
Little Hereford *H & W*	**46**	SO5568
Little Hermitage *Kent*	**28**	TQ7170
Little Horkesley *Essex*	**41**	TL9632
Little Hormead *Herts*	**39**	TL4028
Little Horsted *E Susx*	**16**	TQ4718
Little Horton *W York*	**82**	SE1531
Little Horton *Wilts*	**23**	SU0462
Little Horwood *Bucks*	**38**	SP7930
Little Houghton *Nhants*	**51**	SP8059
Little Houghton *S York*	**83**	SE4205
Little Hucklow *Derbys*	**74**	SK1678
Little Hulton *Gt Man*	**79**	SD7203
Little Hungerford *Berks*	**24**	SU5173
Little Hutton *N York*	**89**	SE4576
Little Ingestre *Staffs*	**73**	SJ9924
Little Irchester *Nhants*	**51**	SP9066
Little Keak *Humb*	**91**	TA0959
Little Keyford *Somset*	**22**	ST7746
Little Kimble *Bucks*	**38**	SP8207
Little Kineton *Warwks*	**48**	SP3350
Little Kingshill *Bucks*	**26**	SU8899
Little Knox *D & G*	**100**	NX8060
Little Langdale *Cumb*	**86**	NY3103
Little Langford *Wilts*	**23**	SU0436
Little Lashbrook *Devon*	**18**	SS4007
Little Laver *Essex*	**39**	TL5409
Little Leigh *Ches*	**71**	SJ6175
Little Leighs *Essex*	**40**	TL7117
Little Lever *Gt Man*	**79**	SD7507
Little Linford *Bucks*	**38**	SP8434
Little Linton *Cambs*	**53**	TL5547
Little Load *Somset*	**21**	ST4624
Little London *Cambs*	**65**	TL4196
Little London *E Susx*	**16**	TQ5720
Little London *Essex*	**39**	TL4729
Little London *Essex*	**53**	TL6835
Little London *Gloucs*	**35**	SO7018
Little London *Hants*	**23**	SU3749
Little London *Hants*	**24**	SU6259
Little London *Lincs*	**65**	TF4323
Little London *Lincs*	**77**	TF3375
Little London *Lincs*	**64**	TF2321
Little London *Norfk*	**65**	TF5620
Little London *Oxon*	**37**	SP6412
Little London *Powys*	**58**	SO0489
Little London *W York*	**82**	SE2039
Little Longstone *Derbys*	**74**	SK1871
Little Madeley *Staffs*	**72**	SJ7745
Little Malvern *H & W*	**47**	SO7740
Little Mancot *Clwyd*	**71**	SJ3266
Little Maplestead *Essex*	**54**	TL8234
Little Marcle *H & W*	**47**	SO6736
Little Marlow *Bucks*	**26**	SU8787
Little Massingham *Norfk*	**66**	TF7924
Little Melton *Norfk*	**66**	TG1607
Little Mill *Gwent*	**34**	SO3203
Little Milton *Oxon*	**37**	SP6100
Little Missenden *Bucks*	**26**	SU9298
Little Mongham *Kent*	**29**	TR3351
Little Moor *Somset*	**21**	ST3232
Little Musgrave *Cumb*	**94**	NY7613
Little Ness *Shrops*	**59**	SJ4019
Little Neston *Ches*	**71**	SJ3076
Little Newcastle *Dyfed*	**30**	SM9829
Little Newsham *Dur*	**96**	NZ1217
Little Norton *Somset*	**10**	ST4815
Little Norton *Staffs*	**60**	SK0208
Little Oakley *Essex*	**41**	TM2129
Little Oakley *Nhants*	**51**	SP8985
Little Odell *Beds*	**51**	SP9557
Little Offley *Herts*	**38**	TL1228
Little Onn *Staffs*	**72**	SJ8315
Little Ormside *Cumb*	**94**	NY7016
Little Orton *Cumb*	**93**	NY3555
Little Oxendon *Nhants*	**50**	SP7184
Little Packington *Warwks*	**61**	SP2184
Little Pattenden *Kent*	**28**	TQ7445
Little Paxton *Cambs*	**52**	TL1862
Little Petherick *Cnwll*	**4**	SW9172
Little Plumpton *Lancs*	**80**	SD3832
Little Plumstead *Norfk*	**67**	TG3112
Little Ponton *Lincs*	**63**	SK9232
Little Posbrook *Hants*	**13**	SU5304
Little Potheridge *Devon*	**19**	SS5214
Little Preston *Nhants*	**49**	SP5854
Little Preston *W York*	**83**	SE3830
Little Raveley *Cambs*	**52**	TL2579
Little Reedness *Humb*	**84**	SE8022
Little Ribston *N York*	**83**	SE3853
Little Rissington *Gloucs*	**36**	SP1819
Little Rollright *Oxon*	**48**	SP2930
Little Rowsley *Derbys*	**74**	SK2566
Little Ryburgh *Norfk*	**66**	TF9628
Little Ryle *Nthumb*	**111**	NU0111
Little Ryton *Shrops*	**59**	SJ4803
Little Salkeld *Cumb*	**94**	NY5636
Little Sampford *Essex*	**40**	TL6533
Little Sandhurst *Berks*	**25**	SU8262
Little Saredon *Staffs*	**60**	SJ9407
Little Saughall *Ches*	**71**	SJ3769
Little Saxham *Suffk*	**54**	TL8063
Little Scatwell *Highld*	**139**	NH3856
Little Sessay *N York*	**89**	SE4674
Little Shelford *Cambs*	**53**	TL4551
Little Silver *Devon*	**9**	SS8601
Little Silver *Devon*	**9**	SS9109
Little Singleton *Lancs*	**80**	SD3739

Little Skipwith Locheilside Station

Little Skipwith N York 83 SE6538
Little Smeaton N York 83 SE5217
Little Snoring Norfk 66 TF9532
Little Sodbury Avon 35 ST7583
Little Sodbury End Avon 35 ST7483
Little Somborne Hants 23 SU3832
Little Somerford Wilts 35 ST9684
Little Soudley Shrops 72 SJ7128
Little Stainforth N York 88 SD8166
Little Stainton Dur 96 NZ3420
Little Stanney Ches 71 SJ4174
Little Staughton Beds 51 TL1062
Little Steeping Lincs 77 TF4362
Little Stoke Staffs 72 SJ9132
Little Stonham Suffk 54 TM1160
Little Stretton Leics 50 SK6600
Little Stretton Shrops 59 SO4492
Little Strickland Cumb 94 NY5619
Little Stukeley Cambs 52 TL2175
Little Sugnall Staffs 72 SJ8031
Little Sutton Ches 71 SJ3776
Little Sutton Shrops 59 SO5182
Little Sypland D & G 99 NX7253
Little Tew Oxon 48 SP3828
Little Tey Essex 40 TL8923
Little Thetford Cambs 53 TL5376
Little Thirkleby N York 89 SE4778
Little Thornage Norfk 66 TG0538
Little Thornton Lancs 80 SD3541
Little Thorpe Dur 96 NZ4242
Little Thurlow Suffk 53 TL6751
Little Thurlow Green Suffk 53 TL6851
Little Thurrock Essex 27 TQ6277
Little Torrington Devon 18 SS4916
Little Totham Essex 40 TL8912
Little Town Ches 79 SJ6494
Little Town Cumb 93 NY2319
Little Town Lancs 81 SD6635
Little Twycross Leics 62 SK3405
Little Urswick Cumb 101 NY2673
Little Wakering Essex 40 TQ9388
Little Walden Essex 39 TL5541
Little Waldingfield Suffk 54 TL9245
Little Walsingham Norfk 66 TF9336
Little Waltham Essex 40 TL7013
Little Warley Essex 40 TQ6090
Little Washbourne Gloucs 47 SO9833
Little Weighton Humb 84 SE9833
Little Weldon Nhants 51 SP9289
Little Welnetham Suffk 54 TL8960
Little Welton Lincs 77 TF3087
Little Wenham Suffk 54 TM0839
Little Wenlock Shrops 59 SJ6407
Little Weston Somset 21 ST6125
Little Whitefield IOW 13 SZ5989
Little Whittington Nthumb 102 NY9869
Little Wilbraham Cambs 53 TL5458
Little Witcombe Gloucs 35 SO9115
Little Witley H & W 47 SO7864
Little Wittenham Oxon 37 SU5693
Little Wolford Warwks 48 SP2635
Little Woodcote Surrey 27 TQ2861
Little Wratting Suffk 53 TL6847
Little Wymington Beds 51 SP9565
Little Wymondley Herts 39 TL2127
Little Wyrley Staffs 60 SK0105
Little Yeldham Essex 53 TL7839
Littlebarn Devon 18 SS4323
Littlebeck N York 90 NZ8704
Littleborough Devon 19 SS8210
Littleborough Gt Man 81 SD9316
Littleborough Notts 75 SK8282
Littlebourne Kent 29 TR2057
Littlebredy Dorset 10 SY5888
Littlebury Essex 39 TL5139
Littlebury Green Essex 39 TL4938
Littlecott Wilts 23 SU1451
Littledean Gloucs 35 SO6713
Littledown Hants 23 SU3558
Littleferry Highld 147 NH8095
Littleham Devon 18 SS4323
Littleham Devon 9 SY0281
Littlehampton W Susx 14 TQ0202
Littleharle Tower Nthumb 103 NZ0183
Littlehempston Devon 7 SX8162
Littlehoughton Nthumb 111 NU2216
Littlemill Gramp 134 NO3295
Littlemill Highld 140 NH9150
Littlemill Strath 107 NS4515
Littlemoor Derbys 74 SK3663
Littlemore Oxon 37 SP5302
Littleover Derbys 62 SK3234
Littleport Cambs 53 TL5686
Littleport Bridge Cambs 53 TL5787
Littler Ches 71 SJ6366
Littlestone-on-Sea Kent 17 TR0824
Littlethorpe Leics 50 SP5496
Littlethorpe N York 89 SE3268
Littleton Avon 21 ST5564
Littleton Ches 71 SJ4466
Littleton D & G 99 NX6355
Littleton Dorset 11 ST8904
Littleton Hants 24 SU4532
Littleton Somset 21 ST4830
Littleton Surrey 25 SU9847
Littleton Surrey 26 TQ0668
Littleton Drew Wilts 35 ST8380
Littleton Pannell Wilts 22 ST9954
Littleton-on-Severn Avon 34 ST5990
Littletown Dur 96 NZ3343
Littletown IOW 13 SZ5390
Littlewick Green Berks 37 SU8379
Littlewindsor Dorset 10 ST4303
Littlewood Staffs 60 SJ9807
Littleworth Bucks 38 SP8823
Littleworth H & W 47 SO9962
Littleworth H & W 47 SO8850
Littleworth Oxon 36 SU3197
Littleworth Staffs 72 SJ9323
Littleworth Staffs 60 SK0112
Littleworth W Susx 15 TQ1920
Littleworth Common Bucks 26 SU9386
Littleworth End Cambs 52 TL2266
Littley Green Essex 40 TL6917
Litton Derbys 74 SK1675
Litton N York 88 SD9074
Litton Somset 21 ST5954
Litton Cheney Dorset 10 SY5490
Liverpool Mersyd 78 SJ3490
Liverton Cleve 97 NZ7115
Liverton Devon 7 SX8075
Liverton Mines Cleve 97 NZ7117
Liverton Street Kent 28 TQ8749
Livesey Street Kent 28 TQ7054
Livingston Loth 117 NT0668
Livingston Village Loth 117 NT0366
Lixton Devon 7 SX6950
Lixwm Clwyd 70 SJ1771
Lizard Cnwll 2 SW7012
Llaingoch Gwynd 68 SH2282
Llaithddu Powys 58 SO0680
Llan-y-pwll Clwyd 71 SJ3752
Llanaber Gwynd 57 SH6018
Llanaelhaearn Gwynd 56 SH3844
Llanafan Dyfed 43 SN6872
Llanafan-fechan Powys 45 SN9750
Llanallgo Gwynd 68 SH5085
Llanarmon Gwynd 56 SH4239
Llanarmon Dyffryn Ceiriog Clwyd 58 SJ1532
Llanarmon-yn-Ial Clwyd 70 SJ1956
Llanarth Dyfed 42 SN4257
Llanarth Gwent 34 SO3710
Llanarthney Dyfed 32 SN5320
Llanasa Clwyd 70 SJ1081
Llanbabo Gwynd 68 SH3786
Llanbadarn Fawr Dyfed 43 SN6080
Llanbadarn Fynydd Powys 45 SO0977
Llanbadarn-y-garreg Powys 45 SO1148
Llanbadoc Gwent 34 ST3799
Llanbadrig Gwynd 68 SH3794
Llanbeder Gwent 34 ST3890
Llanbedr Gwynd 57 SH5826
Llanbedr Powys 45 SO1446
Llanbedr Powys 34 SO2320
Llanbedr-Dyffryn-Clwyd Clwyd 70 SJ1459
Llanbedr-y-cennin Gwynd 69 SH7669
Llanbedrgoch Gwynd 68 SH5180
Llanbedrog Gwynd 56 SH3231
Llanberis Gwynd 69 SH5760
Llanbethery S Glam 20 ST0369
Llanbister Powys 45 SO1073
Llanblethian S Glam 33 SS9873
Llanboidy Dyfed 31 SN2123
Llanbradach M Glam 33 ST1490
Llanbrynmair Powys 57 SH8902
Llancadle S Glam 20 ST2368
Llancarfan S Glam 33 ST0570
Llancayo Gwent 34 SO3603
Llancillo H & W 46 SO3625
Llancloudy H & W 34 SO4920
Llancynfelyn Dyfed 43 SN6492
Llandaff S Glam 33 ST1578
Llandanwg Gwynd 57 SH5728
Llandawke Dyfed 31 SN2811
Llanddaniel Fab Gwynd 68 SH4970
Llanddarog Dyfed 32 SN5016
Llanddeiniol Dyfed 43 SN5572
Llanddeiniolen Gwynd 69 SH5465
Llandderfel Gwynd 58 SH9837
Llanddeusant Dyfed 44 SN7724
Llanddeusant Gwynd 68 SH3485
Llanddewi W Glam 32 SS4685
Llanddewi W Glam 32 SS4689
Llanddewi Brefi Dyfed 44 SN6655
Llanddewi Rhydderch Gwent 34 SO3513
Llanddewi Velfrey Dyfed 31 SN1416
Llanddewi Ystradenni Powys 45 SO1068
Llanddewi'r Cwm Powys 45 SO0348
Llanddoget Gwynd 69 SH8063
Llanddona Gwynd 69 SH5779
Llanddowror Dyfed 31 SN2514
Llanddrew Powys 45 SO0530
Llanddulas Clwyd 69 SH9078
Llanddyfnan Gwynd 68 SH5078
Llandecwyn Gwynd 57 SH6337
Llandefaelog Fach Powy's 45 SO0332
Llandefaelogtrer-graig Powys 45 SO1229
Llandefalle Powys 45 SO1035
Llandegai Gwynd 69 SH5971
Llandegfan Gwynd 69 SH5674
Llandegla Clwyd 70 SJ1952
Llandegley Powys 45 SO1463
Llandegveth Gwent 34 ST3395
Llandegwning Gwynd 56 SH2630
Llandeilo Dyfed 32 SN6322
Llandeilo Graban Powys 45 SO0944
Llandeilo'r Fan Powys 45 SN8934
Llandeloy Dyfed 30 SM8526
Llandenny Gwent 34 SO4104
Llandenny Walks Gwent 34 SO4003
Llandevaud Gwent 34 ST4090
Llandevenny Gwent 34 ST4186
Llandinabo H & W 46 SO5128
Llandinam Powys 58 SO0288
Llandissilio Dyfed 31 SN1221
Llandogo Gwent 34 SO5203
Llandough S Glam 33 SS9972
Llandough S Glam 33 ST1673
Llandovery Dyfed 44 SN7634
Llandow S Glam 33 SS9473
Llandre Dyfed 43 SN6286
Llandre Dyfed 44 SN6741
Llandre Isaf Dyfed 31 SN1328
Llandrillo Clwyd 58 SJ0337
Llandrillo-yn-Rhos Clwyd 69 SH8380
Llandrindod Wells Powys 45 SO0561
Llandrinio Powys 58 SJ2817
Llandudno Gwynd 69 SH7882
Llandudno Junction Gwynd 69 SH7977
Llandudwen Gwynd 56 SH2736
Llandulas Powys 45 SN8841
Llandwrog Gwynd 68 SH4556
Llandybie Dyfed 32 SN6215
Llandyfaelog Dyfed 31 SN4111
Llandyfan Dyfed 32 SN6417
Llandyfriog Dyfed 31 SN3341
Llandyfrydog Gwynd 68 SH4485
Llandygwydd Dyfed 31 SN2443
Llandyrnog Clwyd 70 SJ1065
Llandyssil Powys 58 SO1995
Llandysul Dyfed 31 SN4140
Llanedeyrn S Glam 34 ST2282
Llanedi Dyfed 32 SN5806
Llanegryn Gwynd 57 SH6005
Llanegryn Gwynd 57 SH5905
Llanegwad Dyfed 32 SN5121
Llaneilian Gwynd 68 SH4692
Llanelian-yn-Rhos Clwyd 69 SH8676
Llanelidan Clwyd 70 SJ1150
Llanelieu Powys 45 SO1834
Llanellen Gwent 34 SO3010
Llanelli Dyfed 32 SN5000
Llanelltyd Gwynd 57 SH7119
Llanelly Gwent 34 SO2314
Llanelwedd Powys 45 SO0451
Llanenddwyn Gwynd 57 SH5823
Llanengan Gwynd 56 SH2926
Llanerch Gwynd 57 SH8816
Llanerch Powys 59 SO3094
Llanerchymedd Gwynd 68 SH4184
Llanerfyl Powys 58 SJ0309
Llanfachraeth Gwynd 68 SH3182
Llanfachreth Gwynd 57 SH7522
Llanfaelog Gwynd 68 SH3373
Llanfaelrhys Gwynd 56 SH2227
Llanfaenor Gwent 34 SO4217
Llanfaes Gwynd 69 SH6077
Llanfaes Powys 45 SO0328
Llanfaethlu Gwynd 68 SH3186
Llanfair Gwynd 57 SH5729
Llanfair H & W 46 SO2444
Llanfair Caereinion Powys 58 SJ1006
Llanfair Clydogau Dyfed 44 SN6251
Llanfair Dyffryn Clwyd Clwyd 70 SJ1355
Llanfair Kilgeddin Gwent 34 SO3407
Llanfair P G Gwynd 69 SH5371
Llanfair Talhaiarn Clwyd 69 SH9269
Llanfair Waterdine Shrops 45 SO2376
Llanfair-is-gaer Gwynd 68 SH5267
Llanfair-Nant-Gwyn Dyfed 31 SN1637
Llanfair-y-Cwmmwd Gwynd 68 SH4466
Llanfair-yn-Neubwll Gwynd 68 SH3077
Llanfairfechan Gwynd 69 SH6874
Llanfairynghornwy Gwynd 68 SH3290
Llanfallteg Dyfed 31 SN1520
Llanfallteg West Dyfed 31 SN1419
Llanfaredd M Glam 45 SO0651
Llanfarian Dyfed 43 SN5977
Llanfechain Powys 58 SJ1820
Llanfechelli Gwynd 68 SH3691
Llanfendigaid Gwynd 57 SH5605
Llanferres Clwyd 70 SJ1960
Llanfflewyn Gwynd 68 SH3689
Llanfihangel Tal-y-llyn Powys 45 SO1128
Llanfihangel ar-Arth Dyfed 31 SN4539
Llanfihangel Glyn Myfyr Clwyd 70 SH9849
Llanfihangel Nant Bran Powys 45 SN9434
Llanfihangel Rhydithon Powys 45 SO1566
Llanfihangel Rogiet Gwent 34 ST4487
Llanfihangel yn Nhowyn Gwynd 68 SH3277
Llanfihangel-nant-Melan Powys 45 SO1858
Llanfihangel-uwch-Gwili Dyfed 44 SN4923
Llanfihangel-y-Creuddyn Dyfed 43 SN6675
Llanfihangel-y-pennant Gwynd 57 SH5245
Llanfihangel-y-pennant Gwynd 57 SH6708
Llanfihangel-y-traethau Gwynd 57 SH5935
Llanfihangel-yng-Ngwynfa Powys 58 SJ0816
Llanfilo Powys 45 SO1132
Llanfoist Gwent 34 SO2813
Llanfor Gwynd 58 SH9336
Llanfrechfa Gwent 34 ST3293
Llanfrothen Gwynd 57 SH6241
Llanfrynach Powys 45 SO0725
Llanfwrog Clwyd 70 SJ1157
Llanfwrog Gwynd 68 SH3083
Llanfyllin Powys 58 SJ1419
Llanfynydd Clwyd 70 SJ2756
Llanfynydd Dyfed 44 SN5527
Llanfyrnach Dyfed 31 SN2231
Llangadfan Powys 58 SJ0111
Llangadog Dyfed 31 SN4207
Llangadog Dyfed 44 SN7028
Llangadwaladr Clwyd 58 SJ1830
Llangadwaladr Gwynd 68 SH3869
Llangaffo Gwynd 68 SH4468
Llangain Dyfed 31 SN3815
Llangammarch Wells Powys 45 SN9347
Llangan S Glam 33 SS9577
Llangarron H & W 34 SO5220
Llangasty-Talyllin Powys 45 SO1326
Llangathen Dyfed 32 SN5822
Llangattock Powys 33 SO2117
Llangattock Lingoed Gwent 34 SO3620
Llangattock-Vibon-Avel Gwent 34 SO4515
Llangedwyn Clwyd 58 SJ1824
Llangefni Gwynd 68 SH4675
Llangeinor M Glam 33 SS9187
Llangeinwen Gwynd 68 SH4465
Llangeitho Dyfed 44 SN6259
Llangeler Dyfed 31 SN3739
Llangelynin Gwynd 57 SH5707
Llangendeirne Dyfed 32 SN4514
Llangennech Dyfed 32 SN5601
Llangennith W Glam 31 SS4291
Llangenny Powys 34 SO2418
Llangernyw Clwyd 69 SH8767
Llangian Gwynd 56 SH2928
Llangiwg W Glam 32 SN7205
Llangloffan Dyfed 30 SM9032
Llanglydwen Dyfed 31 SN1827
Llangoed Gwynd 69 SH6079
Llangoedmor Dyfed 42 SN1945
Llangollen Clwyd 70 SJ2141
Llangolman Dyfed 31 SN1127
Llangorse Powys 45 SO1327
Llangovan Gwent 34 SO4505
Llangower Gwynd 58 SH9032
Llangranog Dyfed 42 SN3154
Llangristiolus Gwynd 68 SH4373
Llangrove H & W 34 SO5219
Llangua Gwent 46 SO3925
Llangunllo Powys 45 SO2171
Llangunnor Dyfed 31 SN4320
Llangurig Powys 43 SN9080
Llangwm Clwyd 70 SH9644
Llangwm Dyfed 30 SM9909
Llangwm Gwent 34 ST4299
Llangwm-isaf Gwent 34 SO4300
Llangwyfan Clwyd 70 SJ1266
Llangwyllog Gwynd 68 SH4379
Llangwyryfon Dyfed 43 SN5970
Llangybi Dyfed 44 SN6053
Llangybi Gwent 34 ST3797
Llangybi Gwynd 56 SH4240
Llangyfelach W Glam 32 SS6498
Llangynhafal Clwyd 70 SJ1263
Llangynidr Powys 33 SO1519
Llangynin Dyfed 31 SN2519
Llangynllo Dyfed 42 SN3544
Llangynog Dyfed 31 SN3314
Llangynog Powys 58 SJ0526
Llangynog Powys 45 SO0145
Llangynwyd M Glam 33 SS8588
Llangynwyd M Glam 33 SS8988
Llanhamlach Powys 45 SO0926
Llanharan M Glam 33 ST0083
Llanharry M Glam 33 ST0080
Llanhennock Gwent 34 ST3592
Llanhilleth Gwent 33 SO2100
Llanidan Gwynd 68 SH4966
Llanidloes Powys 58 SN9584
Llaniestyn Gwynd 56 SH2633
Llanigon Powys 45 SO2139
Llanilar Dyfed 43 SN6275
Llanilid M Glam 33 SS9781
Llanina Dyfed 42 SN4059
Llanishen Gwent 34 SO4703
Llanishen S Glam 33 ST1781
Llanllechid Gwynd 69 SH6268
Llanlleonfel Powys 45 SN9350
Llanllowell Gwent 34 ST3998
Llanllugan Powys 58 SJ0502
Llanllwch Dyfed 31 SN3818
Llanllwchaiarn Powys 58 SO1292
Llanllwni Dyfed 44 SN4741
Llanllyfni Gwynd 68 SH4651
Llanmadoc W Glam 32 SS4493
Llanmaes S Glam 20 SS9869
Llanmartin Gwent 34 ST3989
Llanmerewig Powys 58 SO1593
Llanmerewig Powys 58 SO1593
Llanmihangel S Glam 33 SS9872
Llanmiloe Dyfed 31 SN2508
Llanmorlais W Glam 32 SS5294
Llannefydd Clwyd 70 SH9870
Llannon Dyfed 32 SN5308
Llannor Gwynd 56 SH3537
Llanon Dyfed 42 SN5166
Llanover Gwent 34 SO3109
Llanpumsaint Dyfed 31 SN4229
Llanrhaeadr Clwyd 70 SJ0763
Llanrhaeadr-ym-Mochnant Clwyd 58 SJ1226
Llanrhidian W Glam 32 SS4992
Llanrhos Gwynd 69 SH7880
Llanrhychwyn Gwynd 69 SH7761
Llanrhyddlad Gwynd 68 SH3389
Llanrhystud Dyfed 43 SN5369
Llanrian Dyfed 30 SM8131
Llanrothal H & W 34 SO4718
Llanrug Gwynd 69 SH5363
Llanrumney S Glam 34 ST2280
Llanrwst Gwynd 69 SH7961
Llansadurnen Dyfed 31 SN2810
Llansadwrn Dyfed 44 SN6931
Llansadwrn Gwynd 69 SH5575
Llansaint Dyfed 31 SN3808
Llansamlet W Glam 32 SS6897
Llansannan Clwyd 70 SH9365
Llansannor S Glam 33 SS9977
Llansantffraed Powys 45 SO1223
Llansantffraed-Cwmdeuddwr Powys 45 SN9667
Llansantffraed-in-Elvel Powys 45 SO0954
Llansantffraid Dyfed 42 SN5167
Llansantffraid Glan Conwy Gwynd 69 SH8075
Llansantffraid-ym-Mechain Powys 58 SJ2220
Llansawel Dyfed 44 SN6136
Llansilin Clwyd 58 SJ2128
Llansoy Gwent 34 SO4402
Llanspyddid Powys 45 SO0128
Llanstadwell Dyfed 30 SM9505
Llanstephan Dyfed 31 SN3511
Llanstephan Powys 45 SO1141
Llantarnam Gwent 34 ST3093
Llanteg Dyfed 31 SN1810
Llanthewy Skirrid Gwent 34 SO3416
Llanthony Gwent 46 SO2827
Llantilio Pertholey Gwent 34 SO3116
Llantrisant Gwent 34 ST3997
Llantrisant Gwynd 68 SH3683
Llantrisant M Glam 33 ST0483
Llantrithyd S Glam 33 ST0472
Llantwit Fardre M Glam 33 ST0886
Llantwit Major S Glam 20 SS9668
Llantysilio Clwyd 70 SJ1943
Llanuwchllyn Gwynd 57 SH8730
Llanvaches Gwent 34 ST4391
Llanvair Discoed Gwent 34 ST4492
Llanvapley Gwent 34 SO3614
Llanvetherine Gwent 34 SO3617
Llanveynoe H & W 46 SO3031
Llanvihangel Crucorney Gwent 34 SO3220
Llanvihangel Gobion Gwent 34 SO3409
Llanvihangel-Ystern-Llewe Gwent 34 SO4313
Llanwarne H & W 46 SO5027
Llanwddyn Powys 58 SJ0219
Llanwenarth Gwent 34 SO2714
Llanwenog Dyfed 44 SN4945
Llanwern Gwent 34 ST3688
Llanwinio Dyfed 31 SN2626
Llanwnda Dyfed 30 SM9339
Llanwnda Gwynd 68 SH4758
Llanwnen Dyfed 44 SN5347
Llanwnog Powys 58 SO0293
Llanwonno M Glam 33 ST0395
Llanwrda Dyfed 44 SN7131
Llanwrin Powys 57 SH7803
Llanwrthwl Powys 45 SN9763
Llanwrtyd Powys 45 SN8647
Llanwrtyd Wells Powys 45 SN8846
Llanwyddelan Powys 58 SJ0801
Llanyblodwel Shrops 58 SJ2423
Llanybri Dyfed 31 SN3312
Llanybydder Dyfed 44 SN5244
Llanycefn Dyfed 31 SN0923
Llanychaer Bridge Dyfed 30 SM9835
Llanycrwys Dyfed 44 SN6445
Llanymawddwy Gwynd 58 SH9019
Llanymynech Shrops 58 SJ2620
Llanynghenedl Gwynd 68 SH3181
Llanynis Powys 45 SN9950
Llanynys Clwyd 70 SJ1062
Llanyre Powys 45 SO0462
Llanystumdwy Gwynd 56 SH4738
Llanywern Powys 45 SO1028
Llawhaden Dyfed 31 SN0717
Llawnt Shrops 58 SJ2430
Llawryglyn Powys 58 SN9291
Llay Clwyd 71 SJ3355
Llechcynfarwy Gwynd 68 SH3881
Llechfaen Powys 45 SO0828
Llechryd Dyfed 31 SN2243
Llechryd M Glam 33 SO1009
Lledrod Dyfed 43 SN6470
Llidiadnenog Dyfed 44 SN5437
Llidiardau Gwynd 57 SH8738
Llidiart-y-parc Clwyd 70 SJ1243
Llithfaen Gwynd 56 SH3542
Llong Clwyd 70 SJ2662
Llowes Powys 45 SO1941
Llwydcoed M Glam 33 SN9904
Llwydiarth Powys 58 SJ0315
Llwyn-drain Dyfed 31 SN2634
Llwyn-du Gwent 34 SO2816
Llwyn-on M Glam 33 SO0111
Llwyn-y-brain Dyfed 31 SN1914
Llwyn-y-Groes Dyfed 44 SN5956
Llwyncelyn Dyfed 42 SN4459
Llwyndafydd Dyfed 42 SN3755
Llwynderw Powys 58 SJ2004
Llwyndyrys Gwynd 56 SH3740
Llwyngwril Gwynd 57 SH5909
Llwynhendy Dyfed 32 SS5399
Llwynmawr Clwyd 58 SJ2237
Llwynypia M Glam 33 SS9993
Llyn-y-pandy Clwyd 70 SJ2065
Llynclys Shrops 58 SJ2823
Llynfaes Gwynd 68 SH4178
Llys-y-fran Dyfed 30 SN0424
Llysfaen Clwyd 69 SH8977
Llysfaen Clwyd 69 SH8977
Llyswen Dyfed 42 SN4561
Llyswen Powys 45 SO1337
Llysworney S Glam 33 SS9674
Llywel Powys 45 SN8730
Load Brook S York 74 SK2788
Loan Cent 117 NS9675
Loanend Nthumb 119 NT9450
Loanhead Loth 117 NT2865
Loaningfoot D & G 92 NX9656
Loans Strath 106 NS3431
Lobb Devon 18 SS4637
Lobhillcross Devon 5 SX4686
Loceport W Isls 154 NF8563
Loch Katrine Pier Cent 124 NN4907
Loch Loyal Lodge Highld 149 NC6146
Loch Maree Hotel Highld 138 NG9968
Loch Skipport W Isls 154 NF8238
Lochailort Highld 129 NM7682
Lochans D & G 98 NX0656
Lochassynt Lodge Highld 148 NC1727
Lochavich Strath 122 NM9415
Lochawe Strath 123 NN1227
Lochboisdale W Isls 154 NF7820
Lochbuie Strath 121 NM6125
Lochcarron Highld 138 NG8939
Lochdochart House Cent 124 NN4327
Lochdrum Highld 145 NH2585
Lochead Strath 113 NR7778
Lochearnhead Cent 124 NN5823
Lochee Tays 126 NO3731
Locheilside Station Highld 130 NM9978

Lochend Ludag

Lochend *Highld* 140 NH5937
Locherben *D & G* 100 NX9797
Lochfoot *D & G* 100 NX8973
Lochgair *Strath* 114 NR9290
Lochgarthside *Highld* 139 NH5219
Lochgelly *Fife* 117 NT1893
Lochgilphead *Strath* 113 NR8688
Lochgoilhead *Strath* 114 NN2001
Lochieheads *Fife* 126 NO2513
Lochill *Gramp* 141 NJ2964
Lochindorb Lodge *Highld* 140 NH9635
Lochinver *Highld* 145 NC0922
Lochlane *Tays* 125 NN8320
Lochluichart *Highld* 139 NH3363
Lochmaben *D & G* 100 NY0882
Lochmaddy *W Isls* 154 NF9169
Lochmore Lodge *Highld* 148 NC2938
Lochore *Fife* 117 NT1896
Lochranza *Strath* 105 NR9350
Lochside *Gramp* 135 NO7364
Lochside *Highld* 140 NH8152
Lochside *Highld* 147 NH8481
Lochslin *Highld* 147 NH8481
Lochton *Strath* 98 NX2579
Lochty *Fife* 127 NO5208
Lochty *Tays* 134 NO5362
Lochty *Tays* 134 NO5362
Lochuisge *Highld* 122 NM7956
Lochwinnoch *Strath* 115 NS3558
Lochwood *D & G* 100 NY0896
Lochwood *Strath* 116 NS6966
Lockengate *Cnwll* 4 SX0361
Lockerbie *D & G* 100 NY1381
Lockeridge *Wilts* 23 SU1467
Lockerley *Hants* 23 SU3026
Locking *Avon* 21 ST3659
Lockington *Humb* 84 SE9947
Lockington *Leics* 62 SK4627
Lockleywood *Shrops* 72 SJ6928
Lockmaddy *W Isls* 154 NF9168
Locks Heath *Hants* 13 SU5107
Locksbottom *Gt Lon* 27 TQ4265
Locksgreen *IOW* 13 SZ4490
Lockton *N York* 90 SE8490
Loddington *Leics* 63 SK7902
Loddington *Nhants* 51 SP8178
Loddiswell *Devon* 7 SX7148
Loddon *Norfk* 67 TM3698
Lode *Cambs* 53 TL5362
Lode Heath *W Mids* 61 SP1580
Loders *Dorset* 10 SY4994
Lodge Green *W Mids* 61 SP2583
Lodsworth *W Susx* 14 SU9223
Lofhouse Gate *W York* 83 SE3324
Lofthouse *N York* 89 SE1073
Lofthouse *W York* 83 SE3325
Loftus *Cleve* 97 NZ7118
Logan *Strath* 107 NS5820
Loganbeck *Cumb* 86 SD1890
Loganlea *Loth* 117 NS9762
Loggerheads *Staffs* 72 SJ7336
Logie *Fife* 126 NO4020
Logie *Gramp* 141 NJ0150
Logie *Tays* 135 NO6963
Logie Coldstone *Gramp* 134 NJ4304
Logie Pert *Tays* 135 NO6664
Logierait *Tays* 125 NN9752
Login *Dyfed* 31 SN1623
Lolworth *Cambs* 52 TL3664
Lon-las *W Glam* 32 SS7097
Lonbain *Highld* 137 NG6852
Londesborough *Humb* 84 SE8645
London *Gt Lon* 27 TQ2980
London Apprentice *Cnwll* 3 SX0050
London Beach *Kent* 28 TQ8836
London Colney *Herts* 39 TL1803
London End *Nhants* 51 SP9265
Londonderry *N York* 89 SE3087
Londonthorpe *Lincs* 63 SK9537
Londubh *Highld* 144 NG8680
Long Ashton *Avon* 34 ST5470
Long Bank *H & W* 60 SO7674
Long Bennington *Lincs* 63 SK8344
Long Bredy *Dorset* 10 SY5690
Long Buckby *Nhants* 50 SP6367
Long Cause *Devon* 7 SX7461
Long Clawson *Leics* 63 SK7227
Long Common *Hants* 13 SU5014
Long Compton *Staffs* 72 SJ8522
Long Compton *Warwks* 48 SP2832
Long Crendon *Bucks* 37 SP6908
Long Crichel *Dorset* 11 ST9710
Long Ditton *Surrey* 26 TQ1766
Long Drax *N York* 83 SE6828
Long Duckmanton *Derbys* 75 SK4471
Long Eaton *Derbys* 62 SK4933
Long Green *Ches* 71 SJ4770
Long Green *H & W* 47 SO8433
Long Hedges *Lincs* 77 TF3546
Long Itchington *Warwks* 50 SP4165
Long Lane *Shrops* 59 SJ6315
Long Lawford *Warwks* 50 SP4776
Long Load *Somset* 21 ST4623
Long Marston *Herts* 38 SP8915
Long Marston *N York* 83 SE5051
Long Marston *Warwks* 48 SP1548
Long Marton *Cumb* 94 NY6624
Long Meadowend *Shrops* 59 SO4081
Long Melford *Suffk* 54 TL8645
Long Newnton *Gloucs* 35 ST9092
Long Newton *Loth* 118 NT5164
Long Preston *N York* 88 SD8358
Long Riston *Humb* 85 TA1242
Long Sight *Gt Man* 79 SD9207
Long Stratton *Norfk* 67 TM1992
Long Street *Bucks* 38 SP7947
Long Sutton *Hants* 24 SU7347
Long Sutton *Lincs* 65 TF4322
Long Sutton *Somset* 21 ST4625
Long Thurlow *Suffk* 54 TM0168
Long Waste *Shrops* 59 SJ6115
Long Whatton *Leics* 62 SK4723
Long Wittenham *Oxon* 37 SU5493
Longbenton *T & W* 103 NZ2768
Longborough *Gloucs* 48 SP1729
Longbridge *W Mids* 60 SP0177
Longbridge *Warwks* 48 SP2762
Longbridge Deverill *Wilts* 22 ST8640
Longbridgemuir *D & G* 100 NY0669
Longburgh *Cumb* 93 NY3159
Longburton *Dorset* 11 ST6412
Longcliffe *Derbys* 73 SK2255
Longcombe *Devon* 7 SX8359
Longcot *Oxon* 36 SU2790
Longcroft *Cumb* 93 NY2158
Longcross *Surrey* 25 SU9865
Longden *Shrops* 59 SJ4406
Longden Common *Shrops* 59 SJ4404
Longdon *H & W* 47 SO8336
Longdon *Staffs* 61 SK0714
Longdon Green *Staffs* 61 SK0813
Longdon Heath *H & W* 47 SO8338
Longdon upon Tern *Shrops* 59 SJ6116
Longdown *Devon* 9 SX8691
Longdowns *Cnwll* 3 SW7434
Longfield *Kent* 27 TQ6069
Longford *Derbys* 73 SK2137
Longford *Gloucs* 35 SO8320
Longford *Gt Lon* 26 TQ0576
Longford *Kent* 27 TQ5156
Longford *Shrops* 72 SJ6434
Longford *Shrops* 72 SJ7218
Longford *W Mids* 61 SP3583
Longforgan *Tays* 126 NO2929
Longformacus *Border* 119 NT6957
Longframlington *Nthumb* 103 NU1201
Longham *Dorset* 12 SZ0697
Longham *Norfk* 66 TF9415
Longhill *Gramp* 143 NJ9953
Longhirst *Nthumb* 103 NZ2289
Longhope *Gloucs* 35 SO6819
Longhorsley *Nthumb* 103 NZ1494
Longhoughton *Nthumb* 111 NU2415
Longlands *Cumb* 93 NY2636
Longlane *Derbys* 73 SK2538
Longlevens *Gloucs* 35 SO8519
Longley *Kent* 28 TQ8052
Longley *W York* 82 SE0522
Longley *W York* 82 SE1404
Longley Green *H & W* 47 SO7350
Longleys *Tays* 126 NO2643
Longmanhill *Gramp* 142 NJ7462
Longmoor Camp *Hants* 14 SU7931
Longmorn *Gramp* 141 NJ2358
Longmoss *Ches* 79 SJ8974
Longnewton *Border* 110 NT5827
Longnewton *Cleve* 96 NZ3816
Longney *Gloucs* 35 SO7612
Longniddry *Loth* 118 NT4476
Longnor *Shrops* 59 SJ4800
Longnor *Staffs* 74 SK0865
Longparish *Hants* 24 SU4344
Longpark *Cumb* 101 NY4261
Longridge *Lancs* 81 SD6037
Longridge *Loth* 117 NS9562
Longridge *Staffs* 72 SJ9015
Longriggend *Strath* 116 NS8270
Longrock *Cnwll* 2 SW4931
Longsdon *Staffs* 72 SJ9654
Longshaw Common *Gt Man* 78 SD5302
Longside *Gramp* 143 NK0347
Longsleddale *Cumb* 87 NY4902
Longslow *Shrops* 72 SJ6535
Longstanton *Cambs* 52 TL3966
Longstock *Hants* 23 SU3536
Longstone *Dyfed* 31 SN1409
Longstone Wells *Devon* 19 SS7634
Longstowe *Cambs* 52 TL3054
Longstreet *Wilts* 23 SU1451
Longthorpe *Cambs* 64 TL1698
Longthwaite *Cumb* 93 NY4323
Longton *Lancs* 80 SD4825
Longton *Staffs* 72 SJ9143
Longtown *Cumb* 101 NY3768
Longtown *H & W* 46 SO3129
Longueville *Jersey* 152 JS0000
Longville in the Dale *Shrops* 59 SO5494
Longwick *Bucks* 37 SP7805
Longwitton *Nthumb* 103 NZ0788
Longwood *D & G* 99 NX7061
Longwood *Shrops* 59 SJ6007
Longwood House *Hants* 13 SU5424
Longworth *Oxon* 36 SU3899
Longyester *Loth* 118 NT5465
Lonmay *Gramp* 143 NK0159
Lonmore *Highld* 136 NG2646
Looe *Cnwll* 5 SX2553
Loose *Kent* 28 TQ7552
Loosebeare *Devon* 8 SS7105
Loosegate *Lincs* 64 TF3125
Loosley Row *Bucks* 37 SP8100
Lootcherbrae *Gramp* 142 NJ6053
Lopcombe Corner *Wilts* 23 SU2435
Lopen *Somset* 10 ST4214
Loppington *Shrops* 59 SJ4629
Lorbottle *Nthumb* 111 NU0306
Lordington *W Susx* 14 SU7809
Lordsbridge *Norfk* 65 TF5712
Lornty *Tays* 126 NO1746
Loscoe *Derbys* 62 SK4247
Loscombe *Dorset* 10 SY4998
Losonford *Warwks* 48 SP1867
Lossiemouth *Gramp* 141 NJ2370
Lostford *Shrops* 59 SJ6231
Lostock Gralam *Ches* 79 SJ6975
Lostock Green *Ches* 79 SJ6973
Lostock Hall Fold *Gt Man* 79 SD6509
Lostock Junction *Gt Man* 79 SD6708
Lostwithiel *Cnwll* 4 SX1059
Lothbeg *Highld* 147 NC9410
Lothersdale *N York* 82 SD9646
Lothmore *Highld* 147 NC9611
Loudwater *Bucks* 26 SU8990
Loughborough *Leics* 62 SK5319
Loughor *W Glam* 32 SS5798
Loughton *Bucks* 38 SP8337
Loughton *Essex* 27 TQ4296
Loughton *Shrops* 59 SO6183
Lound *Lincs* 64 TF0618
Lound *Notts* 75 SK6986
Lound *Suffk* 67 TM5099
Lounston *Devon* 7 SX7874
Lount *Leics* 62 SK3819
Louth *Lincs* 77 TF3287
Lovaton *Devon* 6 SX5466
Love Clough *Lancs* 81 SD8127
Lovedean *Hants* 13 SU6812
Lover *Wilts* 12 SU2120
Loversall *S York* 75 SK5798
Loves Green *Essex* 40 TL6404
Lovesome Hill *N York* 89 SE3699
Loveston *Dyfed* 31 SN0808
Lovington *Somset* 21 ST5931
Low Ackworth *W York* 83 SE4517
Low Angerton *Nthumb* 103 NZ0984
Low Barbeth *D & G* 98 NX0166
Low Barlings *Lincs* 76 TF0873
Low Barugh *S York* 82 SE3108
Low Bell End *N York* 90 SE7196
Low Biggin *Cumb* 87 SD6078
Low Borrowbridge *Cumb* 87 NY6101
Low Bradfield *S York* 74 SK2691
Low Bradley *N York* 82 SE0048
Low Braithwaite *Cumb* 93 NY4242
Low Brunton *Nthumb* 102 NY9269
Low Burnham *Humb* 84 SE7702
Low Buston *Nthumb* 111 NU2207
Low Catton *Humb* 84 SE7053
Low Coniscliffe *Dur* 89 NZ2513
Low Crosby *Cumb* 93 NY4459
Low Dinsdale *Dur* 89 NZ3411
Low Eggborough *N York* 83 SE5523
Low Ellington *N York* 89 SE1983
Low Fell *T & W* 96 NZ2559
Low Fremington *N York* 88 SE0398
Low Gartachorrans *Cent* 115 NS4685
Low Gate *Nthumb* 102 NY9064
Low Geltbridge *Cumb* 94 NY5259
Low Grantley *N York* 89 SE2370
Low Green *N York* 89 SE2059
Low Habberley *H & W* 60 SO8077
Low Ham *Somset* 21 ST4329
Low Harrogate *N York* 82 SE2855
Low Hartsop *Cumb* 93 NY4013
Low Hawsker *N York* 91 NZ9207
Low Hesket *Cumb* 93 NY4646
Low Hill *H & W* 60 SO8473
Low Hutton *N York* 90 SE7567
Low Knipe *Cumb* 94 NY5219
Low Laithe *N York* 89 SE1963
Low Langton *Lincs* 76 TF1576
Low Leighton *Derbys* 79 SK0085
Low Lorton *Cumb* 92 NY1525
Low Marnham *Notts* 75 SK8069
Low Mill *N York* 90 SE6795
Low Moor *Lancs* 81 SD7341
Low Moor *Lancs* 81 SD7341
Low Moor *W York* 82 SE1629
Low Moorsley *T & W* 96 NZ3346
Low Mowthorpe *N York* 91 SE9066
Low Rogerscales *Cumb* 92 NY1426
Low Row *Cumb* 93 NY3536
Low Row *Cumb* 93 NY1945
Low Row *Cumb* 102 NY5863
Low Row *N York* 88 SD9897
Low Salchrie *D & G* 98 NX0365
Low Salter *Lancs* 87 SD6063
Low Santon *Humb* 84 SE9312
Low Skeog *D & G* 99 NX4540
Low Street *Essex* 28 TQ6677
Low Street *Norfk* 67 TG3424
Low Tharston *Norfk* 66 TM1895
Low Toynton *Lincs* 77 TF2770
Low Valley *S York* 83 SE4003
Low Valleyfield *Fife* 117 NT0086
Low Walworth *Dur* 96 NZ2417
Low Wood *Cumb* 101 NY3483
Low Worsall *N York* 89 NZ3909
Low Wray *Cumb* 93 NY3731
Lowbands *H & W* 47 SO7831
Lowca *Cumb* 92 NX9821
Lowdham *Notts* 63 SK6646
Lowe *Shrops* 59 SJ4930
Lowe Hill *Staffs* 73 SJ9955
Lower Aisholt *Somset* 20 ST2035
Lower Ansty *Dorset* 11 ST7603
Lower Apperley *Gloucs* 47 SO8527
Lower Arncott *Oxon* 37 SP6019
Lower Ashton *Devon* 8 SX8484
Lower Assendon *Oxon* 37 SU7484
Lower Ballam *Lancs* 80 SD3631
Lower Barewood *H & W* 46 SO3956
Lower Bartle *Lancs* 80 SD4933
Lower Bayston *Shrops* 59 SJ4908
Lower Beeding *W Susx* 15 TQ2227
Lower Benefield *Nhants* 51 SP9888
Lower Bentham *N York* 87 SD6469
Lower Bentley *H & W* 47 SO9865
Lower Beobridge *Shrops* 60 SO7891
Lower Berry Hill *Gloucs* 34 SO5711
Lower Birchwood *Derbys* 75 SK4354
Lower Boddington *Nhants* 49 SP4851
Lower Boscaswell *Cnwll* 2 SW3834
Lower Bourne *Surrey* 25 SU8444
Lower Brailes *Warwks* 48 SP3139
Lower Broadheath *H & W* 47 SO8057
Lower Breakish *Highld* 129 NG6723
Lower Bredbury *Gt Man* 79 SJ9191
Lower Buckenhill *H & W* 46 SO6033
Lower Bullingham *H & W* 46 SO5137
Lower Bullingham *H & W* 46 SO5038
Lower Burgate *Hants* 12 SU1515
Lower Burrowton *Devon* 9 SY0096
Lower Burrowton *Devon* 4 SX0097
Lower Burton *H & W* 46 SO4256
Lower Caldecote *Beds* 52 TL1746
Lower Cam *Gloucs* 35 SO7400
Lower Canada *Avon* 21 ST3658
Lower Catesby *Nhants* 49 SP5159
Lower Chapel *Powys* 45 SO0235
Lower Chicksgrove *Wilts* 22 ST9730
Lower Chute *Wilts* 23 SU3153
Lower Clapton *Gt Lon* 27 TQ3486
Lower Clent *H & W* 60 SO9279
Lower Creedy *Devon* 8 SS8402
Lower Crossings *Derbys* 74 SK0480
Lower Cumberworth *W York* 82 SE2209
Lower Cwmtwrch *Powys* 32 SN7610
Lower Dalveen *D & G* 108 NS8807
Lower Darwen *Lancs* 81 SD6825
Lower Dean *Beds* 51 TL0569
Lower Denby *W York* 82 SE2307
Lower Diabaig *Highld* 137 NG7960
Lower Dicker *E Susx* 16 TQ5511
Lower Dinchope *Shrops* 59 SO4584
Lower Down *Shrops* 59 SO3384
Lower Dunsforth *N York* 89 SE4464
Lower Egleton *H & W* 47 SO6245
Lower Elkstone *Staffs* 74 SK0658
Lower Ellastone *Staffs* 73 SK1142
Lower End *Bucks* 37 SP6809
Lower End *Bucks* 38 SP9237
Lower End *Nhants* 51 SP8861
Lower Everleigh *Wilts* 23 SU1854
Lower Exbury *Hants* 13 SZ4298
Lower Eythorne *Kent* 29 TR2749
Lower Failand *Avon* 34 ST5173
Lower Farringdon *Hants* 24 SU7035
Lower Feltham *Gt Lon* 26 TQ0972
Lower Fittleworth *W Susx* 14 TQ0118
Lower Frankton *Shrops* 59 SJ3732
Lower Freystrop *Dyfed* 30 SM9512
Lower Froyle *Hants* 24 SU7644
Lower Gabwell *Devon* 7 SX9169
Lower Gledfield *Highld* 146 NH5890
Lower Godney *Somset* 21 ST4742
Lower Gornal *W Mids* 60 SO9191
Lower Gravenhurst *Beds* 38 TL1034
Lower Green *Essex* 39 TL4334
Lower Green *Gt Man* 79 SJ7099
Lower Green *Herts* 39 TL4232
Lower Green *Herts* 39 TL1832
Lower Green *Kent* 16 TQ5640
Lower Green *Kent* 16 TQ6341
Lower Green *Nhants* 51 SP8159
Lower Green *Norfk* 66 TF9837
Lower Green *Staffs* 60 SJ9007
Lower Green *Suffk* 53 TL7465
Lower Grove Common *H & W* 46 SO5525
Lower Hacheston *Suffk* 55 TM3157
Lower Halliford *Surrey* 26 TQ0867
Lower Halstock Leigh *Dorset* 10 ST5207
Lower Halstow *Kent* 28 TQ8567
Lower Hamworthy *Dorset* 11 SY9990
Lower Hardres *Kent* 29 TR1453
Lower Harpton *H & W* 46 SO2760
Lower Hartshay *Derbys* 74 SK3851
Lower Hartwell *Bucks* 38 SP7912
Lower Hatton *Staffs* 72 SJ8236
Lower Hawthwaite *Cumb* 101 NY2189
Lower Hergest *H & W* 46 SO2755
Lower Heyford *Oxon* 49 SP4824
Lower Heysham *Lancs* 87 SD4160
Lower Higham *Kent* 28 TQ7172
Lower Holbrook *Suffk* 54 TM1835
Lower Hordley *Shrops* 59 SJ3929
Lower Horncroft *W Susx* 14 TQ0017
Lower Howsell *H & W* 47 SO7848
Lower Irlam *Gt Man* 79 SJ7193
Lower Kilburn *Derbys* 62 SK3745
Lower Kilcott *Avon* 35 ST7889
Lower Killeyan *Strath* 104 NR2743
Lower Kingscombe *Dorset* 10 SY5599
Lower Kingswood *Surrey* 26 TQ2453
Lower Kinnerton *Ches* 71 SJ3462
Lower Langford *Avon* 21 ST4560
Lower Largo *Fife* 126 NO4102
Lower Leigh *Staffs* 73 SK0136
Lower Lemington *Gloucs* 48 SP2134
Lower Llanfadog *Powys* 45 SN9567
Lower Lovacott *Devon* 19 SS5326
Lower Loxhore *Devon* 19 SS6137
Lower Lydbrook *Gloucs* 34 SO5916
Lower Lye *H & W* 46 SO4067
Lower Machen *Gwent* 34 ST2288
Lower Maes-coed *H & W* 46 SO3430
Lower Mannington *Dorset* 12 SU0705
Lower Marston *Somset* 22 ST7643
Lower Meend *Gloucs* 34 SO5504
Lower Middleton Cheney *Nhants* 49 SP5041
Lower Milton *Somset* 21 ST5446
Lower Moor *W Mids* 47 SO9747
Lower Morton *Avon* 35 ST6492
Lower Nazeing *Essex* 39 TL3906
Lower Norton *Warwks* 48 SP2364
Lower Nyland *Dorset* 22 ST7421
Lower Penarth *S Glam* 20 ST1869
Lower Penn *Staffs* 60 SO8796
Lower Pennington *Hants* 12 SZ3193
Lower Penwortham *Lancs* 80 SD5327
Lower Peover *Ches* 79 SJ7474
Lower Place *Gt Man* 81 SD9011
Lower Pollicott *Bucks* 37 SP7013
Lower Pond Street *Essex* 39 TL4537
Lower Quinton *Warwks* 48 SP1847
Lower Rainham *Kent* 28 TQ8167
Lower Raydon *Suffk* 54 TM0338
Lower Roadwater *Somset* 20 ST0139
Lower Seagry *Wilts* 35 ST9580
Lower Sheering *Essex* 39 TL4914
Lower Shelton *Beds* 38 SP9942
Lower Shiplake *Oxon* 37 SU7679
Lower Shuckburgh *Warwks* 49 SP4862
Lower Shurlach *Ches* 79 SJ6772
Lower Slaughter *Gloucs* 36 SP1622
Lower Smerlay *Strath* 105 NR7522
Lower Soothill *W York* 82 SE2523
Lower Soothill *W York* 82 SE2523
Lower Soudley *Gloucs* 35 SO6609
Lower Standen *Kent* 29 TR2340
Lower Stanton St. Quintin *Wilts* 35 ST9180
Lower Stoke *Kent* 28 TQ8375
Lower Stone *Gloucs* 35 ST6794
Lower Stonnall *Staffs* 61 SK0803
Lower Stow Bedon *Norfk* 66 TL9694
Lower Street *Dorset* 11 SY8399
Lower Street *E Susx* 16 TQ7012
Lower Street *Norfk* 67 TG2635
Lower Street *Suffk* 53 TL7852
Lower Street *Suffk* 54 TM1052
Lower Stretton *Ches* 79 SJ6281
Lower Stroud *Dorset* 10 SY4598
Lower Sundon *Beds* 38 TL0526
Lower Swanwick *Hants* 13 SU4909
Lower Swell *Gloucs* 48 SP1725
Lower Tadmarton *Oxon* 48 SP4036
Lower Tale *Devon* 9 ST0601
Lower Tean *Staffs* 73 SK0138
Lower Thurlton *Norfk* 67 TM4299
Lower Town *Cnwll* 2 SW6528
Lower Town *Devon* 5 SX7172
Lower Town *Dyfed* 30 SM9637
Lower Town *H & W* 47 SO6342
Lower Tregantle *M Glam* 5 SX3953
Lower Treluswell *Cnwll* 3 SW7735
Lower Tysoe *Warwks* 48 SP3445
Lower Ufford *Suffk* 55 TM2952
Lower Upcott *Devon* 9 SX8880
Lower Upham *Hants* 13 SU5219
Lower Upnor *Kent* 28 TQ7571
Lower Vexford *Somset* 20 ST1135
Lower Walton *Ches* 78 SJ6086
Lower Waterston *Dorset* 11 SY7395
Lower Weare *Somset* 21 ST4053
Lower Welson *H & W* 46 SO2950
Lower Westmancote *H & W* 47 SO9337
Lower Whatcombe *Dorset* 11 ST8401
Lower Whatley *Somset* 22 ST7347
Lower Whitley *Ches* 71 SJ6179
Lower Wick *Gloucs* 35 ST7196
Lower Wick *H & W* 47 SO8352
Lower Wield *Hants* 24 SU6340
Lower Wigginton *Herts* 38 SP9409
Lower Willingdon *E Susx* 16 TQ5803
Lower Winchendon *Bucks* 37 SP7312
Lower Woodend *Bucks* 37 SU8187
Lower Woodford *Wilts* 23 SU1235
Lower Wraxhall *Dorset* 10 ST5700
Lower Wyche *H & W* 47 SO7743
Lower Wyke *W York* 82 SE1425
Lowerhouse *Lancs* 81 SD8032
Lowertown *Devon* 5 SX4584
Lowesby *Leics* 63 SK7207
Lowestoft *Suffk* 67 TM5493
Loweswater *Cumb* 92 NY1420
Lowfield Heath *W Susx* 15 TQ2740
Lowgill *Cumb* 87 SD6297
Lowgill *Cumb* 87 SD6297
Lowgill *Lancs* 87 SD6564
Lowick *Cumb* 86 SD2985
Lowick *Nhants* 51 SP9881
Lowick *Nthumb* 111 NU0139
Lowick Bridge *Cumb* 101 NY2886
Lowick Green *Cumb* 101 NY3085
Lowlands *Dur* 96 NZ1325
Lowlands *Gwent* 34 ST2996
Lowther Castle *Cumb* 94 NY5223
Lowtherton *D & G* 101 NY2566
Lowthorpe *Humb* 91 TA0860
Lowton *Devon* 8 SS6604
Lowton *Gt Man* 78 SJ6197
Lowton Comon *Gt Man* 79 SJ6498
Lowton St. Mary's *Gt Man* 79 SJ6397
Loxbeare *Devon* 9 SS9116
Loxhill *Surrey* 25 TQ0038
Loxhore *Devon* 19 SS6138
Loxhore Cott *Devon* 19 SS6138
Loxley *Warwks* 48 SP2552
Loxley Green *Staffs* 73 SK0630
Loxter *H & W* 47 SO7140
Loxton *Avon* 21 ST3755
Loxwood *W Susx* 14 TQ0331
Lubcroy *Highld* 145 NC3502
Lubenham *Nhants* 50 SP7087
Lucas Green *Surrey* 25 SU9460
Lucasgate *Lincs* 77 TF4147
Luccombe *Somset* 20 SS9144
Luccombe Village *IOW* 13 SZ5880
Lucker *Nthumb* 111 NU1530
Luckett *Cnwll* 5 SX3873
Lucking Street *Essex* 54 TL8134
Luckington *Wilts* 35 ST8383
Lucklawhill *Fife* 127 NO4221
Lucknam *Wilts* 35 ST8272
Luckwell Bridge *Somset* 20 SS9038
Lucott *Somset* 19 SS8645
Lucton *H & W* 46 SO4364
Lucy Cross *N York* 89 NZ2112
Ludag *W Isls* 154 NF7714

Ludborough *Lincs*	77	TF2995
Ludbrook *Devon*	7	SX6654
Ludchurch *Dyfed*	31	SN1411
Luddenden *W York*	82	SE0426
Luddenden Foot *W York*	82	SE0325
Luddenham Court *Kent*	28	TQ9962
Luddesdown *Kent*	28	TQ6766
Luddington *Humb*	84	SE8216
Luddington *Warwks*	48	SP1652
Luddington in the Brook *Nhants*	51	TL1083
Ludford *Lincs*	76	TF1989
Ludford *Shrops*	46	SO5174
Ludgershall *Bucks*	37	SP6517
Ludgershall *Wilts*	23	SU2650
Ludgershall *Wilts*	23	SU2650
Ludgvan *Cnwll*	2	SW5033
Ludham *Norfk*	67	TG3R1R
Ludlow *Shrops*	46	SO5175
Ludney *Somset*	10	ST3812
Ludwell *Wilts*	22	ST9122
Ludworth *Dur*	96	NZ3641
Luffenhall *Herts*	39	TL2928
Luffincott *Devon*	5	SX3394
Lufflands *Devon*	18	SS3209
Luffness *Loth*	118	NT4780
Lugar *Strath*	107	NS5821
Lugg Green *H & W*	46	SO4462
Luggate Burn *Loth*	118	NT6074
Luggiebank *Strath*	116	NS7672
Lugsdale *Ches*	78	SJ5285
Lugton *Strath*	115	NS4152
Lugwardine *H & W*	46	SO5540
Luib *Highld*	137	NG5627
Lulham *H & W*	46	SO4141
Lullington *Derbys*	61	SK2513
Lullington *E Susx*	16	TQ5202
Lullington *Somset*	22	ST7851
Lulsgate Bottom *Avon*	21	ST5165
Lulsley *H & W*	47	SO7455
Lulworth Camp *Dorset*	11	SY8381
Lumb *Lancs*	81	SD8324
Lumb *W York*	82	SE0321
Lumbutts *W York*	82	SD9528
Lumby *N York*	83	SE4830
Lumloch *Strath*	116	NS6370
Lumphanan *Gramp*	134	NJ5804
Lumphinnans *Fife*	117	NT1692
Lumsden *Gramp*	142	NJ4722
Lunan *Tays*	127	NO6851
Lunanhead *Tays*	127	NO4752
Luncarty *Tays*	125	NO0929
Lund *Humb*	84	SE9647
Lund *N York*	83	SE6532
Lundie *Cent*	124	NN7304
Lundie *Tays*	126	NO2836
Lundin Links *Fife*	126	NO4002
Lundy Green *Norfk*	67	TM2392
Lunna *Shet*	155	HU4869
Lunsford *Kent*	28	TQ6959
Lunsford's Cross *E Susx*	17	TQ7210
Lunt *Mersyd*	78	SD3402
Luntley *H & W*	46	SO3955
Luppitt *Devon*	9	ST1606
Lupridge *Devon*	7	SX7153
Lupset *W York*	82	SE3119
Lupton *Cumb*	87	SD5581
Lurgashall *W Susx*	14	SU9327
Lurley *Devon*	9	SS9214
Lusby *Lincs*	77	TF3367
Luscombe *Devon*	7	SX7957
Luskentyre *W Isls*	154	NG0699
Luson *Devon*	6	SX6050
Luss *Strath*	115	NS3692
Lusta *Highld*	136	NG2756
Lustleigh *Devon*	8	SX7881
Luston *H & W*	46	SO4863
Luthermuir *Gramp*	135	NO6568
Luthrie *Fife*	126	NO3319
Lutley *W Mids*	60	SO9483
Luton *Beds*	38	TL0921
Luton *Devon*	9	ST0802
Luton *Devon*	9	SX9076
Luton *Kent*	28	TQ7766
Lutterworth *Leics*	50	SP5484
Lutton *Devon*	6	SX5959
Lutton *Dorset*	11	SY8980
Lutton *Lincs*	65	TF4325
Lutton *Nhants*	52	TL1187
Lutworthy *Devon*	19	SS7615
Luxborough *Somset*	20	SS9738
Luxulyan *Cnwll*	4	SX0458
Luzley *Gt Man*	79	SD9601
Lybster *Highld*	151	ND2435
Lydbury North *Shrops*	59	SO3486
Lydcott *Devon*	19	SS6936
Lydd *Kent*	17	TR0420
Lydden *Kent*	29	TR3567
Lydden *Kent*	29	TR2645
Lyddington *Leics*	51	SP8797
Lyde Green *Hants*	24	SU7057
Lydeard St. Lawrence *Somset*	20	ST1232
Lydford *Devon*	5	SX5084
Lydford on Fosse *Somset*	21	ST5630
Lydgate *Derbys*	74	SK3177
Lydgate *Gt Man*	82	SD9526
Lydgate *W York*	81	SD9225
Lydham *Shrops*	59	SO3391
Lydiard Green *Wilts*	36	SU0885
Lydiard Millicent *Wilts*	36	SU0986
Lydiard Tregoze *Wilts*	36	SU1085
Lydiate *Mersyd*	78	SD3604
Lydiate Ash *H & W*	60	SO9775
Lydlinch *Dorset*	11	ST7413
Lydney *Gloucs*	35	SO6303
Lydstep *Dyfed*	31	SS0898
Lye *W Mids*	60	SO9284
Lye Cross *Avon*	21	ST4962
Lye Green *Bucks*	38	SP9703
Lye Green *E Susx*	16	TQ5034
Lye Green *Warwks*	48	SP1965
Lye Head *H & W*	60	SO7573
Lye's Green *Wilts*	22	ST8246
Lyford *Oxon*	36	SU3994
Lymbridge Green *Kent*	29	TR1244
Lyme Border	109	NT2041
Lyme Regis *Dorset*	10	SY3492
Lyminge *Kent*	29	TR1641
Lymington *Hants*	12	SZ3295
Lyminster *W Susx*	14	TQ0204
Lymm *Ches*	79	SJ6887
Lympne *Kent*	17	TR1135
Lympsham *Somset*	21	ST3454
Lympstone *Devon*	9	SX9984
Lynbridge *Devon*	19	SS7248
Lynch *Somset*	20	SS9047
Lynch Green *Norfk*	66	TG1505
Lynchat *Highld*	132	NH7801
Lyndhurst *Hants*	12	SU2907
Lyndon *Leics*	63	SK9004
Lyndon Green *W Mids*	61	SP1485
Lyne *Surrey*	26	TQ0166
Lyne Down *H & W*	47	SO6530
Lyne Hill *Staffs*	60	SJ9212
Lyne of Gorthleck *Highld*	139	NH6420
Lyne of Skene *Gramp*	135	NJ7610
Lyneal *Shrops*	59	SJ4433
Lynegar *Highld*	151	ND2256

Lyneham *Devon*	8	SX8579
Lyneham *Oxon*	36	SP2720
Lyneham *Wilts*	35	SU0278
Lyneholmford *Cumb*	101	NY5172
Lynemouth *Nthumb*	103	NZ2991
Lyness *Ork*	155	ND3094
Lyng *Norfk*	66	TG0717
Lyng *Somset*	21	ST3328
Lynhales *H & W*	46	SO3255
Lynmouth *Devon*	19	SS7249
Lynn *Shrops*	72	SJ7815
Lynn of Shenval *Gramp*	141	NJ2129
Lynsted *Kent*	28	TQ9460
Lynstone *Cnwll*	18	SS2005
Lynton *Devon*	19	SS7149
Lyon's Gate *Dorset*	11	ST6605
Lyonshall *H & W*	46	SO3355
Lytchett Matravers *Dorset*	11	SY9495
Lytchett Minster *Dorset*	11	SY9593
Lytham *Lancs*	80	SD3627
Lytham St. Anne's *Lancs*	80	SD3427
Lytham Shrops	59	SJ4607
Lythe *Highld*	151	ND2762
Lythe *N York*	90	NZ8413
Lythmore *Highld*	150	ND0566

M

Maaruig *W Isls*	154	NB1906
Mabe Burnthouse *Cnwll*	3	SW7634
Mabie *D & G*	100	NX9570
Mablethorpe *Lincs*	77	TF5085
Macclesfield *Ches*	79	SJ9173
Macclesfield Forest *Ches*	79	SJ9772
Macduff *Gramp*	142	NJ7064
Macharioch *Strath*	105	NR7309
Machen *M Glam*	33	ST2189
Machire *Strath*	112	NR2064
Machrie Farm *Strath*	105	NR9033
Machrihanish *Strath*	104	NR6320
Machrins *Strath*	112	NR3693
Machynlleth *Powys*	57	SH7400
Machynys *Dyfed*	32	SS5198
Mackworth *Derbys*	62	SK3137
Macmerry *Loth*	118	NT4372
Maddaford *Devon*	8	SX5495
Madderty *Tays*	125	NN9522
Maddington *Wilts*	23	SU0643
Maddiston *Cent*	116	NS9476
Madehurst *W Susx*	14	SU9810
Madeley *Shrops*	60	SJ6904
Madeley *Staffs*	72	SJ7744
Madeley Heath *Staffs*	72	SJ7845
Madford *Devon*	9	ST1411
Madingley *Cambs*	52	TL3960
Madley *H & W*	46	SO4238
Madresfield *H & W*	47	SO8047
Madron *Cnwll*	2	SW4532
Maen-y-groes *Dyfed*	42	SN3858
Maenaddwyn *Gwynd*	68	SH4684
Maenclochog *Dyfed*	31	SN0827
Maendy *S Glam*	33	ST0076
Maenporth *Cnwll*	3	SW7829
Maentwrog *Gwynd*	57	SH6640
Maer *Cnwll*	18	SS2008
Maer *Staffs*	72	SJ7938
Maerdy *Clwyd*	70	SJ0144
Maerdy *M Glam*	33	SS9798
Maes-glas *Gwent*	34	ST2986
Maes-y-cwmmer *M Glam*	33	ST1794
Maesbrook *Shrops*	59	SJ3021
Maesbury *Shrops*	59	SJ3026
Maesbury Marsh *Shrops*	59	SJ3125
Maesgwynne *Dyfed*	31	SN2024
Maeshafn *Clwyd*	70	SJ2061
Maeslyn *Dyfed*	42	SN3644
Maesmynis *Powys*	45	SO0350
Maesmynis *Powys*	45	SO0147
Maesteg *M Glam*	33	SS8590
Maesybont *Dyfed*	32	SN5616
Maesycwmmer *M Glam*	33	ST1594
Magdalen Laver *Essex*	39	TL5108
Maggieknockater *Gramp*	141	NJ3145
Maggots End *Essex*	39	TL4727
Magham Down *E Susx*	16	TQ6011
Maghull *Mersyd*	78	SD3703
Magor *Gwent*	34	ST4287
Mahaar *D & G*	98	NX1058
Maiden Bradley *Wilts*	22	ST7938
Maiden Head *Avon*	21	ST5666
Maiden Law *Dur*	96	NZ1749
Maiden Newton *Dorset*	10	SY5997
Maiden Rushett *Gt Lon*	26	TQ1761
Maiden Wells *Dyfed*	30	SR9799
Maidencombe *Devon*	7	SX9268
Maidenhayne *Devon*	10	SY2795
Maidenhead *Berks*	26	SU8980
Maidens *Strath*	106	NS2107
Maidens Green *Berks*	25	SU8972
Maidenwell *Lincs*	77	TF3179
Maidford *Nhants*	49	SP6052
Maids Moreton *Bucks*	49	SP7035
Maidstone *Kent*	28	TQ7555
Maidwell *Nhants*	50	SP7476
Maindee *Gwent*	34	ST3288
Mains of Allardice *Gramp*	135	NO8375
Mains of Bainakettle *Gramp*	134	NO6274
Mains of Bainakettle *Gramp*	134	NO6274
Mains of Balhall *Tays*	134	NO5163
Mains of Cairnbarrow *Gramp*	142	NJ4640
Mains of Dalvey *Highld*	141	NJ1031
Mains of Dillavaird *Gramp*	135	NO7482
Mains of Haulkerton *Gramp*	135	NO7172
Mains of Haulkerton *Gramp*	135	NO7172
Mains of Throsk *Cent*	116	NS8690
Mainsforth *Dur*	96	NZ3131
Mainsriddle *D & G*	92	NX9657
Mainstone *Shrops*	58	SO2787
Maisemore *Gloucs*	35	SO8121
Major's Green *H & W*	61	SP1077
Makeney *Derbys*	62	SK3544
Malborough *Devon*	7	SX7039
Malcoff *Derbys*	74	SK0782
Malden *Surrey*	26	TQ2175
Malden *Surrey*	26	TQ2166
Maldon *Essex*	40	TL8507
Malham *N York*	88	SD9062
Mallaig *Highld*	129	NM6796
Mallaigvaig *Highld*	129	NM6897
Malleny Mills *Loth*	117	NT1665
Mallows Green *Essex*	39	TL4726
Malltraeth *Gwynd*	68	SH4069
Mallwyd *Gwynd*	57	SH8612
Malmesbury *Wilts*	35	ST9387
Malmsmead *Somset*	19	SS7947
Malpas *Ches*	71	SJ4847
Malpas *Cnwll*	3	SW8442
Malpas *Gwent*	34	ST3090
Malshanger House *Hants*	24	SU5652

Maltby *Cleve*	89	NZ4613
Maltby *Lincs*	77	TF3083
Maltby *S York*	75	SK5392
Maltby le Marsh *Lincs*	77	TF4681
Malting Green *Essex*	41	TL9720
Maltman's Hill *Kent*	28	TQ9043
Malton *N York*	90	SE7871
Malvern Link *H & W*	47	SO7847
Malvern Wells *H & W*	47	SO7741
Malzie *D & G*	99	NX3754
Mamble *H & W*	60	SO6991
Mamhilad *Gwent*	34	SO3003
Manaccan *Cnwll*	3	SW7625
Manafon *Powys*	58	SJ1102
Manaton *Devon*	8	SX7581
Manby *Lincs*	77	TF3986
Mancetter *Warwks*	61	SP3296
Manchester *Gt Man*	79	SJ8497
Mancot *Clwyd*	71	SJ3267
Mandally *Highld*	131	NH2900
Manea *Cambs*	53	TL4789
Maneight *Strath*	107	NS5409
Maney *W Mids*	61	SP1295
Manfield *N York*	89	NZ2213
Mangersta *W Isls*	154	NB0131
Mangerton *Dorset*	10	SY4995
Mangotsfield *Avon*	35	ST6676
Mangrove End *Herts*	38	TL1223
Manhay *Cnwll*	2	SW6930
Manish *W Isls*	154	NA9513
Manish *W Isls*	154	NG1089
Mankinholes *W York*	82	SD9623
Mankinholes *W York*	82	SD9623
Manley *Ches*	71	SJ5071
Manmoel *Gwent*	33	SO1803
Manning's Heath *W Susx*	15	TQ2028
Manningford Bohune *Wilts*	23	SU1357
Manningford Bruce *Wilts*	23	SU1359
Manningham *W York*	82	SE1435
Mannington *Dorset*	12	SU0605
Manningtree *Essex*	41	TM1032
Mannofield *Gramp*	135	NJ9204
Manor Park *Gt Lon*	27	TQ4286
Manorbier *Dyfed*	30	SS0697
Manorbier Newton *Dyfed*	30	SN0400
Manorhill *Border*	110	NT6632
Manorowen *Dyfed*	30	SM9336
Mansell Gamage *H & W*	46	SO3944
Mansell Lacy *H & W*	46	SO4245
Mansergh *Cumb*	87	SD6082
Mansfield *Notts*	75	SK5361
Mansfield *Strath*	107	NS6214
Mansfield Woodhouse *Notts*	75	SK5363
Mansriggs *Cumb*	86	SD2880
Manston *Dorset*	11	ST8115
Manston *Kent*	29	TR3466
Manston *W York*	83	SE3634
Manswood *Dorset*	11	ST9708
Manthorpe *Lincs*	63	SK9237
Manthorpe *Lincs*	64	TF0715
Manton *Humb*	84	SE9502
Manton *Leics*	63	SK8704
Manton *Notts*	75	SK6078
Manton *Wilts*	23	SU1768
Manuden *Essex*	39	TL4926
Manwood End *Essex*	39	TL5412
Maolachy *Strath*	122	NM8912
Maperton *Somset*	22	ST6726
Maple Cross *Herts*	26	TQ0392
Maplebeck *Notts*	75	SK7160
Mapledurham *Oxon*	37	SU6776
Mapledurwell *Hants*	24	SU6851
Maplehurst *W Susx*	15	TQ1824
Maplescombe *Kent*	27	TQ5664
Mapleton *Derbys*	73	SK1648
Mapleton *Kent*	16	TQ4649
Mapperley *Derbys*	62	SK4343
Mapperley Park *Notts*	62	SK5742
Mapperton *Dorset*	10	SY5099
Mappleborough Green *Warwks*	48	SP0866
Mappleton *Humb*	85	TA2243
Mappowder *Dorset*	11	ST7105
Marazanvose *Cnwll*	3	SW8050
Marazion *Cnwll*	2	SW5130
Marbury *Ches*	71	SJ5645
March *Cambs*	65	TL4297
March *Strath*	108	NS9914
Marcham *Oxon*	37	SU4596
Marchamley *Shrops*	59	SJ5929
Marchamley Wood *Shrops*	59	SJ5831
Marchington *Staffs*	73	SK1330
Marchington Woodlands *Staffs*	73	SK1128
Marchros *Gwynd*	56	SH3126
Marchwiel *Clwyd*	71	SJ3547
Marchwood *Hants*	12	SU3810
Marcross *S Glam*	20	SS9269
Marden *H & W*	46	SO5146
Marden *Kent*	28	TQ7444
Marden *Wilts*	23	SU0857
Marden Ash *Essex*	27	TL5502
Marden Beech *Kent*	28	TQ7343
Marden Thorn *Kent*	28	TQ7643
Mardens Hill *E Susx*	16	TQ5003
Mardlebury *Herts*	39	TL2618
Mardy *Gwent*	34	SO3015
Mare Green *Somset*	21	ST3326
Marefield *Leics*	63	SK7407
Mareham le Fen *Lincs*	77	TF2761
Mareham on the Hill *Lincs*	77	TF2867
Marehay *Derbys*	74	SK3948
Marehill *W Susx*	14	TQ0618
Maresfield *E Susx*	16	TQ4624
Marfleet *Humb*	85	TA1329
Marford *Clwyd*	59	SJ3655
Margam *W Glam*	32	SS7887
Margaret Marsh *Dorset*	22	ST8218
Margaretting *Essex*	40	TL6701
Margaretting Tye *Essex*	40	TL6801
Margate *Kent*	29	TR3571
Margnaheglish *Strath*	105	NS0332
Margrie *D & G*	99	NX5950
Margrove Park *Cleve*	97	NZ6515
Marham *Norfk*	65	TF7110
Marhamchurch *Cnwll*	18	SS2203
Marholm *Cambs*	64	TF1402
Marian-glas *Gwynd*	68	SH5084
Mariansleigh *Devon*	19	SS7422
Marine Town *Kent*	28	TQ9274
Marionburgh *Gramp*	135	NJ7006
Marishader *Highld*	136	NG4963
Maristow *Devon*	6	SX4764
Marjoriebanks *D & G*	100	NY0883
Mark *D & G*	98	NX1158
Mark *Somset*	21	ST3747
Mark Causeway *Somset*	21	ST3547
Mark Cross *E Susx*	16	TQ5010
Mark's Corner *IOW*	13	SZ4792
Markbeech *Kent*	16	TQ4742
Markby *Lincs*	77	TF4878
Markeaton *Derbys*	62	SK3337
Market Bosworth *Leics*	62	SK4003
Market Deeping *Lincs*	64	TF1310
Market Drayton *Shrops*	72	SJ6734
Market Harborough *Leics*	50	SP7387
Market Lavington *Wilts*	22	SU0154
Market Overton *Leics*	63	SK8816

Market Rasen *Lincs*	76	TF1089
Market Stainton *Lincs*	76	TF2279
Market Street *Norfk*	67	TG2921
Market Weighton *Humb*	84	SE8741
Market Weston *Suffk*	54	TL9877
Markfield *Leics*	62	SK4810
Markham *Gwent*	33	SO1601
Markham Moor *Notts*	75	SK7274
Markinch *Fife*	126	NO2901
Markington *N York*	89	SE2864
Marks Tey *Essex*	40	TL9023
Marksbury *Avon*	22	ST6662
Markshall *Essex*	40	TL8425
Markwell *Cnwll*	5	SX3658
Markyate *Herts*	38	TL0616
Marl Bank *H & W*	47	SO7840
Marlborough *Wilts*	36	SU1869
Marlbrook *H & W*	46	SO5054
Marlbrook *H & W*	60	SO9774
Marlcliff *Warwks*	48	SP0950
Marldon *Devon*	7	SX8663
Marle Green *E Susx*	16	TQ5816
Marlesford *Suffk*	55	TM3258
Marley *Kent*	29	TR1750
Marley *Kent*	29	TR3352
Marley Green *Ches*	71	SJ5745
Marlingford *Norfk*	66	TG1309
Marloes *Dyfed*	30	SM7908
Marlow *Bucks*	26	SU8486
Marlow *H & W*	46	SO4076
Marlpit Hill *Kent*	16	TQ4447
Marlpits *E Susx*	16	TQ4528
Marlpits *E Susx*	16	TQ7013
Marlpool *Derbys*	62	SK4345
Marnhull *Dorset*	22	ST7718
Marnoch *Gramp*	142	NJ5950
Marple *Gt Man*	79	SJ9588
Marple Bridge *Gt Man*	79	SJ9789
Marr *S York*	83	SE5105
Marrel *Highld*	147	ND0117
Marrick *N York*	88	SE0798
Marros *Dyfed*	31	SN2009
Marsden *T & W*	103	NZ4064
Marsden *W York*	82	SE0411
Marsden Height *Lancs*	81	SD8636
Marsett *N York*	88	SD9085
Marsh *Bucks*	38	SP8109
Marsh *Somset*	10	ST2510
Marsh *W York*	82	SE0236
Marsh Baldon *Oxon*	37	SU5699
Marsh Gibbon *Bucks*	37	SP6422
Marsh Green *Devon*	9	SY0493
Marsh Green *Kent*	16	TQ4344
Marsh Green *Shrops*	59	SJ6014
Marsh Green *Staffs*	72	SJ8859
Marsh Lane *Derbys*	74	SK4079
Marsh Lane *Gloucs*	34	SO5807
Marsh Street *Somset*	20	SS9944
Marsh The *Powys*	59	SO3197
Marshall's Heath *Herts*	39	TL1614
Marshalswick *Herts*	39	TL1608
Marsham *Norfk*	67	TG1924
Marshborough *Kent*	29	TR2958
Marshbrook *Shrops*	59	SO4489
Marshchapel *Lincs*	77	TF3599
Marshfield *Avon*	35	ST7773
Marshfield *Gwent*	34	ST2582
Marshgate *Cnwll*	4	SX1592
Marshland Green *Gt Man*	79	SJ6899
Marshland St. James *Norfk*	65	TF5209
Marshside *Mersyd*	80	SD3619
Marshwood *Dorset*	10	SY3899
Marske *N York*	89	NZ1000
Marske-by-the-Sea *Cleve*	97	NZ6322
Marston *Ches*	79	SJ6775
Marston *H & W*	46	SO3557
Marston *Lincs*	63	SK8943
Marston *Oxon*	37	SP5208
Marston *Staffs*	60	SJ8314
Marston *Staffs*	72	SJ9227
Marston *Warwks*	61	SP2195
Marston *Wilts*	22	ST9656
Marston Green *W Mids*	61	SP1785
Marston Jabbet *Warwks*	61	SP3788
Marston Magna *Somset*	21	ST5922
Marston Meysey *Wilts*	36	SU1297
Marston Montgomery *Derbys*	73	SK1338
Marston Moretaine *Beds*	38	SP9941
Marston on Dove *Derbys*	73	SK2329
Marston St. Lawrence *Nhants*	49	SP5342
Marston Stannett *H & W*	46	SO5655
Marston Trussell *Nhants*	50	SP6985
Marstow *H & W*	34	SO5518
Marsworth *Bucks*	38	SP9214
Marten *Wilts*	23	SU2860
Marthall *Ches*	79	SJ8075
Martham *Norfk*	67	TG4518
Martin *Hants*	12	SU0719
Martin *Kent*	29	TR3347
Martin *Lincs*	76	TF2366
Martin *Lincs*	76	TF1259
Martin Dales *Lincs*	76	TF1762
Martin Drove End *Hants*	12	SU0420
Martin Hussingtree *H & W*	47	SO8860
Martindale *Cumb*	93	NY4319
Martinhoe *Devon*	19	SS6648
Martinscroft *Ches*	79	SJ6589
Martinstown *Dorset*	11	SY6488
Martlesham *Suffk*	55	TM2547
Martletwy *Dyfed*	30	SN0310
Martock *Somset*	21	ST4619
Marton *Ches*	71	SJ6267
Marton *Ches*	79	SJ8568
Marton *Cleve*	97	NZ5115
Marton *Humb*	85	TA1839
Marton *Lincs*	75	SK8381
Marton *N York*	89	SE4162
Marton *N York*	90	SE7383
Marton *Shrops*	58	SJ2802
Marton *Warwks*	48	SP4069
Marton-le-Moor *N York*	89	SE3670
Martyr Worthy *Hants*	24	SU5132
Martyr's Green *Surrey*	26	TQ0857
Marwick *Ork*	155	HY2324
Marwood *Devon*	19	SS5437
Mary Tavy *Devon*	5	SX5079
Marybank *Highld*	139	NH4853
Maryburgh *Highld*	139	NH5456
Maryculter *Gramp*	135	NO8599
Maryfield *Cnwll*	4	SX4256
Maryhill *Gramp*	143	NJ8245
Maryhill *Strath*	115	NS5669
Marykirk *Gramp*	135	NO6865
Maryland *Gwent*	34	SO5105
Marylebone *Gt Man*	78	SD5807
Marypark *Gramp*	141	NJ1938
Maryport *Cumb*	92	NY0336
Maryport *D & G*	98	NX1434
Maryton *Tays*	127	NO6856
Marywell *Gramp*	135	NO9399
Marywell *Gramp*	135	NO9399
Marywell *Tays*	127	NO6544
Masham *N York*	89	SE2280
Mashbury *Essex*	40	TL6511

Mason Milton

Mason *T & W* 103 NZ2073
Masongill *N York* 87 SD6675
Mastin Moor *Derbys* 75 SK4575
Matching *Essex* 39 TL5212
Matching Green *Essex* 39 TL5311
Matching Tye *Essex* 39 TL5111
Matfen *Nthumb* 103 NZ0371
Matfield *Kent* 28 TQ6541
Mathern *Gwent* 34 ST5291
Mathon *H & W* 47 SO7345
Mathry *Dyfed* 30 SM8832
Matlaske *Norfk* 66 TG1534
Matlock *Derbys* 74 SK3060
Matlock Bank *Derbys* 74 SK3060
Matlock Bath *Derbys* 74 SK2958
Matlock Dale *Derbys* 74 SK2959
Matson *Gloucs* 35 SO8515
Matterdale End *Cumb* 93 NY3933
Mattersey *Notts* 75 SK6889
Mattersey Thorpe *Notts* 75 SK6889
Mattingley *Hants* 24 SU7357
Mattishall *Norfk* 66 TG0511
Mattishall Burgh *Norfk* 66 TG0512
Mauchline *Strath* 107 NS4927
Maud *Gramp* 143 NJ9247
Maufant *Jersey* 152 JS0000
Maugersbury *Gloucs* 48 SP1925
Maughold *IOM* 153 SC4991
Mauld *Highld* 139 NH4038
Maulden *Beds* 38 TL0538
Maulds Meaburn *Cumb* 94 NY6216
Maunby *N York* 89 SE3486
Maund Bryan *H & W* 46 SO5650
Maundown *Somset* 20 ST0528
Mautby *Norfk* 67 TG4812
Mavesyn Ridware *Staffs* 73 SK0816
Mavis Enderby *Lincs* 77 TF3666
Maw Green *Ches* 72 SJ7157
Maw Green *W Mids* 60 SP0196
Mawbray *Cumb* 92 NY0846
Mawdesley *Lancs* 80 SD4914
Mawdlam *M Glam* 32 SS8081
Mawgan *Cnwll* 2 SW7025
Mawgan Cross *Cnwll* 2 SW7024
Mawgan Porth *Cnwll* 4 SW8467
Mawla *Cnwll* 2 SW7045
Mawnan *Cnwll* 3 SW7827
Mawnan Smith *Cnwll* 3 SW7728
Mawthorpe *Lincs* 77 TF4672
Maxey *Cambs* 64 TF1208
Maxstoke *Warwks* 61 SP2386
Maxted Street *Kent* 29 TR1244
Maxton *Border* 110 NT6130
Maxton *Kent* 29 TR3041
Maxwellheugh *Border* 110 NT7333
Maxwelltown *D & G* 100 NX9676
Maxworthy *Cnwll* 5 SX2593
May Bank *Staffs* 72 SJ8547
May's Green *Oxon* 37 SU7580
May's Green *Surrey* 26 TQ0957
Mayals *W Glam* 32 SS6090
Maybole *Strath* 106 NS2909
Maybury *Surrey* 26 TQ0158
Mayes Green *Surrey* 14 TQ1239
Mayfield *E Susx* 16 TQ5827
Mayfield *Loth* 118 NT3565
Mayfield *Staffs* 73 SK1545
Mayford *Surrey* 25 SU9956
Mayland *Essex* 40 TL9201
Maymore *Strath* 114 NR9986
Maynard's Green *E Susx* 16 TQ5818
Maypole *Gwent* 34 SO4716
Maypole *Kent* 29 TR2064
Maypole *W Mids* 61 SP0878
Maypole Green *Norfk* 67 TM4195
Maypole Green *Suffk* 54 TL9159
Maypole Green *Suffk* 55 TM2767
Mead *Devon* 18 SS2217
Meadgate *Avon* 22 ST6758
Meadle *Bucks* 38 SP8006
Meadowtown *Shrops* 59 SJ3101
Meadwell *Devon* 5 SX4081
Meal Bank *Cumb* 87 SD5495
Mealrigg *Cumb* 92 NY1345
Mealsgate *Cumb* 93 NY2142
Meamskirk *Strath* 115 NS5455
Meanwood *W York* 82 SE2837
Mearbeck *N York* 88 SD8160
Meare *Somset* 21 ST4541
Meare Green *Somset* 20 ST2922
Mears Ashby *Nhants* 51 SP8366
Measham *Leics* 62 SK3312
Meathop *Cumb* 87 SD4380
Meaux *Humb* 85 TA0839
Meavy *Devon* 6 SX5467
Med *Avon* 22 ST7358
Medbourne *Leics* 51 SP8093
Meddon *Devon* 18 SS2717
Meden Vale *Notts* 90 SE5870
Medlam *Lincs* 77 TF3156
Medlar *Lancs* 80 SD4135
Medmenham *Berks* 37 SU8084
Medomsley *Dur* 96 NZ1254
Medstead *Hants* 24 SU6537
Meer Common *H & W* 46 SO3652
Meer End *W Mids* 61 SP2474
Meerbrook *Staffs* 72 SJ9860
Meesden *Herts* 39 TL4322
Meeson *Shrops* 72 SJ6420
Meeth *Devon* 19 SS5408
Meeting Green *Suffk* 53 TL7455
Meeting House Hill *Norfk* 67 TG3028
Meidrim *Dyfed* 31 SN2820
Meifod *Powys* 58 SJ1513
Meigle *Tays* 126 NO2944
Meikle Carco *D & G* 107 NS7813
Meikle Earnock *Strath* 116 NS7053
Meikle Grenach *Strath* 114 NS0760
Meikle Kilmory *Strath* 114 NS0561
Meikle Obney *Tays* 125 NO0337
Meikle Wartle *Gramp* 142 NJ7231
Meikleour *Tays* 126 NO1539
Meinciau *Dyfed* 32 SN4610
Meir *Staffs* 72 SJ9342
Meirheath *Staffs* 72 SJ9240
Melbourn *Cambs* 39 TL3844
Melbourne *Derbys* 62 SK3825
Melbourne *Humb* 84 SE7543
Melbury *Devon* 18 SS3719
Melbury Abbas *Dorset* 22 ST8820
Melbury Bubb *Dorset* 10 ST5906
Melbury Osmond *Dorset* 10 ST5707
Melbury Sampford *Dorset* 10 ST5705
Melchbourne *Beds* 51 TL0365
Melcombe Bingham *Dorset* 11 ST7602
Meldon *Devon* 8 SX5692
Meldon *Nthumb* 103 NZ1183
Meldreth *Cambs* 52 TL3746
Meldrum *Cent* 116 NS7199
Meledon *Cnwll* 3 SW9254
Melfort *Strath* 122 NM8313
Melgund Castle *Tays* 127 NO5455
Meliden *Clwyd* 70 SJ0580
Melin Court *W Glam* 33 SN8201
Melin-byrhedyn *Powys* 57 SN8198
Melin-y-coed *Gwynd* 69 SH8160
Melin-y-ddol *Powys* 58 SJ0907
Melin-y-wig *Clwyd* 70 SJ0448
Melinau *Dyfed* 31 SN1613
Melkinthorpe *Cumb* 94 NY5525
Melkridge *Nthumb* 102 NY7363
Melksham *Wilts* 22 ST9063
Mell Green *Berks* 37 SU4577
Mellangoose *Cnwll* 2 SW6826
Melldalloch *Strath* 114 NR9375
Mellguards *Cumb* 93 NY4446
Melling *Lancs* 87 SD5970
Melling *Mersyd* 78 SD3800
Melling Mount *Mersyd* 78 SD4001
Mellis *Suffk* 54 TM0974
Mellon Charles *Highld* 144 NG8491
Mellon Udrigle *Highld* 144 NG8895
Mellor *Gt Man* 79 SJ9988
Mellor *Lancs* 81 SD6530
Mellor Brook *Lancs* 81 SD6431
Mells *Somset* 22 ST7249
Mells *Suffk* 55 TM4076
Melmerby *Cumb* 94 NY6137
Melmerby *N York* 88 SE0785
Melmerby *N York* 89 SE3376
Melness *Highld* 149 NC5861
Melon Green *Suffk* 54 TL8456
Melplash *Dorset* 10 SY4797
Melrose *Border* 109 NT5434
Melsetter *Ork* 155 ND2689
Melsonby *N York* 89 NZ1908
Meltham *W York* 82 SE0910
Meltham *W York* 82 SE1010
Meltham Mills *W York* 82 SE1010
Melton *Humb* 84 SE9726
Melton *Suffk* 55 TM2850
Melton Constable *Norfk* 66 TG0433
Melton Mowbray *Leics* 63 SK7518
Melton Ross *Humb* 84 TA0610
Meltonby *Humb* 84 SE7952
Melvaig *Highld* 144 NG7486
Melverley *Shrops* 59 SJ3316
Melverley Green *Shrops* 59 SJ3317
Melvich *Highld* 150 NC8764
Membury *Devon* 10 ST2703
Memsie *Gramp* 143 NJ9762
Menabilly *Cnwll* 3 SX0951
Menagissey *Cnwll* 2 SW7146
Menai Bridge *Gwynd* 69 SH5571
Mendham *Suffk* 55 TM2783
Mendlesham *Suffk* 54 TM1065
Mendlesham Green *Suffk* 54 TM0963
Menethorpe *N York* 90 SE7667
Menheniot *Cnwll* 5 SX2862
Menithwood *H & W* 47 SO7069
Mennock *D & G* 108 NS8008
Menston *W York* 82 SE1743
Menstrie *Cent* 116 NS8596
Menthorpe *N York* 83 SE6934
Mentmore *Bucks* 38 SP9019
Meoble *Highld* 129 NM7987
Meole Brace *Shrops* 59 SJ4810
Meonstoke *Hants* 13 SU6119
Meopham *Kent* 27 TQ6466
Meopham Green *Kent* 27 TQ6465
Meopham Station *Kent* 27 TQ6467
Mepal *Cambs* 53 TL4481
Meppershall *Beds* 38 TL1336
Mere *Ches* 79 SJ7281
Mere *Wilts* 22 ST8132
Mere Brow *Lancs* 80 SD4218
Mere Green *H & W* 47 SO9562
Mere Green *W Mids* 61 SP1298
Mere Heath *Ches* 79 SJ6670
Mereclough *Lancs* 81 SD8730
Meresborough *Kent* 28 TQ8264
Mereworth *Kent* 28 TQ6553
Meriden *W Mids* 61 SP2482
Merkadale *Highld* 136 NG3931
Merlin's Bridge *Dyfed* 30 SM9414
Merrifield *Devon* 7 SX8147
Merrington *Shrops* 59 SJ4720
Merriott *Somset* 10 ST4412
Merrivale *Devon* 6 SX5475
Merrow *Surrey* 26 TQ0250
Merry Field Hill *Dorset* 12 SU0201
Merry Hill *Herts* 26 TQ1394
Merry Hill *W Mids* 60 SO9386
Merry Lees *Leics* 62 SK4705
Merryhill *W Mids* 60 SO8897
Merrymeet *Cnwll* 5 SX2766
Mersham *Kent* 28 TR0540
Merstham *Surrey* 27 TQ2953
Merston *W Susx* 14 SU8903
Merstone *IOW* 13 SZ5285
Merther *Cnwll* 3 SW8644
Merthyr *Dyfed* 31 SN3520
Merthyr Cynog *Powys* 45 SN9837
Merthyr Dyfan *S Glam* 20 ST1169
Merthyr Mawr *M Glam* 33 SS8877
Merthyr Tydfil *M Glam* 33 SO0506
Merthyr Vale *M Glam* 33 ST0799
Merthyr Vale *M Glam* 33 ST0899
Merton *Devon* 19 SS5212
Merton *Gt Lon* 27 TQ2570
Merton *Norfk* 66 TL9098
Merton *Oxon* 37 SP5717
Mervinslaw *Border* 110 NT6713
Meshaw *Devon* 19 SS7519
Messing *Essex* 40 TL8919
Messingham *Humb* 84 SE8904
Metcombe *Devon* 9 SY0791
Metfield *Suffk* 55 TM2980
Metherell *Cnwll* 5 SX4069
Metherin *Cnwll* 4 SX1174
Metheringham *Lincs* 76 TF0661
Methil *Fife* 118 NT3799
Methleigh *Cnwll* 2 SW6226
Methley *W York* 83 SE3826
Methley Junction *W York* 83 SE3926
Methlick *Gramp* 143 NJ8537
Methven *Tays* 125 NO0226
Methwold *Norfk* 65 TL7394
Methwold Hythe *Norfk* 65 TL7195
Mettingham *Suffk* 55 TM3690
Metton *Norfk* 67 TG1937
Mevagissey *Cnwll* 3 SX0144
Mexborough *S York* 75 SE4700
Mey *Highld* 151 ND2872
Meyllteyrn *Gwynd* 56 SH2332
Meylltyrn *Gwynd* 56 SH2333
Meysey Hampton *Gloucs* 36 SU1199
Miavaig *W Isls* 154 NB0834
Michaelchurch *H & W* 46 SO5125
Michaelchurch Escley *H & W* 46 SO3134
Michaelchurch-on-Arrow *Powys* 46 SO2450
Michaelston-le-Pit *S Glam* 33 ST1573
Michaelstone-y-Fedw *Gwent* 34 ST2484
Michaelstow *Cnwll* 4 SX0878
Michelcombe *Devon* 7 SX6968
Micheldever *Hants* 24 SU5139
Micheldever Station *Hants* 24 SU5143
Michelmersh *Hants* 23 SU3426
Mickfield *Suffk* 54 TM1361
Mickle Trafford *Ches* 71 SJ4469
Micklebring *S York* 75 SK5194
Mickleby *N York* 90 NZ8012
Micklefield *W York* 83 SE4432
Micklefield Green *Herts* 26 TQ0498
Mickleham *Surrey* 26 TQ1753
Mickleover *Derbys* 73 SK3034
Micklethwaite *Cumb* 93 NY2850
Micklethwaite *W York* 82 SE1041
Mickleton *Dur* 95 NY9623
Mickleton *Gloucs* 48 SP1643
Mickleton *W York* 83 SE4027
Mickley *Derbys* 74 SK3379
Mickley *N York* 89 SE2576
Mickley Green *Suffk* 54 TL8457
Mickley Square *Nthumb* 103 NZ0762
Mid Ardlaw *Gramp* 143 NJ9464
Mid Beltie *Gramp* 134 NJ6200
Mid Bockhampton *Hants* 12 SZ1796
Mid Calder *Loth* 117 NT0767
Mid Clyth *Highld* 151 ND2937
Mid Lavant *W Susx* 14 SU8508
Mid Mains *Highld* 139 NH4239
Mid Sannox *Strath* 105 NS0145
Mid Thorpe *Lincs* 77 TF2572
Mid Yell *Shet* 155 HU5191
Midbea *Ork* 155 HY4444
Middle Assendon *Oxon* 37 SU7385
Middle Aston *Oxon* 49 SP4726
Middle Chinnock *Somset* 10 ST4713
Middle Claydon *Bucks* 49 SP7225
Middle Duntisbourne *Gloucs* 35 SO9806
Middle Handley *Derbys* 74 SK4077
Middle Harling *Norfk* 54 TL9885
Middle Kames *Strath* 114 NR9189
Middle Littleton *H & W* 48 SP0847
Middle Madeley *Staffs* 72 SJ7745
Middle Maes-coed *H & W* 46 SO3333
Middle Mayfield *Staffs* 73 SK1444
Middle Mill *Dyfed* 30 SM8026
Middle Quarter *Kent* 28 TQ8937
Middle Rasen *Lincs* 76 TF0889
Middle Rocombe *Devon* 7 SX9069
Middle Salter *Lancs* 87 SD6063
Middle Stoford *Somset* 20 ST1821
Middle Stoke *Kent* 28 TQ8275
Middle Stoughton *Somset* 21 ST4248
Middle Street *Essex* 39 TL4005
Middle Street *Gloucs* 35 SO7803
Middle Taphouse *Cnwll* 4 SX1763
Middle Town *IOS* 2 SV8808
Middle Tysoe *Warwks* 48 SP3344
Middle Wallop *Hants* 23 SU2938
Middle Winterslow *Wilts* 23 SU2432
Middle Woodford *Wilts* 23 SU1136
Middle Yard *Gloucs* 35 SO8103
Middlebie *D & G* 101 NY2176
Middlecliffe *S York* 83 SE4204
Middlecott *Devon* 8 SX7186
Middlegill *D & G* 108 NT0407
Middleham *N York* 89 SE1287
Middlehill *Cnwll* 5 SX2869
Middlehill *Wilts* 35 ST8169
Middlehope *Shrops* 59 SO4988
Middlemarsh *Dorset* 11 ST6707
Middlemore *Devon* 6 SX5073
Middlesbrough *Cleve* 97 NZ4920
Middlesceugh *Cumb* 93 NY3942
Middleshaw *Cumb* 87 SD5589
Middleshaw *D & G* 100 NY1475
Middlesmoor *N York* 88 SE0973
Middlestone *Dur* 96 NZ2531
Middlestone Moor *Dur* 96 NZ2432
Middlestown *W York* 82 SE2617
Middlethird *Border* 110 NT6743
Middleton *Cumb* 87 SD6285
Middleton *Derbys* 74 SK1963
Middleton *Derbys* 73 SK2756
Middleton *Essex* 54 TL8739
Middleton *Gt Man* 79 SD8705
Middleton *H & W* 46 SO5469
Middleton *Hants* 24 SU4244
Middleton *Lancs* 87 SD4258
Middleton *Loth* 118 NT3758
Middleton *N York* 90 SE7885
Middleton *Nhants* 51 SP8489
Middleton *Norfk* 65 TF6616
Middleton *Nthumb* 111 NU0024
Middleton *Nthumb* 111 NU1035
Middleton *Nthumb* 103 NZ0584
Middleton *Shrops* 59 SJ3129
Middleton *Shrops* 46 SO5477
Middleton *Strath* 120 NL9443
Middleton *Strath* 115 NS3952
Middleton *Suffk* 55 TM4267
Middleton *Tays* 126 NO1206
Middleton *W Glam* 31 SS4287
Middleton *W York* 82 SE1249
Middleton *W York* 82 SE3027
Middleton *Warwks* 61 SP1798
Middleton Cheney *Nhants* 49 SP4941
Middleton Green *Staffs* 73 SJ9935
Middleton Hall *Nthumb* 111 NT9825
Middleton Moor *Suffk* 55 TM4167
Middleton one Tow *Dur* 89 NZ3512
Middleton Priors *Shrops* 59 SO6290
Middleton Quernhow *N York* 89 SE3378
Middleton Scriven *Shrops* 60 SO6887
Middleton St. George *Dur* 89 NZ3412
Middleton Stoney *Oxon* 49 SP5323
Middleton Tyas *N York* 89 NZ2205
Middleton-in-Teesdale *Dur* 95 NY9425
Middleton-on-Lever *N York* 89 NZ4609
Middleton-on-Sea *W Susx* 14 SU9800
Middleton-on-the-Hill *H & W* 46 SO5364
Middleton-on-the-Wolds *Humb* 84 SE9449
Middletown *Avon* 34 ST4571
Middletown *Cumb* 86 NX9908
Middletown *Powys* 59 SJ3012
Middlewich *Ches* 72 SJ7066
Middlewood *Cnwll* 5 SX2775
Middlewood *H & W* 46 SO2844
Middlewood Green *Suffk* 54 TM0961
Middleyard *Strath* 107 NS5132
Middlezoy *Somset* 21 ST3733
Middridge *Dur* 96 NZ2526
Midford *Avon* 22 ST7660
Midge Hall *Lancs* 80 SD5123
Midgeholme *Cumb* 94 NY6359
Midgham *Berks* 24 SU5567
Midgley *W York* 82 SE2714
Midgley *W York* 82 SE0226
Midhopestones *S York* 74 SK2399
Midhurst *W Susx* 14 SU8821
Midlem *Border* 109 NT5227
Midney *Somset* 21 ST4927
Midpark *Strath* 114 NS0259
Midsomer Norton *Avon* 22 ST6654
Midtown *Highld* 144 NG8285
Midtown *Highld* 149 NC5861
Midville *Lincs* 77 TF3756
Midway *Ches* 79 SJ9282
Migvie *Gramp* 134 NJ4306
Milarrochy *Cent* 115 NS4092
Milborne Port *Somset* 22 ST6718
Milborne St. Andrew *Dorset* 11 SY8097
Milborne Wick *Somset* 22 ST6620
Milbourne *Nthumb* 103 NZ1175
Milbourne *Wilts* 35 ST9587
Milburn *Cumb* 94 NY6529
Milbury Heath *Avon* 35 ST6790
Milby *N York* 89 SE4067
Milcombe *Oxon* 49 SP4134
Milden *Suffk* 54 TL9546
Mildenhall *Suffk* 53 TL7174
Mildenhall *Wilts* 36 SU2069
Mile Elm *Wilts* 35 ST9969
Mile End *Essex* 41 TL9927
Mile End *Gloucs* 34 SO5811
Mile End *Suffk* 55 TM3489
Mile Head *Lancs* 87 SD4970
Mile Oak *E Susx* 15 TQ2407
Mile Oak *Kent* 28 TQ6743
Mile Oak *Staffs* 61 SK1802
Mile Town *Kent* 28 TQ9274
Milebrook *Powys* 46 SO3172
Milebush *Kent* 28 TQ7545
Mileham *Norfk* 66 TF9119
Milehead *Highld* 132 NH8406
Miles Hope *H & W* 46 SO5764
Miles Platting *Gt Man* 79 SJ8599
Milesmark *Fife* 117 NT0688
Milfield *Nthumb* 110 NT9333
Milford *Derbys* 62 SK3545
Milford *Devon* 18 SS2322
Milford *Powys* 58 SO0991
Milford *Staffs* 72 SJ9721
Milford *Surrey* 25 SU9442
Milford Haven *Dyfed* 30 SM9006
Milford on Sea *Hants* 12 SZ2891
Milkwall *Gloucs* 34 SO5809
Mill Bank *W York* 82 SE0321
Mill Brow *Gt Man* 79 SJ9889
Mill Common *Norfk* 67 TG3301
Mill Common *Suffk* 55 TM4082
Mill Cross *Devon* 7 SX7361
Mill End *Bucks* 37 SU7885
Mill End *Cambs* 52 TL3180
Mill End *Herts* 39 TL3332
Mill Green *Cambs* 53 TL6245
Mill Green *Essex* 40 TL6301
Mill Green *Herts* 39 TL2410
Mill Green *Lincs* 64 TF2223
Mill Green *Norfk* 54 TM1384
Mill Green *Staffs* 73 SK0821
Mill Green *Suffk* 54 TM1360
Mill Green *Suffk* 55 TM3161
Mill Green *Suffk* 54 TL9957
Mill Green *Suffk* 54 TL9542
Mill Green *W Mids* 61 SK0701
Mill Hill *E Susx* 16 TQ6104
Mill Hill *Gt Lon* 26 TQ2292
Mill Meece *Staffs* 72 SJ8333
Mill of Cammie *Gramp* 135 NO6993
Mill of Drummond *Tays* 125 NN8315
Mill of Grange *Gramp* 141 NJ0460
Mill of Haldane *Strath* 115 NS4083
Mill of Uras *Gramp* 135 NO8680
Mill of Uras *Gramp* 135 NO8680
Mill Side *Cumb* 87 SD4484
Mill Street *Kent* 28 TQ6957
Mill Street *Norfk* 66 TG0118
Mill Street *Norfk* 66 TG0517
Mill Street *Suffk* 54 TM0672
Millais *Jersey* 152 JS0000
Milland *W Susx* 14 SU8328
Milland Marsh *W Susx* 14 SU8326
Millbeck *Cumb* 93 NY2526
Millbrex *Gramp* 143 NK0044
Millbreck *Gramp* 143 NJ8144
Millbridge *Surrey* 25 SU8442
Millbrook *Beds* 38 TL0138
Millbrook *Cnwll* 6 SX4252
Millbrook *Gt Man* 79 SJ9799
Millbrook *Hants* 12 SU3813
Millbrook *Jersey* 152 JS0000
Millbuie *Gramp* 135 NJ7909
Millburn *Strath* 107 NS4429
Millcombe *Devon* 7 SX8050
Millcorner *E Susx* 17 TQ8223
Millcraig *Highld* 146 NH6571
Milldale *Staffs* 73 SK1354
Millend *Gloucs* 34 SO5608
Millend *Gloucs* 35 ST7496
Miller's Dale *Derbys* 74 SK1373
Miller's Green *Essex* 40 TL5808
Millerhill *Loth* 118 NT3269
Millers Green *Derbys* 73 SK2752
Millerston *Strath* 116 NS6467
Millgate *Lancs* 81 SD8819
Millgreen *Shrops* 72 SJ6828
Millhalf *H & W* 46 SO2847
Millhayes *Devon* 9 ST2303
Millheugh *Strath* 116 NS7450
Millholme *Cumb* 87 SD5690
Millhouse *Cumb* 93 NY3637
Millhouse *S York* 74 SK3484
Millhouse *Strath* 114 NR9570
Millhouse Green *S York* 82 SE2203
Millhousebridge *D & G* 100 NY1085
Millhouses *S York* 74 SK3484
Millhouses *S York* 83 SE4204
Millikenpark *Strath* 115 NS4162
Millin Cross *Dyfed* 30 SM9914
Millington *Humb* 84 SE8351
Millisle *D & G* 99 NX4547
Millness *Cumb* 87 SD5383
Millom *Cumb* 86 SD1780
Millook *Cnwll* 18 SX1899
Millpool *Cnwll* 2 SW5730
Millpool *Cnwll* 4 SX1170
Millport *Strath* 114 NS1655
Millthrop *Cumb* 87 SD6691
Milltimber *Gramp* 135 NJ8501
Milltown *D & G* 101 NY3375
Milltown *Derbys* 74 SK3561
Milltown *Devon* 19 SS5539
Milltown *Gramp* 133 NJ2609
Milltown *Gramp* 142 NJ4716
Milltown of Campfield *Gramp* 135 NJ6500
Milltown of Edinvillie *Gramp* 141 NJ2639
Milltown of Learney *Gramp* 134 NJ6303
Milnathort *Tays* 126 NO1204
Milngavie *Strath* 115 NS5574
Milnmark *D & G* 99 NX6582
Milnrow *Gt Man* 81 SD9212
Milnthorpe *Cumb* 87 SD4981
Milnthorpe *W York* 83 SE3317
Milovaig *Highld* 136 NG1550
Milson *Shrops* 47 SO6472
Milsted *Kent* 28 TQ9058
Milston *Wilts* 23 SU1645
Milthorpe *Lincs* 64 TF1030
Milthorpe *Nhants* 49 SP5946
Milton *Avon* 21 ST3462
Milton *Cambs* 53 TL4762
Milton *Cent* 115 NN5001
Milton *Cent* 115 NS4490
Milton *Cumb* 101 NY5560
Milton *D & G* 98 NX2154
Milton *D & G* 100 NX8470
Milton *Derbys* 62 SK3126
Milton *Dyfed* 30 SN0303
Milton *Gramp* 142 NJ5163
Milton *Gwent* 34 ST3688
Milton *Highld* 151 ND3451
Milton *Highld* 139 NH5030
Milton *Highld* 137 NG7134
Milton *Highld* 139 NH4930

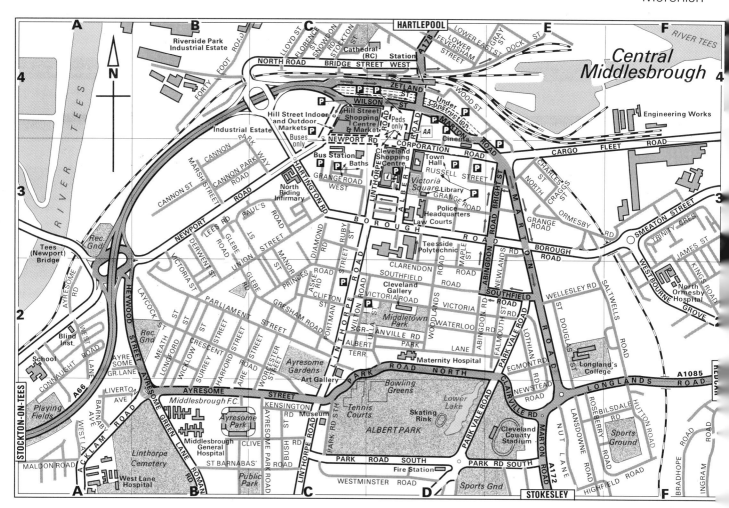

N

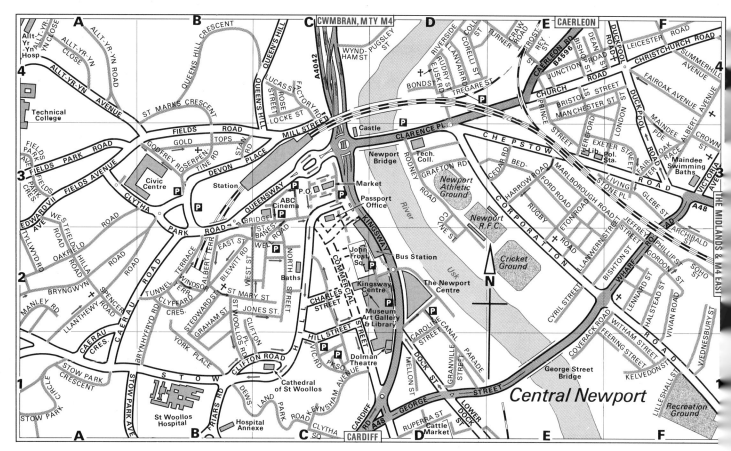

Central Newport

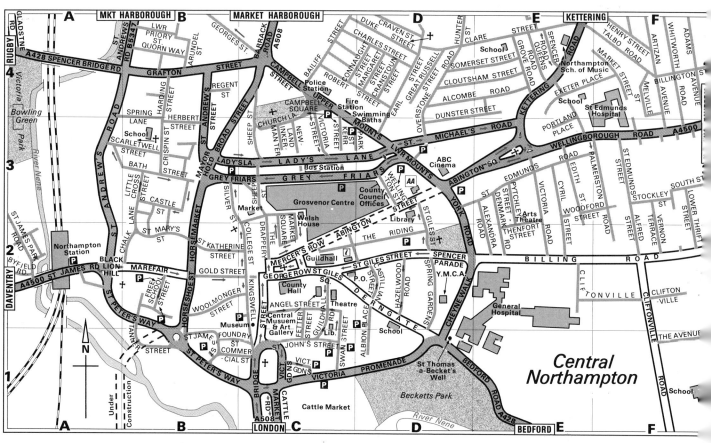

Central Northampton

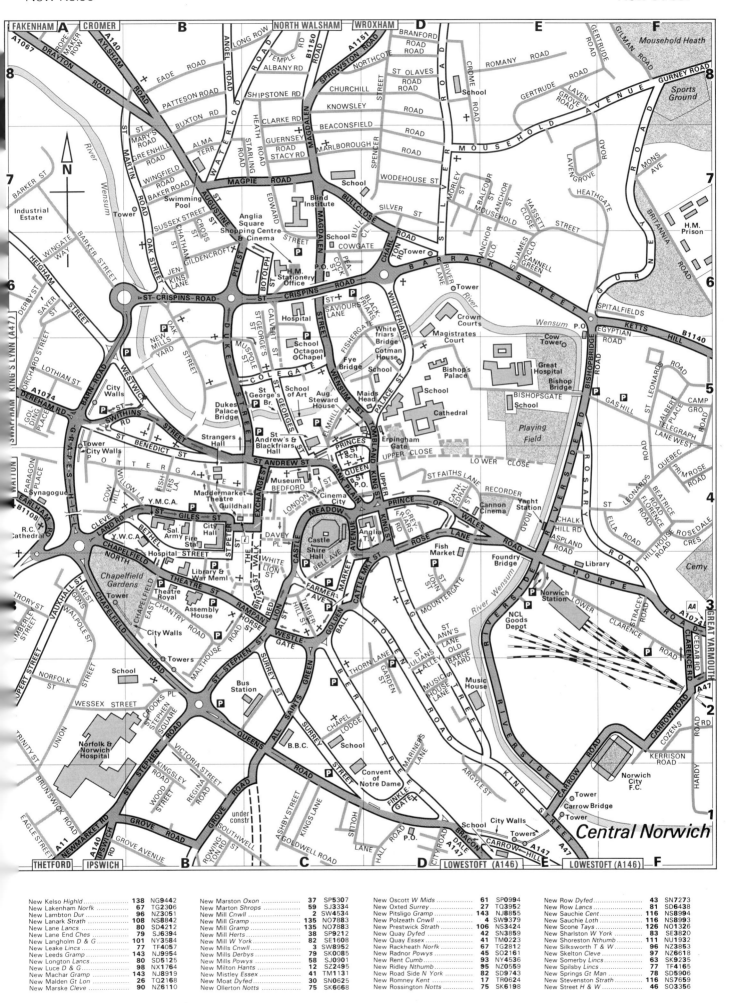

Central Norwich

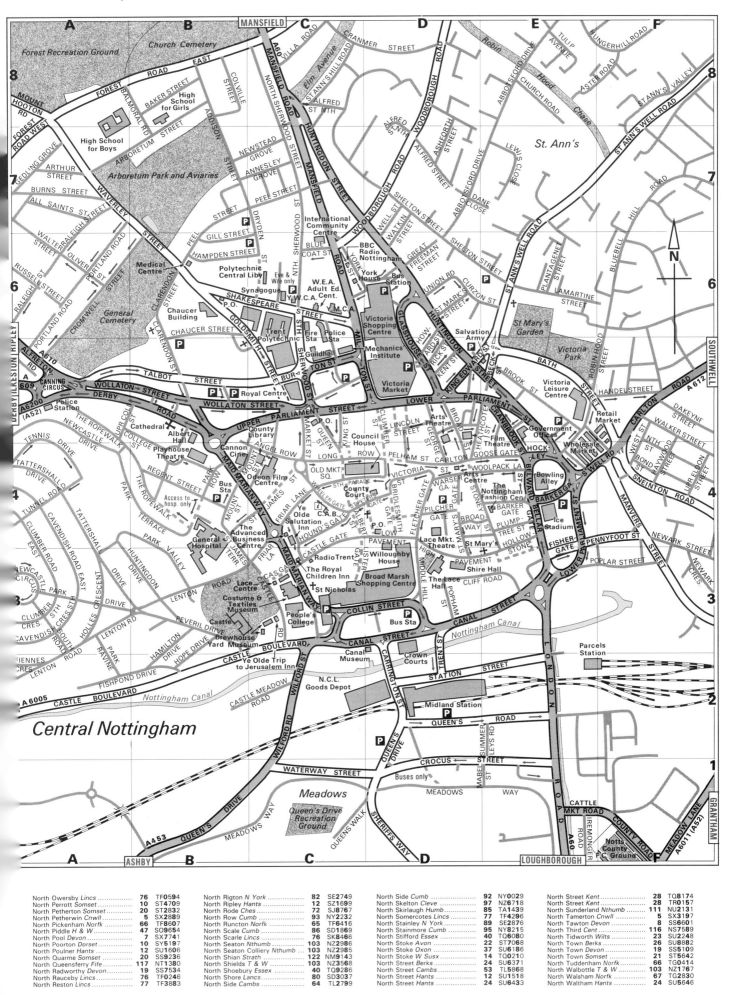

Central Nottingham

North Warnborough

Otterham Quay

North Warnborough *Hants* 24 SU7351
North Weald Basset *Essex* 39 TL4904
North Weston *Avon* 34 ST4674
North Wheatley *Notts* 75 SK7685
North Whilborough *Devon* 7 SX8766
North Wick *Avon* 21 ST5865
North Widcombe *Somset* 21 ST5758
North Willingham *Lincs* 76 TF1688
North Wingfield *Derbys* 74 SK4064
North Witham *Lincs* 63 SK9221
North Wootton *Dorset* 11 ST6614
North Wootton *Norfk* 65 TF6424
North Wootton *Somset* 21 ST5641
North Wraxall *Wilts* 35 ST8175
North Wroughton *Wilts* 36 SU1481
Northacre *Norfk* 66 TL9598
Northall *Bucks* 38 SP9520
Northall Green *Norfk* 66 TF9915
Northallerton *N York* 89 SE3793
Northam *Devon* 18 SS4429
Northam *Hants* 13 SU4312
Northampton *H & W* 47 SO8365
Northampton *Nhants* 49 SP7560
Northaw *Herts* 27 TL2702
Northay *Somset* 10 ST2811
Northborough *Cambs* 64 TF1507
Northbourne *Kent* 29 TR3352
Northbridge Street *E Susx* 17 TQ7423
Northbrook *Hants* 24 SU5139
Northbrook *Oxon* 37 SP4922
Northchapel *W Susx* 14 SU9529
Northchurch *Herts* 38 SP9708
Northcott *Devon* 9 ST0912
Northcott *Devon* 9 ST1109
Northcott *Devon* 5 SX3392
Northcourt *Oxon* 37 SU5098
Northdown *Kent* 29 TR3770
Northedge *Derbys* 74 SK3565
Northend *Bucks* 37 SU7392
Northend *Warwks* 48 SP3852
Northend Woods *Bucks* 26 SU9089
Northenden *Gt Man* 79 SJ8290
Northfield *Gramp* 135 NJ9008
Northfield *Humb* 84 TA0328
Northfield *W Mids* 60 SP0279
Northfields *Lincs* 64 TF0208
Northfleet *Essex* 27 TQ6274
Northiam *E Susx* 17 TQ8324
Northill *Beds* 52 TL1446
Northington *Gloucs* 35 SO7008
Northington *Hants* 24 SU5637
Northlands *Lincs* 77 TF3453
Northleach *Gloucs* 36 SP1114
Northleigh *Devon* 19 SS6034
Northleigh *Devon* 9 SY1995
Northlew *Devon* 19 SX5099
Northload Bridge *Somset* 21 ST4939
Northmoor *Somset* 20 SS9028
Northmoor *Oxon* 36 SP4202
Northmoor Green or Moorla *Somset* 21 ST3332
Northmuir *Tays* 126 NO3854
Northney *Hants* 13 SU7303
Northolt *Gt Lon* 26 TQ1384
Northop *Clwyd* 70 SJ2468
Northop Hall *Clwyd* 70 SJ2667
Northorpe *Lincs* 64 TF2036
Northorpe *Lincs* 76 SK8996
Northorpe *Lincs* 64 TF0917
Northorpe *W York* 82 SE2121
Northover *Somset* 21 ST4838
Northover *Somset* 21 ST5223
Northowram *W York* 82 SE1127
Northport *Dorset* 11 SY9288
Northrepps *Norfk* 67 TG2439
Northton *W Isls* 154 NF9889
Northway *Somset* 20 ST1329
Northway *W Glam* 32 SS5889
Northwich *Ches* 79 SJ6673
Northwick *Avon* 34 ST5686
Northwick *H & W* 47 SO8458
Northwick *Somset* 21 ST3548
Northwold *Norfk* 65 TL7597
Northwood *Derbys* 74 SK2664
Northwood *Gt Lon* 26 TQ0990
Northwood *IOW* 13 SZ4893
Northwood *Shrops* 59 SJ4633
Northwood *Staffs* 72 SJ8948
Northwood End *Beds* 38 TL0941
Northwood Green *Gloucs* 35 SO7216
Norton *Avon* 21 ST3463
Norton *Ches* 78 SJ5582
Norton *Cleve* 96 NZ4421
Norton *Cnwll* 4 SX0869
Norton *E Susx* 16 TQ4601
Norton *Gloucs* 47 SO8524
Norton *Gwent* 34 SO4420
Norton *H & W* 47 SO8751
Norton *H & W* 48 SP0448
Norton *Herts* 39 TL2334
Norton *IOW* 12 SZ3489
Norton *N York* 90 SE7971
Norton *Nhants* 49 SP5963
Norton *Notts* 75 SK5772
Norton *Powys* 46 SO3067
Norton *S York* 83 SE5415
Norton *S York* 74 SK3561
Norton *S York* 74 SK3581
Norton *Shrops* 59 SO4681
Norton *Shrops* 59 SJ5609
Norton *Shrops* 60 SJ7200
Norton *Shrops* 59 SO6482
Norton *Shrops* 59 SO4681
Norton *Suffk* 54 TL9565
Norton *W Glam* 32 SS6188
Norton *W Susx* 14 SU9306
Norton *Wilts* 35 ST8884
Norton Bavant *Wilts* 33 ST9043
Norton Bridge *Staffs* 72 SJ8730
Norton Brook *Staffs* 72 SJ9052
Norton Canes *Staffs* 60 SK0107
Norton Canon *H & W* 46 SO3847
Norton Corner *Norfk* 66 TG0928
Norton Disney *Lincs* 76 SK8859
Norton Ferris *Wilts* 22 ST7936
Norton Fitzwarren *Somset* 20 ST1925
Norton Green *IOW* 12 SZ3388
Norton Green *Staffs* 60 SK0107
Norton Hawkfield *Avon* 21 ST5964
Norton Heath *Essex* 40 TL6004
Norton in Hales *Shrops* 72 SJ7038
Norton in the Moors *Staffs* 72 SJ8951
Norton Lindsey *Warwks* 48 SP2263
Norton Little Green *Suffk* 54 TL9766
Norton Malreward *Avon* 21 ST6065
Norton Mandeville *Essex* 40 TL5804
Norton St. Philip *Somset* 22 ST7755
Norton Subcourse *Norfk* 67 TM4198
Norton sub Hamdon *Somset* 10 ST4615
Norton Wood *H & W* 46 SO3648
Norton-Juxta-Twycross *Leics* 61 SK3207
Norton-le-Clay *N York* 89 SE4071
Norwell *Notts* 75 SK7661
Norwell Woodhouse *Notts* 75 SK7362
Norwich *Norfk* 67 TG2308
Norwick *Shet* 155 HP6514
Norwood *Cent* 116 NS8793
Norwood *Kent* 17 TR0430
Norwood *S York* 75 SK4681
Norwood End *Essex* 40 TL5608
Norwood Green *Gt Lon* 26 TQ1378
Norwood Green *W York* 82 SE1427
Norwood Hill *Surrey* 15 TQ2443
Norwoodside *Cambs* 65 TL4197
Noseley *Leics* 50 SP7398
Noss Mayo *Devon* 6 SX5447
Nosterfield *N York* 89 SE2780
Nosterfield End *Cambs* 53 TL6344
Nostie *Highld* 138 NG8527
Notgrove *Gloucs* 36 SP1020
Nottage *M Glam* 33 SS8278
Notter *M Glam* 5 SX3961
Nottingham *Notts* 62 SK5739
Nottington *Dorset* 11 SY6682
Notton *W York* 83 SE3413
Notton *Wilts* 35 ST9169
Nottswood Hill *Gloucs* 35 SO7018
Nounsley *Essex* 40 TL7910
Noutard's Green *H & W* 47 SO8066
Nox *Shrops* 59 SJ4110
Nuffield *Oxon* 37 SU6687
Nun Monkton *N York* 90 SE5057
Nuncargate *Notts* 75 SK5054
Nunclose *Cumb* 94 NY4945
Nuneaton *Warwks* 61 SP3692
Nuneham Courtenay *Oxon* 37 SU5599
Nunhead *Gt Lon* 27 TQ3475
Nunkeeling *Humb* 85 TA1449
Nunnerie *Strath* 108 NS9612
Nunney *Somset* 22 ST7345
Nunney Catch *Somset* 22 ST7344
Nunnington *H & W* 46 SO5543
Nunnington *N York* 90 SE6679
Nunnykirk *Nthumb* 103 NZ0793
Nuns Moor *T & W* 103 NZ2266
Nunsthorpe *Humb* 85 TA2508
Nunthorpe *N York* 83 SE6050
Nunthorpe Village *Cleve* 90 NZ5313
Nunton *W Isls* 154 NF7653
Nunton *Wilts* 23 SU1525
Nunwick *N York* 89 SE3274
Nunwick *Nthumb* 102 NY8774
Nup End *Bucks* 38 SP8619
Nupdown *Avon* 35 ST6295
Nupend *Gloucs* 35 SO7806
Nuptow *Berks* 25 SU8873
Nursling *Hants* 12 SU3616
Nursted *Hants* 14 SU7621
Nursteed *Wilts* 23 SU0260
Nurton *Staffs* 60 SO8399
Nutbourne *W Susx* 14 SU7705
Nutbourne *W Susx* 14 TQ0718
Nutfield *Surrey* 27 TQ3050
Nuthall *Notts* 62 SK5144
Nuthampstead *Herts* 39 TL4034
Nuthurst *W Susx* 15 TQ1926
Nutley *E Susx* 16 TQ4427
Nutley *Hants* 24 SU6144
Nuttal Lane *Gt Man* 81 SD7915
Nutwell *S York* 83 SE6304
Nybster *Highld* 151 ND3663
Nyetimber *W Susx* 14 SZ8998
Nyewood *W Susx* 14 SU8021
Nymet Rowland *Devon* 19 SS7108
Nymet Tracey *Devon* 8 SS7200
Nympsfield *Gloucs* 35 SO8000
Nynehead *Somset* 20 ST1423
Nyton *W Susx* 14 SU9305

O

Oad Street *Kent* 28 TQ8662
Oadby *Leics* 50 SK6200
Oak Cross *Devon* 8 SX5399
Oakall Green *H & W* 47 SO8161
Oakamoor *Staffs* 73 SK0544
Oakbank *Loth* 117 NT0766
Oakdale *Gwent* 33 ST1898
Oake *Somset* 20 ST1525
Oaken *Staffs* 60 SJ8502
Oakenclough *Lancs* 80 SD5447
Oakengates *Shrops* 60 SJ7010
Oakenholt *Clwyd* 70 SJ2571
Oakenshaw *Dur* 96 NZ1937
Oakenshaw *W York* 82 SE1728
Oaker Side *Derbys* 74 SK2761
Oakerthorpe *Derbys* 74 SK3854
Oakford *Devon* 20 SS9021
Oakford *Dyfed* 42 SN4558
Oakfordbridge *Devon* 20 SS9122
Oakgrove *Ches* 79 SJ9169
Oakham *Leics* 63 SK8608
Oakhanger *Ches* 72 SJ7654
Oakhanger *Hants* 14 SU7635
Oakhill *Somset* 21 ST6347
Oakhurst *Kent* 27 TQ5450
Oakington *Cambs* 52 TL4164
Oaklands *Powys* 45 SO0450
Oakle Street *Gloucs* 35 SO7517
Oakley *Beds* 51 TL0053
Oakley *Bucks* 37 SP6412
Oakley *Dorset* 11 SZ0198
Oakley *Hants* 24 SU5650
Oakley *Oxon* 37 SP7400
Oakley *Suffk* 54 TM1678
Oakley Green *Berks* 26 SU9276
Oakleypark *Powys* 58 SN9886
Oakridge *Gloucs* 35 SO9103
Oaks *Dur* 96 NZ1526
Oaks *Lancs* 81 SD6733
Oaks *Shrops* 59 SJ4204
Oaks Green *Derbys* 73 SK1533
Oaksey *Wilts* 35 ST9893
Oakshaw *Cumb* 101 NY5076
Oakshott *Hants* 13 SU7427
Oakthorpe *Leics* 61 SK3213
Oaktree *Dur* 89 NZ3613
Oakwood *Border* 109 NT4225
Oakwood *Nthumb* 102 NY9465
Oakwoodhill *Surrey* 15 TQ1337
Oakworth *W York* 82 SE0339
Oape *Highld* 146 NC4101
Oare *Kent* 28 TR0063
Oare *Somset* 19 SS8047
Oare *Wilts* 23 SU1563
Oasby *Lincs* 63 TF0039
Oath *Somset* 21 ST3827
Oathlaw *Tays* 127 NO4756
Oatlands Park *Surrey* 26 TQ0865
Oban *Strath* 122 NM8630
Obinan *Highld* 144 NG8796
Obney *Tays* 125 NO0237
Oborne *Dorset* 11 ST6518
Obthorpe *Lincs* 64 TF0915
Occlestone Green *Ches* 72 SJ6962
Occold *Suffk* 54 TM1570
Ochertyre *Tays* 125 NN8323
Ochiltree *Strath* 107 NS5121
Ockbrook *Derbys* 62 SK4235
Ocker Hill *W Mids* 60 SO9793
Ockeridge *H & W* 47 SO7762
Ockham *Surrey* 26 TQ0756
Ockle *Highld* 129 NM5570
Ockley *Surrey* 15 TQ1440
Ocle Pychard *H & W* 46 SO5946
Octon *Humb* 91 TA0369
Odcombe *Somset* 10 ST5015
Odd Down *Avon* 22 ST7462
Oddingley *H & W* 47 SO9159
Oddington *Gloucs* 48 SP2225
Oddington *Oxon* 37 SP5514
Odell *Beds* 51 SP9657
Odham *Devon* 18 SS4703
Odiham *Hants* 24 SU7451
Odsal *W York* 82 SE1529
Odsey *Herts* 39 TL2938
Odstock *Wilts* 23 SU1426
Odstone *Leics* 62 SK3907
Offchurch *Warwks* 48 SP3566
Offenham *H & W* 48 SP0546
Offerton *T & W* 96 NZ3455
Offham *E Susx* 15 TQ4012
Offham *Kent* 28 TQ6557
Offham *W Susx* 14 TQ0208
Offleymarsh *Shrops* 72 SJ7829
Offord Cluny *Cambs* 52 TL2267
Offord Darcy *Cambs* 52 TL2266
Offton *Suffk* 54 TM0649
Offwell *Devon* 9 SY1999
Ogbourne Maizey *Wilts* 36 SU1871
Ogbourne St. Andrew *Wilts* 36 SU1872
Ogbourne St. George *Wilts* 36 SU2074
Ogden *W York* 82 SE0730
Ogle *Nthumb* 103 NZ1378
Oglet *Mersyd* 78 SJ4481
Ogmore *M Glam* 33 SS8876
Ogmore Vale *M Glam* 33 SS9390
Ogmore-by-Sea *M Glam* 33 SS8675
Ogwen Bank *Gwynd* 69 SH6265
Ohelmick *Shrops* 59 SO4791
Okeford Fitzpaine *Dorset* 11 ST8010
Okehampton *Devon* 8 SX5895
Okehampton Camp *Devon* 8 SX5893
Olchard *Devon* 9 SX8776
Old *Nhants* 50 SP7873
Old Aberdeen *Gramp* 135 NJ9407
Old Alresford *Hants* 24 SU5834
Old Auchenbrack *D & G* 107 NX7597
Old Basford *Notts* 62 SK5543
Old Basing *Hants* 24 SU6652
Old Bewick *Nthumb* 111 NU0621
Old Bolingbroke *Lincs* 77 TF3564
Old Bracknell *Berks* 25 SU8668
Old Bramhope *W York* 82 SE2343
Old Brampton *Derbys* 74 SK3371
Old Bridge of Tilt *Tays* 132 NN8866
Old Bridge of Urr *D & G* 100 NX7767
Old Buckenham *Norfk* 66 TM0691
Old Burghclere *Hants* 24 SU4657
Old Byland *N York* 90 SE5485
Old Cassop *Dur* 96 NZ3339
Old Castle *M Glam* 33 SS9079
Old Church Stoke *Powys* 58 SO2894
Old Clee *Humb* 85 TA2808
Old Cleeve *Somset* 20 ST0342
Old Colwyn *Clwyd* 69 SH8678
Old Dailly *Strath* 106 NX2299
Old Dalby *Leics* 63 SK6723
Old Dam *Derbys* 74 SK1179
Old Deer *Gramp* 143 NJ9747
Old Ditch *Somset* 21 ST5049
Old Edington *S York* 75 SK5397
Old Eldon *Dur* 96 NZ2427
Old Ellerby *Humb* 85 TA1637
Old Felixstowe *Suffk* 55 TM3136
Old Fletton *Cambs* 64 TL1997
Old Forge *H & W* 34 SO5518
Old Furnace *H & W* 46 SO4923
Old Glossop *Derbys* 74 SK0494
Old Goole *Humb* 84 SE7422
Old Grimsby *IOS* 2 SV8915
Old Hall Green *Herts* 39 TL3622
Old Hall Street *Norfk* 67 TG3033
Old Harlow *Essex* 39 TL4711
Old Heath *Essex* 41 TM0122
Old Hunstanton *Norfk* 65 TF6842
Old Hutton *Cumb* 87 SD5688
Old Kea *Cnwll* 3 SW8441
Old Kilpatrick *Strath* 115 NS4673
Old Knebworth *Herts* 39 TL2320
Old Lakenham *Norfk* 67 TG2206
Old Langho *Lancs* 81 SD7035
Old Leake *Lincs* 77 TF4050
Old Malton *N York* 90 SE7972
Old Micklefield *W York* 83 SE4432
Old Milton *Hants* 12 SZ2494
Old Milverton *Warwks* 48 SP2967
Old Newton *Suffk* 54 TM0662
Old Quarrington *Dur* 96 NZ3237
Old Radford *Notts* 62 SK5540
Old Radnor *Powys* 46 SO2559
Old Ratray *Gramp* 143 NK0857
Old Rayne *Gramp* 142 NJ6728
Old Romney *Kent* 17 TR0325
Old Scone *Tays* 126 NO1226
Old Shoreham *W Susx* 15 TQ2006
Old Shoremore *Highld* 148 NC2059
Old Soar *Kent* 27 TQ6154
Old Sodbury *Avon* 35 ST7581
Old Somerby *Lincs* 63 SK9633
Old Stratford *Nhants* 49 SP7741
Old Sunnford *W Mids* 60 SO9083
Old Tebay *Cumb* 87 NY6105
Old Thirsk *N York* 89 SE4382
Old Town *Cumb* 93 NY4743
Old Town *Cumb* 87 SD5983
Old Town *E Susx* 16 TV5999
Old Town *IOS* 2 SV9110
Old Town *Nthumb* 102 NY8891
Old Town *W York* 82 SE0028
Old Trafford *Gt Man* 79 SJ8196
Old Tupton *Derbys* 74 SK3865
Old Warden *Beds* 38 TL1343
Old Weston *Cambs* 51 TL0977
Old Wick *Highld* 151 ND3649
Old Windsor *Berks* 25 SU9874
Old Wives Lees *Kent* 29 TR0754
Old Woking *Surrey* 26 TQ0156
Old Wolverton *Bucks* 38 SP8041
Oldany *Highld* 148 NC0932
Oldberrow *Warwks* 48 SP1266
Oldborough *Devon* 8 SS7706
Oldburry *Kent* 27 TQ5956
Oldbury *Shrops* 60 SO7192
Oldbury *W Mids* 60 SO9889
Oldbury *Warwks* 61 SP3194
Oldbury Naite *Avon* 35 ST6293
Oldbury on the Hill *Gloucs* 35 ST8287
Oldbury-on-Severn *Avon* 34 ST6092
Oldcastle *Gwent* 46 SO3224
Oldcastle Heath *Ches* 71 SJ4745
Oldcotes *Notts* 75 SK5888
Oldfield *H & W* 47 SO8465
Oldfield *W York* 82 SE0037
Oldford *Somset* 22 ST7849
Oldhall Green *Suffk* 54 TL8956
Oldham *Gt Man* 81 SD9215
Oldham *Gt Man* 79 SD9204
Oldhamstocks *Loth* 119 NT7470
Oldhurst *Cambs* 52 TL3077
Oldland *Avon* 35 ST6771
Oldley *Shrops* 46 SO3378
Oldmeldrum *Gramp* 143 NJ8027
Oldmill *Cnwll* 5 SX3774
Oldmixon *Avon* 21 ST3358
Oldridge *Devon* 8 SX8295
Oldstead *N York* 90 SE5279
Oldwall *Cumb* 101 NY4761
Oldwalls *W Glam* 32 SS4891
Oldways End *Devon* 19 SS8624
Oldwhat *Gramp* 143 NJ8661
Oldwoods *Shrops* 59 SJ4520
Olive Green *Staffs* 73 SK1118
Oliver *Border* 108 NT0924
Oliver's Battery *Hants* 13 SU4527
Ollaberry *Shet* 155 HU3680
Ollach *Highld* 137 NG5137
Ollerton *Ches* 79 SJ7776
Ollerton *Notts* 75 SK6567
Ollerton *Shrops* 72 SJ6425
Olmarch *Dyfed* 44 SN6255
Olmstead Green *Cambs* 53 TL6341
Olney *Bucks* 38 SP8851
Olney *Nhants* 49 SP6643
Olrig House *Highld* 151 ND1866
Olton *W Mids* 61 SP1382
Olveston *Avon* 34 ST6087
Ombersley *H & W* 47 SO8463
Ompton *Notts* 75 SK6865
Onchan *IOM* 153 SC4078
One House *Suffk* 54 TM0159
Onecote *Staffs* 73 SK0455
Onen *Gwent* 34 SO4314
Ongar Street *H & W* 46 SO3967
Onibury *Shrops* 46 SO4579
Onich *Highld* 130 NN0261
Onllwyn *W Glam* 33 SN8410
Onneley *Staffs* 72 SJ7543
Onslow Village *Surrey* 25 SU9849
Onston *Ches* 71 SJ5973
Openwoodgate *Derbys* 62 SK3647
Opinan *Highld* 137 NG7472
Orbliston *Gramp* 141 NJ3057
Orbost *Highld* 136 NG2543
Orby *Lincs* 77 TF4967
Orchard Portman *Somset* 20 ST2421
Orcheston *Wilts* 23 SU0545
Orcop *H & W* 46 SO4726
Orcop Hill *H & W* 46 SO4828
Ord *Gramp* 142 NJ6259
Ord *Highld* 129 NG6113
Ordhead *Gramp* 135 NJ6610
Ordie *Gramp* 134 NJ4501
Ordiequish *Gramp* 141 NJ3356
Ordley *Nthumb* 95 NY9559
Ordsall *Notts* 75 SK7079
Ore *E Susx* 17 TQ8311
Oreleton Common *H & W* 46 SO4768
Oreton *Shrops* 59 SO6581
Orford *Ches* 78 SJ6190
Orford *Suffk* 55 TM4250
Organford *Dorset* 11 SY9392
Orgreave *Staffs* 73 SK1415
Orlestone *Kent* 17 TR0034
Orleton *H & W* 46 SO4967
Orleton *H & W* 47 SO7067
Orlingbury *Nhants* 51 SP8572
Ormathwaite *Cumb* 93 NY2625
Ormesby *Cleve* 97 NZ5317
Ormesby St. Margaret *Norfk* 67 TG4914
Ormesby St. Michael *Norfk* 67 TG4814
Ormidale *Strath* 114 NS0081
Ormiscaig *Highld* 144 NG8590
Ormiston *Loth* 118 NT4269
Ormsaigmore *Highld* 121 NM4763
Ormsary *Strath* 113 NR7472
Ormskirk *Lancs* 78 SD4108
Ornsby Hill *Dur* 96 NZ1648
Oronsay *Strath* 112 NR3588
Orosay *W Isls* 154 NB3612
Orphir *Ork* 155 HY3405
Orpington *Gt Lon* 27 TQ4666
Orrell *Gt Man* 78 SD5303
Orrell *Mersyd* 78 SJ3496
Orrell Post *Gt Man* 78 SD5305
Orrisdale *IOM* 153 SC3293
Orrisdale Head *IOM* 153 SC3192
Orroland *D & G* 92 NX7746
Orsett *Essex* 40 TQ6482
Orslow *Staffs* 72 SJ8015
Orston *Notts* 63 SK7740
Orthwaite *Cumb* 93 NY2534
Orton *Cumb* 87 NY6208
Orton *Nhants* 51 SP8079
Orton *Staffs* 60 SO8795
Orton Longueville *Cambs* 64 TL1696
Orton Rigg *Cumb* 93 NY3352
Orton Waterville *Cambs* 64 TL1596
Orton-on-the-Hill *Leics* 61 SK3003
Orwell *Cambs* 52 TL3650
Osbaldeston *Lancs* 81 SD6431
Osbaldeston Green *Lancs* 81 SD6432
Osbaldwick *N York* 83 SE6251
Osbaston *Leics* 62 SK4204
Osbaston *Shrops* 59 SJ3222
Osborne *IOW* 13 SZ5194
Osbournby *Lincs* 64 TF0638
Oscroft *Ches* 71 SJ5067
Osgathorpe *Leics* 62 SK4219
Osgodby *Lincs* 76 TF0792
Osgodby *N York* 83 SE6433
Osgodby *N York* 91 TA0584
Oskaig *Highld* 137 NG5438
Oskamull *Strath* 121 NM4540
Osmaston *Derbys* 73 SK1943
Osmington *Dorset* 11 SY7282
Osmington Mills *Dorset* 11 SY7381
Osmondthorpe *W York* 83 SE3333
Osmotherley *N York* 89 SE4596
Osney *Oxon* 37 SP5006
Ospringe *Kent* 28 TR0060
Ossett *W York* 82 SE2720
Ossington *Notts* 75 SK7564
Ostend *Essex* 40 TQ9397
Oswaldkirk *N York* 90 SE6278
Oswaldtwistle *Lancs* 81 SD7327
Oswestry *Shrops* 58 SJ2829
Otford *Kent* 27 TQ5359
Otham *Kent* 28 TQ7954
Otham Hole *Kent* 28 TQ7952
Othery *Somset* 21 ST3831
Otley *Suffk* 55 TM2055
Otley *W York* 82 SE2045
Otley Green *Suffk* 55 TM2156
Otter Ferry *Strath* 114 NR9384
Otterbourne *Hants* 13 SU4523
Otterburn *N York* 88 SD8857
Otterburn *Nthumb* 102 NY8893
Otterham *Cnwll* 4 SX1690
Otterham Quay *Kent* 28 TQ8366

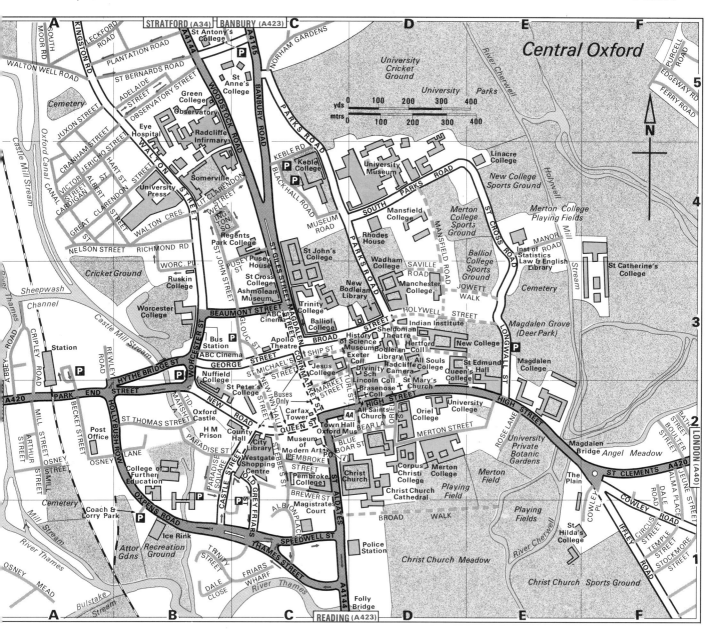

Central Oxford

P

Paignton Peterstone Wentlooge

Paignton *Devon* 7 SX8960
Pailton *Warwks* 50 SP4781
Paincastle *Powys* 45 SO1646
Paine's Cross *E Susx* 16 TQ6223
Painleyhill *Staffs* 73 SK0333
Painshawfield *Nthumb* 103 NZ0560
Painsthorpe *Humb* 90 SE8158
Painswick *Gloucs* 35 SO8609
Painter's Forstal *Kent* 28 TQ9958
Paisley *Strath* 115 NS4864
Pakefield *Suffk* 55 TM5390
Pakenham *Suffk* 54 TL9267
Pale *Gwynd* 58 SH9836
Pale Green *Essex* 53 TL6542
Palestine *Hants* 23 SU2640
Palestine *Hants* 23 SU2640
Paley Street *Berks* 26 SU8770
Palfrey *W Mids* 60 SP0197
Palgrave *Suffk* 54 TM1178
Pallington *Dorset* 11 SY7891
Palmers Green *Gt Lon* 27 TQ3193
Palmersbridge *Cnwll* 5 SX1977
Palmerston *Strath* 107 NS5019
Palmerstown *S Glam* 20 ST1369
Palnackie *D & G* 92 NX8257
Palnure *D & G* 99 NX4563
Palterton *Derbys* 75 SK4768
Pamber End *Hants* 24 SU6158
Pamber Green *Hants* 24 SU6059
Pamber Heath *Hants* 24 SU6162
Pamington *Gloucs* 47 SO9333
Pamphill *Dorset* 11 ST9900
Pampisford *Cambs* 53 TL4948
Panborough *Somset* 21 ST4745
Panbride *Tays* 127 NO5635
Pancrasweek *Devon* 18 SS2905
Pancross *S Glam* 20 ST0469
Pandy *Clwyd* 58 SJ1935
Pandy *Gwent* 34 SO3322
Pandy *Gwynd* 57 SH8729
Pandy *Gwynd* 57 SH6203
Pandy *M Glam* 33 ST1587
Pandy *Powys* 58 SH9004
Pandy Tudur *Clwyd* 69 SH8564
Pandy'r Capel *Clwyd* 70 SJ0850
Panfield *Essex* 40 TL7425
Pangbourne *Berks* 37 SU6376
Pangdean *W Susx* 15 TQ2911
Panks Bridge *H & W* 47 SO6248
Pannal *N York* 82 SE3051
Pannal Ash *N York* 82 SE2853
Pannanich Wells Hotel *Gramp* 134 NO4097
Pant *Shrops* 58 SJ2722
Pant Mawr *Powys* 43 SN8482
Pant-Gwyn *Dyfed* 44 SN5925
Pant-glas *Gwynd* 68 SH4747
Pant-pastynog *Clwyd* 70 SJ0461
Pant-y-dwr *Powys* 45 SN9874
Pant-y-ffridd *Powys* 58 SJ1502
Pant-y-gog *M Glam* 33 SS9090
Pant-y-mwyn *Clwyd* 70 SJ1964
Pant-yr-awel *M Glam* 33 SS9287
Pantasaph *Clwyd* 70 SJ1675
Pantersbridge *Cnwll* 4 SX1667
Pantglas *Powys* 43 SN7797
Panton *Lincs* 76 TF1778
Pantperthog *Gwynd* 57 SH7404
Pantside *Gwent* 34 ST2297
Pantyffynnon *Dyfed* 32 SN6210
Pantygasseg *Gwent* 34 ST2599
Pantygasseg *Gwent* 34 SO2501
Pantymenyn *Dyfed* 31 SN1426
Panxworth *Norfk* 67 TG3513
Papcastle *Cumb* 92 NY1131
Papigoe *Highld* 151 ND3851
Papple *Loth* 118 NT5972
Papplewick *Notts* 75 SK5451
Papworth Everard *Cambs* 52 TL2862
Papworth St. Agnes *Cambs* 52 TL2664
Par *Cnwll* 3 SX0753
Paramour Street *Kent* 27 TQ2861
Paramour Street *Kent* 27 TQ2858
Parbold *Lancs* 80 SD4911
Parbrook *Somset* 21 ST5736
Parbrook *W Susx* 14 TQ0824
Parc *Gwynd* 57 SH8834
Parc Seymour *Gwent* 34 ST4091
Parcllyn *Dyfed* 42 SN2451
Pardshaw *Cumb* 92 NY0925
Parham *Suffk* 55 TM3060
Park *D & G* 100 NX9091
Park *Gramp* 135 NO7898
Park *Nthumb* 102 NY6861
Park Bottom *Cnwll* 2 SW6642
Park Bridge *Gt Man* 79 SD9402
Park Corner *Berks* 26 SU8583
Park Corner *E Susx* 16 TQ5336
Park Corner *Oxon* 37 SU6988
Park End *Beds* 51 SP9853
Park End *Nthumb* 102 NY8675
Park End *Staffs* 72 SJ7851
Park Gate *H & W* 60 SO9371
Park Gate *Hants* 13 SU5108
Park Gate *W York* 82 SE1841
Park Green *Essex* 39 TL4628
Park Green *Suffk* 54 TM1364
Park Head *Derbys* 74 SK3654
Park Head *W York* 82 SE1907
Park Hill *Gloucs* 34 ST5699
Park Royal *Gt Lon* 26 TQ2082
Park Street *W Susx* 14 TQ1131
Parkend *Gloucs* 34 SO6108
Parkers Green *Kent* 16 TQ6138
Parkeston *Essex* 41 TM2332
Parkfield *Bucks* 37 SP8002
Parkfield *M Glam* 6 SX5267
Parkgate *Ches* 70 SJ2878
Parkgate *Ches* 79 SJ7873
Parkgate *Cumb* 93 NY2146
Parkgate *D & G* 100 NY0288
Parkgate *E Susx* 17 TQ7214
Parkgate *Essex* 40 TL6829
Parkgate *Kent* 27 TQ5064
Parkgate *Kent* 17 TQ8534
Parkgate *Surrey* 15 TQ2043
Parkhall *Strath* 115 NS4871
Parkham *Devon* 18 SS3821
Parkham Ash *Devon* 18 SS3620
Parkhead *Cumb* 94 NY5841
Parkhill *Notts* 75 SK6952
Parkhill House *Gramp* 143 NJ8914
Parkhouse *Gwent* 34 SO5002
Parkmill *W Glam* 32 SS5489
Parkside *Clwyd* 71 SJ3855
Parkside *Dur* 96 NZ4148
Parkstone *Dorset* 12 SZ0491
Parley Green *Dorset* 12 SZ1097
Parlington *W York* 83 SE4235
Parmoor *Bucks* 37 SU7989
Parndon *Essex* 39 TL4308
Parr Bridge *Gt Man* 79 SD7001
Parracombe *Devon* 19 SS6645
Parrah Green *Ches* 72 SJ7145
Parrog *Dyfed* 30 SN0439
Parson Drove *Cambs* 64 TF3708
Parson's Cross *S York* 74 SK3491
Parson's Heath *Essex* 41 TM0226
Parson's Hill *Derbys* 73 SK2926
Parsonby *Cumb* 92 NY1438
Partick *Strath* 115 NS5567
Partington *Gt Man* 79 SJ7191
Partney *Lincs* 77 TF4168
Parton *Cumb* 93 NY2715
Parton *Cumb* 92 NX9720
Parton *D & G* 99 NX6970
Partridge Green *W Susx* 15 TQ1919
Partrishaw *Powys* 34 SO2722
Parwich *Derbys* 73 SK1854
Paslow Wood Common *Essex* 27 TL5802
Passenham *Nhants* 38 SP7839
Passfield *Hants* 14 SU8234
Passingford Bridge *Essex* 27 TQ5098
Paston *Cambs* 64 TF1802
Paston *Norfk* 67 TG3234
Pasturefields *Staffs* 73 SJ9925
Patchacott *Devon* 5 SX4798
Patcham *E Susx* 15 TQ3009
Patchetts Green *Herts* 26 TQ1497
Patching *W Susx* 14 TQ0806
Patchole *Devon* 19 SS6142
Patchway *Avon* 34 ST6081
Pateley Bridge *N York* 89 SE1565
Paternoster Heath *Essex* 40 TL9115
Pateshall *H & W* 46 SO5262
Path of Condie *Tays* 125 NO0711
Pathe *Somset* 21 ST3730
Pathhead *Gramp* 135 NO7263
Pathhead *Gramp* 135 NO7263
Pathhead *Loth* 118 NT3964
Pathhead *Strath* 107 NS6114
Pathlow *Warwks* 48 SP1758
Patmore Heath *Herts* 39 TL4425
Patna *Strath* 106 NS4110
Patney *Wilts* 23 SU0758
Patrick *IOM* 153 SC2482
Patrick Brompton *N York* 89 SE2290
Patricroft *Gt Man* 79 SJ7597
Patrington *Humb* 85 TA3122
Patrixbourne *Kent* 29 TR1855
Patterdale *Cumb* 93 NY3915
Pattingham *Staffs* 60 SO8299
Pattishall *Nhants* 49 SP6754
Pattiswick Green *Essex* 40 TL8224
Patton *Shrops* 59 SO5895
Paul *Cnwll* 2 SW4627
Paul's Dene *Wilts* 23 SU1432
Paulerspury *Bucks* 49 SP7144
Paull *Humb* 85 TA1626
Paulton *Avon* 21 ST6456
Pauperhaugh *Nthumb* 103 NZ1099
Pave Lane *Shrops* 72 SJ7516
Pavenham *Beds* 51 SP9955
Pawlett *Somset* 20 ST2942
Pawston *Nthumb* 110 NT8532
Paxford *Gloucs* 48 SP1837
Paxton *Border* 119 NT9353
Payden Street *Kent* 28 TQ9253
Payhembury *Devon* 9 ST0801
Paythorne *Lancs* 81 SD8251
Paytoe *H & W* 46 SO4171
Peacehaven *E Susx* 15 TQ4101
Peak Dale *Derbys* 74 SK0976
Peak Forest *Derbys* 74 SK1179
Peak Hill *Lincs* 64 TF2614
Peakirk *Cambs* 64 TF1606
Pean *Kent* 29 TR1837
Peanmeanach *Highld* 129 NM7180
Pearsie *Tays* 134 NO3659
Pearson's Green *Kent* 28 TQ6943
Pease Pottage *W Susx* 15 TQ2633
Peasedown St. John *Avon* 22 ST7057
Peasehill *Derbys* 74 SK4049
Peaseland *Norfk* 66 TG0516
Peasemore *Berks* 37 SU4576
Peasenhall *Suffk* 55 TM3569
Peaslake *Surrey* 14 TQ0844
Peasley Cross *Mersyd* 78 SJ5294
Peasmarsh *E Susx* 17 TQ8822
Peasmarsh *Somset* 10 ST3313
Peasmarsh *Surrey* 25 SU9946
Peat Inn *Fife* 127 NO4509
Peathill *Gramp* 143 NJ9365
Peatling Magna *Leics* 50 SP5992
Peatling Parva *Leics* 50 SP5989
Peaton *Shrops* 59 SO5385
Pebmarsh *Essex* 40 TL8533
Pebworth *H & W* 48 SP1347
Pecket Well *W York* 82 SD9929
Peckforton *Ches* 71 SJ5356
Peckham *Gt Lon* 27 TQ3476
Peckleton *Leics* 62 SK4701
Pedair-ffordd *Powys* 58 SJ1124
Pedlinge *Kent* 17 TR1335
Pedmore *W Mids* 60 SO9182
Pedwell *Somset* 21 ST4236
Peebles *Border* 109 NT2540
Peel *IOM* 153 SC2484
Peel *Lancs* 80 SD3531
Peel Common *Hants* 13 SU5804
Peening Quarter *Kent* 17 TQ8828
Pegsdon *Beds* 38 TL1130
Pegswood *Nthumb* 103 NZ2287
Pegwell *Kent* 29 TR3664
Peinchorran *Highld* 137 NG5233
Peinlich *Highld* 136 NG4158
Pelaw *T & W* 96 NZ2962
Pelcomb *Dyfed* 30 SM9218
Pelcomb Bridge *Dyfed* 30 SM9317
Peldon *Essex* 41 TL9817
Pell Green *E Susx* 28 TQ6736
Pelsall *W Mids* 60 SK0103
Pelsall Wood *W Mids* 60 SK0103
Pelton *Dur* 96 NZ2553
Pelton Fell *Dur* 96 NZ2552
Pelutho *Cumb* 92 NY1249
Pelynt *Cnwll* 5 SX2055
Pemberton *Devon* 8 SS5300
Pemberton *Dyfed* 32 SN5300
Pemberton *Gt Man* 78 SD5503
Pembles Cross *Kent* 28 TQ8847
Pembrey *Dyfed* 31 SN4201
Pembridge *H & W* 46 SO3958
Pembroke *Dyfed* 30 SM9901
Pembroke Dock *Dyfed* 30 SM9603
Pembury *Kent* 16 TQ6240
Pen Rhiwfawr *W Glam* 32 SN7410
Pen-bont Rhydybeddau *Dyfed* 43 SN6783
Pen-ffordd *Dyfed* 31 SN0722
Pen-groes-oped *Gwent* 34 SO3107
Pen-llyn *Gwynd* 68 SH3482
Pen-lon *Gwynd* 68 SH4364
Pen-Sarn *Gwynd* 56 SH4344
Pen-Sarn *Gwynd* 57 SH5728
Pen-twyn *Gwent* 33 SO2000
Pen-twyn *Gwent* 34 SO2603
Pen-twyn *Gwent* 34 SO5209
Pen-Yr-Heolgerrig *Gwent* 34 SO3006
Pen-y-bont *Clwyd* 58 SJ2123
Pen-y-bryn *Dyfed* 31 SN1743
Pen-y-bryn *M Glam* 33 SS8384
Pen-y-cae *Powys* 33 SN8413
Pen-y-cae-mawr *Gwent* 34 ST4095
Pen-y-cefn *Clwyd* 70 SJ1175
Pen-y-clawdd *Gwent* 34 SO4507
Pen-y-coedcae *M Glam* 33 ST0687
Pen-y-cwn *Dyfed* 30 SM8423
Pen-y-darren *M Glam* 33 SO0506
Pen-y-fai *M Glam* 33 SS8981
Pen-y-felin *Clwyd* 70 SJ1569
Pen-y-Gwryd Hotel *Gwynd* 69 SH6555
Pen-y-garn *Dyfed* 43 SN6285
Pen-y-genffordd *Powys* 45 SO1730
Pen-y-graig *Gwynd* 56 SH1933
Pen-y-lan *S Glam* 33 SS9976
Pen-y-pass *Gwynd* 69 SH6455
Pen-y-stryt *Clwyd* 70 SJ1952
Pen-y-stryt *Clwyd* 70 SJ2052
Pen-yr-Heol *Gwent* 34 SO4311
Pen-yr-Heolgerrig *M Glam* 33 SO0306
Penair *Cnwll* 3 SW8445
Penallt *Gwent* 34 SO5210
Penally *Dyfed* 31 SS1199
Penalt *H & W* 46 SO5629
Penare *Cnwll* 3 SW9940
Penarth *S Glam* 33 ST1872
Penbryn *Dyfed* 42 SN2952
Pencader *Dyfed* 31 SN4436
Pencaitland *Loth* 118 NT4468
Pencalenick *Cnwll* 3 SW8545
Pencarnisiog *Gwynd* 68 SH3573
Pencarreg *Dyfed* 44 SN5345
Pencarrow *Cnwll* 4 SX1082
Pencelli *Powys* 45 SO0925
Penclawdd *W Glam* 32 SS5495
Pencoed *M Glam* 33 SS9681
Pencombe *H & W* 46 SO5952
Pencoyd *H & W* 46 SO5126
Pencraig *H & W* 34 SO5620
Pencraig *Powys* 58 SJ0426
Pendeen *Cnwll* 2 SW3834
Penderyn *M Glam* 33 SN9408
Pendine *Dyfed* 31 SN2308
Pendlebury *Gt Man* 79 SD7802
Pendleton *Lancs* 81 SD7539
Pendock *H & W* 47 SO7832
Pendoggett *Cnwll* 4 SX0279
Pendomer *Somset* 10 ST5210
Pendoylan *S Glam* 33 ST0576
Pendre *M Glam* 33 SS9181
Penegoes *Powys* 57 SH7701
Penelewey *Cnwll* 3 SW8140
Pengam *Gwent* 33 ST1597
Pengam *S Glam* 33 ST2178
Penge *Gt Lon* 27 TQ3570
Pengelly *Cnwll* 3 SW8551
Pengelly *Cnwll* 4 SX0783
Pengorffwysfa *Gwynd* 68 SH4692
Pengover Green *Cnwll* 5 SX2865
Pengrugla *Cnwll* 3 SW9947
Pengwern *Clwyd* 70 SJ0176
Penhale *Cnwll* 2 SW6918
Penhale *Cnwll* 4 SW9257
Penhale *Cnwll* 4 SX0860
Penhale *M Glam* 5 SX4153
Penhallow *Cnwll* 3 SW7651
Penhalurick *Cnwll* 2 SW7038
Penhalvean *Cnwll* 2 SW7037
Penhill *Wilts* 36 SU1588
Penhow *Gwent* 34 ST4290
Penhurst *E Susx* 16 TQ6916
Peniarth *Gwynd* 57 SH6105
Penifiler *Highld* 136 NG4841
Peninver *Strath* 105 NR7524
Penisar Waun *Gwynd* 69 SH5564
Penistone *S York* 82 SE2402
Penjerrick *Cnwll* 3 SW7730
Penkelly *Cnwll* 4 SX1854
Penketh *Ches* 78 SJ5587
Penkill *Strath* 106 NX2398
Penkridge *Staffs* 60 SJ9214
Penlean *Cnwll* 5 SX2098
Penley *Clwyd* 71 SJ4040
Penllergaer *W Glam* 32 SS6198
Penllyn *S Glam* 33 SS9776
Penmachno *Gwynd* 69 SH7950
Penmaen *Gwent* 33 ST1897
Penmaen *W Glam* 32 SS5388
Penmaenan *Gwynd* 69 SH7175
Penmaenmawr *Gwynd* 69 SH7176
Penmaenmawr *Gwynd* 69 SH7176
Penmaenpool *Gwynd* 57 SH6918
Penmark *S Glam* 20 ST0568
Penmon *Gwynd* 69 SH6381
Penmorfa *Gwynd* 57 SH5440
Penmynydd *Gwynd* 68 SH5174
Penn *Bucks* 26 SU9193
Penn Green *Notts* 75 SK5375
Penn Street *Bucks* 26 SU9295
Pennal *Gwynd* 57 SH6900
Pennan *Gramp* 143 NJ8465
Pennant *Clwyd* 58 SJ0234
Pennant *Powys* 43 SN8897
Pennant-Melangell *Powys* 58 SJ0226
Pennard *W Glam* 32 SS5688
Pennerley *Shrops* 59 SO3599
Pennicott *Devon* 9 SS8701
Pennington *Cumb* 86 SD2677
Pennington *Hants* 12 SZ3194
Pennington Green *Gt Man* 79 SD6206
Pennorth *Powys* 45 SO1125
Pennsylvania *Avon* 35 ST7473
Penny Bridge *Cumb* 86 SD3183
Penny Hill *Lincs* 64 TF3626
Pennycross *Strath* 121 NM5025
Pennygate *Norfk* 67 TG3423
Pennyghael *Strath* 121 NM5125
Pennyglen *Strath* 106 NS2710
Pennygown *Strath* 121 NM6042
Pennymoor *Devon* 19 SS8611
Penparc *Dyfed* 42 SN2148
Penparcau *Dyfed* 43 SN5980
Penpedairheol *Gwent* 34 SO3303
Penpedairheol *M Glam* 33 ST1497
Penperlleni *Gwent* 34 SO3204
Penpethy *Cnwll* 4 SX0886
Penpillick *Cnwll* 3 SX0756
Penpol *Cnwll* 3 SW8139
Penpoll *Cnwll* 3 SX1454
Penponds *Cnwll* 2 SW6339
Penpont *D & G* 100 NX8494
Penpont *Powys* 45 SN9728
Penquit *Devon* 7 SX6454
Penrest *M Glam* 5 SX3378
Penrherber *Dyfed* 31 SN2839
Penrhiw *Dyfed* 31 SN2440
Penrhiwceiber *M Glam* 33 ST0597
Penrhiwllan *Dyfed* 31 SN3742
Penrhiwpal *Dyfed* 42 SN3445
Penrhos *Gwent* 34 SO4111
Penrhos *Gwynd* 68 SH2781
Penrhos *Gwynd* 56 SH3433
Penrhos *Powys* 32 SN8011
Penrhos garnedd *Gwynd* 69 SH5670
Penrhyn Bay *Gwynd* 69 SH8281
Penrhyn-side *Gwynd* 69 SH8181
Penrhyncoch *Dyfed* 43 SN6384
Penrhyndeudraeth *Gwynd* 57 SH6138
Penrice *W Glam* 32 SS4987
Penrioch *Strath* 105 NR8744
Penrith *Cumb* 94 NY5130
Penrose *Cnwll* 5 SX2589
Penrose *Cnwll* 4 SW8770
Penruddock *Cumb* 93 NY4227
Penryn *Cnwll* 3 SW7834
Pensarn *Clwyd* 70 SH9478
Pensarn *Dyfed* 31 SN4119
Pensax *H & W* 47 SO7269
Pensby *Mersyd* 78 SJ2782
Penselwood *Somset* 22 ST7531
Pensford *Avon* 21 ST6263
Pensham *H & W* 47 SO9444
Penshaw *T & W* 96 NZ3354
Penshurst *Kent* 16 TQ5243
Penshurst Station *Kent* 16 TQ5246
Pensilva *Cnwll* 5 SX2969
Pensnett *W Mids* 60 SO9189
Pensont *Cnwll* 4 SX0874
Penstone *Devon* 8 SS7700
Penstrowed *Powys* 58 SO0691
Pentewan *Cnwll* 3 SX0147
Pentir *Gwynd* 69 SH5767
Pentire *Cnwll* 4 SW7961
Pentlepoir *Dyfed* 31 SN1105
Pentlow *Essex* 54 TL8146
Pentlow Street *Essex* 54 TL8245
Pentney *Norfk* 65 TF7214
Penton Grafton *Hants* 23 SU3247
Penton Mewsey *Hants* 23 SU3347
Pentraeth *Gwynd* 68 SH5278
Pentre *Clwyd* 71 SJ3267
Pentre *Clwyd* 70 SJ0862
Pentre *Clwyd* 70 SJ2840
Pentre *Gwent* 34 SO3106
Pentre *M Glam* 33 SS9796
Pentre *Powys* 58 SO1589
Pentre *Powys* 58 SO0686
Pentre *Shrops* 59 SJ3617
Pentre Bach *Clwyd* 70 SJ2176
Pentre Berw *Gwynd* 68 SH4772
Pentre bach *Dyfed* 44 SN5547
Pentre chwyth *W Glam* 32 SS6795
Pentre Ffwrndan *Clwyd* 70 SJ2572
Pentre Halkyn *Clwyd* 70 SJ2072
Pentre Hodrey *Shrops* 46 SO3277
Pentre Isaf *Clwyd* 70 SH9871
Pentre Llifior *Powys* 58 SO1598
Pentre Meyrick *S Glam* 33 SS9675
Pentre ty gwyn *Dyfed* 44 SN8135
Pentre'r Felin *Gwynd* 69 SH8069
Pentre'r-felin *Powys* 45 SN9230
Pentre-bach *Powys* 45 SN9133
Pentre-bont *Gwynd* 69 SH7351
Pentre-Cagal *Dyfed* 31 SN3440
Pentre-cagel *Dyfed* 31 SN3340
Pentre-celyn *Clwyd* 70 SJ1453
Pentre-celyn *Powys* 57 SH8905
Pentre-clawdd *Shrops* 59 SJ2931
Pentre-cwrt *Dyfed* 31 SN3838
Pentre-Dolau-Honddu *Powys* 45 SN9943
Pentre-dwr *W Glam* 32 SS6995
Pentre-Gwenlais *Dyfed* 32 SN6116
Pentre-llwyn-llwyd *Powys* 45 SN9654
Pentre-llyn *Dyfed* 43 SN6174
Pentre-llyn-cymmer *Clwyd* 70 SH9752
Pentre-Maw *Powys* 57 SH8903
Pentre-piod *Gwent* 33 SO2602
Pentre-poeth *Gwent* 34 ST2687
Pentre-tafarn-y-fedw *Gwynd* 69 SH8162
Pentrebach *M Glam* 33 SO0604
Pentrebeirdd *Powys* 58 SJ1913
Pentredwr *Clwyd* 70 SJ1946
Pentrefelin *Gwynd* 68 SH4392
Pentrefelin *Gwynd* 57 SH5239
Pentrefoelas *Clwyd* 69 SH8751
Pentregalar *Dyfed* 31 SN1831
Pentregat *Dyfed* 42 SN3551
Pentrich *Derbys* 74 SK3852
Pentridge Hill *Dorset* 12 SU0317
Pentyrch *M Glam* 33 ST1081
Penwithick *Cnwll* 3 SX0256
Penwyllt *Powys* 33 SN8515
Penybanc *Dyfed* 44 SN6124
Penybont *Powys* 45 SO1164
Penybontfawr *Powys* 58 SJ0824
Penybryn *M Glam* 33 ST1395
Penycae *Clwyd* 70 SJ2745
Penycaerau *Gwynd* 56 SH1927
Penyffordd *Clwyd* 71 SJ3061
Penygarnedd *Powys* 58 SJ1023
Penygraig *M Glam* 33 SS9990
Penygroes *Dyfed* 32 SN5813
Penygroes *Gwynd* 68 SH4753
Penysarn *Gwynd* 68 SH4690
Penywaun *M Glam* 33 SN9804
Penywern *W Glam* 32 SN7609
Penzance *Cnwll* 2 SW4730
Peopleton *H & W* 47 SO9350
Peover Heath *Ches* 79 SJ7973
Peper Harow *Surrey* 25 SU9344
Peplow *Shrops* 59 SJ6324
Pepper's Green *Essex* 40 TL6210
Peppershill *Oxon* 37 SP6709
Pepperstock *Beds* 38 TL0817
Percie *Gramp* 134 NO5991
Percyhorner *Gramp* 143 NJ9665
Perelle *Guern* 152 GN0000
Periton *Somset* 20 SS9645
Perivale *Gt Lon* 26 TQ1682
Perkin's Beach *Shrops* 59 SJ3600
Perkins Village *Devon* 9 SY0291
Perkinsville *Dur* 96 NZ2553
Perlethorpe *Notts* 75 SK6471
Permathorn *Loth* 117 NT2459
Perran Wharf *Cnwll* 3 SW7738
Perranarworthal *Cnwll* 3 SW7738
Perranporth *Cnwll* 3 SW7554
Perranuthnoe *Cnwll* 2 SW5329
Perranwell *Cnwll* 3 SW7739
Perranwell *Cnwll* 3 SW7752
Perranzabuloe *Cnwll* 3 SW7752
Perrott's Brook *Gloucs* 35 SP0106
Perry *W Mids* 61 SP0792
Perry Barr *W Mids* 61 SP0791
Perry Green *Essex* 40 TL8122
Perry Green *Herts* 39 TL4317
Perry Green *Somset* 20 ST2738
Perry Green *Wilts* 35 ST9689
Perry Street *Somset* 10 ST3405
Pershall *Staffs* 72 SJ8129
Pershore *H & W* 47 SO9445
Pertenhall *Beds* 51 TL0865
Perth *Tays* 126 NO1123
Perthcelyn *M Glam* 33 ST0595
Perthy *Shrops* 59 SJ3633
Perton *Staffs* 60 SO8699
Pertwood *Wilts* 22 ST8936
Pet Street *Kent* 29 TR0846
Peter Tavy *Devon* 5 SX5177
Peter's Green *Herts* 38 TL1419
Peterborough *Cambs* 64 TL1989
Peterchurch *H & W* 46 SO3438
Peterculter *Gramp* 135 NJ8400
Peterhead *Gramp* 143 NK1246
Peterlee *Dur* 96 NZ4341
Peters Marland *Devon* 18 SS4713
Petersfield *Hants* 13 SU7423
Petersham *Gt Lon* 26 TQ1873
Peterstone Wentlooge *Gwent* 34 ST2679

Peterstonsuper-Ely Potthorpe

Peterstonsuper-Ely S Glam 33 ST0876
Peterstow H & W 46 SO5624
Petham Kent 29 TR1251
Petherwin Gate Cnwll 5 SX2889
Petrockstow Devon 32 SS5190
Petrockstow Devon 19 SS5109
Petsoe End Bucks 38 SP8949
Pett E Susx 17 TQ8714
Pett Bottom Kent 29 TR1552
Pettaugh Suffk 54 TM1659
Petterden Tays 127 NO4240
Pettinain Strath 108 NS9542
Pettistree Suffk 55 TM3055
Petton Devon 20 ST0024
Petton Shrops 59 SJ4326
Petts Wood Gt Lon 27 TQ4567
Pettycur Fife 117 NT2686
Pettymuk Gramp 143 NJ9024
Petworth W Susx 14 SU9721
Pevensey E Susx 16 TQ6405
Pevensey Bay E Susx 16 TQ6504
Pewsey Wilts 23 SU1660
Pheasant's Hill Bucks 37 SU7887
Phepson H & W 47 SO9459
Philadelphia T & W 96 NZ3352
Philham Devon 18 SS2522
Philiphaugh Border 109 NT4327
Phillack Cnwll 2 SW5638
Philleigh Cnwll 3 SW8739
Philpot End Essex 40 TL6118
Philpstoun Loth 117 NT0677
Phocle Green H & W 47 SO6226
Phoenix Green Hants 24 SU7555
Phoines Highld 132 NN7093
Pibsbury Somset 21 ST4326
Pica Cumb 92 NY0222
Piccotts End Herts 38 TL0409
Pickering N York 90 SE7983
Picket Piece Hants 23 SU3947
Picket Post Hants 12 SU1905
Pickford W Mids 61 SP2781
Pickford Green W Mids 61 SP2781
Pickhill N York 89 SE3483
Picklescott Shrops 59 SO4399
Pickmere Ches 79 SJ6977
Pickney Somset 20 ST2128
Pickstock Shrops 72 SJ7223
Pickup Bank Lancs 81 SD7122
Pickwell Devon 18 SS4540
Pickwell Leics 63 SK7811
Pickwick Wilts 35 ST8670
Pickworth Leics 63 SK9913
Pickworth Lincs 64 TF0433
Pict's Cross H & W 46 SO5526
Pictillum Gramp 142 NJ7317
Picton Ches 71 SJ4371
Picton Clwyd 70 SJ1282
Picton N York 89 NZ4107
Picton Ferry Dyfed 31 SN2717
Piddinghoe E Susx 16 TQ4303
Piddington Bucks 37 SU8094
Piddington Nhants 51 SP8054
Piddington Oxon 37 SP6317
Piddlehinton Dorset 11 SY7197
Piddletrenthide Dorset 11 SY7099
Pidley Cambs 52 TL3377
Pie Corner H & W 47 SO6461
Piercebridge Dur 96 NZ2015
Pierowall Ork 155 HY4348
Piff's Elm Gloucs 47 SO8926
Pig Oak Dorset 12 SU0202
Pig Street H & W 46 SO3647
Pigdon Nthumb 103 NZ1588
Pigeon Green Warwks 48 SP2260
Pikehall Derbys 74 SK1959
Pilford Dorset 12 SU0301
Pilgrims Hatch Essex 27 TQ5895
Pilham Lincs 76 SK8693
Pill Avon 34 ST5275
Pillaton Cnwll 5 SX3664
Pillaton Staffs 60 SJ9413
Pillatonmill M Glam 5 SX3063
Pillerton Hersey Warwks 48 SP2948
Pillerton Priors Warwks 48 SP2947
Pilleth Powys 46 SO2667
Pilley Hants 12 SZ3398
Pilley S York 74 SE3300
Pilley Bailey Hants 12 SZ3398
Pillgwenlly Gwent 34 ST3186
Pillhead Devon 18 SS4726
Pilling Lancs 80 SD4048
Pilling Lane Lancs 80 SD3749
Pilning Avon 34 ST5684
Pilot Inn Kent 17 TR0818
Pilsbury Derbys 74 SK1163
Pilsdon Dorset 10 SY4199
Pilsgate Cambs 64 TF0605
Pilsley Derbys 74 SK2471
Pilsley Derbys 74 SK4262
Pilson Green Norfk 67 TG3713
Piltdown E Susx 16 TQ4422
Pilton Leics 63 SK9102
Pilton Nhants 51 TL0284
Pilton Somset 21 ST5940
Pilton Green W Glam 32 SS4487
Pimlico Lancs 81 SD7543
Pimlico Nhants 49 SP6140
Pimperne Dorset 11 ST9009
Pin Green Herts 39 TL2525
Pinchbeck Lincs 64 TF2425
Pinchbeck Bars Lincs 64 TF1905
Pinchbeck West Lincs 64 TF2024
Pincheon Green S York 83 SE6517
Pinchinthorpe Cleve 90 NZ5714
Pincock Lancs 81 SD5517
Pindon End Bucks 38 SP7847
Pineham Kent 29 TR3145
Pinfold Lancs 80 SD3811
Pinford End Suffk 54 TL8559
Pinged Dyfed 31 SN4203
Pingewood Berks 24 SU6969
Pinhoe Devon 9 SX9694
Pinkett's Booth W Mids 61 SP2781
Pinkney Wilts 35 ST8686
Pinley W Mids 61 SP3577
Pinley Green Warwks 48 SP2066
Pinmill Suffk 55 TM2037
Pinminnoch Strath 106 NX1993
Pinmore Strath 106 NX2091
Pinn Devon 4 SX0986
Pinner Gt Lon 26 TQ1289
Pinner Green Gt Lon 26 TQ1290
Pinsley Green Ches 71 SJ5846
Pinvin H & W 47 SO9549
Pinwherry Strath 98 NX2086
Pinxton Derbys 75 SK4555
Pipe and Lyde H & W 46 SO5043
Pipe Gate Shrops 72 SJ7340
Pipehill Staffs 61 SK0908
Piperhill Highld 140 NH8650
Pipers Pool Cnwll 5 SX2584
Pipewell Nhants 51 SP8385
Pippacott Devon 19 SS5237
Pippin Street Lancs 81 SD5824
Pipton Powys 45 SO1637
Pirbright Surrey 25 SU9455
Pirbright Camp Surrey 25 SU9257
Pirnie Border 110 NT6528
Pirton H & W 47 SO8847
Pirton Herts 38 TL1431
Pishill Oxon 37 SU7389
Pistyll Gwynd 56 SH3242
Pitagowan Tays 132 NN8165
Pitblae Gramp 143 NJ9864
Pitcairngreen Tays 125 NO0627
Pitcalnie Highld 147 NH8172
Pitcaple Gramp 142 NJ7225
Pitcarity Tays 134 NO3365
Pitch Green Bucks 37 SP7703
Pitch Place Surrey 25 SU8939
Pitch Place Surrey 25 SU9852
Pitchcombe Gloucs 35 SO8508
Pitchcott Bucks 37 SP7720
Pitcher Row Lincs 64 TF2933
Pitchford Shrops 59 SJ5303
Pitchroy Gramp 141 NJ1738
Pitcombe Somset 22 ST6732
Pitcot M Glam 33 SS8974
Pitcox Loth 118 NT6475
Pitcur Tays 126 NO2437
Pitfichie Gramp 142 NJ6716
Pitfour Castle Tays 126 NO1921
Pitglassie Gramp 142 NJ6943
Pitglassie Gramp 142 NJ6943
Pitgrudy Highld 147 NH7991
Pitkennedy Tays 127 NO5454
Pitlessie Fife 126 NO3309
Pitlochry Tays 132 NN9458
Pitmachie Gramp 142 NJ6728
Pitmain Highld 132 NH7400
Pitmedden Gramp 143 NJ8827
Pitminster Somset 20 ST2119
Pitmuies Tays 127 NO5649
Pitmunie Gramp 142 NJ6615
Pitney Somset 21 ST4428
Pitroddie Tays 126 NO2125
Pitscottie Fife 126 NO4112
Pitsea Essex 40 TQ7488
Pitses Gt Man 79 SD9403
Pitsford Nhants 50 SP7568
Pitsford Hill Somset 20 ST0930
Pitstone Bucks 38 SP9415
Pitt Devon 9 ST0316
Pitt Hants 24 SU4528
Pitt Court Gloucs 35 ST7496
Pitt's Wood Kent 16 TQ6149
Pittarrow Gramp 135 NO7274
Pittarrow Gramp 135 NO7274
Pittenweem Fife 127 NO5502
Pitteuchar Fife 117 NT2899
Pittington Dur 96 NZ3244
Pittodrie Gramp 142 NJ6925
Pitton Wilts 23 SU2131
Pittulie Gramp 143 NJ9567
Pity Me Dur 96 NZ2645
Pityme Cnwll 4 SW9575
Pivington Kent 28 TQ9146
Pixey Green Suffk 55 TM2475
Pixham Surrey 26 TQ1750
Plain Street Cnwll 4 SW9778
Plains Strath 116 NS7966
Plaish Shrops 59 SO5296
Plaistow Derbys 74 SK3556
Plaistow Gt Lon 27 TQ4082
Plaistow H & W 47 SO6939
Plaistow W Susx 14 TQ0030
Plaitford Hants 12 SU2719
Plas Llanfair Gwynd 69 SH5371
Plas Llysyn Powys 58 SN9596
Plastow Green Hants 24 SU5361
Platt Kent 27 TQ6257
Platt Bridge Gt Man 78 SD6002
Platt Lane Shrops 59 SJ5136
Platts Heath Kent 28 TQ8750
Plawsworth Dur 96 NZ2647
Plaxtol Kent 27 TQ6053
Play Hatch Oxon 37 SU7376
Playden E Susx 17 TQ9121
Playford Suffk 55 TM2147
Playing Place Cnwll 3 SW8141
Playley Green Gloucs 47 SO7631
Plealey Shrops 59 SJ4206
Plean Cent 116 NS8386
Pleasance Fife 126 NO2312
Pleasey Hill Notts 80 SE5064
Pleasington Lancs 81 SD6426
Pleasley Derbys 75 SK5064
Pleck Dorset 11 ST7011
Pledgdon Green Essex 40 TL5626
Pledwick W York 83 SE3317
Pleinheaume Guern 152 GN0000
Plemont Jersey 152 JS0000
Plemstall Ches 71 SJ4570
Plenmeller Nthumb 102 NY7162
Pleshey Essex 40 TL6614
Plockton Highld 137 NG8033
Ploughfield H & W 46 SO3841
Plowden Shrops 59 SO3888
Ploxgreen Shrops 59 SJ3604
Pluckley Kent 28 TQ9245
Pluckley Street Kent 28 TQ9243
Pluckley Thorne Kent 28 TQ9644
Plucks Gutter Kent 29 TR2663
Plumbland Cumb 92 NY1539
Plumgarths Cumb 87 SD4994
Plumley Ches 79 SJ7275
Plumpton Cumb 94 NY4937
Plumpton E Susx 15 TQ3613
Plumpton End Nhants 49 SP7245
Plumpton Green E Susx 15 TQ3616
Plumpton Head Cumb 94 NY5035
Plumstead Gt Lon 27 TQ4478
Plumstead Norfk 66 TG1335
Plumstead Green Norfk 66 TG1334
Plumtree Notts 62 SK6133
Plumtree Green Kent 28 TQ8245
Plungar Leics 63 SK7633
Plurenden Kent 28 TQ9237
Plush Dorset 11 ST7102
Plusha Cnwll 5 SX2580
Plushabridge Cnwll 5 SX3072
Plwmp Dyfed 42 SN3652
Plymouth Devon 6 SX4755
Plympton Devon 6 SX5356
Plymstock Devon 6 SX5152
Plymtree Devon 9 ST0502
Pockley N York 90 SE6385
Pocklington Humb 84 SE8048
Pode Hole Lincs 64 TF2121
Podimore Somset 21 ST5424
Podington Beds 51 SP9462
Podmore Staffs 72 SJ7835
Point Clear Essex 41 TM1015
Pointon Lincs 64 TF1131
Pokesdown Dorset 12 SZ1292
Polapit Tamar Cnwll 5 SX3389
Polbae D & G 98 NX2873
Polbain Highld 144 NB9910
Polbathic Cnwll 5 SX3456
Polbeth Loth 117 NT0364
Polbrock Cnwll 4 SX0169
Polchar Highld 132 NH8909
Pole Elm H & W 47 SO8450
Pole Moor W York 82 SE0615
Polebrook Nhants 51 TL0687
Polegate E Susx 16 TQ5804
Polelane Ends Ches 79 SJ6479
Polesworth Warwks 61 SK2602
Polgigga Cnwll 2 SW3723
Polglass Highld 144 NC0307
Polgooth Cnwll 3 SW9950
Polgown D & G 107 NS7104
Poling W Susx 14 TQ0404
Poling Corner W Susx 14 TQ0405
Polkerris Cnwll 3 SX0952
Polla Highld 149 NC3854
Pollard Street Norfk 67 TG3332
Pollington Humb 83 SE6119
Polloch Highld 129 NM7868
Pollokshaws Strath 115 NS5661
Pollokshields Strath 115 NS5773
Polmassick Cnwll 3 SW9745
Polmear Cnwll 3 SX0833
Polmont Cent 116 NS9378
Polnish Highld 129 NM7582
Polperro Cnwll 5 SX2051
Polruan Cnwll 3 SX1250
Polsham Somset 21 ST5142
Polstead Suffk 54 TL9938
Polstead Heath Suffk 54 TL9940
Poltalluch Strath 113 NR8196
Poltescoe Cnwll 3 SW7215
Poltimore Devon 9 SX9696
Polton Loth 117 NT2864
Polwarth Border 119 NT7450
Polyphant Cnwll 5 SX2682
Polzeath Cnwll 4 SW9378
Ponde Powys 45 SO1037
Ponders End Gt Lon 27 TQ3596
Pondersbridge Cambs 64 TL2692
Ponsanooth Cnwll 3 SW7537
Ponsongath Cnwll 3 SW7518
Ponsworthy Devon 7 SX7073
Pont Cyfyng Gwynd 69 SH7357
Pont Morlais Dyfed 32 SN5307
Pont Pen-y-benglog Gwynd 69 SH6460
Pont Rhyd-sarn Gwynd 57 SH8528
Pont Rhyd-y-cyff M Glam 33 SS8788
Pont Robert Powys 58 SJ1112
Pont Walby M Glam 33 SN8906
Pont-ar-gothi Dyfed 32 SN5021
Pont-ar-Hydfer Powys 45 SN8627
Pont-ar-llechau Dyfed 44 SN7224
Pont-Ebbw Gwent 34 ST2986
Pont-faen Powys 45 SN9934
Pont-gareg Dyfed 31 SN1441
Pont-Nedd-Fechan Powys 33 SN9007
Pont-rhyd-y-fen W Glam 32 SS7994
Pont-rug Gwynd 68 SH5162
Pont-y-blew Clwyd 71 SJ3138
Pont-y-pant Gwynd 69 SH7554
Pont-yr-hafod Dyfed 30 SM9026
Pont-yr-Rhyl M Glam 33 SS9089
Pontac Jersey 152 JS0000
Pontamman Dyfed 32 SN6312
Pontantwn Dyfed 32 SN4412
Pontardawe W Glam 32 SN7204
Pontarddulais W Glam 32 SN5903
Pontarsais Dyfed 31 SN4428
Pontblyddyn Clwyd 70 SJ2760
Pontdolgoch Powys 58 SO0193
Pontefract W York 83 SE4521
Ponteland Nthumb 103 NZ1673
Ponterwyd Dyfed 43 SN7481
Pontesbury Shrops 59 SJ3906
Pontesbury Hill Shrops 59 SJ3905
Pontesford Shrops 59 SJ4106
Pontfadog Clwyd 70 SJ2338
Pontfaen Dyfed 30 SN0234
Pontgarreg Dyfed 42 SN3354
Ponthenry Dyfed 32 SN4709
Ponthir Gwent 34 ST3293
Ponthirwaun Dyfed 42 SN2645
Pontllanfraith Gwent 33 ST1895
Pontlliw W Glam 32 SN6101
Pontlottyn M Glam 33 SO1106
Pontlyfni Gwynd 68 SH4352
Pontnewydd Gwent 34 ST2896
Pontnewynydd Gwent 34 SO2701
Pontop Dur 96 NZ1453
Pontrhydfendigaid Dyfed 43 SN7366
Pontrhydygroes Dyfed 43 SN7472
Pontrhydyrun Gwent 34 ST2997
Pontrilas H & W 46 SO3927
Ponts Green E Susx 16 TQ6716
Pontshaen Dyfed 42 SN4446
Pontshill H & W 35 SO6321
Pontsticill M Glam 33 SO0511
Pontwelly Dyfed 31 SN4140
Pontyates Dyfed 32 SN4708
Pontyberem Dyfed 32 SN5011
Pontybodkin Clwyd 70 SJ2659
Pontyclun M Glam 33 ST0381
Pontycymer M Glam 33 SS9091
Pontyglasier Dyfed 31 SN1436
Pontygwaith M Glam 33 ST0094
Pontygynon Dyfed 31 SN1237
Pontymoel Gwent 34 SO2900
Pontypool Gwent 34 SO2800
Pontypool Road Gwent 34 ST3099
Pontypridd M Glam 33 ST0790
Pontywaun Gwent 34 ST2292
Pooksgreen Hants 12 SU3710
Pool Cnwll 2 SW6741
Pool IOS 2 SV8714
Pool W York 82 SE2445
Pool Head H & W 46 SO5550
Pool O' Muckhart Cent 117 NO0000
Pool Quay Powys 58 SJ2511
Pool Street Essex 53 TL7637
Poole Dorset 11 SZ0190
Poole Keynes Wilts 35 ST9995
Poolewe Highld 144 NG8580
Pooley Bridge Cumb 93 NY4724
Pooley Street Norfk 54 TM0581
Poolfold Staffs 72 SJ8959
Poolhill Gloucs 47 SO7329
Poolmill H & W 46 SO5724
Pooting's Kent 16 TQ4449
Popham Hants 24 SU5543
Poplar Gt Lon 27 TQ3780
Poplar Street Suffk 55 TM4465
Porchbrook H & W 60 SO7270
Porchfield IOW 13 SZ4491
Porin Highld 139 NH3155
Porkellis Cnwll 2 SW6933
Porlock Somset 19 SS8846
Porlock Weir Somset 19 SS8647
Port Akaig Strath 112 NR4369
Port Appin Strath 122 NM9045
Port Bannatyne Strath 114 NS0867
Port Carlisle Cumb 101 NY2461
Port Charlotte Strath 112 NR2558
Port Clarence Cleve 97 NZ5022
Port Cornaa IOM 153 SC4787
Port Dinorwic Gwynd 68 SH5267
Port Dolgarrog Gwynd 69 SH7766
Port Driseach Strath 114 NR9973
Port Ellen Strath 104 NR3645
Port Elphinstone Gramp 142 NJ7720
Port Erin IOM 153 SC1969
Port Erroll Gramp 143 NK0935
Port e Vullen IOM 153 SC4793
Port Glasgow Strath 115 NS3274
Port Henderson Highld 137 NG7573
Port Isaac Cnwll 4 SW9980
Port Logan D & G 98 NX0940
Port Mor Highld 128 NM4279
Port Mulgrave N York 97 NZ7917
Port Na-Craig Tays 116 NS9357
Port of Menteith Cent 115 NN5801
Port of Ness W Isls 154 NB5363
Port Quin Cnwll 4 SW9780
Port Ramsay Strath 122 NM8845
Port Soderick IOM 153 SC3472
Port St. Mary IOM 153 SC2067
Port Sunlight Mersyd 78 SJ3384
Port Talbot W Glam 32 SS7589
Port Tennant W Glam 32 SS6893
Port Wemyss Strath 112 NR1751
Port William D & G 98 NX3343
Portachoillan Strath 113 NR7557
Portavadie Strath 114 NR9369
Portbury Avon 34 ST5075
Portchester Hants 13 SU6105
Portencalzie D & G 98 NX0171
Portencross Strath 114 NS1748
Portesham Dorset 10 SY6085
Portessie Gramp 142 NJ4366
Portfield Gate Dyfed 30 SM9115
Portgate Devon 5 SX4285
Portgaverne Cnwll 4 SX0080
Portgordon Gramp 142 NJ3964
Portgower Highld 147 ND0013
Porth Cnwll 4 SW8262
Porth M Glam 33 ST0291
Porth Dinllaen Gwynd 56 SH2740
Porth Mellin Cnwll 2 SW6618
Porth Navas Cnwll 3 SW7527
Porth-y-Waen Shrops 70 SJ2642
Porthallow Cnwll 5 SX2251
Porthallow Cnwll 3 SW7923
Porthcawl M Glam 33 SS8177
Porthcothan Cnwll 4 SW8572
Porthcurno Cnwll 2 SW3822
Porthgain Dyfed 30 SM8132
Porthgwarra Cnwll 2 SW3722
Porthill Staffs 72 SJ8548
Porthkea Cnwll 3 SW8242
Porthkerry S Glam 20 ST0866
Porthleven Cnwll 2 SW6225
Porthmadog Gwynd 57 SH5638
Porthmeor Cnwll 2 SW4337
Portholland Cnwll 3 SW9541
Porthoustock Cnwll 3 SW8021
Porthpean Cnwll 3 SX0350
Porthtowan Cnwll 2 SW6947
Porthyrhyd Dyfed 32 SN5215
Porthyrhyd Dyfed 44 SN7137
Portincaple Strath 114 NS2393
Portinfer Jersey 152 JS0000
Portington Humb 84 SE7830
Portinnisherrich Strath 122 NM9711
Portinscale Cumb 93 NY2524
Portishead Avon 34 ST4675
Portknockie Gramp 142 NJ4868
Portlethen Gramp 135 NO9296
Portloe Cnwll 3 SW9339
Portlooe Cnwll 5 SX2452
Portmahomack Highld 147 NH9184
Portmeirion Gwynd 57 SH5937
Portmellon Cnwll 3 SX0143
Portmore Hants 12 SZ3397
Portnacroish Strath 122 NM9247
Portnaguran W Isls 154 NB5537
Portnahaven Strath 112 NR1652
Portnalong Highld 136 NG3435
Portnancon Highld 149 NC4260
Portneora Highld 137 NG7731
Portobello Loth 117 NT3073
Portobello T & W 96 NZ2755
Portobello W Mids 60 SO9598
Porton Wilts 23 SU1836
Portontown Devon 5 SX4176
Portpatrick D & G 98 NX0054
Portreath Cnwll 4 SW6679
Portreath Cnwll 2 SW6545
Portree Highld 136 NG4843
Portrye Strath 114 NS1757
Portscatho Cnwll 3 SW8735
Portsea Hants 13 SU6300
Portskerra Highld 150 NC8765
Portskewett Gwent 34 ST4988
Portslade E Susx 15 TQ2506
Portslade-by-Sea E Susx 15 TQ2604
Portslogan D & G 98 NW9858
Portsmouth Hants 13 SU6400
Portsmouth W York 81 SD9026
Portsoy Gramp 142 NJ5866
Portswood Hants 13 SU4314
Portuairk Highld 128 NM4468
Portvasgo Highld 149 NC5865
Portway Cnwll 5 SX3553
Portway H & W 45 SO0872
Portway H & W 46 SO4844
Portway H & W 46 SO4935
Portway W Mids 60 SO9788
Portwrinkle Cnwll 5 SX3553
Portyerrerrock D & G 99 NX4738
Posbury Devon 8 SX8197
Posenhall Shrops 59 SJ6501
Poslingford Suffk 53 TL7748
Posonby Cumb 86 NY0505
Posso Border 109 NT2033
Post Green Dorset 11 SY9583
Postbridge Devon 8 SX6579
Postcombe Oxon 37 SU7099
Postling Kent 29 TR1439
Postwick Norfk 67 TG2907
Pothole Cnwll 3 SW9750
Potsgrove Beds 38 SP9529
Pott Row Norfk 65 TF7022
Pott Shrigley Ches 79 SJ9479
Pott's Green Essex 40 TL9122
Potten End Herts 38 TL0109
Potten Street Kent 27 TQ2567
Potter Brompton N York 91 SE9776
Potter Heigham Norfk 67 TG4119
Potter Row Bucks 26 SP9002
Potter Somersal Derbys 73 SK1436
Potter's Cross Staffs 60 SO8484
Potter's Forstal Kent 28 TQ8946
Potter's Green E Susx 16 TQ5023
Potter's Green Herts 39 TL3520
Pottergate Street Norfk 66 TM1591
Potterhanworth Lincs 76 TF0566
Potterhanworth Booths Lincs 76 TF0767
Potterne Wilts 22 ST9958
Potterne Wick Wilts 22 ST9957
Potters Bar Herts 27 TL2501
Potters Brook Lancs 80 SD4952
Potters Crouch Herts 38 TL1105
Potters Green W Mids 61 SP3781
Potters Marston Leics 50 SP4996
Pottersheath Herts 39 TL2318
Potterspury Nhants 49 SP7543
Potterton W York 83 SE4038
Potthorpe Norfk 66 TF9422

Pottle Street Redgrave

Pottle Street *Wilts* 22 ST8141
Potto *N York* 89 NZ4703
Potton *Beds* 52 TL2249
Poughill *Cnwll* 18 SS2207
Poughill *Devon* 19 SS8508
Poulner *Hants* 12 SU1606
Poulshot *Wilts* 22 ST9659
Poulston *Devon* 7 SX7754
Poulton *Gloucs* 36 SP0900
Poulton *Mersyd* 78 SJ3091
Poulton Priory *Gloucs* 36 SP0900
Poulton-le-Fylde *Lancs* 80 SD3439
Pound Bank *H & W* 60 SO7374
Pound Green *E Susx* 16 TQ5123
Pound Green *H & W* 60 SO7579
Pound Green *Hants* 24 SU5759
Pound Hill *W Susx* 15 TQ2937
Pound Street *Hants* 24 SU4561
Poundffald *W Glam* 32 SS5694
Poundgates *E Susx* 16 TQ4918
Poundon *Bucks* 49 SP6425
Poundsbridge *Kent* 16 TQ5341
Poundsgate *Devon* 7 SX7072
Poundstock *Cnwll* 18 SX2099
Pounsley *E Susx* 16 TQ5221
Pouton *D & G* 99 NX4645
Povey Cross *Surrey* 15 TQ2642
Pow Green *H & W* 47 SO7044
Powburn *Nthumb* 111 NU0616
Powderham *Devon* 9 SX9684
Powerstock *Dorset* 10 SY5196
Powfoot *D & G* 100 NY1465
Powhill *Cumb* 93 NY2355
Powick *H & W* 47 SO8351
Powler's Piece *Devon* 18 SS3618
Powmill *Tays* 117 NT0297
Poxwell *Dorset* 11 SY7484
Poyle *Gt Lon* 26 TQ0376
Poynings *W Susx* 15 TQ2612
Poynter's Lane End *Cnwll* 2 SW6743
Poyntington *Dorset* 21 ST6419
Poynton *Ches* 79 SJ9283
Poynton *Shrops* 59 SJ5717
Poynton Green *Shrops* 59 SJ5618
Poys Street *Suffk* 55 TM3570
Poyston Cross *Dyfed* 30 SM9819
Poystreet Green *Suffk* 54 TL9858
Praa Sands *Cnwll* 2 SW5828
Pratt's Bottom *Gt Lon* 27 TQ4762
Prawle Point *Devon* 7 SX7734
Praze-an-Beeble *Cnwll* 2 SW6336
Predannack Wollas *Cnwll* 2 SW6616
Prees *Shrops* 59 SJ5533
Prees Green *Shrops* 59 SJ5531
Prees Heath *Shrops* 71 SJ5538
Prees Higher Heath *Shrops* 59 SJ5636
Prees Lower Heath *Shrops* 59 SJ5732
Preesall *Lancs* 80 SD3647
Pren-gwyn *Dyfed* 42 SN4244
Prendwick *Nthumb* 111 NU0012
Prenteg *Gwynd* 57 SH5841
Prenton *Mersyd* 78 SJ3086
Prescot *Mersyd* 78 SJ4692
Prescott *Devon* 9 ST0814
Prescott *Shrops* 60 SO6681
Prescott *Shrops* 59 SJ4220
Presnerb *Tays* 133 NO1866
Pressen *Nthumb* 110 NT8335
Prestatyn *Clwyd* 70 SJ0682
Prestbury *Ches* 79 SJ9077
Prestbury *Gloucs* 47 SO9723
Presteigne *Powys* 46 SO3164
Prestleigh *Somset* 21 ST6340
Prestolee *Gt Man* 79 SD7505
Preston *Border* 119 NT7957
Preston *Devon* 7 SX8862
Preston *Devon* 7 SX7351
Preston *Devon* 7 SX8574
Preston *Dorset* 11 SY7083
Preston *E Susx* 15 TQ3106
Preston *Gloucs* 47 SO6734
Preston *Gloucs* 36 SP0400
Preston *Herts* 39 TL1824
Preston *Humb* 85 TA1830
Preston *Kent* 28 TR0260
Preston *Kent* 29 TR2561
Preston *Lancs* 80 SD5329
Preston *Leics* 63 SK8602
Preston *Loth* 118 NT5977
Preston *Nthumb* 111 NU1825
Preston *Shrops* 59 SJ5215
Preston *Somset* 20 ST1036
Preston *Suffk* 54 TL9450
Preston *Wilts* 36 SU2774
Preston Bagot *Warwks* 48 SP1766
Preston Bissett *Bucks* 49 SP6529
Preston Bowyer *Somset* 20 ST1326
Preston Brockhurst *Shrops* 59 SJ5324
Preston Brook *Ches* 78 SJ5680
Preston Candover *Hants* 24 SU6041
Preston Capes *Nhants* 49 SP5754
Preston Crowmarsh *Oxon* 37 SU6190
Preston Deanery *Nhants* 50 SP7855
Preston Green *Warwks* 48 SP1665
Preston Gubbals *Shrops* 59 SJ4919
Preston Montford *Shrops* 59 SJ4314
Preston on Stour *Warwks* 48 SP2049
Preston on the Hill *Ches* 78 SJ5780
Preston on Wye *H & W* 46 SO3842
Preston Patrick *Cumb* 87 SD5483
Preston Plucknett *Somset* 10 ST5515
Preston Streeet *Kent* 27 TQ2561
Preston upon the Weald Mo *Shrops* 72 SJ6815
Preston Wynne *H & W* 46 SO5546
Preston-under-Scar *N York* 88 SE0791
Prestonpans *Loth* 118 NT3874
Prestwich *Gt Man* 79 SD8104
Prestwick *Nthumb* 103 NZ1872
Prestwick *Strath* 106 NS3525
Prestwood *Bucks* 26 SP8700
Prestwood *Staffs* 60 SO8686
Price Town *M Glam* 33 SS9392
Prickwillow *Cambs* 53 TL5982
Priddy *Somset* 21 ST5250
Priest Hutton *Lancs* 87 SD5273
Priestacott *Devon* 18 SS4206
Priestcliffe *Derbys* 74 SK1471
Priestcliffe Ditch *Derbys* 74 SK1271
Priestend *Bucks* 37 SP6906
Priestly Green *W York* 82 SE1326
Priestweston *Shrops* 59 SO2997
Priestwood Green *Kent* 27 TQ6464
Primethorpe *Leics* 50 SP5293
Primrose Green *Norfk* 66 TG0616
Primrose Hill *Border* 119 NT7857
Primrose Hill *Cambs* 52 TL3889
Primrose Hill *Derbys* 75 SK4358
Primrose Hill *Lancs* 78 SD3809
Primrose Hill *W Mids* 60 SO9487
Primsidemill *Border* 110 NT8126
Princes Gate *Dyfed* 31 SN1312
Princes Risborough *Bucks* 38 SP8003
Princethorpe *Warwks* 61 SP4070
Princetown *Devon* 6 SX5873
Prinsted *W Susx* 14 SU7605
Prior-Rigg *Cumb* 101 NY4568
Priors Halton *Shrops* 46 SO4975
Priors Hardwick *Warwks* 49 SP4756
Priors Marston *Warwks* 49 SP4957
Priors Norton *Gloucs* 47 SO8624
Priory Wood *H & W* 46 SO2545
Prisk *S Glam* 33 ST0176
Priston *Avon* 22 ST6960
Pristow Green *Norfk* 54 TM1388
Prittlewell *Essex* 40 TQ8687
Privett *Hants* 13 SU6727
Prixton *Devon* 19 SS5436
Probus *Cnwll* 3 SW8947
Prospect *Cumb* 92 NY1041
Prospidnick *Cnwll* 2 SW6431
Protstonhill *Gramp* 143 NJ8163
Providence *Avon* 34 ST5370
Prowse *Devon* 8 SS8405
Prudhoe *Nthumb* 103 NZ0962
Prussia Cove *Cnwll* 2 SW5528
Ptarmigan Lodge *Cent* 115 NN3500
Publow *Avon* 21 ST6264
Puckeridge *Herts* 39 TL3823
Puckington *Somset* 10 ST3718
Pucklechurch *Avon* 35 ST6976
Puckrup *Gloucs* 47 SO8836
Puddinglake *Ches* 79 SJ7269
Puddington *Ches* 71 SJ3273
Puddington *Devon* 19 SS8310
Puddledock *Norfk* 66 TM0592
Puddletown *Dorset* 11 SY7594
Pudleston *H & W* 46 SO5659
Pudsey *W York* 82 SE2232
Pulborough *W Susx* 14 TQ0418
Puleston *Shrops* 72 SJ7322
Pulford *Ches* 71 SJ3759
Pulham *Dorset* 35 ST7080
Pulham *Dorset* 11 ST7008
Pulham Market *Norfk* 55 TM1986
Pulham St. Mary *Norfk* 55 TM2185
Pullens Green *Avon* 34 ST6192
Pulley *Shrops* 59 SJ4809
Pulloxhill *Beds* 38 TL0634
Pumpherston *Loth* 117 NT0669
Pumsaint *Dyfed* 44 SN6540
Puncheston *Dyfed* 30 SN0030
Puncknowle *Dorset* 10 SY5388
Punnett's Town *E Susx* 16 TQ6220
Purbrook *Hants* 13 SU6707
Purbrook Park *Hants* 13 SU6707
Purfleet *Essex* 27 TQ5578
Puriton *Somset* 21 ST3241
Purleigh *Essex* 40 TL8402
Purley *Berks* 37 SU6675
Purley *Gt Lon* 27 TQ3161
Purlogue *Shrops* 46 SO2877
Purlpit *Wilts* 22 ST8766
Purls Bridge *Cambs* 53 TL4787
Purse Caundle *Dorset* 11 ST6917
Purshall Green *H & W* 60 SO8971
Purslow *Shrops* 59 SO3681
Purslow *Shrops* 59 SO3681
Purston Jaglin *W York* 83 SE4319
Purtington *Somset* 10 ST3808
Purton *Gloucs* 35 SO6705
Purton *Gloucs* 35 SO6904
Purton *Wilts* 36 SU0887
Purton Stoke *Wilts* 36 SU0990
Pury End *Nhants* 49 SP7045
Pusey *Oxon* 36 SU3596
Putley *H & W* 47 SO6337
Putley Green *H & W* 47 SO6437
Putloe *Gloucs* 35 SO7809
Putney *Gt Lon* 26 TQ2374
Putron Village *Guern* 152 GN0000
Putsborough *Devon* 18 SS4540
Puttenham *Herts* 38 SP8814
Puttenham *Surrey* 25 SU9347
Puttock End *Essex* 54 TL8140
Puttock's End *Essex* 40 TL5619
Putton *Dorset* 11 SY6480
Puxley *Nhants* 49 SP7542
Puxton *Avon* 21 ST4063
Pwll *Dyfed* 32 SN4800
Pwll Trap *Dyfed* 31 SN2616
Pwll-du *Gwent* 34 SO2411
Pwll-y-glaw *W Glam* 32 SS7993
Pwllcrochan *Dyfed* 30 SM9202
Pwllglas *Clwyd* 70 SJ1154
Pwllgloyw *Powys* 45 SO0333
Pwllheli *Gwynd* 56 SH3734
Pwllmeyric *Gwent* 34 ST5192
Pye Bridge *Derbys* 75 SK4452
Pye Corner *Gwent* 34 ST3485
Pye Corner *Herts* 39 TL4412
Pye Green *Staffs* 60 SJ9814
Pyecombe *W Susx* 15 TQ2912
Pyle *M Glam* 33 SS8282
Pyleigh *Somset* 20 ST1331
Pylle *Somset* 21 ST6038
Pymore *Cambs* 53 TL4986
Pymore *Dorset* 10 SY4694
Pyrford *Surrey* 26 TQ0458
Pyrton *Oxon* 37 SU6896
Pytchley *Nhants* 51 SP8574
Pyworthy *Devon* 18 SS3002

Q

Quabbs *Shrops* 58 SO2080
Quadring *Lincs* 64 TF2233
Quadring Eaudike *Lincs* 64 TF2433
Quainton *Bucks* 37 SP7420
Quaker's Yard *M Glam* 33 ST0996
Quaking Houses *Dur* 96 NZ1850
Quarley *Hants* 23 SU2743
Quarley *Hants* 23 SU2743
Quarndon *Derbys* 62 SK3340
Quarr Hill *IOW* 13 SZ5792
Quarrier's Homes *Strath* 115 NS3666
Quarrington *Lincs* 64 TF0544
Quarrington Hill *Dur* 96 NZ3337
Quarry Bank *W Mids* 60 SO9386
Quarrybank *Ches* 71 SJ5465
Quarrywood *Gramp* 141 NJ1764
Quarter *Strath* 116 NS7251
Quatford *Shrops* 60 SO7391
Quatt *Shrops* 60 SO7588
Quebec *Dur* 96 NZ1743
Quedgeley *Gloucs* 35 SO8113
Queen Adelaide *Cambs* 53 TL5681
Queen Camel *Somset* 21 ST5924
Queen Charlton *Avon* 21 ST6367
Queen Dart *Devon* 19 SS8316
Queen Oak *Dorset* 22 ST7840
Queen Street *Kent* 28 TQ6845
Queen Street *Wilts* 35 SU0287
Queen's Bower *IOW* 13 SZ5784
Queen's Head *Shrops* 59 SJ3327
Queen's Park *Beds* 38 TL0349
Queen's Park *Nhants* 49 SP7662
Queenborough *Kent* 28 TQ9172
Queenborough *Kent* 28 TQ9172
Queenhill *H & W* 47 SO8537
Queensbury *W York* 82 SE1030
Queensferry *Clwyd* 71 SJ3168
Queenzieburn *Strath* 116 NS6977
Quendon *Essex* 39 TL5130
Queniborough *Leics* 63 SK6412
Quenington *Gloucs* 36 SP1404
Quernhow *N York* 89 SE3480
Quernmore *Lancs* 87 SD5160
Quernmore Park Hall *Lancs* 87 SD5162
Queslett *W Mids* 61 SP0695
Quethiock *Cnwll* 5 SX3164
Quick's Green *Berks* 37 SU5876
Quidenham *Norfk* 54 TM0287
Quidhampton *Hants* 24 SU5150
Quidhampton *Wilts* 23 SU1030
Quina Brook *Shrops* 59 SJ5233
Quinberry End *Nhants* 49 SP6250
Quine's Hill *IOM* 153 SC3473
Quinish House *Strath* 121 NM4154
Quinton *Nhants* 49 SP7754
Quinton *W Mids* 60 SO9884
Quinton Green *Nhants* 38 SP7852
Quintrell Downs *Cnwll* 4 SW8460
Quither *Devon* 5 SX4481
Quixhall *Staffs* 73 SK1041
Quixwood *Border* 119 NT7863
Quoditch *Devon* 5 SX4097
Quorndon *Leics* 62 SK5616
Quothquan *Strath* 108 NS9939
Quoyburray *Ork* 155 HY5005
Quoyloo *Ork* 155 HY2421

R

RAF College *Lincs* 76 TF0049
Rabbit's Cross *Kent* 28 TQ7848
Rableyheath *Herts* 39 TL2319
Raby *Cumb* 93 NY1951
Raby *Mersyd* 71 SJ3179
Rachan Mill *Border* 108 NT1134
Rachub *Gwynd* 69 SH6267
Rackenford *Devon* 19 SS8418
Rackham *W Susx* 14 TQ0513
Rackheath *Norfk* 67 TG2814
Racks *D & G* 100 NY0274
Rackwick *Ork* 155 ND2099
Radbourne *Derbys* 73 SK2836
Radcliffe *Gt Man* 79 SD7807
Radcliffe *Nthumb* 103 NU2602
Radcliffe on Trent *Notts* 63 SK6439
Radclive *Bucks* 49 SP6734
Radcot *Oxon* 36 SU2899
Raddington *Somset* 20 ST0225
Radernie *Fife* 127 NO4609
Radford Semele *Warwks* 48 SP3464
Radlet *Somset* 20 ST2038
Radlett *Herts* 26 TL1600
Radley *Devon* 19 SS7323
Radley *Oxon* 37 SU5399
Radley Green *Essex* 40 TL6205
Radmore Green *Ches* 71 SJ5955
Radnage *Bucks* 37 SU7897
Radstock *Avon* 22 ST6854
Radstone *Nhants* 49 SP5840
Radway *Warwks* 48 SP3648
Radway Green *Ches* 72 SJ7754
Radwell *Beds* 51 TL0057
Radwell *Herts* 39 TL2335
Radwinter *Essex* 53 TL6037
Radwinter End *Essex* 53 TL6139
Radyr *S Glam* 33 ST1380
Raecleugh *D & G* 108 NT0311
Rafford *Gramp* 141 NJ0656
Raftra *Cnwll* 2 SW3723
Ragdale *Leics* 63 SK6619
Ragdon *Shrops* 59 SO4591
Raginnis *Cnwll* 2 SW4625
Raglan *Gwent* 34 SO4107
Ragnall *Notts* 75 SK8073
Raigbeg *Highld* 140 NH8128
Rainbow Hill *H & W* 47 SO8656
Rainford *Mersyd* 78 SD4700
Rainham *Gt Lon* 27 TQ5282
Rainham *Kent* 28 TQ8165
Rainhill *Mersyd* 78 SJ4991
Rainhill Stoops *Mersyd* 78 SJ5090
Rainigadale *W Isls* 154 NB2201
Rainow *Ches* 79 SJ9475
Rainsough *Gt Man* 79 SD8002
Rainton *N York* 89 SE3775
Rainworth *Notts* 75 SK5958
Raisbeck *Cumb* 87 NY6407
Raise *Cumb* 94 NY7146
Raisthorpe *N York* 90 SE8561
Rait *Tays* 126 NO2226
Raithby *Lincs* 77 TF3084
Raithby *Lincs* 77 TF3767
Raithwaite *N York* 90 NZ8611
Rake *W Susx* 14 SU8027
Rakewood *Gt Man* 82 SD9414
Ralia *Highld* 132 NN7097
Raltcliff Bridge *Cumb* 93 NY3636
Ram *Dyfed* 44 SN5846
Ram Hill *Avon* 35 ST6779
Ram Lane *Kent* 28 TQ9646
Ramasaig *Highld* 136 NG1644
Rame *Cnwll* 6 SX4249
Rame *Cnwll* 3 SW7233
Rampisham *Dorset* 10 ST5502
Rampside *Cumb* 86 SD2366
Rampton *Cambs* 53 TL4268
Rampton *Notts* 75 SK8078
Ramridge End *Beds* 38 TL1022
Ramsbottom *Gt Man* 81 SD7916
Ramsbury *Wilts* 36 SU2771
Ramscraigs *Highld* 151 ND1427
Ramsdean *Hants* 13 SU7022
Ramsdell *Hants* 24 SU5957
Ramsden *H & W* 47 SO9246
Ramsden *Oxon* 36 SP3515
Ramsden Bellhouse *Essex* 40 TQ7194
Ramsden Heath *Essex* 40 TQ7095
Ramsey *Cambs* 52 TL2885
Ramsey *Essex* 41 TM2130
Ramsey *IOM* 153 SC4594
Ramsey Forty Foot *Cambs* 52 TL3087
Ramsey Heights *Cambs* 52 TL2484
Ramsey Island *Essex* 40 TL9506
Ramsey Mereside *Cambs* 52 TL2889
Ramsey St. Mary's *Cambs* 52 TL2588
Ramsgate *Kent* 29 TR3865
Ramsgill *N York* 89 SE1170
Ramshaw *Dur* 95 NY9547
Ramsholt *Suffk* 55 TM3141
Ramshope *Nthumb* 102 NT7304
Ramshorn *Staffs* 73 SK0845
Ramsley *Devon* 8 SX6493
Ramsnest Common *Surrey* 14 SU9533
Ranby *Lincs* 76 TF2278
Ranby *Notts* 75 SK6580
Rand *Lincs* 76 TF1078
Randwick *Gloucs* 35 SO8206
Ranfurly *Strath* 115 NS3864
Rangemore *Staffs* 73 SK1822
Rangeworthy *Avon* 35 ST6986
Rank's Green *Essex* 40 TL7518
Rankinston *Strath* 107 NS4513
Ranksborough *Leics* 63 SK8310
Rann *Lancs* 81 SD7124
Rannoch Station *Tays* 124 NN4257
Ranochan *Highld* 129 NM8282
Ranscombe *Somset* 20 SS9543
Ranskill *Notts* 75 SK6587
Ranton *Staffs* 72 SJ8524
Ranton Green *Staffs* 72 SJ8423
Ranworth *Norfk* 67 TG3514
Raploch *Cent* 116 NS7894
Rapness *Ork* 155 HY5041
Rapps *Somset* 10 ST3316
Rascarrel *D & G* 92 NX7948
Rashfield *Strath* 114 NS1483
Rashwood *H & W* 47 SO9165
Raskelf *N York* 90 SE4971
Rassau *Gwent* 33 SO1512
Ratagan *Highld* 138 NG9220
Ratby *Leics* 62 SK5105
Ratcliffe Culey *Leics* 61 SP3299
Ratcliffe on Soar *Notts* 62 SK4928
Ratcliffe on the Wreake *Leics* 63 SK6314
Ratfyn *Wilts* 23 SU1642
Rathen *Gramp* 143 NJ9960
Rathhead *Fife* 117 NT2992
Rathillet *Fife* 126 NO3620
Rathmell *N York* 88 SD8059
Ratho *Loth* 117 NT1370
Rathven *Gramp* 142 NJ4465
Ratlake *Hants* 13 SU4123
Ratley *Warwks* 48 SP3847
Ratling *Kent* 29 TR2453
Ratlinghope *Shrops* 59 SO4097
Rattan Row *Norfk* 65 TF5114
Rattar *Highld* 151 ND2673
Ratten Row *Cumb* 93 NY3949
Ratten Row *Cumb* 93 NY3140
Ratten Row *Lancs* 80 SD4241
Rattery *Devon* 7 SX7361
Rattlesden *Suffk* 54 TL9759
Ratton Village *E Susx* 16 TQ5901
Rattray *Tays* 126 NO1845
Raughton *Cumb* 93 NY3948
Raughton Head *Cumb* 93 NY3745
Raunds *Nhants* 51 SP9972
Raven Meols *Mersyd* 78 SD2905
Ravenfield *S York* 75 SK4895
Ravenglass *Cumb* 86 SD0896
Ravenhills Green *H & W* 47 SO7454
Raveningham *Norfk* 67 TM3996
Ravenscar *N York* 91 NZ9801
Ravenscliffe *Staffs* 72 SJ8452
Ravensdale *IOM* 153 SC3592
Ravensden *Beds* 51 TL0754
Ravenshead *Notts* 75 SK5654
Ravensmoor *Ches* 71 SJ6150
Ravensthorpe *Nhants* 50 SP6670
Ravensthorpe *W York* 82 SE2220
Ravenstone *Bucks* 38 SP8450
Ravenstone *Leics* 62 SK4013
Ravenstonedale *Cumb* 88 NY7203
Ravenstruther *Strath* 116 NS9245
Ravensworth *N York* 89 NZ1307
Raw *N York* 91 NZ9305
Rawcliffe *Humb* 83 SE6822
Rawcliffe *N York* 83 SE5854
Rawcliffe *N York* 83 SE5854
Rawcliffe Bridge *Humb* 83 SE6921
Rawdon *W York* 82 SE2139
Rawling Street *Kent* 28 TQ9059
Rawmarsh *S York* 75 SK4396
Rawnsley *Staffs* 60 SK0212
Rawreth *Essex* 40 TQ7893
Rawridge *Devon* 9 ST2006
Rawtenstall *Lancs* 81 SD8123
Raydon *Suffk* 54 TM0438
Raylees *Nthumb* 102 NY9291
Rayleigh *Essex* 40 TQ8090
Raymond's Hill *Devon* 10 SY3396
Rayne *Essex* 40 TL7222
Raynes Park *Gt Lon* 26 TQ2368
Reach *Cambs* 53 TL5666
Read *Lancs* 81 SD7734
Reading *Berks* 24 SU7173
Reading Street *Kent* 29 TR3868
Reading Street *Kent* 17 TQ9230
Reagill *Cumb* 94 NY6017
Rearquhar *Highld* 146 NH7492
Rearsby *Leics* 63 SK6514
Rease Heath *Shrops* 72 SJ6454
Reaster *Highld* 151 ND2565
Reay *Highld* 150 NC9664
Reculver *Kent* 29 TR2269
Red Ball *Devon* 9 ST0917
Red Bull *Ches* 72 SJ8255
Red Cross *Cambs* 53 TL4754
Red Cross *Cnwll* 18 SS2605
Red Dial *Cumb* 93 NY2546
Red Hill *Dorset* 12 SZ0995
Red Hill *Warwks* 48 SP1355
Red Lodge *Suffk* 53 TL6970
Red Lumb *Gt Man* 81 SD8415
Red Rock *Gt Man* 78 SD5809
Red Roses *Dyfed* 31 SN2012
Red Row *T & W* 103 NZ2599
Red Street *Staffs* 72 SJ8251
Red Wharf Bay *Gwynd* 68 SH5281
Redberth *Dyfed* 31 SN0804
Redbourn *Herts* 38 TL1012
Redbourne *Lincs* 76 SK9699
Redbrook *Clwyd* 71 SJ5040
Redbrook *Gloucs* 34 SO5309
Redbrook Street *Kent* 28 TQ9336
Redburn *Highld* 140 NH9447
Redburn *Nthumb* 102 NY7764
Redcar *Cleve* 97 NZ6024
Redcastle *D & G* 100 NX8165
Redcastle *Highld* 139 NH5849
Redcliff Bay *Avon* 34 ST4475
Redding *Cent* 116 NS9278
Reddingmuirhead *Cent* 116 NS9177
Reddish *Gt Man* 79 SJ8993
Redditch *H & W* 48 SP0467
Rede *Suffk* 54 TL8056
Redenhall *Norfk* 55 TM2684
Redenham *Hants* 23 SU3049
Redesmouth *Nthumb* 102 NY8681
Redford *Gramp* 135 NO7570
Redford *Gramp* 135 NO7570
Redford *Tays* 127 NO5644
Redford *W Susx* 14 SU8626
Redfordgreen *Border* 109 NT3616
Redgate *M Glam* 33 ST0188
Redgorton *Tays* 125 NO0828
Redgrave *Suffk* 54 TM0478

Redhill Roughton

Redhill *Avon* 21 ST4963
Redhill *Gramp* 135 NJ7704
Redhill *Herts* 39 TL3032
Redhill *Surrey* 27 TQ2850
Redisham *Suffk* 55 TM4084
Redland *Avon* 34 ST5775
Redland *Ork* 155 HY3724
Redlingfield *Suffk* 54 TM1870
Redlingfield Green *Suffk* 54 TM1871
Redlynch *Somset* 22 ST6933
Redlynch *Wilts* 12 SU2020
Redmain *Cumb* 92 NY1434
Redmarley *H & W* 47 SO7666
Redmarley D'Abitot *Gloucs* 47 SO7531
Redmarshall *Cleve* 96 NZ3821
Redmile *Leics* 63 SK7935
Redmire *N York* 88 SE0491
Redmyre *Gramp* 135 NO7575
Redmyre *Gramp* 135 NO7575
Rednal *Shrops* 59 SJ3628
Rednal *W Mids* 60 SP0076
Redpath *Border* 110 NT5835
Redruth *Cnwll* 2 SW6941
Redstocks *Wilts* 22 ST9362
Redstone *Tays* 126 NO1834
Redvales *Gt Man* 79 SD8008
Redwick *Avon* 34 ST5486
Redwick *Gwent* 34 ST4184
Redworth *Dur* 96 NZ2423
Reed *Herts* 39 TL3636
Reedham *Norfk* 67 TG4101
Reedness *Humb* 84 SE7923
Reeds Holme *Lancs* 81 SD8124
Reedy *Devon* 8 SX8189
Reef *W Isls* 154 NB1134
Reepham *Lincs* 76 TF0373
Reepham *Norfk* 66 TG1023
Reeth *N York* 88 SE0499
Reeves Green *W Mids* 61 SP2677
Regaby *IOM* 153 SC4397
Reiff *Highld* 144 NB9614
Reigate *Surrey* 27 TQ2550
Reighton *N York* 91 TA1375
Reinachait *Highld* 148 NC0430
Reisque *Gramp* 143 NJ8820
Reiss *Highld* 151 ND3354
Rejerrah *Cnwll* 3 SW8056
Releath *Cnwll* 2 SW6633
Relubbus *Cnwll* 2 SW5631
Relugas *Gramp* 141 NH9948
Remenham *Berks* 37 SU7783
Remenham Hill *Berks* 37 SU7882
Remony *Tays* 124 NN7643
Rempstone *Notts* 62 SK5724
Rendcomb *Gloucs* 35 SP0209
Rendham *Suffk* 55 TM3464
Renfrew *Strath* 115 NS4967
Renhold *Beds* 51 TL0953
Renishaw *Derbys* 75 SK4477
Rennington *Nthumb* 111 NU2118
Renton *Strath* 115 NS3878
Renwick *Cumb* 94 NY5943
Repps *Norfk* 67 TG4217
Repton *Derbys* 73 SK3026
Resaurie *Highld* 140 NH7045
Rescassa *Cnwll* 3 SW9842
Rescorla *Cnwll* 3 SW9848
Resipole *Highld* 121 NM7264
Reskadinnick *Cnwll* 2 SW6341
Resolis *Highld* 140 NH6765
Resolven *W Glam* 33 SN8302
Rest and be Thankful *Strath* 123 NN2307
Reston *Border* 119 NT8862
Restronguet *Cnwll* 3 SW8136
Reswallie *Tays* 127 NO5051
Reterth *Cnwll* 4 SW9463
Retew *Cnwll* 3 SW9256
Retford *Notts* 75 SK7081
Retire *Cnwll* 4 SX0064
Rettendon *Essex* 40 TQ7698
Retyn *Cnwll* 4 SW8858
Revesby *Lincs* 77 TF2961
Rew *Devon* 7 SX7570
Rew Street *IOW* 13 SZ4994
Rewe *Devon* 9 SX9499
Rexon *Devon* 5 SX4188
Rexon Cross *Devon* 5 SX4188
Reydon *Suffk* 55 TM4977
Reymerston *Norfk* 66 TG0206
Reynalton *Dyfed* 31 SN0908
Reynoldston *W Glam* 32 SS4890
Rezare *Cnwll* 5 SX3677
Rhadyr *Gwent* 34 SO3602
Rhandirmwyn *Dyfed* 44 SN7843
Rhayader *Powys* 45 SN9768
Rheindown *Highld* 139 NH5147
Rhelonie *Highld* 146 NH5597
Rhes-y-cae *Clwyd* 70 SJ1971
Rhewl *Clwyd* 70 SJ1160
Rhewl *Clwyd* 70 SJ1744
Rhewl Mostyn *Clwyd* 70 SJ1580
Rhewl-fawr *Clwyd* 70 SJ1580
Rhicarn *Highld* 148 NC0825
Rhiconich *Highld* 148 NC2552
Rhicullen *Highld* 146 NH6971
Rhifail *Highld* 150 NC7249
Rhigos *M Glam* 33 SN9205
Rhilochan *Highld* 146 NC7407
Rhireavach *Highld* 144 NH0295
Rhives *Highld* 147 NC8200
Rhiwbina *S Glam* 33 ST1682
Rhiwbryfdir *Gwynd* 57 SH6946
Rhiwderyn *Gwent* 34 ST2687
Rhiwen *Gwynd* 69 SH5763
Rhiwinder *M Glam* 33 ST0287
Rhiwlas *Clwyd* 58 SJ1932
Rhiwlas *Gwynd* 69 SH5765
Rhiwlas *Gwynd* 58 SH9237
Rhiwsaeson *M Glam* 33 ST0682
Rhode *Somset* 20 ST2734
Rhoden Green *Kent* 28 TQ6745
Rhodes *Gt Man* 79 SD8505
Rhodes Minnis *Kent* 29 TR1542
Rhodesia *Notts* 75 SK5680
Rhodiad-y-brenin *Dyfed* 30 SM7627
Rhonehouse or Kelton Hill *D & G* 99 NX7459
Rhoose *S Glam* 20 ST0666
Rhos *Clwyd* 70 SJ1261
Rhos *Dyfed* 31 SN3835
Rhos *Powys* 45 SO1731
Rhos *W Glam* 32 SN7403
Rhos Haminiog *Dyfed* 43 SN5364
Rhos Lligwy *Gwynd* 68 SH4986
Rhos y-brithdir *Powys* 58 SJ1323
Rhos-fawr *Gwynd* 56 SH3838
Rhos-hill *Dyfed* 31 SN1940
Rhos-on-Sea *Clwyd* 69 SH8480
Rhos-y-garth *Dyfed* 43 SN6373
Rhos-y-gwaliau *Gwynd* 58 SH9434
Rhos-y-llan *Gwynd* 56 SH2337
Rhos-y-meirch *Powys* 46 SO2769
Rhosaman *Dyfed* 32 SN7214
Rhoscefnhir *Gwynd* 68 SH5276
Rhoscolyn *Gwynd* 56 SH2735
Rhoscrowther *Dyfed* 30 SM9002
Rhosesmor *Clwyd* 70 SJ2168
Rhosgadfan *Gwynd* 68 SH5057
Rhosgoch *Gwynd* 68 SH4189
Rhosgoch *Powys* 45 SO1847
Rhoshirwaun *Gwynd* 56 SH1930
Rhoslan *Gwynd* 56 SH4841
Rhosllanerchrugog *Clwyd* 71 SJ2946
Rhosmaen *Dyfed* 44 SN6423
Rhosmeirch *Gwynd* 68 SH4677
Rhosneigr *Gwynd* 68 SH3172
Rhosnesni *Clwyd* 71 SJ3450
Rhosrobin *Clwyd* 71 SJ3452
Rhossili *W Glam* 31 SS4188
Rhostryfan *Gwynd* 68 SH4958
Rhostyllen *Clwyd* 71 SJ3148
Rhosybol *Gwynd* 68 SH4288
Rhosygadfa *Shrops* 59 SJ3234
Rhosymedre *Clwyd* 70 SJ2842
Rhu *Strath* 115 NS2783
Rhuallt *Clwyd* 70 SJ0774
Rhuban *W Isls* 154 NF7811
Rhubodach *Strath* 114 NS0273
Rhuddall Heath *Ches* 71 SJ5562
Rhuddlan *Clwyd* 70 SJ0277
Rhulen *Powys* 45 SO1349
Rhunahaorine *Strath* 105 NR7048
Rhyd *Gwynd* 57 SH6341
Rhyd-Ddu *Gwynd* 69 SH5652
Rhyd-lydan *Clwyd* 69 SH8950
Rhyd-uchaf *Gwynd* 58 SH9037
Rhyd-y pennau *Dyfed* 43 SN6386
Rhyd-y-clafdy *Gwynd* 56 SH3234
Rhyd-y-foel *Clwyd* 70 SH9176
Rhyd-y-groes *Gwynd* 69 SH5867
Rhyd-y-meirch *Gwent* 34 SO3107
Rhyd-y-sarn *Gwynd* 57 SH6842
Rhyd-yr-onnen *Gwynd* 57 SH6102
Rhydargaeau *Dyfed* 31 SN4326
Rhydcymerau *Dyfed* 44 SN5738
Rhydd *H & W* 47 SO8345
Rhydding *W Glam* 32 SS7499
Rhyddlan *Dyfed* 44 SN4943
Rhydgaled *Clwyd* 70 SH9964
Rhydlanfair *Gwynd* 69 SH8252
Rhydlewis *Dyfed* 42 SN3447
Rhydlios *Gwynd* 56 SH1830
Rhydowen *Dyfed* 42 SN4445
Rhydrosser *Dyfed* 43 SN5667
Rhydspence *H & W* 46 SO2447
Rhydtalog *Clwyd* 70 SJ2354
Rhydwyn *Gwynd* 68 SH3188
Rhydycroesau *Shrops* 58 SJ2430
Rhydyfelin *Dyfed* 43 SN5979
Rhydyfelin *M Glam* 33 ST0988
Rhydyfro *W Glam* 32 SN7105
Rhydymain *Gwynd* 57 SH7821
Rhydymwyn *Clwyd* 70 SJ2067
Rhyl *Clwyd* 70 SJ0181
Rhymney *M Glam* 33 SO1107
Rhynd *Tays* 126 NO1520
Rhynie *Gramp* 142 NJ4927
Rhynie *Highld* 147 NH8479
Ribbesford *H & W* 60 SO7874
Ribbleton *Lancs* 81 SD5631
Ribby *Lancs* 80 SD4031
Ribchester *Lancs* 81 SD6535
Riber *Derbys* 74 SK3059
Ribigill *Highld* 149 NC5854
Riby *Lincs* 85 TA1807
Riccall *N York* 83 SE6237
Riccarton *Border* 101 NY5495
Riccarton *Strath* 107 NS4236
Richards Castle *H & W* 46 SO4969
Richings Park *Bucks* 26 TQ0278
Richmond *N York* 89 NZ1701
Richmond *S York* 74 SK4085
Richmond Fort *Guern* 152 GN0000
Richmond upon Thames *Gt Lon* 26 TQ1874
Richs Halford *Somset* 20 ST1534
Rickerscote *Staffs* 72 SJ9220
Rickford *Avon* 21 ST4859
Rickham *Devon* 7 SX7437
Rickham *Devon* 7 SX7437
Rickinghall Inferior *Suffk* 54 TM0475
Rickinghall Superior *Suffk* 54 TM0375
Rickinghall Superior *Suffk* 54 TM0475
Rickling *Essex* 39 TL4931
Rickling Green *Essex* 39 TL5029
Rickmansworth *Herts* 26 TQ0694
Riddell *Border* 109 NT5124
Riddings *Cumb* 101 NY4075
Riddings *Derbys* 74 SK4252
Riddlecombe *Devon* 19 SS6013
Riddlesden *W York* 82 SE0742
Ridge *Avon* 21 ST5555
Ridge *Dorset* 11 SY9386
Ridge *Herts* 26 TL2100
Ridge *Wilts* 22 ST9531
Ridge Green *Surrey* 15 TQ3048
Ridge Lane *Warwks* 61 SP2994
Ridge Row *Kent* 29 TR2042
Ridgebourne *Powys* 45 SO0560
Ridgehill *Avon* 21 ST5362
Ridgeway *Derbys* 74 SK3551
Ridgeway *Derbys* 74 SK4081
Ridgeway *H & W* 48 SP0461
Ridgeway Cross *H & W* 47 SO7147
Ridgewell *Essex* 53 TL7340
Ridgewood *E Susx* 16 TQ4719
Ridgmont *Beds* 38 SP9736
Riding Mill *Nthumb* 103 NZ0161
Ridley *Kent* 27 TQ6164
Ridley *Nthumb* 102 NY7963
Ridley Green *Ches* 71 SJ5554
Ridlington *Leics* 63 SK8402
Ridlington *Norfk* 67 TG3431
Ridlington Street *Norfk* 67 TG3430
Ridsdale *Nthumb* 102 NY9084
Rievaulx *N York* 90 SE5785
Rigg *D & G* 101 NY2966
Riggend *Strath* 116 NS7670
Righoul *Highld* 140 NH8851
Rigmadon Park *Cumb* 87 SD6185
Rigsby *Lincs* 77 TF4375
Rigside *Strath* 108 NS8735
Riley Green *Lancs* 81 SD6225
Rileyhill *Staffs* 73 SK1115
Rilla Mill *Cnwll* 5 SX2973
Rillaton *Cnwll* 5 SX2973
Rillington *N York* 90 SE8574
Rimington *Lancs* 81 SD8045
Rimpton *Somset* 21 ST6021
Rimswell *Humb* 85 TA3028
Rinaston *Dyfed* 30 SM9826
Rindleford *Shrops* 60 SO7395
Ring O'Bells *Lancs* 78 SD4510
Ring's End *Cambs* 65 TF3902
Ringford *D & G* 99 NX6857
Ringinglow *Derbys* 74 SK2983
Ringland *Norfk* 66 TG1314
Ringles Cross *E Susx* 16 TQ4722
Ringlestone *Kent* 28 TQ8755
Ringley *Gt Man* 79 SD7605
Ringmer *E Susx* 16 TQ4412
Ringmore *Devon* 7 SX9272
Ringmore *Devon* 7 SX6545
Ringorm *Gramp* 141 NJ2644
Ringsfield *Suffk* 55 TM4088
Ringsfield Corner *Suffk* 55 TM4087
Ringshall *Bucks* 38 SP9814
Ringshall *Suffk* 54 TM0453
Ringshall Stocks *Suffk* 54 TM0551
Ringstead *Nhants* 51 SP9875
Ringstead *Norfk* 65 TF7040
Ringwood *Hants* 12 SU1405
Ringwould *Kent* 29 TR3548
Rinsey *Cnwll* 2 SW5927
Rinsey Croft *Cnwll* 2 SW6028
Ripe *E Susx* 16 TQ5110
Ripley *Derbys* 74 SK3950
Ripley *Hants* 12 SZ1698
Ripley *N York* 89 SE2860
Ripley *Surrey* 26 TQ0556
Riplingham *Humb* 84 SE9631
Riplington *Hants* 13 SU6623
Ripon *N York* 89 SE3171
Rippingale *Lincs* 64 TF0927
Ripple *H & W* 47 SO8737
Ripple *Kent* 29 TR3550
Ripponden *W York* 82 SE0319
Risabus *Strath* 104 NR3143
Risbury *H & W* 46 SO5454
Risby *Humb* 84 SE9114
Risby *Suffk* 53 TL7966
Risca *Gwent* 34 ST2391
Rise *Humb* 85 TA1542
Riseden *E Susx* 16 TQ6130
Risedown *Kent* 28 TQ7036
Risegate *Lincs* 64 TF2129
Riseholme *Lincs* 76 SK9670
Risehow *Cumb* 92 NY0335
Riseley *Beds* 51 TL0462
Riseley *Berks* 24 SU7263
Rishangles *Suffk* 54 TM1668
Rishton *Lancs* 81 SD7230
Rishworth *W York* 82 SE0318
Rising Bridge *Lancs* 81 SD7825
Risley *Ches* 79 SJ6592
Risley *Derbys* 62 SK4635
Risplith *N York* 89 SE2468
Rivar *Wilts* 23 SU3161
Rivenhall End *Essex* 40 TL8416
River *Kent* 29 TR2943
River *W Susx* 14 SU9322
River Bank *Cambs* 53 TL5368
Riverford *Highld* 139 NH5455
Riverhead *Kent* 27 TQ5156
Rivers Corner *Dorset* 11 ST7712
Rivington *Lancs* 81 SD6214
Roa Island *Cumb* 86 SD2364
Roachhill *Devon* 19 SS8422
Road Ashton *Wilts* 22 ST8856
Road Green *Norfk* 67 TM2694
Road Weedon *Nhants* 49 SP6359
Roade *Nhants* 49 SP7551
Roadhead *Cumb* 101 NY5175
Roadmeetings *Strath* 116 NS8649
Roadside *Highld* 151 ND1560
Roadside *Strath* 107 NS5717
Roadside of Catterline *Gramp* 135 NO8678
Roadside of Catterline *Gramp* 135 NO8678
Roadside of Kinneff *Gramp* 135 NO8477
Roadwater *Somset* 20 ST0238
Roag *Highld* 136 NG2744
Roan of Craigoch *Strath* 106 NS2904
Roast Green *Essex* 39 TL4632
Roath *S Glam* 33 ST1977
Roberton *Border* 109 NT4214
Roberton *Strath* 108 NS9428
Robertsbridge *E Susx* 17 TQ7423
Roberttown *W York* 82 SE1922
Robeston Wathen *Dyfed* 31 SN0815
Robgill Tower *D & G* 101 NY2471
Robin Hill *Staffs* 72 SJ9057
Robin Hood *Lancs* 80 SD5211
Robin Hood *W York* 83 SE3227
Robin Hood's Bay *N York* 91 NZ9505
Robinhood End *Essex* 53 TL7036
Roborough *Devon* 19 SS5717
Roby *Mersyd* 78 SJ4390
Roby Mill *Lancs* 78 SD5107
Rocester *Staffs* 73 SK1039
Roch *Dyfed* 30 SM8821
Roch Gate *Dyfed* 30 SM8720
Rochdale *Gt Man* 81 SD8913
Roche *Cnwll* 4 SW9860
Rochester *Kent* 28 TQ7468
Rochester *Nthumb* 102 NY8298
Rochford *Essex* 40 TQ8790
Rochford *H & W* 47 SO6368
Rochville *Strath* 114 NS2390
Rock *Cnwll* 4 SW9476
Rock *H & W* 60 SO7371
Rock *Nthumb* 111 NU2020
Rock *W Glam* 32 SS7893
Rock *W Susx* 14 TQ1214
Rock Ferry *Mersyd* 78 SJ3386
Rock Hill *H & W* 47 SO9569
Rockbeare *Devon* 9 SY0195
Rockbourne *Hants* 12 SU1118
Rockcliffe *Cumb* 101 NY3561
Rockcliffe *D & G* 92 NX8553
Rockcliffe Cross *Cumb* 101 NY3463
Rockesta *Cnwll* 2 SW3722
Rockfield *Gwent* 34 SO4814
Rockfield *Highld* 147 NH9283
Rockford *Devon* 19 SS7547
Rockford *Hants* 12 SU1608
Rockgreen *Shrops* 46 SO5275
Rockhampton *Gloucs* 35 ST6593
Rockhead *Cnwll* 4 SX0784
Rockhill *Shrops* 46 SO2879
Rockingham *Nhants* 51 SP8691
Rockland All Saints *Norfk* 66 TL9996
Rockland St. Mary *Norfk* 67 TG3104
Rockland St. Peter *Norfk* 66 TL9897
Rockley *Notts* 75 SK7174
Rockley *Wilts* 36 SU1571
Rockliffe *Lancs* 81 SD8722
Rockwell End *Bucks* 37 SU7988
Rockwell Green *Somset* 20 ST1320
Rodborough *Gloucs* 35 SO8304
Rodbourne *Wilts* 36 SU1485
Rodbourne *Wilts* 35 ST9383
Rodd *H & W* 46 SO3262
Roddam *Nthumb* 111 NU0220
Rodden *Dorset* 10 SY6184
Roddymoor *Dur* 96 NZ1536
Rode *Somset* 22 ST8053
Rode Heath *Ches* 72 SJ8767
Rode Heath *Ches* 72 SJ8057
Rodel *W Isls* 154 NG0483
Roden *Shrops* 59 SJ5716
Rodhuish *Somset* 20 ST0139
Rodington *Shrops* 59 SJ5814
Rodington Heath *Shrops* 59 SJ5814
Rodley *Gloucs* 35 SO7411
Rodley *W York* 82 SE2236
Rodmarton *Gloucs* 35 ST9497
Rodmell *E Susx* 15 TQ4106
Rodmersham *Kent* 28 TQ9261
Rodmersham Green *Kent* 28 TQ9161
Rodney Stoke *Somset* 21 ST4849
Rodono *Border* 109 NT2321
Rodsley *Derbys* 73 SK2040
Rodway *Somset* 20 ST2540
Roe Cross *Gt Man* 79 SJ9896
Roe Green *Gt Man* 79 SD7501
Roe Green *Herts* 39 TL2107
Roe Green *Herts* 39 TL3133
Roecliffe *N York* 89 SE3765
Roehampton *Gt Lon* 26 TQ2273
Roewen *Gwynd* 69 SH7672
Roffey *W Susx* 15 TQ1932
Rogart *Highld* 146 NC7304
Rogate *W Susx* 14 SU8023
Roger Ground *Cumb* 101 NY3597
Rogerstone *Gwent* 34 ST2788
Rogiet *Gwent* 34 ST4587
Roke *Oxon* 37 SU6293
Roker *T & W* 96 NZ4059
Rollesby *Norfk* 67 TG4415
Rolleston *Leics* 50 SK7300
Rolleston *Notts* 75 SK7452
Rolleston *Staffs* 73 SK2327
Rolston *Humb* 85 TA2145
Rolstone *Avon* 21 ST3862
Rolvenden *Kent* 17 TQ8431
Rolvenden Layne *Kent* 17 TQ8530
Romaldkirk *Dur* 95 NY9921
Romanby *N York* 89 SE3693
Romanno Bridge *Border* 117 NT1647
Romansleigh *Devon* 19 SS7220
Romden Castle *Kent* 28 TQ8941
Romesdal *Highld* 136 NG4033
Romford *Dorset* 12 SU0709
Romford *Gt Lon* 27 TQ5188
Romiley *Gt Man* 79 SJ9490
Romney Street *Kent* 27 TQ5461
Romsey *Hants* 12 SU3521
Romsley *H & W* 60 SO9679
Romsley *Shrops* 60 SO7883
Ronachan *Strath* 113 NR7454
Ronague *IOM* 153 SC2472
Rookhope *Dur* 95 NY9342
Rookley *IOW* 13 SZ5084
Rookley Green *IOW* 13 SZ5083
Rooks Bridge *Somset* 21 ST3752
Rooks Nest *Somset* 20 ST0339
Rookwith *N York* 89 SE2086
Roos *Humb* 85 TA2830
Roosebeck *Cumb* 101 NY2567
Roothams Green *Beds* 51 TL1057
Ropley *Hants* 24 SU6431
Ropley Dean *Hants* 24 SU6332
Ropley Soke *Hants* 24 SU6533
Ropsley *Lincs* 63 SK9934
Rora *Gramp* 143 NK0650
Rorrington *Shrops* 59 SJ3000
Rosarie *Gramp* 141 NJ3850
Roscroggan *Cnwll* 2 SW6542
Rose *Cnwll* 3 SW7754
Rose Ash *Devon* 19 SS7821
Rose Green *Essex* 40 TL9028
Rose Green *Suffk* 54 TL9337
Rose Green *Suffk* 54 TL9744
Rose Green *W Susx* 14 SZ9099
Rose Hill *E Susx* 16 TQ4516
Rose Hill *Lancs* 81 SD8231
Rose Lands *E Susx* 16 TQ6200
Roseacre *Lancs* 80 SD4336
Rosebank *Strath* 116 NS8049
Rosebush *Dyfed* 31 SN0729
Rosecare *Cnwll* 4 SX1695
Rosecliston *Cnwll* 4 SW8159
Rosedale Abbey *N York* 90 SE7296
Roseden *Nthumb* 111 NU0321
Rosehall *Highld* 146 NC4701
Rosehearty *Gramp* 143 NJ9367
Rosehill *Shrops* 59 SJ4717
Roseisle *Gramp* 141 NJ1466
Rosemarket *Dyfed* 30 SM9508
Rosemarkie *Highld* 140 NH7357
Rosemary Lane *Devon* 9 ST1514
Rosemount *Tays* 126 NO1843
Rosenannon *Cnwll* 4 SW9566
Rosenithon *Cnwll* 3 SW8021
Roser's Cross *E Susx* 16 TQ5420
Rosevean *Cnwll* 4 SX0258
Rosevine *Cnwll* 3 SW8736
Rosewarne *Cnwll* 2 SW6137
Rosewell *Loth* 117 NT2862
Roseworth *Cleve* 96 NZ4121
Roseworthy *Cnwll* 2 SW6139
Rosgill *Cumb* 94 NY5316
Roshven *Highld* 129 NM7078
Roskhill *Highld* 136 NG2745
Roskorwell *Cnwll* 3 SW7923
Roskrow *Cnwll* 3 SW7635
Rosley *Cumb* 93 NY3245
Roslin *Loth* 117 NT2763
Rosliston *Derbys* 73 SK2416
Rosneath *Strath* 114 NS2583
Ross *D & G* 99 NX6444
Ross *Nthumb* 111 NU1337
Ross *Tays* 124 NN7621
Ross-on-Wye *H & W* 46 SO6024
Rossett *Clwyd* 71 SJ3657
Rossett Green *N York* 82 SE2952
Rossie Orchill *Tays* 125 NO0912
Rossington *Notts* 75 SK6298
Rosskeen *Highld* 146 NH6869
Rossland *Strath* 115 NS4370
Roster *Highld* 151 ND2639
Rostherne *Ches* 79 SJ7483
Rosthwwaite *Cumb* 93 NY2514
Roston *Derbys* 73 SK1241
Rosudgeon *Cnwll* 2 SW5529
Rosyth *Loth* 117 NT1182
Rothbury *Nthumb* 103 NU0501
Rotherby *Leics* 63 SK6716
Rotherfield *E Susx* 16 TQ5529
Rotherfield Greys *Oxon* 37 SU7282
Rotherfield Peppard *Oxon* 37 SU7082
Rotherham *S York* 75 SK4392
Rothersthorpe *Nhants* 49 SP7156
Rotherwick *Hants* 24 SU7156
Rothes *Gramp* 141 NJ2749
Rothesay *Strath* 114 NS0864
Rothiebrisbane *Gramp* 142 NJ7437
Rothiemay *Gramp* 142 NJ5448
Rothienorman *Gramp* 142 NJ7235
Rothley *Leics* 62 SK5812
Rothley *Nthumb* 103 NZ0488
Rothmaise *Gramp* 142 NJ6832
Rothwell *Lincs* 76 TF1499
Rothwell *Nhants* 51 SP8181
Rothwell *W York* 83 SE3428
Rothwell Haigh *W York* 83 SE3328
Rotsea *Humb* 84 TA0651
Rottal *Tays* 134 NO3769
Rottingdean *E Susx* 15 TQ3602
Rottington *Cumb* 92 NX9613
Roucan *D & G* 100 NY0277
Roud *IOW* 13 SZ5180
Rough Close *Staffs* 72 SJ9239
Rough Common *Kent* 29 TR1359
Rougham *Norfk* 66 TF8320
Rougham Green *Suffk* 54 TL9061
Roughlee *Lancs* 81 SD8440
Roughley *W Mids* 61 SP1399
Roughton *Lincs* 76 TF2364

Roughton Scholey Hill

Roughton Norfk 67 TG2237
Roughton Shrops 60 SO7594
Roughway Kent 27 TQ6153
Round Bush Herts 26 TQ1498
Round Green Suffk 53 TL7154
Round Street Kent 28 TQ6568
Roundbush Essex 40 TL8601
Roundbush Green Essex 40 TL5815
Roundham Somset 10 ST4209
Roundhay W York 83 SE3235
Rounds Green W Mids 60 SO9889
Roundstone Foot D & G 108 NT1308
Roundstreet Common W Susx 14 TQ0528
Roundway Wilts 22 SU0163
Roundyhill Tays 126 NO3750
Rous Lench H & W 47 SP0153
Rousdon Devon 10 SY2990
Rousham Oxon 49 SP4724
Rout's Green Bucks 37 SU7899
Routenbeck Cumb 93 NY1930
Routenburn Strath 114 NS1961
Routh Humb 85 TA0942
Row Cnwll 4 SX0976
Row Cumb 94 NY6235
Row Cumb 87 SD4589
Row Ash Hants 13 SU5413
Row Green Essex 40 TL7420
Rowanburn D & G 101 NY4177
Rowardennan Cent 115 NS3698
Rowarth Derbys 79 SK0189
Rowberrow Somset 21 ST4558
Rowborough IOW 13 SZ4685
Rowde Wilts 22 ST9762
Rowden Devon 8 SX6499
Rowfield Derbys 73 SK1949
Rowfoot Nthumb 102 NY6860
Rowford Somset 20 ST2327
Rowhedge Essex 41 TM0321
Rowhook W Susx 14 TQ1234
Rowington Warwks 48 SP2069
Rowland Derbys 74 SK2172
Rowland's Castle Hants 13 SU7310
Rowland's Gill T & W 96 NZ1658
Rowledge Surrey 25 SU8243
Rowley Dur 95 NZ0848
Rowley Humb 84 SE9732
Rowley Shrops 59 SJ3006
Rowley Green W Mids 61 SP3483
Rowley Hill W York 82 SE1915
Rowley Regis W Mids 60 SO9787
Rowlstone H & W 46 SO3727
Rowly Surrey 14 TQ0441
Rowner Hants 13 SU5801
Rowney Green H & W 61 SP0471
Rownhams Hants 12 SU3817
Rows of Trees Ches 79 SJ8379
Rowsham Bucks 38 SP8418
Rowsley Derbys 74 SK2566
Rowstock Oxon 37 SU4788
Rowston Lincs 76 TF0856
Rowthorne Derbys 75 SK4864
Rowton Ches 71 SJ4564
Rowton Shrops 59 SO4180
Rowton Shrops 59 SJ3612
Rowton Shrops 59 SJ6120
Rowtown Surrey 26 TQ0363
Roxburgh Border 110 NT6930
Roxby Humb 84 SE9217
Roxby N York 97 NZ7616
Roxton Beds 52 TL1554
Roxwell Essex 40 TL6408
Roy Bridge Highld 131 NN2681
Royal Leamington Spa Warwks 48 SP3265
Royal Oak Dur 96 NZ2023
Royal Oak Lancs 78 SD4103
Royal Tunbridge Wells Kent 16 TQ5839
Royal's Green Ches 71 SJ6242
Roydhouse W York 82 SE2112
Roydon Essex 39 TL4009
Roydon Norfk 65 TF7023
Roydon Norfk 54 TM0980
Roydon Hamlet Essex 39 TL4107
Royston Herts 39 TL3540
Royston S York 83 SE3611
Royton Gt Man 79 SD9107
Rozel Jersey 152 JS0000
Ruabon Clwyd 71 SJ3043
Ruaig Strath 120 NM0747
Ruan Lanihorne Cnwll 3 SW8942
Ruan Major Cnwll 2 SW7016
Ruan Minor Cnwll 2 SW7215
Ruardean Gloucs 34 SO6117
Ruardean Hill Gloucs 35 SO6317
Ruardean Woodside Gloucs 35 SO6215
Rubery H & W 60 SO9877
Ruckcroft Cumb 94 NY5344
Ruckhall Common H & W 46 SO4539
Ruckinge Kent 17 TR0233
Ruckland Lincs 77 TF3378
Ruckley Shrops 59 SJ5300
Rudby N York 89 NZ4706
Rudchester Nthumb 103 NZ1167
Ruddington Notts 62 SK5733
Ruddle Gloucs 35 SO6811
Ruddlemoor Cnwll 3 SX0054
Rudford Gloucs 35 SO7721
Rudge Somset 22 ST8252
Rudgeway Avon 35 ST6386
Rudgwick W Susx 14 TQ0833
Rudhall H & W 47 SO6225
Rudheath Ches 79 SJ7471
Rudley Green Essex 40 TL8303
Rudry M Glam 33 ST2086
Rudston Humb 91 TA0967
Rudway Barton Devon 9 SS9301
Rudyard Staffs 72 SJ9558
Ruecastle Border 110 NT6120
Rufford Lancs 80 SD4615
Rufforth N York 83 SE5251
Rug Clwyd 70 SJ0543
Rugby Warwks 50 SP5075
Rugeley Staffs 73 SK0418
Ruggaton Devon 19 SS5645
Ruishton Somset 20 ST2624
Ruislip Gt Lon 26 TQ0987
Ruletown Head Border 110 NT6113
Rumbach Gramp 141 NJ3852
Rumbling Bridge Tays 117 NT0199
Rumburgh Suffk 55 TM3481
Rumby Hill Dur 96 NZ1634
Rumford Cent 116 NS9377
Rumford Cnwll 4 SW8970
Rumney S Glam 33 ST2179
Rumwell Somset 20 ST1923
Runcorn Ches 78 SJ5182
Runcton W Susx 14 SU8802
Runcton Holme Norfk 65 TF6109
Runfold Surrey 25 SU8747
Runhall Norfk 66 TG0507
Runham Norfk 67 TG5108
Runham Norfk 67 TG4610
Running Waters Dur 96 NZ3340
Runnington Somset 20 ST1121
Runsell Green Essex 40 TL7905
Runshaw Moor Lancs 80 SD5319
Runswick N York 97 NZ8016
Runtaleave Tays 133 NO2867
Runwell Essex 40 TQ7594
Ruscombe Berks 37 SU8076
Rush Green Ches 79 SJ6987
Rush Green Essex 41 TM1615
Rush Green Gt Lon 27 TQ5187
Rush Green Herts 39 TL3325
Rush Green Herts 39 TL2123
Rushall H & W 47 SO6435
Rushall Norfk 55 TM1982
Rushall W Mids 60 SK0201
Rushall Wilts 23 SU1255
Rushbrooke Suffk 54 TL8961
Rushbury Shrops 59 SO5092
Rushden Herts 39 TL3031
Rushden Nhants 51 SP9566
Rushenden Kent 28 TQ9071
Rusher's Cross E Susx 16 TQ6028
Rushett Common Surrey 14 TQ0242
Rushford Devon 5 SX4476
Rushford Norfk 54 TL9281
Rushlake Green E Susx 16 TQ6218
Rushmere Suffk 55 TM4987
Rushmere St. Andrew Suffk 55 TM1946
Rushmoor Surrey 25 SU8740
Rushock H & W 46 SO3058
Rushock H & W 60 SO8871
Rusholme Gt Man 79 SJ8595
Rushton Ches 71 SJ5864
Rushton Nhants 51 SP8483
Rushton Shrops 59 SJ6008
Rushton Spencer Staffs 72 SJ9362
Rushwick H & W 47 SO8254
Rushyford Dur 96 NZ2828
Ruskie Cent 116 NN6200
Ruskington Lincs 76 TF0850
Rusland Cumb 87 SD3488
Rusper W Susx 15 TQ2037
Ruspidge Gloucs 35 SO6611
Russ Hill Surrey 15 TQ2340
Russel's Green Suffk 55 TM2572
Russell Green Essex 40 TL7413
Russell's Green E Susx 16 TQ7011
Russell's Water Oxon 37 SU7089
Rusthall Kent 16 TQ5639
Rusthall Kent 16 TQ5639
Rustington W Susx 14 TQ0502
Ruston N York 91 SE9583
Ruston Parva Humb 91 TA0661
Ruswarp N York 90 NZ8809
Ruthall Shrops 59 SO5990
Rutherford Border 110 NT6430
Rutherglen Strath 116 NS6162
Ruthernbridge Cnwll 4 SX0166
Ruthin Clwyd 70 SJ1258
Ruthrieston Gramp 135 NJ9204
Ruthven Gramp 142 NJ5046
Ruthven Highld 132 NN7699
Ruthven Highld 140 NH8132
Ruthven Tays 126 NO2848
Ruthven House Tays 126 NO3047
Ruthvoes Cnwll 4 SW9260
Ruthwaite Cumb 93 NY2336
Ruthwell D & G 100 NY1067
Ruxley Corner Gt Lon 27 TQ4770
Ruxton Green H & W 34 SO5419
Ruyton-XI-Towns Shrops 59 SJ3922
Ryal Nthumb 103 NZ0174
Ryall Dorset 10 SY4094
Ryall H & W 47 SO8640
Ryarsh Kent 28 TQ6660
Rycote Oxon 37 SP6705
Rydal Cumb 87 NY3606
Ryde IOW 13 SZ5992
Rye E Susx 17 TQ9220
Rye Cross H & W 47 SO7735
Rye Foreign E Susx 17 TQ8922
Rye Harbour E Susx 17 TQ9319
Rye Street H & W 47 SO7835
Ryebank Shrops 59 SJ5131
Ryeford H & W 35 SO6322
Ryeish Green Nhants 24 SU6267
Ryhall Leics 64 TF0310
Ryhill W York 83 SE3814
Ryhope T & W 96 NZ4152
Rylah Derbys 75 SK4667
Ryland Lincs 76 TF0179
Rylands Notts 62 SK5336
Rylstone N York 88 SD9658
Ryme Intrinseca Dorset 10 ST5810
Ryther N York 83 SE5539
Ryton N York 90 SE7975
Ryton Shrops 60 SJ7602
Ryton T & W 103 NZ1564
Ryton Warwks 61 SP3986
Ryton Woodside T & W 96 NZ1462
Ryton-on-Dunsmore Warwks 61 SP3874

S

Sabden Lancs 81 SD7837
Sabine's Green Essex 27 TQ5496
Sacombe Herts 39 TL3319
Sacombe Green Herts 39 TL3419
Sacriston T & W 96 NZ2447
Sadberge Dur 96 NZ3416
Saddell Strath 105 NR7832
Saddington Leics 50 SP6591
Saddle Bow Norfk 65 TF6015
Saddlescombe W Susx 15 TQ2711
Sadgilk Cumb 87 NY4805
Saffron Walden Essex 39 TL5438
Sageston Dyfed 30 SN0503
Saham Hills Norfk 66 TF9003
Saham Toney Norfk 66 TF9001
Saighton Ches 71 SJ4462
Saint Hill Devon 9 ST0908
Saint Hill W Susx 15 TQ3835
Saintbury Gloucs 48 SP1139
Salachail Strath 123 NN0551
Salcombe Devon 7 SX7338
Salcombe Regis Devon 9 SY1588
Salcott Essex 40 TL9413
Sale Gt Man 79 SJ7991
Sale Green H & W 47 SO9358
Saleby Lincs 77 TF4578
Salehurst E Susx 17 TQ7424
Salem Dyfed 44 SN6236
Salem Dyfed 43 SN6684
Salem Gwynd 69 SH5456
Salen Highld 121 NM6864
Salen Strath 121 NM5743
Salesbury Lancs 81 SD6832
Salford Beds 38 SP9339
Salford Gt Man 79 SJ8198
Salford Oxon 48 SP2828
Salford Priors Warwks 48 SP0751
Salfords Surrey 15 TQ2846
Salhouse Norfk 67 TG3014
Saline Fife 117 NT0292
Salisbury Wilts 23 SU1429
Salkeld Dykes Cumb 94 NY5437
Sall Norfk 66 TG1025
Sallachy Highld 146 NC5408
Sallachy Highld 138 NG9130
Salmonby Lincs 77 TF3273
Salmond's Muir Tays 127 NO5838
Salperton Gloucs 36 SP0720
Salph End Beds 38 TL0852
Salsburgh Strath 116 NS8262
Salt Staffs 72 SJ9527
Salt Cotes Cumb 93 NY1853
Salta Cumb 92 NY0845
Saltaire W York 82 SE1337
Saltash Cnwll 6 SX4258
Saltburn Highld 146 NH7270
Saltburn-by-the-Sea Cleve 97 NZ6621
Saltby Leics 63 SK8526
Saltcoats Cumb 86 SD0797
Saltcoats Lancs 80 SD3728
Saltcoats Strath 106 NS2441
Saltdean E Susx 15 TQ3802
Salter Lancs 87 SD6063
Salterbeck Cumb 92 NX9926
Salterbeck Cumb 92 NX9926
Salterforth IOM 81 SD8845
Salterswall Ches 71 SJ6266
Salterton Wilts 23 SU1236
Salterton Wilts 23 SU1236
Saltfleet Lincs 77 TF4593
Saltfleetby All Saints Lincs 77 TF4590
Saltfleetby St. Clements Lincs 77 TF4591
Saltfleetby St. Peter Lincs 77 TF4489
Saltford Avon 22 ST6867
Salthouse Norfk 66 TG0743
Saltley W Mids 61 SP0987
Saltmarsh Gwent 34 ST3483
Saltmarshe Humb 84 SE7824
Saltney Ches 71 SJ3865
Salton N York 90 SE7179
Saltrens Devon 18 SS4521
Saltwick Nthumb 103 NZ1780
Saltwood Kent 29 TR1535
Salvington W Susx 15 TQ1305
Salwarpe H & W 47 SO8762
Salwayash Dorset 10 SY4596
Sambourne Warwks 48 SP0662
Sambrook Shrops 72 SJ7124
Samlesbury Lancs 81 SD5930
Samlesbury Bottoms Lancs 81 SD6229
Sampford Arundel Somset 20 ST1018
Sampford Brett Somset 20 ST0941
Sampford Courtnay Devon 8 SS6301
Sampford Moor Somset 20 ST1118
Sampford Peverell Devon 9 ST0214
Sampford Spiney Devon 6 SX5372
Samson's Corner Essex 41 TM0818
Samsonlane Ork 155 HY6525
Samuelston Loth 118 NT4870
Sanaigmore Strath 112 NR2370
Sancreed Cnwll 2 SW4129
Sancton Humb 84 SE8939
Sand Somset 21 ST4346
Sand Cross E Susx 16 TQ5820
Sand Hills W York 83 SE3739
Sand Hole Humb 84 SE8037
Sand Hutton N York 90 SE6958
Sand Side Cumb 86 SD2282
Sandaig Highld 129 NG7102
Sandal Magna W York 83 SE3417
Sandale Cumb 93 NY2440
Sandavore Highld 128 NM4785
Sandbach Ches 72 SJ7560
Sandbank Strath 114 NS1580
Sandbanks Dorset 12 SZ0487
Sandend Gramp 142 NJ5566
Sanderstead Gt Lon 27 TQ3461
Sandford Avon 21 ST4159
Sandford Cumb 94 NY7216
Sandford Devon 8 SS8202
Sandford Dorset 11 SY9289
Sandford Hants 12 SU1601
Sandford IOW 13 SZ5481
Sandford Shrops 59 SJ3423
Sandford Shrops 59 SJ5834
Sandford Strath 107 NS7143
Sandford Batch Avon 21 ST4158
Sandford Orcas Dorset 21 ST6220
Sandford St. Martin Oxon 49 SP4226
Sandford-on-Thames Oxon 37 SP5301
Sandgate Kent 29 TR2035
Sandhaven Gramp 143 NJ9667
Sandhead D & G 98 NX0949
Sandhill S York 75 SK4496
Sandhills Dorset 10 ST5800
Sandhills Dorset 11 ST6710
Sandhills Oxon 37 SP5507
Sandhills Staffs 61 SK0604
Sandhills Surrey 25 SU9438
Sandhoe Nthumb 102 NY9666
Sandhole Strath 114 NS0098
Sandholme Humb 84 SE8230
Sandholme Lincs 64 TF3337
Sandhurst Berks 25 SU8361
Sandhurst Gloucs 47 SO8223
Sandhurst Kent 17 TQ8028
Sandhurst Cross Kent 17 TQ7827
Sandhutton N York 89 SE3881
Sandiacre Derbys 62 SK4736
Sandilands Lincs 77 TF5280
Sandiway Ches 71 SJ6070
Sandleheath Hants 12 SU1214
Sandley Dorset 22 ST7724
Sandling Kent 28 TQ7557
Sandlow Green Ches 72 SJ7865
Sandness Shet 155 HU1957
Sandon Essex 40 TL7404
Sandon Herts 39 TL3234
Sandon Staffs 72 SJ9429
Sandon Bank Staffs 72 SJ9428
Sandown IOW 13 SZ5984
Sandplace Cnwll 5 SX2556
Sandridge Herts 39 TL1710
Sandridge Wilts 22 ST9465
Sandringham Norfk 65 TF6928
Sands Bucks 37 SU8393
Sandsend N York 90 NZ8612
Sandside House Highld 150 NC9565
Sandtoft Humb 84 SE7408
Sandwich Kent 29 TR3358
Sandwick Cumb 93 NY4219
Sandwick Shet 155 HU4323
Sandwith Cumb 92 NX9615
Sandwith Newtown Cumb 92 NX9614
Sandy Beds 52 TL1649
Sandy Bank Lincs 77 TF2654
Sandy Cross H & W 47 SO6757
Sandy Haven Dyfed 30 SM8507
Sandy Lane Clwyd 71 SJ4040
Sandy Lane W York 82 SE1136
Sandy Lane Wilts 22 ST9668
Sandy Park Devon 8 SX7189
Sandycroft Clwyd 71 SJ3366
Sandyford D & G 101 NY2093
Sandygate Devon 7 SX8674
Sandygate IOM 153 SC3797
Sandylands Lancs 87 SD4163
Sandylane Staffs 72 SJ7035
Sandylane W Glam 32 SS5589
Sandystones Border 110 NT5926
Sandyway H & W 46 SO4925
Sangobeg Highld 149 NC4266
Sangomore Highld 149 NC4067
Sankey Bridges Ches 78 SJ5887
Sankyn's Green H & W 47 SO7964
Sanna Bay Highld 128 NM4469
Santon Cumb 86 NY1001
Santon IOM 153 SC3171
Santon Bridge Cumb 86 NY1101
Santon Downham Suffk 54 TL8187
Sapcote Leics 50 SP4893
Sapey Common H & W 47 SO7064
Sapiston Suffk 54 TL9175
Sapley Cambs 52 TL2474
Sapperton Derbys 73 SK1834
Sapperton Gloucs 35 SO9403
Sapperton Lincs 64 TF0133
Saracen's Head Lincs 64 TF3427
Sarclet Highld 151 ND3443
Sarisbury Hants 13 SU5008
Sarn Gwynd 56 SH2432
Sarn Gwynd 56 SH2432
Sarn M Glam 33 SS9184
Sarn Powys 58 SN9597
Sarn Powys 58 SO2091
Sarn-bach Gwynd 56 SH3026
Sarn-wen Powys 58 SJ2718
Sarnau Dyfed 42 SN3151
Sarnau Dyfed 31 SN3318
Sarnau Gwynd 70 SH9739
Sarnau Powys 58 SJ2315
Sarnau Powys 45 SO0232
Sarnesfield H & W 46 SO3750
Saron Dyfed 31 SN3737
Saron Dyfed 32 SN6012
Saron Gwynd 69 SH5365
Sarratt Herts 26 TQ0499
Sarre Kent 29 TR2565
Sarsden Oxon 36 SP2822
Sarson Hants 23 SU3044
Sartfield IOM 153 SC3599
Satley Dur 95 NZ1143
Satmar Kent 29 TR2539
Satron N York 88 SD9397
Satterleigh Devon 19 SS6622
Satterthwaite Cumb 86 SD3392
Satwell Oxon 37 SU7083
Sauchen Gramp 135 NJ7011
Saucher Tays 126 NO1933
Sauchieburn Gramp 135 NO6669
Saughtree Border 101 NY5696
Saul Gloucs 35 SO7409
Saundby Notts 75 SK7888
Saundersfoot Dyfed 31 SN1304
Saunderton Bucks 37 SP7901
Saunton Devon 18 SS4637
Sausthorpe Lincs 77 TF3868
Saveock Water Cnwll 3 SW7645
Saverley Green Staffs 72 SJ9638
Savile Town W York 82 SE2420
Sawbridge Warwks 50 SP5065
Sawbridgeworth Herts 39 TL4814
Sawdon N York 91 SE9485
Sawley Derbys 62 SK4731
Sawley Lancs 81 SD7746
Sawley N York 89 SE2467
Sawry Cumb 87 SD3795
Sawston Cambs 53 TL4849
Sawtry Cambs 52 TL1683
Saxby Leics 63 SK8219
Saxby Lincs 76 TF0086
Saxby W Susx 14 SU9604
Saxby All Saints Humb 84 SE9816
Saxelbye Leics 63 SK7021
Saxham Street Suffk 54 TM0861
Saxilby Lincs 76 SK8875
Saxlingham Norfk 66 TG0239
Saxlingham Green Norfk 67 TM2496
Saxlingham Nethergate Norfk 67 TM2397
Saxlingham Thorpe Norfk 67 TM2198
Saxmundham Suffk 55 TM3863
Saxon Street Cambs 53 TL6579
Saxondale Notts 63 SK6839
Saxtead Suffk 55 TM2665
Saxtead Green Suffk 55 TM2564
Saxtead Little Green Suffk 55 TM2566
Saxthorpe Norfk 66 TG1130
Saxton N York 83 SE4736
Sayers Common W Susx 15 TQ2618
Scackleton N York 90 SE6472
Scaftworth Notts 75 SK6691
Scagglethorpe N York 90 SE8372
Scalasaig Strath 112 NR3994
Scalby Humb 84 SE8530
Scalby N York 91 TA0190
Scald End Beds 51 TL0457
Scaldwell Nhants 50 SP7672
Scale Houses Cumb 94 NY5845
Scaleby Cumb 101 NY4463
Scalebyhill Cumb 101 NY4363
Scales Cumb 93 NY3427
Scales Cumb 86 SD2772
Scales Lancs 80 SD4531
Scalesceough Cumb 93 NY4450
Scalford Leics 63 SK7624
Scaling N York 90 NZ7413
Scaling Dam N York 90 NZ7412
Scalloway Shet 155 HU4039
Scalpay W Isls 154 NG2395
Scamblesby Lincs 77 TF2778
Scammonden W York 82 SE0515
Scamodala Highld 129 NM8373
Scampston N York 90 SE8575
Scampton Lincs 76 SK9479
Scancroft Hill W York 83 SE3741
Scaniport Highld 140 NH6239
Scapegoat Hill W York 82 SE0916
Scarborough N York 91 TA0388
Scarcewater Cnwll 3 SW9154
Scarcliffe Derbys 75 SK4968
Scarcroft W York 83 SE3540
Scarfskerry Highld 151 ND2674
Scargill Dur 88 NZ0510
Scarinish Strath 120 NM0444
Scarisbrick Lancs 80 SD3813
Scarness Cumb 93 NY2130
Scarning Norfk 66 TF9512
Scarrington Notts 63 SK7341
Scarth Hill Lancs 78 SD4206
Scarthingwell N York 83 SE4837
Scartho Humb 85 TA2606
Scawby Humb 84 SE9605
Scawsby S York 83 SE5305
Scawthorpe S York 83 SE5506
Scawton N York 90 SE5483
Scayne's Hill W Susx 15 TQ3623
Scethrog Powys 45 SO1025
Scholar Green Staffs 72 SJ8357
Scholes Gt Man 78 SD5905
Scholes S York 74 SK3896
Scholes W York 82 SE1507
Scholes W York 82 SE1726
Scholes W York 83 SE3736
Scholey Hill W York 83 SE3825

Stanley *W York* 83 SE3422
Stanley Common *Derbys* 62 SK4142
Stanley Crook *Dur* 96 NZ1638
Stanley Gate *Lancs* 78 SD4405
Stanley Moor *Staffs* 72 SJ9251
Stanley Pontlarge *Gloucs* 47 SO9930
Stanmer *E Susx* 15 TQ3309
Stanmore *Berks* 37 SU4778
Stanmore *Gt Lon* 26 TQ1692
Stanmore *Hants* 24 SU4628
Stannersburn *Nthumb* 102 NY7286
Stanningley *W York* 82 SE2234
Stannington *Nthumb* 103 NZ2179
Stannington *S York* 74 SK2988
Stansbatch *H & W* 46 SO3461
Stansfield *Suffk* 53 TL7852
Stanshope *Staffs* 73 SK1254
Stanstead *Suffk* 54 TL8449
Stanstead Abbots *Herts* 39 TL3811
Stanstead Street *Suffk* 54 TL8448
Stansted *Kent* 27 TQ6062
Stansted Mountfitchet *Essex* 39 TL5125
Stanton *Derbys* 73 SK2719
Stanton *Devon* 7 SX7050
Stanton *Gloucs* 48 SP0634
Stanton *Gwent* 34 SO3021
Stanton *Nthumb* 103 NZ1390
Stanton *Staffs* 73 SK1246
Stanton *Suffk* 54 TL9673
Stanton Butts *Cambs* 52 TL2372
Stanton by Bridge *Derbys* 62 SK3627
Stanton by Dale *Derbys* 62 SK4637
Stanton Drew *Avon* 21 ST5963
Stanton Fitzwarren *Wilts* 36 SU1790
Stanton Harcourt *Oxon* 36 SP4105
Stanton Hill *Notts* 75 SK4760
Stanton in Peak *Derbys* 74 SK2464
Stanton Lacy *Shrops* 46 SO4979
Stanton Long *Shrops* 59 SO5691
Stanton on the Wolds *Notts* 63 SK6330
Stanton Prior *Avon* 22 ST6762
Stanton St. Bernard *Wilts* 23 SU0962
Stanton St. John *Oxon* 37 SP5709
Stanton St. Quintin *Wilts* 35 ST9079
Stanton Street *Suffk* 54 TL9566
Stanton under Bardon *Leics* 62 SK4610
Stanton upon Hine Heath *Shrops* 59 SJ5624
Stanton Wick *Avon* 21 ST6162
Stantway *Gloucs* 35 SO7313
Stanwardine in the Field *Shrops* 59 SJ4124
Stanwardine in the Wood *Shrops* 59 SJ4227
Stanway *Essex* 40 TL9424
Stanway *Gloucs* 48 SP0632
Stanway Green *Essex* 41 TL9623
Stanway Green *Suffk* 55 TM2470
Stanwell *Surrey* 26 TQ0574
Stanwell Moor *Surrey* 26 TQ0474
Stanwick *Nhants* 51 SP9871
Stanwix *Cumb* 93 NY3957
Stape *N York* 90 SE7994
Stapehill *Dorset* 12 SU0500
Stapeley *Ches* 72 SJ6749
Stapenhill *Staffs* 73 SK2521
Staple *Kent* 29 TR2756
Staple *Somset* 20 ST1141
Staple Cross *Devon* 20 ST0320
Staple Cross *E Susx* 17 TQ7822
Staple Fitzpaine *Somset* 10 ST2618
Staple Hill *H & W* 60 SO9773
Staplefield *W Susx* 15 TQ2728
Stapleford *Cambs* 53 TL4751
Stapleford *Herts* 39 TL3117
Stapleford *Leics* 63 SK8018
Stapleford *Lincs* 76 SK8857
Stapleford *Notts* 62 SK4837
Stapleford *Wilts* 23 SU0637
Stapleford Abbotts *Essex* 27 TQ5194
Stapleford Tawney *Essex* 27 TQ5099
Staplegrove *Somset* 20 ST2126
Staplehay *Somset* 20 ST2121
Staplehurst *Kent* 28 TQ7843
Staplers *IOW* 13 SZ5189
Staplestreet *Kent* 29 TR0660
Stapleton *H & W* 46 SO3265
Stapleton *Leics* 50 SP4398
Stapleton *N York* 89 NZ2612
Stapleton *Shrops* 59 SJ4604
Stapleton *Somset* 21 ST4621
Stapley *Somset* 9 ST1813
Staploe *Beds* 52 TL1560
Staplow *H & W* 47 SO6941
Star *Dyfed* 31 SN2435
Star *Fife* 126 NO3103
Star *Somset* 21 ST4358
Star Hill *Gwent* 34 SO4702
Starbeck *N York* 83 SE3255
Starbotton *N York* 88 SD9574
Starcross *Devon* 9 SX9781
Stareton *Warwks* 61 SP3371
Starkholmes *Derbys* 74 SK3058
Starklin *H & W* 60 SO8574
Starling *Gt Man* 79 SD7710
Starlings Green *Essex* 39 TL4531
Starr's Green *E Susx* 17 TQ7615
Starston *Norfk* 55 TM2384
Start *Devon* 7 SX8144
Start Point *Devon* 7 SX8337
Startforth *Dur* 95 NZ0415
Startley *Wilts* 35 ST9482
Statenborough *Kent* 29 TR3155
Statham *Ches* 79 SJ6787
Stathe *Somset* 21 ST3728
Stathern *Leics* 63 SK7731
Station Town *Dur* 96 NZ4036
Staughton Green *Cambs* 52 TL1365
Staughton Highway *Cambs* 52 TL1364
Staunton *Gloucs* 34 SO5512
Staunton *Gloucs* 47 SO7929
Staunton Green *H & W* 46 SO3661
Staunton on Arrow *H & W* 46 SO3760
Staunton on Wye *H & W* 46 SO3644
Staveley *Cumb* 87 SD3786
Staveley *Cumb* 87 SD4698
Staveley *Derbys* 75 SK4374
Staveley *N York* 89 SE3662
Staverton *Devon* 7 SX7964
Staverton *Gloucs* 47 SO8923
Staverton *Nhants* 49 SP5461
Staverton *Wilts* 22 ST8560
Staverton Bridge *Gloucs* 35 SO8722
Stawell *Somset* 21 ST3638
Stawley *Somset* 20 ST0622
Staxigoe *Highld* 151 ND3852
Staxton *N York* 91 TA0179
Staylittle *Dyfed* 43 SN6489
Staylittle *Powys* 43 SN8892
Staynall *Lancs* 80 SD3643
Staythorpe *Notts* 75 SK7554
Stead *W York* 82 SE1446
Stean *N York* 89 SE0973
Steane *Nhants* 49 SP5538
Stearsby *N York* 90 SE6071
Steart *Somset* 20 ST2745
Stebbing *Essex* 40 TL6624
Stebbing Green *Essex* 40 TL6823

Stebbing Park *Essex* 40 TL6524
Stechford *W Mids* 61 SP1387
Stede Quarter *Kent* 28 TQ8737
Stedham *W Susx* 14 SU8622
Steel Cross *E Susx* 16 TQ5331
Steel Heath *Shrops* 59 SJ5436
Steele Road *Border* 101 NY5292
Steen's Bridge *H & W* 46 SO5357
Steep *Hants* 13 SU7425
Steep Lane *W York* 82 SE0223
Steephill *IOW* 13 SZ5477
Steeple *Dorset* 11 SY9080
Steeple *Essex* 40 TL9303
Steeple Ashton *Wilts* 22 ST9056
Steeple Aston *Oxon* 49 SP4725
Steeple Barton *Oxon* 49 SP4424
Steeple Bumpstead *Essex* 53 TL6841
Steeple Claydon *Bucks* 49 SP7026
Steeple Gidding *Cambs* 52 TL1381
Steeple Langford *Wilts* 23 SU0337
Steeple Morden *Cambs* 39 TL2842
Steeton *W York* 82 SE0344
Stein *Highld* 136 NG2656
Stella *T & W* 103 NZ1763
Stelling Minnis *Kent* 29 TR1447
Stembridge *Somset* 21 ST4220
Stenalees *Cnwll* 4 SX0157
Stenhouse *D & G* 107 NX7993
Stenhousemuir *Cent* 116 NS8682
Stenigot *Lincs* 77 TF2481
Stenscholl *Highld* 136 NG4767
Stenton *Loth* 118 NT6274
Stepaside *Dyfed* 31 SN1307
Stepney *Gt Lon* 27 TQ3581
Stepping Hill *Gt Man* 79 SJ9187
Steppingley *Beds* 38 TL0135
Stepps *Strath* 116 NS6568
Sternfield *Suffk* 55 TM3861
Sterridge *Devon* 19 SS5546
Stert *Wilts* 23 SU0259
Stetchworth *Cambs* 53 TL6459
Steven's Crouch *E Susx* 17 TQ7115
Stevenage *Herts* 39 TL2325
Stevenston *Strath* 106 NS2742
Steventon *Hants* 24 SU5447
Steventon *Oxon* 37 SU4691
Steventon End *Essex* 53 TL5942
Stevington *Beds* 51 SP9853
Stewartby *Beds* 38 TL0142
Stewarton *Strath* 105 NR6919
Stewarton *Strath* 115 NS4246
Stewkley *Bucks* 38 SP8525
Stewley *Somset* 10 ST3118
Stewton *Lincs* 77 TF3687
Steyne Cross *IOW* 13 SZ6487
Steyning *W Susx* 15 TQ1711
Steynton *Dyfed* 30 SM9108
Stibb *Cnwll* 18 SS2210
Stibb Cross *Devon* 18 SS4314
Stibb Green *Wilts* 23 SU2262
Stibbard *Norfk* 66 TF9828
Stibbington *Cambs* 51 TL0998
Stichill *Border* 110 NT7138
Sticker *Cnwll* 3 SW9750
Stickford *Lincs* 77 TF3560
Sticklepath *Devon* 8 SX6494
Sticklepath *Somset* 20 ST0435
Stickling Green *Essex* 39 TL4732
Stickney *Lincs* 77 TF3456
Stidd *Lancs* 81 SD6536
Stiff Green *Kent* 28 TQ8761
Stiffkey *Norfk* 66 TF9743
Stifford's Bridge *H & W* 47 SO7448
Stile Bridge *Kent* 28 TQ7547
Stileway *Somset* 21 ST4640
Stilligarry *W Isls* 154 NF7638
Stillingfleet *N York* 83 SE5940
Stillington *Cleve* 96 NZ3723
Stillington *N York* 90 SE5867
Stilton *Cambs* 52 TL1689
Stinchcombe *Gloucs* 35 ST7398
Stinsford *Dorset* 11 SY7191
Stirchley *Shrops* 60 SJ6906
Stirchley *W Mids* 61 SP0581
Stirling *Cent* 116 NS7993
Stirling *Gramp* 143 NK1242
Stirtloe *Cambs* 52 TL1966
Stirton *N York* 82 SD9753
Stisted *Essex* 40 TL8024
Stitchcombe *Wilts* 36 SU2369
Stithians *Cnwll* 3 SW7336
Stittal *Humb* 84 SE7652
Stittenham *N York* 90 SE6767
Stivichall *W Mids* 61 SP3376
Stixwould *Lincs* 76 TF1765
Stoak *Ches* 71 SJ4273
Stobo *Border* 109 NT1838
Stoborough *Dorset* 11 SY9286
Stoborough Green *Dorset* 11 SY9285
Stobs Castle *Border* 109 NT5008
Stobswood *Nthumb* 103 NZ2195
Stock *Avon* 21 ST4561
Stock *Essex* 40 TQ6999
Stock Gifford *Avon* 35 ST6279
Stock Green *H & W* 47 SO9859
Stock Wood *H & W* 47 SP0058
Stockbridge *Hants* 23 SU3535
Stockbriggs *Strath* 107 NS7936
Stockbury *Kent* 28 TQ8461
Stockcross *Berks* 24 SU4368
Stockdale *Cnwll* 3 SW7837
Stockdalewath *Cumb* 93 NY3845
Stocker's Hill *Kent* 28 TQ9650
Stockerston *Leics* 51 SP8397
Stocking *H & W* 47 SO6230
Stocking Green *Bucks* 38 SP8047
Stocking Pelham *Herts* 39 TL4529
Stockingford *Warwks* 61 SP3391
Stockland *Devon* 9 ST2404
Stockland Bristol *Somset* 20 ST2443
Stockland Green *Kent* 16 TQ5642
Stockleigh English *Devon* 8 SS8406
Stockleigh Pomeroy *Devon* 9 SS8703
Stockley *Wilts* 22 ST9967
Stockley Hill *H & W* 46 SO3738
Stocklinch *Somset* 10 ST3817
Stockmoor *H & W* 46 SO3954
Stockmoor *H & W* 46 SO3954
Stockport *Gt Man* 79 SJ8990
Stocksbridge *S York* 74 SK2698
Stocksfield *Nthumb* 103 NZ0561
Stockstreet *Essex* 40 TL8322
Stockton *H & W* 46 SO5261
Stockton *Norfk* 67 TM3894
Stockton *Shrops* 72 SJ7716
Stockton *Shrops* 60 SO7399
Stockton *Shrops* 58 SJ2601
Stockton *Shrops* 60 SO7299
Stockton *Warwks* 49 SP4364
Stockton *Wilts* 22 ST9738
Stockton Brook *Staffs* 72 SJ9152
Stockton Heath *Ches* 78 SJ6186
Stockton on Teme *H & W* 47 SO7167
Stockton on the Forest *N York* 83 SE6556
Stockton-on-Tees *Cleve* 96 NZ4419
Stockwell *Gloucs* 35 SO9414
Stockwell End *W Mids* 60 SJ8800

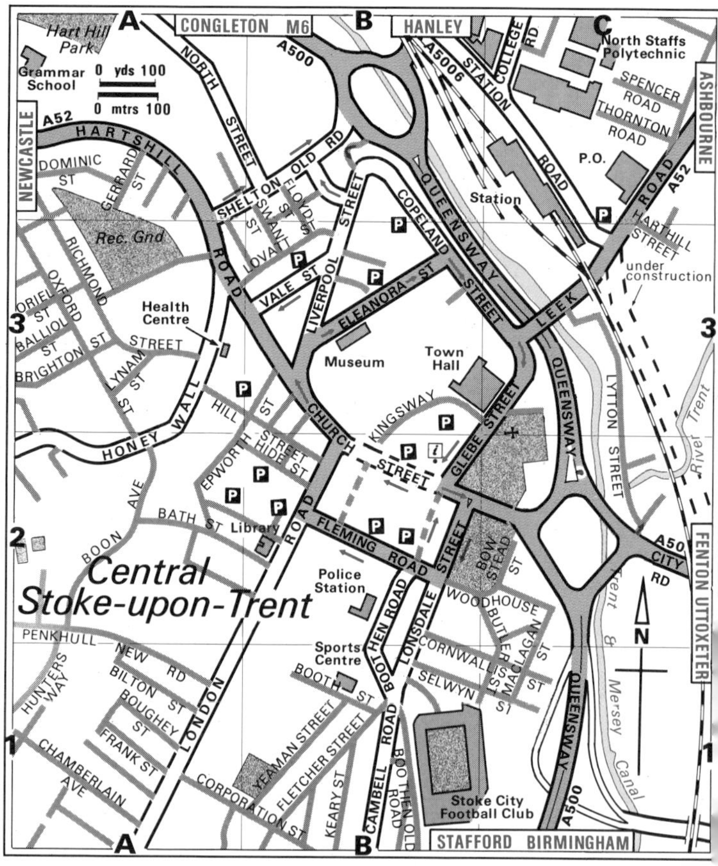

Stockwell Heath *Staffs* 73 SK0521
Stockwood *Avon* 21 ST6268
Stockwood *Dorset* 10 ST5806
Stodday *Lancs* 87 SD4658
Stodmarsh *Kent* 29 TR2160
Stody *Norfk* 66 TG0535
Stoer *Highld* 148 NC0428
Stoford *Somset* 10 ST5613
Stoford *Wilts* 23 SU0835
Stogumber *Somset* 20 ST0937
Stogumber *Somset* 20 ST0936
Stogursey *Somset* 20 ST2042
Stogursey *Somset* 20 ST1942
Stoke *Devon* 18 SS2324
Stoke *Hants* 24 SU4051
Stoke *Hants* 13 SU7202
Stoke *Kent* 28 TQ8274
Stoke *W Mids* 61 SP3678
Stoke Abbott *Dorset* 10 ST4500
Stoke Albany *Nhants* 51 SP8088
Stoke Ash *Suffk* 54 TM1170
Stoke Bardolph *Notts* 63 SK6441
Stoke Bliss *H & W* 47 SO6563
Stoke Bruerne *Nhants* 49 SP7449
Stoke by Clare *Suffk* 53 TL7443
Stoke Canon *Devon* 9 SX9397
Stoke Charity *Hants* 24 SU4839
Stoke Climsland *Cnwll* 5 SX3574
Stoke Cross *H & W* 47 SO6250
Stoke D'Abernon *Surrey* 26 TQ1259
Stoke Doyle *Nhants* 51 TL0286
Stoke Dry *Leics* 51 SP8596
Stoke End *Warwks* 61 SP1696
Stoke Farthing *Wilts* 23 SU0525
Stoke Ferry *Norfk* 65 TF7000
Stoke Fleming *Devon* 7 SX8648
Stoke Gabriel *Devon* 7 SX8557
Stoke Gabriel *Devon* 7 SX8457
Stoke Golding *Leics* 61 SP3997
Stoke Goldington *Bucks* 38 SP8348
Stoke Green *Bucks* 26 SU9882
Stoke Hammond *Bucks* 38 SP8829
Stoke Heath *H & W* 47 SO9468
Stoke Heath *Shrops* 72 SJ6529
Stoke Heath *W Mids* 61 SP3580
Stoke Holy Cross *Norfk* 67 TG2301
Stoke Lacy *H & W* 46 SO6149
Stoke Lyne *Oxon* 49 SP5628
Stoke Mandeville *Bucks* 38 SP8310
Stoke Newington *Gt Lon* 27 TQ3386
Stoke Orchard *Gloucs* 47 SO9128
Stoke Poges *Bucks* 26 SU9783
Stoke Pound *H & W* 47 SO9667
Stoke Prior *H & W* 46 SO5256
Stoke Prior *H & W* 47 SO9467
Stoke Rivers *Devon* 19 SS6335
Stoke Rochford *Lincs* 63 SK9127
Stoke Row *Oxon* 37 SU6884
Stoke St. Gregory *Somset* 21 ST3426
Stoke St. Mary *Somset* 20 ST2622
Stoke St. Michael *Somset* 22 ST6646
Stoke St. Milborough *Shrops* 59 SO5682
Stoke sub Hamdon *Somset* 10 ST4717
Stoke Talmage *Oxon* 37 SU6799
Stoke Trister *Somset* 22 ST7328
Stoke upon Tern *Shrops* 59 SJ6328
Stoke Wake *Dorset* 11 ST7606
Stoke Wharf *H & W* 47 SO9567
Stoke-by-Nayland *Suffk* 54 TL9836
Stoke-on-Trent *Staffs* 72 SJ8745
Stoke-upon-Trent *Staffs* 72 SJ8745
Stokeford *Dorset* 11 SY8787
Stokeham *Notts* 75 SK7876
Stokeinteignhead *Devon* 7 SX9170
Stokenchurch *Bucks* 37 SU7696
Stokenham *Devon* 7 SX8042
Stokesay *Shrops* 59 SO4381
Stokesby *Norfk* 67 TG4310

Stokesley *N York* 90 NZ5208
Stolford *Somset* 20 ST2245
Stolford *Somset* 20 ST0332
Ston Easton *Somset* 21 ST6253
Stondon Massey *Essex* 27 TL5800
Stone *Bucks* 37 SP7812
Stone *Gloucs* 35 ST6895
Stone *H & W* 60 SO8675
Stone *Kent* 27 TQ5774
Stone *Kent* 17 TQ9427
Stone *S York* 75 SK5589
Stone *Somset* 21 ST5834
Stone *Staffs* 72 SJ9034
Stone Allerton *Somset* 21 ST3950
Stone Bridge Corner *Cambs* 64 TF2700
Stone Chair *W York* 82 SE1227
Stone Cross *E Susx* 16 TQ5128
Stone Cross *E Susx* 16 TQ6431
Stone Cross *E Susx* 16 TQ6104
Stone Cross *Kent* 16 TQ5239
Stone Cross *Kent* 28 TR0236
Stone Cross *Kent* 29 TR3257
Stone Hill *S York* 83 SE6809
Stone House *Cumb* 88 SD7785
Stone Rows *Leics* 61 SK3214
Stone Street *Kent* 27 TQ5754
Stone Street *Suffk* 55 TM3882
Stone Street *Suffk* 54 TM0143
Stone Street *Suffk* 54 TL9639
Stone-edge-Batch *Avon* 34 ST4671
Stonea *Cambs* 65 TL4693
Stonebridge *Avon* 21 ST3959
Stonebridge *Norfk* 54 TL9290
Stonebridge *W Mids* 61 SP2182
Stonebroom *Derbys* 74 SK4159
Stonebury *Herts* 39 TL3828
Stonechrubie *Highld* 145 NC2419
Stonecross Green *Suffk* 54 TL8257
Stonecrouch *Kent* 16 TQ7033
Stoneferry *Humb* 85 TA1231
Stonefield *Strath* 113 NR8671
Stonegarthside *Cumb* 101 NY4780
Stonegate *E Susx* 16 TQ6628
Stonegate *N York* 90 NZ7709
Stonegrave *N York* 90 SE6577
Stonehall *H & W* 47 SO8848
Stonehaugh *Nthumb* 102 NY7976
Stonehaven *Gramp* 135 NO8786
Stonehill Green *Gt Lon* 27 TQ4870
Stonehouse *Ches* 71 SJ5070
Stonehouse *D & G* 100 NX8268
Stonehouse *Devon* 6 SX4653
Stonehouse *Gloucs* 35 SO8005
Stonehouse *Nthumb* 94 NY6958
Stonehouse *Strath* 116 NS7546
Stoneleigh *Warwks* 61 SP3372
Stoneley Green *Ches* 71 SJ6151
Stonely *Cambs* 52 TL1167
Stoner Hill *Hants* 13 SU7225
Stones Green *Essex* 41 TM1626
Stonesby *Leics* 63 SK8224
Stonesfield *Oxon* 36 SP3917
Stonethwaite *Cumb* 93 NY2613
Stonetree Green *Kent* 29 TR0637
Stonewells *Gramp* 141 NJ2865
Stonewood *Kent* 27 TQ5972
Stoney Cross *Hants* 12 SU2511
Stoney Middleton *Derbys* 74 SK2275
Stoney Stanton *Leics* 50 SP4994
Stoney Stoke *Somset* 22 ST7032
Stoney Stratton *Somset* 21 ST6539
Stoney Stretton *Shrops* 59 SJ3809
Stoneybridge *W Isls* 154 NF7433
Stoneyburn *Loth* 117 NS9862
Stoneygate *Leics* 62 SK6002
Stoneyhills *Essex* 40 TQ9597
Stoneykirk *D & G* 98 NX0853
Stoneywood *Cent* 116 NS7982

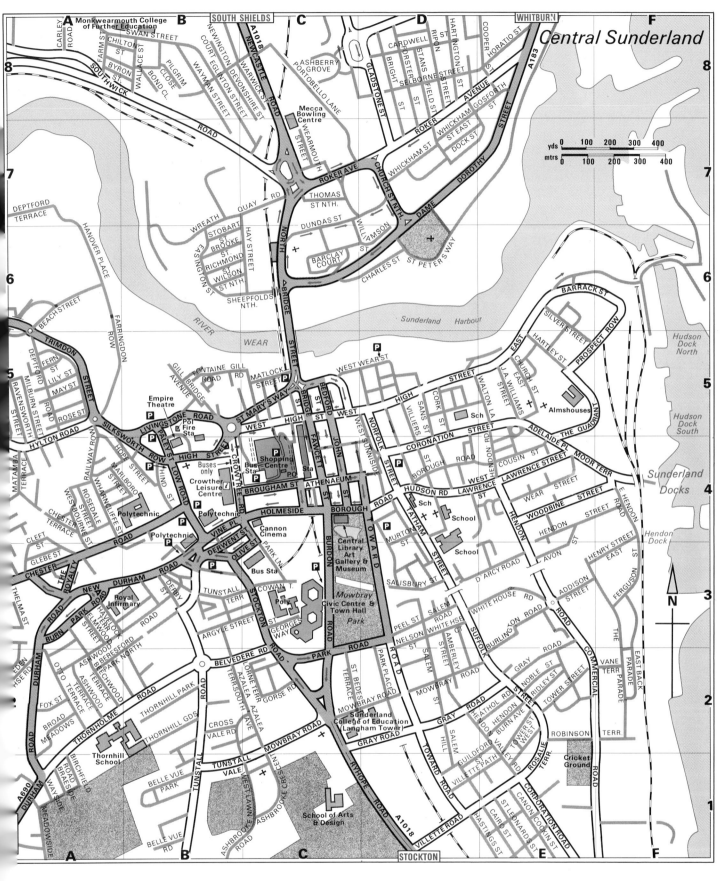

Central Sunderland

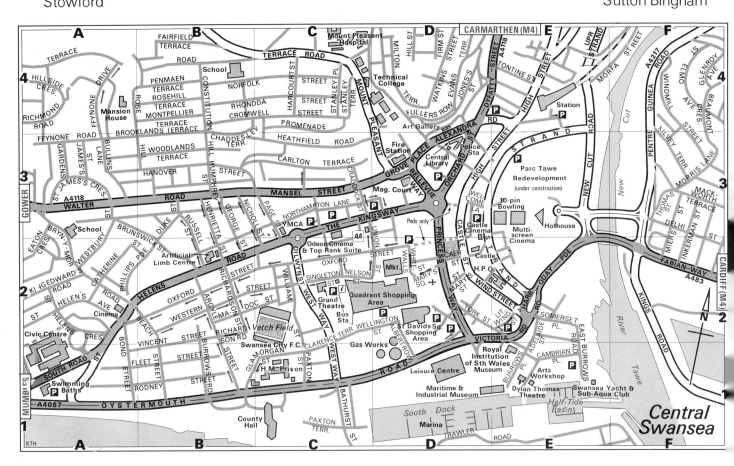

Central Swansea

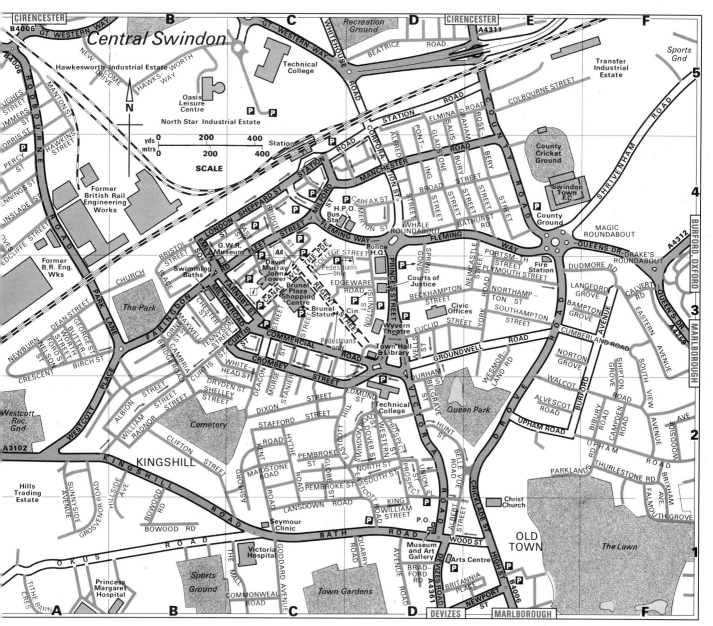

Tabley Hill

Threehammer Common

T

Tabley Hill *Ches* 79 SJ7379
Tackley *Oxon* 37 SP4720
Tacolneston *Norfk* 66 TM1495
Tadcaster *N York* 83 SE4843
Taddington *Derbys* 74 SK1471
Taddiport *Devon* 18 SS4818
Tadley *Hants* 24 SU6061
Tadlow *Cambs* 52 TL2847
Tadmarton *Oxon* 48 SP3937
Tadwick *Avon* 35 ST7470
Tadworth *Surrey* 26 TQ2356
Tafarn-y-bwlch *Dyfed* 31 SN0834
Tafarn-y-Gelyn *Clwyd* 70 SJ1961
Tafarnaubach *Gwent* 33 SO1210
Tafarnaubach *M Glam* 33 SO1110
Taff Merthyr Garden Villa *M Glam* 33 ST1198
Taff's Well *M Glam* 33 ST1283
Tafolwern *Powys* 57 SH8902
Tai'n-lon *Gwynd* 68 SH4450
Tai'r Bull *Powys* 45 SN9926
Taibach *W Glam* 32 SS7788
Tain *Highld* 151 ND2266
Tain *Highld* 147 NH7781
Takeley *Essex* 40 TL5621
Takeley Street *Essex* 39 TL5421
Tal-y-Bont *Gwynd* 69 SH7668
Tal-y-Bont *Gwynd* 69 SH7668
Tal-y-bont *Gwynd* 57 SH5921
Tal-y-bont *Gwynd* 69 SH6070
Tal-y-cafn *Gwynd* 69 SH7971
Tal-y-coed *Gwent* 34 SO4115
Tal-y-garn *M Glam* 33 ST0379
Tal-y-llyn *Gwynd* 57 SH7109
Tal-y-Waun *Gwent* 34 SO2604
Talachddu *Powys* 45 SO0833
Talacre *Clwyd* 70 SJ1283
Talaton *Devon* 9 SY0699
Talbenny *Dyfed* 30 SM8412
Talbot Village *Dorset* 12 SZ0793
Taleford *Devon* 4 SX0996
Talerddig *Powys* 58 SH9300
Talgarreg *Dyfed* 42 SN4251
Talgarth *Gwynd* 57 SN6899
Talgarth *Powys* 45 SO1533
Taliesin *Dyfed* 43 SN6591
Talisker *Highld* 136 NG3230
Talke *Staffs* 72 SJ8253
Talke Pits *Staffs* 72 SJ8352
Talkin *Cumb* 94 NY5457
Talla Linnfoots *Border* 108 NT1320
Talladale *Highld* 144 NG9270
Tallaminnoc *Strath* 106 NX4098
Tallarn Green *Clwyd* 71 SJ4444
Tallentire *Cumb* 92 NY1045
Talley *Dyfed* 44 SN6332
Tallington *Lincs* 64 TF0908
Tallwrn *Clwyd* 71 SJ2947
Talmine *Highld* 149 NC5863
Talog *Dyfed* 31 SN3325
Talsarn *Dyfed* 44 SN5456
Talsarnau *Gwynd* 57 SH6135
Talskiddy *Cnwll* 4 SW9165
Talwrn *Clwyd* 71 SJ3847
Talwrn *Gwynd* 68 SH4877
Talybont *Dyfed* 43 SN6589
Talybont-on-Usk *Powys* 33 SO1122
Talysarn *Gwynd* 68 SH4852
Talywern *Powys* 57 SH8200
Tamer Lane End *Gt Man* 79 SD6401
Tamerton Foliot *Devon* 6 SX4761
Tamworth *Staffs* 61 SK2004
Tamworth Green *Lincs* 64 TF3842
Tan Hill *N York* 88 NY8907
Tan Office Green *Suffk* 53 TL7858
Tan-y-Bwlch *Gwynd* 57 SH6540
Tan-y-fron *Clwyd* 71 SJ2952
Tan-y-fron *Clwyd* 70 SH9664
Tan-y-groes *Dyfed* 42 SN2849
Tancred *N York* 89 SE4558
Tancredston *Dyfed* 30 SM8826
Tandlemuir *Strath* 115 NS3361
Tandridge *Surrey* 27 TQ3750
Tanfield *Dur* 96 NZ1855
Tanfield Lea *Dur* 96 NZ1854
Tangiers *Dyfed* 30 SM9518
Tangley *Hants* 23 SU3252
Tangmere *W Susx* 14 SU9006
Tangusdale *W Isls* 154 NF6500
Tankerness *Ork* 155 HY5108
Tankersley *S York* 74 SK3499
Tankerton *Kent* 29 TR1167
Tannach *Highld* 151 ND3247
Tannachie *Gramp* 135 NO7884
Tannadice *Tays* 134 NO4758
Tanner Green *H & W* 61 SP0874
Tannington *Suffk* 55 TM2467
Tannochside *Strath* 116 NS6962
Tansley *Derbys* 74 SK3259
Tansor *Nhants* 51 TL0590
Tantobie *Dur* 96 NZ1754
Tanton *N York* 90 NZ5210
Tanwood *H & W* 60 SO8974
Tanworth in Arden *Warwks* 61 SP1170
Tanygrisiau *Gwynd* 56 SH4945
Taplow *Bucks* 26 SU9182
Tarbert *Strath* 113 NR6182
Tarbert *Strath* 113 NR6551
Tarbert *Strath* 113 NR8668
Tarbert *W Isls* 154 NB1500
Tarbet *Highld* 148 NC1649
Tarbet *Highld* 129 NM7992
Tarbet *Strath* 123 NN3104
Tarbock Green *Mersyd* 78 SJ4687
Tarbolton *Strath* 107 NS4327
Tarbrax *Strath* 117 NT0255
Tardebigge *H & W* 47 SO9969
Tardy Gate *Lancs* 80 SD5426
Tarfside *Tays* 134 NO4979
Tarland *Gramp* 134 NJ4804
Tarleton *Lancs* 80 SD4520
Tarlscough *Lancs* 80 SD4314
Tarlton *Gloucs* 35 ST9599
Tarnock *Somset* 21 ST3852
Tarns *Cumb* 92 NY1247
Tarnside *Cumb* 87 SD4390
Tarporley *Ches* 71 SJ5562
Tarr *Somset* 20 ST1030
Tarr *Somset* 19 SS8632
Tarrant Crawford *Dorset* 11 ST9203
Tarrant Gunville *Dorset* 11 ST9212
Tarrant Hinton *Dorset* 11 ST9310
Tarrant Keynston *Dorset* 11 ST9204
Tarrant Launceston *Dorset* 11 ST9409
Tarrant Monkton *Dorset* 11 ST9408
Tarrant Rawston *Dorset* 11 ST9306
Tarrant Rushton *Dorset* 11 ST9305
Tarring Neville *E Susx* 16 TQ4404
Tarrington *H & W* 47 SO6240
Tarrylin *Strath* 105 NR9621
Tarskavaig *Highld* 129 NG5810
Tarves *Gramp* 143 NJ8631
Tarvie *Tays* 133 NO0164
Tarvin *Ches* 71 SJ4966
Tarvin Sands *Ches* 71 SJ4967
Tasburgh *Norfk* 67 TM2096
Tasley *Shrops* 60 SO6894
Taston *Oxon* 36 SP3621
Tatenhill *Staffs* 73 SK2022
Tathall End *Bucks* 38 SP8246
Tatham *Lancs* 87 SD6069
Tathwell *Lincs* 77 TF3281
Tatsfield *Surrey* 27 TQ4156
Tattenhall *Ches* 71 SJ4858
Tatterford *Norfk* 66 TF8628
Tattersett *Norfk* 66 TF8429
Tattershall *Lincs* 76 TF2157
Tattershall Bridge *Lincs* 76 TF1956
Tattershall Thorpe *Lincs* 76 TF2159
Tattingstone *Suffk* 54 TM1337
Tattingstone White Horse *Suffk* 54 TM1338
Tatworth *Somset* 10 ST3205
Tauchers *Gramp* 141 NJ3649
Taunton *Somset* 20 ST2324
Taverham *Norfk* 66 TG1614
Taverners Green *Essex* 40 TL5618
Tavernspite *Dyfed* 31 SN1812
Tavistock *Devon* 6 SX4774
Taw green *Devon* 8 SX6597
Tawstock *Devon* 19 SS5529
Taxal *Derbys* 79 SK0079
Taychreggan Hotel *Strath* 123 NN0421
Tayinloan *Strath* 105 NR7044
Taynish *Strath* 113 NR7282
Taynton *Gloucs* 35 SO7222
Taynton *Oxon* 36 SP2313
Taynuilt *Strath* 122 NN0031
Tayport *Fife* 127 NO4628
Tayvallich *Strath* 113 NR7487
Tealby *Lincs* 76 TF1590
Teangue *Highld* 129 NG6609
Teanord *Highld* 140 NH5964
Tebay *Cumb* 87 NY6104
Tebworth *Beds* 38 SP9926
Tedburn St. Mary *Devon* 8 SX8194
Teddington *Gloucs* 47 SO9632
Teddington *Gt Lon* 26 TQ1671
Tedstone Delamere *H & W* 47 SO6958
Tedstone Wafer *H & W* 47 SO6759
Teeton *Nhants* 50 SP6970
Teffont Evias *Wilts* 22 ST9831
Teffont Magna *Wilts* 22 ST9832
Tegryn *Dyfed* 31 SN2233
Teigh *Leics* 63 SK8615
Teign Village *Devon* 8 SX8381
Teigncombe *Devon* 8 SX6787
Teigngrace *Devon* 7 SX8474
Teignmouth *Devon* 7 SX9473
Telford *Shrops* 60 SJ6908
Tellisford *Somset* 22 ST8055
Telscombe *E Susx* 15 TQ4003
Telscombe Cliffs *E Susx* 15 TQ4001
Tempar *Tays* 124 NN6857
Templand *D & G* 100 NY0886
Temple *Cnwll* 4 SX1473
Temple *Loth* 117 NT3158
Temple *Strath* 115 NS5469
Temple Balsall *W Mids* 61 SP2076
Temple Bar *Dyfed* 44 SN5354
Temple Cloud *Avon* 21 ST6157
Temple End *Suffk* 53 TL6650
Temple Ewell *Kent* 29 TR2844
Temple Grafton *Warwks* 48 SP1255
Temple Guiting *Gloucs* 48 SP0928
Temple Hirst *N York* 83 SE6024
Temple Normanton *Derbys* 74 SK4167
Temple Pier *Highld* 139 NH5330
Temple Sowerby *Cumb* 94 NY6127
Templecombe *Somset* 22 ST7022
Templehall *Tays* 127 NO4936
Templeton *Devon* 19 SS8813
Templeton *Dyfed* 31 SN1111
Templeton Bridge *Devon* 19 SS8714
Templetown *Dur* 95 NZ1049
Tempsford *Beds* 52 TL1653
Ten Mile Bank *Norfk* 65 TL5996
Tenbury Wells *H & W* 46 SO5968
Tenby *Dyfed* 31 SN1300
Tendring *Essex* 41 TM1424
Tendring Green *Essex* 41 TM1326
Tendring Heath *Essex* 41 TM1326
Tenpenny Heath *Essex* 41 TM0820
Tenterden *Kent* 17 TQ8833
Terling *Essex* 40 TL7715
Tern *Shrops* 59 SJ6216
Ternhill *Shrops* 59 SJ6332
Terregles *D & G* 100 NX9377
Terrington *N York* 90 SE6670
Terrington St. Clement *Norfk* 65 TF5520
Terrington St. John *Norfk* 65 TF5314
Terry's Cross *W Susx* 15 TQ2314
Terry's Green *Warwks* 61 SP1073
Teston *Kent* 28 TQ7053
Testwood *Hants* 12 SU3514
Tetbury *Gloucs* 35 ST8993
Tetbury Upton *Gloucs* 35 ST8795
Tetchill *Shrops* 59 SJ3932
Tetcott *Devon* 5 SX3396
Tetford *Lincs* 77 TF3374
Tetney *Lincs* 77 TA3100
Tetney Lock *Lincs* 85 TA3402
Tetsworth *Oxon* 37 SP6801
Tettenhall *W Mids* 60 SJ8800
Tettenhall Wood *W Mids* 60 SO8799
Tetworth *Cambs* 52 TL2253
Teversal *Notts* 75 SK4861
Teversham *Cambs* 53 TL4958
Teviothead *Border* 109 NT4005
Tewel *Gramp* 135 NO8085
Tewinbury *Herts* 39 TL2714
Tewkesbury *Gloucs* 47 SO8933
Teynham *Kent* 28 TQ9562
Thackley *W York* 82 SE1739
Thackthwaite *Cumb* 93 NY4225
Thackthwaite *Cumb* 92 NY1423
Thakeham *W Susx* 14 TQ1017
Thame *Oxon* 37 SP7005
Thames Ditton *Surrey* 26 TQ1567
Thamesmead *Gt Lon* 27 TQ4780
Thanington *Kent* 29 TR1356
Thankerton *Strath* 108 NS9737
Tharston *Norfk* 66 TM1894
Thatcham *Berks* 24 SU5167
Thatto Heath *Mersyd* 78 SJ5093
Thaxted *Essex* 40 TL6131
The Abbey *Gwynd* 69 SH7865
The Bank *Ches* 72 SJ8457
The Bank *Shrops* 59 SO6199
The Beeches *Gloucs* 35 SP0201
The Biggins *Cambs* 53 TL4788
The Bourne *H & W* 47 SO9856
The Bratch *Staffs* 60 SO8693
The Broad *H & W* 46 SO4961
The Brunt *Loth* 118 NT6873
The Bryn *Gwent* 34 SO3309
The Bungalow *IOM* 153 SC3987
The Bush *Kent* 28 TQ6649
The Butts *Gloucs* 35 SO8916
The Chart *Surrey* 27 TQ4251
The Chequer *Clwyd* 71 SJ4840
The City *Beds* 52 TL1159
The City *Bucks* 37 SU7896
The Common *Oxon* 48 SP2927
The Common *Wilts* 35 SU0285
The Corner *Kent* 28 TQ7041
The Corner *Shrops* 59 SO4387
The Crossways *H & W* 46 SO3538
The Den *Strath* 115 NS3251
The Fence *Gloucs* 34 SO5405
The Forge *H & W* 46 SO3459
The Forstal *E Susx* 27 TQ5455
The Forstal *Kent* 28 TR0439
The Fouralls *Shrops* 72 SJ6831
The Green *Essex* 40 TL7719
The Grove *H & W* 47 SO8740
The Haven *W Susx* 14 TQ0830
The Haw *Gloucs* 47 SO8427
The Hirsel *Border* 110 NT8240
The Holt *Berks* 37 SU8078
The Horns *Kent* 17 TQ7429
The Howe *IOM* 153 SC1967
The Leacon *Kent* 17 TQ9833
The Lee *Bucks* 38 SP9004
The Lochs *Gramp* 141 NJ3020
The Marsh *Ches* 72 SJ8463
The Middles *Dur* 96 NZ2051
The Mound *Highld* 147 NH7798
The Mumbles *W Glam* 32 SS6187
The Mythe *Gloucs* 47 SO8934
The Nant *Clwyd* 70 SJ2850
The Narth *Gwent* 34 SO5206
The Neuk *Gramp* 135 NO7397
The Pill *Gwent* 34 ST4887
The Quarry *Gloucs* 35 ST7399
The Quarter *Kent* 28 TQ8844
The Reddings *Gloucs* 35 SO9021
The Rookery *Staffs* 72 SJ8555
The Rowe *Staffs* 72 SJ8238
The Sands *Surrey* 25 SU8846
The Shoe *Wilts* 35 ST8074
The Smithies *Shrops* 60 SO6897
The Spike *Cambs* 53 TL4848
The Spring *Warwks* 61 SP2873
The Square *Gwent* 34 ST2796
The Stair *Kent* 16 TQ6037
The Stocks *Kent* 17 TQ9127
The Straits *Hants* 25 SU7839
The Thrift *Herts* 39 TL3139
The Towans *Cnwll* 2 SW5538
The Vauld *H & W* 46 SO5349
The Wrythe *Gt Lon* 27 TQ2765
Thealby *Humb* 84 SE8917
Theale *Berks* 24 SU6471
Theale *Somset* 21 ST4646
Thearne *Humb* 85 TA0736
Theberton *Suffk* 55 TM4365
Thedden Grange *Hants* 24 SU6839
Theddingworth *Leics* 50 SP6685
Theddlethorpe All Saints *Lincs* 77 TF4688
Theddlethorpe St. Helen *Lincs* 77 TF4788
Thelbridge Barton *Devon* 19 SS7812
Thelbridge Cross *Devon* 19 SS7812
Thelnetham *Suffk* 54 TM0178
Thelveton *Norfk* 54 TM1681
Thelwall *Ches* 79 SJ6587
Themelthorpe *Norfk* 66 TG0524
Thenford *Nhants* 49 SP5241
Theobald's Green *Wilts* 23 SU0268
Therfield *Herts* 39 TL3337
Thetford *Norfk* 54 TL8783
Thetwaite *Cumb* 93 NY3744
Theydon Bois *Essex* 27 TQ4499
Thicket Prior *Humb* 83 SE6943
Thickwood *Wilts* 35 ST8272
Thimbleby *Lincs* 76 TF2369
Thimbleby *N York* 89 SE4495
Thingwall *Mersyd* 78 SJ2884
Thirkleby *N York* 89 SE4778
Thirlby *N York* 90 SE4883
Thirlestane *Border* 118 NT5647
Thirlspot *Cumb* 93 NY3118
Thirn *N York* 89 SE2185
Thirsk *N York* 89 SE4282
Thirtleby *Humb* 85 TA1634
Thistleton *Lancs* 80 SD4037
Thistleton *Leics* 63 SK9117
Thistley Green *Suffk* 53 TL6776
Thixendale *N York* 90 SE8461
Thockrington *Nthumb* 102 NY9578
Tholomas Drove *Cambs* 65 TF4006
Tholthorpe *N York* 89 SE4766
Thomas Chapel *Dyfed* 31 SN1008
Thomas Close *Cumb* 93 NY4340
Thomas Town *Warwks* 45 SO0763
Thomastown *Gramp* 142 NJ5737
Thompson *Norfk* 66 TL9296
Thomshill *Gramp* 141 NJ2157
Thong *Kent* 28 TQ6770
Thongsleigh *Devon* 9 SS9011
Thoralby *N York* 88 SE0086
Thoresby *Notts* 75 SK6371
Thoresthorpe *Lincs* 77 TF4578
Thoresway *Lincs* 76 TF1696
Thorganby *Lincs* 76 TF2097
Thorganby *N York* 83 SE6841
Thorgill *N York* 90 SE7096
Thorington *Suffk* 55 TM4174
Thorington Street *Suffk* 54 TM0135
Thorlby *N York* 82 SD9653
Thorley *Herts* 39 TL4719
Thorley *IOW* 12 SZ3688
Thorley Houses *Herts* 39 TL4620
Thorley Street *IOW* 12 SZ3788
Thormanby *N York* 90 SE4974
Thorn's Flush *Surrey* 14 TQ0440
Thornaby-on-Tees *Cleve* 97 NZ4518
Thornage *Norfk* 66 TG0536
Thornborough *Bucks* 49 SP7433
Thornborough *N York* 89 SE2979
Thornbury *Avon* 35 ST6490
Thornbury *Devon* 18 SS4008
Thornbury *H & W* 46 SO6159
Thornbury *W York* 82 SE1933
Thornby *Cumb* 93 NY2951
Thornby *Nhants* 50 SP6675
Thorncliff *Staffs* 73 SK0158
Thorncombe *Dorset* 10 ST3703
Thorncombe Street *Surrey* 25 TQ0042
Thorncott Green *Beds* 52 TL1547
Thorncross *IOW* 13 SZ4381
Thorndon *Suffk* 54 TM1469
Thorndon Cross *Devon* 5 SX5293
Thorne *S York* 83 SE6813
Thorne *Somset* 10 ST5217
Thorne St. Margaret *Somset* 20 ST0920
Thornecroft *Devon* 7 SX7767
Thornehillhead *Devon* 18 SS4116
Thorner *W York* 83 SE3740
Thornes *Staffs* 61 SK0703
Thornes *W York* 83 SE3219
Thorney *Bucks* 26 TQ0379
Thorney *Cambs* 64 TF2804
Thorney *Notts* 76 SK8572
Thorney *Somset* 21 ST4222
Thorney Hill *Hants* 12 SZ2099
Thorney Toll *Cambs* 64 TF3404
Thornfalcon *Somset* 20 ST2723
Thornford *Dorset* 10 ST6013
Thorngrafton *Nthumb* 102 NY7865
Thorngrove *Somset* 21 ST3632
Thorngumbald *Humb* 85 TA2026
Thornham *Norfk* 65 TF7343
Thornham Magna *Suffk* 54 TM1071
Thornham Parva *Suffk* 54 TM1072
Thornhaugh *Cambs* 64 TF0600
Thornhill *Cent* 116 NN6600
Thornhill *D & G* 100 NX8795
Thornhill *Derbys* 74 SK1983
Thornhill *Hants* 13 SU4612
Thornhill *M Glam* 33 ST1584
Thornhill *W York* 82 SE2418
Thornhill Lees *W York* 82 SE2419
Thornhills *W York* 82 SE1523
Thornholme *Humb* 91 TA1163
Thornicombe *Dorset* 11 ST8703
Thornington *Nthumb* 110 NT8833
Thornley *Dur* 95 NZ1137
Thornley *Dur* 96 NZ3639
Thornley Gate *Cumb* 95 NY8356
Thornliebank *Strath* 115 NS5459
Thorns *Suffk* 53 TL7455
Thorns Green *Gt Man* 79 SJ7984
Thornsett *Derbys* 79 SK0187
Thornthwaite *Cumb* 93 NY2225
Thornthwaite *N York* 83 SE5618
Thornthwaite *N York* 89 SE1758
Thornton *Bucks* 49 SP7435
Thornton *Cleve* 89 NZ4713
Thornton *Dyfed* 30 SM9007
Thornton *Fife* 117 NT2897
Thornton *Humb* 84 SE7545
Thornton *Lancs* 80 SD3342
Thornton *Leics* 62 SK4607
Thornton *Lincs* 77 TF2467
Thornton *Mersyd* 78 SD3301
Thornton *Nthumb* 111 NT9547
Thornton *Tays* 126 NO3946
Thornton *W York* 82 SE0932
Thornton Curtis *Humb* 85 TA0817
Thornton Dale *N York* 90 SE8383
Thornton Green *Ches* 71 SJ4473
Thornton Heath *Gt Lon* 27 TQ3168
Thornton Hough *Mersyd* 78 SJ3081
Thornton le Moor *Lincs* 76 TF0490
Thornton Rust *N York* 88 SD9689
Thornton Steward *N York* 89 SE1786
Thornton Watlass *N York* 89 SE2385
Thornton-in-Craven *N York* 81 SD9048
Thornton-in-Lonsdale *N York* 87 SD6879
Thornton-le-Beans *N York* 89 SE3990
Thornton-le-Clay *N York* 90 SE6875
Thornton-le-Moor *N York* 89 SE3988
Thornton-le-Moors *Ches* 71 SJ4474
Thornton-le-Street *N York* 89 SE4186
Thorntonhall *Strath* 115 NS5955
Thorntonloch *Loth* 119 NT7574
Thornwood Common *Essex* 39 TL4604
Thornydyes *Border* 110 NT6148
Thornythwaite *Cumb* 93 NY3922
Thoroton *Notts* 63 SK7642
Thorp Arch *W York* 83 SE4346
Thorpe *Derbys* 73 SK1550
Thorpe *Humb* 84 SE9946
Thorpe *Lincs* 77 TF4981
Thorpe *N York* 88 SE0161
Thorpe *Norfk* 67 TM4398
Thorpe *Notts* 75 SK7649
Thorpe *Surrey* 26 TQ0168
Thorpe Abbotts *Norfk* 55 TM1979
Thorpe Acre *Leics* 62 SK5120
Thorpe Arnold *Leics* 63 SK7720
Thorpe Audlin *W York* 83 SE4715
Thorpe Bassett *N York* 90 SE8673
Thorpe Bay *Essex* 40 TQ9185
Thorpe by Water *Leics* 51 SP8996
Thorpe Common *S York* 74 SK3895
Thorpe Constantine *Staffs* 61 SK2508
Thorpe End *Norfk* 67 TG2811
Thorpe Green *Essex* 41 TM1623
Thorpe Green *Lancs* 81 SD5823
Thorpe Green *Suffk* 54 TL9354
Thorpe Hesley *S York* 74 SK3796
Thorpe in Balne *S York* 83 SE5910
Thorpe in the Fallows *Lincs* 76 SK9180
Thorpe Langton *Leics* 50 SP7492
Thorpe Larches *Dur* 96 NZ3826
Thorpe Lea *Surrey* 26 TQ0270
Thorpe le Street *Humb* 84 SE8343
Thorpe Malsor *Nhants* 51 SP8378
Thorpe Mandeville *Nhants* 49 SP5344
Thorpe Market *Norfk* 67 TG2435
Thorpe Morieux *Suffk* 54 TL9453
Thorpe on the Hill *Lincs* 76 SK9065
Thorpe on the Hill *W York* 82 SE3125
Thorpe Perrow *N York* 89 SE2685
Thorpe Salvin *S York* 75 SK5281
Thorpe Satchville *Leics* 63 SK7311
Thorpe St. Andrew *Norfk* 67 TG2608
Thorpe St. Peter *Lincs* 77 TF4860
Thorpe Thewles *Cleve* 96 NZ4023
Thorpe Tilney *Lincs* 76 TF1257
Thorpe Underwood *N York* 89 SE4659
Thorpe Underwood *Nhants* 50 SP7880
Thorpe Waterville *Nhants* 51 TL0281
Thorpe Willoughby *N York* 83 SE5731
Thorpe-le-Soken *Essex* 41 TM1722
Thorpeness *Suffk* 55 TM4759
Thorpland *Norfk* 65 TF6108
Thorrington *Essex* 41 TM0920
Thorverton *Devon* 9 SS9202
Thrales End *Beds* 38 TL1116
Thrandeston *Suffk* 54 TM1176
Thrapston *Nhants* 51 SP9978
Threapland *Cumb* 92 NY1539
Threapland *N York* 88 SD9860
Threapwood *Ches* 71 SJ4344
Threapwood Head *Staffs* 73 SK0342
Threave *Strath* 106 NS3406
Threawood *Staffs* 73 SK1342
Three Ashes *H & W* 46 SO5123
Three Bridges *W Susx* 15 TQ2837
Three Burrows *Cnwll* 3 SW7446
Three Chimneys *Kent* 28 TQ8238
Three Cocks *Powys* 45 SO1737
Three Crosses *W Glam* 32 SS5794
Three Cups Corner *E Susx* 16 TQ6320
Three Gates *H & W* 47 SO6862
Three Hammers *Cnwll* 5 SX2387
Three Holes *Norfk* 65 TF5000
Three Lane Ends *Gt Man* 79 SD8309
Three Leg Cross *E Susx* 16 TQ6831
Three Legged Cross *Dorset* 12 SU0806
Three Mile Cross *Berks* 24 SU7167
Three Mile Stone *Cnwll* 3 SW7745
Three Miletown *Loth* 117 NT0675
Three Oaks *E Susx* 17 TQ8314
Threehammer Common *Norfk* 67 TG3419

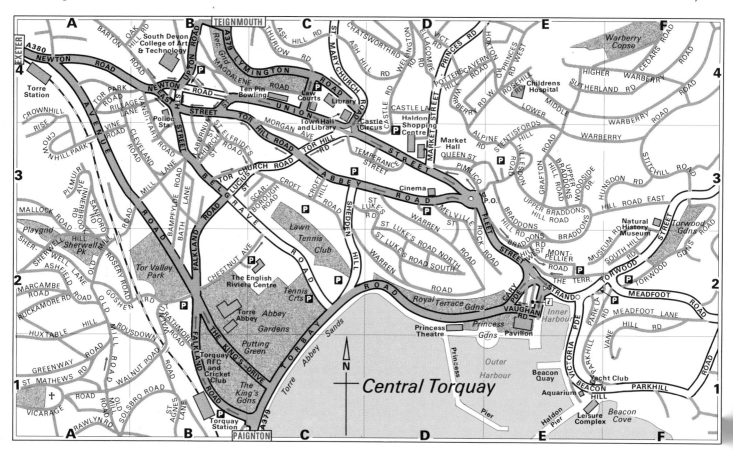

Central Torquay

Tregatta *Cnwll* 4 SX0587	Trembraze *Cnwll* 5 SX2565	Trevaughan *Dyfed* 31 SN1915	Trimdon Colliery *Dur* 96 NZ3835
Tregawne *Cnwll* 4 SX0066	Tremeirchion *Clwyd* 70 SJ0773	Treveal *Cnwll* 2 SW4740	Trimdon Grange *Dur* 96 NZ3635
Tregear *Cnwll* 3 SW8750	Tremethick Cross *Cnwll* 2 SW4430	Treveal *Cnwll* 4 SW7858	Trimingham *Norfk* 67 TG2738
Tregeare *Cnwll* 5 SX2486	Tremollett *Cnwll* 5 SX2975	Treveale *Cnwll* 3 SW8751	Trimley *Suffk* 55 TM2737
Tregeiriog *Clwyd* 58 SJ1733	Tremore *Cnwll* 5 SX0165	Treveighan *Cnwll* 4 SX0779	Trimley Heath *Suffk* 55 TM2738
Tregele *Gwynd* 68 SH3592	Trenance *Cnwll* 2 SW6718	Trevellas *Cnwll* 3 SW7452	Trimley Lower Street *Suffk* 55 TM2636
Tregellist *Cnwll* 4 SX0177	Trenance *Cnwll* 3 SW8022	Trevelmond *Cnwll* 5 SX2063	Trimpley *H & W* 60 SO7978
Tregenna *Cnwll* 3 SW8743	Trenance *Cnwll* 4 SW9270	Trevemper *Cnwll* 4 SW8159	Trimsaran *Dyfed* 32 SN4504
Tregenna *Cnwll* 4 SX0973	Trenance *Cnwll* 4 SW8567	Treveneague *Cnwll* 2 SW5432	Trimstone *Devon* 19 SS5043
Tregeseal *Cnwll* 2 SW3832	Trenarren *Cnwll* 3 SX0348	Treveor *Cnwll* 3 SW9841	Trinafour *Tays* 132 NN7264
Tregew *Cnwll* 3 SW8034	Trenault *Cnwll* 5 SX2683	Treverbyn *Cnwll* 3 SW8849	Trinant *Gwent* 33 ST2099
Tregidden *Cnwll* 3 SW7523	Trench *Shrops* 60 SJ6913	Treverbyn *Cnwll* 4 SX0157	Trinant *Gwent* 33 SO2000
Tregiddle *Cnwll* 2 SW6723	Trench Green *Oxon* 37 SU6877	Treverva *Cnwll* 3 SW7531	Tring *Herts* 38 SP9211
Tregidgeo *Cnwll* 3 SW9647	Trencreek *Cnwll* 4 SW8260	Trevescan *Cnwll* 2 SW3524	Tring Wharf *Herts* 38 SP9212
Tregiskey *Cnwll* 3 SX0146	Trencreek *Cnwll* 5 SX1896	Trevethin *Gwent* 34 SO2802	Tringford *Herts* 38 SP9113
Treglemais *Dyfed* 30 SM8229	Trendeal *Cnwll* 3 SW8952	Trevia *Cnwll* 4 SX0983	Trinity *Jersey* 152 JS0000
Tregole *Cnwll* 5 SX1998	Trendrine *Cnwll* 2 SW4739	Trevigro *Cnwll* 5 SX3369	Trinity *Tays* 134 NO6061
Tregolls *Cnwll* 3 SW7335	Treneague *Cnwll* 4 SW9871	Trevilla *Cnwll* 3 SW8239	Trinity Gask *Tays* 108 NS9618
Tregonce *Cnwll* 4 SW9373	Trenear *Cnwll* 2 SW6831	Trevilledor *Cnwll* 4 SW8967	Triscombe *Somset* 20 ST1535
Tregonetha *Cnwll* 4 SW9563	Treneglos *Cnwll* 5 SX2088	Trevilson *Cnwll* 3 SW8455	Triscombe *Somset* 20 SS9237
Tregony *Cnwll* 3 SW9244	Trenerth *Cnwll* 2 SW6035	Trevine *Dyfed* 30 SM8432	Trislaig *Highld* 130 NN0874
Tregoodwell *Cnwll* 4 SX1183	Trenewan *Cnwll* 4 SX1753	Treviscoe *Cnwll* 3 SW9455	Trispen *Cnwll* 3 SW8450
Tregoose *Cnwll* 2 SW6823	Trenewth *Cnwll* 4 SX0778	Treviskey *Cnwll* 3 SW9340	Tritlington *Nthumb* 103 NZ2092
Tregoss *Cnwll* 4 SW9660	Trengothal *Cnwll* 2 SW3724	Trevissick *Cnwll* 3 SX0248	Troan *Cnwll* 4 SW8957
Tregowris *Cnwll* 3 SW7523	Trengune *Cnwll* 4 SX1893	Trevithal *Cnwll* 2 SW4626	Trochry *Tays* 125 NN9740
Tregoyd *Powys* 45 SO1937	Treninnick *Cnwll* 4 SW8160	Trevithick *Cnwll* 4 SW8662	Trodigal *Strath* 104 NR6420
Tregrehan Mills *Cnwll* 3 SX0453	Trenowah *Cnwll* 4 SW7959	Trevithick *Cnwll* 3 SW9645	Troedrhiwfuwch *M Glam* 33 SO1204
Tregullon *Cnwll* 4 SX0664	Trenoweth *Cnwll* 4 SW7533	Trevivian *Cnwll* 4 SX1785	Troedyraur *Dyfed* 42 SN3245
Tregunna *Cnwll* 4 SW9673	Trent *Dorset* 10 ST5918	Trevoll *Cnwll* 4 SW8358	Troedyrharn *Powys* 45 SO0630
Tregunnon *Cnwll* 5 SX2283	Trent *Lincs* 76 SK8381	Trevone *Cnwll* 4 SW8975	Troedyrhiw *M Glam* 33 SO0702
Tregurrian *Cnwll* 4 SW8465	Trent Vale *Staffs* 72 SJ8643	Trevor *Clwyd* 70 SJ2642	Trofarth *Clwyd* 69 SH8571
Tregustick *Cnwll* 4 SW9966	Trentham *Staffs* 72 SJ8641	Trevor *Gwynd* 56 SH3746	Trois Bois *Jersey* 152 JS0000
Tregynon *Powys* 58 SO1099	Trentishoe *Devon* 19 SS6448	Trevorgans *Cnwll* 2 SW4025	Troon *Cnwll* 2 SW6638
Trehafod *M Glam* 33 ST0490	Trentlock *Derbys* 62 SK4831	Trevorrick *Cnwll* 4 SW8672	Troon *Strath* 106 NS3230
Trehan *Cnwll* 5 SX4058	Treoes *S Glam* 33 SS9478	Trevorrick *Cnwll* 4 SW8273	Troquhain *D & G* 99 NX6879
Treharris *M Glam* 33 ST0996	Treorchy *M Glam* 33 SS9597	Trevose *Cnwll* 4 SW8675	Trossachs Hotel *Cent* 124 NN5107
Treharrock *Cnwll* 4 SX0178	Trequite *Cnwll* 4 SX0277	Trew *Cnwll* 2 SW6129	Troston *Suffk* 54 TL8972
Trehemborne *Cnwll* 4 SW8773	Trerhyngyll *S Glam* 33 ST0077	Trewalder *Cnwll* 4 SX0782	Troswell *Cnwll* 5 SX2592
Treherbert *Cnwll* 44 SN5847	Trerulefoot *Cnwll* 5 SX3258	Trewalkin *Powys* 45 SO1531	Trots Hill *H & W* 47 SO8856
Treherbert *M Glam* 33 SS9498	Tresahor *Cnwll* 3 SW7431	Trewarlett *M Glam* 5 SX3379	Trottiscliffe *Kent* 27 TQ6460
Treheveras *Cnwll* 3 SW8146	Tresawle *Cnwll* 3 SW8946	Trewarmett *Cnwll* 4 SX0686	Trotton *W Susx* 14 SU8322
Trehunist *Cnwll* 5 SX3163	Trescott *Staffs* 60 SO8597	Trewarthenick *Cnwll* 3 SW9044	Trough Gate *Lancs* 81 SD8821
Trekelland *M Glam* 5 SX3480	Trescowe *Cnwll* 2 SW5731	Trewassa *Cnwll* 4 SX1486	Troughend *Nthumb* 102 NY8692
Trekenner *Cnwll* 5 SX3478	Tresean *Cnwll* 4 SW7858	Trewaves *Cnwll* 2 SW5926	Troutbeck *Cumb* 87 NY4002
Treknow *Cnwll* 4 SX0586	Tresham *Avon* 35 ST7991	Treween *Cnwll* 5 SX2282	Troutbeck Bridge *Cumb* 87 NY4000
Trelan *Cnwll* 3 SW7418	Tresillian *Cnwll* 3 SW8646	Trewellard *Cnwll* 2 SW3733	Trow Green *Gloucs* 34 SO5706
Trelash *Cnwll* 4 SX1081	Tresinney *Cnwll* 4 SX1081	Trewen *Cnwll* 4 SX0577	Troway *Derbys* 74 SK3879
Trelassick *Cnwll* 3 SW8752	Treskinnick Cross *Cnwll* 5 SX2098	Trewennack *Cnwll* 2 SW6828	Trowbridge *Wilts* 22 ST8557
Trelawne *Cnwll* 5 SX2154	Treslea *Cnwll* 4 SX1368	Trewent *Dyfed* 30 SS0197	Trowell *Notts* 62 SK4839
Trelawnyd *Clwyd* 70 SJ0879	Tresmeer *Cnwll* 5 SX2387	Trewern *Powys* 58 SJ2811	Trowle Common *Wilts* 22 ST8358
Trelech *Dyfed* 31 SN3821	Tresparrett *Cnwll* 5 SX1491	Trewetha *Cnwll* 4 SX0080	Trowse Newton *Norfk* 67 TG2406
Treleaver *Cnwll* 3 SW7716	Tressait *Tays* 132 NN8160	Trewethern *Cnwll* 4 SX0076	Troy *W York* 82 SE2438
Trelech *Dyfed* 31 SN2830	Tresta *Shet* 155 HU3651	Trewidland *Cnwll* 5 SX2560	Trudoxhill *Somset* 22 ST7443
Trelech a'r Betws *Dyfed* 31 SN3026	Tresta *Shet* 155 HU6190	Trewillis *Cnwll* 3 SW7717	Trull *Somset* 20 ST2122
Treleddyd-fawr *Dyfed* 30 SM7528	Treswell *Notts* 75 SK7779	Trewince *Cnwll* 3 SW8633	Trumfleet *S York* 83 SE6012
Trelew *Cnwll* 33 SW8035	Treswithian *Cnwll* 2 SW6241	Trewint *Cnwll* 4 SX1072	Trumisgarry *W Isls* 154 NF8674
Trelewis *M Glam* 33 ST1096	Trethawle *Cnwll* 5 SX2662	Trewint *Cnwll* 5 SX2180	Trumpan *Highld* 136 NG2261
Treligga *Cnwll* 4 SX0584	Trethevey *Cnwll* 4 SX0789	Trewint *Cnwll* 5 SX2963	Trumpet *H & W* 47 SO6539
Trelights *Cnwll* 4 SW9979	Trethewey *Cnwll* 2 SW3824	Trewirgie *Cnwll* 3 SW8845	Trumpington *Cambs* 53 TL4454
Trelill *Cnwll* 4 SX0478	Trethomas *M Glam* 33 ST1888	Trewithian *Cnwll* 3 SW8737	Trumpington *Cambs* 53 TL4754
Trelion *Cnwll* 4 SW9252	Trethosa *Cnwll* 3 SW9454	Trewithian *Cnwll* 3 SW8737	Trumpsgreen *Surrey* 25 SU9967
Trelissick *Cnwll* 3 SX0355	Trethurgy *Cnwll* 3 SX0355	Trewoodloe *M Glam* 5 SX3271	Trunch *Norfk* 67 TG2834
Trelleck *Gwent* 34 SO5005	Tretio *Dyfed* 30 SM7828	Trewoon *Cnwll* 2 SW4425	Trunnah *Lancs* 80 SD3442
Trelleck Grange *Gwent* 34 SO4901	Tretire *H & W* 46 SO5123	Trewoon *Cnwll* 2 SW6819	Truro *Cnwll* 3 SW8244
Trelminoe *M Glam* 5 SX3181	Tretower *Powys* 33 SO1821	Trewoon *Cnwll* 3 SW9952	Truscott *Cnwll* 5 SX2985
Trelogan *Clwyd* 70 SJ1180	Tretower *Powys* 33 SO1821	Treworgan *Cnwll* 3 SW8349	Trusham *Devon* 8 SX8582
Trelonk *Cnwll* 3 SW8941	Treuddyn *Clwyd* 70 SJ2557	Treworlas *Cnwll* 3 SW8938	Trusley *Derbys* 73 SK2535
Trelow *Cnwll* 4 SW9269	Trevadlock *Cnwll* 5 SX2679	Treworld *Cnwll* 4 SX1190	Trysull *Staffs* 60 SO8594
Trelowarren *Cnwll* 2 SW7124	Trevague *Cnwll* 5 SX2379	Treworthal *Cnwll* 3 SW8838	Tubney *Oxon* 36 SU4398
Trelowia *Cnwll* 5 SX2956	Trevalga *Cnwll* 4 SX0890	Treyarnon *Cnwll* 4 SW8673	Tuckenhay *Devon* 7 SX8156
Treluggan *Cnwll* 4 SW8838	Trevalyn *Clwyd* 71 SJ3856	Treyford *W Susx* 14 SU8218	Tuckhill *Shrops* 60 SO7888
Trelystan *Powys* 58 SJ2503	Trevanger *Cnwll* 4 SW9577	Triangle *Gloucs* 34 SO5401	Tuckingmill *Cnwll* 2 SW6540
Tremadog *Gwynd* 57 SH5640	Trevanson *Cnwll* 4 SW9772	Triangle *W York* 82 SE0422	Tuckingmill *Wilts* 22 ST9329
Tremail *Cnwll* 4 SX1686	Trevarrack *Cnwll* 2 SW4831	Trickett's Cross *Dorset* 12 SU0801	Tuckton *Dorset* 12 SZ1492
Tremain *Dyfed* 42 SN2348	Trevarren *Cnwll* 4 SW9160	Triermain *Cumb* 102 NY5967	Tucoyse *Cnwll* 3 SW9646
Tremaine *Cnwll* 5 SX2388	Trevarrian *Cnwll* 4 SW8566	Triffleton *Dyfed* 30 SM9724	Tuddenham *Suffk* 55 TL7371
Tremar *Cnwll* 5 SX2568	Trevarrick *Cnwll* 3 SW9843	Trillacott *Cnwll* 5 SX2689	Tuddenham *Suffk* 55 TM1948
Trematon *Cnwll* 5 SX3959	Trevarth *Cnwll* 3 SW7240	Trimdon *Dur* 96 NZ3634	Tudeley *Kent* 16 TQ6245

Tudhoe Usworth

Tudhoe *Dur* **96** NZ2535
Tudweiloig *Gwynd* **56** SH2336
Tuesley *Surrey* **25** SU9642
Tuffley *Gloucs* **35** SO8314
Tufton *Dyfed* **30** SN0428
Tufton *Hants* **24** SU4546
Tugby *Leics* **63** SK7601
Tugford *Shrops* **59** SO5587
Tughall *Nthumb* **111** NU2126
Tullibody *Cent* **116** NS8595
Tullich *Highld* **140** NH6328
Tullich *Highld* **147** NH8576
Tullich *Strath* **123** NN0815
Tullich Muir *Highld* **146** NH7273
Tulliemet *Tays* **125** NO0052
Tulloch *Cent* **124** NN5120
Tulloch *Gramp* **143** NJ7931
Tulloch *Gramp* **135** NO7671
Tulloch Station *Highld* **131** NN3580
Tullochgorm *Strath* **114** NR9695
Tullybeagles Lodge *Tays* **125** NO0136
Tullynessle *Gramp* **142** NJ5519
Tumble *Dyfed* **32** SN5411
Tumbler's Green *Essex* **40** TL8025
Tumby *Lincs* **76** TF2359
Tumby Woodside *Lincs* **77** TF2757
Tummel Bridge *Tays* **132** NN7659
Tungate *Norfk* **67** TG2629
Tunstall *Humb* **85** TA3031
Tunstall *Kent* **28** TQ8961
Tunstall *Lancs* **87** SD6073
Tunstall *N York* **89** SE2195
Tunstall *Norfk* **67** TG4108
Tunstall *Staffs* **72** SJ7727
Tunstall *Staffs* **72** SJ8551
Tunstall *Suffk* **55** TM3655
Tunstall *T & W* **96** NZ3953
Tunstead *Derbys* **74** SK1175
Tunstead *Norfk* **67** TG3022
Tunstead Milton *Derbys* **74** SK0280
Tunworth *Hants* **24** SU6748
Tupsley *H & W* **46** SO5340
Tur Langton *Leics* **50** SP7194
Turgis Green *Hants* **24** SU6959
Turin *Tays* **127** NO5352
Turkdean *Gloucs* **36** SP1017
Turleigh *Wilts* **22** ST8060
Turleygreen *Shrops* **60** SO7685
Turn *Lancs* **81** SD8118
Turnastone *H & W* **46** SO3536
Turnberry *Strath* **106** NS2005
Turnchapel *Devon* **6** SX4952
Turnditch *Derbys* **73** SK2946
Turner Green *Lancs* **81** SD6030
Turner's Green *E Susx* **16** TQ6218
Turner's Green *Warwks* **48** SP1969
Turner's Hill *W Susx* **15** TQ3435
Turners Puddle *Dorset* **11** SY8394
Turnworth *Dorset* **11** ST8107
Turriff *Gramp* **142** NJ7250
Turton Bottoms *Gt Man* **81** SD7315
Turvey *Beds* **38** SP9452
Turville *Bucks* **37** SU7691
Turville Heath *Bucks* **37** SU7490
Turweston *Bucks* **49** SP6037
Tushielaw Inn *Border* **109** NT3017
Tushingham cum Grindley *Ches* **71** SJ5246
Tutbury *Staffs* **73** SK2128
Tutnall *H & W* **60** SO9970
Tutshill *Gloucs* **34** ST5495
Tuttington *Norfk* **67** TG2227
Tutwell *Cnwll* **5** SX3876
Tuxford *Notts* **75** SK7471
Twatt *Ork* **155** HY2624
Twatt *Shet* **155** HU3253
Twechar *Strath* **116** NS6975
Tweedmouth *Nthumb* **119** NT9952
Tweedsmuir *Border* **108** NT1024
Twelve Oaks *E Susx* **16** TQ6820
Twelveheads *Cnwll* **3** SW7642
Twemlow Green *Ches* **79** SJ7868
Twenty *Lincs* **64** TF1520
Twerton *Avon* **22** ST7264
Twickenham *Gt Lon* **26** TQ1673
Twigworth *Gloucs* **35** SO8422
Twineham *W Susx* **15** TQ2519
Twineham Green *W Susx* **15** TQ2520
Twinhoe *Avon* **22** ST7359
Twinstead *Essex* **54** TL8636
Twiss Green *Ches* **79** SJ6595
Twitchen *Devon* **19** SS7830
Twitchen *Shrops* **46** SO3779
Twitham *Kent* **29** TR2556
Two Bridges *Devon* **6** SX6075
Two Dales *Derbys* **74** SK2762
Two Gates *Staffs* **61** SK2101
Two Mile Oak Cross *Devon* **7** SX8467
Two Pots *Devon* **19** SS5344
Two Waters *Herts* **38** TL0505
Twycross *Leics* **62** SK3305
Twyford *Berks* **37** SU7976
Twyford *Bucks* **49** SP6626
Twyford *Derbys* **62** SK3228
Twyford *Hants* **13** SU4824
Twyford *Leics* **63** SK7210
Twyford *Lincs* **63** SK9323
Twyford *Norfk* **66** TG0124
Twyford Common *H & W* **46** SO5035
Twyn-carno *M Glam* **33** SO1108
Twyn-y-Sheriff *Gwent* **34** SO4005
Twyn-yr-Odyn *S Glam* **33** ST1173
Twynholm *D & G* **99** NX6654
Twyning *Gloucs* **47** SO8936
Twyning Green *Gloucs* **47** SO9036
Twynllanan *Dyfed* **44** SN7524
Twynmynydd *Dyfed* **32** SN6614
Twywell *Nhants* **51** SP9578
Ty Rhiw *M Glam* **33** ST1283
Ty'n-dwr *Clwyd* **70** SJ2341
Ty'n-y-bryn *M Glam* **30** SS0087
Ty'n-y-coedcae *M Glam* **33** ST1988
Ty'n-y-groes *Gwynd* **69** SH7771
Ty-nant *Clwyd* **70** SH9845
Ty-nant *Gwynd* **58** SH9026
Tyberton *H & W* **46** SO3839
Tyburn *W Mids* **61** SP1391
Tycroes *Dyfed* **32** SN6010
Tycrwyn *Powys* **58** SJ1018
Tydd Gote *Lincs* **65** TF4518
Tydd St. Giles *Cambs* **65** TF4216
Tydd St. Mary *Lincs* **65** TF4418
Tye *Hants* **13** SU7302
Tye Green *Essex* **39** TL5424
Tye Green *Essex* **40** TL7821
Tye Green *Essex* **53** TL5935
Tyersal *W York* **82** SE1932
Tyldesley *Gt Man* **79** SD6802
Tyler Hill *Kent* **29** TR1461
Tyler's Green *Essex* **39** TL5005
Tylers Green *Bucks* **26** SU9093
Tylers Green *Surrey* **27** TQ3552
Tylorstown *M Glam* **33** ST0095
Tylwch *Powys* **58** SN9780
Tyn-y-graig *Powys* **45** SO0149
Tyn-y-nant *M Glam* **33** ST0685
Tynant *M Glam* **33** ST0684
Tyndrum *Cent* **123** NN3330
Tyneham *Dorset* **11** SY8880
Tynemouth *T & W* **103** NZ3669
Tynewydd *M Glam* **33** SS9399
Tyninghame *Loth* **118** NT6179
Tynron *D & G* **100** NX8093
Tyntesfield *Avon* **34** ST5071
Tynygongl *Gwynd* **68** SH5082
Tynygongl *Gwynd* **68** SH5182
Tynygraig *Dyfed* **43** SN6969
Tyringham *Bucks* **38** SP8546
Tyseley *W Mids* **61** SP1184
Tythecott *Devon* **18** SS4117
Tythegston *M Glam* **33** SS8578
Tytherington *Avon* **35** ST6788
Tytherington *Ches* **79** SJ9175
Tytherington *Somset* **22** ST7744
Tytherington *Wilts* **22** ST9140
Tytherleigh *Devon* **10** ST3203
Tywardreath *Cnwll* **3** SX0854
Tywardreath Highway *Cnwll* **3** SX0755
Tywyn *Gwynd* **69** SH5790
Tywyn *Gwynd* **69** SH7978

U

Uachdar *W Isls* **154** NF7955
Ubbeston Green *Suffk* **55** TM3272
Ubley *Avon* **21** ST5257
Uckerby *N York* **89** NZ2402
Uckfield *E Susx* **16** TQ4721
Uckinghall *H & W* **47** SO8637
Uckington *Gloucs* **47** SO9224
Uckington *Shrops* **59** SJ5709
Uddingston *Strath* **116** NS6960
Uddington *Strath* **108** NS8633
Udimore *E Susx* **17** TQ8719
Udny Green *Gramp* **143** NJ8726
Uffcott *Wilts* **36** SU1277
Uffculme *Devon* **20** ST0620
Uffculme *Devon* **9** ST0612
Uffington *Oxon* **36** SU3089
Uffington *Shrops* **59** SJ5314
Ufford *Cambs* **64** TF0904
Ufford *Suffk* **55** TM2952
Ufton *Warwks* **48** SP3762
Ufton Nervet *Berks* **24** SU6367
Ugadale *Strath* **105** NR7828
Ugborough *Devon* **7** SX6755
Uggeshall *Suffk* **55** TM4480
Ugglebarnby *N York* **90** NZ8807
Ughill *Derbys* **74** SK2590
Ugley *Essex* **39** TL5228
Ugley Green *Essex* **39** TL5227
Ugthorpe *N York* **90** NZ7911
Uig *Highld* **136** NG1952
Uig *Highld* **136** NG3963
Uig *Strath* **120** NM1754
Uig *W Isls* **154** NB0534
Uigshader *Highld* **136** NG4346
Uisken *Strath* **121** NM3919
Ulbster *Highld* **151** ND3241
Ulcat Row *Cumb* **93** NY4022
Ulceby *Humb* **85** TA1014
Ulceby *Lincs* **77** TF4272
Ulceby Skitter *Humb* **85** TA1014
Ulcombe *Kent* **28** TQ8448
Uldale *Cumb* **93** NY2437
Uley *Gloucs* **35** ST7898
Ulgham *Nthumb* **103** NZ2392
Ullapool *Highld* **145** NH1294
Ullceby Cross *Lincs* **77** TF4173
Ullenhall *Warwks* **48** SP1267
Ullenwood *Gloucs* **35** SO9416
Ulleskelf *N York* **83** SE5139
Ullesthorpe *Leics* **50** SP5087
Ulley *S York* **75** SK4687
Ullingswick *H & W* **46** SO5950
Ullinish *Highld* **136** NG3237
Ullock *Cumb* **92** NY0724
Ulpha *Cumb* **87** SD3581
Ulpha *Cumb* **86** SD1993
Ulrome *Humb* **85** TA1656
Ulsta *Shet* **155** HU4680
Ulting Wick *Essex* **40** TL8009
Ulverley Green *W Mids* **61** SP1381
Ulverston *Cumb* **86** SD2878
Ulwell *Dorset* **12** SZ0280
Umachan *Highld* **137** NG6150
Umberleigh *Devon* **19** SS6023
Under Burnmouth *D & G* **101** NY4783
Under River *Kent* **27** TQ5552
Underbarrow *Cumb* **87** SD4692
Undercliffe *W York* **82** SE1834
Underdale *Shrops* **59** SJ5013
Underley Hall *Cumb* **87** SD6179
Underling Green *Kent* **28** TQ7546
Underwood *Gwent* **34** ST3888
Underwood *Notts* **75** SK4750
Undley *Suffk* **53** TL6981
Undy *Gwent* **34** ST4386
Union Mills *IOM* **153** SC3578
Union Street *E Susx* **16** TQ7031
Unstone *Derbys* **74** SK3777
Unstone Green *Derbys* **74** SK3776
Unsworth *Gt Man* **79** SD8207
Unthank *Cumb* **93** NY3948
Unthank *Cumb* **94** NY6050
Unthank *Cumb* **93** NY3948
Unthank *Nthumb* **111** NT9848
Unthank End *Cumb* **93** NY4535
Up Cerne *Dorset* **11** ST6502
Up Exe *Devon* **9** SS9302
Up Holland *Lancs* **78** SD5105
Up Marden *W Susx* **14** SU7914
Up Mudford *Somset* **10** ST5718
Up Nately *Hants* **24** SU6951
Up Somborne *Hants* **23** SU3932
Up Sydling *Dorset* **10** ST6201
Upavon *Wilts* **23** SU1354
Upchurch *Kent* **28** TQ8467
Upcott *Devon* **19** SS5739
Upcott *Devon* **19** SS7529
Upcott *H & W* **46** SO3250
Upcott *Somset* **20** SS9025
Updown Hill *Surrey* **25** SU9363
Upend *Cambs* **53** TL7058
Upgate *Norfk* **66** TG1418
Upgate Street *Norfk* **66** TM0992
Upgate Street *Norfk* **67** TM2891
Uphall *Dorset* **10** ST5502
Uphall *Loth* **117** NT0671
Upham *Devon* **19** SS8808
Upham *Hants* **13** SU5320
Uphampton *H & W* **47** SO8364
Uphampton *H & W* **46** SO3963
Uphill *Avon* **21** ST3158
Uplawmoor *Strath* **115** NS4355
Upleadon *Gloucs* **47** SO7527
Upleatham *Cleve* **97** NZ6319
Uplees *Kent* **17** TR0004
Uploders *Dorset* **10** SY5093
Uplowman *Devon* **9** ST0115
Uplyme *Devon* **10** SY3293
Upminster *Gt Lon* **27** TQ5686
Upottery *Devon* **9** ST2007
Uppark *W Susx* **14** SU7717
Upparthong *W York* **82** SE1208
Uppat House *Highld* **147** NC8702
Uppaton *Devon* **5** SX4380
Upper Affcot *Shrops* **59** SO4486
Upper Ardchronie *Highld* **146** NH6188
Upper Arley *H & W* **60** SO7680
Upper Arncott *Oxon* **37** SP6017
Upper Astrop *Nhants* **49** SP5137
Upper Basildon *Berks* **37** SU5976
Upper Batley *W York* **82** SE2325
Upper Beeding *W Susx* **15** TQ1910
Upper Benefield *Nhants* **51** SP9789
Upper Bentley *H & W* **47** SO9966
Upper Bighouse *Highld* **150** NC8857
Upper Birchwood *Derbys* **75** SK4355
Upper Boat *M Glam* **33** ST1087
Upper Boddington *Nhants* **49** SP4853
Upper Borth *Dyfed* **43** SN6088
Upper Brailes *Warwks* **48** SP3040
Upper Breakish *Highld* **129** NG6823
Upper Breinton *H & W* **46** SO4640
Upper Broadheath *H & W* **47** SO8056
Upper Broughton *Notts* **63** SK6826
Upper Bucklebury *Berks* **24** SU5468
Upper Burgate *Hants* **12** SU1516
Upper Bush *Kent* **28** TQ6966
Upper Cairmie *Tays* **105** NS0319
Upper Cairn *D & G* **107** NS6912
Upper Caldecote *Beds* **52** TL1645
Upper Canada *Avon* **21** ST3658
Upper Canterton *Hants* **12** SU2612
Upper Catesby *Nhants* **49** SP5259
Upper Catshill *H & W* **60** SO9674
Upper Chapel *Powys* **45** SO0040
Upper Cheddon *Somset* **20** ST2328
Upper Chickgrove *Wilts* **22** ST9730
Upper Chute *Wilts* **23** SU2953
Upper Chute *Wilts* **23** SU2953
Upper Clapton *Gt Lon* **27** TQ3487
Upper Clatford *Hants* **23** SU3543
Upper Clynnog *Gwynd* **56** SH4746
Upper Coberley *Gloucs* **35** SO9815
Upper Cokeham *W Susx* **15** TQ1705
Upper Cotton *Staffs* **73** SK0547
Upper Cound *Shrops* **59** SJ5505
Upper Cudworth *S York* **83** SE3908
Upper Cumberworth *W York* **82** SE2008
Upper Cwmtwrch *Powys* **32** SN7611
Upper Dallachy *Gramp* **141** NJ3662
Upper Deal *Kent* **29** TR3651
Upper Dean *Beds* **51** TL0467
Upper Denby *W York* **82** SE2307
Upper Denton *Cumb* **102** NY6165
Upper Dicker *E Susx* **16** TQ5509
Upper Dinchope *Shrops* **59** SO4583
Upper Dovercourt *Essex* **41** TM2331
Upper Drumbane *Cent* **124** NN6606
Upper Dunsforth *N York* **89** SE4463
Upper Eashing *Surrey* **25** SU9543
Upper Egleton *H & W* **47** SO6345
Upper Elkstone *Staffs* **74** SK0559
Upper Ellastone *Staffs* **73** SK1143
Upper Elmers End *Gt Lon* **27** TQ3667
Upper End *Derbys* **74** SK0876
Upper Enham *Hants* **23** SU3649
Upper Ethrie *Highld* **140** NH7662
Upper Farmcote *Shrops* **60** SO7792
Upper Farringdon *Hants* **24** SU7135
Upper Framilode *Gloucs* **35** SO7510
Upper Froyle *Hants* **24** SU7542
Upper Godney *Somset* **21** ST4842
Upper Gravenhurst *Beds* **38** TL1136
Upper Green *Berks* **23** SU3763
Upper Green *Essex* **53** TL5935
Upper Green *Gwent* **34** SO3818
Upper Green *Suffk* **53** TL7464
Upper Grove Common *H & W* **46** SO5526
Upper Hackney *Derbys* **74** SK2861
Upper Hale *Surrey* **25** SU8449
Upper Halliford *Surrey* **26** TQ0968
Upper Halling *Kent* **28** TQ6964
Upper Hambleton *Leics* **63** SK9007
Upper Harbledown *Kent* **29** TR1158
Upper Hardres Court *Kent* **29** TR1550
Upper Hardwick *H & W* **46** SO4057
Upper Hartfield *E Susx* **16** TQ4634
Upper Hartshay *Derbys* **74** SK3850
Upper Hatherley *Gloucs* **35** SO9221
Upper Hatton *Staffs* **72** SJ8337
Upper Haugh *S York* **74** SK4297
Upper Hayton *Shrops* **59** SO5281
Upper Heaton *W York* **82** SE1719
Upper Helmsley *N York* **83** SE6956
Upper Hergest *H & W* **46** SO2654
Upper Heyford *Nhants* **49** SP6659
Upper Heyford *Oxon* **49** SP4925
Upper Hill *H & W* **46** SO4753
Upper Hockenden *Kent* **27** TQ5069
Upper Hopton *W York* **82** SE1918
Upper Howsell *H & W* **47** SO7748
Upper Hulme *Staffs* **73** SK0160
Upper Ifold *Surrey* **14** TQ0033
Upper Inglesham *Wilts* **36** SU2096
Upper Keith *Loth* **118** NT4562
Upper Kilcott *Avon* **35** ST7988
Upper Killay *W Glam* **32** SS5892
Upper Kinchrackine *Strath* **123** NN1627
Upper Lambourn *Berks* **36** SU3180
Upper Landywood *Staffs* **60** SJ9805
Upper Langford *Avon* **21** ST4659
Upper Langwith *Derbys* **75** SK5169
Upper Largo *Fife* **127** NO4203
Upper Leigh *Staffs* **73** SK0136
Upper Ley *Gloucs* **35** SO7217
Upper Littleton *Avon* **21** ST5564
Upper Lochton *Gramp* **135** NO6997
Upper Longdon *Staffs* **61** SK0614
Upper Ludstone *Shrops* **60** SO8095
Upper Lybster *Highld* **151** ND2537
Upper Lydbrook *Gloucs* **34** SO6015
Upper Lyde *H & W* **46** SO4944
Upper Lye *H & W* **46** SO3965
Upper Maes-coed *H & W* **46** SO3334
Upper Midhope *Derbys* **74** SK2199
Upper Milton *H & W* **60** SO8072
Upper Minety *Wilts* **35** SU0091
Upper Moor *H & W* **47** SO9747
Upper Mulben *Gramp* **141** NJ2551
Upper Nesbet *Border* **110** NT6727
Upper Netchwood *Shrops* **59** SO6192
Upper Nobut *Staffs* **73** SK0435
Upper Norwood *W Susx* **14** SU9317
Upper Ollach *Highld* **137** NG5137
Upper Padley *Derbys* **74** SK2478
Upper Pennington *Hants* **12** SZ3095
Upper Pickwick *Wilts* **35** ST8571
Upper Pollicott *Bucks* **37** SP7013
Upper Pond Street *Essex* **39** TL4536
Upper Poppleton *N York* **83** SE5554
Upper Pulley *Shrops* **59** SJ4808
Upper Quinton *Warwks* **48** SP1846
Upper Ratley *Hants* **23** SU3223
Upper Rochford *H & W* **47** SO6367
Upper Ruscoe *D & G* **99** NX5661
Upper Sapey *H & W* **47** SO6863
Upper Seagry *Wilts* **35** ST9480
Upper Shelton *Beds* **38** SP9843
Upper Sheringham *Norfk* **66** TG1441
Upper Shuckburgh *Warwks* **49** SP4961
Upper Slaughter *Gloucs* **48** SP1523
Upper Soudley *Gloucs* **35** SO6510
Upper Spond *H & W* **46** SO3153
Upper Standen *Kent* **29** TR2240
Upper Staploe *Beds* **52** TL1459
Upper Stepford *D & G* **100** NX8681
Upper Stoke *Norfk* **67** TG2502
Upper Stondon *Beds* **39** TL1535
Upper Stowe *Nhants* **49** SP6456
Upper Street *Hants* **12** SU1418
Upper Street *Norfk* **67** TG3217
Upper Street *Norfk* **67** TG3617
Upper Street *Norfk* **54** TM1779
Upper Street *Suffk* **53** TL7851
Upper Street *Suffk* **54** TM1434
Upper Street *Suffk* **54** TM1051
Upper Sundon *Beds* **38** TL0427
Upper Swell *Gloucs* **48** SP1726
Upper Tankersley *S York* **74** SK3399
Upper Tasburgh *Norfk* **67** TM2095
Upper Tean *Staffs* **73** SK0139
Upper Threapwood *Ches* **71** SJ4345
Upper Town *Avon* **21** ST5265
Upper Town *Derbys* **73** SK2351
Upper Town *Derbys* **74** SK2462
Upper Town *Dur* **95** NZ0737
Upper Town *H & W* **46** SO5848
Upper Town *Suffk* **54** TL9267
Upper Tysoe *Warwks* **48** SP3343
Upper Ufford *Suffk* **55** TM2953
Upper Upham *Wilts* **36** SU2277
Upper Upnor *Kent* **28** TQ7570
Upper Victoria *Tays* **127** NO5336
Upper Vobster *Somset* **22** ST7049
Upper Wardington *Oxon* **49** SP4945
Upper Weald *Bucks* **38** SP8037
Upper Weedon *Nhants* **49** SP6158
Upper Wellingham *E Susx* **16** TQ4313
Upper Weston *Avon* **22** ST7266
Upper Weybread *Suffk* **55** TM2379
Upper Whiston *S York* **75** SK4588
Upper Wick *H & W* **47** SO8252
Upper Wield *Hants* **24** SU6238
Upper Winchendon *Bucks* **37** SP7414
Upper Witton *W Mids* **61** SP0892
Upper Woodford *Wilts* **23** SU1237
Upper Wootton *Hants* **24** SU5854
Upper Wraxall *Wilts* **35** ST8074
Upper Wyche *H & W* **47** SO7643
Upperby *Cumb* **93** NY4153
Upperglen *Highld* **136** NG3151
Uppermill *Gt Man* **82** SD9905
Uppermoorside *W York* **82** SE2430
Upperthorpe *Derbys* **75** SK4580
Upperthorpe *Humb* **84** SE7426
Upperton *Derbys* **74** SK3264
Upperton *W Susx* **14** SU9522
Uppertown *Highld* **151** ND3576
Upperup *Gloucs* **36** SU0396
Upperwood *Derbys* **74** SK2957
Uppincott *Devon* **9** SS9106
Uppingham *Leics* **51** SP8699
Uppington *Dorset* **11** SU0106
Uppington *Shrops* **59** SJ5909
Upsall *N York* **89** SE4586
Upsettlington *Border* **110** NT8846
Upshire *Essex* **27** TL4100
Upstreet *Kent* **29** TR2263
Upthorpe *Suffk* **54** TL9772
Upton *Berks* **26** SU9779
Upton *Bucks* **37** SP7711
Upton *Cambs* **64** TF1000
Upton *Cambs* **52** TL1778
Upton *Ches* **78** SJ5087
Upton *Ches* **71** SJ4169
Upton *Cnwll* **18** SS2004
Upton *Cnwll* **5** SX2772
Upton *Cumb* **93** NY3139
Upton *Devon* **9** ST0902
Upton *Devon* **7** SX7042
Upton *Dorset* **11** SY7483
Upton *Dorset* **11** SY9893
Upton *Dyfed* **30** SN0204
Upton *Hants* **23** SU3555
Upton *Hants* **12** SU3717
Upton *Humb* **85** TA1454
Upton *Leics* **61** SP3699
Upton *Lincs* **76** SK8686
Upton *Mersyd* **78** SJ2788
Upton *Nhants* **49** SP7159
Upton *Norfk* **67** TG3912
Upton *Notts* **75** SK7354
Upton *Notts* **75** SK7476
Upton *Oxon* **36** SP2312
Upton *Oxon* **37** SU5186
Upton *Somset* **20** SS9928
Upton *Somset* **21** ST4526
Upton *W York* **83** SE4713
Upton *Warwks* **48** SP1257
Upton Bishop *H & W* **47** SO6527
Upton Cheyney *Avon* **35** ST6970
Upton Cressett *Shrops* **59** SO6592
Upton Crews *H & W* **47** SO6527
Upton Cross *Cnwll* **5** SX2872
Upton End *Beds* **38** TL1234
Upton Grey *Hants* **24** SU6948
Upton Heath *Ches* **71** SJ4169
Upton Hellions *Devon* **8** SS8303
Upton Lovell *Wilts* **22** ST9440
Upton Magna *Shrops* **59** SJ5512
Upton Noble *Somset* **22** ST7139
Upton Pyne *Devon* **9** SX9197
Upton Scudamore *Wilts* **22** ST8647
Upton Snodsbury *H & W* **47** SO9454
Upton St. Leonards *Gloucs* **35** SO8615
Upton Towans *Cnwll* **2** SW5740
Upton upon Severn *H & W* **47** SO8540
Upton Warren *H & W* **47** SO9367
Upton Wood *Kent* **29** TR2546
Upwaltham *W Susx* **14** SU9413
Upware *Cambs* **53** TL5470
Upwell *Norfk* **65** TF5002
Upwey *Dorset* **11** SY6684
Upwick Green *Herts* **39** TL4524
Upwood *Cambs* **52** TL2582
Urchany *Highld* **140** NH8849
Urchfont *Wilts* **23** SU0356
Urdimarsh *H & W* **46** SO5248
Ure Bank *N York* **89** SE3172
Urlay Nook *Cleve* **96** NZ3816
Urmston *Gt Man* **79** SJ7694
Urquhart *Gramp* **141** NJ2862
Urra *N York* **90** NZ5601
Urray *Highld* **139** NH5052
Ushaw Moor *Dur* **96** NZ2242
Usk *Gwent* **34** SO3700
Usselby *Lincs* **76** TF0993
Usworth *T & W* **96** NZ3058

Utley
Weeton

Utley *W York* 82 SE0543
Uton *Devon* 8 SX8298
Utterby *Lincs* 77 TF3093
Uttoxeter *Staffs* 73 SK0933
Uwchmynydd *Gwynd* 56 SH1525
Uxbridge *Gt Lon* 26 TQ0584
Uyeasound *Shet* 155 HP5901
Uzmaston *Dyfed* 30 SM9714

V

Vale *Guern* 152 GN0000
Valley *Gwynd* 68 SH2979
Valley End *Surrey* 25 SU9564
Valley Truckle *Cnwll* 4 SX1082
Valtos *Highld* 137 NG5163
Valtos *W Isls* 154 NB0936
Van *M Glam* 33 ST1686
Vange *Essex* 40 TQ7187
Vardre *W Glam* 32 SN6902
Varteg *Gwent* 34 SO2606
Vatsetter *Shet* 155 HU5389
Vatten *Highld* 136 NG2843
Vaynor *M Glam* 33 SO0410
Velindre *Dyfed* 31 SN1039
Velindre *Dyfed* 31 SN3538
Velindre *Powys* 45 SO1836
Vellow *Somset* 20 ST0938
Velly *Devon* 18 SS2924
Venn *Devon* 7 SX8550
Venn Ottery *Devon* 9 SY0791
Venngreen *Devon* 18 SS3711
Vennington *Shrops* 59 SJ3309
Venny Ten Burn *Devon* 8 SX8297
Venterdow *M Glam* 5 SX3675
Ventnor *IOW* 13 SZ5677
Venton *Devon* 6 SX5856
Vernham Dean *Hants* 23 SU3456
Vernham Street *Hants* 23 SU3457
Vernolds Common *Shrops* 59 SO4780
Verwig *Dyfed* 42 SN1849
Verwood *Dorset* 12 SU0908
Veryan *Cnwll* 3 SW9139
Veryan Green *Cnwll* 3 SW9240
Vicarage *Devon* 9 SY2088
Vickerstown *Cumb* 86 SD1868
Victoria *Cnwll* 4 SW9861
Victoria *Gwent* 33 SO1707
Victoria *S York* 82 SE1605
Vidlin *Shet* 155 HU4765
Viewfield *Gramp* 141 NJ2864
Viewpark *Strath* 116 NS7061
Villavin *Devon* 19 SS5816
Ville la Bas *Jersey* 152 JS0000
Villiaze *Guern* 152 GN0000
Vine's Cross *E Susx* 16 TQ5917
Vinehall Street *E Susx* 17 TQ7520
Virginia Water *Surrey* 14 TQ0007
Virginstow *Devon* 5 SX3792
Virley *Essex* 40 TL9414
Vobster *Somset* 22 ST7048
Voe *Shet* 155 HU4063
Vowchurch *H & W* 46 SO3636
Vulcan Village *Ches* 78 SJ5894

W

Wackerfield *Dur* 96 NZ1522
Wacton *Norfk* 66 TM1791
Wadborough *H & W* 47 SO9047
Waddesdon *Bucks* 37 SP7416
Waddeton *Devon* 7 SX8756
Waddicar *Mersyd* 78 SJ3999
Waddingham *Lincs* 76 SK9896
Waddington *Lancs* 81 SD7343
Waddington *Lincs* 76 SK9764
Waddon *Dorset* 10 SY6185
Wadebridge *Cnwll* 4 SW9972
Wadeford *Somset* 10 ST3110
Wadenhoe *Nhants* 51 TL0183
Wadesmill *Herts* 39 TL3517
Wadhurst *E Susx* 16 TQ6431
Wadshelf *Derbys* 74 SK3171
Wadswick *Wilts* 22 ST8467
Wadworth *S York* 75 SK5697
Waen *Clwyd* 70 SJ0062
Waen *Clwyd* 70 SJ1166
Waen *Powys* 58 SJ2320
Waen Fach *Powys* 58 SJ2017
Waen-pentir *Gwynd* 69 SH5766
Waen-wen *Gwynd* 69 SH5768
Wagbeach *Shrops* 59 SJ3602
Wainfelin *Gwent* 34 SO2701
Wainfleet All Saints *Lincs* 77 TF4959
Wainfleet Bank *Lincs* 77 TF4759
Wainford *Norfk* 55 TM3490
Wainhouse Corner *Cnwll* 4 SX1895
Wains Hill *Avon* 34 ST3970
Wainscott *Kent* 28 TQ7470
Wainstalls *W York* 82 SE0428
Waitby *Cumb* 88 NY7508
Waithe *Lincs* 77 TA2800
Wake Green *W Mids* 61 SP0882
Wakefield *W York* 83 SE3320
Wakerley *Nhants* 51 SP9599
Wakes Colne *Essex* 40 TL8928
Wal-wen *Clwyd* 70 SJ2076
Walberswick *Suffk* 55 TM4974
Walberton *W Susx* 14 SU9706
Walbottle *T & W* 103 NZ1666
Walbutt *D & G* 99 NX7468
Walby *Cumb* 101 NY4460
Walcombe *Somset* 21 ST5546
Walcot *Humb* 84 SE8720
Walcot *Lincs* 64 TF0635
Walcot *Lincs* 76 TF1356
Walcot *Shrops* 59 SO3485
Walcot *Shrops* 59 SJ5912
Walcot *Warwks* 48 SP1358
Walcot *Wilts* 36 SU1684
Walcot Green *Norfk* 54 TM1280
Walcote *Leics* 50 SP5783
Walcott *Norfk* 67 TG3632
Walden *N York* 88 SE0082
Walden Head *N York* 88 SD9880
Walden Stubbs *N York* 83 SE5516
Walderslade *Kent* 28 TQ7663
Walderton *W Susx* 14 SU7910
Walditch *Dorset* 10 SY4892
Waldley *Derbys* 73 SK1237
Waldridge *Dur* 96 NZ2549
Waldringfield *Suffk* 55 TM2845
Waldron *E Susx* 16 TQ5419
Wales *S York* 75 SK4882
Wales *Somset* 21 ST5925
Walesby *Lincs* 76 TF1392
Walesby *Notts* 75 SK6870
Walford *H & W* 46 SO3872
Walford *H & W* 34 SO5820
Walford *Shrops* 59 SJ4320
Walford *Staffs* 72 SJ8134
Walford Heath *Shrops* 59 SJ4519
Walgherton *Ches* 72 SJ6949
Walgrave *Nhants* 51 SP8071
Walhampton *Hants* 12 SZ3395
Walk Mill *Lancs* 81 SD8729
Walkden *Gt Man* 79 SD7303
Walker *T & W* 103 NZ2964
Walker *T & W* 103 NZ2964
Walker Fold *Lancs* 81 SD6741
Walker's Green *H & W* 46 SO5247
Walker's Heath *W Mids* 61 SP0578
Walkerburn *Border* 109 NT3637
Walkeringham *Notts* 75 SK7692
Walkerith *Notts* 75 SK7892
Walkern *Herts* 39 TL2826
Walkerton *Fife* 126 NO2301
Walkhampton *Devon* 6 SX5369
Walkington *Humb* 84 SE9937
Walkley *S York* 74 SK3388
Walkwood *H & W* 48 SP0364
Wall *Border* 109 NT4623
Wall *Cnwll* 2 SW6036
Wall *Nthumb* 102 NY9168
Wall *Staffs* 61 SK0906
Wall End *Cumb* 101 NY2383
Wall End *H & W* 46 SO4457
Wall Heath *W Mids* 60 SO8889
Wallaceton *D & G* 100 NX8487
Wallacetown *Strath* 106 NS2703
Wallacetown *Strath* 106 NS3422
Wallands Park *E Susx* 15 TQ4010
Wallasey *Mersyd* 78 SJ2991
Wallend *Kent* 28 TQ8775
Waller's Green *H & W* 47 SO6738
Wallfield *Fife* 126 NO1909
Wallhead *Cumb* 101 NY4661
Wallingford *Oxon* 37 SU6089
Wallington *Gt Lon* 27 TQ2864
Wallington *Hants* 13 SU5806
Wallington *Herts* 39 TL2933
Wallington Heath *W Mids* 60 SJ9902
Wallis *Dyfed* 30 SN0125
Wallisdown *Dorset* 12 SZ0694
Walliswood *W Susx* 14 TQ1238
Walls *Shet* 155 HU2449
Wallsend *T & W* 103 NZ2966
Wallthwaite *Cumb* 93 NY3526
Wallyford *Loth* 118 NT3671
Walmer *Kent* 29 TR3750
Walmer Bridge *Lancs* 80 SD4824
Walmersley *Gt Man* 81 SD8013
Walmestone *Kent* 29 TR2559
Walmley *W Mids* 61 SP1393
Walmley Ash *W Mids* 61 SP1392
Walmsgate *Lincs* 77 TF3677
Walpole *Somset* 20 ST3042
Walpole *Suffk* 55 TM3674
Walpole Cross Keys *Norfk* 65 TF5119
Walpole Highway *Norfk* 65 TF5113
Walpole St. Andrew *Norfk* 65 TF5017
Walpole St. Peter *Norfk* 65 TF5016
Walrow *Somset* 21 ST3347
Walsall *W Mids* 60 SP0198
Walsall Wood *W Mids* 61 SK0403
Walsden *W York* 81 SD9321
Walsgrave on Sowe *W Mids* 61 SP3881
Walshall Green *Herts* 39 TL4430
Walsham le Willows *Suffk* 54 TM0071
Walshaw *Gt Man* 81 SD7711
Walshaw *W York* 82 SD9731
Walshford *N York* 83 SE4153
Walsoken *Norfk* 65 TF4710
Walston *Strath* 117 NT0545
Walsworth *Herts* 39 TL1930
Walter Ash *Bucks* 37 SU8398
Walters Green *Kent* 16 TQ5140
Walterston *S Glam* 33 ST0771
Walterstone *H & W* 46 SO3425
Waltham *Humb* 85 TA2503
Waltham *Kent* 29 TR1048
Waltham Abbey *Essex* 27 TL3800
Waltham Chase *Hants* 13 SU5615
Waltham Cross *Herts* 27 TL3600
Waltham on the Wolds *Leics* 63 SK8024
Waltham St. Lawrence *Berks* 37 SU8276
Waltham's Cross *Essex* 40 TL6930
Walthamstow *Gt Lon* 27 TQ3689
Walton *Bucks* 38 SP8936
Walton *Cambs* 64 TF1702
Walton *Cumb* 101 NY5264
Walton *Derbys* 74 SK3568
Walton *Leics* 50 SP5987
Walton *Powys* 46 SO2559
Walton *Shrops* 46 SO4679
Walton *Shrops* 59 SJ5818
Walton *Somset* 21 ST4636
Walton *Staffs* 72 SJ8528
Walton *Staffs* 72 SJ8933
Walton *Suffk* 55 TM2935
Walton *W Susx* 14 SU8104
Walton *W York* 83 SE4447
Walton *W York* 83 SE3516
Walton *Warwks* 48 SP2853
Walton Cardiff *Gloucs* 47 SO9032
Walton East *Dyfed* 30 SN0223
Walton Elm *Dorset* 11 ST7717
Walton Grounds *Nhants* 49 SP5135
Walton Lower Street *Suffk* 55 TM2834
Walton on the Hill *Surrey* 26 TQ2255
Walton on the Naze *Essex* 41 TM2622
Walton on the Wolds *Leics* 62 SK5919
Walton Park *Avon* 34 ST4172
Walton West *Dyfed* 30 SM8613
Walton-in-Gordano *Avon* 34 ST4273
Walton-on-Thames *Surrey* 26 TQ1066
Walton-on-Trent *Derbys* 73 SK2118
Walton-on-the-Hill *Staffs* 72 SJ9520
Walwen *Clwyd* 70 SJ1771
Walwen *Clwyd* 70 SJ1179
Walwick *Nthumb* 102 NY9070
Walworth *Dur* 96 NZ2318
Walworth Gate *Dur* 96 NZ2320
Walwyn's Castle *Dyfed* 30 SM8711
Wambrook *Somset* 10 ST2907
Wamphray *D & G* 100 NY1295
Wampool *Cumb* 93 NY2454
Wanborough *Surrey* 25 SU9348
Wanborough *Wilts* 36 SU2082
Wanclon End *Herts* 38 TL1322
Wandel *Strath* 108 NS9427
Wangford *Suffk* 55 TM4679
Wanlip *Leics* 62 SK5910
Wanlockhead *D & G* 108 NS8712
Wannock *E Susx* 16 TQ5703
Wansford *Cambs* 64 TL0799
Wansford *Humb* 84 TA0656
Wanshurst Green *Kent* 28 TQ7645
Wanstead *Gt Lon* 27 TQ4088
Wanstrow *Somset* 22 ST7141
Wanswell *Gloucs* 35 SO6801
Wantage *Oxon* 36 SU3988
Wants Green *H & W* 47 SO7557
Wapley *Avon* 35 ST7179
Wappenbury *Warwks* 48 SP3769
Wappenham *Nhants* 49 SP6245
Warbister *Ork* 155 HY3933
Warbleton *E Susx* 16 TQ6018
Warborough *Oxon* 37 SU5993
Warbourne Ford *Devon* 7 SX7162
Warboys *Cambs* 52 TL3080
Warbreck *Lancs* 80 SD3238
Warbstow *Cnwll* 5 SX2090
Warburton *Gt Man* 79 SJ7089
Warcop *Cumb* 94 NY7415
Ward End *W Mids* 61 SP1188
Ward Green *Suffk* 54 TM0564
Warden *Kent* 28 TR0271
Warden *Nthumb* 102 NY9166
Warden Law *T & W* 96 NZ3649
Warden Street *Beds* 38 TL1244
Wardhedges *Beds* 38 TL0635
Wardington *Oxon* 49 SP4946
Wardle *Ches* 71 SJ6057
Wardle *Gt Man* 81 SD9116
Wardley *Gt Man* 79 SD7602
Wardley *Leics* 51 SK8300
Wardlow *Derbys* 74 SK1874
Wardsend *Ches* 79 SJ9382
Wardy Hill *Cambs* 53 TL4782
Ware *Herts* 39 TL3514
Ware Street *Kent* 28 TQ7856
Wareham *Dorset* 11 SY9287
Warehorne *Kent* 17 TQ9832
Waren Mill *Nthumb* 111 NU1434
Warenford *Nthumb* 111 NU1328
Warenton *Nthumb* 111 NU1030
Wareside *Herts* 39 TL3915
Waresley *Cambs* 52 TL2454
Waresley *H & W* 60 SO8470
Warfield *Berks* 25 SU8872
Warfleet *Devon* 7 SX8750
Wargate *Lincs* 64 TF2330
Wargrave *Berks* 37 SU7978
Warham *H & W* 46 SO4838
Warham All Saints *Norfk* 66 TF9441
Warham St. Mary *Norfk* 66 TF9441
Wark *Nthumb* 110 NT8238
Wark *Nthumb* 102 NY8576
Warkleigh *Devon* 19 SS6422
Warkton *Nhants* 51 SP8979
Warkworth *Nhants* 49 SP4840
Warkworth *Nthumb* 111 NU2406
Warlaby *N York* 89 SE3591
Warland *W York* 82 SD9420
Warleggan *Cnwll* 4 SX1569
Warleigh *Avon* 22 ST7964
Warley Town *W York* 82 SE0524
Warlingham *Surrey* 27 TQ3658
Warmanbie *D & G* 101 NY1968
Warmbrook *Derbys* 73 SK2853
Warmfield *W York* 83 SE3720
Warmfield *W York* 83 SE3720
Warmingham *Ches* 72 SJ7161
Warmington *Nhants* 51 TL0791
Warmington *Warwks* 49 SP4147
Warminster *Wilts* 22 ST8644
Warmley *Avon* 35 ST6673
Warmsworth *S York* 75 SE5400
Warmwell *Dorset* 11 SY7585
Warndon *H & W* 47 SO8856
Warnford *Hants* 13 SU6223
Warnham *W Susx* 15 TQ1533
Warnham Court *W Susx* 15 TQ1633
Warningcamp *W Susx* 14 TQ0307
Warninglid *W Susx* 15 TQ2526
Warren *Ches* 79 SJ8870
Warren *Dyfed* 30 SR9397
Warren Row *Berks* 37 SU8180
Warren Street *Kent* 28 TQ9253
Warren's Green *Herts* 39 TL2628
Warrenby *Cleve* 97 NZ5755
Warrenhill *Strath* 108 NS9439
Warrington *Bucks* 51 SP8953
Warrington *Ches* 78 SJ6088
Warriston *Loth* 117 NT2575
Warsash *Hants* 13 SU4906
Warslow *Staffs* 74 SK0858
Warsop *Notts* 75 SK5667
Warsop Vale *Notts* 90 SE5467
Warter *Humb* 84 SE8750
Warter Priory *Humb* 84 SE8449
Warthermaske *N York* 89 SE2078
Warthill *N York* 83 SE6755
Wartling *E Susx* 16 TQ6509
Wartnaby *Leics* 63 SK7123
Warton *Lancs* 80 SD4128
Warton *Lancs* 87 SD4972
Warton *Nthumb* 103 NU0003
Warton *Warwks* 61 SK2803
Warwick *Cumb* 93 NY4656
Warwick *Warwks* 48 SP2865
Warwick Bridge *Cumb* 93 NY4657
Warwicksland *Cumb* 101 NY4477
Wasdale Head *Cumb* 86 NY1808
Wash *Derbys* 74 SK0682
Wash *Devon* 7 SX7765
Washaway *Cnwll* 4 SX0369
Washbourne *Devon* 7 SX7954
Washbrook *Somset* 21 ST4150
Washbrook *Suffk* 54 TM1142
Washfield *Devon* 9 SS9315
Washfold *N York* 88 NZ0502
Washford *Somset* 20 ST0441
Washford Pyne *Devon* 19 SS8111
Washingborough *Lincs* 76 TF0170
Washington *T & W* 96 NZ2956
Washington *W Susx* 14 TQ1212
Washwood Heath *W Mids* 61 SP1088
Wasing *Berks* 24 SU5764
Waskerley *Dur* 95 NZ0445
Wasperton *Warwks* 48 SP2659
Wasps Nest *Lincs* 76 TF0764
Wass *N York* 90 SE5579
Watchet *Somset* 20 ST0743
Watchfield *Oxon* 36 SU2490
Watchfield *Somset* 21 ST3446
Watchgate *Cumb* 87 SD5399
Watchill *Cumb* 93 NY1842
Watcombe *Devon* 7 SX9267
Watendlath *Cumb* 93 NY2716
Watendlath *Cumb* 93 NY2716
Water *Devon* 8 SX7580
Water *Lancs* 81 SD8425
Water Eaton *Oxon* 37 SP5112
Water Eaton *Staffs* 60 SJ9011
Water End *Beds* 38 TL0637
Water End *Beds* 38 TL1047
Water End *Beds* 52 TL1151
Water End *Essex* 53 TL5840
Water End *Herts* 38 TL0310
Water End *Herts* 39 TL2304
Water End *Humb* 84 SE7938
Water Fryston *W York* 83 SE4626
Water Newton *Cambs* 51 TL1097
Water Orton *Warwks* 61 SP1791
Water Stratford *Bucks* 49 SP6534
Water Street *M Glam* 32 SS8083
Water Yeat *Cumb* 86 SD2889
Water's Nook *Gt Man* 79 SD6605
Waterbeach *Cambs* 53 TL4965
Waterbeach *W Susx* 14 SU8908
Waterbeck *D & G* 101 NY2477
Watercombe *Dorset* 11 SY7585
Waterden *Norfk* 66 TF8836
Waterend *Cumb* 92 NY1122
Waterfall *Staffs* 73 SK0851
Waterfoot *Lancs* 81 SD8322
Waterfoot *Strath* 115 NS5655
Waterford *Herts* 39 TL3114
Watergate *Cnwll* 4 SX1181
Waterhead *Cumb* 87 NY3703
Waterhead *Cumb* 87 NY3804
Waterhead *Strath* 107 NS5411
Waterhead *Strath* 107 NS5411
Waterheads *Border* 117 NT2451
Waterhouses *Dur* 96 NZ1841
Waterhouses *Staffs* 73 SK0850
Wateringbury *Kent* 28 TQ6853
Waterlane *Gloucs* 35 SO9204
Waterloo *Cnwll* 4 SX1072
Waterloo *Derbys* 74 SK4163
Waterloo *Dorset* 11 SZ0194
Waterloo *Dyfed* 30 SM9803
Waterloo *H & W* 46 SO3447
Waterloo *Highld* 129 NG6623
Waterloo *Mersyd* 78 SJ3298
Waterloo *Norfk* 67 TG2219
Waterloo *Strath* 116 NS8054
Waterloo *Strath* 116 NS8054
Waterloo *Tays* 125 NO0537
Waterloo Cross *Devon* 9 ST0514
Waterloo Port *Gwynd* 68 SH4964
Waterlooville *Hants* 13 SU6809
Watermillock *Cumb* 93 NY4422
Waterperry *Oxon* 37 SP6206
Waterrow *Somset* 20 ST0525
Waters Upton *Shrops* 59 SJ6319
Watersfield *W Susx* 14 TQ0115
Waterside *Bucks* 26 SP9600
Waterside *Cumb* 93 NY2445
Waterside *Lancs* 81 SD7123
Waterside *S York* 83 SE6714
Waterside *Strath* 107 NS4308
Waterside *Strath* 107 NS4843
Waterside *Strath* 116 NS6773
Waterside *Surrey* 15 TQ3945
Waterstock *Oxon* 37 SP6305
Waterston *Dyfed* 30 SM9306
Watford *Herts* 26 TQ1196
Watford *Nhants* 50 SP6069
Wath *N York* 89 SE1467
Wath *N York* 89 SE3276
Wath Upon Dearne *S York* 75 SE4300
Watlington *Norfk* 65 TF6211
Watlington *Oxon* 37 SU6894
Watnall Chaworth *Notts* 62 SK5046
Watten *Highld* 151 ND2454
Wattisfield *Suffk* 54 TM0074
Wattisham *Suffk* 54 TM0151
Watton *Dorset* 10 SY4592
Watton *Humb* 84 TA0150
Watton *Norfk* 66 TF9100
Watton Green *Norfk* 66 TF9301
Watton Green *Norfk* 66 TF9301
Watton-at-Stone *Herts* 39 TL3019
Wattons Green *Essex* 27 TQ5295
Wattstown *M Glam* 33 ST0193
Wattsville *Gwent* 33 ST2091
Wauldby *Humb* 84 SE9629
Waulkmill *Gramp* 135 NO6492
Waunarlwydd *W Glam* 32 SS6095
Waunfawr *Dyfed* 43 SN6081
Waunfawr *Gwynd* 68 SH5259
Waungron *W Glam* 32 SN5901
Waunlwyd *Gwent* 33 SO1807
Wavendon *Bucks* 38 SP9037
Waverbridge *Cumb* 93 NY2249
Waverton *Ches* 71 SJ4663
Waverton *Cumb* 93 NY2247
Waverton *Cumb* 93 NY2247
Wawne *Humb* 85 TA0936
Waxham *Norfk* 67 TG4426
Waxholme *Humb* 85 TA3229
Way *Kent* 29 TR3265
Way Village *Devon* 19 SS8810
Way Wick *Avon* 21 ST3862
Waye *Devon* 7 SX7771
Wayford *Somset* 10 ST4006
Waytown *Devon* 18 SS3622
Waytown *Dorset* 10 SY4698
Weacombe *Somset* 20 ST1140
Weald *Cambs* 52 TL2259
Weald *Oxon* 36 SP3002
Wealdstone *Gt Lon* 26 TQ1589
Wear Head *Dur* 95 NY8539
Weardley *W York* 82 SE2944
Weare *Somset* 21 ST4152
Weare Giffard *Devon* 18 SS4721
Wearne *Somset* 21 ST4228
Weasdale *Cumb* 87 NY6904
Weasenham All Saints *Norfk* 66 TF8421
Weasenham St. Peter *Norfk* 66 TF8522
Weasle *Gt Man* 79 SJ8098
Weatheroak Hill *H & W* 61 SP0674
Weaverham *Ches* 71 SJ6174
Weaverslake *Staffs* 73 SK1319
Weaverthorpe *N York* 91 SE9670
Webb's Heath *Avon* 35 ST6873
Webbington *Somset* 21 ST3855
Webheath *H & W* 48 SP0266
Webton *H & W* 46 SO4136
Wedderlairs *Gramp* 143 NJ8532
Wedding Hall Fold *N York* 82 SD9446
Weddington *Kent* 29 TR2959
Weddington *Warwks* 61 SP3693
Wedhampton *Wilts* 23 SU0557
Wedmore *Somset* 21 ST4347
Wednesbury *W Mids* 60 SO9895
Wednesfield *W Mids* 60 SJ9400
Weecar *Notts* 75 SK8267
Weedon *Bucks* 38 SP8118
Weedon Lois *Nhants* 49 SP6046
Weeford *Staffs* 61 SK1404
Week *Devon* 19 SS7316
Week *Devon* 19 SS5726
Week *Devon* 7 SX7862
Week *Somset* 20 SS9133
Week St. Mary *Cnwll* 5 SX2397
Weeke *Devon* 8 SS7606
Weeke *Hants* 24 SU4631
Weekley *Nhants* 51 SP8881
Weel *Humb* 84 TA0039
Weeley *Essex* 41 TM1422
Weeley Heath *Essex* 41 TM1520
Weem *Tays* 125 NN8449
Weeping Cross *Staffs* 72 SJ9421
Weethley Hamlet *Warwks* 48 SP0555
Weeting *Norfk* 53 TL7788
Weeton *Humb* 77 TA3600
Weeton *Lancs* 80 SD3834
Weeton *W York* 82 SE2846

Weetwood
Weston-in-Gordano

Weetwood *W York*	82	SE2737
Weir *Lancs*	81	SD8625
Weir Quay *Devon*	6	SX4365
Weirbrook *Shrops*	59	SJ3524
Welbeck Abbey *Notts*	75	SK5574
Welborne *Norfk*	66	TG0610
Welbourn *Lincs*	76	SK9654
Welburn *N York*	90	SE7168
Welbury *N York*	89	NZ3902
Welby *Lincs*	63	SK9738
Welches Dam *Cambs*	53	TL4786
Welcombe *Devon*	18	SS2218
Welford *Berks*	24	SU4072
Welford *Nhants*	50	SP6480
Welford-on-Avon *Warwks*	48	SP1442
Welham *Leics*	50	SP7692
Welham *Notts*	75	SK7382
Welham Green *Herts*	39	TL2305
Well *Hants*	24	SU7646
Well *Lincs*	77	TF4473
Well *N York*	89	SE2681
Well End *Bucks*	26	SU8888
Well End *Herts*	26	TQ2098
Well Fold *W York*	82	SE2024
Well Head *Herts*	39	TL1727
Well Hill *Kent*	27	TQ4963
Well Town *Devon*	20	SS9050
Welland *H & W*	47	SO7940
Wellbank *Tays*	127	NO4737
Wellbury *Herts*	38	TL1328
Wellesbourne *Warwks*	48	SP2755
Wellesbourne Mountford *Warwks*	48	SP2855
Wellfield *Dur*	96	NZ4137
Wellhouse *Berks*	24	SU5272
Welling *Gt Lon*	27	TQ4575
Wellingborough *Nhants*	51	SP8968
Wellingham *Norfk*	66	TF8722
Wellingore *Lincs*	76	SK9856
Wellington *Cumb*	86	NY0704
Wellington *H & W*	46	SO4948
Wellington *Shrops*	59	SJ6511
Wellington *Somset*	20	ST1521
Wellington *Somset*	20	ST1320
Wellington Heath *H & W*	47	SO7140
Wellington Marsh *H & W*	46	SO4946
Wellow *Avon*	22	ST7358
Wellow *IOW*	12	SZ3887
Wellow *Notts*	75	SK6666
Wellpond Green *Herts*	39	TL4122
Wells *Somset*	21	ST5445
Wells Green *Ches*	72	SJ6853
Wells Head *W York*	82	SE0833
Wells of Ythan *Gramp*	142	NJ6338
Wells-Next-The-Sea *Norfk*	66	TF9143
Wellsborough *Leics*	62	SK3602
Wellstye Green *Essex*	40	TL6318
Welltree *Tays*	108	NS9622
Wellwood *Fife*	117	NT0988
Welney *Norfk*	65	TL5294
Welsh End *Shrops*	59	SJ5035
Welsh Frankton *Shrops*	59	SJ3633
Welsh Hook *Dyfed*	30	SM9327
Welsh Newton *H & W*	34	SO4918
Welsh St. Donats *S Glam*	33	ST0276
Welshampton *Shrops*	59	SJ4335
Welshpool *Powys*	58	SJ2207
Welton *Cumb*	93	NY3544
Welton *Humb*	84	SE9527
Welton *Lincs*	76	TF0079
Welton *Nhants*	50	SP5865
Welton le Marsh *Lincs*	77	TF4768
Welton le Wold *Lincs*	77	TF2787
Welwick *Humb*	85	TA3421
Welwyn *Herts*	39	TL2316
Welwyn Garden City *Herts*	39	TL2312
Wem *Shrops*	59	SJ5129
Wembdon *Somset*	20	ST2837
Wembley *Gt Lon*	26	TQ1885
Wembury *Devon*	6	SX5148
Wembworthy *Devon*	19	SS6609
Wemyss Bay *Strath*	114	NS1969
Wenallt *Dyfed*	43	SN6771
Wendens Ambo *Essex*	39	TL5136
Wendlebury *Oxon*	37	SP5519
Wendling *Norfk*	66	TF9312
Wendover *Bucks*	38	SP8607
Wendron *Cnwll*	2	SW6731
Wendy *Cambs*	52	TL3247
Wenfordbridge *Cnwll*	4	SX0875
Wenhaston *Suffk*	55	TM4275
Wennington *Cambs*	52	TL2379
Wennington *Gt Lon*	27	TQ5381
Wennington *Lancs*	87	SD6169
Wensley *Derbys*	74	SK2661
Wensley *N York*	89	SE0989
Wentbridge *W York*	83	SE4817
Wentnor *Shrops*	59	SO3892
Wentworth *Cambs*	53	TL4878
Wentworth *S York*	74	SK3898
Wentworth Castle *S York*	82	SE3102
Wenvoe *S Glam*	33	ST1272
Weobley *H & W*	46	SO4051
Weobley Marsh *H & W*	46	SO4151
Wepham *W Susx*	14	TQ0408
Wereham *Norfk*	65	TF6801
Wergs *Staffs*	60	SJ8701
Wern *Powys*	58	SH9612
Wern *Powys*	58	SJ2513
Wern *Powys*	33	SO1217
Wern *Shrops*	58	SJ2734
Wern-y-gaer *Clwyd*	70	SJ2068
Werneth Low *Gt Man*	79	SJ9592
Wernffrwd *W Glam*	32	SS5194
Wernrheolydd *Gwent*	34	SO3913
Werrington *Cambs*	64	TF1603
Werrington *Cnwll*	5	SX3287
Werrington *Staffs*	72	SJ9447
Wervin *Ches*	71	SJ4271
Wesham *Lancs*	80	SD4133
Wessington *Derbys*	74	SK3757
West Aberthaw *S Glam*	20	ST0266
West Acre *Norfk*	65	TF7715
West Allerdean *Nthumb*	111	NT9646
West Allotment *T & W*	103	NZ3170
West Alvington *Devon*	7	SX7243
West Amesbury *Wilts*	23	SU1341
West Anstey *Devon*	19	SS8527
West Appleton *N York*	89	SE2294
West Ashby *Lincs*	77	TF2672
West Ashling *W Susx*	14	SU8107
West Ashton *Wilts*	22	ST8755
West Auckland *Dur*	96	NZ1826
West Ayton *N York*	91	SE9884
West Bagborough *Somset*	20	ST1633
West Balsdon *Cnwll*	5	SX2798
West Bank *Ches*	78	SJ5184
West Bank *Gwent*	33	SO2105
West Barkwith *Lincs*	76	TF1580
West Barnby *N York*	90	NZ8112
West Barnham *W Susx*	14	SU9505
West Barns *Loth*	118	NT6578
West Barsham *Norfk*	66	TF9033
West Bay *Dorset*	10	SY4690
West Beckham *Norfk*	66	TG1439
West Bedfont *Surrey*	26	TQ0674
West Bergholt *Essex*	40	TL9527
West Bexington *Dorset*	10	SY5386
West Bilney *Norfk*	65	TF7115
West Blatchington *E Susx*	15	TQ2706
West Bolden *T & W*	96	NZ3462
West Boldon *T & W*	96	NZ3443
West Bourton *Dorset*	22	ST7629
West Bowling *W York*	82	SE1630
West Brabourne *Kent*	29	TR0742
West Bradenham *Norfk*	66	TF9208
West Bradford *Lancs*	81	SD7444
West Bradley *Somset*	21	ST5536
West Bretton *W York*	82	SE2813
West Bridgford *Notts*	62	SK5837
West Briscoe *Dur*	95	NY9619
West Bromwich *W Mids*	60	SP0091
West Buckland *Devon*	19	SS6531
West Buckland *Somset*	20	ST1720
West Burnside *Gramp*	135	NO7070
West Burnside *Gramp*	135	NO7070
West Burton *N York*	88	SE0186
West Burton *W Susx*	14	TQ0014
West Butsfiel *Dur*	95	NZ0945
West Butterwick *Humb*	84	SE8305
West Cairngaan *D & G*	98	NX1232
West Caistor *Norfk*	67	TG5111
West Calder *Loth*	117	NT0163
West Camel *Somset*	21	ST5724
West Causeway-head *Cumb*	92	NY1253
West Chaldon *Dorset*	11	SY7783
West Challow *Oxon*	36	SU3688
West Charleton *Devon*	7	SX7542
West Chelborough *Dorset*	10	ST5405
West Chevington *Nthumb*	103	NZ2297
West Chiltington *W Susx*	14	TQ0918
West Chinnock *Somset*	10	ST4613
West Chisenbury *Wilts*	23	SU1352
West Clandon *Surrey*	26	TQ0452
West Cliffe *Kent*	29	TR3444
West Coker *Somset*	10	ST5113
West Combe *Devon*	7	SX7662
West Compton *Dorset*	10	SY5694
West Compton *Somset*	21	ST5942
West Cottingwith *N York*	83	SE6942
West Cowick *Humb*	83	SE6521
West Craigneuk *Strath*	116	NS7765
West Cross *W Glam*	32	SS6189
West Curry *Cnwll*	5	SX2893
West Curthwaite *Cumb*	93	NY3249
West Dean *Hants*	23	SU2526
West Dean *W Susx*	14	SU8512
West Dean *Wilts*	23	SU2526
West Deeping *Lincs*	64	TF1008
West Derby *Mersyd*	78	SJ3993
West Dereham *Norfk*	65	TF6500
West Down *Devon*	19	SS5142
West Drayton *Gt Lon*	26	TQ0679
West Drayton *Notts*	75	SK7074
West Dunnet *Highld*	151	ND2171
West Ella *Humb*	84	TA0029
West End *Avon*	21	ST4569
West End *Avon*	35	ST7188
West End *Beds*	51	SP9853
West End *Berks*	37	SU8275
West End *Cambs*	52	TL3168
West End *Cumb*	93	NY3258
West End *Gwent*	33	ST2195
West End *Hants*	24	SU6335
West End *Hants*	13	SU4614
West End *Herts*	39	TL2608
West End *Herts*	39	TL3306
West End *Humb*	84	SE9131
West End *Humb*	85	TA1830
West End *Humb*	85	TA2627
West End *Lancs*	81	SD7328
West End *Lincs*	77	TF3598
West End *N York*	83	SE5140
West End *N York*	89	SE1457
West End *Norfk*	66	TF9109
West End *Norfk*	67	TG5011
West End *Oxon*	37	SU5886
West End *Somset*	22	ST6735
West End *Surrey*	26	TQ1364
West End *Surrey*	25	SU9461
West End *W Susx*	15	TQ2016
West End *W York*	82	SE2238
West End *Wilts*	22	ST9123
West End *Wilts*	22	ST9824
West End *Wilts*	35	ST9777
West End Green *Hants*	24	SU6661
West Ewell *Surrey*	26	TQ2063
West Farleigh *Kent*	28	TQ7152
West Farndon *Nhants*	49	SP5251
West Felton *Shrops*	59	SJ3425
West Firle *E Susx*	16	TQ4707
West Firsby *Lincs*	76	SK9784
West Flotmanby *N York*	91	TA0779
West Garforth *W York*	83	SE3833
West Garforth *W York*	83	SE3932
West Garty *Highld*	147	NC9912
West Geirnish *W Isls*	154	NF7741
West Ginge *Oxon*	37	SU4486
West Grafton *Wilts*	23	SU2460
West Green *Hants*	24	SU7456
West Grimstead *Wilts*	23	SU2026
West Grinstead *W Susx*	15	TQ1720
West Haddlesey *N York*	83	SE5626
West Haddon *Nhants*	50	SP6371
West Hagbourne *Oxon*	37	SU5187
West Hagley *H & W*	60	SO9080
West Hallam *Derbys*	62	SK4341
West Hallam Common *Derbys*	62	SK4241
West Halton *Humb*	84	SE9020
West Ham *Gt Lon*	27	TQ3983
West Handley *Derbys*	74	SK3977
West Hanney *Oxon*	36	SU4092
West Hanningfield *Essex*	17	TQ7300
West Harnham *Wilts*	23	SU1229
West Harptree *Avon*	21	ST5556
West Harting *W Susx*	14	SU7821
West Hatch *Somset*	20	ST2820
West Hatch *Wilts*	22	ST9228
West Head *Norfk*	65	TF5705
West Heath *Hants*	24	SU5858
West Heath *W Mids*	60	SP0277
West Helmsdale *Highld*	147	ND0115
West Hendred *Oxon*	37	SU4488
West Herrington *T & W*	96	NZ3352
West Heslerton *N York*	91	SE9175
West Hewish *Avon*	21	ST3964
West Hill *Devon*	9	SY0694
West Hoathly *W Susx*	15	TQ3632
West Holme *Dorset*	11	SY8885
West Holywell *T & W*	103	NZ3072
West Horndon *Essex*	40	TQ6288
West Horrington *Somset*	21	ST5747
West Horsley *Surrey*	26	TQ0752
West Horton *Nthumb*	111	NU0230
West Hougham *Kent*	29	TR2640
West Howe *Dorset*	12	SZ0595
West Howetown *Somset*	20	SS9135
West Huntspill *Somset*	20	ST3044
West Hyde *Beds*	38	TL1117
West Hyde *Herts*	26	TQ0391
West Hythe *Kent*	17	TR1234
West Ilkerton *Devon*	19	SS7046
West Ilsley *Berks*	37	SU4782
West Itchenor *W Susx*	14	SU7900
West Keal *Lincs*	77	TF3663
West Kennet *Wilts*	23	SU1168
West Kilbride *Strath*	114	NS2048
West Kingsdown *Kent*	27	TQ5763
West Kington *Wilts*	35	ST8077
West Kirby *Mersyd*	78	SJ2186
West Knapton *N York*	90	SE8775
West Knighton *Dorset*	11	SY7387
West Knoyle *Wilts*	22	ST8532
West Lambrook *Somset*	10	ST4118
West Langdon *Kent*	29	TR3247
West Langwell *Highld*	146	NC6909
West Laroch *Highld*	130	NN0758
West Lavington *W Susx*	14	SU8920
West Lavington *Wilts*	22	SU0052
West Layton *N York*	89	NZ1410
West Leake *Notts*	62	SK5226
West Learmouth *Nthumb*	110	NT8437
West Lees *N York*	89	NZ4702
West Leigh *Devon*	8	SS6805
West Leigh *Devon*	7	SX7557
West Leigh *Somset*	20	ST1231
West Lexham *Norfk*	66	TF8417
West Lilling *N York*	90	SE6465
West Linton *Border*	117	NT1551
West Littleton *Avon*	35	ST7675
West Lockinge *Oxon*	36	SU4187
West Luccombe *Somset*	19	SS8946
West Lulworth *Dorset*	11	SY8280
West Lutton *N York*	91	SE9369
West Lydford *Somset*	21	ST5632
West Lyn *Devon*	19	SS7248
West Lyng *Somset*	21	ST3228
West Lynn *Norfk*	65	TF6120
West Malling *Kent*	28	TQ6857
West Malvern *H & W*	47	SO7646
West Marden *W Susx*	14	SU7713
West Markham *Notts*	75	SK7272
West Marsh *Humb*	85	TA2509
West Marton *N York*	81	SD8950
West Melta *S York*	83	SE4001
West Meon *Hants*	13	SU6424
West Meon Hut *Hants*	13	SU6526
West Meon Woodlands *Hants*	13	SU6426
West Mersea *Essex*	41	TM0112
West Milton *Dorset*	10	SY5096
West Minster *Kent*	28	TQ9073
West Monkton *Somset*	20	ST2528
West Moors *Dorset*	12	SU0802
West Morden *Dorset*	11	SY9095
West Morton *W York*	82	SE0942
West Mudford *Somset*	21	ST5620
West melbury *Dorset*	22	ST8720
West Ness *N York*	90	SE6879
West Newbiggin *Dur*	96	NZ3518
West Newton *Humb*	85	TA2037
West Newton *Norfk*	65	TF6928
West Newton *Somset*	20	ST2829
West Norwood *Gt Lon*	27	TQ3171
West Ogwell *Devon*	7	SX8170
West Orchard *Dorset*	11	ST8216
West Overton *Wilts*	23	SU1267
West Panson *Devon*	5	SX3491
West Parley *Dorset*	12	SZ0997
West Peckham *Kent*	27	TQ6452
West Pelton *Dur*	96	NZ2352
West Pennard *Somset*	21	ST5438
West Pentire *Cnwll*	4	SW7760
West Perry *Cambs*	52	TL1466
West Porlock *Somset*	33	SS8797
West Prawle *Devon*	7	SX7637
West Preston *W Susx*	14	TQ0502
West Pulham *Dorset*	11	ST7008
West Putford *Devon*	18	SS3616
West Quantoxhead *Somset*	20	ST1142
West Raddon *Devon*	9	SS8902
West Rainton *T & W*	96	NZ3246
West Rasen *Lincs*	76	TF0589
West Ravendale *Humb*	76	TF2299
West Raynham *Norfk*	66	TF8725
West Retford *Notts*	75	SK6981
West Rounton *N York*	89	NZ4103
West Row *Suffk*	53	TL6775
West Rudham *Norfk*	66	TF8128
West Runton *Norfk*	66	TG1842
West Safford *Dorset*	11	SY7289
West Saltoun *Loth*	118	NT4667
West Sandford *Devon*	8	SS8102
West Sandwick *Shet*	155	HU4588
West Scrafton *N York*	88	SE0783
West Sleekburn *Nthumb*	103	NZ2884
West Somerton *Norfk*	67	TG4720
West Stoke *W Susx*	14	SU8308
West Stonesdale *N York*	88	NY8802
West Stoughton *Somset*	21	ST4149
West Stour *Dorset*	22	ST7822
West Stourmouth *Kent*	29	TR2562
West Stow *Suffk*	54	TL8171
West Stowell *Wilts*	23	SU1362
West Stratton *Hants*	24	SU5240
West Street *Kent*	28	TQ7376
West Street *Kent*	29	TR3254
West Street *Kent*	28	TQ9054
West Street *Suffk*	54	TL9871
West Tanfield *N York*	89	SE2678
West Taphouse *Cnwll*	4	SX1463
West Tarbert *Strath*	113	NR8467
West Tarring *W Susx*	14	TQ1203
West Thorney *W Susx*	14	SU7602
West Thorpe *Notts*	62	SK6225
West Thurrock *Essex*	27	TQ5877
West Tilbury *Essex*	28	TQ6677
West Tisted *Hants*	24	SU6529
West Torrington *Lincs*	76	TF1381
West Town *Avon*	21	ST5160
West Town *Avon*	21	ST4868
West Town *Devon*	18	SS3221
West Town *H & W*	46	SO4361
West Town *Hants*	13	SZ7099
West Town *Somset*	22	ST7041
West Town *Somset*	21	ST5335
West Tytherley *Hants*	23	SU2730
West Tytherley *Hants*	23	SU2730
West Tytherton *Wilts*	35	ST9474
West Walton *Norfk*	65	TF4713
West Walton Highway *Norfk*	65	TF4913
West Weetwood *Nthumb*	111	NU0029
West Wellow *Hants*	12	SU2918
West Wellow *Hants*	12	SU2818
West Wembury *Devon*	6	SX5249
West Wemyss *Fife*	118	NT3294
West Wick *Avon*	21	ST3762
West Wickham *Cambs*	53	TL6149
West Wickham *Gt Lon*	27	TQ3766
West Williamston *Dyfed*	30	SN0305
West Winch *Norfk*	65	TF6316
West Winterslow *Wilts*	23	SU2232
West Wittering *W Susx*	14	SZ7898
West Witton *N York*	88	SE0588
West Woodburn *Nthumb*	102	NY8986
West Woodhay *Berks*	23	SU3962
West Woodlands *Somset*	22	ST7743
West Worldham *Hants*	24	SU7437
West Worthing *W Susx*	15	TQ1302
West Wratting *Essex*	53	TL6052
West Wycombe *Bucks*	37	SU8294
West Wylam *Nthumb*	103	NZ1063
West Yatton *Wilts*	35	ST8575
West Yoke *Kent*	27	TQ5965
West Youlstone *Cnwll*	18	SS2615
Westbere *Kent*	29	TR1961
Westborough *Lincs*	63	SK8544
Westbourne *W Susx*	13	SU7507
Westbrook *Berks*	24	SU4272
Westbrook *Kent*	29	TR3470
Westbrook *Wilts*	22	ST9565
Westbury *Bucks*	49	SP6235
Westbury *Shrops*	59	SJ3509
Westbury *Wilts*	22	ST8751
Westbury Leigh *Wilts*	22	ST8649
Westbury on Severn *Gloucs*	35	SO7114
Westbury-on-Trym *Avon*	34	ST5777
Westbury-on-trym *Avon*	34	ST5877
Westbury-sub-Mendip *Somset*	21	ST5049
Westby *Lancs*	80	SD3831
Westcliff-on-Sea *Essex*	40	TQ8686
Westcombe *Somset*	22	ST6739
Westcote *Gloucs*	36	SP2120
Westcott *Bucks*	37	SP7117
Westcott *Devon*	9	ST0204
Westcott *Somset*	19	SS8720
Westcott *Surrey*	15	TQ1448
Westcott Barton *Oxon*	49	SP4325
Westcourt *Wilts*	23	SU2261
Westdean *E Susx*	16	TV5299
Westdown Camp *Wilts*	23	SU0447
Westdowns *Cnwll*	4	SX0582
Wested *Kent*	27	TQ5166
Westend *Gloucs*	35	SO7807
Westend Town *Nthumb*	102	NY7865
Westenhanger *Kent*	29	TR1237
Wester Causewayend *Loth*	117	NT0861
Wester Drumashie *Highld*	140	NH6032
Wester Ellister *Strath*	112	NR2053
Wester Essenside *Border*	109	NT4320
Wester Ochiltree *Loth*	117	NT0374
Wester Pitkierie *Fife*	127	NO5505
Wester Rarichie *Highld*	147	NH8374
Westerdale *Highld*	151	ND1251
Westerdale *N York*	90	NZ6605
Westerfield *Suffk*	54	TM1747
Westergate *W Susx*	14	SU9305
Westerham *Kent*	27	TQ4454
Westerhope *T & W*	103	NZ1966
Westerland *Devon*	7	SX8662
Westerleigh *Avon*	35	ST6979
Westerloch *Highld*	151	ND3258
Westerton *Tays*	127	NO6754
Westfield *Avon*	22	ST6753
Westfield *E Susx*	17	TQ8115
Westfield *Loth*	116	NS9472
Westfield *Norfk*	66	TF9909
Westfield Sole *Kent*	28	TQ7761
Westfields *Dorset*	11	ST7206
Westfields *H & W*	46	SO4941
Westfields of Rattray *Tays*	126	NO1846
Westford *Somset*	20	ST1120
Westgate *Dur*	95	NY9038
Westgate *Humb*	84	SE7707
Westgate *Norfk*	66	TF9740
Westgate Hill *W York*	82	SE2029
Westgate on Sea *Kent*	29	TR3270
Westgate Street *Norfk*	67	TG1921
Westhall *Gramp*	142	NJ6826
Westhall *Suffk*	55	TM4280
Westham *Dorset*	11	SY6579
Westham *E Susx*	16	TQ6404
Westham *Somset*	21	ST4046
Westhampnett *W Susx*	14	SU8806
Westhay *Somset*	21	ST4342
Westhead *Lancs*	78	SD4407
Westhide *H & W*	46	SO5843
Westhill *Gramp*	135	NJ8307
Westholme *Somset*	21	ST5642
Westhope *H & W*	46	SO4651
Westhope *Shrops*	59	SO4786
Westhorp *Nhants*	49	SP5152
Westhorpe *Lincs*	64	TF2231
Westhorpe *Suffk*	54	TM0568
Westhoughton *Gt Man*	79	SD6506
Westhouse *N York*	87	SD6673
Westhouses *Derbys*	74	SK4257
Westhumble *Surrey*	26	TQ1651
Westlake *Devon*	6	SX6253
Westland Green *Herts*	39	TL4222
Westleigh *Devon*	18	SS4728
Westleigh *Devon*	9	ST0517
Westleton *Suffk*	55	TM4469
Westley *Shrops*	59	SJ3607
Westley *Suffk*	54	TL8264
Westley Heights *Essex*	40	TQ6887
Westley Waterless *Cambs*	53	TL6156
Westlington *Bucks*	37	SP7610
Westlinton *Cumb*	101	NY3964
Westmarsh *Kent*	29	TR2761
Westmeston *E Susx*	15	TQ3313
Westmill *Herts*	39	TL3627
Westmoor *T & W*	103	NZ2670
Westmuir *Tays*	126	NO3652
Westnewton *Cumb*	92	NY1344
Westoe *T & W*	103	NZ3765
Weston *Avon*	22	ST7366
Weston *Berks*	36	SU3973
Weston *Ches*	78	SJ5080
Weston *Ches*	72	SJ7252
Weston *Devon*	9	ST1500
Weston *Devon*	9	SY1688
Weston *Dorset*	11	SY6871
Weston *H & W*	46	SO3656
Weston *Hants*	13	SU7221
Weston *Herts*	39	TL2530
Weston *Lincs*	64	TF2925
Weston *Nhants*	49	SP5846
Weston *Notts*	75	SK7767
Weston *Shrops*	46	SO3373
Weston *Shrops*	59	SJ2927
Weston *Shrops*	59	SJ5629
Weston *Staffs*	72	SJ9727
Weston *W York*	82	SE1747
Weston Beggard *H & W*	46	SO5841
Weston by Welland *Nhants*	50	SP7791
Weston Colley *Hants*	24	SU5039
Weston Colville *Cambs*	53	TL6153
Weston Corbett *Hants*	24	SU6846
Weston Coyney *Staffs*	72	SJ9343
Weston Favel *Nhants*	50	SP7962
Weston Favell *Nhants*	50	SP7962
Weston Green *Cambs*	53	TL6252
Weston Heath *Shrops*	60	SJ7713
Weston Hills *Lincs*	64	TF2720
Weston in Arden *Warwks*	61	SP3886
Weston Jones *Staffs*	72	SJ7624
Weston Longville *Norfk*	66	TG1115
Weston Lullingfields *Shrops*	59	SJ4224
Weston Patrick *Hants*	24	SU6946
Weston Rhyn *Shrops*	58	SJ2835
Weston Subedge *Gloucs*	48	SP1240
Weston Turville *Bucks*	38	SP8510
Weston Underwood *Bucks*	38	SP8650
Weston Underwood *Derbys*	73	SK2942
Weston under Penyard *H & W*	35	SO6322
Weston under Wetherley *Warwks*	48	SP3669
Weston-in-Gordano *Avon*	34	ST4474

Weston-on-Trent Windmill

Weston-on-Trent Derbys 62 SK4028
Weston-on-the-Green Oxon 37 SP5318
Weston-Super-Mare Avon 21 ST3261
Weston-under-Lizard Staffs 60 SJ8010
Westonbirt Gloucs 35 ST8589
Westoning Beds 38 TL0332
Westoning Woodend Beds 38 TL0232
Westonzoyland Somset 21 ST3534
Westover Hants 23 SU3640
Westow N York 90 SE7565
Westpeek Devon 5 SX3493
Westport Somset 21 ST3820
Westport Strath 104 NR6526
Westquarter Cent 116 NS9178
Westra S Glam 33 ST1471
Westridge Green Berks 37 SU5679
Westrigg Loth 116 NS9067
Westrop Wilts 36 SU1992
Westruther Border 110 NT6349
Westry Cambs 65 TL3998
Westthope Derbys 75 SK4579
Westward Cumb 93 NY2744
Westward Ho Devon 18 SS4329
Westwell Kent 28 TQ9847
Westwell Oxon 36 SP2210
Westwell Leacon Kent 28 TQ9547
Westwick Cambs 53 TL4265
Westwick Dur 95 NZ0715
Westwick Norfk 67 TG2726
Westwood Devon 9 SY0199
Westwood Kent 27 TQ6070
Westwood Kent 29 TR3667
Westwood Notts 75 SK4551
Westwood Wilts 22 ST8059
Westwood Heath W Mids 61 SP2776
Westwoodside Humb 75 SE7400
Wetham Green Kent 28 TQ8467
Wetheral Cumb 93 NY4654
Wetherby W York 83 SE4048
Wetherden Suffk 54 TM0062
Wetheringsett Suffk 54 TM1266
Wethersfield Essex 40 TL7131
Wetherup Street Suffk 54 TM1464
Wetley Rocks Staffs 72 SJ9649
Wettenhall Ches 71 SJ6261
Wetton Staffs 73 SK1055
Wetwang Humb 91 SE9358
Wetwood Staffs 72 SJ7733
Wexcombe Wilts 23 SU2658
Wexham Bucks 26 SU9882
Wexham Street Bucks 26 SU9883
Weybourne Norfk 66 TG1143
Weybread Suffk 55 TM2480
Weybread Street Suffk 55 TM2479
Weybridge Surrey 26 TQ0764
Weycroft Devon 10 ST3099
Weydale Highld 151 ND1564
Weyhill Hants 23 SU3146
Weymouth Dorset 11 SY6778
Whaddon Bucks 38 SP8034
Whaddon Cambs 52 TL3546
Whaddon Gloucs 35 SO8313
Whaddon Wilts 22 ST8861
Whaddon Wilts 23 SU1926
Whale Cumb 94 NY5221
Whaley Derbys 75 SK5171
Whaley Bridge Derbys 79 SK0180
Whaley Thorns Notts 75 SK5271
Whaligoe Highld 151 ND3140
Whalley Lancs 81 SD7336
Whalley Banks Lancs 81 SD7335
Whalton Nthumb 103 NZ1281
Wham N York 88 SD7762
Whamley Nthumb 102 NY8766
Whaplode Lincs 64 TF3224
Whaplode Drove Lincs 64 TF3113
Wharf Warwks 49 SP4352
Wharfe N York 88 SD7869
Wharles Lancs 80 SD4435
Wharley End Beds 38 SP9342
Wharncliffe Side S York 74 SK2995
Wharram le Street N York 90 SE8665
Wharton Ches 72 SJ6666
Wharton H & W 46 SO5055
Whashton Green N York 89 NZ1405
Whasset Cumb 87 SD5181
Whaston N York 89 NZ1506
Whatcote Warwks 48 SP2944
Whateley Warwks 61 SP2299
Whatfield Suffk 54 TM0246
Whatley Somset 10 ST3607
Whatley Somset 22 ST7347
Whatley's End Avon 35 ST6581
Whatlington E Susx 17 TQ7618
Whatsole Street Kent 29 TR1144
Whatstandwell Derbys 74 SK3354
Whatton Notts 63 SK7439
Whauphill D & G 99 NX4049
Whaw N York 88 NY9804
Wheal Rose Cnwll 3 SW7244
Wheatacre Norfk 67 TM4694
Wheatfield Oxon 37 SU6899
Wheathampstead Herts 39 TL1714
Wheathill Shrops 59 SO6282
Wheathill Somset 21 ST5830
Wheatley Hants 25 SU7840
Wheatley Oxon 37 SP5905
Wheatley W York 82 SE0726
Wheatley Hill Dur 96 NZ3738
Wheatley Hills S York 83 SE5905
Wheatley Lane Lancs 81 SD8337
Wheaton Aston Staffs 60 SJ8512
Wheatsheaf Clwyd 71 SJ3253
Wheddon Cross Somset 20 SS9238
Wheel Inn Cnwll 2 SW6921
Wheelbarrow Town Kent 29 TR1445
Wheeler End Common Bucks 37 SU8093
Wheeler's Green Oxon 24 SU7672
Wheeler's Street Kent 28 TQ8444
Wheelerstreet Surrey 25 SU9440
Wheelock Ches 72 SJ7559
Wheelock Heath Ches 72 SJ7457
Wheelton Lancs 81 SD6021
Wheldale W York 83 SE4426
Wheldrake N York 83 SE6844
Whelpley Hill Bucks 38 TL0004
Whelpo Cumb 93 NY3139
Whelston Clwyd 70 SJ2076
Whemstead Herts 39 TL3121
Whenby N York 90 SE6369
Whepstead Suffk 54 TL8358
Wherstead Suffk 54 TM1540
Wherwell Hants 23 SU3941
Wheston Derbys 74 SK1376
Whetsted Kent 28 TQ6546
Whetstone Gt Lon 27 TQ2693
Whetstone Leics 50 SP5597
Wheyrigg Cumb 93 NY1948
Whicham Cumb 86 SD1382
Whichford Warwks 48 SP3134
Whickham T & W 96 NZ2061
Whiddon Devon 18 SX4799
Whiddon Down Devon 8 SX6992
Whight's Corner Suffk 54 TM1242
Whigstreet Tays 127 NO4844
Whiligh E Susx 16 TQ6431
Whilton Nhants 49 SP6364
Whim Border 117 NT2153
Whimble Devon 18 SS3403
Whimple Devon 9 SY0497
Whimpwell Green Norfk 67 TG3829
Whin Lane End Lancs 80 SD3941
Whinburgh Norfk 66 TG0009
Whinnie Liggate D & G 99 NX7152
Whinnow Cumb 93 NY3051
Whinny Hill Cleve 96 NZ3818
Whipcott Devon 20 ST0718
Whippingham IOW 13 SZ5193
Whipsnade Beds 38 TL0108
Whipton Devon 9 SX9493
Whisby Lincs 76 SK9067
Whissendine Leics 63 SK8214
Whissonsett Norfk 66 TF9123
Whistley Green Berks 25 SU7974
Whiston Mersyd 78 SJ4791
Whiston Nhants 51 SP8460
Whiston S York 75 SK4490
Whiston Staffs 73 SK0347
Whiston Staffs 60 SJ8914
Whiston Cross Shrops 60 SJ7903
Whiston Eaves Staffs 73 SK0446
Whiston Lane End Mersyd 78 SJ4690
Whitacre Fields Warwks 61 SP2592
Whitbeck Cumb 86 SD1184
Whitbourne H & W 47 SO7156
Whitburn Loth 116 NS9464
Whitburn T & W 96 NZ4062
Whitby Ches 71 SJ3975
Whitby N York 91 NZ8910
Whitbyheath Ches 71 SJ3974
Whitchurch Avon 21 ST6167
Whitchurch Bucks 38 SP8020
Whitchurch Devon 6 SX4972
Whitchurch Dyfed 30 SM8025
Whitchurch H & W 34 SO5417
Whitchurch Hants 24 SU4648
Whitchurch Oxon 37 SU6377
Whitchurch S Glam 33 ST1579
Whitchurch Shrops 71 SJ5441
Whitchurch Canonicorum Dorset 10 SY3995
Whitchurch Hill Oxon 37 SU6378
Whitcombe Dorset 11 SY7188
Whitcot Shrops 59 SO3791
Whitcott Keysett Shrops 58 SO2782
White Chapel H & W 48 SP0740
White Chapel Lancs 81 SD5541
White Colne Essex 40 TL8830
White Coppice Lancs 81 SD6119
White Cross Cnwll 2 SW6821
White End H & W 47 SO7834
White Kirkley Dur 95 NZ0255
White Lackington Dorset 11 SY7198
White Ladies Aston H & W 47 SO9252
White Notley Essex 40 TL7818
White Ox Avon 22 ST7258
White Pit Lincs 77 TF3777
White Roding Essex 40 TL5613
White Stake Lancs 80 SD5125
White Stone H & W 46 SO5642
White Stone Cross Devon 9 SX8993
White Waltham Berks 26 SU8577
White-le-Head Dur 96 NZ1754
Whiteacre Kent 29 TR1148
Whiteacre Heath Warwks 61 SP2292
Whiteash Green Essex 40 TL7931
Whitebirk Lancs 81 SD7028
Whitebridge Highld 139 NH4815
Whitebrook Gwent 34 SO5306
Whitecairns Gramp 143 NJ9218
Whitechapel Gt Lon 27 TQ3381
Whitechurch Dyfed 31 SN1536
Whitecliffe Gloucs 34 SO5609
Whitecraig Loth 118 NT3470
Whitecroft Gloucs 34 SO6106
Whitecrook D & G 98 NX1656
Whitecross Cnwll 2 SW5234
Whitecross Cnwll 4 SW9672
Whiteface Highld 146 NH7088
Whitefarland Strath 105 NR8642
Whitefield Devon 19 SS7035
Whitefield Gt Man 79 SD8006
Whitefield Lane End Mersyd 78 SJ4589
Whiteford Gramp 142 NJ7126
Whitegate Ches 71 SJ6269
Whitehall Hants 24 SU7452
Whitehall Ork 155 HY6528
Whitehall W Susx 15 TQ1321
Whitehaven Cumb 92 NX9718
Whitehill Hants 14 SU7934
Whitehill Kent 29 TR0950
Whitehills Gramp 142 NJ6565
Whitehouse Gramp 142 NJ6114
Whitehouse Strath 113 NR8161
Whitehouse Common W Mids 61 SP1397
Whitekirk Loth 118 NT5981
Whitelackington Somset 10 ST3815
Whiteley Bank IOW 13 SZ5581
Whiteley Green Ches 79 SJ9278
Whiteley Village Surrey 26 TQ0962
Whitemans Green W Susx 15 TQ3025
Whitemire Gramp 140 NH9854
Whitemoor Cnwll 4 SW9757
Whitemoor Derbys 74 SK3648
Whitemoor Notts 62 SK5442
Whitemoor Staffs 72 SJ8861
Whitenap Hants 12 SU3721
Whiteoak Green Oxon 36 SP3414
Whiteparish Wilts 23 SU2423
Whiterashes Gramp 143 NJ8523
Whiterow Gramp 141 NJ0257
Whiterow Highld 151 ND3648
Whiteshill Gloucs 35 SO8407
Whitesmith E Susx 16 TQ5214
Whitestaunton Somset 10 ST2810
Whitestone Devon 9 SX8694
Whitestreet Green Suffk 54 TL9739
Whitewall Corner N York 90 SE7969
Whiteway Avon 22 ST7263
Whitewell Lancs 81 SD6646
Whitewell-on-the-Hill N York 90 SE7265
Whiteworks Devon 6 SX6171
Whitfield Avon 35 ST6791
Whitfield Kent 29 TR3045
Whitfield Nhants 49 SP6039
Whitfield Nthumb 94 NY7758
Whitfield Hall Nthumb 94 NY7756
Whitford Clwyd 70 SJ1478
Whitford Devon 10 SY2595
Whitgift Humb 84 SE8122
Whitgift Humb 84 SE8022
Whitgreave Staffs 72 SJ8928
Whithorn D & G 99 NX4440
Whiting Bay Strath 105 NS0425
Whitington Norfk 65 TL7199
Whitkirk W York 83 SE3634
Whitland Dyfed 31 SN1916
Whitlaw Border 109 NT5012
Whitletts Strath 106 NS3623
Whitley Berks 24 SU7270
Whitley Ches 71 SJ6178
Whitley N York 83 SE5620
Whitley S York 74 SK3494
Whitley Wilts 22 ST8866
Whitley Bay T & W 103 NZ3572
Whitley Chapel Nthumb 95 NY9357
Whitley Heath Staffs 72 SJ8126
Whitley Lower W York 82 SE2217
Whitley Row Kent 27 TQ4952
Whitlieburn Strath 114 NS2163
Whitlock's End W Mids 61 SP1076
Whitlow S York 74 SK3182
Whitminster Gloucs 35 SO7708
Whitmore Dorset 12 SU0609
Whitmore Staffs 72 SJ8041
Whitnage Devon 9 ST0215
Whitnash Warwks 48 SP3263
Whitney H & W 46 SO2747
Whitrigg Cumb 93 NY2038
Whitrigg Cumb 93 NY2257
Whitrigglees Cumb 93 NY2457
Whitsbury Hants 12 SU1218
Whitsford Devon 19 SS6633
Whitsome Border 119 NT8650
Whitson Gwent 34 ST3883
Whitstable Kent 29 TR1066
Whitstone Cnwll 5 SX2698
Whittingham Nthumb 111 NU0612
Whittingslow Shrops 59 SO4388
Whittington Derbys 74 SK3875
Whittington Gloucs 35 SP0120
Whittington H & W 47 SO8752
Whittington Lancs 87 SD5976
Whittington Shrops 59 SJ3231
Whittington Staffs 61 SK1508
Whittington Staffs 60 SO8682
Whittington Warwks 61 SP2999
Whittle-le-Woods Lancs 81 SD5821
Whittlebury Nhants 49 SP6943
Whittlesey Cambs 64 TL2697
Whittlesford Cambs 53 TL4748
Whittlestone Head Lancs 81 SD7119
Whitton Cleve 96 NZ3921
Whitton Humb 84 SE9024
Whitton Powys 46 SO2767
Whitton Shrops 46 SO5772
Whitton Suffk 54 TM1447
Whittonditch Wilts 36 SU2872
Whittonstall Nthumb 95 NZ0757
Whitway Hants 24 SU4559
Whitwell Derbys 75 SK5276
Whitwell Herts 39 TL1820
Whitwell IOW 13 SZ5277
Whitwell Leics 63 SK9208
Whitwell N York 89 SE2899
Whitwell Street Norfk 66 TG1022
Whitwick Leics 62 SK4316
Whitwood W York 83 SE4124
Whitworth Lancs 81 SD8818
Whixall Shrops 59 SJ5134
Whixley N York 89 SE4458
Whorlton Dur 95 NZ1014
Whorlton N York 90 NZ4802
Whyle H & W 46 SO5561
Whyteleafe Surrey 27 TQ3358
Wibdon Gloucs 34 ST5797
Wibsey W York 82 SE1430
Wibtoft Warwks 50 SP4887
Wichenford H & W 47 SO7860
Wichling Kent 28 TQ9256
Wick Avon 35 ST7072
Wick Devon 9 ST1604
Wick Dorset 12 SZ1591
Wick H & W 47 SO9645
Wick Highld 151 ND3650
Wick M Glam 33 SS9272
Wick Somset 21 ST4027
Wick Somset 20 ST2144
Wick W Susx 14 TQ0203
Wick Wilts 12 SU1621
Wick End Beds 38 SP9850
Wick Rissington Gloucs 36 SP1821
Wick St. Lawrence Avon 21 ST3665
Wicken Cambs 53 TL5770
Wicken Nhants 49 SP7439
Wicken Bonhunt Essex 39 TL4933
Wickenby Lincs 76 TF0882
Wicker Street Green Suffk 54 TL9742
Wickersley S York 75 SK4791
Wickford Essex 40 TQ7593
Wickham Berks 36 SU3971
Wickham Hants 13 SU5711
Wickham Bishops Essex 40 TL8412
Wickham Green Berks 24 SU4072
Wickham Green Suffk 54 TM0969
Wickham Heath Berks 24 SU4169
Wickham Market Suffk 55 TM3055
Wickham Skeith Suffk 54 TM0969
Wickham St. Paul Essex 54 TL8336
Wickham Street Suffk 53 TL7654
Wickham Street Suffk 54 TM0869
Wickhambreaux Kent 29 TR2158
Wickhambrook Suffk 53 TL7554
Wickhamford H & W 48 SP0641
Wickhampton Norfk 67 TG4205
Wicklewood Norfk 66 TG0702
Wickmere Norfk 66 TG1733
Wickstreet E Susx 16 TQ5308
Wickwar Avon 35 ST7288
Widdington Essex 39 TL5331
Widdop Lancs 81 SD9333
Widdrington Nthumb 103 NZ2595
Widdrington Station T & W 103 NZ2494
Wide Open T & W 103 NZ2372
Widecombe in the Moor Devon 8 SX7176
Widegates Cnwll 5 SX2857
Widemouth Bay Cnwll 18 SS2002
Widford Essex 40 TL6905
Widford Herts 39 TL4116
Widford Oxon 36 SP2712
Widham Wilts 36 SU0988
Widmer End Bucks 26 SU8796
Widmerpool Notts 63 SK6327
Widmore Gt Lon 27 TQ4268
Widnes Ches 78 SJ5184
Widworthy Devon 18 SX2199
Wigan Gt Man 78 SD5805
Wigborough Somset 10 ST4415
Wiggaton Devon 9 SY1093
Wiggenhall St. Germans Norfk 65 TF5914
Wiggenhall St. Mary Magda Norfk 65 TF5911
Wiggenhall St. Mary the V Norfk 65 TF5814
Wiggens Green Essex 53 TL6642
Wiggenstall Staffs 74 SK0960
Wiggington Shrops 59 SJ3335
Wigginton Herts 38 SP9310
Wigginton N York 90 SE5958
Wigginton Oxon 48 SP3833
Wigginton Staffs 61 SK2106
Wigglesworth N York 88 SD8157
Wiggold Gloucs 36 SP0404
Wiggonby Cumb 93 NY2953
Wiggonholt W Susx 14 TQ0616
Wigham Devon 19 SS7508
Wighill N York 83 SE4746
Wighton Norfk 66 TF9439
Wigley Hants 12 SU3217
Wigmore H & W 46 SO4169
Wigmore Kent 28 TQ7964
Wigsley Notts 76 SK8570
Wigsthorpe Nhants 51 TL0482
Wigston Leics 50 SP6199
Wigston Fields Leics 50 SK6000
Wigston Parva Leics 50 SP4689
Wigthorpe Notts 75 SK5983
Wigtoft Lincs 64 TF2636
Wigton Cumb 93 NY2548
Wigtown D & G 99 NX4355
Wigtwizzle S York 74 SK2495
Wike W York 83 SE3342
Wilbarston Nhants 51 SP8188
Wilberfoss Humb 84 SE7350
Wilburton Cambs 53 TL4785
Wilby Nhants 51 SP8666
Wilby Norfk 54 TM0389
Wilby Suffk 55 TM2472
Wilcot Wilts 23 SU1360
Wilcrick Gwent 34 ST4088
Wilday Green Derbys 74 SK2274
Wildboarclough Ches 79 SJ9868
Wilden Beds 51 TL0955
Wilden H & W 60 SO8272
Wildhern Hants 23 SU3550
Wildhill Herts 39 TL2606
Wildmanbridge Strath 116 NS8253
Wildmoor H & W 60 SO9575
Wildsworth Lincs 75 SK8097
Wilford Notts 62 SK5637
Wilkesley Ches 71 SJ6241
Wilkhaven Highld 147 NH9486
Wilkieston Fife 117 NT1268
Wilkin's Green Herts 39 TL1907
Wilksby Lincs 77 TF2862
Willand Devon 9 ST0310
Willards Hill E Susx 17 TQ7124
Willaston Ches 71 SJ3377
Willaston Ches 72 SJ6752
Willcott Shrops 59 SJ3718
Willen Bucks 38 SP8741
Willenhall W Mids 60 SO9698
Willenhall W Mids 61 SP3676
Willerby Humb 84 TA0230
Willerby N York 91 TA0079
Willersey Gloucs 48 SP1039
Willersley H & W 46 SO3147
Willesborough Kent 28 TR0441
Willesborough Lees Kent 28 TR0342
Willesden Gt Lon 26 TQ2284
Willesleigh Devon 19 SS6033
Willesley Wilts 35 ST8588
Willett Somset 20 ST1033
Willey Shrops 60 SO6799
Willey Warwks 50 SP4984
Willey Green Surrey 25 SU9351
Williamscot Oxon 49 SP4745
Williamstown M Glam 33 ST0090
Willian Herts 39 TL2230
Willingale Essex 40 TL5907
Willingdon E Susx 16 TQ5902
Willingham Cambs 52 TL4070
Willingham Lincs 76 SK8784
Willingham Green Cambs 53 TL6254
Willington Beds 52 TL1150
Willington Derbys 73 SK2928
Willington Dur 96 NZ1935
Willington Kent 28 TQ7853
Willington Warwks 48 SP2638
Willington Corner Ches 71 SJ5366
Willington Quay T & W 103 NZ3167
Willitoft Humb 84 SE7434
Williton Somset 20 ST0740
Willoughbridge Staffs 72 SJ7440
Willoughby Lincs 64 TF0537
Willoughby Lincs 77 TF4771
Willoughby Warwks 50 SP5167
Willoughby Hills Lincs 64 TF3545
Willoughby Waterleys Leics 50 SP5792
Willoughby-on-the-Wolds Notts 63 SK6325
Willoughton Lincs 76 SK9293
Willow Green Ches 71 SJ6076
Willows Green Essex 40 TL7219
Willsbridge Avon 35 ST6670
Willsworthy Devon 8 SX5381
Willtown Somset 21 ST3924
Wilmcote Warwks 48 SP1658
Wilmington Avon 22 ST6962
Wilmington Devon 9 SY2199
Wilmington E Susx 16 TQ5404
Wilmington Kent 27 TQ5371
Wilmslow Ches 79 SJ8481
Wilnecote Staffs 61 SK2201
Wilpshire Lancs 81 SD6832
Wilsden W York 82 SE0936
Wilsford Lincs 63 TF0042
Wilsford Wilts 23 SU1057
Wilsford Wilts 23 SU1339
Wilsham Devon 19 SS7548
Wilshaw W York 82 SE1109
Wilsill N York 89 SE1864
Wilsley Green Kent 28 TQ7737
Wilsley Pound Kent 28 TQ7837
Wilson H & W 46 SO5523
Wilson Leics 62 SK4024
Wilsontown Strath 116 NS9455
Wilstead Beds 38 TL0643
Wilsthorpe Lincs 64 TF0913
Wilstone Herts 38 SP9014
Wilstone Green Herts 38 SP9013
Wilton Cleve 97 NZ5819
Wilton Cleve 97 NZ5819
Wilton Cumb 86 NY0411
Wilton H & W 46 SO5824
Wilton N York 90 SE8582
Wilton Wilts 23 SU0931
Wilton Wilts 23 SU2661
Wilton Dean Border 109 NT4914
Wimbish Essex 53 TL5936
Wimbish Green Essex 53 TL6035
Wimblebury Staffs 60 SK0111
Wimbledon Gt Lon 26 TQ2370
Wimblington Cambs 65 TL4192
Wimborne Minster Dorset 11 SZ0199
Wimborne St. Giles Dorset 12 SU0212
Wimbotsham Norfk 65 TF6205
Wimpstone Warwks 48 SP2148
Wincanton Somset 22 ST7128
Winceby Lincs 77 TF3268
Wincham Ches 79 SJ6775
Winchburgh Loth 117 NT0974
Winchcombe Gloucs 48 SP0228
Winchelsea E Susx 17 TQ9017
Winchelsea Beach E Susx 17 TQ9115
Winchester Hants 24 SU4829
Winchet Hill Kent 28 TQ7340
Winchfield Hants 24 SU7654
Winchmore Hill Bucks 26 SU9395
Winchmore Hill Gt Lon 27 TQ3194
Wincle Ches 72 SJ9666
Wincobank S York 74 SK3891
Winder Cumb 92 NY0417
Windermere Cumb 87 SD4198
Winderton Warwks 48 SP3240
Windhill Highld 139 NH5348
Windlehurst Gt Man 79 SJ9586
Windlesham Surrey 25 SU9264
Windmill Cnwll 4 SW8975
Windmill Derbys 74 SK1677

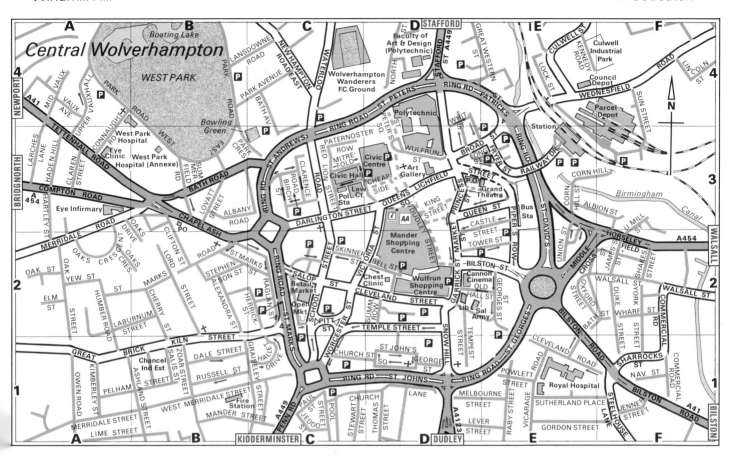

Woodend *Cumb* 86 SD1696
Woodend *Highld* 130 NM7861
Woodend *Loth* 116 NS9269
Woodend *Nhants* 49 SP6149
Woodend *Staffs* 73 SK1726
Woodend *W Susx* 14 SU8108
Woodend Green *Essex* 39 TL5528
Woodfalls *Wilts* 12 SU1920
Woodford *Devon* 7 SX7950
Woodford *Gloucs* 35 ST6996
Woodford *Gt Lon* 27 TQ4092
Woodford *Gt Man* 79 SJ8882
Woodford *Nhants* 51 SP9676
Woodford Bridge *Gt Lon* 27 TQ4291
Woodford End *Bucks* 49 SP6148
Woodford Halse *Nhants* 49 SP5452
Woodford Wells *Gt Lon* 27 IQ4093
Woodgate *Devon* 9 ST1015
Woodgate *H & W* 47 SO9666
Woodgate *Norfk* 66 TF8915
Woodgate *Norfk* 66 TG0216
Woodgate *W Mids* 60 SO9982
Woodgate *W Susx* 14 SU9304
Woodgreen *Hants* 12 SU1717
Woodgreen *Oxon* 36 SP3610
Woodhall *N York* 88 SD9790
Woodhall Hill *W York* 82 SE1935
Woodhall Spa *Lincs* 76 TF1962
Woodham *Bucks* 37 SP7018
Woodham *Dur* 96 NZ2826
Woodham *Lincs* 76 TF2367
Woodham Ferrers *Essex* 40 TQ7999
Woodham Mortimer *Essex* .. 40 TL8104
Woodham Walter *Essex* 40 TL8107
Woodhaven *Fife* 126 NO4126
Woodhead *Gramp* 143 NJ7938
Woodhill *Shrops* 60 SO7384
Woodhill *Somset* 21 ST3527
Woodhorn *Nthumb* 103 NZ2988
Woodhorn Demesne *Nthumb* 103 NZ3088
Woodhouse *Cumb* 93 NY3252
Woodhouse *Leics* 62 SK5315
Woodhouse *S York* 74 SK4284
Woodhouse *W York* 83 SE3821
Woodhouse *W York* 82 SE2932
Woodhouse Eaves *Leics* 62 SK5214
Woodhouse Green *Staffs* 72 SJ9162
Woodhouse Mill *S York* 75 SK4385
Woodhouselee *Fife* 117 NT2364
Woodhouses *Gt Man* 79 SD9100
Woodhouses *Staffs* 61 SK0809
Woodhouses *Staffs* 73 SK1519
Woodhuish *Devon* 7 SX9162
Woodhurst *Cambs* 52 TL3176
Woodingdean *E Susx* 15 TQ3505
Woodkirk *W York* 82 SE2725
Woodland *Devon* 6 SX6250
Woodland *Devon* 7 SX7968
Woodland *Dur* 95 NZ0726
Woodland *Gramp* 143 NJ8723
Woodland *Kent* 29 TR1441
Woodland *Strath* 106 NX1795
Woodland Head *Devon* 8 SX7796
Woodland Street *Somset* 21 ST5437
Woodland View *S York* 74 SK3188
Woodlands *Dorset* 12 SU0508
Woodlands *Gramp* 135 NO7895
Woodlands *Hants* 12 SU3211
Woodlands *Kent* 27 TQ5660
Woodlands *S York* 83 SE3255
Woodlands *S York* 83 SE5308
Woodlands Park *Berks* 26 SU8678
Woodlands St. Mary *Berks* . 36 SU3375
Woodlands St. Mary *Berks* . 36 SU3375
Woodleigh *Devon* 7 SX7348
Woodlesford *W York* 83 SE3629
Woodley *Berks* 25 SU7773
Woodley *Gt Man* 79 SJ9492
Woodley Green *Berks* 26 SU8480
Woodlords *Strath* 117 NT0056
Woodmancote *Gloucs* 47 SO9727
Woodmancote *Gloucs* 35 SP0008
Woodmancote *Gloucs* 35 ST7697
Woodmancote *H & W* 47 SO9142
Woodmancote *W Susx* 14 SU7707
Woodmancote *W Susx* 15 TQ2314
Woodmancott *Hants* 24 SU5642
Woodmansey *Humb* 84 TA0538
Woodmansgreen *W Susx* ... 14 SU8627
Woodmansterne *Surrey* 27 TQ2759
Woodmanton *Devon* 4 SX0185
Woodmarsh *Wilts* 22 ST8555
Woodmill *Staffs* 73 SK1321
Woodminton *Wilts* 22 SU0122
Woodnesborough *Kent* 29 TR3157
Woodnewton *Nhants* 51 TL0394
Woodnook *Notts* 75 SK4752
Woodplumpton *Lancs* 80 SD5034
Woodrising *Norfk* 66 TF9803
Woodrow *H & W* 60 SO8875
Woodseaves *Shrops* 72 SJ6831
Woodseaves *Staffs* 72 SJ7925
Woodsend *Wilts* 36 SU2275
Woodsetts *S York* 75 SK5483
Woodsford *Dorset* 11 SY7690
Woodside *Berks* 25 SU9371
Woodside *Cumb* 92 NY0434
Woodside *D & G* 100 NY0475
Woodside *Dyfed* 31 SN1406
Woodside *Essex* 39 TL4704
Woodside *Fife* 127 NO4207
Woodside *Gt Lon* 27 TQ3467
Woodside *Hants* 12 SZ3294
Woodside *Herts* 39 TL2406
Woodside *Tays* 126 NO2037
Woodside Green *Kent* 28 TQ9053
Woodstock *Dyfed* 30 SN0325
Woodstock *Oxon* 37 SP4416
Woodston *Cambs* 64 TL1897
Woodthorpe *Derbys* 75 SK4574
Woodthorpe *Leics* 62 SK5417
Woodthorpe *Lincs* 77 TF4380
Woodton *Norfk* 67 TM2994
Woodtown *Devon* 18 SS4123
Woodtown *Devon* 18 SS4926
Woodvale *Mersyd* 80 SD3011
Woodville *Derbys* 62 SK3119
Woodwall Green *Staffs* 72 SJ7831
Woody Bay *Devon* 19 SS6748
Woodyates *Dorset* 12 SU0219
Woofferton *Shrops* 46 SO5268
Wookey *Somset* 21 ST5145
Wookey Hole *Somset* 21 ST5347
Wool *Dorset* 11 SY8486
Woolacombe *Devon* 18 SS4643
Woolage Green *Kent* 29 TR2349
Woolage Village *Kent* 26 TQ2250
Woolaston *Gloucs* 34 ST5899
Woolaston Common *Gloucs*. 34 SO5801
Woolavington *Somset* 21 ST3441
Woolbeding *W Susx* 14 SU8722
Woolbrook *Devon* 4 SX1289
Woolcotts *Somset* 20 SS9731
Wooldale *W York* 82 SE1508
Wooler *Nthumb* 111 NT9928
Wooley Bridge *Derbys* 79 SK0195
Woolfardisworthy *Devon* 19 SS8208

Woolfardisworthy *Devon* 18 SS3321
Woolfold *Gt Man* 81 SD7812
Woolhampton *Berks* 24 SU5766
Woolhanger *Devon* 19 SS6945
Woolhope *H & W* 46 SO6135
Woolland *Dorset* 11 ST7707
Woollard *Avon* 21 ST6364
Woollaton *Devon* 18 SS4712
Woollensbrook *Herts* 39 TL3609
Woolley *Avon* 22 ST7468
Woolley *Cambs* 52 TL1474
Woolley *Cnwll* 18 SS2516
Woolley *Derbys* 74 SK3760
Woolley *W York* 82 SE3113
Woolmer Green *Herts* 39 TL2518
Woolmere Green *H & W* 47 SO9663
Woolmerston *Somset* 20 ST2533
Woolminstone *Somset* 10 ST4008
Woolpack *Kent* 28 TQ8537
Woolpack Inn *Cumb* 86 NY1901
Woolpit *Suffk* 54 TL9762
Woolpit Green *Suffk* 54 TL9761
Woolscott *Warwks* 50 SP4968
Woolsgrove *Devon* 8 SS7902
Woolsgrove *Devon* 8 SS7902
Woolsington *T & W* 103 NZ1870
Woolstaston *Shrops* 59 SO4598
Woolsthorpe *Lincs* 63 SK8333
Woolsthorpe *Lincs* 63 SK9224
Woolston *Ches* 79 SJ6589
Woolston *Devon* 7 SX7150
Woolston *Devon* 7 SX7141
Woolston *Hants* 13 SU4410
Woolston *Shrops* 59 SJ3224
Woolston *Shrops* 59 SO4287
Woolston *Somset* 20 ST1139
Woolston *Somset* 21 ST6528
Woolston Green *Devon* 7 SX7765
Woolstone *Bucks* 38 SP8738
Woolstone *Gloucs* 47 SO9530
Woolstone *Oxon* 36 SU2987
Woolton *Mersyd* 78 SJ4286
Woolton Hill *Hants* 24 SU4261
Woolvers Hill *Avon* 21 ST3860
Woolverstone *Suffk* 54 TM1838
Woolverton *Somset* 22 ST7853
Woolwich *Gt Lon* 27 TQ4478
Woonton *H & W* 46 SO5562
Woonton *H & W* 46 SO3552
Wooperton *Nthumb* 111 NU0420
Woore *Shrops* 72 SJ7342
Wooston *Devon* 8 SX7689
Wootten Breadmead *Beds* .. 38 TL0243
Wootten Green *Suffk* 55 TM2373
Wootton *Beds* 38 TL0045
Wootton *H & W* 46 SO3252
Wootton *Hants* 12 SZ2498
Wootton *Humb* 85 TA0815
Wootton *IOW* 13 SZ5492
Wootton *Kent* 29 TR2246
Wootton *Nhants* 49 SP7656
Wootton *Oxon* 36 SP4319
Wootton *Oxon* 37 SP4701
Wootton *Shrops* 59 SJ3327
Wootton *Staffs* 72 SJ8227
Wootton *Staffs* 73 SK1045
Wootton Bassett *Wilts* 36 SU0782
Wootton Bridge *IOW* 13 SZ5492
Wootton Common *IOW* 13 SZ5391
Wootton Courtenay *Somset* 20 SS9343
Wootton Fitzpaine *Dorset* ... 10 SY3695
Wootton Rivers *Wilts* 23 SU1963
Wootton St. Lawrence *Hants* 24 SU5953
Wootton Wawen *Warwks* 48 SP1563
Worbarrow *Dorset* 11 SY8779
Worcester *H & W* 47 SO8555
Worcester Park *Gt Lon* 26 TQ2165
Wordsley *W Mids* 60 SO8987
Worfield *Shrops* 60 SO7596
Worgret *Dorset* 11 SY9087
Workington *Cumb* 92 NX9928
Worksop *Notts* 75 SK5879
Worlaby *Humb* 84 TA0113
Worlaby *Lincs* 77 TF3476
World's End *Berks* 37 SU4876
Worlds End *Bucks* 38 SP8609
Worlds End *Hants* 13 SU6312
Worlds End *W Susx* 15 TQ3220
Worle *Avon* 21 ST3563
Worleston *Ches* 72 SJ6556
Worlingham *Suffk* 55 TM4489
Worlington *Devon* 19 SS7713
Worlington *Suffk* 53 TL6973
Worlingworth *Suffk* 55 TM2368
Wormald Green *N York* 89 SE3065
Wormbridge *H & W* 46 SO4230
Wormegay *Norfk* 65 TF6611
Wormelow Tump *H & W* 46 SO4930
Wormhill *Derbys* 74 SK1274
Wormhill *H & W* 46 SO4239
Wormingford *Essex* 40 TL9332
Worminghall *Bucks* 37 SP6308
Wormington *Gloucs* 48 SP0336
Worminster *Somset* 21 ST5742
Wormiston *Border* 117 NT2345
Wormit *Fife* 126 NO3926
Wormleighton *Warwks* 49 SP4453
Wormley *Herts* 39 TL3605
Wormley *Surrey* 25 SU9438
Wormley Hill *S York* 83 SE6616
Wormleybury *Herts* 39 TL3506
Wormshill *Kent* 28 TQ8857
Wormsley *H & W* 46 SO4247
Worplesdon *Surrey* 25 SU9753
Worrall *S York* 74 SK3092
Worsbrough *S York* 83 SE3503
Worsbrough Bridge *S York* .. 83 SE3403
Worsbrough Dale *S York* 83 SE3402
Worsley *Gt Man* 79 SD7500
Worsley Mesnes *Gt Man* 78 SD5703
Worstead *Norfk* 67 TG3026
Worsthorne *Lancs* 81 SD8732
Worston *Devon* 6 SX5952
Worston *Lancs* 81 SD7742
Worswell *Devon* 6 SX5447
Worth *Kent* 29 TR3356
Worth *Somset* 21 ST5145
Worth *W Susx* 15 TQ3036
Worth Abbey *Surrey* 15 TQ3134
Worth Matravers *Dorset* 11 SY9777
Wortham *Suffk* 54 TM0877
Worthen *Shrops* 59 SJ3204
Worthenbury *Clwyd* 71 SJ4246
Worthing *Norfk* 66 TF9919
Worthing *W Susx* 15 TQ1402
Worthington *Leics* 62 SK4020
Worthybrook *Gwent* 34 SO4711
Worting *Hants* 24 SU5952
Wortley *S York* 74 SK3099
Wortley *W York* 82 SE2732
Worton *N York* 88 SD9589
Worton *Wilts* 22 ST9757
Wortwell *Norfk* 55 TM2784
Wotherton *Shrops* 58 SJ2800
Wothorpe *Cambs* 64 TF0205
Wotter *Devon* 6 SX5562
Wotton *Surrey* 14 TQ1247

Wotton Under Edge *Gloucs* . 35 ST7593
Wotton Underwood *Bucks* ... 37 SP6816
Woughton on the Green *Bucks* 38 SP8737
Wouldham *Kent* 28 TQ7164
Woundale *Shrops* 60 SO7793
Wrabness *Essex* 41 TM1731
Wrafton *Devon* 18 SS4935
Wragby *Lincs* 76 TF1378
Wragby *W York* 83 SE4014
Wramplingham *Norfk* 66 TG1106
Wrangaton *Devon* 7 SX6757
Wrangbrook *W York* 83 SE4013
Wrangle *Lincs* 77 TF4250
Wrangle Common *Lincs* 77 TF4253
Wrangle Lowgate *Lincs* 77 TF4451
Wrangway *Somset* 9 ST1217
Wrantage *Somset* 20 ST3022
Wrawby *Humb* 84 TA0108
Wraxall *Avon* 34 ST4871
Wraxall *Somset* 21 ST6036
Wray *Lancs* 87 SD6067
Wray Castle *Cumb* 93 NY3730
Wraysbury *Berks* 25 TQ0074
Wrayton *Lancs* 87 SD6172
Wrea Green *Lancs* 80 SD3931
Wreaks End *Cumb* 101 NY2186
Wrecclesham *Surrey* 25 SU8245
Wrekenton *T & W* 96 NZ2758
Wrelton *N York* 90 SE7886
Wrenbury *Ches* 71 SJ5947
Wrench Green *N York* 91 SE9689
Wreningham *Norfk* 66 TM1699
Wrentham *Suffk* 55 TM4982
Wrentnall *Shrops* 59 SJ4203
Wressing *Devon* 9 ST0508
Wressle *Humb* 84 SE7099
Wressle *Humb* 84 SE7031
Wrestlingworth *Beds* 52 TL2547
Wretton *Norfk* 65 TF6900
Wrexham *Clwyd* 71 SJ3350
Wribbenhall *H & W* 60 SO7975
Wrickton *Shrops* 59 SO6486
Wright's Green *Essex* 39 TL5017
Wrightington Bar *Lancs* 80 SD5313
Wrinehill *Staffs* 72 SJ7547
Wrington *Avon* 21 ST4762
Wringworthy *Cnwll* 5 SX2658
Writhlington *Somset* 22 ST7054
Writtle *Essex* 40 TL6706
Wrockwardine *Shrops* 59 SJ6212
Wroot *Humb* 84 SE7103
Wrose *W York* 82 SE1636
Wrotham *Kent* 27 TQ6159
Wrotham Green *Kent* 27 TQ6357
Wrottesley *Staffs* 60 SJ8201
Wroughton *Wilts* 36 SU1480
Wroxall *IOW* 13 SZ5579
Wroxall *Warwks* 61 SP2271
Wroxeter *Shrops* 59 SJ5608
Wroxham *Norfk* 67 TG3017
Wroxton *Oxon* 49 SP4141
Wyaston *Derbys* 73 SK1842
Wyatt's Green *Essex* 27 TQ5999
Wyberton *Lincs* 64 TF3240
Wyboston *Beds* 52 TL1656
Wybunbury *Ches* 72 SJ6949
Wych *Dorset* 10 SY4791
Wych Cross *E Susx* 15 TQ4331
Wychbold *H & W* 47 SO9266
Wychnor *Staffs* 73 SK1716
Wyck *Hants* 24 SU7539
Wycliffe *Dur* 95 NZ1114
Wycoller *Lancs* 81 SD9339
Wycomb *Leics* 63 SK7724
Wycombe Marsh *Bucks* 26 SU8892
Wyddial *Herts* 39 TL3731
Wye *Kent* 28 TR0546
Wyesham *Gwent* 34 SO5111
Wyfordby *Leics* 63 SK7918
Wyke *Devon* 5 SX2996
Wyke *Devon* 8 SX8799
Wyke *Dorset* 22 ST7926
Wyke *Shrops* 59 SJ6402
Wyke *Surrey* 25 SU9251
Wyke *W York* 82 SE1526
Wyke Champflower *Somset* . 22 ST6634
Wyke Regis *Dorset* 11 SY6677
Wyke The *Shrops* 60 SJ7306
Wykeham *N York* 90 SE8175
Wykeham *N York* 91 SE9683
Wyken *Shrops* 60 SO7695
Wyken *W Mids* 61 SP3680
Wykey *Shrops* 59 SJ3925
Wykin *Leics* 61 SP4095
Wylam *Nthumb* 103 NZ1164
Wylde Green *W Mids* 61 SP1294
Wyllie *Gwent* 33 ST1794
Wylye *Wilts* 22 SU0037
Wymeswold *Leics* 62 SK6023
Wymington *Beds* 51 SP9564
Wymondham *Leics* 63 SK8518
Wymondham *Norfk* 66 TG1101
Wymondham *M Glam* 33 SS9392
Wynds Point *H & W* 47 SO7640
Wynford Eagle *Dorset* 10 SY5895
Wyre Piddle *H & W* 47 SO9647
Wysall *Notts* 62 SK6027
Wyson *H & W* 46 SO5267
Wythall *H & W* 61 SP0774
Wytham *Oxon* 37 SP4708
Wythborn *Cumb* 93 NY3214
Wythenshawe *Gt Man* 79 SJ8386
Wythop Mill *Cumb* 93 NY1729
Wyton *Cambs* 52 TL2772
Wyton *Humb* 85 TA1733
Wyverstone *Suffk* 54 TM0468
Wyverstone Street *Suffk* 54 TM0367
Wyville *Lincs* 63 SK8729
Wyvis Lodge *Highld* 146 NH4873

Y

Y Rhiw *Gwynd* 56 SH2227
Y-Ffrith *Clwyd* 70 SJ0483
Yaddlethorpe *Humb* 84 SE8806
Yafford *IOW* 13 SZ4481
Yafforth *N York* 89 SE3494
Yalberton *Devon* 7 SX8658
Yalding *Kent* 28 TQ7050
Yalverton *Devon* 6 SX5267
Yanworth *Gloucs* 36 SP0713
Yapham *Humb* 84 SE7851
Yapton *W Susx* 14 SU9703
Yarborough *Avon* 21 ST3858
Yarbridge *IOW* 13 SZ6086

Yarburgh *Lincs* 77 TF3493
Yarcombe *Devon* 9 ST2408
Yard *Devon* 19 SS7721
Yarde *Somset* 20 ST0538
Yardley *W Mids* 61 SP1386
Yardley Gobion *Nhants* 49 SP7644
Yardley Hastings *Nhants* 51 SP8656
Yardley Wood *W Mids* 61 SP1080
Yardro *Powys* 45 SO2258
Yarford *Somset* 20 ST2029
Yarkhill *H & W* 46 SO6042
Yarlet *Staffs* 72 SJ9129
Yarley *Somset* 21 ST5045
Yarlington *Somset* 21 ST6529
Yarlsber *N York* 87 SD7072
Yarm *Cleve* 89 NZ4111
Yarmouth *IOW* 12 SZ3589
Yarnacott *Devon* 19 SS6230
Yarnbrook *Wilts* 22 ST8654
Yarnfield *Staffs* 72 SJ8632
Yarnscombe *Devon* 19 SS5523
Yarnton *Oxon* 37 SP4712
Yarpole *H & W* 46 SO4664
Yarrow *Border* 109 NT3528
Yarrow *Somset* 21 ST3747
Yarrow Feus *Border* 109 NT3325
Yarrowford *Border* 109 NT4030
Yarsop *H & W* 46 SO4047
Yarwell *Nhants* 51 TL0797
Yate *Avon* 35 ST7082
Yateley *Hants* 25 SU8260
Yatesbury *Wilts* 36 SU0671
Yattendon *Berks* 24 SU5574
Yatton *Avon* 21 ST4365
Yatton *H & W* 46 SO4367
Yatton *H & W* 47 SO6330
Yatton Keynell *Wilts* 35 ST8676
Yaverland *IOW* 13 SZ6185
Yawl *Devon* 10 SY3194
Yawthorpe *Lincs* 76 SK8992
Yaxham *Norfk* 66 TG0010
Yaxley *Cambs* 64 TL1892
Yaxley *Suffk* 54 TM1274
Yazor *H & W* 46 SO4046
Yeading *Gt Lon* 26 TQ1182
Yeadon *W York* 82 SE2040
Yealand Conyers *Lancs* 87 SD5074
Yealand Redmayne *Lancs* ... 87 SD4975
Yealand Redmayne *Lancs* ... 87 SD5075
Yealand Stores *Lancs* 87 SD5075
Yealmpton *Devon* 6 SX5751
Yearby *Cleve* 97 NZ5921
Yearngill *Cumb* 92 NY1343
Yearsley *N York* 90 SE5874
Yeaton *Shrops* 59 SJ4319
Yeaveley *Derbys* 73 SK1840
Yedingham *N York* 91 SE8979
Yelford *Oxon* 36 SP3504
Yelland *Devon* 18 SS4932
Yelling *Cambs* 52 TL2662
Yelvertoft *Nhants* 50 SP6075
Yelvertoft *Nhants* 50 SP5975
Yelverton *Norfk* 67 TG2902
Yenston *Somset* 22 ST7120
Yeo Mill *Somset* 19 SS8426
Yeo Park *Devon* 6 SX5852
Yeo Vale *Devon* 18 SS4223
Yeoford *Devon* 8 SX7898
Yeolmbridge *Cnwll* 5 SX3187
Yeovil *Somset* 10 ST5515
Yeovil Marsh *Somset* 10 ST5418
Yeovilton *Somset* 21 ST5422
Yerbeston *Dyfed* 30 SN0609
Yesnaby *Ork* 155 HY2215
Yetlington *Nthumb* 111 NU0209
Yetminster *Dorset* 10 ST5910
Yetson *Devon* 7 SX8056
Yettington *Devon* 9 SY0585
Yetts O'Muckhart *Cent* 117 NO0001
Yew Green *Warwks* 48 SP2367
Yews Green *W York* 82 SE1030
Yielden *Beds* 51 TL0167
Yieldingtree *H & W* 60 SO8977
Yieldshields *Strath* 116 NS8750
Yiewsley *Gt Lon* 26 TQ0680
Ynysboeth *M Glam* 33 ST0695
Ynysddu *Gwent* 33 ST1792
Ynysforgan *W Glam* 32 SS6799
Ynyshir *M Glam* 33 ST0292
Ynyslas *Dyfed* 43 SN6293
Ynysmaerdy *M Glam* 33 ST0383
Ynysmeudwy *W Glam* 32 SN7305
Ynyswen *M Glam* 33 SS9597
Ynyswen *Powys* 33 SN8313
Ynysybwl *M Glam* 33 ST0594
Ynysymaengwyn *Gwynd* 57 SH5902
Yockenthwaite *N York* 88 SD9078
Yockleton *Shrops* 59 SJ3910
Yokefleet *Humb* 84 SE8124
Yoker *Strath* 115 NS5169
Yonder Bognie *Gramp* 142 NJ6046
Yondertown *Devon* 6 SX5958
York *Lancs* 81 SD7133
York *N York* 83 SE6052
York Town *Hants* 25 SU8660
Yorkletts *Kent* 29 TR0963
Yorley Gloucs 35 SO6307
Yorton Heath *Shrops* 59 SJ5022
Youlgreave *Derbys* 74 SK2164
Youlthorpe *Humb* 84 SE7655
Youlton *N York* 90 SE4963
Young's End *Essex* 40 TL7419
Youngsbury *Herts* 39 TL3618
Yoxall *Staffs* 73 SK1418
Yoxford *Suffk* 55 TM3968
Yoxford Little Street *Suffk* ... 55 TM3869
Ysbyty Cynfyn *Dyfed* 43 SN7578
Ysbyty Ifan *Gwynd* 69 SH8448
Ysbyty Ystwyth *Dyfed* 43 SN7371
Ysceifiog *Clwyd* 70 SJ1571
Ysgubor-y-Coed *Dyfed* 43 SN6895
Ystalyfera *W Glam* 32 SN7708
Ystrad *M Glam* 33 SS9895
Ystrad Aeron *Dyfed* 44 SN5256
Ystrad Meurig *Dyfed* 43 SN7067
Ystrad Mynach *M Glam* 33 ST1494
Ystrad-ffyn *Dyfed* 44 SN7846
Ystradgynlais *Powys* 32 SN7910
Ystradowen *Dyfed* 32 SN7512
Ystradowen *S Glam* 33 ST0177
Ystumtuen *Dyfed* 43 SN7378